Making Places Special

Stories of Real Places
Made Better by Planning

By
Gene Bunnell, AICP

PLANNERS PRESS
AMERICAN PLANNING ASSOCIATION
Chicago, Illinois
Washington, D.C.

Copyright 2002 by the American Planning Association
122 S. Michigan Ave., Suite 1600, Chicago, IL 60603

ISBN (paperback edition): 1-884829-57-0
ISBN (hardbound edition): 1-884829-58-9
Library of Congress Catalog Number 2001 131721
Printed in the United States of America
All rights reserved

Interior composition and copyediting by Joanne Shwed, Backspace Ink
Art scans by Charles Eaton
CD-ROM composition by Silicon Publishing, Inc. and Backspace Ink
Cover photograph by Richard Benjamin
Cover design by Susan Deegan

Contents

5.   CHARLESTON, SOUTH CAROLINA   212
Making a Very Special Place

6.   DULUTH, MINNESOTA   299
Making a Special Place in the Face of Decline

ADDITIONAL CD-ROM CASE STUDIES

*(These chapters are numbered on the CD-ROM
as Chapters 8, 9, 10 and 11, respectively)*

WESTMINSTER, COLORADO

TWO NEW ENGLAND PLANNERS TELL THEIR OWN STORIES

Acknowledgements

This book contains a series of stories and accounts describing the positive changes that people in 10 very different kinds of places achieved by planning. It would not have been possible to compile a book such as this without the cooperation and assistance of literally hundreds of people, only some of whom I am able to thank by name here.

I want to thank Frank So and Sylvia Lewis of the American Planning Association (APA) for responding favorably to my book proposal, and the APA staff in Chicago for their assistance in sending out the survey instrument that provided the basis for selecting case-study communities and for identifying specific qualities and outcomes that have been achieved by planning. I also want to thank the 136 APA members who mailed back completed questionnaires, and the 37 other planning and design professionals who agreed to be interviewed by telephone during the survey phase. The thoughtful responses and comments conveyed by those 173 individuals provided a solid foundation for beginning work on this book.

Edward Jepson analyzed and tabulated the results of the completed surveys, developed profiles of the respective case-study communities, conducted a number of interviews with principals in communities that were not chosen as case-study communities, and read and critiqued early drafts of the manuscript. Ed's keen interest in the project, and the comments and advice he offered throughout the three and one-half years of work on the book, were immensely valuable and greatly appreciated.

I also want to express my heartfelt thanks to the 116 individuals who agreed to be interviewed, often at considerable length, in connection with the research I carried out in the eight case-study communities. Truly, it is *their* cooperation and assistance that made it possible for me to compile the planning stories in this book, and it is their words and accounts that make these stories so important and instructive. The names of the people I contacted and interviewed in each case-study community are listed at the end of each chapter. The fact that so many people were willing to take the time to speak to me about the impact planning had on their community is, in itself, a testament to the importance people place on the outcomes that planning has helped achieve.

To those individuals who served as my principal local contacts in the eight case-study communities—who provided me with needed information; put me in touch with key local informants; helped me obtain copies of relevant plans, documents and supporting materials like photographs; and in many other ways helped make the task of documenting the impacts of planning in specific communities more manageable—I owe a special debt of gratitude.

I am especially grateful to those individuals who took the time to read drafts of the manuscript for accuracy, and who offered thoughtful comments and suggestions. I would particularly like to acknowledge the contributions of the following individuals: T. D. Harden, Ann Coulter, Jerry Pace and Jim Bowen in Chattanooga; Samuel J. Shamoon, Tina Regan and William D. Warner regarding Providence; George Austin and David V. Mollenhoff in Madison; Marvin S. Krout in Wichita; Joseph P. Riley and Robert Behre in Charleston; Gerald M. (Jerry) Kimball in Duluth; John Carpenter in Westminster; and Michael Stepner in San Diego. Related to the Chattanooga case study, I would also like to express my thanks to Professor Ron Foresta of the University of Tennessee at Knoxville for sharing photocopies of Chattanooga newspaper articles from the 1950s and 1960s that he compiled on the Golden Triangle urban renewal project.

On both a personal and professional level, I would like to thank David B. Musante, Jr. (mayor of Northampton, Massachusetts from 1980 to 1992); Marcia Burick, his former administrative assistant; and the people of Northampton for giving me the opportunity to be that city's director of planning and development in the 1980s. The experiences and satisfaction I gained from working in that capacity gave me the deep appreciation of the positive difference planning can make in communities that ultimately inspired me to take on the task of writing this book.

Last, but certainly not least, I want to express my profound gratitude to my wife, Lynne, who read, edited and critiqued drafts of every chapter, often in the early stages when my thoughts and words were far from polished. It was her support and encouragement throughout the years it took to complete this project that gave me the strength to press on when the light at the end of the tunnel seemed so far away.

—GENE BUNNELL
FEBRUARY 2002

Definitions of Planning

To plan: *To realize the achievement of . . .*
                 To arrange the parts of . . .
                 To intend . . .

—OXFORD ENGLISH DICTIONARY

Planning is a process of preparing in advance, and in a reasonably systematic fashion, recommendations for programs and courses of action to attain the common objectives of the community . . .

—ANTHONY CATANESE

Planning is the use of reason and understanding to reduce collective uncertainty about the future.

—CHARLES HOCH

By planning, I mean a method and process of decision-making which includes the proper formulation of the problems which [a] city needs to solve (or of the goals it wishes to achieve); the determination of the causes of those problems; and the formulation of those policies, action programs, and decisions which will deal with the causes to solve the problem, and will do so democratically . . .

—HERBERT GANS

Planning is a practical activity that is done in places to solve particular problems . . . Local allegiances and local perspectives are essential to solving environmental and social problems.

—GREG LINDSEY

Planners typically ask three questions: What is likely to happen without specific intervention? What should happen? And how can the desired state be brought about?

—JOHN FRIEDMAN

Planning is what planners do.

—ANONYMOUS

List of Acronyms

ACP   American Community Partnerships
AIA   American Institute of Architects
APA   American Planning Association
BAR   Board of Architectural Review
BART   Bay Area Rapid Transit
C3   Citizens Coordinate for Century Three
CAH   Charleston Affordable Housing, Inc.
Caltrans   California Department of Transportation
CARTA   Chattanooga Area Regional Transportation Authority
CBD   central business district
CCDC   Centre City Development Corporation
CDA   Community Development Authority
CDBG   Community Development Block Grant
CEO   Chief Executive Officer
CIP   capital improvement plan
CNE   Chattanooga Neighborhood Enterprise, Inc.
CPO   Comprehensive Planning Organization
CRF   Capital Revolving Fund
DARE   Downtown Area Redevelopment Effort
DASH   Downtown Area Shuttle
DCD   Department of Community Development
DECC   Duluth Entertainment and Convention Center
DNR   Department of National Resources
DPD   Department of Planning and Development (Duluth)
DPD   Department of Planning and Development (Madison)
DPUD   Department of Planning and Urban Development (Charleston)
DPUD   Department of Planning and Urban Development (Providence)

DPW	Department of Public Works
DRC	Development Resource Center (Chattanooga)
DRC	Development Review Committee (Westminster)
EDA	Economic Development Administration
EIS	Environmental Impact Statement
EOA	Economic Opportunity Area
EPA	U. S. Environmental Protection Agency
ETA	Economic Target Area
ETVI	Electric Transit Vehicle Institute
FHA	Federal Housing Administration
FHWA	Federal Highway Administration
FRA	Federal Railroad Administration
GE	General Electric Corporation
GIPC	Greater Indianapolis Progress Committee
GIS	geographic information system
HOME	Home Investment Partnerships [program]
HRA	Housing and Redevelopment Agency
HTF	Housing Trust Fund
HUD	[U.S. Department of] Housing and Urban Development
IPCDG	Inland Pacific Colorado Development Group
IRB	Industrial Revenue Bond
IRS	Internal Revenue Service
ISTEA	Intermodal Surface Transportation Efficiency Act
KDHE	Kansas Department of Health and Environment
L & N	Louisville and Nashville [Railroad]
LAX	Los Angeles International airport
LSPI	Lake Superior Paper Industries
MAPD	Metropolitan Area Planning Department
MBTA	Massachusetts Bay Transportation Authority
MG & E	Madison Gas and Electric
MNDOT	Minnesota Department of Transportation
MPO	Metropolitan Planning Organization
MPPDA	Madison Park and Pleasure Drive Association
MSCP	*Multiple Species Conservation Program*
MTDB	Metropolitan Transit Development Board
MTS	Metropolitan Transit System
NAACP	National Association for the Advancement of Colored People
NAHB	National Association of Homebuilders
NEA	National Endowment for the Arts
OPD	Office of Planning and Development
P & W	Providence and Worcester [Railroad]
PLAN	Prevent Los Angelization Now

PRA	Providence Redevelopment Agency
PUD	Planned Unit Development
RFP	Request for Proposals
RFQ	Request for Qualifications
RIDEM	Rhode Island Department of Environmental Management
RIDOT	Rhode Island Department of Transportation
RISD	Rhode Island School of Design
RP	Responsible Party
RPA	Regional Planning Agency
RTC	Resolution Trust Corporation
SANDAG	San Diego Association of Governments
SDHC	San Diego Housing Commission
SNOB	Slightly North of Broad
SOM	Skidmore, Owings & Merrill LLP
SRO	single-room-occupancy
SVNDA	Spirit Valley Neighborhood Development Association
SWAP	Stop Wasting Abandoned Properties
TD	Tourist Development [zone]
TDA	Transportation Development Act
TEA-21	Transportation Efficiency Act—21st century
TIF	Tax Increment Financing
TOD	transit-oriented development
TOT	transient occupancy tax
TransNet	Transportation Sales Tax Initiative
TVA	Tennessee Valley Authority
UDAG	Urban Development Action Grant
UDC	Urban Design Commission
ULI	Urban Land Institute
UMD	University of Minnesota at Duluth
UTC	University of Tennessee at Chattanooga
WCI	Wisconsin Centennial, Inc.
WI/SE	Wichita-Sedgwick County
WPA	Works Progress Administration

Preface

This book is not just for planners or people who have had experience in planning, although I hope that planners will want to read the book and be invigorated and inspired by the case studies. This book is written for anyone who loves cities and cares about the quality and livability of communities. It is for people who, when they look at how communities are growing and changing, sense that far too little thought is being given to the long-term impacts of land use and development decisions. It is for anyone who senses that communities, and the places we call home, are not well served when the form and nature of development are left largely to chance, and when little thought is given to what we want our communities to be and look like in the future. It is for anyone who sits on a local planning commission, or who thinks they might someday serve on a local planning commission. It is also for anyone who holds an elected office, who thinks they might run for office sometime in the future, or who has thought about taking a leadership role in their community. Most of all, it is for anyone who, over the years, has lost hope in the possibility that carefully prepared plans—and thoughtful public policies consistent with those plans—can actually make communities better.

The case studies contained in this book are not meant to tell you *how* planning should be carried out in your particular community, or what tools or processes you should use to achieve planning objectives. Rather, their purpose is to communicate the message that it *is* possible to make places better, and preserve and strengthen the qualities that make places special, by planning.

CHAPTER

1

The Direction of Change

At the heart of the struggle to determine the direction any city will take is the question of how its land is to be used. It can either be treated primarily as a source of profit, to be packaged, bought and sold, or else, as the holistic perspective teaches, as a resource that in an interrelated manner serves the spiritual as well as the material needs of the people who live upon it.

—JOHN GUINTHER (*THE DIRECTION OF CITIES*, 1996, 20)

1-1   Directional sign in Pioneer Square (Portland, Oregon) showing distances from other places in the world.

Source: Gene Bunnell

GRAPPLING WITH CHANGE

The cities, villages and towns we call home and experience in our daily lives are constantly changing. Change is most obvious in communities experiencing rapid growth and development. The signs of change can be equally evident in communities that are losing jobs and population. Even communities that appear relatively stable, whose populations have remained roughly the same, experience change. To maintain the same level of population, new people must be attracted to take the place of those who have moved away. New businesses must be started, and existing businesses must grow to take the place of those that have gone out of business and gotten smaller. To maintain the *appearance* of staying the same, communities must undergo a significant amount of change.

Having for many years observed and studied how and why communities change, I have come to the following basic conclusions:

- There is almost always a direction to community change. At any given time, some places are becoming better and others are becoming worse.
- Contrary to what many people believe, the direction of change (whether a community becomes better or worse over time) is remarkably unaffected by growth. Many communities that have experienced negative growth (*i.e.*, lost jobs and population) are actually much better places than they were when they were growing and booming. Positive things can happen in places that have shrunk in size. Although many communities have been negatively affected by rapid growth, rapid growth need not destroy the positive qualities that make places special. Some communities that have experienced high rates of growth have nevertheless succeeded in preserving valued qualities and in becoming better than they were before they experienced rapid growth.
- The direction of change in the past is no guarantee of the direction of change in the future. The fortunes of communities, and the direction of change, can vary markedly over time. Many communities that were "down" are now on their way "up." Conversely, communities that seemed destined to prosper forever have seen their circumstances sour as the qualities that once made them desirable have disappeared.

Viewed from afar, the direction of change in communities often seems determined more by luck than design. Some communities just seem to have been in the right place at the right time. San Jose, California prospered in the 1980s and 1990s because it was located in the heart of "Silicon Valley" where the high-tech industrial revolution unfolded. The fact that major corporations like Boeing, Microsoft, Starbucks and Amazon.com were based in and around Seattle, Washington is undoubtedly a major reason why downtown Seattle and the Puget Sound region prospered to such a great extent during the 1990s.

Other cities have not been nearly as lucky. Pittsburgh, Pennsylvania lost 120,000 steel industry jobs in a six-year period. At one time, General Electric employed over 60,000 people in Schenectady, New York; today it employs only 4,000. Clearly, communities that have sustained such devastating blows to their local economies have faced a daunting task in attempting to achieve and sustain a positive direction of change.

The external forces working *for* or *against* particular communities at any given point in time are formidable and cannot be completely negated, and attempting to blunt their effects can require tremendous effort. Does that mean that communities are entirely incapable of influencing the *direction* and amplitude of change? I don't think so.

If you look closely at the recent histories of a number of U.S. cities, you will find that the direction of change—and the nature and quality of change—have often been altered to a significant extent by plan-based public policy choices. Good places rarely come about entirely by chance. Special places never retain the qualities that made them special without a good deal of conscious effort.

USING PLACES UP AND MOVING ON

Massive, multistory office and apartment buildings can now be brought down into a pile of dust and rubble in a matter of seconds. The artistry and precision of modern demolition techniques, orchestrated by teams of highly skilled demolition specialists, makes it awe-inspiring to watch. Years ago, the Travelers Insurance Office Building in downtown Boston—surrounded on three sides by other office towers and on the fourth side by the Central Artery Expressway—was neatly imploded without inflicting damage to any adjacent buildings or property.

In order to minimize collateral damage, demolition experts try to cause tall structures to collapse like a falling tree in a favored direction. In Australia, a number of people in boats on a nearby river, who were watching a building being blown up, were injured—and some killed—by flying bricks that were mistakenly propelled outward by the blast. However, in most cases, it all works so perfectly that demolitions are accomplished with what seems like surgical precision.

Like many Americans, my fascination in seeing buildings being demolished has been nourished by watching television film replays of large buildings being leveled as if they were simply made of toy blocks. Indeed, as building demolition technology has become increasingly sophisticated, preparations for filming demolitions have also become increasingly sophisticated and elaborate, so that films and videotapes have become more entertaining.

The videotaped demolition of the old Sands Hotel in Las Vegas, Nevada was staged at night on New Year's Eve, and was watched by thousands of New Year's Eve revelers with the same glee they might have felt watching a Fourth of July fireworks display. The implosion of the Seattle Kingdome on a Sunday in March 2000 was also turned into a major entertainment event. Not only was it observed live by tens of thousands of Seattle residents, but the demolition was also videotaped from various angles and from the air, and replays of the implosion were shown on nightly television news broadcasts across the country. Watching buildings and places being brought down has attained the same entertainment value as watching sports highlight films of football players crashing into one another, of baseball players running into outfield walls and of high-speed crashes of racing cars.

It is hard not to be impressed by the skill of those who masterfully carry out the demolition of major buildings and make it all happen so smoothly. Having said this, it must also be said that there is something terribly amiss when the work of people who obliterate buildings and places is so admired, and when we have so little appreciation and understanding of the planning skills required to create and maintain livable communities.

On April 9, 1998, during the same week that the national conference of the American Planning Association (APA) was held in Boston, the lead story on the front page of *The Boston Globe* was that Boston's mayor, Thomas M. Menino, recommended that the city sell Boston City Hall and the adjoining City Hall Plaza, and build a new city hall elsewhere. "The building is 30 years old," Menino said. "There's not enough room."

The mayor's words seemed to suggest that he was more concerned with finding better office space than he was about what would happen to Government Center when and if city offices moved out of the area. When asked by a reporter what he thought should happen to the site, Menino seemed to suggest that he hadn't thought much about it. "I don't know what it could be used for. Some parts of it would make a great handball court," quipped the mayor. Adopting a somewhat more serious tone, Menino said that it might actually be a good idea to tear the building down and clear the way for a new hotel and/or office complex. Then again, recalling Boston City Hall's solid poured concrete construction, the mayor admitted that the building might be difficult to take down. "I'm not sure it could be imploded," the mayor said.

People in other parts of the world must find it hard to imagine that a major American city would seriously consider abandoning a city hall building that was only 30 years old. British prime ministers have been housed at 10 Downing Street for over 200 years.

Boston City Hall, the building Mayor Menino seemed so willing to leave behind, was not a run-of-the-mill public building, but rather the centerpiece of Government Center—an area of the city that was redeveloped in the 1960s based on a master plan prepared by architect I. M. Pei. In fact, a great deal of care and forethought went into its planning and design. An international design competition was held to select the best design for the new Boston City Hall. For many years, the design and plan for Boston City Hall (submitted by Gerhard Kallmann and Michael McKinnell) were widely regarded as a stunning success. In a poll of historians and architects, sponsored by the American Institute of Architects (AIA) in 1976, Boston City Hall was voted the sixth greatest building in American history.

Ada Louise Huxtable, long-time architectural writer for *The New York Times*, was particularly effusive in her praise of the building. In her book, *Will They Ever Finish Bruckner Boulevard?*, Huxtable writes, "Boston can celebrate with the knowledge that it has produced a superior public building in an age that values cheapness over quality as a form of public virtue . . . A powerful focus for the new Government Center that has replaced the sordid charms of the old Scollay Square, it makes a motley collection of very large, very average new buildings around it look good. It confers . . . an instant image of progressive excellence on a city government traditionally known for something less than creativity and quality. That is an old trick of architecture called symbolism." (Huxtable 1970, 168-169)

Robert Campbell, whose columns on architecture and urban planning in Boston have appeared regularly in *The Boston Globe*, notes that Boston City Hall is not as highly regarded now as it was before. Just as people were once turned off by elaborate Victorian-style architecture, the modern "brutal" appearance of the building that people in the 1960s and 1970s found so appealing now turns many people off. Nevertheless, as Campbell noted, "City Hall's so-called brutalism . . . may look awful today. But styles of architecture fall in and out of fashion. You have to be careful. Harvard's great Victorian Memorial Hall was slated for eventual demolition. Now it's regarded as a precious landmark. I don't think there's any question that the modernist grandeur of City Hall will regain favor at some point. If we take care of it, that is." (Campbell, April 10, 1998, A1)

I myself have always thought that the brutal architectural features of Boston City Hall were part of its appeal. I was therefore aghast at the thought that such an important public building, which not so long ago had been considered bold and inspiring, could be so cavalierly abandoned. What troubled me *even more* about the mayor's proposal was that he was apparently prepared to write off an entire centrally located area that had been planned and built expressly for the purpose of serving as the center of public life in the city.

When Government Center and Boston City Hall were built in the 1960s, they symbolized the "New Boston." To create this new place, a large section of the city's downtown (a heavily congested area of old, low-rise buildings fronting narrow streets known as Scollay Square) was cleared away. Except for the 227-gallon steaming tea kettle—"the most beloved sign in Boston" (Southworth and Southworth 1992, 28)—there is little left to remind us of what the area was like before. Now, just 30 years after obliterating Scollay Square, the mayor seemed to be saying, "Oops, we shouldn't have done that!"

What Mayor Menino was suggesting was what Americans have done for generations. When presented with problems (first the decay of inner cities,

1-2   Government Center Plaza and Boston City Hall in 1978. The spire of the Old North Church is visible in the distance on the left.

Source: Gene Bunnell

1-3   Steaming tea kettle, hanging off the corner of the 1848 Sears Crescent Building overlooking Government Center Plaza—virtually all that remains of old Scollay Square.

Source: Gene Bunnell

then the decline and deterioration of inner-ring suburbs, and later the decline of second-generation suburbs), we retreat and move on—and leave the mess we have made behind.

Robert Campbell's response to what the mayor proposed was carried on the front page of the next day's edition of *The Boston Globe*. Campbell decried the proposal as yet another "depressing manifestation of a throwaway society. . . . We're always quicker to buy the latest fad than to nurture what we've got, and taking care of City Hall is something the city hasn't been good at." (Campbell, April 10, 1998, A1) Even the best-planned, best-designed places need a little attention paid to them.

The fact that we have become so pessimistic about our ability to make places better—and that our first instinct whenever things are no longer working quite right is to flee—is really quite sad. Happily, Mayor Menino's press conference proved to be nothing more than a "trial balloon," and the mayor backed off from his call for abandoning Boston City Hall. The mayor's ill-considered remarks should teach us an important lesson: *Places are forever, and walking away is not the answer.*

The exodus of growing numbers of Americans to deed-restricted "gated communities" is the latest, and in many ways the most troubling, manifestation of the retreat response. An economist viewing the growth and popularity of gated communities might be inclined to say that gated communities are simply responding to consumer preferences and that people are "voting with their feet." However, an alternative explanation might be that growing numbers of Americans have become fed up with living in communities where there is little or no planning and where development is entirely out of control.

Indeed, the rise of deed-restricted communities seems to have been particularly pronounced in areas where state and local approaches to land use planning and growth management have been fairly weak, and where citizens have been fiercest in asserting the primacy of the "rights" of private property owners over the rights of communities to plan and regulate land use and development in the public interest. In Phoenix, Arizona—one of the fastest growing metropolitan areas in the country—Joel Garreau reported that virtually all of the new, high-quality housing developments in the metropolitan area were deed-restricted communities.

The retreat of large numbers of Americans to deed-restricted communities is ironic. A major reason that many people have given for being unwilling to support public planning and land use regulation is that they haven't wanted someone telling them what they can (or can't) do with their property. However, when people move to deed-restricted communities, they are almost always subjected to a much higher degree of control and regulation than they would ever have been subjected to had they remained in a more traditional, publicly governed community.[1] Moreover, when people buy into deed-restricted com-

1-4   Entrance to deed-restricted community in Tampa, Florida.

Source: Gene Bunnell

munities, they give up the opportunity to shape the rules that govern the community in which they live, because the restrictions are written by developers and their lawyers before any residents have appeared on the scene, and are virtually impossible to change once they have already been placed on the deed. As a result, people living in deed-restricted communities are much less able to shape their community than people living in traditional communities where planning is undertaken through publicly established institutions and processes, and where residents are able to openly observe and participate in the crafting of policies and regulations that will shape their future.

CHOOSING TO BE A PLANNER

Each of us brings to our conversations and interactions a point of view shaped by our own personal backgrounds and experiences. It is therefore useful when reading a book to know something about the background and life experiences of the person whose words and ideas we are digesting. It is especially important when that person is presenting us with ideas that are controversial and make us uncomfortable. At the very least, it can help us understand why that person has come to believe certain things and hold certain views. Let me therefore tell you a little about how I became involved in urban planning and about some of the experiences that have shaped my point of view.

When I was in college in the 1960s, the subject of urban planning was very much in the news. Books and articles about the planning and design of cities were everywhere. National magazines such as *Time* and *Newsweek* had major cover stories focusing on cities. *Scientific American* published a book entitled *Cities* (1965) that drew attention to problems associated with the growth of cities throughout the world, and described how urban planners and policymakers were responding to those problems. Revitalization and renewal of cities were high priorities at state and local levels, and planners such as Ed Logue in Boston and Ed Bacon in Philadelphia were playing important and highly visible roles in reshaping their respective cities. Logue and Bacon were almost as well known as the mayors under which they served.

The fact that urban and regional planning was being viewed so positively undoubtedly influenced my choice of a career, as well as the career choices of many other young people in the 1960s. Graduate professional programs in urban planning were expanding and attracting some of the brightest and most idealistic college students. I applied and was accepted to the Harvard Graduate School of Design, and began a three-year program of study toward earning a master's degree in city and regional planning.

My first real-world planning experience began in 1973 when I was hired by the Massachusetts Department of Community Affairs' Office of Local Assistance to provide planning assistance to small- and medium-sized communities. Over a seven-year period, I worked with planning boards and local officials in dozens of Massachusetts communities on a wide range of land use and development issues. I also helped a number of communities prepare comprehensive plans, district improvement and downtown revitalization plans, and historic preservation plans.

In 1980, I became planning and development director of Northampton, Massachusetts (a city of roughly 30,000 people in western Massachusetts), a position I held for another seven years. In retrospect, I consider the work I did in Northampton the most important of my career. The work was particularly satisfying because I could readily discern the difference planning was making in Northampton, and how the plans and policies adopted and implemented in the city were making it a better place. Plans and policies often take many years to be fully realized, and more than 10 years after I left the employment of the city, projects and initiatives were still unfolding that were conceived and planned when I was planning director.

After working for two years as a planning consultant and teaching planning-related courses at Smith College, Hampshire College and the University of

Massachusetts at Amherst, I began studying for a Ph.D. degree in planning studies at the London School of Economics and Political Science. For the better part of three years, I studied British versus American approaches to shifting infrastructure costs to private developers, and earned a Ph.D. degree in 1993. In the fall of 1992, I joined the faculty of the University of Wisconsin at Madison, where I taught planning between 1992 and 1998.

The University of Wisconsin at Madison is a huge university with a total student enrollment of nearly 40,000, but its Department of Urban and Regional Planning was quite small. The department, which offered a two-year graduate master's degree program, was housed in Old Music Hall, a Victorian-style sandstone building (circa 1870) with a quaint charm and personality. (There were musical bars in the ancient blackboards—a reminder of when the building had been occupied by the music department before it moved to larger and more modern quarters.) On the other hand, there was no denying that the Department of Urban and Regional Planning had inherited one of the oldest and smallest buildings on campus. Worse still was the fact that the building was poorly equipped, had meager computer facilities for students, and the department existed on a shoe-string budget that provided a bare minimum for basic supplies and materials. Other schools and departments in the university did not seem to be suffering from the same low level of support.

Right next door to Old Music Hall, the Law School built a $16.5 million addition that tripled the size of the school's facilities. State money paid for $10 million of the cost; money donated by Law School alumni paid for $6.5 million. Around the same time and only a short distance away, an even grander building was built to house the School of Business at a cost of $40 million. In this case, private donors contributed $17.5 million. One family—the Grainger family—contributed $10 million.[2]

Upon entering Grainger Hall, the first thing one notices is a spacious atrium in the center that extends to the top of the building. Walkways on each level surround the atrium, providing people on upper levels with dramatic views of the hustle and bustle on the ground floor—reminiscent of many Hyatt Regency Hotels. Another prominent feature one sees upon entering the atrium is a row of clocks that give the time in New York, London, Paris, Frankfurt, Hong Kong and Tokyo—something one might expect to find on the trading floors of the stock exchanges in those international financial capitals or at Lloyds of London, but not in a university building.

Grainger Hall's comfortable lecture and seminar rooms are lavishly provided with all the latest high-tech equipment and have all the "bells and whistles" one could possibly imagine. The building even has its own gracious dining room, which provides a cozy, club-like atmosphere in which Business School faculty and students can host luncheon meetings in a business-like atmosphere. Indeed, these and many other features found in Grainger Hall were even more stunning when compared to the austere accommodations of the Department of Urban and Regional Planning.

In 1999, 46 students were enrolled in the two-year master's degree program at Wisconsin's Department of Urban and Regional Planning. Meanwhile, the University of Wisconsin Law School had an enrollment of 850 students, and 2,300 students were enrolled in undergraduate and graduate courses at the Business School.[3]

I do not mean to criticize those who have chosen to study law or business and pursue careers in those fields. Many lawyers have used their skills to fight for environmental protection and defend disadvantaged groups and communities. Likewise, some of the most innovative and successful approaches to problem-solving and organization-building have come out of schools of business and management.

I *am* suggesting, however, that the *imbalance* between the number of people studying law and business and the number of people we are training as community planners is indicative of a societal imbalance. Do we really need *quite* so many more lawyers? (We already have more lawyers per capita than any other country in the world.) Certainly, taking people to court—or threatening to take people to court—is not the only way of solving problems. Aren't there other ways of encouraging economic development than by simply producing more and more individuals with MBA degrees? The time has come to say something truly heretical: Perhaps it would be a good idea if we valued and encouraged planning a little more, and if a few more young people wanted to be urban and regional planners.

HOW LITTLE WE ARE INVESTING IN PLANNING

One of the unavoidable risks associated with being an urban planner is that I often find myself at social gatherings listening to people recite long lists of land use-related complaints which almost invariably end with something like, "There should have been better planning!" When I hear people say that, I find myself wondering if they have any idea how little is being invested in planning by their communities.

At the state and local levels, billions of dollars are spent each year on building roads and transportation facilities, schools, water and sewer systems, parks and recreation facilities, libraries and other community facilities. When we make these expenditures, we are in effect determining where development will occur and what the future will look like. However, these major infrastructure investments are frequently made with very little advance planning, and without considering the long-term impacts such investments are likely to have on land use and development at the local and regional levels. As Charles Siemon put it, ". . . we must invest in planning before we invest in any more infrastructure. We as a nation have the cart before the horse, and the trail of manure we have left behind the planning cart is beginning to pile up." (Siemon 1997, 246)

Rummaging through my files from when I was planning director in Northampton, I came across a piece of paper that listed the annual assessment that Northampton paid in the mid-1980s to the Lower Pioneer Valley Regional Planning Commission for regional planning services: $4,500 (equivalent to roughly 15 cents per resident). There are two ways of looking at that figure: (1) regional planning is a real bargain; or (2) the small sum paid to the regional planning agency is an indication of the low importance that city residents placed on regional planning. (I fear the latter is closer to the truth.)

Only a minority of American local governments (counties, cities, villages and towns) seriously engages in planning on an ongoing basis. Even in communities that have engaged in planning, planning has often been sporadic and undertaken in response to crises, and then forgotten about until the next crisis arises. A large proportion of the 81,000+ local governments in this country have never prepared or adopted a comprehensive plan. Additionally, a large proportion of local governments has not employed a full-time professional planner, nor have they ever hired a private planning consultant.

Wisconsin is generally regarded as being a fairly progressive state in terms of land use planning and environmental protection. It was one of the first states to adopt a state zoning-enabling legislation for cities and villages (1917), and was the first state to adopt zoning-enabling legislation for rural areas (1923). It was also the home of Aldo Leopold, the well-known conservationist whose book, *a Sand County almanac* (1949), written in and about the central sands area of Wisconsin, had an enormous influence over the years on the way people think about land and how it is used. Among the many notions communicated by Leopold was the importance of living "lightly" on the land, and of developing a land "ethic"—ideas that have strengthened the resolve of people in states across the country to work for the adoption of more responsible land use policies.

However, when I arrived in Wisconsin in 1992, I soon discovered that a majority of counties and local governments employed no land use planners, and that a substantial proportion of local governments had no zoning whatsoever. To many rural Wisconsin residents, the words "plan" and "zone" were *four-letter words*—more reviled than common swear words.

According to a large proportion of the people I met in Wisconsin, land use decisions were best left to individual private property owners, and *any* limitation whatsoever that was imposed on the ability of landowners to use their land as they wished was an unconstitutional infringement on the rights of private property owners. I also got the distinct sense that a large proportion of the people in Wisconsin, particularly those who lived outside of cities and villages, actually believed that having *no* plans and *no* land use controls produced better land use and better communities. Most were entirely comfortable with the idea of allowing changes in land use to be instituted at the whim of private property owners, without considering the impact those changes might have on neighboring properties, and the cumulative effects of individually made land use decisions on the community at large and on future generations.

Many Americans who are uncomfortable with the idea of planning seem to feel that planning is out of place in a free and democratic society. To their way of thinking, planning is a step down the slippery slope toward central government control and a loss of personal freedom. Indeed, this view seems to have become even more prevalent since the fall of communist regimes in Russia and eastern Europe—a turning point in world history that many interpret as having rendered the final judgment regarding the supreme wisdom and dominance of "the market" and the inadvisability of planning.

This perception misreads what planning in this country is all about. Planning is not a way of centralizing power or of taking important decision-making control away from the people; nor is it an activity that is conducted in secret, behind closed doors and out of public view. Quite the contrary, planning as practiced in most communities typically brings decision-making into the light

1-5   Sign in Indiana countryside. In the minds of many Americans, planning and zoning is un-American and communistic.

Source: James Segedy, Ball State University, Muncie, Indiana

of day, informs people about available choices and alternative courses of action, and provides a structured process that allows people to take part and make their views known.

When I was planning director in Northampton, I was amazed by how much coverage the local *Daily Hampshire Gazette* gave to the meetings of the city's planning board and zoning board of appeals, Historical Commission and Design Review Committee, and to zoning and land use issues in general. Most meetings were also televised and rebroadcast by the local cable access channel. The plus side of so much coverage was that people were kept informed about what their local government was doing—and thinking about doing—related to land use and development. On the other hand, it also gave people the impression that local government boards and commissions were very powerful and controlled a great deal of what was happening in the community, which was *not* true. In fact, most key decisions affecting land use and development in the city were being made privately, out of public view, and the vast majority of the development that was occurring was taking place "by right" without requiring any public approval whatsoever. The issues and matters with which local government agencies and boards were dealing, while important in individual cases, represented only the tip of the iceberg.

The real reason so much local news coverage was devoted to local government meetings was *not* that public plans and decisions were controlling land use and development; rather, it was because local government meetings were *easy* for the local press to cover because they were (and are) conducted out in the open, whereas meetings of landowners, developers and/or private businesses that result in decisions that affect land use and development are conducted in private. To cover such private decision-making sessions requires investigative-style reporting, which is extremely difficult and time-consuming. In fact, it was the very *transparency* of local government proceedings that made them so attractive as the subject of local reporting.

The fear that many people in this country have of planning is curious given how little inherent power planners have to insist that the policies they recommend be adopted and implemented. (In only a few states, local governments are *required* by state statute to prepare plans; in even fewer states are local governments required to follow and implement officially adopted plans.) A close examination of the distribution of power and authority in most local governments reveals that planning agencies typically have considerably less power than other city agencies and departments. The only way planners in this country can influence the future is through their ability to inspire and persuade.

In my opinion, one reason why Americans have been blind to planning successes is that, in a perverse way and on a possibly unconscious level, we have *wanted* planning to fail. Not that we are necessarily conscious of wanting planning to fail, but believing that planning rarely succeeds does validate and reinforce the widely held American belief that market forces, and minimal governmental intervention and regulation, produce the best outcomes.

THE BELIEF THAT PLANNING NEVER WORKS

Everywhere you look, there is evidence that unplanned and unregulated development often produces outcomes that are contrary to the long-term best interests of communities and are damaging to the environment. Still, many people remain hesitant to endorse or support public sector planning. Essentially, their rationale for *not* planning is, "Yes, in an ideal world, it would be nice if we could make communities better by planning, but plans never work. Not only that, they often end up making things worse."

Even people who have taught and written about planning have contributed to the notion that planning never works. One of the people whose writings I have most admired over the years is John W. Reps, a long-time professor of urban planning and planning history at Cornell University. Among Reps' many books and articles on planning, my favorite is *The Making of Urban America—A History of City Planning in the United States* (1965). Nevertheless, reading through a volume of scholarly papers published under the title of *Environment and Change* in 1968, I read a paper quoting Reps as having said that, "Nowhere in this country can one find a major city or a major sector of an important city which in the present era has been developed as planned. It is not a case of an occasional departure from an officially adopted plan. It is not even a situation where a majority of cities do not grow as planned. It is, rather, a record of complete and consistent failure." (Feiss 1968, 218)

Admittedly, many American cities have not grown and developed according to plan. I would even agree that a majority of American cities that have prepared plans have not adhered to them. However, the statement reportedly made by Reps (as quoted above) is just plain wrong. Any number of cities in this country has been shaped by plans and planning. In fact, the planning case studies presented in this book are proof.

One reason why people tend to believe that planning never works is because the term "plan" is so egregiously overused and misapplied. Almost every time a problem arises in a community, someone will almost immediately step forward to propose a "plan" to solve it. In most cases, what is being presented is *not* a plan. There can be no "plan" if there has been no *planning*—no gathering of data, no defining of a community's long-range goals, and no identification and evaluation of alternative courses of action.

More often than not, what is being called a "plan" is nothing more than a preconceived solution to a predefined problem (or, to put it more honestly, a solution in *search* of an application). Some recognized "experts," who are very successful as consultants, unfortunately engage in this practice by peddling their favored solutions to communities eager for quick, simple answers. For such individuals—experts at marketing a single idea or approach—every community presents an opportunity for applying their favored solution. In certain cases, the single answer or approach offered may do some good, but it isn't *planning* in the true sense of the word. Real planning involves devising unique solutions for unique places.

Another reason why people might be led to believe that planning never succeeds is that they have gotten the impression that the aim of planning is to make communities perfect; that if it falls short of that, then planning has failed. The purpose of planning is *not* to make communities perfect, nor is it reasonable to expect or require that *everything* unfold according to plan. Rather, the real reason for planning is to make communities better than they would have been in the absence of planning.

Another reason for believing that planning never or rarely produces desirable outcomes is that planning failure stories attract much more attention than planning success stories, just as "bad news" catches our attention more than "good news." Peter Hall knew that when he wrote the book *Great Planning Disasters* (1982), a title virtually guaranteed to attract attention. (It certainly caught mine when I was browsing in a bookstore.)

When I read Hall's book, I found that few of the seven case studies presented shed much light on the planning issues most American communities are facing. One case focused on the flawed decision-making process that led Britain and France to develop and produce the Supersonic Concorde airplane—despite clear evidence that the plane would not be economical to operate, and that there was little worldwide need or demand for it. While the case study on the Concorde reveals how easy it is for countries to invest immense amounts in costly and wasteful undertakings simply out of a desire to enhance national pride, it has little to do with the kinds of problems and issues with which urban planners deal.

Two case studies in Hall's book focus on proposed major transportation infrastructure projects in Britain. One describes the conflicting interests and political posturing that made it impossible to reach a rational decision on the siting and development of a third London airport; the other describes the difficulties encountered in planning limited access highways around and through London.

Two additional case studies in *Great Planning Disasters* will be of greater interest to American readers. One tells about the planning of the San Francisco Bay Area Rapid Transit (BART) system—the highly automated rapid transit system which was planned in the 1950s and first began operating in 1973. According to Hall, the operational failures that plagued BART in its early years were largely due to the obsession of transportation engineers with untested new technologies. He also faults the project for major cost overruns.

Three decades later, Hall's criticisms seem almost like nit-picking and pale into insignificance when viewed in light of the longer term impacts and benefits of the BART system. Ask today's citizens of the San Francisco Bay Area to try to imagine what moving about the city would be like without BART on city streets and highways or by public transit, and ask them if they believe that the Bay Area would be a better place today if BART had not been built.

In *Transit Villages in the 21st Century*, Michael Bernick and Robert Cervero report that, "When BART was first conceived in the early 1950s, planners hoped a modern-era rail system would guide future population and employment growth in the region ... and that BART [would] strengthen the Bay Area's urban centers while guiding suburban growth along radial corridors, leading to a star-shaped, multicentered metropolitan form." (Bernick and Cervero 1997, 164) Indeed, a BART impact study undertaken 25 years after the system began operating found that BART transit stations had served as magnets for development. Job growth in zip codes with BART stations was nearly three times as great as in zip codes without BART stations, and population and housing densities in areas in proximity to BART stations were considerably higher than in areas not served by BART. If the goal was to combat sprawl and create concentrated, mixed-use, transit-oriented communities, BART most certainly was not a disaster.

The other case in Hall's *Great Planning Disasters* I found revealing described the planning, design and construction of the Sydney Opera House in Sydney, Australia. The process of planning Sydney's opera house began in 1954, and 30 different sites were evaluated before a final site was selected. In 1955, a worldwide design competition for the design of the opera house was announced, which attracted 233 submissions from 32 countries. In January 1957, the winning design by John Utzon (a 38-year-old Danish architect) was announced.

As in the BART case, Hall is critical of the failure to foresee technical problems and cost overruns that resulted from trying to do something innovative. Indeed, the soaring roof of the Sydney Opera House designed by Utzon (which gave the appearance of a series of sails of varying heights and sizes) was so complicated that no one at the time (including Utzon himself) could be sure it could actually be built. Constructing the building was so difficult that the opera house wasn't completed and dedicated until October 1973—nearly 20 years after the project began.

Once again, the passage of time allows us to step back and view the outcome from a longer term perspective. The decision to place an innovatively designed structure on the most prominent site on Sydney Harbor now looks like a stroke of genius, and I suspect few people would agree with Hall's assertion that the undertaking was a planning disaster. Far from it, the Sydney Opera House is one of the most widely recognized and admired buildings in the world today. As I write this in the year 2000 (the year of the 2000 Sydney Olympics), magazines, newspapers and television programs are filled with pictures and representations of the Sydney Opera House. When people see a picture of the unique sail-like outlines of the opera house, they automatically think of Sydney, Australia; the building has come to symbolize the place. If one of the important aims of planning is to create a sense of place, then the process that led to the design and development of the Sydney Opera House must be regarded as a smashing success.

FAILING TO RECOGNIZE THE VALUE OF PLANNING

In November 1980 (two months after I became planning and development director in Northampton, Massachusetts), voters in the state passed Proposition 2-1/2 (a statewide ballot measure that imposed stringent limits on what local governments could spend and on the amount of money they could collect in local property taxes).[4] As a result of Proposition 2-1/2, local governments in most cities and towns in Massachusetts faced the need to sharply reduce their total level of local spending. A crisis atmosphere prevailed in Northampton and across the state, as city officials looked for programs and activities they could cut or eliminate. One of the *first* places where cuts were proposed was in the area of planning.

Other municipal departments that provided services and operated facilities, which were easily discernible and highly valued (schools and education, roads, garbage collection, street lighting, water and sewer, parks and recreation, police and fire), had a core of vocal supporters who could be relied upon to insist that funding be maintained for those particular services and facilities. Although planning potentially affected all of those service areas, planning was not solely identified with any one of them and therefore lacked a core constituency of supporters. Planning is a relatively invisible activity, and the difference planning makes in communities is often qualitative, subtle and unclear until after many years have passed.

In the highly political, crisis-ridden atmosphere that prevailed, city officials obviously felt great pressure to maintain funding for departments that produced the most obvious and immediate benefits (and whose absence or reduction would be most quickly noticed). A number of city councilors were therefore attracted to the idea of significantly reducing the budget of the planning department. One city councilor even called for the total elimination of the planning department. (Ironically, the amount of funding the city was investing in planning was so small that cutting the *entire* planning budget would have done little to alleviate the budget shortfall. The city's planning department at the time was composed only of the director, a senior planner and a secretary.)

As I watched the proceedings and pondered the fate of the planning department, I realized the importance of documenting and communicating the positive difference planning makes in communities, and of reminding people that planning, when done well, produces value and benefits that far exceed its costs. Planning is the *last* thing—not the *first* thing—that a community should cut from the local budget.

Around the time I began working in Northampton, the city's Main Street, which ran through the center of the city's downtown historic district, was about to be reconstructed as part of a federally funded "Urban Systems" highway project. The city agency primarily responsible for the project was the Engineering Division of the Department of Public Works (DPW), which in turn had hired a Boston-based engineering firm to prepare the detailed plan. I was new on the job, but it did not take long for me to realize that, as the city's planning director, I had little or no authority related to the planning of the highway project, and that the engineers at the DPW were not terribly interested in any thoughts or suggestions I might have regarding the project.

Even so, I thought I should at least review the plan. I contacted the engineering firm in Boston and they agreed to review the plan with me at their office. When I did, I noticed that it called for widening Main Street just north of its intersection with State Route 5/10 (Pleasant and King Streets). Main Street was already very wide at this point (wider than anywhere else on what was already a very wide street), and widening it further struck me as altogether unnecessary. Widening the road was also going to make the sidewalk in front of the Hampshire County courthouse narrower. A bus stop and bus shelter were located in front of the courthouse, and the road widening was going to make the sidewalk so narrow that it was going to be impossible to place the bus shelter the way it had previously been placed (back a few feet from the curb, with the opening of the shelter facing toward the street).

The only way to widen the road and leave pedestrians enough room to walk behind the bus shelter was to push the shelter forward toward the street—up to the edge of the curb—and turn the shelter completely around so that its opening faced *away* from the street. Otherwise, people would have had to walk into the street to enter the shelter. I could imagine people standing in the shelter, peering out through its scratched Plexiglas side walls, straining to see if a bus was coming and then, when the bus arrived, backing out and circling around the shelter to get to the bus.

I asked the highway engineer at the consulting firm whether it was absolutely necessary to widen Main Street so much and make the sidewalk in front of the courthouse so narrow. "Could you add back 3 or 4 feet to the width of the sidewalk in front of the courthouse?" I asked. He said he would try, and that is what ultimately happened. Some months later, I was told by an engineer at the DPW, "That's not how things are supposed to be done. You had no authority to ask for the change." He was right, but I'm still glad I spoke up.

Probably no one else who walks down the sidewalk, or waits for a bus in front of the courthouse, thinks anything of it. After all, it's really not very different than what it was before Main Street was reconstructed, except that I know what would have happened had I not been the city's planning director. It is a small difference, but small differences can add up over time and end up making a big difference in communities.

A year or two later, a ribbon-cutting ceremony was held opening a 3.5-mile-long bikeway constructed along an abandoned railroad right of way that ran from downtown Northampton to the village of Florence and Look Park (a large public park). The mayor and the chairman of the DPW presided over the ceremony, which was covered by the local newspapers, the local radio station and a Springfield TV station. Prior to cutting the ribbon, the mayor thanked many of the people who had played a role in making the bikeway a reality, such as the state representative who supported the project *once it was conceived and planned* and the DPW that built the bike path. Standing toward the back of the audience, I noticed the lack of any mention of the planners who conceived the project, conducted the studies that established the feasibility of the project and sold it to local officials, and prepared the grant application that qualified the project for state funding.

1-6 Sidewalk and bus shelter in front of the Hampshire County courthouse on Main Street in downtown Northampton, Massachusetts.

Source: Gene Bunnell

Most of the planning work related to the Look Park bike path was done long before I became Northampton's planning director, so I deserved very little credit for the project. However, planners who preceded me in Northampton (such as York Phillips and Nancy Stack) and planners at the Pioneer Valley Regional Planning Commission did. Unfortunately, planning typically takes many years to bear fruit. As a result, when plans are finally realized, the people who did the planning are often no longer on the scene to accept some small measure of credit.

An even lengthier planning process (requiring the cooperation of planners working for the City of Northampton, the Town of Amherst and the Pioneer Valley Regional Planning Commission) helped bring about the 8.5-mile-long Norwottuck bike trail that connects Northampton and Amherst. An essential step toward making the Norwottuck bike trail possible was taken when the Massachusetts Department of Environmental Management agreed to purchase an abandoned Boston and Maine Railroad right of way leading from the City of Northampton on the west, across the Connecticut River, through the Town of Hadley, to just south of the center of the Town of Amherst.

However, the Norwottuck bike trail would not have been possible had it not been for Northampton's farsighted acquisition of land along the western shoreline of the Connecticut River—an acquisition that ultimately provided the toe hold and embarkation point and parking area for the bikeway. That critical conservation property acquisition (a negotiated purchase from the Elwell family) brought into public ownership a tract of land along the western shore of the Connecticut River north of the Coolidge Bridge and the intersection of Route 9, Damon Road and Interstate 91, as well as an island just off-shore in the river, which someday (as a result of sedimentation processes) will be joined to the western shore. The impetus for acquiring the Elwell property came from Northampton's planning staff working with the city's Conservation Commission.[5]

Planners working for the city succeeded in obtaining state and federal grant commitments to pay for 90% of the cost of acquiring the Elwell property. All the City of Northampton had to do was to pay 10% of the cost ($3,000). Today, looking back, it seems inconceivable that the city might have turned down the opportunity to secure and preserve a key parcel of Connecticut River shoreline when all it had to pay was $3,000 (the total budget of the City of Northampton at the time was roughly $35 million). Nevertheless, getting the city council to agree to appropriate $3,000 to acquire a parcel of land for conservation purposes was extremely difficult.

I remember being at the city council meeting and observing how strongly opposed some city councilors were to the idea of acquiring land for conservation purposes and "taking it off the tax roles." I also recall how skeptical many were as to the value of providing a dedicated right of way for bicyclists and pedestrians. Many openly questioned whether anyone would ever use it. After prolonged discussion and bickering, the council grudgingly approved the expenditure. The Elwell property now serves as the beginning point (and end point) of the bike path in Northampton. Crews of rowers, who row on the Connecticut River, also use the property as their embarkation point and store their "shells" in a storage facility on the property.

A few years ago, I returned to Northampton with my wife. We brought along our bicycles so we could ride the bike path from Northampton to Amherst and back. (The bike path was completed after we had moved away, and this was our first opportunity to see and experience it first-hand.) Along the way we saw people on bicycles, people walking, young and old couples arm in arm, and young families with small children in tow and infants in strollers. It was an experience I will never forget—a quiet, personal reminder that planning does make a difference. At the same time, I could not help thinking that probably only a few of the people who were using and enjoying the bike path realized that it was brought about by planning.[6]

I mention this, and the previous matter of the sidewalk and bus shelter in front of the county courthouse, to illustrate a simple point. Planning *does* make a positive difference and the difference is often readily visible "on the ground." Indeed, within the 35-square-mile area of the City of Northampton, I can iden-

1-7   Western segment of Norwottuck bike trail crossing the Connecticut River on a restored former railroad bridge.

Source: Gene Bunnell

tify any number of projects and land use outcomes that either owe their existence to planning or were made better as a result of planning.

One of the reasons why the benefits of planning are so easily overlooked is that they are often best measured in terms of the things that *didn't* happen and the developments that *didn't* get built. (In this regard, measuring the benefits of planning is somewhat like trying to count the number of people who don't walk through a door.) In other cases, the benefits of planning are even subtler and harder to recognize. Many of the development projects that are reviewed and ultimately approved by local planning bodies are far from perfect. However, having sat through many long planning meetings, I know how much *worse* many of these developments would have turned out had the citizen members of the planning board not taken their responsibilities so seriously.

AMERICANS' YEARNING FOR SPECIAL PLACES

During the years I lived in Madison, Wisconsin, I got in the habit of listening to a weekly radio program called "Whad'YaKnow?" that originated from Madison, hosted by Michael Feldman. While listening to this program on a regular basis, I realized how attached most people in this country were to the places they called "home."

A regular feature on "Whad'YaKnow?" was the "Town of the Week." Each week, a new "Town of the Week" was selected by having someone in the audience throw a dart at a map of the United States. The town closest to where the dart landed automatically became "Town of the Week." Someone was selected at random from the local phone directory and was asked to describe what people did there for fun and what they especially liked about living there.

Many of the places chosen as "Town of the Week" were pretty small and ordinary places and, on the surface, seemed to possess little that was special or exceptional. Nevertheless, people almost always found something positive to say about their communities and many actually succeeded in making them sound perfectly delightful—even though the reality in many cases may have fallen far short of their rosy descriptions.

Most Americans want the places they call "home" to be special. Unfortunately, simply *wanting* communities to be special is often not enough to *make* them special. The nub of the problem is that, although most Americans *want* their communities to have the kind of qualities that stand the test of time, they have been remarkably hesitant to support the development of plans and policies that could create and preserve those qualities. As Peter Hall put it, planning in the United States is almost a "contradiction in terms." (Hall 1975, 247)

Americans are enthusiastic tourists and love to travel to places that are unique. Driven by a hunger to see and experience special places, large numbers of Americans travel each year to Europe to experience cities and see landscapes that are a welcome relief from the ones we experience on a daily basis in this country. When Americans come back from European vacations, they frequently rave about the compact, pedestrian-oriented city centers they visited and experienced, and about the lack of sprawl. Indeed, something simple and wonderful strikes most Americans about European cities and landscapes: there is a generally clear distinction between urban and rural places. That simple fact was powerfully driven home to me when I was traveling on a train out of London through miles of dense urban development. Then, all of a sudden, we were traveling through lush green countryside, speeding through the 5-mile-wide Greenbelt that surrounds London (the product of the 1943 Greater London plan).[7]

Listening to friends who have returned from European vacations tell about what they saw, I have often wondered how many of them have thought about *why* European cities and countrysides are so different from those in the U.S. How many people who appreciate the beauty of the English countryside have stopped to wonder how a country as densely populated as England has been able to preserve so much open countryside?

One of the biggest mistakes we make in this country is to frame the debate over the advisability of planning in partisan political and ideological terms. Many Americans assume that people who support planning are liberal and people who oppose planning are conservative. During the three years I spent in England doing Ph.D. research, I learned how very wrong this stereotype is. When former Prime Minister Margaret Thatcher sought to implement a series of measures designed to weaken the power of local authority plans and planning controls, she faced strong opposition from within her own Conservative party. In Britain, land use planning is not a partisan issue. Indeed, there was as much support for planning among Conservatives as among members of the Labour party. Ms. Thatcher's attempts to weaken the British planning system were largely unsuccessful. Planning was not just supported by people on the "loony left" (a favorite expression of hers), but rather enjoyed broad-based support across the political spectrum, for sound and practical reasons.

SO MANY BOOKS, BUT SOMETHING IS MISSING

Many books have been written over the years addressing various aspects of the broad subject of urban planning and urban design. Remarkably few books, however, have been written for a general readership to help people understand and appreciate how particular places have been positively shaped by planning.

Admittedly, many books have been written about specific land use problems and issues such as growth management, open space and farmland preservation, etc. Books that focus on a single problem can be very informative and bring to light creative solutions that are potentially applicable to many different communities. However, when people focus on a single issue, they can tend to forget that good places are rarely created or maintained by focusing on just one issue or problem. To create and maintain livable communities, it is necessary to think about the *whole* community, and to develop and implement plans and strategies that address multiple problems and issues simultaneously.

Many "how to" books have been published—for professional planners as well as citizen planners—promoting particular planning processes, methods and regulatory tools. These books have sought to improve the quality of community planning and design by highlighting "best practices," and by showcasing successful development approaches and solutions as models to be replicated in other communities. However, citizens in communities have to *want* developers to do better—and have to *believe* they *can do* better—for such books to be used as a resource.

Recent books provide encouraging evidence that positive change *is* possible in cities. However, none of these books, in my opinion, adequately focus on and/or describe the role that state and local planning have played in reviving cities and communities.

In *Comeback Cities—A Blueprint for Urban Neighborhood Revival* (2000), Paul Grogan and Tony Proscio report that positive changes are occurring in cities across the country, and that prospects for the future of American cities are brighter than they have been in decades. The rebirth of cities and urban neighborhoods, they say, has been brought about by a surprising convergence of four trends: (1) grassroots organizing efforts and the formation of neighborhood-based, nonprofit development corporations; (2) the reappearance of functioning, inner-city real estate markets, due in large part to federal immigration policies that have allowed large numbers of people from other countries to migrate to America and settle in cities; (3) dropping crime rates (due in large part, Grogan and Proscio believe, to altered methods of community policing); and (4) the tide of reform in public education, public housing and welfare prompted by the previous failures of government programs and policies in those areas. On the last point, the authors applaud the steps that have been taken to force public school systems to compete with charter, private and religious schools for public funding and students, and take strong ideological positions on welfare and public housing reform.

My intent here is not to respond to or critique the specific arguments Grogan and Proscio put forward, but rather to note that the social and demographic changes, political changes and reform movements about which they have written have little to do with the issues that urban planners and planning agencies at the state and local levels have been empowered to deal—except perhaps indirectly and after the fact.

In *Cities Back From the Edge—new life for downtown* (1998), Roberta Grandes Gratz and Norman Mintz provide brief descriptions of a large number of urban success stories intermixed with tales of ill-advised actions in other cities and towns that have produced outcomes that they regard as utterly horrible. Unfortunately, the accounts they provide are abbreviated and sketchy, and not detailed enough for the reader to understand why *some* communities were able to make wise land use and development decisions but not others. In addition, not enough background information is provided to enable the reader to judge the significance of the various outcomes they describe, because they are largely presented as isolated events rather than as part of a much broader historical, social, economic, political and institutional context.[8]

Alexander Garvin's *The American City—What Works, What Doesn't* (1996) is an impressive volume that describes a remarkable number of land use and development outcomes in American cities, ranging from slum clearance to historic preservation projects, and from parks and playgrounds to downtown development and revitalization projects. All of the places and projects described in the book are places that Garvin has personally seen and experienced, and most of the photographs in the book were taken by the author. *The American City— What Works, What Doesn't* is therefore an extremely important contribution to the literature on urban growth and change.

Nevertheless, despite its stunning range and the richness of its place descriptions, the book leaves many important aspects of planning practice—and the full range of impacts that planning and urban design policies and plans can have on communities—largely unilluminated. Garvin defines planning as a public action that is intended to produce a sustained and widespread private market reaction. This way of defining planning suggests that the efficacy of planning is best established when profit-motivated real estate developers respond to plans by providing something that consumers want and buy. It specifically ignores the possibility that plans and policies might run *counter* to what developers want and still produce a positive outcome. Indeed, Edward Jepson—who used *The American City—What Works and What Doesn't* as the text for an urban planning course he taught at the University of Wisconsin at Milwaukee—reports (through personal communication in 2000) that, "Throughout the book, there are subtle comments and inferences that public plans and policies are often an obstacle to the development of good cities."

One book I expected would provide hard evidence of the value of planning was *Planning America's Communities—Paradise Found? Paradise Lost?* (1991) by Herbert H. Smith, which had a lengthy chapter on "Four Cities That Made Planning Work," and another describing the experiences of four other cities that "Tried."[9] Upon rereading the book, however, I realized that *Planning America's Communities* was "preaching to the choir." Smith assumed that his readers already agreed with him that planning was a good idea and that, if cities would plan, good things would happen. He failed to grasp the fact that the logic of planning is not obvious to most Americans. Planning is not an *end* in itself; rather, it is a necessary *means* for achieving outcomes that people value in communities. For people to accept the notion that planning is worthwhile and necessary, they have to believe that planning can make a positive difference.

One book that does convey an appreciation of the positive qualities that planning can achieve in all kinds of communities (those that are stagnant and in decline as well as those that are growing) is *Save Our Land, Save Our Towns* (1995) by Thomas Hylton. This well-written book, subtitled *A Plan for Pennsylvania*, is filled with beautiful color photographs of people and places, and provides a remarkably comprehensive overview of the varied landscapes and community characteristics that planning can benefit, protect and strengthen.

Many books have been written over the years expressing outrage at the mess we are making of the American landscape, and the extent to which we seem to be bent on eradicating everything special and unique about particular places. The publication of *God's Own Junkyard* (1964) by Peter Blake was one such outburst: "This book is not written in anger. It is written in fury—though not, I trust, in blind fury. It is a deliberate attack upon all those who have already befouled a large portion of this country for private gain, and are engaged in befouling the rest." (Blake 1964, 7)

Blake's fiery rhetoric got people's attention and *God's Own Junkyard* became a best seller, but it didn't change what was happening to the American landscape. Over 35 years later, it is still going on.

The latest writer to try to shame people into caring more about what our communities look like is James Howard Kunstler, the author of *Geography of Nowhere* (1993) and *Home From Nowhere* (1996). Kunstler is a strong advocate of the New Urbanist approach to community design—a philosophy with which most planners I know agree. However, you would never know that from reading Kunstler, who repeatedly blames planners for foisting zoning ordinances on communities that have mandated sprawl, and for just about every terrible thing that has happened to cities and suburbs since World War II. People who work on the staffs of local government planning departments are singled out for especially harsh criticism. In Kunstler's opinion, any planner who works in a government planning department rather than as a private consultant must, by definition, be incompetent. Thus he urges, whenever possible, to "bypass the inevitable incompetence of government agencies . . ." (Kunstler 1996, 158)

In addition to castigating planners, Kunstler also condemns builders, developers and bankers, and questions the motives and intelligence of people who hold elected office and citizens who serve on local boards and commissions. He also blames ordinary citizens for not insisting on higher standards of civic design. After lambasting planners in Cleveland for allowing a suburban-style strip mall in an inner-city neighborhood, Kunstler blames neighborhood citizens as well. "My guess is that they may be doing this because the impoverished and uneducated citizens of the inner city see these things on television and demand stuff like it." (*ibid.,* 163)

Throughout *Home from Nowhere*, Kunstler criticizes the rigidity of zoning rules and calls for the abolition of zoning. Ironically, because he has so little faith in people, he can't trust them to see the wisdom of the new community order he is advocating. "In the absence of a new widespread consensus about how to build a better everyday environment, we'll have to replace the old set of rules with an explicit set of new rules." (*ibid.*, 114)

Kunstler's style of writing is very engaging and amusing, and his books have drawn attention to some important planning issues. In my experience, however, insulting people is not the way to win them over. The best way to win people over is to respect their intelligence and good intentions, and appeal to their best instincts.

As the above discussion illuminates, there is no shortage of books on urban planning and development-related topics and issues. The problem is that there are few case-study accounts of the process of deliberate community change that shed light on the motivations and intentions of groups and individuals who have engaged in planning. The six case studies presented by Neal R. Peirce and Robert Guskind in *Breakthroughs: Re-Creating the American City* (1993) come the closest to what I think we need more of in the planning literature—accounts that are sufficiently detailed to provide an understanding of *how* and *why* specific outcomes have resulted in specific communities. The value of case studies is twofold: (1) they provide an understanding of the local context, which is essential to understanding the significance of particular outcomes; and (2) they can help explain not only *what* happened but also *why* things happened, by shedding light on people's motivations and on what they intended when they took certain actions and made certain decisions.

FILLING THE GAP

A number of years ago, I wrote a book to convince people that preserving and reusing old buildings had practical advantages. The message of the book was simply this: *reusing old buildings is not just a nice idea*. The value of saving and reusing old and historic buildings now seems fairly obvious to most people but, back in the 1970s when I wrote the book, many people (including elected officials and developers) considered it unnecessary and impractical. To many, preserving and reusing old buildings was a luxury, not a necessity, and was of no importance whatsoever except to "little old rich ladies in tennis shoes."

My book, *Built To Last* (1977), was not written for "little old rich ladies in tennis shoes" or for people who were already convinced of the value of historic preservation. Instead, I set out to write a book directed at people who had never before thought about the importance of preserving and renovating old buildings, as well as at people who were fundamentally opposed to the idea.

Twenty-five years later, a similar book is needed to remind Americans of something else that should be equally obvious but that is also generally overlooked: *planning can and does make a positive difference in communities.* This book, therefore, presents a series of "planning stories" about *real* places that have been positively shaped by planning. These stories do more than describe beneficial changes and outcomes that communities have achieved. They also describe the planning processes that produced those positive outcomes.

NOTES

1. For an excellent description of the controls and restrictions imposed on residents living in deed-restricted communities, see *Privatopia—Homeowner Associations and the Rise of Residential Private Government* (1994) by Evan McKenzie.

2. Most students who earn master's degrees in urban and regional planning go on to work for local or state government agencies, or for consulting firms that provide planning services to those agencies on a contract basis. Because the amount of money that planners earn is largely dependent upon what local, county and state governments spend on planning (which, in most cases, is the bare minimum they can get away with), planners tend to earn considerably less than people who enter the fields of law or business, and are rarely in a position to make major financial gifts to the schools of urban and regional planning that trained them. A $10 million gift from a single donor, such as the one that helped build the University of Wisconsin's new Grainger School of Business, is highly unlikely.

3. A central tenet of business school education is the importance of corporate planning and of developing a solid business plan. There is therefore a certain irony in the fact that schools of business have become so popular at a time when schools of planning have fallen out of favor.

4. Once Proposition 2-1/2 was approved, no municipality in Massachusetts could levy and collect property taxes that exceeded 2-1/2% of the total assessed value of property in the municipality. Any subsequent increase in the property tax levy thereafter was limited to a maximum

of 2-1/2% per year. The only way a local government could increase its property tax levy more than 2-1/2% in a given year was by holding a referendum and obtaining *two-thirds* voter approval for the tax increase.

5. Some of the most bitter criticism I received as Northampton's planning director resulted from my efforts to prevent a parcel of private land adjacent to the Elwell property from being developed as a Friendly's Ice Cream restaurant, and discourage the Hampshire County Commission from making the restaurant development more likely by discontinuing a part of what had been an old county road. Had the restaurant been built, the Norwottuck bike trail would probably not have come to fruition, and congestion problems at the intersection of Damon Road and Route 9, already serious, would have become appreciably worse.

6. At the time this was written, a quarter-mile gap remains between the end of the Look Park bike path and the beginning of the Norwottuck bike trail. Planners at the City of Northampton and the Pioneer Valley Regional Planning Commission have developed preliminary plans to link the two bikeways, but the funding needed for this expensive bikeway segment has not yet been found.

7. The 1943 Greater London plan, developed by Patrick Abercrombie, imposed a Greenbelt around London, 5 miles wide on average, at the point where the outward spread of development had stopped at the outbreak of war in 1939. The Greenbelt, according to Hall, provided "an effective barrier to growth, and also . . . a valuable recreational tract for Londoners." (Hall 1975, 96) The imposition of the Greenbelt also helped achieve Ebenezer Howard's planning vision, put forward a half century earlier, of accommodating future population growth in completely new, self-contained, planned "New Towns" with housing and employment 20 to 35 miles from London. If and when you visit England, you will find a number of planned New Towns just outside of the Greenbelt (such as Stevenage, Hatfield, Welwyn, Harlow, Bracknell, Crawley and Basildon).

8. At one point in *Cities Back From the Edge—new life for downtown* (1998), Gratz and Mintz applaud Guilford, Connecticut's decision to reject nearly $1 million in federal and state highway money that could have been used to widen a state highway through the town. Highway-widening projects have been carried out in countless communities across the country with nary a whimper out of the local citizenry. What made Guilford different? Was this an isolated event, or was there a fairly long history in Guilford of attempting to manage and control growth in order to maintain the character of the town? Who in the community helped mobilize opposition to the highway-widening project and convinced local officials that they should reject the state and federal funding? The brief description that Gratz and Mintz provide does not answer these questions. Simply reporting that a Connecticut town turned back state and federal funds to widen a highway does not enable the reader to judge whether it was an enlightened action based on a broadly framed, inclusive vision of the future, or a narrowly conceived action by a privileged suburban community desirous of maintaining its privilege. Only by understanding more about a place, and the nature and extent of the planning that has gone on in that community, can one understand the significance and meaning of such an action, and the motives and intentions underlying them.

9. The four cities, according to Smith, "That Made Planning Work" were: Portland, Oregon; Charlotte, North Carolina; Minneapolis, Minnesota; and Pittsburgh, Pennsylvania. The four cities that Smith suggests "Tried" but fell short were: Baltimore, Maryland; San Diego, California; Denver, Colorado; and St. Paul, Minnesota.

2

Good Places

We ought to know how to assemble a human habitat of high quality that equitably allows citizens of all classes to get around in a dignified, comfortable, even pleasurable manner, that gives children and old people equal access to society's civic institutions, that produces safe neighborhoods for the well-off and the less well-off, that promotes a sense of belonging to a community, that honors what is beautiful, and which doesn't destroy its rural and agricultural surroundings.

—JAMES HOWARD KUNSTLER (*HOME FROM NOWHERE*, 1996, 78)

INTRODUCTION

It is impossible to engage in planning without making value judgments concerning the relative desirability or undesirability of possible future outcomes. If all possible future outcomes were equally desirable, then we would have no reason to plan. Outcomes related to the issues of how land is used and how communities are developed can be very different and do matter a great deal. Indeed, the main reason people in communities are motivated to plan is that they hope to shift future changes in the direction of certain outcomes rather than others.

What qualities and characteristics should we try to introduce and strengthen in order to make better communities? What qualities and characteristics have planners valued and sought to strengthen in communities? What kinds of outcomes have planners sought to achieve and what outcomes have they sought to avoid? This chapter addresses these important questions.

During the mid-1980s, a development boom swept through New England as it did through many other parts of the country. Cities and towns in New England that had seen little or no development for decades—and even generations—absorbed a large amount of new development in a remarkably short period of time. Most communities were caught completely unprepared.

The "boom" left a permanent mark on many communities. Its most noticeable physical effect was a more sprawling and disorganized pattern of land use and development. A less visible—but no less important—impact was on the quality of people's lives. People found themselves driving longer distances between home and work, and spending more time on the road stuck in traffic.

I was planning director in Northampton, Massachusetts at the time and I recall how long the planning board meetings lasted during that period, as the board reviewed one new subdivision proposal after another. I also recall how distressed people were when forests and wooded hillsides behind their homes were cleared, and when new homes on large lots started popping up in large numbers in previously remote rural areas.

Prior to the development boom, there had been very little vocal public support for the work of Northampton's planning department, and some city officials had even proposed disbanding the department. Once development had accelerated, however, people quickly became very interested in planning. The problem was that they wanted something done *right away.* They didn't recognize that, to manage growth successfully and achieve a desired pattern of land use and development, it is necessary to *plan ahead* and develop plans and policies *before* development has manifested itself. Once applications for subdivision approval and building permits have been submitted in accordance with existing regulatory provisions, there is really very little a community can do to change the rules of the game.

The total population of Northampton in 1990 was not very different from what it was in 1980, because the increase in the number of housing units in the city was offset by a decrease in household size. Nevertheless, the city underwent tremendous change during the decade of the 1980s. Housing became much more expensive and the pattern of development favored by developers (large, single-family detached homes on increasingly large lots) was very different from the compact development pattern in the city's traditional neighborhoods. The changes that occurred in Northampton (and many other New England communities) not only changed the physical form of communities, but also made people more disillusioned and resigned.

As the development boom was nearing its peak (just before the New England economy plunged into recession, and banks and savings and loan associations across the country began to fail), I attended a conference at the University of New Hampshire on "planning for growth management." At one point during the session, a woman stood up and asked people in the audience to close their eyes and think about what their town had been like 10 years ago, and how their communities had changed during the past 10 years. "Now, imagine you are back in your community 10 years ago," she suggested, "in a planning commission meeting. Is what you see now what you would have wished for?" Everybody at the meeting shook their heads "no."

Getting people to agree *ahead of time* on what they want to happen—or not happen—in the future is a very different matter, and certainly much more difficult than looking back with the benefit of 20-20 hindsight at what *should* and *could* have been done. Still, the woman's point was well taken. If people *had* engaged in a planning process that enabled them to reach agreement on some basic principles to guide development, a very different pattern of land use and development could have evolved—one that most of today's New England residents might have preferred.

When I talk with people about land use and development issues, I am struck by how often people bemoan the changes that have occurred in their communities. When I pursue this point, I find that these same people are also uncertain whether even good planning could have avoided the negative outcomes they decry. Although deeply disturbed by the land use and development trends they see occurring, few seem sufficiently convinced of the value of planning to support the establishment of planning processes in situations that could counteract those trends and bring about different outcomes in the future.

YEARNING FOR GOOD PLACES

Given the enormous size and varied geography of the U.S., it seemed inconceivable until very recently that communities in the northeast, southeast, midwest, northwest and southwest would come to look the same; nevertheless, that is exactly what is happening. With national franchise operations and chain stores proliferating along highways, and with residential developers increasingly favoring standardized approaches to residential development, places are becoming less and less distinctive and more and more like the "nowhere" to which James Howard Kunstler refers in *Geography of Nowhere* (1993) and *Home from Nowhere* (1996). Now, whether you are on the outskirts of Auburn (Maine), Janesville (Wisconsin), Atlanta (Georgia) or Denver (Colorado), it all looks and feels pretty much the same.

Despite this increasing sameness and dreariness, Americans continue to yearn to live in places that are unique and special and have a sense of place. Indeed, the yearning now seems more intense than ever. In a book titled *A Good Place to Live* (1995), Terry Pindell recounts his search for a good place for his family to live. He began by reading a number of "Places Rated" surveys and almanacs.[1]

In this way, he identified a dozen communities in different parts of the country that seemed to possess the qualities for which he was looking, and then traveled to each community to experience them first-hand. He spent about a week in each place, speaking to people about how and why they had come to live there, and what they especially liked about the place.[2] Many of the people to whom he spoke were long-time residents. However, in each place that he visited, he also encountered a large number of recent arrivals—people whose desire for a good place to live had led them to migrate there from somewhere else. The more people to whom he talked, the more Pindell realized that he was not alone in his search for a good place—an observation that led him to subtitle his book *America's Last Migration*.

Almost all of us at one time or another have been in places that have seemed special, and where we have wished we could stay longer and perhaps relocate. However, identifying the precise qualities of a place that make it special, and putting them into words, is difficult. Kevin Lynch, the author of many books such as *The Image of the City* (1960), *What Time Is This Place?* (1972) and *Managing the Sense of a Region* (1980), spent his life studying and writing about peoples' perceptions and "mental maps" of places, and why some places evoke a more positive response than others. When he asked people to draw maps of places, he found that some places and locations were so firmly fixed in people's minds that they were almost always shown on the maps people drew. Moreover, people had a very clear idea of how these important and valued places connected to other parts of the city. The places people emphasized in the maps they drew had meaning and played an important part in their lives.

2-1　People *want* their communities to be special. "Berkshire Days" celebration and parade in North Adams, Massachusetts in 1984.

Source: Gene Bunnell

On the other hand, large areas of the urban landscape were so unremarkable and unimportant in people's lives that they were almost invisible, and were rarely (if ever) shown on the maps people drew. Indeed, if one were to repeat Lynch's research today and ask people to draw maps of areas through which they pass, glance at or otherwise experience on a fairly frequent basis, I suspect that many would find it difficult to identify and locate many truly memorable places (memorable in a positive sense) and that, other than locating where they happen to work and live and the highway corridors on which they drive between those two points, large areas of their maps would be blank.

Terry Pindell has probably spent considerably less time studying and analyzing the qualities of places than Kevin Lynch, but the qualities he sought in communities are ones that I suspect Kevin Lynch (were he alive today) would have little difficulty endorsing. They were:

- local identity and a sense of place
- escape from the "suburban paradigm" (the ability to come and go without using the automobile)[3]
- a strong, vital, densely developed, pedestrian-oriented downtown with a mixture of uses and activities that makes it the focal point of the community
- good neighborhoods and well-kept older housing adjacent to and surrounding the downtown
- gathering places (so-called "third places") where people can interact with one another and have the sense of being part of a community
- environmental, scenic and open space resources integrated within the city and/or close at hand. Pindell playfully calls this the "cake factor": the ability to live in a vital, urban place while still remaining in touch with nature, and being able to appreciate scenic and environmental qualities (*i.e.,* to have one's cake and eat it, too).

Pindell is not a professional planner and did not set out to write about the impact of planning on communities, or to necessarily explain *how* the communities he visited had become good places; he was just looking for a good place to live. Nevertheless, he indicates several times that the qualities that made the places he visited distinctive and special apparently did not come about by chance. In most of the places, having a strong downtown was "part of a community's vision" and had come about as a result of efforts that amounted to "nothing less than a crusade." He was, for example, impressed by the four-block-long pedestrian mall in Burlington, Vermont that was created in 1981—a project widely credited with having helped revitalize the downtown.

Pindell was particularly explicit in describing how the "community vision" developed and officially adopted in Corvallis, Oregon had helped to make that city a better place. According to Pindell's interview with Neil Mann, Corvallis' director of the city's Department of Community Development (DCD), the city's vision for community development had specific aims such as to:

- site small, high-tech industries on land set aside for that purpose
- channel all major development into downtown
- develop small "pocket" commercial zones in residential areas and within walking distance of private homes, confining strip development to the one north-south corridor where it was established years ago, and absolutely prohibiting it from the pristine east and west entrances to the city

In his chapter on Burlington, Pindell also notes another necessary ingredient to achieving good places: the ability of citizens to engage in constructive debate regarding land use and development issues. During his stay there, Pindell learned that the question of whether or not a key downtown parcel of land located along Lake Champlain should be developed (and if so, how) had been a subject of long-standing local debate. Many people were apparently in favor of developing the waterfront parcel in some way, while many others felt that the parcel should be kept open and undeveloped to provide open space and public access to the lake.[4] The strength of Burlington, it seemed to Pindell, lay in the fact that "People didn't hunker down in ideological enclaves to share their prejudices exclusively with their own kind in Burlington. Instead, they debated their differences publicly and spiritedly with ideological opponents and discovered diverse friendships in the process. If Americans [are] ever going to return to living together in their cities, that's one thing they would have to learn to do." (Pindell 1995, 272)

Finally, Pindell's accounts underscore the importance of local leadership in bringing about positive change. In Missoula, Montana, much of the leadership and vision was provided by the city's mayor, Dan Kemmis. In Oregon's Willamette Valley, the governmental leadership and vision were provided by former Oregon governor, Tom McCall, and the private sector leadership was provided by a farmer named Hector McPherson. In Burlington, Vermont, the person who drew attention to land use and development policy questions and who served as a lightning rod for public and private initiatives and actions, which revitalized the city's downtown, was the city's mayor, Bernard Sanders, now a member of Congress. In Wilmington, North Carolina, the energizing vision was provided by key members of the Downtown Wilmington business community who spearheaded what they called the Downtown Area Redevelopment Effort (DARE).

PLACES PLANNERS ADMIRE AND QUALITIES THEY VALUE

At one point I thought I might follow Pindell's approach, and identify good places by compiling a list of the "best places" from various "Places Rated" catalogs. What better way to prove that planning has helped create good places than to research the extent to which the most highly rated communities in the country had been shaped by planning?

However, the more I looked at various "Places Rated" surveys and catalogs, the less appropriate this approach seemed. An important goal of urban planning, I believe, is to preserve and strengthen the special qualities of places so that each city has a unique character and identity; however, most of the "Places Rated" surveys and almanacs I examined rated cities according to a single, one-size-fits-all formula. Moreover, when I looked at the criteria used for rating cities (ranking them hierarchically from "best" to "worst"), I realized that many of the criteria were totally irrelevant to the *aims* of planning.

For example, "Places Rated" almanacs typically ranked communities in terms of their climate (communities that had warm climates and mild winters were favored). Likewise, cities that happened to be located in scenic locations (along seacoasts, and/or in close proximity to mountains and ski resorts) were given a boost in the rankings.[5] This implicitly biased way of ranking communities was ill suited to my purposes because I felt it important to be able to show that planning can make a positive difference in all kinds of communities, not just in places with warm climates and/or other special environmental qualities. There is nothing planning can do to change the weather or affect where cities are located; those facts of geography are simply "givens."

In some cases, the criteria used in ranking cities appeared downright contradictory. The criteria used by *Money Magazine*, for example, ranked cities highly if they had *low* housing costs, *rising* house prices *and* high-paying jobs.[6] Likewise, cities were ranked highly if they had *good public schools, high-quality public facilities* and *low taxes*. I can understand people wanting to pay low taxes, but you usually get what you pay for!

I noticed another quality about the rankings of cities published in almanacs and magazines that made them unsuitable: although they almost always included criteria that placed a high value on natural beauty, they placed little or no importance on the design, aesthetics, appearance and "feel" of man-made environments. This omission confirms another of Kevin Lynch's astute observations that, although a great deal of data has been collected describing the quantitative and technical aspects of places, little attention has been devoted to analyzing and describing how environments impact the everyday lives of the people who use them "in an immediate sense, through their eyes, ears, nose, and skin." (Lynch 1980, 3)

I ultimately decided to ask members of APA to help select the case-study communities. With the help of APA's staff in Chicago, 1,400 individuals who had been APA members for 10 years or more were randomly selected and sent a survey questionnaire. To obtain geographically representative responses, and avoid receiving disproportionately large numbers of responses from highly populated states where large numbers of APA members were based (such as

California, Florida and New York), the continental U.S. was divided into seven regions (northeast, southeast, Gulf states, midwest, central/mountain, northwest and southwest) and equal numbers of planners in each of those regions were sent the questionnaire, which asked the following questions:

- Thinking as a planner, keeping in mind the kinds of qualities and outcomes that planning seeks to achieve (and that you value), what would you say are the best places, cities or communities in the U.S.? When answering, try to focus on places that are good places to live and work, not just good places to visit.
- What qualities and/or features did you have in mind when you chose these communities?
- What cities or places in the U.S. would you say have been positively shaped by planning (*i.e.*, they are "better places" today because of planning)?
- In what specific ways were the above-mentioned communities made better by planning?
- Related to the communities you identified as "best places" and places positively shaped by planning, what people do you recommend be contacted for further information regarding the positive effects of planning?
- Is there a planner you particularly admire whose work has had a positive effect on a particular community?
- What specific planning approaches and tools have you found to be the most important in creating good places?

While waiting for surveys to be returned, I made 25 telephone calls to planners, educators, architects and urban designers whom I knew and respected, and asked them the same questions. My research assistant, Edward Jepson, conducted telephone interviews with another dozen planners.

One hundred thirty-six completed questionnaires were returned over a three-month period, and the responses from the questionnaires were tabulated and analyzed along with the responses obtained from the above-mentioned telephone interviews.[7] Thus, a total of 173 planners and people in planning-related professions had input in the identification of the "best cities," cities positively shaped by planning and the qualities that planning seeks to achieve in communities.

The question asking people to identify the "best cities" in the country elicited the names of 170 cities and one county (Montgomery County, Maryland). Many of the places named were mentioned only once by a single respondent, although a large proportion of cities mentioned were in fact identified by multiple respondents. Large cities tended to receive the largest number of multiple votes, which is probably due to the fact that survey respondents were more familiar with, and were more likely to have visited, large cities than small- and medium-sized cities. Nevertheless, a remarkable number of small- and medium-sized cities did receive relatively large numbers of multiple votes.

Far and away the city of any size that planners cited most frequently as the "best city" was Portland, Oregon. The second most often-named city was San Francisco. Other *large* cities most frequently cited as "best cities" (in descending order) were: Seattle, Washington; Boston, Massachusetts; Minneapolis-St. Paul, Minnesota; Austin, Texas; San Diego, California; Chicago, Illinois; New York City, New York; Washington, DC; and San Antonio, Texas.

Among *medium-sized and small cities*, the city most frequently mentioned as being the best place was Charleston, South Carolina. Other most frequently mentioned medium-sized and small cities (in descending order) were: Boulder, Colorado; Madison, Wisconsin; and San Luis Obispo, California.

Responses to the question asking planners to identify cities that had been "positively shaped by planning" mirrored somewhat the responses to the first question—which is noteworthy since it suggests that respondents recognized that many of the "best cities" in the country had achieved that distinction by planning. Once again, the city that was mentioned most often as having been positively shaped by planning was Portland, Oregon, followed by San Francisco, California and Boston, Massachusetts, which were tied for second. Other frequently mentioned *large* cities were: Seattle, Washington; Washington, DC; Philadelphia, Pennsylvania; Chicago, Illinois; Minneapolis-St. Paul, Minnesota; New York City, New York; San Diego, California; Baltimore, Maryland; Pittsburgh, Pennsylvania; Cleveland, Ohio; Kansas City, Missouri; Orlando, Florida; and San Jose, California. Montgomery County, Maryland (a county rather than a city or town) was also mentioned multiple times.

The *medium- or small-sized* city most frequently mentioned by respondents as having been positively shaped by planning was Boulder, Colorado. Tied for second were Charleston, South Carolina; Providence, Rhode Island; and Madison, Wisconsin. Other medium- and small-sized cities mentioned multiple times included: Chattanooga, Tennessee; Columbia, Maryland; Celebration, Florida; Davis, California; Lancaster, Pennsylvania; Lawrence, Kansas; Palo Alto, California; Raleigh and Durham, North Carolina; San Luis Obispo, California; Santa Barbara, California; and Santa Fe, New Mexico.

The vast majority of communities identified by respondents (long-time members of APA) as "best cities" and "places positively shaped by planning" are distinctly urban in character. Most are central cities. Only two of the frequently mentioned places could be characterized as "suburban" (Columbia, Maryland and Celebration, Florida), yet even these communities have a relatively compact pattern of development and have little in common with sprawling, unplanned suburbs.

The answers that APA members surveyed in 1998 provided to the question about specific qualities respondents had in mind when they made their choices were especially helpful in shedding light on the qualities planners value. Those qualities were:

- compact development that doesn't sprawl, enabling urban and rural areas to be clearly differentiated from one another
- urban places with a strong center, where multiple uses and activities (such as housing, employment, retail and shopping, government offices and local institutions, cultural resources, performing arts and entertainment) are clustered in fairly close proximity
- pedestrian-friendly environments (in mixed-use and commercial areas, a pattern of development that supports and encourages sidewalk pedestrian activity; in less densely developed areas and neighborhoods, a pattern of development that encourages and enables people to reach stores, public institutions such as schools and libraries, recreational resources, playfields and open space areas, public transit stops, etc., on foot or by bicycle, without having to travel by car)
- high-quality and convenient public transit coordinated with land use and development, and concentrated development along transit corridors and in proximity to transit stops
- vital, distinctive and varied neighborhoods in close proximity to the urban center
- a mixture of housing types that meets the needs of a variety of households with different income levels
- environmental resources, natural amenities, scenic qualities and open space that are preserved and are consciously integrated into the fabric of the community (cities most highly prized by planners, and thought of as having been positively shaped by planning, are not just dense concentrations of urban development, but are places where one is aware of a connection with nature and with the environmental qualities of the surrounding region)
- historic and cultural resources consciously preserved and integrated into contemporary settings
- well-designed public buildings and public spaces that strengthen community identity and sense of place, often reinforced and enlivened by works of art and sculpture

The above qualities of places identified by planners nationally are largely consistent with the results obtained from a survey of members of the Wisconsin Chapter of APA that I helped devise and administer in 1993. Unlike the more recent 1998 survey of nationwide APA members, which was open-ended, the Wisconsin survey presented a specified list of planning objectives, and asked respondents to choose those that they believed were most important and rank them in order of importance.[8] The most highly ranked planning objectives, according to Wisconsin planners, were:

Not the kind of qualities planners had in mind when they described the qualities planning seeks to achieve in communities.

2-2 Pedestrian experience in downtown Los Angeles, California. View at sidewalk level at the base of an office tower complex built on top of an enclosed, multilevel parking structure.

Source: Gene Bunnell

2-3 Acres of paved surface parking lots in downtown Kansas City, Missouri.

Source: Gene Bunnell

1. to strengthen village and city centers
2. to preserve farmland, open space, wildlife habitats and environmental corridors
3. to encourage infill development and city-centered redevelopment
4. to curtail sprawl
5. to limit very low-density residential development on the urban fringe
6. to enhance and strengthen local character, community identity and a sense of place
7. to achieve a closer integration of housing with employment centers and shopping areas, so that communities contain places to live, work and shop, and contain a full range of facilities
8. to coordinate land use and development with the larger network of roads and public transportation, and to assure that as many activities as possible are located within easy walking distance of transit stops

At the 2000 APA conference in New York City, Mark Hinshaw gave a presentation that zeroed in even more on the aesthetic qualities of good places that planning can help to strengthen. Hinshaw is director of urban design at LMN Architects in Seattle, and writes a column on urban planning and design issues for *The Seattle Times*. According to Hinshaw, the key attributes of the places to which we are instinctively drawn, and which planning can and should aim to introduce and strengthen in communities, are:

- *connectivity:* vehicular, pedestrian and transit connectivity and ease of movement from one part of the community to another
- *drama and dignity:* landmarks and building façades providing evidence that it is a real place, not just superficial
- *variety and whimsy:* as expressed in architectural forms and design details
- *reflection of local values:* appropriate architectural styles, materials and vegetation
- *sociable settings:* public spaces and squares, with areas for seating
- *many choices and many things to do:* not just consumerism and shopping; not just a workplace or a bedroom community

The fact that planners list *so many different* physical attributes and outcomes as being associated with good places, and as desired outcomes of planning, is itself significant. Cities that people most admire possess a number of positive attributes. When you look at these places closely, you will find that they have become great because they have done a number of different things, which were complementary and mutually reinforcing (*i.e.,* they had a plan).

Admittedly, most of the qualities listed by APA survey respondents and Mark Hinshaw are *urban* qualities. Does that mean that planners don't care about rural areas, and don't recognize the importance of preserving and protecting environmental resources and open land from development? I don't think it does. How *do* we go about protecting and conserving environmental

2-4   *Drama and dignity:* Milwaukee City Hall and Pabst Theater in Milwaukee, Wisconsin.

Source: Gene Bunnell

2-5   *Variety and whimsy in a sociable setting:* sitting on a bench in Fanieul Hall Marketplace in Boston, next to a sculpture of former Boston Celtics General Manager "Red" Auerbach with "victory cigar" in hand.

Source: Gene Bunnell

resources and preserving rural places, wilderness areas and areas of prime agricultural land? The only way to preserve environmental resources and rural areas in the long run is by confronting development head on—by planning, building and maintaining urban communities in which people want to live.

SELECTION OF CASE-STUDY COMMUNITIES

Analysis of survey and interview responses related to "best cities" and "places shaped positively by planning" produced a short list of 56 frequently mentioned cities. However, deciding *which* communities to select as case studies was difficult, because I needed to take account of and weigh a number of different considerations.

First of all, I felt it was important to choose different types and sizes of communities in different parts of the country. I also wanted to select communities that had faced different kinds of planning issues and challenges, such as strong and sustained growth, alternating periods of boom and bust, moderate growth, and no growth or negative growth (loss of population and economic base).

I also decided *not* to write about planned new communities developed after World War II (such as Columbia, Maryland; Reston, Virginia; Celebration and Seaside, Florida). Excluding totally planned communities from a book aimed at documenting the positive impact planning has had on communities may seem contradictory. However, most Americans do not live in fully planned communities. Moreover, I suspect that if you asked people if they would like to live in a place where *everything* had been centrally planned, most would probably say, "No, thanks!" Most of us, if given the choice, would probably choose to live in a place where there is a balance between planning and *not* planning. The challenge, of course, is to learn how to strike the *right* balance. The best way of getting at the heart of that important issue, it seemed to me, was to focus on communities that had evolved and changed over time and been shaped by planning, but were not completely planned.

Another reason for not choosing totally planned communities as case studies is the fact that the process of planning a thoroughly planned community is very different from the kind of planning processes one is likely to find in most communities. When a community is planned "from scratch," it is almost always the case that all of the land is owned by one person or development corporation, giving that individual or development entity nearly total control of what gets built. The developer may be enlightened, and may hire a qualified and creative urban designer and architect, who in turn may introduce desirable features into the planning and design of the community. Still, the process of bringing such a community into being is very different from the open and largely democratic (and often "messy") planning processes undertaken in communities where land ownership is highly fragmented, and where existing residents and property owners are active participants.

Second, I wanted to try to select places that had sought to achieve the kind of outcomes and qualities that planners had said were present in the "best cities" and in places "positively shaped by planning." This meant, for example, that I wanted to select communities with a mixture of land uses, where people both lived and worked, and that were reasonably socioeconomically balanced and "home" to people of different ages and incomes. Likewise, I made a conscious effort to select communities that had sought to balance the need for development with the need for conservation, and that had been mindful of the importance of not pursuing land use and development policies that excluded low- and moderate-income residents.

A third consideration was that I needed to be able to identify someone in each case-study community who was knowledgeable of past planning efforts and their impacts, and was willing to serve as my principal local contact. Having a principal local contact was crucial, since I needed to rely on this person to help orient me to the community, gather background materials and past plans and forward them to me, and identify people that would be helpful to contact and interview.

One final consideration which affected the selection of case-study communities was that I wanted to draw attention to some cities whose positive qualities as places, and planning successes, have not necessarily received a great deal of attention. In other words, I decided to try to not write about "the usual suspects"—cities whose qualities and successful planning efforts have already been widely written about elsewhere.

Taking into account the various considerations described above and striving to come up with a representative cross-section of communities, I decided *not* to include Portland, San Francisco and Boulder as case studies, even though they were frequently mentioned by survey respondents not only as "best cities" but as having been "positively shaped by planning." The decision not to study and write about Portland and San Francisco was largely due to the fact that the special qualities of these cities are already fairly widely recognized, and the planning initiatives and land use policies that have contributed to those qualities have already been written about elsewhere.[9]

Boulder's strong commitment to managing growth and preserving open space has also drawn a great deal of national attention. More than 40,000 acres of undeveloped land have been publicly bought and permanently protected as open space by the city. Not only is there an extensive network of parks and open spaces within the city, but the city is also completely encircled by a greenbelt of publicly owned land that the city has no intention of ever releasing for development.

Clearly, something of major significance has been accomplished in Boulder and yet, when I conducted telephone interviews, a number of planners expressed reservations concerning Boulder's one-sided approach to managing growth, and about the city's highly restrictive development policies. According to the planners to whom I spoke, the city's obsession with limiting development and acquiring land as open space had reduced the amount of land available for development so much as to make housing in the city prohibitively expensive for many people. As a result, large numbers of people employed at the University of Colorado (the region's largest employer) and elsewhere in the city must commute long distances from communities where housing costs are lower.

In many ways, the situation in Boulder (described above) illustrates just how difficult it is in the U.S. to be regarded as successful in terms of planning and managing growth. On the one hand, if planners fail to achieve the purposes local citizens want to achieve, then planning is judged a failure. On the other hand, when planning succeeds in achieving what people want it to achieve—as it has so clearly been done in Boulder—it can be criticized for increasing housing costs. In a largely market-based country where most land is privately owned, when planning succeeds in making one place more attractive and desirable than another, people bid up the price of housing in that place. Viewed in that light, there does seem to be a degree of unfairness in blaming planning for Boulder's high housing costs. As one Colorado planner shared, "If there were more communities like Boulder, the problem of increased housing costs wouldn't be nearly so great because there would be other nearby communities people could choose to live in that offered many of the same amenities." I think this planner had a good point. I nevertheless decided to put Boulder aside, and focus attention on some other community that had sought to balance development and conservation, and was less well known.

The eight communities I chose to study and write about, after weighing all of the above-mentioned considerations, were: (1) Chattanooga, Tennessee; (2) Providence, Rhode Island; (3) Charleston, South Carolina; (4) Duluth, Minnesota; (5) San Diego, California; (6) Madison, Wisconsin; (7) Wichita, Kansas; and (8) Westminster, Colorado. To round out the book, I invited two other people (Philip Herr and Terry Szold), both of whom have had extensive experience as planning practitioners and taught planning courses at the Massachusetts Institute of Technology, to submit independent case studies drawn from their own experience. The case study Terry Szold chose to contribute describes the difference planning made in Burlington, Massachusetts—an "edge city" suburb north of Boston—where she worked as the director of planning before establishing her own private consulting firm. The case study Philip Herr chose to contribute describes a positive outcome associated with citizen-led planning in Block Island, Rhode Island.

The 10 communities whose stories are told in this book range in size from San Diego (population 1,223,400 in 2000) to Block Island (year-round population approximately 850). They are also different from one another in other ways. Providence and Charleston are among the oldest cities in this country. Chattanooga and Duluth are rustbelt cities that, although not as old as Providence and Charleston, also have long and rich histories. San Diego and Westminster are remarkably young cities and grew rapidly during the latter half of the 20th century. The explosive growth that has occurred in those two young cities has made the task of land use planning and growth management especially daunting. Duluth, on the other hand, has faced an equally difficult planning challenge: how to maintain the positive qualities people value in the face of a significant loss of population and jobs. Wichita and Madison have experienced moderate but steady growth for nearly 50 years.

While most of the case studies tell about what planning can achieve in cities, two tell about what planning can achieve in suburban communities (Westminster and Burlington). One tells about the special case of planning on an island only 10 square miles in area (Block Island) where the limits of growth are especially obvious.

One other factor that I believe increases the relevance and applicability of the case studies is that they involve communities with different forms of local government. Burlington and Block Island both have a town form of government. Among the municipalities with a city form of government, two (Wichita and Westminster) have a city manager form of government and the others have a mayor-council form of government.

Profiles of each case-study community (in a standard format) are provided in the Appendix at the end of the book. These profiles provide an easy way of identifying and comparing the varied characteristics of the 10 case-study communities.

RESEARCH APPROACH

Prior to embarking on this project, I had never been in Chattanooga, Wichita, Westminster or Charleston, and had never been in Providence (except for passing through while on trains traveling between Boston and New York). I had briefly been in Duluth and San Diego while attending professional meetings, but otherwise knew very little about those cities. The one city I knew well was Madison, where I lived for six years between 1992 and 1998.

Since I was living in Madison when I began writing this book, I was able to gather information related to that city over an extended period of time. However, gathering material and conducting interviews related to the seven other case-study communities required a more compressed approach.

Once the case-study communities were selected, I contacted the person who had agreed to serve as a local contact (in many cases, the current or former planning director) and engaged in back-and-forth conversations to identify past plans and planning processes that had a positive impact on the community, and specific geographic areas that had benefited from planning. I also obtained the names, addresses and telephone numbers of additional people who had played important roles in past planning efforts, and/or were knowledgeable about those efforts and their effects.

With this background information in hand, I made a series of weeklong trips to each of the seven case-study communities with which I was not familiar. During the week I spent in each place, I obtained copies of past plans, planning studies and other relevant planning documents. I walked through and photographed areas that had been targeted by past planning efforts. I also interviewed people who had first-hand knowledge of local planning activities and their impacts to reconstruct various strands of the planning story.

Many of the people I interviewed had been personally involved in the local planning efforts I wanted to learn about. Many were professional planners who had worked as staff planners or planning consultants. Others were citizen planners whose workdays were spent in other careers but who served on local planning commissions, and/or on ad-hoc planning committees and groups formed in relation to specific planning initiatives.

I also interviewed people who, while not personally involved in plan-making, could judge the significance of changes that had occurred in the community, and could offer informed opinions from various perspectives regarding how and why those changes occurred. People interviewed included newspaper reporters and editors, professors at local universities and colleges, developers and property owners, bankers and realtors, chamber of commerce representatives and staff, local business leaders, as well as representatives and members of local nonprofit organizations, historic preservation organizations, neighborhood associations and environmental groups. To learn how planning was perceived by local government officials, I interviewed past and present mayors and city council members in cities with mayor-council forms of government, and the city managers in communities which had city manager forms of government.

Most interviews conducted in the field lasted roughly an hour, although some were much longer. A number of individuals were interviewed more than once (once in person and again by phone). Each interview was tape recorded and subsequently transcribed for later reference and analysis. In all, I interviewed more than 116 individuals in the eight case-study communities. All of the interviews I conducted in the field were between January 1998 and December 2000. Follow-up telephone interviews to update and verify information were carried out up until August 2001.

At the end of each of the case studies, I provide a list of the names and positions of people I interviewed in connection with that case study. Please note that the titles/positions were the ones these individuals held when I interviewed them; they may be different when you read these accounts.

◆

When I began this project, there was no way to know that I would find that planning had produced positive outcomes in all of the case-study communities, nor could I be sure that the planning outcomes I was going to uncover were going to be significant or even interesting. An isolated success here and there, intermixed with planning failures that failed to fit a pattern or tell a coherent story, did not seem likely to provide very engaging reading.

After completing the field research in all of the case-study cities, however, I realized that the problem was not going to be having too little to write about, but rather having too much. As I constructed the planning chronologies of each place from the transcribed interviews and from the scores of documents, reports, studies, memoranda, plans and ordinances that I had collected, each story seemed to take on its own richness and coherence. Just as none of the places was like any of the others, none of the stories or accounts was like any other story. Even more intriguing was the extent to which the various planning purposes and outcomes reflected the characteristics and features that distinguished each place. The planning aims and outcomes that I uncovered were so closely connected to local history, geography and politics that it was impossible to fully grasp their significance without understanding the geography, history, politics, economic base and social culture of each place.

When the planning stories about all of the places were completed, it became clear that the complexity and length of the case studies were far greater than could be encompassed in a single book. One way of meeting the space constraints might have been to excise major sections from each of the case studies; however, that would have meant presenting incomplete accounts of the planning stories of each place. Readers with a special interest in particular strategies, approaches or outcomes would have found no mention of them in the case studies. Also, many of the extended quotes obtained from transcribed interviews and planning documents, which add local flavor and meaning to the story lines, would have had to be omitted.

The idea of reducing the size of the book by publishing only half of the case studies was an even less attractive option, inasmuch as the methodology that guided this undertaking at the outset specified that a cross-section of case-study communities would be selected, that field research would be conducted in each place, and that an honest and complete account of the difference that planning had made in each place would be written and published. Deleting the stories of a number of the preselected case-study communities violated the integrity of that chosen approach.

A compromise solution made it possible to publish a book of a manageable size, to keep all of the case studies intact and to provide them in a readily accessible form to interested readers. The solution was to publish a book containing half of the case studies, plus an accompanying CD-ROM containing all of the case studies with the accompanying photographs and illustrations *in color* (images in the book are reproduced in black and white).

In the course of conducting field research and gathering material for this book, I developed a deep affection and appreciation of the special qualities of all eight cities that I personally studied. In writing each of the stories, I have tried to do justice to the individuality and unique challenges presented in each planning context. Because the planning contexts and challenges faced in each place are different and unique, each of the stories contains its own important lessons and insights. I therefore urge readers not to presume that the stories of the five places which found their way into the book, and which comprise

Chapters 3 through 7, are more instructive and/or interesting than the stories found only on the CD-ROM. I suspect there will be many readers, for example, who will be very interested in reading the planning stories of Madison (Wisconsin), Westminster (Colorado) and Wichita (Kansas)—and the contributed case studies of Block Island, Rhode Island (by Philip Herr) and of Burlington, Massachusetts (by Terry Szold)—that are not included in the book but can be found on the CD-ROM.

Chapters 3 through 7 in the book present the planning stories of Chattanooga (Tennessee), Providence (Rhode Island), Charleston (South Carolina), Duluth (Minnesota) and San Diego (California), respectively. The concluding chapter in the book (Chapter 8, *Lessons Learned*) draws conclusions and insights from all 10 of the case studies, including the five additional case studies found only on the CD-ROM.

THE NATURE OF THESE PLANNING STORIES

The case studies that are presented in this book, and on the accompanying CD-ROM, do not make a theoretical argument for planning. Rather, they describe, in specific and concrete terms, the positive changes that have been brought about by planning in 10 real communities.

The stories I present have been shaped by what I saw with my own eyes and experienced first-hand, and by the voices of the people I interviewed. Because of the emphasis on first-hand accounts, it is possible that relatively minor inaccuracies may have found their way into the text. I have not independently verified the accuracy of every fact and statistic that people I interviewed passed on to me. If someone I interviewed said that some particular event happened in 1974, for example, that is what I have reported, although it is conceivable that detailed research might reveal that it happened in 1975 or 1973. The truth of these case studies does not hinge on any particular date or statistic, but on the narrative story line embedded within each case study that sets out the *sequence* of events and decisions related to local planning processes, and describes the motivations and intentions of people who were key players in those processes.

It is possible that the people I interviewed may have failed to mention the names of all the people who played important roles in shaping the community outcomes I describe and who deserve credit. If that is the case, I do apologize. I have simply reported as faithfully as possible (from transcribed, tape-recorded interviews) the honest recollections and perceptions of the people I interviewed, and interwoven them with the information gleaned from the hundreds of planning documents, studies, reports, memoranda, plans, maps and ordinances I succeeded in gathering together from each place. It is in the hands of you, the reader, to decide whether the composite stories constitute credible evidence of the value and efficacy of planning.

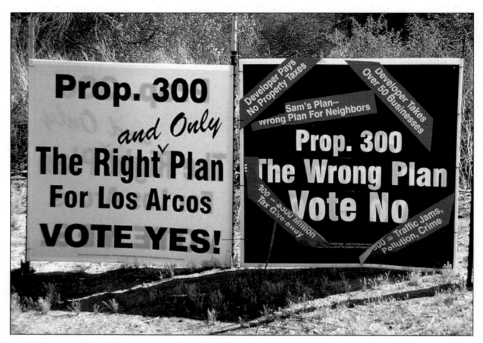

2-6 Competing signs related to an upcoming referendum on a proposed plan in Scottsdale, Arizona. Planning can be controversial—but *not* planning can produce even more intense and prolonged controversy.

Source: Gene Bunnell

♦

People do not engage in planning because it is fun. Planning is hard work. Planning can also stir up controversy by bringing to light conflicting opinions, views and interests that, in the absence of planning, might have been able to be ignored. However, *not* planning and *not* confronting problems and issues can also be controversial, and in the end can be even more divisive if problems become worse because of the failure to plan.

People engage in planning when they recognize that it is *necessary* to achieve the outcomes they desire, and to preserve the qualities they value in their communities. Planning is not an end in itself; it is a means for achieving and preserving the qualities and features we value in our communities, and that make them good places in which to live and work.

NOTES

1. The almanacs Pindell looked at included *The Places Rated Almanac* (Savageu and Loftus 1995), *The Rating Guide to Life in America's Small Cities* (G. Scott Thompson 1990), and *The Livable Cities Almanac* (J. T. Marlin 1992).

2. The places Pindell visited and wrote about were: Wilmington, North Carolina; Asheville, North Carolina; Charlottesville, Virginia; Portsmouth, New Hampshire; Burlington, Vermont; Ithaca, New York; Minneapolis, Minnesota; Missoula, Montana; Santa Fe, New Mexico; San Luis Obispo, California; and Portland/Corvallis, Oregon.

3. To reinforce this point, Pindell quotes Andres Duany and Elizabeth Plater-Zyberk as follows: "The structure of the suburb tends to confine people to their houses and cars; it discourages strolling, walking, mingling with neighbors. The suburb is the last word in privatization . . ." (Pindell 1995, 5)

4. In 1990, a plan for the property was finalized and agreed to, and the land became what is now known as Waterfront Park.

5. Nashua, New Hampshire—*Money Magazine's* #1 rated city in 1997—was highly rated in part because it was relatively close to mountains and ski resorts, Lake Winnipesaukee and the ocean, although none of those environmental and recreational amenities were actually present in Nashua itself.

6. Each year, *Money Magazine* ranks 300 cities based on 41 quality-of-life factors. The relative importance and weight given to each of these quality-of-life factors are determined by annually surveying a representative sample of *Money Magazine* readers and asking them to rate each of the quality-of-life factors in terms of importance on a scale from 10 to 1 (with 10 being most important and 1 being least important). Thus, the relative weight given to the various quality-of-life factors can vary from year to year, which explains why Madison, Wisconsin was ranked #1 in 1996 and #7 in 1997. Madison's seven-place drop in the rankings from one year to the next says more about the variability of *Money Magazine's* ranking criteria than it does about how Madison changed between 1996 and 1997.

7. The overall rate of response was disappointingly low. The main reason for the low rate of response, I am certain, was that the questionnaire required respondents to take the time to provide thoughtful and original written answers, which was asking a great deal. A multiple-choice questionnaire, requiring less time and effort, would undoubtedly have resulted in a much higher rate of response. However, the answers obtained from such a questionnaire would have been much less revealing and informative. The 136 thoughtful and often lengthy written responses obtained from the completed questionnaires made it worth sacrificing numbers for quality.

8. Wisconsin planners who responded to the survey had an average of 18 years of planning experience; 71% had a professional degree in planning; 75% worked for a public or governmental agency (city, village, town, county, state or regional planning agency); and 25% were private planning consultants.

9. Many books have been written about the impact of planning on Portland and the Willamette Valley in Oregon. *Breakthroughs: Re-Creating The American City* (1993) by Neal R. Peirce and Robert Guskind includes a lengthy, detailed account of Portland's 1972 Downtown plan and how it (along with other state-supported land use planning policies) brought about the rebirth of that city. Alexander Garvin's *The American City— What Works, What Doesn't* (1996) includes an extended section on "The Transformation of Portland, Oregon" (pp. 456-459). *Profiles in Growth Management: An Assessment of Current Programs and Guidelines for*

Effective Management (1996) by Douglas R. Porter et al. includes an excellent and concise overview of growth-management policies and initiatives in the Portland region. Terry Pindell's book, *A Good Place to Live—America's Last Migration* (1995) also includes a revealing chapter on Portland and the Willamette Valley (Chapter 4, "Getting It Right This Time").

Books are also available that provide insights into the role planning has played in maintaining San Francisco's unique urban and environmental qualities. Bernick and Cervero's book, *Transit Villages in the 21st Century* (1997), devotes considerable space to describing how the coordi-

nation of land use planning and transit extensions has helped produce a multinucleated region composed of relatively high-density, mixed-use "transit villages." San Francisco's urban design plan and the innovative Office-Housing Linkage Program (no longer in force) have also been discussed in the planning literature. To this day, one of the best accounts of what planners do, and of the difference that planning can make in communities, is Allan Jacobs' *Making City Planning Work* (1980), a first-hand account of the planning principles and aims he sought to advance and defend when he was director of planning in San Francisco.

3

Chattanooga, Tennessee

A Dramatic Turnaround
and a Work in Progress

THE WAY THINGS WERE AND THE WAY THINGS ARE

Not that long ago, Chattanooga was in the national headlines and the publicity it was attracting was not the kind that cities like to receive. In 1969, the city was cited as having the most badly polluted air in the United States. In 1980, *The New York Times* published an article that focused attention on Chattanooga's lagging economy. At a time when most other major southern cities were growing and prospering, Chattanooga stood out as a notable exception.

According to *The New York Times*, when businesses were looking to locate and expand their operations in the south, the one city they hardly ever considered was Chattanooga. At one point in the article, Jack Lupton was quoted as saying, "This is a very cliquish place." (Rawls, Jr., July 27, 1980, 20) Later in *The New York Times* article, a local executive (who asked to remain unidentified) was quoted as saying that there was "a backwardness and a resistance to growth and change and progress by a relatively small group of economically powerful people. There is not enough new blood infused into this city to produce new ideas, new approaches. Major decisions here always seem to be based on how things have been done in the past or else how some other city has done them. Original thinking is rare. Very few people seem willing to take any kind of business risk." (*ibid.*)

By the 1990s, Chattanooga was again in the news, but the headlines had turned decidedly positive. The following headlines were typical: "Chattanooga Turnaround," "Chattanooga Reborn," "Cinderella Story," "Tennessee Triumph" and "Back from the Brink." Not only was Chattanooga no longer the poster city for pollution and environmental degradation (every year since 1988, the air in Chattanooga has met all applicable standards for air quality set by the U.S. Environmental Protection Agency (EPA), but it also had fashioned itself into a laboratory for testing and demonstrating model approaches to becoming an environmentally sustainable city. It had also transformed and revitalized the center of the city. In *The Ecology of Place: Planning for Environment, Economy and Community* (1997), Timothy Beatley and Kristy Manning highlight a number of Chattanooga's accomplishments, and praise the city for having turned environmental resources and amenities into economic assets. Indeed, they go so far as to say that, "One of the most dramatic examples of a U.S. city that has recast itself in terms of green principles is Chattanooga, Tennessee." (Beatley and Manning 1997, 97)

In January 1998, I traveled to Chattanooga to see what this city had accomplished, and to learn how these positive changes occurred, by interviewing individuals who had played a part in achieving the city's transformation. Getting to Chattanooga these days is not quite as easy as it used to be (unless you travel there by car). In 1948, 27 passenger trains arrived and departed at the city's two railroad stations each day[1]; now there are none. Airline service to Chattanooga (the fourth largest city in Tennessee) is also less than one would

3-1   Chattanooga, Tennessee, looking south across the Tennessee River, with Lookout Mountain in the distance. The sharp bend in the Tennessee River (upper right) is known as Moccasin Bend.

Source: State of Tennessee Photo Services, courtesy of Chattanooga News Bureau

expect, mostly because of the tendency of airlines under deregulation to concentrate service in major hubs like Atlanta and the proximity of Chattanooga to
Atlanta.[2]

I arrived in Chattanooga late on a rainy Sunday night, and all I saw while
driving a rental car into the city was a blur of headlights. The next morning
when I walked out the front door of the newly completed Riverfront Residence
Inn, the first thing I saw was a massive, seven-story structure directly across
the street, with display windows and awnings at sidewalk level, a multiscreen
cinema complex called the Bijou and decks of parking above. An unusual-look-
ing electric bus drove by and turned into the large opening at the north end of
the structure where people were waiting to board. Every 5 or 10 minutes,
another bus would arrive and depart. Walking north toward the river, I passed
an attractive IMAX®-3D Theater. When I rounded the corner, I found myself
facing a broad plaza leading up to the Tennessee State Aquarium.

3-2   Electric Shuttle bus passing in front of IMAX-3D Theater.

Source: Courtesy of Electric Transit Vehicle Institute

I was expected at the Regional Planning Agency (RPA) at 9:30 AM and had no time to explore the area more fully at that moment, so I rode one of the electric buses (for free) up to 11th Street and walked a short distance to the offices of the Chattanooga-Hamilton County RPA. Jerry Pace, a planner who by that time had worked at the RPA for 31 years, was there to greet me, and offered to take me on a driving tour of the city and its environs to get me oriented.

In the days that followed, I learned a great deal more about the city. I explored different parts of the downtown on foot (like the Bluff View Art District overlooking the Tennessee River) and made my way from the Hunter Museum of Art down an elegantly designed serpentine stairway to the Tennessee Riverwalk. I walked across the restored Walnut Street Bridge (at approximately three-quarters of a mile in length, the longest pedestrian bridge in the country) to the North Shore area of the city. I also visited a number of city neighborhoods where significant numbers of older housing units have been rehabilitated and where new homes have been built.

I found that I could either walk or take the Electric Shuttle bus to most of the places I wanted to go, including the former Terminal Railroad Station in the city's South Central Business District (referred to as the Southside), which has

3-3   The Tennessee State Aquarium.

Source: Gene Bunnell

3-4   Serpentine staircase leading from the Bluff View Art District downtown to the Tennessee Riverwalk.

Source: 2000 Robert Boyer/Shoot the Works

3-5   The restored Walnut Street Bridge, linking downtown Chattanooga and the city's North Shore area.

Source: State of Tennessee Photo Services, courtesy of Chattanooga News Bureau

3-6   Electric Shuttle turning into Shuttle Park South next to the Chattanooga Choo Choo Holiday Inn Hotel. The main lobby and dining and lounge areas of the hotel are in the former Terminal Railroad Station, which has been restored.

Source: Courtesy of Electric Transit Vehicle Institute

been renovated and converted into the Chattanooga Choo Choo Holiday Inn Hotel ("the Chattanooga Choo Choo").[3]

Most of my time was spent interviewing people who had played, and/or were continuing to play, an important role in the process of remaking the city. Toward the end of the week, I decided to give the rental car some use by driving out of the city to see the Chickamauga Dam. I also drove south to Lookout Mountain to ride the Incline Railway—the steepest passenger railway in the world with a 72.7% grade on the upper half—that runs up to the top of Lookout Mountain.[4]

A PLACE SHAPED BY GEOGRAPHY AND HISTORY

Chattanooga, Tennessee is situated in the Tennessee River Valley in the southeast corner of Tennessee, near the Georgia/Tennessee state border—an area with a very distinctive geography and history. The Tennessee River winds its way through the valley and passes through the heart of the city. Just west of the downtown core, the river loops dramatically in a U shape to form a large peninsula called Moccasin Bend (because its shape was thought to be reminiscent of the contours of a moccasin); further west, the river cuts through Tennessee River Gorge, known as the "Grand Canyon" of Tennessee. The city itself lies on a fairly flat plain surrounded by mountains and steep ridges on all sides (Signal Mountain to the north, Lookout Mountain to the south, Missionary Ridge on the east, and Elder Mountain to the west).

Chattanooga began when a trading post was built along the Tennessee River in the 1830s by John Ross, in an area that became known as Ross's Landing. Years later, when the railroads began to replace rivers and canals as the principal mode of transportation, a number of rail lines were built to and through Chattanooga, placing the city along major rail corridors leading to midwest cities like Chicago and Cincinnati. When the interstate highway system was built after World War II, Chattanooga once again found itself occupying a strategically important geographic position. Three interstate highways (I-59, I-24 and I-75) converge on Chattanooga, placing it squarely along major travel routes between Nashville and Atlanta, and between Knoxville and Birmingham.

Because of Chattanooga's strategic location in relation to transportation routes, it became a favored place for industries and manufacturing companies to locate. From the 1860s through the 1960s, the city was known for its iron and steel products; over the years, other industries located in the Chattanooga area flourished, such as chemical plants and factories producing synthetic yarn for the area's carpet industry.

In the 1960s, the largest employer in Chattanooga was Combustion Engineering, a firm that manufactured the vessels used in nuclear power plants. The city was also the home of the largest manufacturing plant of ammunition and TNT in the country, and of a glass factory that manufactured glass bottles for the Chattanooga Coca-Cola bottling plant. The city still has hundreds of factories that manufacture everything from plumbing and heating equipment to plastics, clothing and food products. While I was in Chattanooga, I bought a bottle of Norwich aspirin. When I looked at the label, I discovered that it was manufactured in Chattanooga!

Before discussing how Chattanooga's transformation came about, it is important to keep in mind two major events or turning points in Chattanooga's history: (1) the Civil War; and (2) the establishment of the Tennessee Valley Authority (TVA) in the 1930s.

In September 1863, 66,000 Confederate soldiers and 60,000 Union soldiers clashed in a large-scale battle on a heavily wooded plain near Chickamauga Creek. At the end of two days, roughly 40,000 Confederate and Union soldiers were dead or wounded. Two months later in November, another bloody battle (called "The Battle Above the Clouds") was fought for control of elevated positions along Missionary Ridge and on top of Lookout Mountain. The areas where those horrific battles took place are now preserved as the Chickamauga and Chattanooga National Military Park and Cemetery—the largest Civil War park and cemetery in the country and the second largest military cemetery in the U.S. after Arlington National Cemetery.

3-7   The Tennessee River Gorge—the "Grand Canyon" of Tennessee.

Source: State of Tennessee Photo Services, courtesy of Chattanooga News Bureau

Adolph Ochs, who is perhaps best known as the long-time publisher of *The New York Times*, was the founding owner and publisher of *The Chattanooga Times*, and played a key role in establishing a Civil War memorial park. Ochs not only gave editorial support to the establishment of a Civil War memorial park in his newspaper, but also personally bought land on Lookout Mountain and donated it to the public for that purpose. The park, with its over 1,400 monuments and historical markers, is one of the most often-visited sites in Chattanooga.

The deep divisions that came to a head during the Civil War left scars on Chattanooga that were slow to heal. It is therefore not surprising that when so-called "carpetbaggers" from the north came to Chattanooga to establish and run Chattanooga's iron and steel factories, they tended to settle in their own neighborhoods. "We had a north and south faction," said Pamela Glaser, an associate planner at the Planning and Design Center. "People tell me that the southerners lived on Cameron Hill and the northerners lived in Fort Wood."

The second major event that had a profound impact on Chattanooga took place in the 1930s. With the country mired in the Depression, President Franklin Delano Roosevelt created the TVA only a few months after he took office. Entire books have been written about the TVA and its impact on the Tennessee Valley region and, for the purposes of this book, I will touch on some of its most salient features.

The most obvious reason for establishing the TVA was to tame the Tennessee River, which John Gunther called America's "worst river . . . an obstreperous angry river with an angry history." (Gunther 1947, 733) However, the TVA was established to accomplish more than just flood control. The public law that established the TVA called upon the agency to also generate abundant electric power, maintain and improve navigation on the river, bring about the proper use of marginal lands, reforest all land suitable for reforestation, and maximize the economic and social well-being of the people living in the river basin. Indeed, a good indication of the impact the TVA had on the Tennessee Valley region is that the establishment of the TVA coincided with the beginning of the period of Chattanooga's most rapid growth as a city.

The scope of the plan that the TVA developed and implemented was truly monumental in scale, and involved the construction of a total of 39 dams, including nine major dams along the main stream of the Tennessee River, creating a chain of lakes stretching from Paducah, Kentucky to Knoxville, Tennessee. Execution of this project required acquisition of significant amounts of privately owned land by eminent domain, which was extremely controversial at the time. Nevertheless, roughly a dozen years after the TVA had begun, John Gunther wrote that a conservative politician told him that if a vote on TVA were taken back then, the pros would have won by 95%.

3-8   The historic Dome Building in downtown Chattanooga—the first home of
The Chattanooga Times newspaper. *The Chattanooga Times* occupied the building until
the 1940s, at which time the paper's offices were moved to East 10th Street.

Source: Gene Bunnell

3-9   The massive Tennessee Valley Authority office headquarters complex in downtown Chattanooga.

Source: Gene Bunnell

One of the benefits produced by the system of dams constructed by the TVA was that downtown Chattanooga was saved from repeated flooding. "Before the dams were constructed on the river," remarked Jerry Pace, "there were repeated floods in downtown Chattanooga. The water would get up into the first and second floors of stores on Market Street. Since the dams were constructed in the 1930s, we haven't had any major flooding in downtown Chattanooga." As planner Steven Leach observed, "If it weren't for the flood control provided by the TVA, we wouldn't have downtown Chattanooga."

The dams and flood control facilities constructed and managed by the TVA also helped reduce soil erosion and thereby strengthen agriculture. "When the TVA came in, there were counties in the valley more than half destroyed by erosion; some few spots were totally destroyed. The authority has so far saved something like three million acres. . . . The gullies are being healed, the scars of erosion are on the mend. . . . What a transformation! The neat terraced fields once deserted, were growing corn; the nontilled land was resting; part was 'under cover' with soil-protecting and water-holding crops, like crimson clover." (Gunther 1947, 742)

When I arrived in Chattanooga in January 1998, it did not take long to be reminded of the fact that, even though many decades have passed, the TVA still exerts a powerful influence over the city and region. The first thing that caught my attention, when Jerry Pace and I began our tour of the city, was the massive headquarters building of the TVA—an elongated structure 700 feet in length (three parallel buildings grouped together in a stepwise fashion) that Pace said people in Chattanooga refer to as "the biggest dam without water."

Good places don't happen by accident, nor do bad places. We tend to get the kind of communities we deserve.

—JACK MURRAH

We really do have a story to tell as a community. It's not just a story about a particular project or economic trend, or a story about the achievements of a particular political administration. It's a story of a community at large that learned to plan, and was able to build on what it learned.

—ANN COULTER[5]

THE 1960s AND 1970s: THE CITY HITS BOTTOM

When Ralph Kelly was elected mayor of Chattanooga in 1962, he was 34 years old. To the surprise of many, he had narrowly defeated P. R. Olgiati—a long-time, old-style politician who was the incumbent mayor.[6] The slogan of Kelly's campaign was, "It's time for a change."

The 1960s were not an easy time to be the mayor of any major American city—particularly a southern city. One hundred years after the Civil War, blacks were still struggling to gain equality and break down laws of segregation that prevented them from staying in "white-only" hotels and restaurants, sitting at lunch counters, and from drinking out of public water fountains. "When I became mayor," said Ralph Kelly, "every water fountain in the city had a sign that said either 'colored' or 'white' on it. Black people couldn't go to a hotel. They couldn't go to a theater."

"Freedom Marches" (such as the famous one from Selma to Montgomery, Alabama led by Reverend Martin Luther King, Jr.) were taking place in cities throughout the south. Pictures frequently appeared in newspapers of blacks and white civil rights supporters being dispersed by fire hoses, attack dogs and club-swinging police, and these confrontations were occurring in places near Chattanooga.

"I knew this city could not go on that way in the 20th century," Kelly continued. "I formed a commission on race relations and brought leaders of the black and white communities together to talk and air issues. At my urging, our city commission [the City of Chattanooga at the time had a commission form of government] passed what we called 'An Open City Resolution,' which declared that every restaurant, every hotel, and every public place was available to everybody, regardless of race ... My mother received anonymous phone calls from people who said 'That #*!*%*#-loving son of yours doesn't deserve to live. We're going to shoot him by four o'clock today' and then hung up. I figured that if they were going to do it, they weren't going to call ahead of time to tell me, so I put it out of my mind. My wife was very supportive, but it was hard on her."

In part because of Ralph Kelly's leadership at a crucial time, Chattanooga escaped the kind of violent conflicts and confrontations that were occurring in other southern cities. "You never saw any police dogs or fire hoses used in Chattanooga because we didn't have any disturbances," said Kelly. Nevertheless, Chattanooga in the 1960s and 1970s was still very much divided along lines of race and class. Blacks and whites lived in separate neighborhoods. The social fabric of the community was further strained by bitter conflicts between labor and management, frequent strike threats and work stoppages. Most managers, senior executives and professionals (who were mostly white) lived outside the city, many of them on hillsides and mountaintops overlooking the valley. Living in homes built on elevated sites enabled well-to-do people to disassociate themselves from the city's urban problems—and also to escape the dense pollution that was contained at lower elevations in the valley.[7]

Meanwhile, a large portion of the west side of the city's downtown core looked like a war zone in the wake of a 407-acre urban renewal clearance project carried out by the Chattanooga Housing Authority between 1957 and 1962, which demolished over 1,200 buildings and displaced over 1,500 households. One of the areas cleared away was a neighborhood of old Victorian homes on Cameron Hill that overlooked downtown Chattanooga. Had that neighborhood been retained and preserved, it very easily could have done for Chattanooga what the preservation and restoration of the College Hill neighborhood did for Providence: provide a distinctive and attractive residential neighborhood within walking distance of the downtown.

Unfortunately, not only was the Cameron Hill neighborhood demolished, but Cameron Hill itself was virtually eliminated as a landscape feature when 3,750,000 cubic yards of dirt were taken from the hill to be used as "fill" to construct a raised interstate freeway connector highway (U.S. 27) through the so-called Golden Gateway urban renewal project area.[8] Progress in committing and selling cleared land in the urban renewal area for redevelopment was extremely slow. By the middle of the 1960s, hundreds of acres of cleared land stood vacant and undeveloped.

Kelly recognized that something needed to be done, but he also knew that it made little sense to undertake individual projects without an overall plan. A joint city-county planning agency had been created in 1955, but up until then had been meagerly funded and staffed and had accomplished relatively little. Kelly set out to upgrade the planning capacity of the RPA.

Sometime in 1964, a "blind ad" was placed in *Jobs in Planning* seeking a qualified individual to direct the planning department of an unnamed southern city. One of the people who saw the advertisement was Thordis ("T. D.") Harden, a 33-year-old planner who was working at the time in Hartford, Connecticut. Harden had grown up in the south and the idea of returning appealed to him. When he answered the ad, Harden didn't know the location of the position, but guessed it might be Winston-Salem, North Carolina.

Six months went by and Harden didn't hear anything. Out of the blue, Harden received a call from the city's personnel director asking him if he was still available and interested. Harden said he was, and a few days later got a call from Mayor Kelly saying that he was going to be in New York City for a meeting. Would Harden be willing to come down to New York City to meet him? Harden traveled down to New York City, met Kelly and, in Harden's words, they "hit it off." Harden was subsequently invited to come to Chattanooga at the city's expense and was formally offered the chief planning position. "I met everybody and felt very comfortable," said Harden.

Within roughly a year from the time Harden arrived in Chattanooga, Kelly had managed to gain joint city and county approval of a sales tax measure that increased the city and county sales tax a fraction of a cent, and dedicated the increased revenue to fund joint city-county agencies—notably the library system and the RPA. Prior to this sales tax measure being approved, the director of the RPA had to go "hat in hand" to each of the 10 municipalities in Hamilton County to seek a modest annual appropriation (calculated by means of a formula largely based on population) from each municipality. Once the sales tax measure was approved, the RPA had a steady core of funding that allowed it to concentrate its attention on the most pressing planning issues of the time. Having a reliable and predictable core of funding also had the advantage of somewhat insulating the RPA from political pressure, and threats from city council members and elected officials in member local communities who disagreed with particular policy recommendations made by the agency.

Harden enjoyed a close working relationship with Mayor Kelly. "We lived fairly close," recalled Harden, "and he would often call me in the evening and say, 'I've got an idea. Come over and let's talk about it.' Often we'd end up talking till 1 AM. Quite often on weekends he'd say, 'Why don't you come up to the lake with us and we'll talk about some things.' And so I'd go up and spend the weekend, or Sunday at least, on his houseboat, and while we were fishing, we'd be brainstorming. It was marvelous."

Still, Harden had his work cut out for him because the direction of change in Chattanooga in those early years was far from positive. The city's downtown retail core was steadily losing market share to stores on the periphery, and no new commercial office building of any appreciable size had been built in the downtown since before World War II (except a small, four-story building for Pioneer Bank). Moreover, as noted earlier, most of the land that had been cleared away by the Golden Gateway urban renewal project was vacant and undeveloped. "The area was known as Hiroshima Flats," quipped Harden.

The area of the downtown south of 9th Street where the city's two railroad terminals were located—the fairly small, Victorian Louisville and Nashville

(L & N) Railroad Station, and the larger Terminal Railroad Station further south—was filled with run-down warehouses and factory buildings. Tracks crisscrossed major downtown streets at grade level, so that traffic was often cut off as trains wound their way slowly in and out of the city.

One building in the South Market area had special historic and architectural qualities that made it a treasured landmark in the minds and hearts of Chattanoogans: the L & N Railroad Station and its associated train shed. "The tracks curved into the L & N Railroad Station from the south," Harden described,

3-10 Aerial view of downtown Chattanooga in the 1950s, looking north toward the Tennessee River. Railroad tracks entered the city at grade level, crossing Market and Broad Streets (the city's main north-south arteries). The railroad terminal on the left is the old Louisville and Nashville Railroad Station.

Source: Courtesy of the Chattanooga-Hamilton County Bicentennial Library

"and the area closest to the station was covered by a huge pre-Civil War train shed, which was magnificent—a real engineering feat. Everybody was in love with the little Victorian station, but the train shed was the real gem."

Otherwise, the South Market area was pretty much a mishmash of undistinguished and run-down buildings. According to Harden, "The bus station occupied the block bounded by 10th, 11th, Broad and Market Streets. . . . South of the L & N Railroad Station Building, where the tracks curved away, there was a tire company with its roof caved in, a little gas station that was on a triangular parcel only 50 feet deep—just enough room for two cars and a pump—and a couple of bars. In the small, triangular-shaped block bounded by Georgia Avenue and 10th and Market Streets, there was an old Railway Express building."

Oddly enough, a five-block area in Chattanooga's downtown was owned by the State of Georgia because, about 20 years before the Civil War, the State of Georgia financed and built the rail line that came into Chattanooga from Atlanta. "If you went in the double door of the station," remembered Harden, "the left-hand side belonged to the State of Georgia, [while] the right-hand side belonged to the L & N Railroad. Unfortunately, unlike most property owners, the State of Georgia had little incentive to invest in improving its properties to benefit a city in another state. "The properties were rented out on long-term leases and the tenants occupying the buildings couldn't do anything with them," said Harden. As a result, after decades of neglect and disinvestment, the buildings fell into considerable disrepair.

CHATTANOOGA'S POLLUTED AIR

Chattanooga suffered from yet another problem that business leaders and citizens had been ignoring for years: its badly polluted air. Chattanooga's air quality problems were aggravated not only by the fact that industries in Chattanooga released significant amounts of pollution, but also because Chattanooga lay in a "bowl" surrounded by mountains, which kept the pollutants contained within the valley. Tuberculosis rates in Chattanooga were three times the national average and the sky was often dark at noon. "Pittsburgh had dirty air back then, but ours was dirtier," said T. D. Harden. "I used to drive into the city to work, through the tunnels from Brainard, and leave the sun on the other side of the ridge. When I got into town, I'd have to turn my headlights on because the pollution was so thick. It was awful."

Everyone who lived in Chattanooga back then has vivid memories of what it was like. Jerry Pace, who grew up in the 1960s in south Chattanooga, told me that, despite living in close proximity to Lookout Mountain, "On most days, we couldn't see the mountain." Ann Coulter, who succeeded Harden as executive director of the RPA, recalled the color of the sky at the beginning and end of the day. "I grew up in Chattanooga and have lived here all my life. When I was a child, I thought orange-pink sunrises and sunsets were normal and that

3-11   Chattanooga in the 1960s. Air quality was so poor that cars drove with their headlights on during the daytime.

Source: Courtesy of Chattanooga-Hamilton County Air Pollution Control Bureau

3-12   View looking down on Chattanooga from Lookout Mountain on a bad air day in the 1960s.

Source: Courtesy of Chattanooga-Hamilton County Air Pollution Control Bureau

they happened everywhere. I remember how colorful and pretty they were, but I know now they were not normal. I can remember my mother hanging clothes on the clothesline and then bringing them in some days in disgust. They were dirtier than when she put them in the washing machine and she had to start all over again because they were full of soot. Sometimes there would even be holes in them caused by the stuff in the air." Reportedly, the pollutants in Chattanooga's air were so corrosive that women who wore nylon stockings outside were apt to have their stockings disintegrate.

For a long time, business leaders in Chattanooga (like their counterparts in Pittsburgh) took pride in the city's gritty image and its reputation as the "Dynamo of Dixie." As Dave Crockett (city council member and director of the Chattanooga Institute) observed, "We were prosperous in the heyday of dirty air and dark skies," and the city's sooty air was evidence of the city's prosperity. "We didn't look at things in a holistic and integrated way, or at the unintended consequences of what we were doing. We didn't think long term," said Crockett.

Not everyone was ignoring the problem, however. Ralph Kelly had an administrative assistant, Bob Elmore, who was very concerned about the city's air pollution problems.[9] According to Kelly, Elmore was his chief advisor on the subject of air pollution and, with his help, the city applied for and received its first grant to study and identify the various pollutants and pollution sources causing the city's poor air quality. Meanwhile, Kelly tried to persuade the heads of major industries in the city to reduce their air emissions. "Wheland Foundry was one of our large employers," stated Kelly. "I sat down with Gordon Street, the Chief Executive Officer (CEO) of the company, and tried to convince him that, for the good of the community, he just had to address this issue. I reminded him that he had children and grandchildren who were going to be living in this community for a long time."

In 1969, the U.S. Department of Health, Education and Welfare declared that Chattanooga had the dirtiest air in the entire United States. Although people in Chattanooga already knew the city's air was polluted, the fact that Chattanooga had the *most* polluted air in the U.S. did come as a shock. Overnight, the name "Chattanooga" came to epitomize exactly what you *didn't* want your city to become. "It's not what you want to put on a bumper sticker," observed Ann Coulter. "It made people wake up and realize that you *can* do things that ultimately ruin a place and make it unlivable. It was pretty sobering."

In that same year (1969), midway through his second four-year term, Ralph Kelly was forced to leave office because of illness (ulcers) and was replaced by Chuck Bender, who served as mayor until 1971. Ralph Kelly had been Chattanooga's mayor for six years, and there were few visible signs that much progress had been made in tackling the city's many problems; nevertheless, a considerable amount of progress *had* been made. The city's planning capacity had been strengthened and leaders of the community's private sector had joined together with representatives of city and county government and planners at the RPA, and had begun to think more critically and realistically about the city's future. Moreover, on at least two fronts, plans had been developed that were aimed at making a concerted effort to move the city in a more positive direction.

Spurred on by the shame of having been cited as having the dirtiest air in the country, members of Chattanooga's business community finally galvanized behind the effort to dramatically reduce pollution in the city. Through the forceful efforts of the chamber of commerce, the Chattanooga Air Pollution Control Board was formed, which began to push local businesses and industries to curtail their emissions, even though it had no legal power to compel them to do so. "The chamber really took the lead, and took a lot of heat and criticism for its efforts," said Harden.

Slowly but surely, changes in industrial operations reduced the amount of industrial pollutants going into Chattanooga's air. Throughout older neighborhoods, home furnaces that burned Tennessee soft coal were also removed and were replaced with less polluting gas burners or electric heaters (electricity being relatively cheap in Chattanooga because of the TVA). The process of cleaning up the city's air took years of steady and persistent effort but, by 1988, the air in Chattanooga met all applicable federal air quality standards.[10]

COMPLETION OF THE FIRST PLAN

In 1967, two years after Harden arrived in Chattanooga, the first plan for Chattanooga and Hamilton County was completed, and was called *Toward a Better Environment—A Beautification Program for the City of Chattanooga and Hamilton County, Tennessee* ("the 1967 Better Environment plan"). Harden didn't just go off on his own to prepare the plan, but was savvy enough to get business and civic leaders involved in the planning process. In this case, Harden found an important ally in Ruth Holmberg (then Mrs. Ruth S. Golden), the chairman of the board of *The Chattanooga Times*, who chaired the Area Beautification Committee of the Greater Chattanooga Chamber of Commerce.[11]

According to Harden, Holmberg was "the force" behind the 1967 Better Environment plan. She not only helped choose the consulting firm that prepared the plan (Simonds and Simonds, Landscape Architects and Planners in Pittsburgh), but also put up most of the money needed for the consultant contract. Along with T. D. Harden, Holmberg was also involved in every step of the process leading to the plan's completion. On a number of occasions, Harden and Holmberg flew back and forth to Pittsburgh to meet with the consultants to avoid the additional cost of bringing the consultant team to Chattanooga.

The 1967 Better Environment plan marked an important turning point because it was the first planning document to focus on the environmental and aesthetic qualities of the city and region, and on the importance of protecting those qualities. Moreover, there was a tone of urgency in the plan's message: "This beautiful landscape is threatened . . . It is being disrupted and despoiled at an alarming rate. Forested areas are being slashed. Hillsides are being gouged back by heavy construction equipment, exposing ugly barren soil which is left open to erosion. Valley floors are being leveled, marshes filled with litter and trash and streams and rivers polluted . . . The people of Chattanooga and Hamilton County, as they move from home to work or to shop or play, are faced with jarring contradictions of scenic splendor and visual blight. From wooded residential areas one drives past automobile junkyards, through uncontrolled sign clutter and down bleak unshaded streets laced with overhead utility wires. . . . It is not too late . . . That which has been harmful must be corrected. That which is threatened should be protected. And that which is needed and has not been provided should be provided—now!"

The 1967 Better Environment plan was also the first planning document to advocate restoring the city's connection to the Tennessee River, which the plan recognized was an overlooked environmental and recreational amenity. "The Tennessee River, Chickamauga Lake, and the Chattanooga and Chickamauga Creeks, comprise the major waterways of the region. Few urban areas of the country have so inviting a potential for water-related living and recreation. Yet the city to date has almost ignored its water courses and their possibilities. There is little access to or enjoyment of the river. There is not one riverside park, developed and useful to the public. Views of the river are rare and occur only when one is well elevated. Even potential river views from the city's bridges are obscured by the side rails."

Viewed with the benefit of hindsight, it is clear that the plan's specific recommendations related to water and waterway resources predicted what ultimately took place some 20 or more years later. The 1967 Better Environment plan's specific recommendations were to:

- develop the full potential of the Tennessee River
- assure clean, usable water [by launching] a major attack . . . on river and stream pollution
- control the use of adjacent land
- include as much of the riverbank and streamside land as possible in the public domain
- incorporate recreational uses along the riverbanks
- construct a major riverside park and marina, and possibly an aquarium

Put simply, the 1967 Better Environment plan laid the groundwork for a fundamentally different way of thinking about and treating the environment, and

3-13   One of many billboards subsequently removed as a result of the adoption of the city's first comprehensive sign ordinance—a result of the 1967 Better Environment plan.

Source: Courtesy of the Chattanooga-Hamilton County Regional Planning Agency

planted the seeds for many of the "big" ideas that reshaped the city in later decades.

Most of the specific actions called for in the 1967 Better Environment plan were subsequently implemented. For example, the plan urged that "forceful measures" be taken to remove the large number of billboards that had proliferated throughout the valley, especially those that cluttered the entrances to the city, and that marred and obscured views of Lookout and Signal Mountains. In line with that recommendation, the city's first comprehensive sign ordinance was adopted. The number and size of signs and billboards along major corridors approaching the city, and leading to major tourist destinations (such as Ruby Falls, Rock City, the Incline Railway, and the Chattanooga and Chickamauga National Park) were significantly reduced. Additionally, Dallas Road (a major entrance to the city) was reconstructed with a planted median strip and measures were adopted to improve the appearance of the Cherokee Boulevard approach to the city.

TWO DOWNTOWN PLANS

While work was proceeding on the 1967 Better Environment plan, Harden was also working with local business leaders to prepare the first comprehensive plan for downtown Chattanooga. Again, Harden recognized that no plan was going to be successfully implemented unless leaders of the city's private sector and people having a financial interest in downtown were involved in the planning process. Harden approached the head of the area chamber of commerce and asked him to appoint a committee of citizens and business leaders who would be willing to serve on a Downtown Development Committee "to review everything and make recommendations."

The people who eventually made up the committee included the CEOs of all the banks, insurance companies and corporations that were based in Chattanooga, the owners of the city's department stores, the publishers of the city's two local newspapers, and the owners of major downtown buildings and properties.

Having the right person named chairman of the committee was especially important. "The chairman of the committee had to be the one person in the community who could say 'no' and make it stick," said Harden. That person was Robert Maclellan, the CEO of Provident Insurance Company.[12] "When Maclellan got the committee together," Harden remembered, "he established several rules. They would try to hold the meetings when everyone could attend, but if you were not there, you couldn't send someone else to vote for you. You just lost your vote, which meant that the major players made a point of being there, and of not sending someone else to attend to simply report on what happened."

The first plan for downtown Chattanooga was completed in 1968 and was called *Downtown Chattanooga—An Urban Design Plan and Improvements Program* ("the 1968 Downtown plan"). At the time the plan was prepared, the city still had four major downtown department stores (Miller Brothers, Lovemans, J. C. Penny and Sears). Nevertheless, retail sales in downtown Chattanooga had been steadily declining since 1958 (the first suburban-style shopping mall—Eastgate Mall—had just opened on the outskirts of the city in 1967), and the importance of downtown Chattanooga as a retail shopping center was clearly in jeopardy. The plan called for a major restructuring and reorganization of functions within the core of the city. It recommended that retail shopping be concentrated and strengthened along Broad and Market Streets between 6th and 9th Streets—in effect, compressing the retail shopping district into a somewhat smaller and more clearly defined geographic area than in the past. "Like most downtowns at the time, Chattanooga's retail business was shrinking," said Harden. "The task of the 1968 Downtown plan was to shrink the retail area to get the maximum amount of synergy out of what remained."

To reinforce the contraction of the retail district, the plan recommended that the area north of 6th Street (between 6th Street and the river) be redeveloped for housing, and that the area south of 9th Street (referred to as Market Street South) be redeveloped for offices, a convention center and hotel, a new central public library[13] and various other public uses.

Another important aspect of the 1968 Downtown plan, pertinent to these land use recommendations, was that it recognized the paramount importance of retaining the TVA's offices in downtown Chattanooga. At the time the 1968 Downtown plan was developed, the TVA's offices were scattered throughout the downtown area in various buildings, and the TVA was giving serious consideration to the possibility of building a new main office facility adjacent to the Chickamauga Dam, miles away from downtown Chattanooga. By anticipating and addressing the TVA's need to consolidate its offices, and urging that a new TVA headquarters building be built in downtown Chattanooga, the 1968 Downtown plan gave Mayor Kelly the ammunition he needed to derail the TVA's plans to move out of the city.

When I examined the 1968 Downtown plan, I was disappointed to discover that it did not recommend the preservation of the old L & N Railroad Station Building which, by Harden's own account, was very much treasured by Chattanooga residents. The plan did, however, call for preserving the pre-Civil War train shed, and for enclosing it and using it as an exhibition hall associated with the Convention and Trade Center. Unfortunately, any possibility of carrying out that planning recommendation was sabotaged by a private developer who had other ideas for the property. To put an end to the possibility that he might have to preserve and reuse the train shed, he drove a big pickup truck next to the train shed one night, tied a rope or chain to a key structural support and pulled it down.

A second plan for downtown Chattanooga, called *Downtown Chattanooga— An Urban Design Plan and Improvements Program* ("the 1976 Downtown plan"), was completed in 1976.[14] In the intervening years between the 1968 Downtown plan and the 1976 Downtown plan, a second peripheral mall (Northgate Mall) had opened in 1972 and, between 1972 and 1975, retail sales in downtown Chattanooga dropped by $33 million. Billed as a "survival kit" for downtown, the 1976 Downtown plan proposed a program of design changes and aesthetic improvements that, it was hoped, would make downtown Chattanooga a more attractive and inviting place.

For example, the plan proposed that sidewalks along Market Street be widened and that rows of trees be planted to create a more pedestrian-oriented environment. Down the middle of Broad Street (the widest north-south street in the downtown), the plan called for constructing a 10-foot-wide raised and landscaped median, and for planting trees down the center of the median to break up the vast paved area. Improvements were also recommended for High

Street to strengthen the connection between the downtown and the Bluff View Art District. Other actions called for in the 1976 Downtown plan included improved street graphics, the removal of downtown billboards, and control of the size and proliferation of protruding signs.

The 1976 Downtown plan did not put forward any bold new ideas for downtown but was, in effect, a further elaboration of the earlier 1968 Downtown plan; however, the tone and emphasis of the plan was different in a subtle but important way. Whereas the emphasis of the 1968 Downtown plan was on clearance and on building new structures, the 1976 Downtown plan devoted lengthy sections to "rehabilitation opportunities" and "design guidelines for rehabilitation."

OUTCOMES OF THE 1968 AND 1976 DOWNTOWN PLANS

In the late 1960s and early 1970s, the city established a federal urban renewal district in the South Market area that included blocks of privately owned property as well as the five-block area around the old L & N Railroad Station owned by the State of Georgia, and began the process of publicly acquiring properties. The properties owned by the State of Georgia were not taken by eminent domain; rather, purchase prices were negotiated that took into account the value of the outstanding leases. Also, rather than use federal urban renewal money to acquire the state-owned properties, the city used federal Community Development Block Grant (CDBG) funding that became available in the late 1970s. By 1979, all the properties previously owned by the State of Georgia had been conveyed to the city and the city proceeded to buy out the leaseholds.

Many of the physical developments and improvements called for in the two downtown plans can be seen in downtown Chattanooga today. The large, new Central Public Library recommended in the 1968 Downtown plan was constructed at 10th and Broad Streets, in the same general area as recommended in the plan. A block east of the Central Public Library, a new downtown park (Miller Park) was developed at Market Street and Martin Luther King, Jr. Boulevard. Mayor Robert Kirk Walker (who served as Chattanooga's mayor from 1971 to 1975) and his wife championed the cause of creating Miller Park and helped raise the money needed to build it after he left office. A block south of the library, a Convention and Trade Center (and associated hotel) were also built in accordance with recommendations contained the 1968 Downtown plan.[15]

One of the 1968 Downtown plan's important planning aims was to keep the TVA's offices in downtown Chattanooga. That aim was achieved when construction began in the early 1980s on a new TVA headquarters building just south of the Central Public Library, on a 9-acre site bounded by Chestnut, Market, 11th and 12th Streets (in the same general area recommended for it in the 1968 Downtown plan). The new TVA headquarters building, which contains

3-14   Central Public Library at 10th and Broad Streets, called for in the 1968 Downtown plan.

Source: Gene Bunnell

3-15   Miller Park—the first significant public open space in downtown Chattanooga.

Source: Gene Bunnell

3-16 The glistening TVA headquarters building, which opened in 1985, as viewed from the upper level of the Electric Shuttle Park South in 1998. In addition to providing a sense of the scale of the TVA complex, this view also provides a sense of the somewhat bleak and run-down state of Chattanooga's industrial Southside.

Source: Gene Bunnell

3-17 View looking south down Broad Street from the aquarium toward the TVA headquarters complex in the distance. The trees planted down the raised median reinforce the major north-south axis between the aquarium and the downtown core, and create a more comfortable, pedestrian-friendly streetscape.

Source: Gene Bunnell

1.3 million square feet of office space (equivalent to 200 football fields), cost $163 million and took nearly five years to build. An added advantage of keeping the TVA's 4,000-5,000 jobs in downtown Chattanooga is that it made it feasible for the city to bring about the renovation and conversion of a former furniture warehouse (across the street from the new TVA headquarters) into a mixed-use development known as Warehouse Row, composed of ground-floor shops and restaurants and upper-floor office space.[16]

Aesthetic improvements specifically outlined in the 1976 Downtown plan, such as the landscaped median strip down the middle of Broad Street, were also implemented. The pear trees planted down the median of Broad Street not only provide visual relief within a wide highway corridor, but also reinforce the axis between the downtown core and the river.

One other very positive outcome can also be traced back to the planning efforts of the late 1960s and early 1970s. While members of the Downtown Development Committee were working with T. D. Harden on planning for the downtown, it was learned that the University of Tennessee system had prepared a plan that called for the establishment of a new branch campus of the state university outside of Chattanooga. Had such a state university campus been built outside of Chattanooga, it undoubtedly would have represented the death knell for Chattanooga College—a private college in the heart of the city that was struggling even then to compete with state-subsidized colleges and universities. Had the campus in the city closed, it would have been a major blow to the core of the city. In an attempt to head off the branch campus plan, an alternative plan was developed with the involvement and approval of Chattanooga College officials calling for the existing college to be absorbed into the state university system, and for the existing campus to become a state university campus—the University of Tennessee at Chattanooga (UTC).

The fact that local leaders in Chattanooga were able to anticipate a potential threat, and develop a counterplan that turned that threat into an opportunity, epitomizes the very essence of planning. As a result of the forward thinking of the Downtown Development Committee, UTC—with its roughly 8,600 students and 1,000 faculty and staff—is now operating in the heart of the city.

The 1968 and 1976 Downtown plans did not reverse the decline of the city's downtown retail shopping district. The economic trends and forces that were operating nationally and at the regional level were simply too powerful to be totally negated. With the benefit of hindsight, it is easy to say that the planners' efforts to reassert downtown Chattanooga's dominance as a center of retail activity represented little more than wishful thinking. On the other hand, the plan did encourage owners of downtown department stores to invest in renovations and building improvements. By helping to stabilize conditions, the plans helped avert what could easily have been a much more precipitous decline. Downtown was not cured of its ills, but it was better off than it might otherwise have been. In the words of T. D. Harden, "We bought time. Downtown Chattanooga did not sink as low as the downtowns in Nashville, Knoxville and Memphis did back then. Downtown Chattanooga still had some life left in it. There were still retail stores and department stores, and downtown Chattanooga held on to roughly 75-80% of the class A office space in the whole region."

One major recommendation contained in the 1968 Downtown plan was thankfully *not* followed: namely, that the area between 4th Street and the river be cleared of existing buildings and be replaced entirely by housing. Had the housing scheme envisioned in the 1968 Downtown plan been implemented, it would have foreclosed a number of land use and development opportunities of which the city skillfully took advantage in the 1980s and 1990s. Moreover, the type of housing depicted in the 1968 Downtown plan would have been disastrous.

The plan envisioned row upon row of regularly spaced, rectangular housing blocks, interspersed with high-rise tower apartment buildings—the kind of massive, impersonal and sterile housing blocks that architects of the period under the influence of the Modern Architectural Movement were pro-

3-18   High-rise office buildings built on the site of the demolished L & N Railroad Station. Central Public Library on the left.

Source: Gene Bunnell

posing for cities across the country (and for which public housing authorities across the country were receiving federal funds to build for low-income residents). Indeed, the only way it would have been possible to construct the housing scheme suggested in the 1968 Downtown plan was if the project had received federal funding (because the housing market in Chattanooga at the time was far too weak to support privately financed, market-rate housing development).[17]

A LOCAL FOUNDATION INVESTS IN CHATTANOOGA BY INVESTING IN PLANNING

In 1980, the results of a six-month survey commissioned by Chattanooga's Civic Forum (a group of business leaders associated with the chamber of commerce) were released. The purpose of the survey was to find out why so few businesses considered locating in Chattanooga. Respondents to the survey basically said that Chattanooga had "no image," and that Chattanooga was seen as nothing more than an "industrial backwater, a stop along the highway." (Rawls, Jr., July 27, 1980, 20)

By most objective measures, Chattanooga's decline continued well into the 1980s; some statistics even appeared to indicate that the city's decline was accelerating. Between 1980 and 1990, Chattanooga lost over 10% of its population, the ninth greatest percentage population loss of any American city with a population of more than 100,000.[18] Also in the mid-1980s, the city's last downtown department stores closed.

Despite these discouraging trends, something happened in 1980 that would subsequently move the city in a more positive direction. At the urging of the Chattanooga Chapter of the AIA, the University of Tennessee College of Architecture and Planning, which was based in Knoxville, agreed to use Chattanooga as a "laboratory" for engaging students in addressing real-world planning and design issues. Professor Stroud Watson volunteered to direct the Chattanooga program and the Chattanooga-based Lyndhurst Foundation agreed to fund a major share of the cost of the planning initiative.[19]

The Lyndhurst Foundation was created in 1938 by John Lupton, the son of Cartter Lupton, who amassed a substantial fortune by opening the world's first Coca-Cola bottling plant in Chattanooga in 1899. Upon Cartter Lupton's death in 1977, an additional $50 million was bequeathed to the foundation, bringing its total assets to approximately $65 million. In that same year, John T. "Jack" Lupton became the new chairman of the foundation and Rick Montague was named its first full-time executive director.

With the funding provided by the Lyndhurst Foundation, Stroud Watson was able to open the Urban Design Studio in 1981 in a storefront on Vine Street. The studio was 20 feet wide by 50 feet deep, was heated with a wood stove, and soon turned into a beehive of activity as the first class of fourth-year undergraduate students, enrolled in the University of Tennessee's School of Architecture and Planning, began studying Chattanooga.

THE FIRST-YEAR PROJECT AT THE PLANNING AND DESIGN STUDIO: A STRUCTURE PLAN

The first year of work at the studio focused on studying the history, character and "inherited footprint" of the city. "What we found was a classic 9 to 5 downtown," Watson recalled. "I mean, classic. This place was empty at 7:30 AM and 5:30 PM. Zero activity. The city had a very urban past (unlike Knoxville, for instance, where I was living at the time), but its diversity had been undermined after the war by outward mobility and urban renewal."

At the end of the 1981-82 academic year, the students completed "Images of the City" ("the 1982 Structure plan") that described and communicated the basic structure of the downtown, and how various parts of the city were inter-related. An important reason for preparing this plan was to provide the kind of foundation that would make it possible to prepare more detailed plans in the future focusing on subareas of the city. Watson called it developing "a common vocabulary and understanding of the city. . . . It's a relatively hard concept to sell, I know, but you really don't have freedom unless you have an underpinning structure [or underlying set of values]. You don't have freedom until you have a constitution. You don't have a basis for making good, understandable choices until you have such a framework. If you start from zero every time, you just don't make any progress or get anywhere."

In the back of Watson's mind, there were two other reasons for developing a plan that focused on the "inherited footprint" of the city: (1) he recognized that reinhabiting the inherited footprint of the city provided the key to creating a vital and sustainable city in Chattanooga; and (2) he wanted to draw attention to the importance of strengthening and reinvigorating "the public realm" of the city and, to do that, it was essential to be able to identify and define the "center" of the city. "Every good city has a center," said Watson.

Identifying the center of great places is usually a relatively simple exercise, but in Chattanooga it was no longer obvious. The city's retail shopping district, which used to be seen as the heart of the city, was shrinking and shifting, and the downtown as a whole was very much in flux. The sad reality was that the city no longer had a center. "The city began on the river but had totally turned its back to the river," observed Watson.

After much study and analysis, Watson and his team of students concluded that Miller Park (the city park that had just been created in the 1970s) should be defined and strengthened as the center of the city. One reason for reinforcing the Miller Park area as the center of the city was that it was where key north-south and east-west arteries converged. "Nevertheless, the area had the visual appearance of a war zone."

The logic of choosing to define Miller Park as the center of the civic life of the city was strengthened by the fact that it was in close proximity to the Central Public Library, the post office, city hall, the courthouse and the city's largest downtown office buildings. The fact that the TVA's massive new headquarters was in the process of being constructed on a site just south of Miller Park further reinforced the importance of the location.

The 1982 Structure plan also identified two key focal points, or subcenters of activity, at opposite ends of the downtown. The northern focal point was at the northern end of Broad Street, overlooking the Tennessee River. The southern focal point was the southern entrance into the downtown, in the vicinity of the Chattanooga Choo Choo on Market Street. Once these north and south focal points were defined, anchoring the downtown at opposite ends, it became clear that one of the major features of downtown Chattanooga was a strong north-south axis that ran from the southern entrance to the city, through Miller Plaza, to the river. One way to create a more coherent and imageable downtown was therefore to strengthen that north-south axis.

To reinforce the southern focal point, the 1982 Structure plan recommended that the Market Street Depot and other older industrial buildings in the area be renovated for commercial occupancy (stores, restaurants and offices)—what today is known as Warehouse Row. To reinforce the northern focal point, the students proposed that both a public park and an aquarium be developed alongside the river that would celebrate the city's origins and generate riverfront activity. The 1982 Structure plan also proposed that housing be developed north of 5th Street and near the river but, unlike the 1968 Downtown plan, recommended that new housing be built only in selected pockets rather than covering the entire area—reasoning that more limited new residential development in selected areas "would provide a variety of desirable opportunities for urban living *and* would help support necessary downtown commerce," the plan said.

A major effort was made to publicly communicate the central findings and concepts of the 1982 Structure plan. First, a printed report called "Images of the City" was published and widely distributed. Second, the students constructed a public exhibit, which was open for public viewing throughout the summer of 1982 in the old S & W Cafe. The exhibit, which was formally opened by Mayor Pat Rose, was visited and seen by over 5,000 people.

The fact that the idea of developing what eventually became the Tennessee State Aquarium was first put forward by students at Watson's Urban Design Studio in 1982 is a stunning reminder of the power of a good idea. Back in 1982, the notion of building an aquarium seemed wacky and "off the wall" to many people. "Early on, it was 'those crazy students and the funny guy with the beard,'" quipped Watson.

THE LYNDHURST FOUNDATION
FOCUSES ON CHATTANOOGA

From the time the Lyndhurst Foundation was established in 1938 until the end of the 1970s, its practice had been to await the receipt of grant proposals, review the proposals on an annual basis and then decide which proposals it would fund. However, under the leadership of Jack Lupton and Rick Montague, the mission of the foundation was reassessed, and the decision was made to give priority to investing in activities and projects aimed at rejuvenating and revitalizing Chattanooga. "We started by making some reasonably small grants and sent a message to institutions in town that we wanted them to think about how to revitalize the city . . ." said Montague. (as quoted by Morris, February 1996, 4 tl)

Early on, the foundation decided that one of the best ways to help regenerate and revitalize the city was to invest in planning. Indeed, the grant provided to the Urban Design Studio was the first of many grant awards the foundation would go on to make in the 1980s and 1990s for the specific purpose of supporting planning efforts and processes focused on Chattanooga.

The foundation also sought to broaden public support for the city's revitalization by reminding people of the value of having a vital central city. It did that by sponsoring a downtown music festival called "Five Nights in Chattanooga." The idea of holding a five-day downtown music celebration was suggested by Gianni Longo, a planning consultant based in New York City (a principal in the firm of American Community Partnerships (ACP), which specializes in participatory Planning and Visioning) to whom Rick Montague had turned for advice.

The "Five Nights in Chattanooga" program, which was aggressively promoted and could be attended free of charge, brought a number of big-name blues and country music artists to perform on successive Tuesday evenings in a vacant lot in the heart of the city. Bluesman B. B. King was the featured performer on the first of the Five Nights and attracted a crowd of roughly 6,000. The Fifth Night program, featuring Hank Williams, Jr., attracted a crowd of 12,000. "It was enormously important," said Stroud Watson. "For the first time in a long time, people from all kinds of different backgrounds came together to celebrate the *communitas* of the downtown."

THE URBAN DESIGN STUDIO GAINS CITY FUNDING
AND BECOMES ASSOCIATED WITH THE RPA

During the first four years of operation, the Urban Design Studio's main funding source was the Lyndhurst Foundation and Stroud Watson was the only full-time professional staff person at the studio. "I was alone all the way up until 1984, except for my students. It makes me tired just thinking of it," remembered Watson.

In 1983, Gene Roberts was elected mayor of Chattanooga, and in 1984 he signed a contract in which the city agreed to join the Lyndhurst Foundation in funding the Urban Design Studio for six years (until 1990). One other significant provision of the contract was that, for the first time, Stroud Watson was officially recognized as a consultant to city government. With the funding provided by the city, Watson was able, for the first time, to hire an assistant. The person Watson hired was Karen Hundt.[20]

Each semester, the students at the Urban Design Studio studied a particular district, block or building in Chattanooga and, at the end of the term, made a public presentation attended by elected officials, realtors, bankers and business people. William Sudderth attended many of the student presentations over the years and came to appreciate the effect the students' ideas had on Chattanooga's experienced, and somewhat jaded, leaders. "What's fascinating to me is how the students approach projects. Unlike me, they come in thinking there's nothing you *can't* do—that there are really no hurdles that can't be overcome. I, on the other hand, come in with a very different mindset. No matter what building or block or district one might choose to study, I could tell you five reasons, based on my 30 years of experience, why you *can't* do something worthwhile there. You've got bad owners; it's got environmental problems or a bad image; traffic patterns aren't right, etc. People in government are also affected by the same kind of negative mindset. They're famous for knowing all the reasons you can't do something. The students, on the other hand, come in and will have none of that! They propose this and that, change roads and move traffic lights, and I think to myself, 'Wow!' There's no question: the students have had an inspirational effect on the leaders of this community."

At some point in the early 1980s, the boards of directors of both the Lyndhurst Foundation and the Tonya Foundation (another Chattanooga-based foundation) got together and decided they would join forces to fund the expansion of Miller Park. However, Stroud Watson was not convinced that simply making the park bigger was going to do much to strengthen the center of the city. "What the city center needed was a clarity of urban structure that produced a memorable place," said Watson. During the 1984-85 academic year, the Urban Design Studio therefore turned its attention to developing a detailed urban design plan for a nine-block area around Miller Park, which was called the Miller Park District. To provide added professional expertise related to the urban design planning effort, Fred Koetter (of Koetter, Kim and Associates of Boston and who, in 1998, became the Dean of Architecture School at Yale) was hired as a consultant to the studio.

The *Urban Design Study of the Miller Park District* ("the Miller Park District plan"), which was completed in July 1985, recommended that an enlarged, public open space be created, but that the area added to the park (which the plan called "Miller Plaza") be of a more urban character. Whereas Miller Park was an informal and "serene" park space, the plan called for Miller Plaza to be a more active space that included a public use Plaza Pavilion and an outdoor space designed for performances and events. To further define the plaza and generate activity befitting the center of the city, the plan also called for the northern edge of the plaza to be framed by a two-story structure accommodating a mixture of stores and offices.

The Miller Park District plan also urged that "high priority" be given to establishing a shuttle bus or trolley line running north and south along the Market Street Corridor, connecting the Chattanooga Choo Choo, Miller Park, the Market Street commercial area and the Tennessee riverfront. In fact, the shuttle bus service that now operates in downtown Chattanooga (which, in 1992, began using emission-free electric buses) follows the same route recommended in the Miller Park District plan.

Miller Plaza was completed in 1990 and, like many other outcomes in Chattanooga, was produced by a combined public and private effort. The city assembled the land, and the Tonya and Lyndhurst Foundations provided the $6.5 million in private funding to pay the cost of designing and constructing the public plaza, public use pavilion and adjoining commercial space. The two-story commercial structure that was built as part of the plaza has been rented out and provides space for various businesses and offices, including the office of the Chattanooga Downtown Partnership, which promotes and markets downtown Chattanooga, organizes downtown programs, concerts, festivals and entertainment, and works with the city and the chamber of commerce to raise funding for seasonal flowers, banners and streetscaping.[21]

Miller Plaza has become a focal point for a wide variety of public events and activities. "The plaza and pavilion have been a great social success," reported Stroud Watson. "There has been everything from weddings to receptions to political rallies to car shows. It did create a center." Each Friday night for 17 weeks during the summer, the "Nightfall" series of musical performances is held at Miller Plaza, featuring local and regional artists and sometimes well-known, big-name performers. "On a typical Friday night, there are 1,500 to 2,000 people down there, and it's all free," said Jim Bowen, vice president of the RiverCity Company.

The completion of Miller Plaza in 1990 marked the beginning of a new era for Stroud Watson's nine-year-old Urban Design Studio. That same year, the studio was renamed the Riverfront/Downtown Planning and Design Center ("the Planning and Design Center"), and officially became an office of the Chattanooga-Hamilton County RPA. It also moved to more spacious quarters on the second floor of the Miller Plaza commercial building, and the RPA assumed responsibility for a major portion of the operating budget of the cen-

3-19 Miller Plaza (Plaza Pavilion in background)—a tangible outcome of the 1982 Structure plan and Miller Park District plan prepared by the Urban Design Studio.

Source: Courtesy of the Chattanooga News Bureau

ter. Two planners on the RPA's planning staff were permanently assigned to the center. The RiverCity Company paid for a third staff member; by 1998, the center had a professional staff of four.

I spent a good deal of time at the Planning and Design Center when I was in Chattanooga in 1998 and conducted a number of interviews there. What I found was an open, undivided space with maps, plans, illustrations and renderings on every wall, and a few three-dimensional models scattered about. There were lots of tables, chairs and movable dividers upon which drawings and maps could be pinned, which could be rearranged to provide a setting for small group meetings or moved aside to accommodate a large group meeting. There was a medium-sized conference room in a corner of the center, enclosed by floor-to-ceiling fixed partitions, and the door to the conference room contained a large area of glass, which made the interior of the conference room visible from the rest of the center. In short, it was impossible to hold a meeting out of the view of others. As Stroud Watson said, "The Planning and Design Center is meant to be a civic forum, where people meet out in the open. The reason there's glass on this door is so everyone can see what's going on. You can go in there and have a quiet meeting, but you can't do it without being seen."

Far from being an impediment, the openness of the Planning and Design Center created an atmosphere that encouraged more people to attend planning-related meetings and increased the diversity of attendees. Indeed, local elected officials like City Councilman Dave Crockett have come to realize that having representatives of all segments of the community is essential for successful problem-solving. "When I'm sitting around a conference table at a meeting, I often look under the table and ask, 'How are we doing on the shoe test? Is it all wing-tips, or are there some tennis shoes and sandals and hiking boots or hunting boots and loafers and pumps and kids' shoes and everything in between?' If we've got the right mix of shoes, then we've probably got the right mix of people at this table so that we can get something done."

Another valuable quality of the Planning and Design Center was the fact that it was *not* a city, county or state government building; neither was it owned by a private business or corporation. In other words, it was "neutral territory." Indeed, the largely unaffiliated nature of the center was tremendously liberating, and helped break down the kind of institutional and ideological boundaries that can tend to divide public and private sector actors. "I don't think the mayor would ever consider having an important meeting [related to the planning and development of the city] anywhere else, as long as the center is big enough," said Stroud Watson.

PLANNING FOR THE CITY-RIVER CONNECTION: THE MOCCASIN BEND TASK FORCE

Wise old cities . . . have always known that the river is more than a thoroughfare for the passage of goods. A city's river is also a spiritual artery, a place for the citizens to stroll and think, reflect, remember, and exercise. The river focuses the soul of a city.

—Andrei Codrescu
(*Hail Babylon—In Search of the American City at the End of the Millennium*, 1998, 105)

The City of Chattanooga began at Ross's Landing, but had turned its back on the river. A city that loses touch with its beginnings loses touch with the whole.

—Stroud Watson

In 1982, while Watson's Urban Design Studio was working on the 1982 Structure plan and "Images of the City" exhibit, the first step was taken toward developing a plan for lands along the Tennessee River. The Chattanooga-Hamilton County RPA asked the Urban Land Institute (ULI) to send an advisory panel of experts to Chattanooga to advise the city on potential alternative uses that could be developed on a roughly 600-acre tract of publicly owned land (city, county and state) along the Tennessee River in the area called Moccasin Bend. The Lyndhurst Foundation paid for the $25,000 cost of bringing the ULI advisory panel to Chattanooga.

The 10 members of the ULI advisory panel spent five full days in the city (April 25-30, 1982).[22] The week began with a briefing by T. D. Harden on existing conditions and trends in the city, the status of current plans, and a tour of the city and the Moccasin Bend property. During the next few days, the panel conducted a large number of interviews with opinion leaders and representatives of various interest groups in the city regarding how they felt the property should be used. They also analyzed pertinent data regarding the market for various kinds of uses. At the end of the week, the panel held a public press conference at which they delivered their main findings and recommendations. A 69-page formal report was subsequently prepared and delivered to the city.

Despite the fact that the ULI advisory panel was composed predominantly of business executives, real estate consultants and property managers (who might be expected to be "pro-development"), the primary message of the ULI advisory panel was that the Moccasin Bend area was a unique and valuable environmental resource that should be largely preserved, and that housing and industry were particularly inappropriate for the property. If development were to take place, the uses the panel felt were most appropriate were related to recreation and tourism (hiking trails, a small marina, riverfront activities, and a few restaurants and specialty shops). Another idea, put forward in the panel's report, was that part of the area could developed with period houses and cabins depicting early life in Chattanooga.

Particular emphasis was given in the report to the importance of preserving "Stringer's Ridge." According to the ULI advisory panel (1982), "It is a beautiful, mature forest area that can be enhanced by the addition of tastefully constructed hiking trails and bikeways and preservation of the remnants of gun placements and other signs of the Civil War. A bikeway system connecting Stringer's Ridge with the recreation and nature areas could substantially increase the number of people using and enjoying the area."

Perhaps the panel's most important recommendation related to the Moccasin Bend area was that the city and county create a Moccasin Bend Commission to implement the recommended program, and that the commission work to develop a long-range plan with a 20-year time horizon.

Not long after the ULI advisory panel's visit and report to Chattanooga, an eight-member Moccasin Bend Task Force was created to carry out further studies, to hire an outside consultant and to develop a long-range master plan. Five members of the task force were citizens (two of them appointed by the city and two by the county). Rick Montague, the executive director of the Lyndhurst

Foundation and the fifth citizen member, was appointed jointly by the city and the county, and was named the chairman of the task force. At Montague's request, Stroud Watson was made an advisor to the task force. Jim Bowen, who worked for the city at the time, served as liaison between the task force and city government.

One of the first things the task force did was develop and issue a Request for Proposals (RFP) to begin the process of selecting a consultant. After reviewing the proposals and qualifications of a large number of consulting firms, the decision was made to hire the firm of Carr, Lynch Associates, Inc. from Cambridge, Massachusetts (headed by Steve Carr and Kevin Lynch). Unfortunately, a day or so after the contract with Carr, Lynch was signed, Kevin Lynch died and responsibility for the planning effort fell entirely on the shoulders of Steve Carr.

By all accounts, the planning process overseen by Rick Montague and the Moccasin Bend Task Force marked the beginning of a much more open and participatory style of planning in Chattanooga. "It was a remarkably open process," said Stroud Watson. "Literally hundreds of public meetings were held, and thousands of people turned out to contribute their ideas and try to rethink what could happen along the river," said Jim Bowen. "About six months into the planning process, we were having community meetings and we were thinking of Disney World North and lots of other riverfront-related schemes. We then realized that many of the projects that were being thought about for Moccasin Bend might be better placed somewhere else along the river, or in the downtown."

When the Moccasin Bend Task Force began its planning process, the idea had been to develop a plan solely for Moccasin Bend—a large tract of publicly owned land that represented a major opportunity but was nevertheless on the opposite side of the river and somewhat remote from downtown Chattanooga. From the beginning, however, Watson had believed that it made little sense to treat the Moccasin Bend property as an isolated planning problem, and that the only way to understand what should occur at Moccasin Bend was to study and plan for a much longer stretch of the river. Looking at a longer stretch of the river was also essential to develop a plan that would succeed in reconnecting the city to the river.

Watson's point of view eventually prevailed and the task force voted to request the city and county government's permission to develop a master plan for a 22-mile stretch of the river from the Chickamauga Dam to the Marion County line. The city and Hamilton County granted that permission and also agreed to join the Lyndhurst Foundation in providing the increased funding for the expanded master planning effort. The total cost of the expanded planning effort was about $300,000, of which a third was paid by city government, a third by the county and a third by the Lyndhurst Foundation. Roughly a year after the Moccasin Bend Task Force began meeting, the aims of the planning effort had become much more ambitious and intertwined with the goal of revitalizing downtown Chattanooga. It took another year for *Tennessee Riverpark: Chattanooga* ("the 1985 Riverpark master plan") to be completed.

THE FIRST INTER-CITY VISIT

One result of the increased planning activity focusing on downtown Chattanooga and the Tennessee River was that leaders of the city's private sector became increasingly interested in learning about what *other* cities had done to revitalize *their* downtowns and riverfront/waterfront areas. The chamber of commerce therefore got the idea of arranging for a large delegation of people to travel to Indianapolis, Indiana to see the city's revitalized downtown, and the 19th century Central Canal that had been reclaimed and rebuilt into an attractive and popular Canal Walk. Roughly 50 community leaders from Chattanooga went on that first inter-city visit to Indianapolis in the fall of 1983—a group that included the "movers and shakers" of the city's private sector as well as Mayor Gene Roberts, Mai Bell Hurley (a citizen activist), the Lyndhurst Foundation's Rick Montague and Jack Murrah, T. D. Harden and Stroud Watson.

After being given a tour of the center city and Canal Walk, the group from Chattanooga had a lengthy meeting with Indianapolis' mayor, Bill Hudnut. During the course of the meeting, Mayor Hudnut gave a great deal of the credit for the city's revitalization to the Greater Indianapolis Progress Committee (GIPC)—a combination "blue ribbon committee" and "think-tank." "When an issue needed to be addressed or a task undertaken, the mayor could ask the GIPC to consider the matter and recommend what should be done," said Ronald C. Littlefield, a person who was part of the group that went to Indianapolis, and who subsequently played a key role in helping organize the *Vision 2000* planning process that trip to Indianapolis inspired.

Jack Murrah and all the others who made the trip to Indianapolis were impressed. "We saw how various interests in Indianapolis had come together for a shared purpose," Murrah commented. "We also realized the importance of devising new institutions and partnerships. We realized that none of the existing institutions in Chattanooga were properly structured for the task or broad enough in their representation."

The first inter-city visit had a profound effect on the people who were part of it, both in terms of stimulating ideas and of generating enthusiasm for the task of replanning the city. Each succeeding year, at around the same time, a large group from Chattanooga traveled to another city, and the "inter-city visit" became an annual event. Among the cities visited after Indianapolis were San Antonio, Texas; St. Louis, Missouri; Portland, Oregon; Pittsburgh, Pennsylvania; Baltimore, Maryland; and Charlotte, North Carolina. "The trips to other cities were very important, especially that first trip to Indianapolis, because at the time we were a fractured community," said Murrah.

Soon after arriving back in Chattanooga, Mai Bell Hurley, Rick Montague, Ronald C. Littlefield, Stroud Watson and a number of others started meeting at the Urban Design Studio on Vine Street. "We met every Thursday afternoon for about four or five months and invited people who hadn't gone on the trip to Indianapolis. The number of people who came would range from 30 to 60 people," said Hurley. One of the first things that came out of those meetings was the idea that an organization like the GIPC was needed in Chattanooga. "We came to the realization that we could develop the best plans in the world, but nothing would happen unless there was broad-based community support for implementing those plans," said Hurley.

The decision was therefore made to form a new, private, nonprofit entity called Chattanooga Venture, with a 60-member board of directors appointed by the mayor. "We worked very hard to create a board of directors that was representative of all the diverse interests and elements in the community," said Hurley. "We didn't call them representatives of any particular segment of the community because they didn't get elected by their peers." As Ron Littlefield noted, "The only charge the mayor gave the Chattanooga Venture board was to look beyond their own agendas, and come up with ideas and recommendations that were in the best interests of the community as a whole. Chattanooga Venture was intended to be the vehicle for bringing the community together."

Ron Littlefield (who had previously worked at the RPA, later for the chamber of commerce and then the mayor's office) was named executive director and worked out of a small room in the mayor's office. Mai Bell Hurley, who had chaired the group meetings at the Urban Design Studio, was elected chairperson and worked as a full-time volunteer.[23] Three vice chairpersons were also named: the CEO of the Krystal Company (a Chattanooga-based, regional fast-food company); the pastor of the African Methodist Episcopal church who was active in Chattanooga's black community (Reverend Robert Keesee); and a representative of organized labor. ("Labor/management relations were perceived as bad back then and there was a lot of publicity about labor strife," said Ron Littlefield.) Both Mayor Roberts and the county executive issued formal statements supporting the efforts of Chattanooga Venture.

VISION 2000

There were good ideas floating all around, but those ideas will only take root and grow if they get beyond the minds of a few to the minds of many.

—Ronald C. Littlefield

Soon after it was officially formed, Chattanooga Venture began setting the stage for a lengthy and elaborate "visioning process" called *Vision 2000* that was aimed at involving large numbers of Chattanooga residents and at building public support for an agreed-upon, action-oriented planning agenda. Once again, the Lyndhurst Foundation invested in planning by providing external funding to Chattanooga Venture and by agreeing to pay the costs associated with *Vision 2000*, including the cost of hiring an outside consultant.[24]

Gianni Longo of ACP was hired to help Chattanooga Venture plan, organize and orchestrate the *Vision 2000* process. "He was a real animator and came up with lots of ideas to make the process fun," said Littlefield. During the months leading up to and during the *Vision 2000* process, Chattanooga Venture published and distributed a newsletter describing and promoting the process. "It was a very high-profile process. The local TV station did a one-half hour program on it, and we at the paper were very involved in promoting and encouraging people to participate in the *Vision 2000* process," said Pat Wilcox, an editorial writer and editor at *The Chattanooga Times*.

Vision 2000 kicked off with a big meeting that was held in September 1984 on the UTC campus. A number of task forces were formed, and everyone was invited and encouraged to join. According to Pat Wilcox, "You could join any task force you wanted—or you could join and go to all of them because the task forces met regularly on different nights in different parts of the city."

When people came to task force meetings, they were challenged to think about the future. Each task force meeting focused on a different question (such as "What gives Chattanooga a unique sense of place?" or "What do we want Chattanooga to look like in 2000?"), and small groups were formed to respond to the questions from different perspectives: Future Alternatives, People, Places, Work, Play and Government. To insure that everyone had an opportu-

3-20   *Vision 2000*, large group meeting, 1984.

nity to express their views (and that no individuals dominated the sessions, which can sometimes happen), each small group meeting was conducted using a "nominal group process" and was overseen by a trained facilitator. "The facilitators wrote down exactly what people said, or asked people to put their own words on the board, and kept a high level of intensity going in the sessions," said Littlefield.

More than 1,700 people participated in the many "visioning" sessions, which were held in different parts of the city over a six-month period. "It was a marathon process—and was both exhausting and exhilarating," said Littlefield. Equally as important as the sheer numbers of people who participated was the diversity of the participation. Pat Wilcox commented, "The validity and the value of the process were directly related to the extent and representativeness of the participation. For a long time in Chattanooga, there was the idea that the people with the money and power controlled everything. We needed to break out of that shell, and did."

3-21   *Vision 2000,* small group meeting with facilitator.

Source: Courtesy of Chattanooga Venture

WHAT *VISION 2000* PRODUCED

At the end of the six-month *Vision 2000* process, participants had produced 40 goal statements and had identified specific activities, projects and/or initiatives that, if carried out, would help achieve each goal and make the city a better place. Staff and volunteers of Chattanooga Venture, in turn, compiled these goal statements and recommended activities into what was called a Portfolio of Commitments.[25] According to Mai Bell Hurley, it was never the aim of *Vision 2000* to try to prioritize the goal statements or recommended activities in terms of their relative importance. Rather, the aim was simply to identify desirable projects, initiatives and actions that people agreed should be undertaken.

Some of the goal statements formulated during *Vision 2000* were very specific and could be achieved by undertaking a single project, such as to:

- restore, renovate and update the Tivoli Theater, a once-grand, 1,700-seat movie house built in 1921, for musical performances and other events as a downtown activity anchor
- plan future use of the Soldiers and Sailors Memorial Auditorium to provide space for events needing facilities between the size of the Tivoli Theater and UTC's arena
- identify the location and create a management organization related to the development of Bessie Smith Preservation Hall on Martin Luther King, Jr. Boulevard[26]
- develop a major outdoor, multipurpose sports facility

Other goal statements were much broader and called for sustained efforts on a number of fronts, such as to:

- reinforce Chattanooga's role as a center for small conventions and family tourism
- program cultural events to celebrate the diverse segments of the population and bring them together, giving special emphasis to the involvement of children
- expand arts activity, and strengthen support and recognition of local artists through neighborhood and city festivals
- develop a coordinated, economically sound, public/private transportation system
- implement a comprehensive plan to alleviate substandard housing through neighborhood revitalization
- provide an additional supply of diverse, high-quality housing in and near the city's center through investment in preservation, new construction and adaptive reuse
- create a coordinated approach to solve existing problems and reduce future problems in air, water, toxic waste and noise pollution

Not long after the *Vision 2000* process was completed, $7 million was raised to restore and renovate the Tivoli Theater.[27] The restored Tivoli Theater reopened in 1989 and has become the home of Chattanooga's Symphony Orchestra.

Another *Vision 2000* goal was achieved when the Soldiers and Sailors Memorial Auditorium was renovated and modified to accommodate performances and productions that were too large to be staged at the Tivoli. Before its renovation, the auditorium contained approximately 7,000 seats and had been used primarily for wrestling. During the renovation, its floor was elevated and the seating was reduced to between 4,000 and 5,000 to accommodate Broadway theater shows and other large-scale productions. The annual operations of both the Tivoli Theater and the Soldiers and Sailors Memorial Auditorium are subsidized by the city at a total cost of about $300,000 per year.[28]

In August 1991, ground was broken for the construction of Bessie Smith Preservation Hall—a multiuse educational, cultural and entertainment facility on Martin Luther King, Jr. Boulevard. The $3.8 million needed to complete the facility was raised from a combination of public and private sources. The facility, which opened in 1996, contains exhibits describing and celebrating the life and singing career of Bessie Smith, a listening room features tapes of her and other artists, and a 264-seat performance hall where local and regional blues musicians and singers can perform. Nationally known jazz and blues artists, as well as regional and local artists, have been featured in concerts at the hall, and experts in the study of blues and jazz have presented lectures, workshops and musical demonstrations.

In pursuit of the *Vision 2000* goal of developing a coordinated, economically sound, public/private transportation system, a shuttle bus service began running between the riverfront and the Chattanooga Choo Choo. As of 1992, all of the buses operating on the shuttle route were emission-free, electric vehicles operated under a lease arrangement with the Chattanooga Area Regional Transportation Authority (CARTA).[29]

Two large and attractive multilevel parking structures, with covered areas on the ground level for departing/arriving buses and waiting passengers, were constructed by CARTA at the southern and northern ends of the shuttle bus route. Revenues collected from the parking structures are used by CARTA to cover the cost of operating the Electric Shuttle, thereby allowing people to ride the Electric Shuttle for free. The northern terminal structure was combined with a seven-screen movie theater complex. (Up until then, there were no movie theaters in downtown Chattanooga.) The southern terminal and parking structure built by CARTA next to the Chattanooga Choo Choo contains a conference center, an educational exhibit and a bus maintenance facility. "The exhibits tell about how the electric buses work, and you can look through the glass and see people working on the buses," said Ann Coulter.

Converting the shuttle bus operation to emission-free buses actually met a number of *Vision 2000* goals at the same time. It improved transportation in the

3-22   The restored Tivoli Theater on Broad Street.

Source: Gene Bunnell

3-23   People boarding Electric Shuttle at southern terminus, Shuttle Park South.

Source: Courtesy of Electric Transit Vehicle Institute

city, and also helped reduce air *and* noise pollution (the new buses operate so quietly that one can hardly hear them at all). It advanced the goal of local economic development by making it possible to establish a locally based company to manufacture the buses. Because of their novelty, the electric buses have proven to be popular with visitors and have added to Chattanooga's appeal as a tourist destination.

Vision 2000 wasn't just concerned with the physical development of the city. By asking the task forces and small groups to address each goal from the perspectives of Future Alternatives, People, Places, Work, Play and Government, the people who organized the *Vision 2000* process consciously encouraged participants to integrate social, economic and political concerns into the action agenda. Pat Wilcox recalled, "There was a woman who actively participated in *Vision 2000* who was very concerned about domestic violence and made sure that issue got highlighted. Within a few months of the end of *Vision 2000*, she had the beginnings of a shelter for battered women."

Another of the goal statements approved during the *Vision 2000* process called for changing the structure and form of government in Chattanooga. When the *Vision 2000* process was held, Chattanooga had a commission form of government, with commissioners elected at large and the mayor elected by majority vote of the city commission. It was generally acknowledged that the effect of this form of government was to minimize political representation of minorities.

To remedy that situation, *Vision 2000* participants approved a goal statement calling for the design of "a new government structure for the City of Chattanooga . . . with legislative powers vested in individuals elected primarily or wholly by district and with a single chief executive representing the entire community." This goal was achieved—although not without a struggle. In 1989, a referendum calling for adoption of a new city charter to change Chattanooga's commission form of government to a mayor-council form was defeated. In the wake of that defeat, many participants in *Vision 2000*, claiming that the at-large system of voting was discriminatory, filed a lawsuit. After months of trial and testimony, Judge Allen Edgar found in favor of the plaintiffs, and the system of government was changed to reflect almost exactly what was proposed in the *Vision 2000* process—namely the election of city councilors by district and the election of the city's mayor by voters city-wide (rather than by a vote of the city's commissioners). The new mayor-council form of government took effect in 1990.

In 1993, Chattanooga Venture organized and ran a second community-wide visioning exercise, called *ReVision 2000*. During a series of nine meetings, more than 2,600 people participated. The ideas generated during this second round of sessions led to the formulation of 27 new goals for the city. As was done in the 1984 *Vision 2000* process, a steering committee oversaw the process, and compiled the input from task forces into goal statements and recommended activities.[30]

ASSESSING THE IMPACT OF CHATTANOOGA VENTURE AND *VISION 2000*

Almost everyone I interviewed is convinced that the *Vision 2000* process carried out by Chattanooga Venture played a key role in bringing about Chattanooga's rebirth. A year after the *Vision 2000* process was completed (in 1985), a well-connected and influential individual who didn't participate in the process came up to Hurley and said, "If I'd known it was going to be that important, I would have come."

"It was a community experience that laid the foundation for everything that followed," noted Pat Wilcox. "The *Vision 2000* process made people realize that many of us want very much the same thing. In addition, it instilled a 'can-do' attitude and made people realize that we can have the kind of community we want to have. It made us realize that we could turn our community around, but to do that we needed to plan as a community."

A survey conducted in 1992 found that 37 of the 40 goals set out and approved during the 1984 *Vision 2000* process had been fully or partially completed. Admittedly, some of the positive outcomes that came about after *Vision 2000* might have come about anyway; on the other hand, most of the outcomes probably would *not* have, and most certainly would not have come about as quickly, had *Vision 2000* not occurred. "Many of the things that were included in the Portfolio of Commitments had been talked about for a long time—like renovating and restoring the Tivoli Theater for live theater and musical performances," stated Mai Bell Hurley. "No one can say for sure, absent Chattanooga Venture and *Vision 2000*, whether or not it would have happened. The fact is that it was identified as an important undertaking in the Portfolio of Commitments and now it's a reality. None of us [associated with Chattanooga Venture] ever thought it was important to claim credit. What was important to us was getting things done."

As both Hurley and Littlefield readily acknowledge, many of the goals and activities endorsed and validated by the *Vision 2000* process had been considered before; they just hadn't been implemented. The purpose of the process was not necessarily to produce new ideas; rather, it was to promote the dispersion of ideas and *energize* the community. Its real contribution was that it brought about a shared vision and mobilized the collective will of the community.

CHATTANOOGA NEIGHBORHOOD ENTERPRISE, INC. —HOUSING INITIATIVES

It got started as a result of the community-based visioning, goal setting, agenda-setting Vision 2000 *process.*

—Leigh M. Ferguson

Two of the most important goal statements set out in the *Vision 2000* Portfolio of Commitments focused on housing—on the need to reduce substandard housing, revitalize neighborhoods and provide a diverse supply of high-quality housing in and near the center of the city. As Leigh Ferguson remembered, "Basically, people recognized that the condition and availability of affordable housing in Chattanooga was a big problem."

Following the *Vision 2000* process, James Rouse (the nationally known developer) was brought to Chattanooga to conduct a housing needs assessment study. The results of Rouse's study confirmed people's worst fears. "Rouse determined that over half of the housing units in the city were substandard," said Ferguson, "and, once the report was released, people rallied 'round the flag and committed to the goal of eliminating substandard housing in Chattanooga within 10 years."

Rouse recommended that a nonprofit 501c3 public/private partnership organization be created in Chattanooga. Such an organization, he argued, could receive public as well as private funding, and could directly intervene to increase the quality and quantity of affordable housing in the city by rehabilitating existing homes and constructing new housing. It could also operate more flexibly than a governmental entity and in a business-like fashion.

A new nonprofit corporation was therefore created in 1986 called Chattanooga Neighborhood Enterprise, Inc. (CNE). It began with about $4 million of federal CDBG money that the city had committed to affordable housing (including money that had been committed in earlier years and was "in the pipeline") and a major grant from the Lyndhurst Foundation. Each year thereafter, the city turned over a major share of its annual federal CDBG allocation to CNE, and also provided CNE with an additional $2 million a year from the city's general fund for CNE's housing programs. In addition, CNE received approximately $1 million each year from the Lyndhurst Foundation. Additional funding was obtained by applying for state and federal funding, and by taking advantage of various state and federal housing programs (such as low-income housing tax credits and historic preservation credits). With this core of local, state, federal and foundation funding, CNE was able to leverage an even greater amount of private investment and mortgage commitments from private lending institutions. "A $5 million grant of public or foundation funding can often leverage $30-40 million worth of conventional market rate capital investment in housing," said Leigh Ferguson, the president of CNE.

In the Lincoln Park neighborhood (in the vicinity of Erlanger Hospital), a member of CNE's board undertook an effort to stop the hospital from tearing down all the houses and CNE stepped forward to provide financing for housing rehabilitation. In the vicinity of the university, CNE renovated three dilapidated houses (each over 100 years old) using low-income housing tax credit finance. The structures now contain a number of lovely apartments that, because of the provisions of the low-income housing tax credit program, now rent for less than they did before.

By the end of 1999, CNE had invested over $180 million in building, financing or rehabilitating more than 5,600 housing units.[31] In 1999 alone, CNE made 198 home improvement loans totaling $3,966,000, financed 330 home purchases ($18,158,000), and produced 211 new rental housing units by acquiring and renovating run-down and abandoned properties ($9,207,000). When viewed in light of the modest size of Chattanooga, with a total housing supply of only 69,500 housing units in 1990, CNE's accomplishments were truly remarkable. Indeed, Beatley and Manning report that, by 1995, CNE had become the largest single producer of affordable housing in the country. (Beatley and Manning 1997, 191)

A unique aspect of CNE's approach is that it recognizes that the people who benefit from its housing investments are partners in the process. "When we make a rehabilitation loan in a neighborhood," commented Leigh Ferguson, "we discuss with the homeowner the things that need to be done to bring a

3-24 Housing units in Lincoln Park neighborhood, before renovation by CNE.

Source: Courtesy of Chattanooga Neighborhood Enterprise, Inc.

3-25 Housing units in Lincoln Park neighborhood, after renovation by CNE.

Source: Courtesy of Chattanooga Neighborhood Enterprise, Inc.

3-26 Orchard Village neighborhood where new housing units were developed by CNE.

Source: Courtesy of Chattanooga Neighborhood Enterprise, Inc.

home up to code, but also ask if there are any other things he or she would like to have done. We suggest that the project be put out to bid, but ask the homeowner to select the contractor, make the inspections along with CNE's inspector and authorize when the contractor is going to get paid, because the homeowner is the one who is going to live in the home and pay off the loan."

CNE has also emphasized the importance of preparing people for successful home ownership by requiring that prospective homebuyers take an eight-hour homebuyer education program covering such subjects as loan qualifications, maintaining a good credit rating, budgeting and home maintenance. During its first years of operation, CNE actually paid prospective homebuyers $500 to take the homebuyer education course; CNE now requires prospective homebuyers to pay $100 to take the homebuyer education course. (When people pay to take the course, they are likely to place more value on it than if it is provided for free.) The $100 fee for the course is then credited toward the down payment on the home.

CNE housing rehabilitation loans are made at graduated rates of interest, depending on the loan recipient's income and circumstances. "If a person has a very low income," Ferguson stated, "the loan may be at 0% interest. Or another way we might structure the loan would be to say that the loan only has to be paid off when the house is sold or at the time of the owner's death. If the applicant has a somewhat higher income, the rate of interest might be 6%. Whatever rate of interest is charged, the money is eventually repaid, and the money recycles [in the form of additional loans]."

Given the fact that CNE must try to operate in a business-like manner, and depends on loan repayments to provide funding for additional loans, it has been remarkably courageous in extending financing to people with very low incomes who have traditionally been regarded by banks as "high risks." According to Ferguson, "A person making about $15,000 a year in Chattanooga can own their own home. For example, a single female head of household, maybe with one child, can buy a $50,000 house. We could loan her $15,000 on a second mortgage at 2% interest, with the remainder of the mortgage financing provided by a conventional FHA [Federal Housing Administration] or Tennessee Housing Development Agency loan at a market rate. The blended rate would end up being about 4.5 or 5%. The total cash she would have to come up with at closing is only 2% of the purchase price, or $1,000, which includes a $100 payment for the homebuyer education program and which is credited toward the down payment. On a monthly basis, the cost of owning that home will be cheaper than renting an apartment, but now she's a homeowner with a vested interest in the community." Despite such aggressive lending practices, Ferguson reported that CNE's loan delinquency and default rate have been "below the national average."

As more of the city's existing housing units have been renovated, CNE has become more involved in constructing new housing. One of CNE's most notable new construction projects to date involved the development of 49 single-family homes in an intimately scaled neighborhood called Orchard Village (five minutes from the downtown). Homes in Orchard Village are on relatively small lots of roughly 5,000 square feet, and front on a street of modest width. (Ann Coulter, RPA director at that time, strongly supported the zoning variances that were required for the project.) The project won the ULI 1994 Award of Excellence for Small-Scale Residential Development.

Prior to becoming the director of the RPA, Ann Coulter had been the director of the city's Community Development Office, and in that capacity worked with Leigh Ferguson on the administration of the city's CDBG allocation and on various grant applications. This good working relationship continued after Coulter moved on to become the RPA director. Leigh Ferguson stated, "There's been a collaborative approach. We're submitting a major grant application to the Fannie Mae Foundation and a lot of the data we needed had to come from the planning agency. So we picked up the phone, faxed the forms over and they faxed back what we needed. We may wear different hats, but we are all working as if we were part of the same organization working with the common goal of improving the quality of life in our community."

A close working relationship between the city staff and CNE has often made it possible for CNE investments targeted on particular neighborhoods to be coordinated with and reinforced by city-financed neighborhood improvements and capital investments (*e.g.,* utility improvements, street repairs and repaving, reconstruction of curbs and sidewalks, streetscape improvements, tree planting, and the creation of neighborhood parks and/or children's play areas). "Ideally, it should be, and often is, done all at once, like a developer would plan a new subdivision," said Ferguson.

Decisions on where and how CNE invests its resources are made by its board of directors, three of whom are ex officio voting members (the mayor, the county executive and the chairman of the Chattanooga Housing Authority). Other members are elected by the board of directors. "We've got a 30-member board of directors," Ferguson continued. "In addition to the three ex-officio members, we have the CEOs or chairmen of six of the nine banks in town and other private sector representatives. Approximately six board members are what I would call representatives of the neighborhoods we serve. We also have several people on the board who happen to be university professors, or what I would call community volunteers, such as the assistant executive director of Children's and Family Services, a 50-year-old single female head of household with a master's degree in social work. The president and vice president of the NAACP [National Association for the Advancement of Colored People] also sit on our board. The city's director of general services, who heads the city department that handles the federal block grant program and the housing funding the city receives from the federal government, is also on the board."

As the housing market in Chattanooga gradually improved, largely as a result of CNE's housing investments, CNE adjusted its lending practices. According to Leigh Ferguson, "We have reduced second mortgage loan amounts because we found ourselves fueling artificial price inflation. We saw houses go from $40,000 to $60,000 in a neighborhood in a period of a year and one-half. When I first came nine years ago, we were giving out $15,000 second mortgages at no interest that people did not have to begin repaying for 10 years. Now, we might loan that same customer a second mortgage of up to $7,500 at 2%, which they must begin repaying immediately."

THE 1985 RIVERPARK MASTER PLAN

"One thing that really came out loud and clear from almost all the task forces during the *Vision 2000* process was the great desire to do something with the river," said Pat Wilcox. "It was a forgotten part of the city." With so much importance placed on reclaiming the city's connection to the river, there was therefore considerable public anticipation regarding the completion and unveiling of the 1985 Riverpark master plan.

According to Jim Bowen, "When Steve Carr came down in 1985 and gave a full-blown presentation of the plan with slides and music, 1,500 people came out to see the presentation. After the presentation, a number of people stood up and gave testimonials in support of the plan, saying 'We've just got to do this.'"

The 1985 Riverpark master plan called for developing a continuous, 22-mile-long parkway and riverwalk along both sides of the Tennessee River from the Chickamauga Dam to the Tennessee River Gorge. A key element of the plan was that the Riverpark would be physically connected to the downtown, to encourage economic development in the city as a whole and mixed-use development in the area of Ross's Landing. The 1985 Riverpark master plan summary states, "The plan places special emphasis on River's Bend, which will be the gateway to the entire system because of its direct connection to downtown. New mixed-use development here will include offices, a hotel, housing, specialty shops, eating places, museums, an aquarium and plazas overlooking the river. A visitor's center will provide orientation to the entire Riverpark."

The 1985 Riverpark master plan publicly unveiled in 1985 was so ambitious that it was almost audacious. As Jim Bowen frankly observed, "I'm sure 99-44/100% of the folks in Chattanooga probably thought it would never happen." The project was not only incredibly expensive ($750 million), but it was a long-term project that was going to take 20 years to complete.

However, the Moccasin Bend Task Force and the team of consultants it hired were not interested in just putting forth a plan with pretty pictures that ended up being put on the shelf. One of the most noteworthy features of the plan is that it directly addressed the issue of implementation. The planners recognized that achieving "an appropriate balance of riverfront uses, with an emphasis on public and commercial recreation, will require a comprehensive implementation strategy." The plan therefore called for the creation of a nonprofit public/private development corporation that would be responsible for "the overall coordination and management of the development process as well as the long-term administration of the Riverpark system."[32]

The corporation the plan had in mind would be in a position to ". . . design, fund, build and manage the system," coordinate public and private resources, and maintain the integrity and high standards of the plan. Indeed, the plan recommended that the jurisdiction of the corporation should "go beyond the trails and parks to include the stimulation and oversight of all development within the project area . . . [including] in some cases, actual land acquisition, land sales or leasing and direct involvement in some construction projects."

To effectively carry out such broad responsibilities, the plan recommended that the corporation be staffed by a management director, program coordinator, architect, landscape architect and planner, and that the corporation also be in a position to hire specialists (such as archaeologists, environmentalists, museum designers and housing specialists) as consultants on an as-needed basis.

EVERYTHING COMES TOGETHER

Creation of the RiverCity Company and Implementation of the 1985 Riverpark Master Plan

Not only did you have an understanding of why the river was important, an overall vision of what it should be like and a detailed plan for what should happen, but you also had an entity that was created to see that it did happen. That's how the Riverpark happened.

—Ann Coulter

If you're armed with a good plan and even a good staff, but no money, you won't get much accomplished. You can have all of the good planning in the world, but if you don't have a vehicle or institution with resources capable of acting on and implementing what planning calls for, nothing will happen.

—William P. Sudderth

The first important step toward implementing the 1985 Riverpark master plan was taken when a nonprofit development corporation (the RiverCity Company) was created along the lines recommended in the plan. The company was separate from city and county government, and had a 12-member board of directors that included the mayor, the county executive and the chair of the city commission. Also on the board were the chairman of the state legislative delegation, a person appointed by local black elected officials, and six other citizens and private sector leaders. Rick Montague, who had chaired the Moccasin Bend Task Force, was one of the citizen members of the board of directors and, according to Stroud Watson, was "the conscience of the corporation."

The RiverCity Company was initially capitalized with about $12 million raised from seven local financial institutions and eight local foundations. William Sudderth was the first president of the RiverCity Company; Jim Bowen, who was the first staff person at RiverCity and who guided the organization before Sudderth came on board, became the organization's vice president.[33] During the two years Sudderth was president, the RiverCity Company went from a 5- to a 21-person organization.

The RiverCity Company began by acquiring and assembling key parcels of land along the Tennessee River. In July 1987, construction began on the first phase of the Tennessee Riverpark—a 3-mile-long segment near the C. B. Robinson Bridge. Construction began there because much of the land in that area was owned by either the city, county or state. Other properties needed for this segment were owned by the TVA, a community college, a railroad and three other private owners. "We convinced every one of them to gift us the land," said Jim Bowen.[34]

Construction of that first segment of the Riverwalk helped create the momentum needed to push on with additional segments. "The community fell in love with it," said Bowen, and this sentiment produced a ground swell of public support for further extensions.

The RiverCity Company made two policy decisions designed to assure that public support for the Riverwalk remained strong. "We decided early on that, since we were a nonprofit, private company, we were not going to ask for or exercise any governmental powers," Bowen continued. "If we needed to get land by eminent domain, we would go to the city government and ask them to do that. The other thing we decided from day one was that we would pay taxes on all of our property."

Bowen admitted that it sometimes felt "almost foolish" to be paying property taxes to the city and county when the RiverCity Company was receiving public funding from the city and county to enable them to carry out various economic development activities. "Annually, we used to get $400,000 from the city government and $400,000 from the county government in our budget. Then we'd turn around at the end of the year and give them about $250,000 in property taxes," said Bowen. Nevertheless, in a "conservative" community like Chattanooga, the fact that the RiverCity Company has paid property taxes on its land has been politically and symbolically important. "We were a new entity in town and there was going to be some political rumbling anyway. If we had started out purchasing land and taking it off the tax rolls, there probably would have been a good deal more political rumbling," said Bowen.

The Tennessee State Aquarium

As noted earlier, the idea of developing an aquarium at Ross's Landing was first put forward in the 1982 Structure plan prepared by students at Stroud Watson's Urban Design Studio. However, moving the aquarium idea forward and getting people to commit to it proved difficult. "Everybody recognized that we needed things to make Ross's Landing a destination, but developing an aquarium there was a tough sell," said Watson.

One factor that made it difficult to get people excited about locating and investing in a major facility at Ross's Landing was the fact that the northern area of the downtown (adjoining the river) was so neglected and forlorn. "There was nothing but two tire stores, a radiator shop and a car wash," recalled Jim Bowen. "The area closest to the river . . . was an absolute dump," said Dave Crockett. "It was a good place to train public works rookies on picking up garbage, wine bottles and tires."

By the time the three-year planning process of the Moccasin Bend Task Force had ended, it almost seemed like the idea of an aquarium had fallen off the radar screen. The final Riverpark master plan delivered by Carr, Lynch makes no mention of the possibility of developing an aquarium at Ross's Landing. It briefly mentions the possibility that an aquarium might be developed somewhere on Moccasin Bend, as part of a strategy to develop the recreational potential of the area, but it almost seemed like an afterthought, and certainly was not the centerpiece of a coordinated effort to revitalize downtown Chattanooga.

Had it not been for Jack McDonald, who had been a member of the Moccasin Bend Task Force, the aquarium idea might have been set aside and forgotten about. However, McDonald never let go of the idea of the aquarium and its potential for advancing other goals. According to Bill Sudderth, "McDonald went around giving talks, telling people how great an aquarium would be in revitalizing the downtown, and how it could knit the city and the river back together." He talked to anyone who would listen and eventually was able to make a presentation to the board of RiverCity. As Sudderth tells it, "McDonald told RiverCity's board, 'I've taken this about as far as I can. If this thing is going to go forward, RiverCity needs to take it on to the next step.' The story I've been told is that Jack Lupton, who was on the RiverCity board and at the meeting, said, 'That's the dumbest idea I've ever heard!' I don't know for certain whether that's true, but that's what I've been told. So the idea of developing an aquarium kind of stopped at that point."

Rick Montague, executive director of the Lyndhurst Foundation and who had chaired the Moccasin Bend Task Force, was not nearly so skeptical. Montague knew that Jack Lupton was soon going to go out to Monterey, California (he went out there every year to see friends) and suggested that, while he was there, he make a point of visiting the aquarium. Bill Sudderth remembered, "Jack, like everybody else, I think, was thinking that an aquarium is a big fishbowl, with four sides, like you see in dental offices. What's the big deal about that? So we build a bigger one, so what?' So he goes out to Monterey and has an incredible time, and sees school buses full of kids and people coming to the aquarium from everywhere. He calls back and says, 'Okay, I see what you're talking about.' When he comes back, Lupton made sure that some of the seed money the foundation had committed to downtown Chattanooga went to the aquarium."

The net result was that the RiverCity Company took on the aquarium project and, between 1986 and 1989, acquired 10 acres of land in the Ross's Landing area at a cost of $4.5 million, including more than enough land for the aquarium. In May 1987, Cambridge Seven Architects (Cambridge, Massachusetts) began work on designing the aquarium and the surrounding public plaza. The principal architect in charge of the project for the firm was Peter Chermayeff. Every two weeks or so, Bill Sudderth (president of RiverCity), Jim Bowen (RiverCity's vice president) and Stroud Watson traveled to Cambridge to review the progress of the plans, and Chermayeff came down to Chattanooga about as frequently. In November 1987, an economic feasibility study concluded that the aquarium could become the linchpin for the entire Riverpark and an economic catalyst for regenerating the entire northern area of downtown Chattanooga.

Initial estimates were that it would cost roughly $20-25 million to build an aquarium. Funding for the project was therefore sought from the State of Tennessee, and Tennessee Governor Lamar Alexander set aside approximately $7 million for the aquarium in the state budget, even though many people expressed opposition to the idea of using public tax dollars to build an aquarium. A concerted effort was therefore made to try to raise a substantial amount of the money needed for the aquarium from private donations. "Jack Lupton basically took it on as his personal objective," recalled Sudderth.

Meanwhile, the cost of the aquarium project was steadily increasing (the final total cost reached $45 million) and opposition to using public funds for the project was intensifying. "There were some people out there really fighting against the project like crazy," Bill Sudderth commented. "Meanwhile, I was struggling, trying to raise the money needed for the project and, at the same time, working on the design plans. I can remember at one point calling Jim Hall, who had been a lawyer and developer here years ago and was the head of the Transportation Safety Board. I said, 'I just can't get this thing going. I've got people hitting me from every direction.' His response was this: 'Go down there and break ground!' I said, 'But the aquarium folks don't even technically own the site, we don't have the plans finished and we don't have the money.' Hall said, 'You'll be amazed at what happens once you break ground.' So, in November, we broke ground. It was truly amazing! From that point on, all the opposition just evaporated and the opponents shifted their attention to projects that hadn't broken ground. Overnight, the 'proposed aquarium' became 'the aquarium' and another wave of private donations came in."

The land needed for the footprint of the aquarium was donated by the RiverCity Company to Tennessee Aquarium, Inc. (a new nonprofit corporation set up to operate and manage the aquarium) and, in November 1989, construction began. The state funding that was initially committed by Governor Alexander to the project was not put toward the cost of the aquarium itself, but was used instead to offset the cost of constructing a public plaza surrounding the aquarium. Construction of the public plaza and supporting infrastructure and roads began in December 1990, and was completed at a total cost of $10,500,000. In addition to $7,350,000 in state funding (from two separate state grants), $2,500,000 in local government funding was committed to the public plaza and associated infrastructure, which was raised from local hotel and motel taxes. The balance of the money needed to construct the aquarium was raised from private sources.

In May 1992, the 12-story Tennessee State Aquarium, holding 400,000 gallons of water (the largest freshwater aquarium in the world), and the adjoining Ross's Landing Park and Public Plaza, were opened. During the first year of operation, the Tennessee State Aquarium attracted 1,500,000 visitors—more than double the projected number. The Ross's Landing Park and Public Plaza and the River Place Visitor's Center became a major destination and city amenity. Each year since that first year, the aquarium has attracted more than a million visitors a year, and the revenue generated as a result of this heavy attendance has been more than enough to cover operating expenses and outstanding debt service.[35]

In 1993, two more projects were completed in the Ross's Landing area that complemented and enhanced the Tennessee State Aquarium and surrounding Ross's Landing Park and Public Plaza as a major destination. In May 1993, the $4.5 million restoration and conversion of the Walnut Street Bridge into a pedestrian bridge was completed. A $2 million federal grant covered a little less than half the cost of the project, while the City of Chattanooga committed $2.1 million (the amount it would have had to spend to demolish the structure). Another $400,000 was obtained from private contributions—much of it raised

3-27 Tennessee State Aquarium and Ross's Landing Park and Public Plaza— a popular visitor destination.

Source: Courtesy of Electric Transit Vehicle Institute

by selling brass plates, engraved with the donors' names, and placing them on the bridge's wooden plank floor. Two months later (July 1993), the $7 million, 38,000-square-foot River Place Visitors Center opened adjacent to the Ross's Landing Public Plaza and the aquarium. The design of the two-story River Place Visitors Center is reminiscent of the manufacturing sheds once common to the Ross's Landing area.

Once the Walnut Street Bridge was reopened as a pedestrian bridge, the amount of pedestrian activity along both sides of the river increased exponentially. "While it was a car bridge, the areas on both sides of the bridge were deader than a doornail," said Dave Crockett. The situation was particularly bleak in north Chattanooga along Frazier Avenue (on the opposite side of the Tennessee River from downtown) where businesses were struggling and many of the storefronts were empty. "You couldn't give property away over there—it just wasn't a very viable district," said Crockett. However, within a short time of opening the Walnut Street Bridge as a pedestrian bridge, a number of new, small businesses opened along Frazier Avenue. Today, there is a new air of vitality and spirit in the area. "Just the simple act of making that area accessible by foot has brought the area back to life," said Pamela Glaser.

3-28   Brass plate, engraved with name of the donor, embedded in a plank of the Walnut Street Bridge.

Source: Gene Bunnell

3-29 River Place Visitors Center at Ross's Landing Public Plaza.

Source: Gene Bunnell

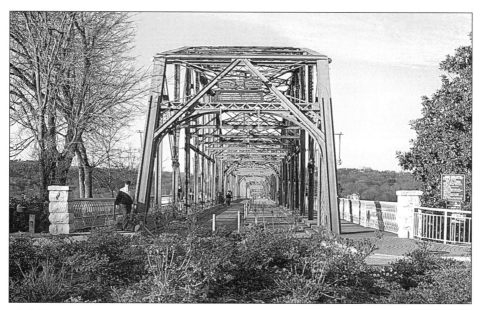

3-30 Landscaped entrance to the Walnut Street Bridge.

Source: Gene Bunnell

The reopening of the bridge also made north Chattanooga an increasingly desirable place to live, because people can easily walk back and forth between downtown Chattanooga and north Chattanooga via the bridge. "We've discovered that the more we made this town pedestrian, the better off the city was going to be in every respect," said Crockett.

In the meantime, the RiverCity Company was adding to its property holdings in the Ross's Landing area, including some old trolley barns and vacant lots, as well as 16 acres from the campus of the former Kirkman High School. By 1993, the RiverCity Company had acquired about $5 million worth of property.[36]

Because the RiverCity Company owned most of the land surrounding the aquarium, and had established a set of development guidelines for the area, it was in a strong position to decide what kinds of development should take place and where it should occur.[37] "Because we were not-for-profit, we were not in the business of maximizing cost per square foot," said Bowen. "We were trying to get projects that fit best with the total environment down there." Also, the fact that the RiverCity Company had an appropriation of funding from the city and county, as well as a steady stream of income from parking lots and other leased properties around the aquarium, it could take its time and did not have to accept the first development proposals that came along. "We received some pretty wacky development proposals that would have brought a lot of money to the company in land sales, but they just weren't right. We were able to hold out until we got projects that we thought best fit in," said Bowen.

A big reason why many of these potentially profitable—but "wacky"— development schemes didn't get built is because of the strong involvement of Stroud Watson (the head of the Planning and Design Center) and the development guidelines Watson helped the RiverCity Company draft for the area. As William Sudderth explained, "Stroud insisted that, in every decision, we made certain the pedestrian character of the area was not only taken into consideration but made paramount in the built environment and along the river. If you didn't make it a friendly place for people to walk and enjoy, then the area wasn't going to succeed. Second, he insisted that whatever was built in the Ross's Landing area should be modest in scale and create pedestrian-friendly spaces . . . Early plans for Ross's Landing [developed by the RiverCity Company] had called for a six- to 10-story office building and a six- to 10-story hotel to be built right in front of the aquarium. Stroud looked at those plans and spent a lot of time over here looking at models of what that would mean and what that would look like—and basically convinced everyone that a lower scaled environment [other than the aquarium itself] was most appropriate and desirable."

"Everybody had become enthralled with the idea of 'going to the river,'" said Stroud Watson, "and some private consultants and developers were predicting that up to 500,000 square feet of office space could be developed around Ross's Landing. However, what we would have ended up with is what I call 'musical offices,' with new office developments draining tenants from existing office buildings elsewhere in the downtown. We managed to stop that idea, and have been very careful to limit commercial development to uses that clearly benefit from or require a riverfront location and reinforce the riverfront as a destination."

In 1995, the Creative Discovery Museum opened at the corner of Chestnut and 4th Streets (two blocks away from the Tennessee State Aquarium) with "hands-on" exhibits that have proven to be a popular attraction for young children, such as an artist's studio, an inventor's workshop, a field scientist's lab and a musician's studio. The city made the land on which the Creative Discovery Museum was built available, and the $16,500,000 needed to construct the museum was raised from private sources.

A year later (1996), the $14 million, 400-seat IMAX-3D Theater, with its six-story screen and state-of-the-art digital sound system, opened diagonally

3-31 Creative Discovery Museum.

Source: Gene Bunnell

across from the aquarium. The RiverCity Company made the land for the IMAX-3D Theater available and the same corporation that manages the Tennessee State Aquarium operates the theater.

A significant test of the RiverCity Company's commitment to high-quality design and development came when a set of plans was presented for a hotel on a site between the IMAX-3D Theater and the Creative Discovery Museum. The RiverCity Company wanted a hotel and had specifically marketed the site for one. In addition to being between the theater and the museum, the site was within one block of the aquarium and across the street from where CARTA had built a multilevel parking structure, the ground floor of which housed the northern passenger terminus of the Electric Shuttle and a seven-screen downtown movie complex.

However, the design plan with which RiverCity was presented was "the typical, cookie-cutter, suburban residential model, like you see in cities around the country," said Jim Bowen. "We told them it wasn't good enough, and to go down to the Planning and Design Center and work with Stroud Watson to come up with a new plan." Getting the Riverfront Residence Inn developer to agree to completely redo their plan was made easier by the fact that development and design guidelines were already in place that applied to all developments in the Ross's Landing District. "They realized that they were building in a special place. That's the value of having a land use plan in place," said Bowen.

The design of the 76-suite Riverfront Residence Inn that was built is much more appropriate to the Ross's Landing area than what was originally proposed. The brick-faced building is sited close to the street (with parking in the rear), giving it an urban character and framing the street in a way that maintains a pedestrian scale. The articulated exterior of the building also gives it visual interest, conveying the impression that the building is a series of attached structures, rather than just one building.

William Sudderth resigned as president of the RiverCity Company in 1996 to form his own for-profit development company, Chattanooga Land Company. Roughly a year later, Chattanooga Land Company purchased six properties from the RiverCity Company for approximately $6 million. One of the properties was an old trolley car barn, which Sudderth's company redeveloped and converted into the Big River Brewing Works and Grille.

The other five properties purchased by Chattanooga Land Company were parking lots that the RiverCity Company wanted to see developed. "The purchase agreement we signed with RiverCity stipulates that at least four of the five surface parking lots we purchased won't be parking lots 10 years from now," Sudderth told me. "They will be developed, probably for housing and some retail, and we have to submit the plans and get them approved by the Planning and Design Studio."

3-32 Riverfront Residence Inn on Chestnut Street, between the Creative Discovery Museum and IMAX-3D Theater.

Source: Gene Bunnell

3-33 Restored trolley car barn, now housing the Big River Brewing Works and Grille.

Source: Gene Bunnell

A MAJOR BOOST FOR IMPLEMENTATION

In 1995, the board of the Lyndhurst Foundation decided, for the first time, to develop a five-year spending plan, rather than simply making decisions on grant allocations on a year-to-year basis. "Developing a five-year plan allows you to think bigger and about longer term effects," said Jack Murrah. "It also allows you to think about allocating larger sums of money to particular activities," he added. The total amount of money the foundation was prepared to allocate over five years was $10 million.

An advisory committee was formed to advise the foundation about how the money should be allocated. Among the people named to the advisory committee were Stroud Watson, Ruth Holmberg (chairman of the board of *The Chattanooga Times*), Leigh Ferguson (president of CNE at that time), Ann Coulter (executive director of the RPA at the time), William Sudderth (president of the RiverCity Company at that time), Sally Robinson (Downtown Partnership) and James Kennedy (head of the chamber of commerce).

The foundation identified four general areas in which it wanted to invest (the Riverwalk, Downtown Housing, Historic Preservation and the Southside) and asked the advisory committee to strategize on how the money should be specifically allocated among and within those areas. The advisory committee deliberated for almost a year, and in the end recommended that *half* of the $10 million be invested in helping develop a diverse supply of housing in the downtown (market-rate housing as well as housing for low- and moderate-income residents). "We felt that one of the most important things that could be done was to develop the widest possible range of in-town housing to create a diverse downtown citizenry," said Watson.

As Leigh Ferguson put it, "We could repopulate the downtown in a heartbeat by building housing exclusively for people with incomes less than 80% of the median income in the city, but if we did that we would be creating a new ghetto where nobody really wanted to live. Nobody *chooses* to live in a purely low-income neighborhood—even poor people. What we and everyone wanted to create in Chattanooga was a downtown that was an attractive, decent and desirable mixed-income community . . . where people *wanted* to live."

Up until then, CNE had concentrated almost exclusively on loaning money for housing rehabilitation and on building new housing solely for people with low and moderate incomes. However, achieving the goal of repopulating downtown Chattanooga with people of varied incomes and backgrounds necessitated the creation of more market-rate housing (*i.e.*, a broader approach). It also required a much greater emphasis on new construction. Two neighborhood areas were specifically identified by the advisory committee for the development of new housing—one in the north and one in the south.

Leigh Ferguson and the board of CNE struggled over whether and how to redefine the nonprofit corporation's mission. CNE also had to seek a ruling from the Internal Revenue Service (IRS) allowing it to build market-rate housing and still retain its nonprofit, tax-exempt status. The resulting IRS ruling said that CNE could maintain its nonprofit status and build market-rate housing as long as at least 20% of the units in each development was affordable to people with incomes of less than 80% of the area's median income. Once these issues were resolved, all of the money that the advisory committee recommended be allocated for housing was turned over to CNE for the development of mixed-income housing.[38]

In addition to the $5 million granted to CNE for the development of in-town housing, the advisory committee recommended that the Lyndhurst Foundation make a matching grant award to help further expand the Riverwalk, that a substantial amount of funding be committed to support planning and development projects aimed at revitalizing the city's Southside, and that a grant be awarded to help establish a new nonprofit entity ("Cornerstones") to work to bring about the preservation and reuse of historic buildings.

By the end of 2000, Cornerstones had secured and stabilized two historic downtown buildings in danger of being abandoned (the old St. John's Hotel— a flatiron-type building at 13th and Market Streets, and the ornate 1880s Central Block at 7th and Market Streets). As this is written, the St. John's Building is being renovated into 14,000 square feet of commercial/retail space on the first floor, and 15 market-rate apartments on the upper floors; the Central Block is being renovated for occupancy as the new headquarters of the United Way of Greater Chattanooga.

In 1998, the RiverCity Company put another major segment of the 1985 Riverpark master plan out to bid—a roughly $7 million bid package calling for the construction of a 1.5-mile-long Riverwalk extension on the south side of the river and the development of a 12-acre park in north Chattanooga near the north end of the Walnut Street Bridge. In 1999, bonds were issued to extend the Riverwalk to the Chickamauga Dam by 2002—a distance of 18-19 miles.

A special feature of the 12-acre park in north Chattanooga ("Coolidge Park") is a restored historic carousel housed in a structure that was specifically designed for that purpose and constructed at a cost of $1 million. The antique frame of the carousel was purchased from Grant Park in Atlanta and was restored in Mansfield, Ohio prior to its installation in north Chattanooga. The riding horses and animals of the carousel were designed, carved and painted by a local Chattanooga artist and craftsman, which gives the carousel a local connection. In addition to the carousel, the park also includes a riverside stage, a multipurpose pavilion, a privately operated floating restaurant, a kayak launch, and inland and riverfront trails.

3-34   Coolidge Park—structure specially designed and built for restored carousel on left.

Source: 2000 Robert Boyer/Shoot the Works

3-35   View of north shore area, Frazier Avenue Business District and Coolidge Park looking south across the Tennessee River toward Ross's Landing area.

Source: 2000 Robert Boyer/Shoot the Works

3-36 Coolidge Park carousel.

Source: 2000 Robert Boyer/Shoot the Works

PROGRESS IN DEVELOPING DOWNTOWN HOUSING

As a result of the various public/private projects and improvements described above, downtown Chattanooga has become an increasingly attractive and appealing place to live. The first step in expanding downtown housing opportunities was taken when the RiverCity Company developed a 41-unit apartment complex (Riverset Apartments) overlooking the Riverwalk and the aquarium—the first new housing development in downtown Chattanooga in over 20 years. Eighty-percent of the units was leased at market rates, while 20%

3-37   Mixed-use housing and retail development at 1st and Market Streets, developed by Chattanooga Neighborhood Enterprise, Inc.

Source: 2000 Robert Boyer/Shoot the Works

was set aside for low- and moderate-income households.[39] Riverset Apartments were fully occupied within eight months of opening. Another downtown residential development (a $55 million condominium project called Heritage Landing) was built not long thereafter. A marketing ad for Heritage Landing that I saw in a local newspaper in January 1998 was headlined, "Last units available on the Riverwalk."

CNE has also begun developing housing in downtown Chattanooga, including a number of projects that also include nonresidential uses. In January 1998, CNE began renovating the old Robinson apartment building at 620 Georgia Avenue at Fountain Square. The building, originally built in 1910, had been empty for several years and suffered significant deterioration. The renovation of the building, which was completed at a cost of $2 million, produced 18 new rental housing units, which were quickly rented out and occupied. The renovated Robinson apartment building also includes 8,000 square feet of ground-floor office space. In February 1999, just as the Robinson apartment building project was being completed, CNE undertook an even more ambitious construction project at 1st and Market Streets, directly across from the River Place Visitors Center and Tennessee State Aquarium: a $4 million development composed of 12 market-rate condominium flats, eight townhomes and 3,500 square feet of retail space on the lower floor. It was the first newly constructed, mixed-use retail and residential development in downtown Chattanooga in 75 years (since 1926).

When I was in Chattanooga in January 1998, the RiverCity Company was about to hire a private consulting firm to help it prepare an updated plan for the Ross's Landing area. "Every decision that has been made up until now has been based on a plan that was made in the 1980s, years before the aquarium was opened. So that plan is pretty dog-eared," said Sudderth. Later in 1998, LDR International (based in Columbia, Maryland) was hired to prepare the updated master plan for the Ross's Landing District. The cost of updating the master plan (roughly $70,000) was shared by the RiverCity Company, the Tennessee State Aquarium and the Chattanooga Land Company.

MANY PLANS AND MANY PLANNERS

The positive changes that occurred in Chattanooga in the 1980s and 1990s did not happen as a result of the efforts of just one person—one great or charismatic political leader, or one particularly gifted or dedicated professional planner. There were many planners (both professional and citizen planners) and many people, from many different walks of life, who played important roles. Nor did positive changes come about because of one single plan or planning process.

In 1994, a new round of planning began when the RPA, the Chattanooga Housing Authority, CNE and the RiverCity Company joined forces to sponsor a planning process to develop the *Southside Area Redevelopment Plan* ("the Southside plan") for an 800-acre area bounded by 12th Street and the Chattanooga Choo Choo on the north, Interstate 24 on the south, U.S. Highway 27 on the west and Houston Street (extended) on the east. Conditions within this 800-acre area were among the worst in Chattanooga. Between 1980 and 1990, the population of the Southside had declined 47% and the percentage of persons living in poverty in the neighborhood increased from 26.8 to 33%. Over 300 parcels, totaling 178 acres of land, were vacant.

Among the consultants hired and brought to Chattanooga for this major planning endeavor was Peter Calthorpe, who led and facilitated a weeklong planning charette.[40] "All the stakeholders in the community, business people and residents, came to a huge meeting," remembered Jim Bowen. "We divided up after the presentation into eight different groups. Each group was given a map of the Southside area and was asked to come up with their own plan for the area. Each team was given a set of little colored templates designating different kinds of uses, so if you wanted to have housing in a particular section, you put the little housing template there. After working for most of the day on their plan, a spokesperson for each team was chosen and each group presented

3-38   Meeting at the Downtown/Riverfront Planning and Design Center—
part of the week-long charette process undertaken in 1994 to develop a plan for
Chattanooga's South Central Business District. Matt Taecker (with Calthorpe
Associates) is writing at the board.

Source: Robert Boyer/Shoot the Works

their plan to everyone. For the next two days, the team of professionals locked
themselves in a room with those eight different plans and eventually came up
with a single plan that contained elements of all eight plans."

The plan for Chattanooga's Southside was eventually completed and
adopted as an amendment to the *Downtown Area Improvement Plan* in May
1997, the stated goal of the plan being to "build a new community whose functioning and livability embodies the fundamental principles of Sustainable
Development . . ." Among the proposed land use changes called for in the plan
were to:

- increase the land area devoted exclusively to housing from 27 to 66 acres
- develop a mixture of commercial and housing in two areas (along Market
  Street north of Main Street, and along the Main Street east-west corridor)
- establish a gateway commercial district, a commercial services district,
  and three industrial districts (including a model industrial district), but
  reduce the land area devoted to commercial and industrial land uses
  from 398 acres to 318 acres
- provide a focus for the community's civic life by developing a residential
  neighborhood center in the middle of the Southside
- increase the land area designated for and converted to public parks and
  greenways from 4.2 acres to 96 acres

By the end of the 1990s, a number of the actions called for in the Southside plan had been carried out. One of the important changes was the development of a linear park along 17th Street (between Market and Broad Streets) to enhance the residential character of the area and make it a more appealing place to live. The linear park was created by completely redesigning and reconstructing 17th Street, reducing the number of traffic lanes, increasing the width of the sidewalk along the northern side of the street to 14 feet, and planting long rows of trees to frame the sidewalk and give the street a parkway-like quality. A stormwater drainage and filtering system was constructed as part of the project that filters and recycles stormwater to irrigate park and greenspace in the area.

An important aim of the Southside plan was to encourage new housing development in selected areas of the Southside, and that has begun to happen. One of the first such projects to be completed was a three-story, mixed-use, private residential development on Williams Street near Main Street. The project, which was completed in the summer of 1999, has nine flats and five townhomes, with retail space on the lower level.

One of the first investments CNE made in the Southside was to renovate the former Grand Hotel, across from the Chattanooga Choo Choo, into 36 one-bedroom rental housing units. "The structure was abandoned and derelict for about 10 years and had no roof on it," said Ferguson. The first floor of the structure was reserved for commercial use and now houses the English Rose Tea Room.

CNE made an even greater investment in the Southside by undertaking a major new construction project at Cowart Place, which will be the city's first planned, mixed-use, market-rate residential community. The first phase of this development—a $3 million project which produced 19 two-story townhomes and three cottage-style, single-family homes—was completed at the end of 2000 on a 2-acre site bordered by 17th, 18th, Williams and Cowart Streets. Occupancy of these units began in early 2001.

CNE offered special financing packages to early buyers that included assistance with the down payment. Second mortgages of up to $25,000 at reduced interest rates were also offered for property enhancements such as the construction of garages and custom landscaping. Additional phases of the residential community at Cowart Place are planned to create a substantially sized neighborhood capable of supporting local shops and restaurants.

Slowly but surely, Chattanooga's once derelict Southside, with its large tracts of vacant land and abandoned buildings, is being reclaimed and filled in. To help accelerate the process, the city made a conscious policy decision to locate a number of major publicly financed projects in the Southside, which would encourage spin-off private investment in the district.

3-39   Rear view of dilapidated former Grand Hotel, with roof caved in.

Source: Courtesy of Chattanooga Neighborhood Enterprise, Inc.

A new 20,000-seat, open-air stadium (Finley Stadium) was constructed on a contaminated Southside industrial property (which was cleaned up). The new stadium, which opened in 1997, replaces Chamberlain Field as the UTC's football arena, and is also used for other local and regional sporting, entertainment and civic events. The idea of building a new outdoor stadium was actually first put forward as a goal in the 1984 *Vision 2000* process, but it took a number of years to raise the necessary money to build the stadium. By the time the money

3-40   Former Grand Hotel Building, completely renovated and restored to accommodate 36 affordable, one-bedroom rental housing units.

Source: Courtesy of Chattanooga Neighborhood Enterprise, Inc.

3-41   English Rose Tea Room on ground floor of renovated Grand Hotel.

Source: Courtesy of Chattanooga Neighborhood Enterprise, Inc.

3-42   New townhomes at Cowart Place, on Chattanooga's Southside, developed by Chattanooga Neighborhood Enterprise, Inc.

Source: Courtesy of Chattanooga-Hamilton County Regional Planning Agency

3-43   Cottage-style, single-family homes at Cowart Place.

Source: Courtesy of Chattanooga-Hamilton County Regional Planning Agency

3-44   Former Ross-Meehan Foundries Building on Chattanooga's Southside, before the area was redeveloped to accommodate Finley Stadium and an open-air Cricket Pavilion across the street from the stadium.

Source: 1996 Robert Boyer/Shoot the Works

was in place for the stadium, the Southside planning effort had been completed and the stadium became a key element in advancing the Southside plan's aim of introducing new life into the Southside.

More than one-third of the $28.5 million needed to build the 20,000-seat stadium was raised from private citizens and corporations, while municipal bonds issued by the city and county paid for $13 million of the project cost. Approximately $1 million of the project budget was used for site improvements, landscaping and extensive tree planting of the large stadium parking area. The surface of the parking area was made permeable to contain and filter all stormwater runoff on site. (In fact, the city has installed over 2,000 oil-skimming devices in parking lots throughout the city to reduce the extent to which stormwater runoff pollutes rivers and streams.)

3-45   Aerial view of Chattanooga's Southside in process of being redeveloped. Finley Stadium and its extensive landscaped parking area are visible in the upper left of the photo. An open-air Cricket Pavilion was constructed on the site of the former Ross-Meehan Foundry, to the right of the stadium end zone. The Chattanoogan, a specialized conference center and hotel complex, is under construction (arched structure at bottom center of photo).

Source: 2000 Robert Boyer/Shoot the Works

The second major publicly financed project sited in the South Central Business District in support of the aims of the Southside plan was a uniquely designed conference center and 202-room hotel called the Chattanoogan. The unusual conference center and hotel—with 20 specially equipped meeting spaces as well as a restaurant, bar and retail space—was built on a site at 12th and Broad Streets, just south of the TVA's headquarters building. It opened in the spring of 2001.[41]

REASONS BEHIND CHATTANOOGA'S
SUCCESSFUL TURNAROUND

Willingness to Invest in Planning

Cities often adopt slogans intended to express their essence, communicate a message or promote an ideal. In Portland, Oregon, it is "The City That Works"; in Baltimore, Maryland, it is "The City That Reads." Prominently displayed in bold letters on the back cover of every packet of information sent out by the RiverCity Company highlighting Chattanooga's accomplishments is the following slogan: "Invest in a city that invests in itself. Chattanooga." Of all the city slogans I've come across, none rings more true than this one. Chattanoogans *have* invested in making their city a better place, and one of the areas in which they have invested most heavily, and that has paid off handsomely, has been in the area of planning.

Ann Coulter's account of what happened when she went before the county commission seeking funding for a "visual preference" survey is a good indication of how far people in Chattanooga and Hamilton County have come in terms of their willingness to invest in planning.

"I had been the director of the RPA for about a year," Coulter explained, "and found myself standing in front of the county commission, which is a rather conservative body, asking for $25,000 in a very tight budget year for a 'visual preference' survey. They were skeptical about the value of the study, and I couldn't say for sure what the outcome of it would be or what it would lead to. However, they provided the funding we asked for, because we have developed a strong track record and have built up some momentum of positive expectations."

In 2000, the City of Chattanooga and Hamilton County provided a total of $1,410,155 in funding to support the work of the RPA and the Planning and Design Center (half from the city and half from the county). That amount of *local* funding for planning—roughly equivalent to $4.86 for every man, woman and child in Hamilton County—represents a fairly substantial local investment in planning compared to what most other American communities invest.[42] Moreover, that figure does not include other investments in planning made by the Lyndhurst Foundation, the RiverCity Company, CNE and other nongovernmental entities.

Another sign of the area's willingness to invest in planning is the City of Chattanooga's decision to finance and construct a new $11.5 million Development Resource Center (DRC) to house all city and county departments, and agencies with responsibilities related to planning and development (including permitting and building inspections), in one location. Like Finley Stadium and the Chattanoogan Conference Center, the DRC was sited on the city's Southside (on South Market Street, roughly halfway between Miller Park and the

Chattanooga Choo Choo). The center, which opened in December 2001, houses the offices of the RPA and provides a new home for the Planning and Design Center, relocated to the DRC from its previous home at Miller Plaza.

Willingness to Invest in Projects to Achieve Planning Objectives

In 1996, voters in Chattanooga approved a half-cent sales tax increase, with one-quarter cent dedicated to education and one-quarter cent to economic development. Another source of revenue for public investments was created in 1998, when the state legislature approved a Tourist Development (TD) zone for the Southside area. Under the legislation, increased sales tax revenue collected in the TD zone as a result of the many public and private investments in the area has been dedicated to help finance continuing public investments in the area.

Meanwhile, hotel room tax revenue earmarked for economic development (which has grown significantly over the years) has been used to help finance the Convention and Trade Center expansion, the new conference center (the Chattanoogan), the DRC and other public investments in the Southside.[43] Sales tax revenue earmarked for education has also been committed to help finance the construction of two new neighborhood elementary schools in downtown Chattanooga as a way of encouraging more people to live downtown.

Private Sector Support for Planning

Members of Chattanooga's business community recognized the need for planning, and actively supported and participated in many planning processes. The chamber of commerce helped lead the public/private effort that reduced air pollution levels and improved air quality. It also organized the first inter-city visit to Indianapolis, which generated new ideas and enthusiasm for the task of replanning and revitalizing Chattanooga, and led to the formation of Chattanooga Venture and the *Vision 2000* process. The Downtown Leadership Group, which worked with T. D. Harden on the 1968 and 1976 Downtown plans, was composed largely of key members of the downtown business community.

Needless to say, the Lyndhurst Foundation, another private sector institution, also played a critical role in supporting planning efforts that transformed downtown Chattanooga. The foundation provided grant support for the establishment of the Urban Design Studio (later renamed the Riverfront/Downtown Planning and Design Center), financially supported a number of other important planning efforts, and made grants that enabled key recommendations put forward in various plans to be implemented. Having said this, I think it is also possible to exaggerate the importance of the Lyndhurst Foundation, and to mistakenly assume that, because the Lyndhurst Foundation played such a critical role, Chattanooga had a built-in advantage that other cities do not have, which assured its success.

William Sudderth told me about a conversation he had with a man who had come to Chattanooga from New Haven. "By the time he got to me," Sudderth explained, "he had conducted a lot of interviews. I was the last person in his three or four days of interviews. We were sitting right here in the Planning and Design Center and he started off the conversation with 'You know, I think I've got this figured out. I think if we just had the Lyndhurst Foundation in New

3-46   Aerial view of the redeveloped Ross's Landing area in 2000. The massive CARTA Shuttle Park/Cinema complex is in the center of the photo; the Tennessee State Aquarium and surrounding public plaza are at center, right. The street running diagonally behind the Shuttle Park North complex is Chestnut Street, along which are aligned, from left to right (south to north) the Creative Discovery Museum, the Riverfront Residence Inn and the IMAX-3D Theater. Behind the Riverfront Residence Inn and IMAX-3D Theater is the new 6,000-seat Bell South Baseball Stadium, the new home of the Chattanooga Lookouts (a Cincinnati Reds farm team), which opened in April 2000. The construction crane in the center of the photo is on the site of the new 120-room, seven-story Courtyard Marriott Hotel, then under construction, which opened in 2001.

Source: Robert Boyer/Shoot the Works

Haven, we could make it happen.' I said, 'I'll tell you what. The staff of the Lyndhurst Foundation consists of four or five people, and over the last couple of years I've gotten to know them pretty well. Maybe I could persuade them to move the foundation's staff, and transfer all its money, to New Haven on one condition: you send Yale University to Chattanooga. Lyndhurst's economic resources and influence pale when compared against those of Yale's. The reason Lyndhurst has made such an impact here is not because of its size or wealth, but because of *how* they have chosen to direct their resources and investments in getting things to happen.'"

Sudderth made essentially the same point when he was invited to Augusta, Georgia to speak to various groups there who wanted to revitalize their downtown. "After I finished my speech," Sudderth continued, "a woman raised her hand and said, 'If we had the Lyndhurst Foundation, we could do the same thing.' I said, 'I'll tell you what. I'll swap you the Lyndhurst Foundation for the Medical College of Georgia, which is a huge generator of funds for research and education and is sitting right in your downtown, but it might as well have a wall around it because there's no interaction between the Medical College of Georgia and the rest of your downtown."

Sudderth's point is an important one. There are major institutions and corporations in cities across the country—many much wealthier than the Lyndhurst Foundation—that could be involved in revitalizing and improving the quality of life in their host communities, but are not. Simply having the Lyndhurst Foundation in Chattanooga did not assure Chattanooga's success. Even the Lyndhurst Foundation's decision to direct its grants toward supporting projects in Chattanooga did not assure Chattanooga's successful turnaround. What *was* crucially important was the decision the Lyndhurst Foundation made regarding *how* it was going to invest its resources (*i.e.,* that it was going to give priority to planning and make it possible to bring the best planners, architects, designers and other consultants in the country to Chattanooga to work on and assist with various planning processes). "You can't target resources effectively without having a plan," observed William Sudderth.

It is also important to recognize that foundations are limited in what they can do. As David Rusk has cogently observed, "Foundations can support but they cannot lead. Foundations cannot fill the leadership gap." (Rusk 1999, 312) The leadership must come from elsewhere within the community—and it *did* in Chattanooga.

Public/Private Partnerships

Perhaps the best indication of private sector acceptance of planning in Chattanooga has been the creation of new nonprofit institutions for the purpose of implementing publicly approved planning recommendations. The 1984 *Vision 2000* process put forward two major goals aimed at strengthening city neighborhoods: (1) to increase the supply and quality of affordable housing; and (2) to increase housing in the downtown. Those two goals were met by forming CNE, whose remarkable success story is told in the previous pages. Likewise, the 1985 Riverpark master plan, which called for developing a 22-mile River-walk and Ross's Landing as a visitor destination and gateway to the River-walk, was implemented by creating the nonprofit organization called the RiverCity Company.

The RiverCity Company and CNE have both played key roles in the process of planning for the revitalization of the city's Southside, as called for in the 1997 Southside plan. The RiverCity Company helped organize the planning process that produced the Southside plan, and has played an important role in implementing it (playing very much the same role it did in implementing the 1985 Riverpark master plan). As noted earlier, CNE is also playing a key role in implementing the Southside plan by focusing its resources on developing new housing in the area (an example being the housing development at Cowart Place and 17th Street).

The way the Electric Shuttle bus in downtown Chattanooga has been approached is another example of Chattanooga's penchant for forming public/private partnerships. There are a number of complementary public and private components to the electric bus operation. CARTA, a public agency, operates the Electric Shuttle (as well as other bus lines in and around the city), and receives an annual operating subsidy from the city and county. Meanwhile, AVS, a local for-profit company, manufactures the emission-free electric buses. It began exporting buses to Costa Rica in 1997 and hopes to sell them to cities throughout the world. The Electric Transit Vehicle Institute (ETVI)—a research laboratory, independent from AVS—tests the operating efficiency, reliability and service records of different models of electric buses.[44]

Although ETVI and AVS are entirely separate, the research findings of ETVI have been extremely valuable to AVS and other manufacturers in helping to refine and perfect the technology. An important breakthrough in this regard was AVS's development of a power system (unique in a regular-duty transit bus) of a hybrid electric vehicle that uses a natural gas-powered turbine to recharge the batteries while the bus is operating, significantly extending the vehicle's range.

Citizen Involvement in Planning

I just came from a meeting at the chamber of commerce with a lot of people who would not call themselves planners or designers, but everyone there was. Literally everyone in the city is a planner and designer. If you develop that kind of culture of planning, you will have a well-planned city.

—DAVE CROCKETT

From the time that T. D. Harden arrived in Chattanooga in 1965, Chattanooga has benefited from having hired skilled and dedicated staff planners who have worked full time on the city's behalf. The city has also hired some of the most highly respected planners and architects in the country as private consultants. Examples also abound of widespread citizen involvement in planning—beginning with the open planning process conducted by the Moccasin Bend Task Force (1983-86), the citizen-led *Vision 2000* planning process (1984) and the way the Planning and Design Center functioned throughout the 1990s.

Ron Foresta is a professor at the University of Tennessee at Knoxville who, prior to moving to Knoxville, lived in Chattanooga. As a geographer interested in cities, Foresta has closely followed Chattanooga's post-World War II planning and development, and is impressed by how Chattanooga's planners have involved and consulted neighborhood residents in the development of neighborhood plans.

"Planners in Chattanooga have 'got religion,'" claimed Foresta, "and have worked well with neighborhood groups and in devising open public planning processes. For a while, I lived in the Fort Wood area of the city, west of the UTC campus. Planners [from the RPA] came to meet and work with the neighborhood. It was a real eye-opener. They had learned how to facilitate and enable creative thinking and problem-solving. They asked what people wanted and listened to what people said. They asked, 'What do you think of this as a possibility?' They pointed out things that could be done if people wanted them done, and pointed out problems and consequences people might have overlooked. Then [once things were agreed to] they promised to try to get those things done."

The effort planners made to reach out and involve citizens in the Futurescape survey is another example of how planners at the RPA and the Planning and Design Center have welcomed and encouraged citizens to be involved in planning. In 1997, the Chattanooga-Hamilton County RPA hired planning consultant Anton C. Nelessen to assist the RPA in conducting a comprehensive visual preference survey called "Futurescape." A grant from the Lyndhurst Foundation paid for half of the $100,000 cost of the Futurescape survey process, with the city and county each contributing $25,000. The aim of the survey, according to Ann Coulter, was to try to achieve consensus on "what we want our community to look like in the future."

The Futurescape survey wasn't just administered once, or during only one week, but rather over a three-month period. "We held 80 different survey sessions," said Karen Hundt, the comprehensive planning director at the RPA. "Some we held at about 20 public and private schools scattered throughout the county, and some we gave to chamber of commerce groups. We called senior centers and said, 'Please let us come administer this survey.' We called businesses and industries, like the Eureka Foundry, and said, 'Will you let your employees take an hour off during the day to take this survey?' and some of them agreed. Giving the survey in so many different places, to so many different groups of people, increased the level of participation and gave us a better diversity of people. Had we just relied on open public meetings, we probably would have gotten the same people who always come to public meetings. In this way, we got people who probably would never have participated otherwise."

The Chattanooga Times, which devoted a full-page editorial to describing the Futurescape survey process and its results, described the process as follows: "The vehicle for consensus-building was the Futurescape survey itself. More than 2,500 participants rated 240 slides on a scale of minus-10 to plus-10, according to whether they liked what they saw. And thanks largely to diligent outreach by the RPA, the survey participants were a pretty close demographic match to our community as a whole . . . Every part of the county was represented: 54% of respondents lived in suburban areas, 19% in rural areas and 27% in the urban core. Racial breakdown was almost exact: 18% of respondents were black, compared to a 29% black population county-wide; 76% were white, compared to a 79% white population county-wide. . . . In other words, they were 'us.' So the report on Futurescape results, published by the planning agency this fall, tells us a lot about ourselves." (Editorial, *The Chattanooga Times*, December 26, 1997, A10)[45]

The Chattanooga Times editorial went on to report the key findings produced by the Futurescape survey, which were that:

- as a community, we cherish the beauty of nature, both undisturbed and as a part of our built environment . . .
- we value historic buildings and respond to architecture that is beautiful as well as functional . . .
- we appreciate places created with humans rather than automobiles in mind . . .
- we are willing to set standards for development that will protect the things we value.

In a written survey, 90% of Futurescape respondents agreed or strongly agreed there should be development restrictions to protect forests, creeks, rivers and other natural areas. And 87% agreed or strongly agreed that there should be standards for location and design of buildings."

"The connecting thread running through these consultations . . .," *The Chattanooga Times* editorial concluded, "is a public desire for quality, desire to preserve the quality of our natural surroundings and to meet a standard of quality in what we build, whether it be streets or stores, workplaces or homes."[46] (*ibid.*)

When there is little planning in a community, and citizens have had little or no previous involvement in planning and visioning processes, it is understandable that they might not feel inclined to engage in or support such processes. Yet once planning processes have drawn people in as participants, they are much more likely to be willing to participate in such processes in the future and to participate more effectively. "If people hadn't gone through the previous planning processes and exercises," Ann Coulter explained, "the Futurescape visual preference survey wouldn't have been half as successful. Through the previous planning processes and visioning exercises we conducted, people learned to expect to be involved in planning, to have their opinions asked and to do a little bit of work. In other words, they've learned they can't just be armchair critics, and need to be involved in trying to look ahead and figure out what the best thing is to do."

The Urban Design Studio/Planning and Design Center

Some of the most creative and influential planning ideas that have reshaped and revitalized Chattanooga have come out of the Planning and Design Center (or out of the Urban Design Studio that Stroud Watson opened on Vine Street in the early 1980s). As William Sudderth put it, having the center has been "like having an idea factory. Somebody described the center very well the other day as the place where dreams are kept. The dreams are all around you on the walls—whether it's the dream of a revitalized Southside, or a dream of what Ross's Landing could become. You can come over here at any time and simply walk around these walls and pick a dream. If you want to go and pursue it, it's there to be pursued. Every time I come to the center, I see ideas and concepts displayed on the walls and I say, 'I never thought about doing something like that there.' . . . I don't know how to measure the impact of the studio exactly. All I know is that Chattanooga wouldn't be what it is today without it. It's made a huge difference in this community."

The important role played by the Planning and Design Center (and the Urban Design Studio before it) in bringing about the transformation of Chattanooga has not gone unnoticed at the national level. According to Jim Bowen, "Over the last couple of years, we've had delegations of people from probably a hundred different cities come to Chattanooga to see some of the high-profile projects completed in the city and to try to find out Chattanooga's secret. Most of them are drawn to Chattanooga because they've heard about the aquarium and the Riverwalk. Once they get here, it's interesting to watch how the focus of their interest often shifts. They will go through the aquarium and through the plaza at Ross's Landing, and along the Riverwalk. Then they'll come to the Planning and Design Center and start looking around. Invariably in a meeting at the center, someone will say, 'We really like your aquarium, but how do you get one of these? How do we go about getting something like the Planning and Design Center in our community?'"

Jim Bowen admitted that he has often had a hard time answering that question. He'd like to tell them that it's fairly easy, but then so much of the success of the studio has been due to Stroud Watson. "Could you do this studio in Des Moines and not have Stroud Watson?," Bowen pondered. "I just don't know. His personal role can't be underestimated. His approach to urban planning, and emphasis on creating pedestrian-oriented public spaces that encourage human interaction, has had an enormous impact in Chattanooga. He also has the unique ability to push, to make you think, to make you try to get everything you can out of something."

PLANNING AS A COLLECTIVE LEARNING PROCESS

When people engage in planning, they inevitably think about future possibilities and alternatives. However, people's ability to think about what is possible is often constrained by the limits of their knowledge and experience. Planning offers a marvelous learning opportunity because it encourages people to expose themselves to new ideas and think about possibilities they have never before considered.

Inviting outside experts and leaders to share insights gained from experiences in other cities is one way of stimulating local imaginations and expanding local understanding of what might be possible. One of the first examples of such a collective learning process in Chattanooga was when groups of people began making yearly trips to other cities to learn what they had done. When people from Chattanooga traveled to other cities, they brought back new ideas, which they subsequently modified and adapted to create something totally new in Chattanooga. For example, when the people went to Indianapolis and learned about a group called GIPC, they came back to Chattanooga and formed an organization called Chattanooga Venture that went on to perform a function that was very different from that which GIPC performed in Indianapolis.

The *Vision 2000* process presented another opportunity for people in Chattanooga to be exposed to new ideas. With the help of a grant from the Lyndhurst Foundation, a local arts and cultural organization sponsored a lecture series that brought three noted experts to speak to large audiences at the Tivoli Theater. The three speakers who came to Chattanooga were James Rouse (who spoke about housing), William H. Whyte (who talked about urban design and the design of public spaces) and Weiming Wu (who spoke about the work of the Lowertown Redevelopment Corporation in redeveloping riverfront areas of St. Paul, Minnesota).

Planners at the RPA have also recognized that planning is an opportunity to learn, and that creative solutions can emerge when you approach problem-solving with an open and inquisitive mind. Indeed, as Chattanooga's planners have taken on ever more complex planning problems, they have increasingly recognized the value and importance of seeking new ideas and perspectives from outside sources.

Planning for the coordination of land use and transportation is one of the most challenging tasks that communities face, yet the method to achieving the best integration of development and transportation is not at all clear—like the proverbial problem of the chicken and the egg. Ann Coulter provided the following account of what staff planners at the RPA did to generate ideas and stimulate discussion, when they realized that they didn't have all the answers.

"One day," Coulter recalled, "planners at the RPA got together to talk about the problem of integrating land use and transportation, and shared their frustrations with each other. Many were frustrated by their inability to do a better job of linking land use and transportation. Others were frustrated by the lack of public understanding related to the importance of coordinating land use and transportation, and still others were frustrated by their lack of knowledge of what other communities were doing in this area and their inability to spread that knowledge around. The outcome of the meeting was this: 'Let's call some people together and brainstorm about what we could do to increase general understanding of these issues.' We asked eight or 10 people to join us—people from two major engineering firms in Chattanooga, somebody from city government, somebody from county government, somebody from the Lyndhurst Foundation, a downtown real estate developer, somebody from the chamber of commerce, somebody from the city council and somebody from CARTA. They came, we fed them lunch and we talked at length. By the time they left, we had created the broad outlines of what we called the Transportation Design Institute. Everybody agreed to put some money into the project and we were able to come up with a budget of $25,000."

The Transportation Design Institute was a program of six daylong sessions in Chattanooga (one every two months) during which nationally recognized experts addressed a number of subjects related to land use and transportation. They shared their thoughts, observations and experience with a cross-section of people—planners, elected officials, surveyors, homebuilders and developers, engineers and others.

For the first session of the Transportation Design Institute, Walter Kulash was brought to Chattanooga to address the broad topic of the "Transportation Land Use Link." As Ann Coulter remembered, "At the morning session we tried to get everybody we could, from greenway activists to neighborhood people, to the chamber of commerce. Then, Kulash had an intensive, one and one-half hour lunch presentation that was limited to city and county elected officials. Then he gave an afternoon session targeted more toward practitioners: highway engineers, Tennessee Department of Transportation, Georgia Department of Transportation, and so forth."

For the second session of the institute, Allan Jacobs came to Chattanooga to do a daylong session on "Great Street Design." "Allan spent the morning giving a wonderful slide presentation about why streets are important and how we need to think about them," Coulter continued. "Then, during lunch and all through the afternoon, we basically did a design charette. We selected four different types of streets around the county (a rural, two-lane road; the access road to the airport; a six- or seven-lane highway lined with strip commercial; and a downtown street) and asked people who were stakeholders in those areas to come up with ideas for redesigning those streets based on what they had learned from Allan Jacobs during the morning session. So we got their drawings."

Other sessions of the institute focused on additional topics such as Pedestrianization, Parking and Public Transportation. After each session, the RPA staff prepared and published a Position Paper summarizing the content of each expert's presentation and of discussions held during the day. Publication and distribution of the Position Papers provided a way of reaching people who were unable to attend the institute sessions in person.

People in Chattanooga continue to seek out the advice of talented and respected experts and practitioners in their fields even though, when they do, they find themselves being called upon (and wanting) to take on still more challenges. "It takes nerve to invite the best consultant planners and designers," commented Jack Murrah. "You just know they're going to recommend something bold and original—something that isn't going to be easy or simple." Indeed, the list of outside experts and consulting firms brought to work in Chattanooga over the course of two decades reads like a *Who's Who* of urban planning, design and development.

CONCLUDING COMMENTS

Chattanooga today is far from perfect. There are still polluted sites that haven't been cleaned up, and run-down buildings and vacant lots that are in need of development. Nevertheless, there is no denying the fact that Chattanooga is now a far better place than it was in the 1960s and 1970s. The positive physical changes that have occurred in the city are only part of the story. Also important is how people's feelings about the city have changed, and how much more optimistic most people are about the city's future and about their ability to shape the future in positive ways.

"In the 1960s and 1970s," Jim Bowen explained, "we were a community that did not believe in itself. Now we're bulging with pride. When you bring a relative into town, you can't wait to drive them around town and show them what's been accomplished since they were here last. For years and years, we sent our kids away to college and they didn't return. Now they're coming back because it's a more exciting place to live and there's things happening."

The positive changes that have occurred in Chattanooga did not just happen by chance. They came about because people came together and planned: first to identify and agree on what kind of city they wanted Chattanooga to be, and then to decide how best to achieve that desired outcome.

INTERVIEWEES

Jim Bowen, vice president, the RiverCity Company

Ann Coulter, executive director, Chattanooga-Hamilton County Regional Planning Agency (1995-2000)

Dave Crockett, city council member and director, the Chattanooga Institute

Leigh M. Ferguson, president, Chattanooga Neighborhood Enterprise, Inc.[47]

Ron Foresta, professor of geography, University of Tennessee at Knoxville

Pamela Glaser, associate planner for historic preservation, Planning and Design Center

Thordis ("T. D.") Harden, AICP, former executive director, Chattanooga-Hamilton County Regional Planning Commission (1965-1995)[48]

Ruth Holmberg, chairman of the board, *The Chattanooga Times*

Karen Hundt, director of comprehensive planning, Chattanooga-Hamilton County Regional Planning Agency

Jim Hunt, former executive director, Chattanooga Area Chamber of Commerce

Mai Bell Hurley, city council member, major organizer of and participant in *Vision 2000* process

Judge Ralph Kelly, mayor of Chattanooga (1963-1969)

John Kinsey, mayor of Chattanooga (1997-2001)

Steven Leach, AICP, director of administration, Chattanooga-Hamilton County Regional Planning Agency

Ronald C. Littlefield, AICP, planner at Chattanooga-Hamilton County Regional Planning Agency (1968-1974); economic development coordinator for Chattanooga and Hamilton County (1974-1980s); executive director of Chattanooga Venture (1983-1986)

Woodley Murphy, executive director, the Chattanooga Institute (retired DuPont executive)

Jack Murrah, president, the Lyndhurst Foundation

Jerry Pace, senior planner, Comprehensive Planning Section, Chattanooga-Hamilton County Regional Planning Agency

William P. Sudderth, president, the Chattanooga Land Company, former president of the RiverCity Company

Carla Thomure, Electric Transit Vehicle Institute, Chattanooga

Stroud Watson, professor, founder and director of the Riverfront/Downtown Planning and Design Center

Pat Wilcox, editorial writer and editor, *The Chattanooga Times*

PLANNING STORY CHRONOLOGY

1930s   The Tennessee Valley Authority is created, headquartered in Chattanooga.

1965   T. D. Harden is hired—the city's first professionally trained director of planning. The Downtown Leadership Group is formed.

1966   A sales tax measure, proposed by Mayor Ralph Kelly, is passed that provides funding for joint city/county agencies such as the Chattanooga-Hamilton County Regional Planning Commission.

1967   The first plan for Chattanooga and Hamilton County is completed: *Toward a Better Environment—A Beautification Program for the City of Chattanooga and Hamilton County, Tennessee* ("the 1967 Better Environment plan").

1968   The first plan for downtown Chattanooga is completed: *Chattanooga Downtown Development Plan* ("the 1968 Downtown plan").

1969   Chattanooga is cited by the U.S. Department of Health, Education and Welfare for having the worst air pollution of any city in the U.S.

1976   *Downtown Chattanooga—An Urban Design Plan and Improvements Program* ("the 1976 Downtown plan") is completed.

1980   Stroud Watson opens a small Urban Design Studio in a storefront on Vine Street, using students from the University of Tennessee's School of Architecture and Planning.

1982   An Urban Land Institute planning advisory panel of outside experts comes to Chattanooga and issues a report evaluating land use alternatives and strategies for the Moccasin Bend area.
Images of the City ("the 1982 Structure plan") is completed by the Urban Design Studio and put on public display.
"Five Nights in Chattanooga" celebration is held during the summer in downtown Chattanooga.
The Moccasin Bend Task Force is formed and begins meeting.

1983   The first inter-city visit is made to Indianapolis. Chattanooga Venture is formed

1984   The *Vision 2000* process is carried out over a six-month period. More than 1,700 individuals participate. Forty goals, to be accomplished by the year 2000, are approved and compiled into a Portfolio of Commitments.
The City of Chattanooga enters into a six-year contract with the University of Tennessee and starts funding the Planning and Design Studio.

1985   *Urban Design Study of the Miller Park District* ("the Miller Park District plan") is prepared.
The firm of Carr, Lynch Associates, Inc. is hired to develop *Tennessee Riverpark: Chattanooga* ("the 1985 Riverpark master plan").

The RiverCity Company is formed as the vehicle for implementing the 1985 Riverpark master plan.

Chattanooga Neighborhood Enterprise, Inc. is formed.

1987   *Horizon Plan 2010 /General Plan for Chattanooga-Hamilton County* is completed (prepared by Chattanooga-Hamilton County Regional Planning Agency (RPA)).

1990   The Planning and Design Center formally becomes part of the RPA, and the RPA assumes full responsibility for funding its operations.

Chattanooga's structure of government is changed from a commission form of government to a city council/district form of government.

Miller Plaza opens.

The Planning and Design Studio relocates to second floor office space at Miller Plaza and becomes the city's "Idea Factory."

1992   The Tennessee Aquarium and Ross's Landing Park and Public Plaza open.

The first battery-powered buses are purchased by the Electric Transit Vehicle Institute and are leased to the Chattanooga Area Regional Transportation Authority.

A survey finds that 37 of the 40 goals set in the 1984 Vision 2000 process had been fully or at least partially accomplished.

1993   The restored Walnut Street Bridge across the Tennessee River opens as a pedestrian bridge. Chattanooga Venture facilitates a second community-wide visioning process (*ReVision 2000*). More than 2,600 people attend and participate in the series of nine meetings.

1995   A comprehensive ordinance regulating outdoor advertising and signage is adopted.

1997   A Visual Preference Survey ("FutureScape") is conducted by consultant Anton C. Nelessen. During the process, over 2,500 residents are surveyed regarding their visual preferences.

The *Southside Area Redevelopment Plan* ("the Southside plan") is completed covering an 800-acre area south of the central business district.

LDR International is hired by the RiverCity Company to prepare a Strategic Planning and Development Assessment of the Ross's Landing area.

NOTES

1. The oldest of the two railroad stations was the Louisville and Nashville Railroad Station at 9th Street (later renamed Martin Luther King, Jr. Boulevard) and Broad Street, which, at the time the station was built, terminated at 9th Street. The second larger and newer railroad station built in Chattanooga (1909) was the Terminal Railroad Station, which served the Southern Railroad system.

2. Chattanooga has a beautiful, new $20 million Airport Terminal Building. Nevertheless, when I traveled to Chattanooga in January 1998, there were only 14 scheduled flights per day in and out of Chattanooga, most of them small commuter planes operated by regional carriers flying to and from Atlanta and Memphis. (During the week I spent in Chattanooga, I saw advertisements in the local newspaper by Delta Airlines offering Chattanooga residents a free bus ticket to the Atlanta airport if they bought a ticket to fly out of Atlanta.) Walking through the Airport Terminal Building, I found myself entering a grand, brightly lit space with an extraordinarily high ceiling capped by a large dome in the center. A day or two later, I entered the Terminal Railroad Station in downtown Chattanooga (now the lobby of the Chattanooga Choo Choo Holiday Inn Hotel) and realized that the dome at the airport terminal was a conscious historical reference to the long-admired, free-standing, 85-foot dome in the central lobby of the old Terminal Railroad Station, the former gateway to the city.

3. A unique feature of the Chattanooga Choo Choo Holiday Inn Hotel is that four dozen old railroad passenger cars have been restored and converted into unique, Victorian-style overnight accommodations, with queen-sized beds and day beds. The rail cars are lined up on the tracks leading into the station, giving the sense that there are indeed trains in the station. The Wabash Cannonball Club Car serves as a cocktail lounge.

4. The Incline Railway at Lookout Mountain was built in 1895 and is listed on the National Register of Historic Places.

5. Ann Coulter resigned as executive director of the Chattanooga-Hamilton County RPA in February 2000 to take a position with the RiverCity Company.

6. The Olgiati Bridge—an important highway bridge that spans the Tennessee River linking Chattanooga and north Chattanooga—is named after former Chattanooga mayor, P. R. Olgiati.

7. For many years, the loss of population occurring in older neighborhoods of Chattanooga was masked by annexations of land that added to the total population of the city and made it look like the population of the city was more stable than it actually was.

8. The removal of so much fill lowered the height of Cameron Hill by approximately 158 feet.

9. Ralph Kelly had two administrative assistants in the mayor's office. According to Kelly, one's job was to deal with the "political side" (with daily issues and crises) and the other's was to think more creatively and long range. The staff assistant whose job it was to think long range was Bob Elmore, who Kelly referred to as his "thinker."

10. One year after Chattanooga was cited for having the most badly polluted air in the country, the first federal Clean Air Act was passed in 1970, which authorized the U.S. EPA to set standards for six airborne pollutants affecting human health: lead, sulfur oxides, ozone, particulates, nitrogen dioxide and carbon monoxide. Given the timing of this important legislation, some might surmise that the Clean Air Act was the main reason why Chattanooga's air was cleaned up. However, Ann Coulter and others to whom I spoke suggest that isn't the case. The actions that were taken to clean up Chattanooga's air went well beyond what the federal Clean Air Act required. In the 1990s, roughly one-fifth of all Americans lived in cities or metropolitan areas where the air did not meet at least one of the national air quality standards (Daniels 1999, 121), but Chattanooga was not one of those places.

11. Ruth Holmberg is the granddaughter of Adolph Ochs, the founding publisher of *The Chattanooga Times* and subsequent long-time publisher of *The New York Times*.

12. Maclellan, in addition to being widely respected, was well known for his conservative views and for opposing government intervention in various land use matters. For example, Maclellan had opposed the Golden Gateway urban renewal project, and also strongly opposed the development of publicly financed and operated parking structures.

13. At the time the 1968 Downtown plan was prepared, the city's public library was on the campus of Chattanooga College—subsequently the campus of the University of Tennessee at Chattanooga.

14. Seay and Ridenour, Inc., Landscape Architects and Planners of Pittsburgh, prepared the plan.

15. The Convention and Trade Center proved so successful that a bond issue was authorized in 2000 to finance a $56 million expansion of the facility, which added another 188,000 square feet to the 110,000 square feet of existing floor space.

16. All of the aforementioned projects, including the $163 million TVA office complex, were aided by federal Urban Development Action Grants (UDAGs), which were made to the city either as outright grants or low-interest loans. The UDAG for the TVA office project amounted to $10 million. According to Jim Bowen of the RiverCity Company, "We were able to convince HUD [U.S. Department of Housing and Urban Development] officials that even though the TVA is a quasi-governmental body, it sells

electricity just like General Motors sells cars. So from that point, it was a private venture."

17. Maps and illustrations in the 1976 Downtown plan that illustrate the area north of 4th Street show the outlines of existing buildings rather than the new buildings shown in the 1968 Downtown plan, which suggests that the idea of building a large-scale housing project along the river (put forward in the 1976 Downtown plan) was dropped in the intervening eight years.

18. Only eight cities experienced greater percentage population losses during the 1980s than Chattanooga: Newark, New Jersey; Gary, Indiana; Detroit, Michigan; Pittsburgh, Pennsylvania; St. Louis, Missouri; Cleveland, Ohio; Flint, Michigan; and New Orleans, Louisiana.

19. Lyndhurst's grant support paid for 60% of Professor Watson's salary and benefits, travel and publications. It also paid for 60% of the operating costs of the Urban Design Center.

20. Karen Hundt was hired by the RPA on a personal services contract and worked with Stroud Watson at the Urban Design Studio for three years. She subsequently went on to become the RPA's director of comprehensive planning.

21. A question was initially raised as to whether it was legal to have rental office and commercial space on a parcel of land that was condemned by the city for purposes of developing a public park. T. D. Harden researched the matter and concluded that it *was* legal, as long as the income from the rental space in the building was used solely for the maintenance of the park, which is how the project was structured.

22. The ULI advisory panel sent to Chattanooga was the 119th panel assignment undertaken by ULI since the program was first initiated in 1947. The 10 members of the advisory panel were chosen for their expertise and experience in dealing with urban land use and development issues somewhat comparable to those that faced Chattanooga. The chairman of the panel was Ernest O. Perry, Jr. The other nine members of the ULI panel were Christopher B. Leinberger, C. Ronald Hoisington, Ed McDowell, Jr., M. Wayne Redeker, Malcolm D. Rivkin, J. Leonard Rogers, Louis Shepard, Philip Stukin and Lewis Tilghman.

23. Mai Bell Hurley later went on to run for and be elected to the Chattanooga City Council representing north Chattanooga, a position she held when I interviewed her in 1998.

24. From 1984 through 1992, the Lyndhurst Foundation funded the efforts and activities of Chattanooga Venture at an average of $350,000 per year, which meant that the new entity could concentrate on managing the planning process rather than on fund raising. "It was very liberating," admitted Mai Bell Hurley. "If you've ever worked for a nonprofit organization, you know that seven-tenths of your time is spent just trying to raise money."

25. A single page of the Portfolio of Commitments was devoted to each goal statement. Under each goal statement were listed the recommended activities to fulfill that goal, as well as "Potential Venturers" (actors, agencies and institutions) in a position to carry out those activities. Goal statement pages were grouped together under the same generic headings as they were discussed during the *Vision 2000* process itself: Future Alternatives, People, Places, Work, Play and Government.

26. Born in Chattanooga in 1894, Bessie Smith began her career collecting nickels and dimes tossed at her in appreciation as she sang on Chattanooga's streets. In 1923, Bessie Smith's "Down-Hearted Blues" sold 750,000 records in the first month—an unprecedented number of record sales in those days. She went on to be one of the most widely acclaimed blues singers and became known as the "Empress of Blues."

27. Ruth Holmberg spearheaded the fund-raising drive that raised the $7 million needed to restore and reopen the theater.

28. The Tivoli Theater and the Soldiers and Sailors Memorial Auditorium are owned by the City of Chattanooga, and are managed and operated by the city's Park and Recreation Department. In addition to accommodating concerts and performances, both facilities are frequently used for civic purposes such as school graduations and other locally sponsored events.

29. Ann Coulter points out that electric-powered buses are particularly appropriate in Chattanooga, given "the importance of electricity generation and the TVA to the area's history and economy."

30. The head of Chattanooga Venture at the time this is written is James Catanzaro, president of Chattanooga State Technical Community College.

31. CNE's total budget in 1998 was approximately $25 million—one quarter of which came from public sources and grants, and three quarters of which came from mortgages, bank lending and the conventional investment market.

32. As an example of the kind of nonprofit development corporation it had in mind, the plan cited the Lowertown Redevelopment Corporation, which managed and orchestrated over $24 million in new development, and stimulated over $117 million of additional projects during its first two years of operation in redeveloping the downtown and riverfront areas in St. Paul, Minnesota. According to the 1985 Riverpark master plan, the Lowertown Redevelopment Corporation provided gap financing, conducted design review and carried out an extensive marketing program for the area.

33. Prior to becoming the RiverCity Company's vice president, Bowen had worked for city government in the city's Economic and Community Development Department from 1971 to 1985.

34. The TVA initially granted a temporary license allowing improvements to be constructed on its land and subsequently granted a permanent conservation easement.

35. The city's decision to use $2.5 million in hotel/motel room tax revenues to construct the public plaza leading up to the aquarium proved to be a wise investment. By August 2000, 10 million visitors had been attracted to the aquarium. As a result, hotel room occupancy rates increased steadily throughout the 1990s, and hotel/motel tax receipts increased from $1.87 million in 1991 to $3.2 million in 1999. As a result of the increased demand for hotel rooms in Chattanooga, two new hotels opened in 2001 in the vicinity of the aquarium—a 120-unit, seven-story Courtyard Marriott Hotel across from the Tennessee State Aquarium and IMAX-3D Theater, and a 94-room Hilton Garden Hotel on Chestnut Street next to the Creative Discovery Museum.

36. That same year (1993), the River-City Company merged with Partners for Economic Progress (the county-wide economic development organization) to create a larger entity with much broader responsibilities for community and economic development. The merged entity took on a new name—RiverValley Partners. However, in 2000, the organization reverted to its original name, the River-City Company, and refocused its mission back on the core area of Chattanooga. To avoid confusion, throughout the main text of the book, I refer to the RiverCity Company (including during the 1993-2000 period) without making reference to the temporary name change.

37. Among the projects for which the merged organization assumed responsibility was the development and management of a 125,000-square-foot small business incubator in a renovated former ceramic manufacturing factory in north Chattanooga. The factory, which was donated to Hamilton County by the 3M Corporation, was subsequently renovated at a cost of $2.3 million. In 1998, roughly 65 different small businesses, employing more than 375 people, rented space in the north Chattanooga business incubator.

38. In the years prior to receiving the $5 million grant, CNE had been receiving roughly $750,000 a year from the Lyndhurst Foundation to support its various housing initiatives. Thus, the $5 million grant (to cover housing projects over a five-year period) represented a substantial increase in its funding level.

39. To make the project economically feasible, the Chattanooga Housing Authority bought the land upon which the project was built from the RiverCity Company, to enable unpaid property taxes on the property to be abated prior to the development of the housing by RiverCity.

40. A document titled *The South Central Business District Plan: A Comprehensive Revitalization Strategy*, prepared by Calthorpe Associates and William McDonough Architects, was completed and delivered to the RiverCity Company (a.k.a. RiverValley Partners) and the city in 1995.

41. The Chattanoogan has been planned and designed to cater specifically to small conferences and corporate business meetings ranging from 15 to 200 people. The facility is managed by Benchmark Hospitality, which also manages a number of similar conference facilities throughout the country; however, all of those other facilities are in rural and nonurban settings. The Chattanoogan is the first conference facility Benchmark has managed that is located in a downtown. The reason for making an exception in the case of Chattanooga, according to Ann Coulter, is that, "Our downtown is the attraction."

42. In 2000, the RPA also received $447,509 in federal and state funding for transportation-related planning from the FHA, Federal Transit Administration and the Georgia Department of Transportation—bringing the total *public* investment in planning up to approximately $6.12 per person.

43. This revenue source was also used to purchase the Volunteer Army Ammunition Plant site from the U.S. Army for future economic development by the city and county.

44. ETVI monitors and evaluates all kinds of prototypical models of electric buses under a contract with the U.S. Department of Transportation, not just those manufactured by AVS. According to Carla Thomure of ETVI, 75% of all electric buses operating in Chattanooga and other cities in the U.S. are prototypes (meaning that there are fewer than 10 of those particular kind in operation).

45. In January 1999, *The Chattanooga Times* published its last issue, and was taken over by its evening rival, *The Chattanooga Free Press*. The newspaper created by the merger is called *The Chattanooga Times Free Press*.

46. According to *The Chattanooga Times* editorial, local zoning and land use regu-

lations should help a community like Chattanooga "get what we want." With that aim in mind, soon after the Futurescape survey was completed, the staff of the RPA began comprehensively reviewing and rewriting the city's zoning and land use regulations, using the Futurescape survey results as a guide.

47. In 2000, David L. Berry replaced Leigh Ferguson as president of Chattanooga Neighborhood Enterprise, Inc.

48. The Chattanooga-Hamilton County Regional Planning Commission became the Chattanooga-Hamilton County Regional Planning Agency (effective January 3, 1996).

4

Providence, Rhode Island

An Old City Reconnects
With Its Past and Finds Its Future

INTRODUCTION

Providence is one of the oldest cities in the United States. It was first settled in 1636 by a group of people led by Roger Williams, who came to Rhode Island to escape the theologically rigid and repressive Puritan society of the Massachusetts Bay Colony in Salem. They came to Providence in search of change, and established a very different kind of community based on the principles of religious freedom and the separation of church and state.

The way Providence was initially laid out also differed from traditional Massachusetts Bay communities, which were built around a town green or commons dominated by the meeting house and church. In Providence, a series of long, narrow lots were platted extending east from the Providence River and up what was later called "College Hill." A public way was established about a quarter mile from the river (paralleling the river), connecting all the lots to one another and enabling people and goods to move freely throughout the community. This first public way was laid out for the benefit of all the residents of the community and was appropriately named "Benefit Street."

For roughly 100 years, the settlement remained confined to the east side of the Providence River. The area west of the river, where the city's central business and financial districts were eventually built (which Providence residents now refer to as "Downcity"), remained undeveloped because the area was surrounded by marshy lowlands and was traversed by Muddy Dock Creek, and the eastern end of the area was hemmed in by the steep Weybosset Hill. Nevertheless, once a bridge was built over the Providence River, the area west of the river also began to be parceled out and developed. Around 1724, work began on leveling Weybosset Hill, which provided soil to fill in low-lying areas as well as a rich source of clay for brick-making. Over the course of many years, the "Old Cove" (a body of tidal water that had existed in the center of the downtown, in the area between Downcity and the State House) was completely filled in.

Providence remained relatively small and unimportant throughout the 18th century and the first quarter of the 19th century. By 1824, the population of the city was still only about 15,000. Up until that time, Providence's main claim to fame was that it was a shipping port; however, its harbor was fairly narrow and shallow and, as ships grew in size, the city's harbor proved to be increasingly inadequate, and the bulk of shipping activity shifted to the ports of Boston and New York.

The industrial revolution changed Providence and caused it to become a major urban center. From 1825-1830, scores of factories were built up and down the Blackstone and Pawtuxet Valleys, harnessing water power and employing the recently invented technologies that made mass production possible. Before long, Rhode Island had become the most highly industrialized state in the nation, and waves of European immigrants came to Providence and surrounding Rhode Island communities to work in the newly built factories.

Another new technology associated with the industrial revolution that caused Providence to grow in the 19th and early 20th centuries was the development of rail transportation. The Boston-to-Providence rail line—the city's first railway—opened in 1835. A second railroad, running from Providence to Stonington, Connecticut, opened two years later. In 1844, the Providence and Worcester (P & W) Railroad was incorporated and an additional rail line between those two cities was built.

Over time, the center of the city was increasingly claimed for railroad use. A freight yard was developed at the southern terminus of the P & W rail line and a passenger depot was built at Exchange Place in 1848. A new Union Railroad Station was later built east of the first rail depot on a portion of the land area created by filling in the Old Cove. When the present-day Rhode Island State House Building was built (between 1895 and 1900) on a prominent and elevated downtown site, it overlooked the railroad lines and freight yards.

The Downcity area of Providence prospered as a center for retail shopping for the region. By 1900, there were three major department stores in downtown Providence, on or near Westminster Street. The first (the "Boston Store") opened in the early 1870s at the corner of Westminster and Union Streets. The Shepard Co. department store was founded in 1880 and proved so popular that it expanded to occupy an entire city block. The third downtown department store was the Outlet Company, which opened in 1891. Like the Boston Store and Shepard's, the Outlet Company rapidly expanded and, before long, had built a building (168-176 Weybosset Street) that also occupied an entire city block. Other department stores, such as Albert and Peerless, followed and did an equally brisk business.

The city's economy and future seemed assured. By virtue of being the state capital, the city had a solid core of state government jobs that offered stability and insurance against recession. The city was also home to a number of major institutions—schools of higher education such as Brown University, the Rhode Island School of Design (RISD) and Bryant College, and hospitals such as Rhode Island Hospital—that also provided a large number of recession-proof jobs. Students drawn to Providence to attend colleges represented a significant proportion of the city's overall population, and money brought into the community by students helped to sustain the city's economy. By 1930, the population of Providence had grown to 253,000. The high point in the city's population was attained in 1949 when the population of the city reached 257,000.

Economic conditions in Providence specifically and Rhode Island in general weakened in the years following World War II. Sectors such as the jewelry and silver industries, which had provided substantial numbers of relatively high-paying jobs and propelled the regional economy, entered a prolonged period of decline and worker layoffs. Many firms went out of business or moved elsewhere. Before long, Providence was suffering from the same conditions and trends that were plaguing many other rust-belt cities in the northeast: loss of jobs and population, and consequent disinvestment in inner-city housing stock.

Equally troubling was the sharp decline in retail activity in downtown Providence. In 1968, the first large suburban shopping mall in Rhode Island opened in Warwick—only 20 minutes from downtown Providence. Within a few short years, retail stores up and down Westminster Street were closing their doors. The Outlet Store closed its doors in 1975 and, by the middle of the 1980s, Providence had lost its last downtown department store.

Fortunately, there were people in Providence who were not willing to give up on downtown Providence. When a local developer wanted to tear down the Loew's State Theater (the city's last remaining downtown theater) to put in a parking lot, a group of people in the business community came together to form the private, nonprofit Providence Foundation, named Ron Marsella as its first executive director, and launched a campaign to save the theater. Their efforts proved successful; today, the theater (now known as the "Providence Performing Arts Center") is a popular venue for concerts and traveling Broadway shows. When the city's last downtown hotel was about to close, private sector business people, including the owners of *The Providence Journal* newspaper, injected money into the Biltmore Hotel to renovate it and keep it open.

As positive as these privately initiated rescue efforts were, the benefits gained from them were limited because they were largely ad hoc undertakings aimed at saving specific buildings and institutions associated with the city's more prosperous past. They were not part of an overall, forward-looking, integrated plan for downtown, and therefore were not in and of themselves enough to create the kind of synergistic effect that could turn downtown Providence around.

A COMPACT BUT PHYSICALLY DIVIDED CITY

Another reason why Providence was having such a difficult time in maintaining a vital and coherent downtown was that the city had allowed what was really a very compact downtown area to be cut up and divided by major transportation corridors. The downtown wasn't working because rail lines and busy highways divided parts of the downtown that would otherwise have complemented and reinforced each other. When rail lines and interstate highways were first pushed through Providence, little thought was given to the spin-off effects of those projects on the fabric and function of the city as a whole. Minimal consideration was given to alternative alignments. In short, there was little or no planning.

Providence community leaders were all too happy to approve whatever alignment the railroad companies considered to be most commercially advantageous. The result was the separation of the State House and Capital District on one side of the tracks from the city's downtown commercial core on the other. A large tract of land at the base of the State House hill was taken up by rail freight yards and switching facilities of the P & W Railroad, and the College Hill area was cut off from the State House area.

Likewise, when federal and state highway engineers began laying out interstate highways through Providence, it was all done with a single-minded purpose, and with little thought to the negative impacts such highways would have on the downtown area and inner-city neighborhoods. The interstate highways constructed through Providence in the 1950s and 1960s cut wide swaths through the city's downtown and older neighborhoods, clearing away everything in their path. Properties that were left standing were condemned to endure not only visual ugliness, but also the constant noise, vibration and soot generated by the large numbers of cars and trucks that soon made use of the new highways through the city.

Downtown Providence was given over to the automobile. Large tracts of land in the center of the city were devoted to surface parking, and the three rivers that ran into and through the downtown were decked over to provide additional surface parking. To make matters worse, interstate highway interchanges at the northwest and southeast corners of the downtown dumped large numbers of cars into Providence's highly circumscribed city center. One

4-1   Downtown Providence (October 1949) looking north, with the Rhode Island State House (top, center of photo) overlooking railroad tracks and freight yards. Memorial Square ("Suicide Circle") is in the center of the photo. The Woonasquatucket and Moshassuck Rivers (which flow into the downtown from the northwest and north, respectively) are covered over, and only a portion of the Providence River (south of Memorial Square) is uncovered. The western edge of the College Hill neighborhood can be seen in the extreme right of the photo.

Source: *The Providence Journal*

4-2   Downtown Providence (October 1949) looking south. Memorial Square is in center of photo. To the right of Memorial Square is the post office, which was built over the Providence River. Further south (above Memorial Square in the photo), an uncovered portion of the Providence River is visible, but is lined with parked cars.

Source: *The Providence Journal*

point where the convergence of car traffic frequently created serious problems was Memorial Square—known to citizens of Providence as "Suicide Circle," because pedestrians took their lives in their hands whenever they attempted to cross it on foot.

SAVING A NEIGHBORHOOD—
THE FIRST STEP IN SAVING A CITY

It is both wonderful and incredible that it happened the way it did.

—Tina Regan

4-3   Downtown Providence (February 1968). By now, much of the land formerly occupied by railroad freight yards (center right of photo) had been converted into a large surface parking lot. The other large surface parking area (center left of photo) is where the Old Cove used to be before it was filled in during the late 19th century.

Source: *The Providence Journal*

4-4 Historic home across from a gate to the campus of Brown University being stripped of building materials prior to its demolition.

Source: *The Providence Journal*

At one time, the College Hill area (where Roger Williams and his followers first settled) was regarded as the finest place in Providence in which to live. However, by the 1950s, College Hill had become one of the worst slums in the city— an area of badly run-down and overcrowded tenements. Five and six families lived in each tenement. Most of the heating was by space heaters and it was common for one basement bathroom to serve the entire building.

Ironically, some of the forces that contributed to the destabilization and decline of College Hill came from the venerable educational institutions located there. According to my contacts in Providence, it was Brown University's heavy-handed institutional expansion that largely prompted the formation of the Providence Preservation Society in 1957—an organization formed for the initial and sole purpose of preserving the College Hill neighborhood. As planner Lachlan F. Blair succinctly put it, "Brown was the devil."

During the 1950s and 1960s, under a new president, Brown University was intent on expanding, and began acquiring property on which to build new university buildings and parking lots. As one historic building after another on the edge of the campus was demolished, concerns increased. Concerns intensified more when massive new buildings of modern design, which clashed horribly with the low-scaled, historic character of the surrounding neighborhood, began to rise on cleared sites.[1] Property acquisitions and demolitions conducted by RISD further destabilized the neighborhood. In the fall of 1959, RISD demolished the historic Pearce House at 225-227 Benefit Street, despite receiving offers from individuals associated with the Providence Preservation Society to purchase and restore the building. An article in *The Providence Journal* (published on September 30, 1959) quoted John R. Frazier, president of RISD, as saying that the school could see no alternative to removing the building, and was not interested in selling or leasing the property to outside interests.

The future of the College Hill neighborhood was threatened from yet another direction. In the 1950s and 1960s, many American cities undertook federally funded urban renewal projects that led to the clearance of large portions of their downtowns. Whole inner-city neighborhoods were designated as "blighted" and were cleared away, and College Hill may have been one of them. Indeed, it seemed almost inevitable that urban renewal land acquisition and clearance activities, already underway elsewhere in the downtown, would extend well into the College Hill neighborhood. After all, College Hill was essentially part of the downtown, and there was no denying that its housing stock was badly run down.

THE EFFORT TO SAVE COLLEGE HILL

Few people in Providence are more knowledgeable or in a better position to tell about the efforts and actions that saved the College Hill neighborhood than Tina Regan. In addition to being an active member of the Providence Preserva-

4-5 Historic brick dwelling at 225-227 Benefit Street, just before falling to the wreckers' hammers. The structure was ordered demolished by the Rhode Island School of Design despite the Providence Preservation Society's pleas that it be preserved.

Source: *The Providence Journal*

tion Society since 1975, and staffing their offices, she is also chairperson of the city's College Hill Historic District Commission, and sits as a member of the Downcity Design Review Committee. When I was in Providence researching this case study, I made a point of contacting Tina Regan, and was pleased when she said I could come to the Providence Preservation Society's offices to speak with her.

Walking through the College Hill area for the first time, and heading north on Benefit Street to the society's offices in a restored historic building at 21 Meeting Street, I saw beautifully restored and maintained old buildings. However, Tina Regan was quick to remind me that College Hill was a very different place back in the 1950s and 1960s. "When I came from the west side to take art lessons on Saturday mornings at RISD here on College Hill, my mother made it a point of always saying as I went out the door, 'Don't go down Benefit Street.' So you can imagine what it had become."

The possibility that the entire College Hill neighborhood might be leveled was very real. Part of the city's downtown area (the Weybosset area) was already in the process of being bulldozed and more extensive clearance was being considered. "Because of the age of the city," Tina Regan continued, "you could have cleared away the entire city. Here was this very old city, with no zoning to speak of, and with this cluster of residential homes on College Hill, right next to old industrial buildings and warehouses. Here comes this tool, 'urban renewal,' that could clear away this clutter and these blighted buildings."

Regan recalls going to some of the meetings where large-scale clearance schemes were presented and discussed. From attending those meetings, she formed the definite impression that the people who were behind those massive clearance schemes did not have a clear vision of the kind of city they wanted to create, once everything was cleared away. "The main impression I got was that the people who were administering urban renewal in Providence back then had no planning training or background in planning, and didn't know what to do with all the urban renewal money they were getting. They knew there was an opportunity to do something major, but really had no idea how to carry out the project."

During the 1950s and 1960s, Providence had a citizen-member City Plan Commission and a small staff that was headed by Frank Malley, whose background was that of an engineer rather than a planner. The City Plan Commission was ostensibly responsible for the overall planning of the city; however, the real power and control over land use and development resided in the Providence Redevelopment Agency (PRA), which had a large staff of its own and which focused on carrying out specific redevelopment projects. It wasn't until the early 1970s that Joseph Doorley, the mayor at that time, established the Department of Planning and Urban Development (DPUD), and folded the PRA into the DPUD (making the DPUD director also the director of the PRA).

Had it not been for the fact that urban renewal and highway building were having such a devastatingly negative effect on Providence, Tina Regan probably would not have become involved in the fight to save College Hill. She became involved because of what urban renewal and interstate highway building had done to the west side of Providence, where she lived. She knew there had to be a different and better way of remaking the city.

Tina Regan is modest and self-effacing about the role she played in the overall effort. She points out that she joined the College Hill effort and became active in the Providence Preservation Society in 1975, midway through the process. The people, she insists, who deserve the most credit for stabilizing and

renewing College Hill were long-time residents of the College Hill neighborhood—such as John Nicholas Brown, Beatrice "Happy" Chace, Elizabeth G.
Allen, Frances S. Sloan, Mary Elizabeth Sharpe and others—who, with the help
and encouragement of architectural historian Antoinette F. Downing, formed
the Providence Preservation Society in 1956, and initiated a remarkably well-
organized and successful planning effort.[2]

In most places where citizens have organized to oppose publicly financed
urban renewal and/or highway projects, the central aim has been to *stop* something from happening. However, from the beginning in the College Hill area,
the goal that people had in mind was not just to *stop* something from happening, but rather to *bring about* positive change within the College Hill neighborhood. From the very beginning, organizers and leaders of the effort to save
College Hill did something else that proved to be crucially important: they
emphasized the importance of planning, and of developing a coherent, overall
development strategy rather than simply pursuing a series of ad hoc, crisis-
driven actions. People in the neighborhood did not simply speak out *against*
the plans of Brown and the city; they also put forward a positive message of
their own. In the words of Tina Regan, "They said, 'We have to slow down. We
have to develop a plan and carry that plan through.'"

The group of people who first came together to try to save College Hill was
mostly composed of long-time citizens of Providence and residents of College
Hill. Over time, however, professionals became more involved and played an
increasingly important role. The first "outside" consultant to be brought in was
Lachlan F. Blair, who was hired to help the group write an application for a
"demonstration planning grant" from the U.S. Department of Housing and
Urban Development (HUD). Prior to founding a private consulting firm along
with Stewart Stein in 1957, Blair had been state planning chief for the State of
Rhode Island, and deputy planning director of Providence. The application
was successful, and the HUD demonstration planning grant of $40,000 was
matched by an additional $20,000 from the Providence Preservation Society.
Blair's newly established consulting firm got the job.

It was Blair and Stein's responsibility to direct the overall planning effort, the
purpose of which was to document and describe significant historic and architectural resources, and develop a detailed plan and implementation strategy
for the area. To accomplish that, Blair and Stein assembled an interdisciplinary
team of professionals, including architectural historian Antoinette F. Downing
and architect/planner William D. Warner. Another person drawn into the
project was Martin Adler, who had just earned a master's degree in planning
and was awarded a student internship from the American Society of Planning
Officials to work on the College Hill project.[3]

The next thing Blair and Stein did, which was required under the contract,
was to study and learn from the experience of other cities that had been leaders

in preservation planning. This helped the team generate ideas concerning how they would approach their task in Providence. "It also helped us avoid the mistakes that others had made," Blair pointed out. Cities which had conducted surveys of historic buildings and/or which had adopted city ordinances regulating land use and structures in historic areas were identified and studied.[4]

Antoinette F. Downing, a tenacious advocate of historic preservation and a highly respected scholar in the field, also became increasingly involved in a professional consultant capacity.[5] It was Downing who developed the innovative survey tools and methods that were used at College Hill—the system of classes and categories used to describe and classify properties, the numerical system used to rate properties in terms of their significance and importance, and the actual survey forms that were used in the field.

After conducting the survey and analyzing the results, and after a thorough study of the neighborhood (including an analysis of traffic, parking, institutional land uses, public schools and open space), a final report was prepared. The process of writing the final report, like the conduct of the entire planning process, was a team effort. The report, titled *College Hill: A Demonstration Study and Plan for Historic Area Renewal* ("the 1959 College Hill plan"), was over 200 pages in length and contained scores of maps, photographs and illustrations.

The first part of the 1959 College Hill plan, which was largely written by Blair and titled "Preservation Elsewhere," provided a succinct but thorough overview and analysis of preservation efforts in other cities throughout the U.S. (This section of the 1959 College Hill plan, in fact, is an excellent distillation of the status of planning for preservation—of historic property surveys, and of land use controls and regulations designed to protect and preserve historic districts—as of the end of the 1950s.) The second part of the report, written primarily by Downing, describes the history of College Hill and the various architectural styles that were associated with different periods in the area's development. Techniques used in surveying the area's architectural and historic resources, and criteria used in judging the historic significance of buildings and the methodology used for scoring buildings (*i.e.*, taking into account their physical condition and the degree of alteration) were also described.

The third and final part of the report, written by Warner, addressed the question of "What should and can be done?" In this section of the report, detailed proposals for nine different subareas within College Hill were presented and tied together into what was called a "25-Year Plan." The recommended implementation strategy was complex and multifaceted, calling for actions to be taken on a number of different levels:

- Establish a permanent committee or organization to guide and oversee development efforts related to the 1959 College Hill plan.

- Undertake an urban renewal project in the College Hill area including selective clearance, rehabilitation and conservation, as well as public infrastructure improvements.
- Establish an historic trail along Benefit Street.
- Develop a national historic park at the site of the Roger Williams Spring on North Main Street.
- Adopt special zoning regulations for the protection of the historic area of College Hill. (The 1959 College Hill plan included a draft of proposed state-enabling legislation authorizing the establishment of an historic district and the adoption of historic district zoning, as well as the wording of a proposed local zoning ordinance.)

4-6   Architectural historian and preservationist Antoinette F. Downing speaking to a group in Providence.

Source: Courtesy of the Providence Preservation Society

- Stimulate private investment in College Hill by alerting individuals and groups to opportunities for investment in the area.
- Urge institutions of higher education located in the College Hill area to be guided by the recommendations contained in the 1959 College Hill plan, and to cooperate with the city and with each other when planning for the physical development of their campuses.
- Plant street trees in renewal areas designated for rehabilitation, particularly along the "Benefit Street Trail."
- Adopt and enforce municipal regulations related to zoning and housing codes.
- Undertake carefully planned publicity, education and information programs to increase public understanding of and support for the aims of the 1959 College Hill plan.

When I interviewed Blair, he said that many people have told him that one of the most important things to come out of the College Hill effort was a structured methodology for inventorying and evaluating historic properties. In fact, the building form and methodology used at College Hill were subsequently adopted by the National Trust for Historic Preservation, and have been used across the country as the basis for surveying and inventorying properties for historic district designation. In Blair's opinion, what happened at College Hill provides two other important lessons: "First, it demonstrated the importance of structuring a task. Second, it demonstrated that planning and preservation go hand in glove."

THE IMPACT OF THE 1959 COLLEGE HILL PLAN

One year after the 1959 College Hill plan was completed, the city passed an historic district zoning ordinance creating the College Hill Historic District and establishing the College Hill Historic District Commission.[6] Under the ordinance, the commission was given some extremely important powers to safeguard historic buildings in the district. No building in the district can be demolished and no exterior remodeling or alteration of any building in the district can take place without the specific permission of the commission.

It did not take long for the power and resolve of the commission to be tested. RISD came before the commission seeking permission to tear down the old Woods-Gerry Mansion at 62 Prospect Street. According to the college, the building was badly run down and the property needed to be demolished to accommodate future college expansion.

The college was not without support in the community, and the question of whether or not to allow the building's demolition became controversial. In an attempt to find a compromise, the commission found a person who was willing to repair the house and live in it, if the college would give him a 20-year lease. The college said no and the issue was forced to a vote. Antoinette F. Downing, who was chairman of the College Hill Historic District Commission, recalled in a 1979 newspaper interview that she went to the climactic meeting at which the vote was taken, and was so uncertain of the outcome that she had prepared a minority opinion. The vote of the commission was unanimous and the demolition application was turned down. For many years, RISD did nothing with the Woods-Gerry Mansion; eventually, the college restored the mansion, and today it houses an art gallery and faculty offices.

Because it was the first test of the commission's powers, and because a revered local college was the applicant, the decision in the case of the Woods-Gerry Mansion was one of the toughest decisions the commission ever made and created a good deal of bitterness in some quarters. However, as the standards imposed by the commission gradually transformed the district over time, public acceptance and approval of the importance of the commission's role in overseeing and controlling land use changes has grown.

A Follow-up Study of the Effects of the 1959 College Hill Plan

One reason why people remain unaware of the extent to which plans shape subsequent events is that, once a particular plan is prepared and recommendations are offered, the investment in planning typically ends. Studies are rarely conducted and reports are rarely prepared that inform citizens on the extent to which planning recommendations have been carried out, and the extent to which the goals and objectives of a plan have been achieved. That was not the case in Providence.

Two years after the 1959 College Hill plan was completed, a follow-up report was prepared documenting the progress that had been made in implementing the various recommendations. The report was titled *College Hill 1961—progress after planning* ("the 1961 College Hill report") and was prepared by Martin Adler for two reasons. First, because the 1959 College Hill plan called for conserving most of the existing fabric of the neighborhood, visible signs of the neighborhood's renewal would be slow in coming. Such subtle and gradual changes could easily be overlooked, whereas major clearance projects (which were in vogue at the time) were attracting headlines and news coverage because they were visually dramatic. Second, it was hoped that reminding people of what had been accomplished in the immediate aftermath of the 1959 College Hill plan would help to maintain and build public support for carrying through with the rest of the program.

According to the 1961 College Hill report, the following actions called for in the 1959 College Hill plan had been implemented:

- A College Hill Coordinating Committee of 20 persons had been organized to oversee the implementation of the plan.
- A federally assisted, preservation-oriented urban renewal program had begun in the College Hill area and deteriorated properties, which did not

significantly contribute to the character of the neighborhood, had been cleared.

- A state-enabling act for historic area zoning had been enacted in 1959, and an historic district zoning ordinance was adopted for the College Hill area in 1960. A seven-member Historic District Commission had also been established to administer and enforce the provisions of the historic district zoning ordinance.

- The Providence Preservation Society had developed educational materials and maps related to the Benefit Street Historic Trail (also called the "Historic Mile"), and guided tours of the College Hill area had been organized and conducted to enhance public appreciation of the architectural and historic resources of the area.

- Legislation was drafted and submitted for congressional approval establishing a national historic park along the western edge of College Hill, at the site of the spring which provided water for Roger Williams and his settlers.

- Private individuals and corporations had bought approximately 30 pre-1840 houses with the intention of restoring them.

- The Episcopal Diocese of Rhode Island had acquired three houses on Benefit Street, and restored and converted them into apartments for elderly persons.

As is evident from the 1961 College Hill report, a great deal was accomplished in a relatively short period of time in terms of implementing the recommendations contained in the 1959 College Hill plan. Much had also been accomplished in terms of changing public attitudes toward College Hill, and in gaining acceptance of the idea that old neighborhoods like College Hill have value and should be preserved rather than cleared away wholesale.

Nevertheless, the neighborhood still looked run down, and there was little visible evidence that the neighborhood was changing for the better. In the minds of realtors, developers and bankers, as well as prospective homebuyers, College Hill remained a risky place in which to invest. Because of these perceived risks (which were made worse by the precariousness of the downtown real estate market just across the river), few people were prepared to buy run-down College Hill properties, and then spend the considerable sums required to restore them and make them livable. Practically everyone was sitting on the sidelines waiting for someone else to make the first move and assume the risk.

Eventually, someone did step forward and did what most people at the time still thought was risky and even foolhardy. That person was Beatrice "Happy" Chace—a long-time resident of Providence, a founding member of the Providence Preservation Society, and a strong supporter of the College Hill planning process. Ms. Chace purchased 15 structures—primarily in the block bounded by Benefit, Jenckes, Halsey and Pratt Streets—and proceeded to restore their exteriors. Through the Burnside Corporation, which she formed in the 1960s, she also erected new infill housing on Pratt Street on land that had been cleared of severely deteriorated structures that were incapable of being renovated.

These positive physical changes in a concentrated area dramatically improved the appearance of that area, and helped to stem the cycle of disinvestment that had plagued College Hill for so long. By doing what she did, Ms. Chace hoped to entice others to purchase and renovate other historic structures in College Hill. She also hoped that, once they saw the renovated exteriors of historic properties she owned, people would become interested in buying them and renovating their interiors so that they could live in them. Nevertheless, few people stepped forward to buy the properties Ms. Chace had rescued. For many years, Ms. Chace continued to own and maintain a large number of properties in the College Hill area—waiting for others to follow.

It is impossible to underestimate the significance of what "Happy" Chace did and its importance in helping to fulfill the aims of the 1959 College Hill plan. Had she not stepped forward and made a significant investment in College Hill, when the market for property in College Hill was extremely weak, the physical renewal of College Hill would undoubtedly have taken even longer than it did—and might not have happened at all.

In 1967, a second edition of the 1959 College Hill plan was published that included an additional section not included in the original plan. Part IV of the second edition, titled "Progress Since 1959," reported on the progress that had been made over an eight-year period in implementing the nine key actions recommended in the 1959 College Hill plan. It reported, for example, that an urban renewal program had been formulated for the area by the PRA that was substantially as recommended in the original report. It also reported that progress was being made in creating Roger Williams Spring National Park between Canal and North Main Streets. Although Congress had still not voted the necessary appropriation, the National Parks Service was proceeding with detailed planning and had estimated the total cost of the project, including the cost of moving the Thomas Clemence House (circa 1680) to the site to serve as the Visitors' Center.[7]

A map was included in the second edition of the 1959 College Hill plan, issued in 1967, showing the locations of 28 properties that had been burned or torn down between 1956 and 1967, half of which had been lost since 1960 when the historic area zoning provisions went into effect. The battle was still being fought and the final judgment on whether College Hill would finally be saved was still somewhat up in the air. To encourage and support those willing to take on the task of restoring old homes, the 1967 second edition of the plan reported that the Providence Preservation Society had organized a Consultant Bureau composed of professionals who were working on a volunteer basis to supply expert advice and guidance upon request.

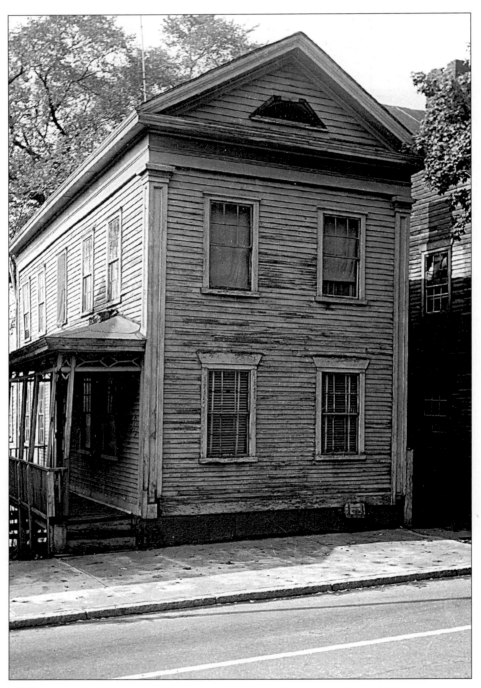

4-7   College Hill home, before restoration.

Source: Courtesy of the Providence Preservation Society

4-8 College Hill home, after restoration.

Source: Courtesy of the Providence Preservation Society

RECONCILING NEIGHBORHOOD
AND INSTITUTIONAL INTERESTS

In the decades that followed, progress was made in establishing a regulatory mechanism to help avoid the kind of head-on conflicts that were sparked when Brown University and RISD acquired and demolished buildings without regard for the effect such actions were having on the surrounding neighborhood. The 1959 College Hill plan specifically addressed this problem by recommending that "the Rhode Island School of Design, Brown University and Bryant College work jointly with the Providence City Planning Commission to plan the future growth of the community and the institutions." In an action which met the spirit and intent of that recommendation, the city's DPUD drafted and the city council adopted a special institutional overlay zoning district in 1986, which imposed special requirements and obligations on the city's seven major colleges and seven hospitals, over and above those specified by the underlying, preexisting zoning.

The boundaries of the new institutional overlay zoning district were drawn to conform exactly to the boundaries of the city's institutions *as they existed in 1986*. In effect, the new zoning ordinance declared that universities or hospitals were allowed in areas where they currently existed, but were prohibited outside those areas. The only way universities or hospitals could expand in the future was to request that adjoining properties be rezoned to be included in the institutional zone—and that, in turn, meant coming before the city council and having a public hearing that neighborhood people could attend. At the same time, the city also adopted a "master plan" requirement that called upon colleges and hospitals to prepare and file a master plan as a public document with the city. According to Samuel J. Shamoon, Providence's associate director for planning, "It was basically a disclosure statement designed to inform the city of what they intended to do, so that we could plan for it as well."

Unfortunately, experience proved that simply requiring institutions to "disclose" their plans was not sufficient to achieve the purpose and intent of the ordinance, and that the master plan provisions needed to be strengthened. In 1991, a revised master plan provision was adopted requiring institutions to prepare a formal, printed master plan document, and to submit it to the City Plan Commission for its approval, which can only be given after a formal public hearing on the plan is held. Furthermore, the institutions are required to prepare and file updated master plans, and to go through the process of holding a public hearing and gaining City Plan Commission approval every five years. Each institutional master plan must contain certain elements and conform to a standardized format. For example, each plan must provide a complete inventory (by location) of all properties owned by the institution, with a description of each building and property's use. It must also describe anticipated facility changes and construction projects, and identify specific areas the institution expects to expand into in the next five years.

Although the master plan requirements imposed on institutions may seem demanding, their imposition has helped avoid the kind of conflicts and antagonisms that arose when local colleges and institutions kept their intentions secret and acted unilaterally without consultation. Colleges and hospitals have also not found it overly difficult to comply with the master plan requirements. When I met with Sam Shamoon in his office, he showed me a box full of institutional master plans that had been submitted to and approved by the city— including a master plan that had recently been submitted by RISD. "We now realize that these institutions were doing their own internal planning all along; we [and others in the community] just didn't know what they were planning."

COLLEGE HILL TODAY

As a result of the 1959 College Hill plan, hundreds of historically and architecturally significant structures have been restored. However, in the broader context of urban and regional planning, there was another important and extremely positive outcome of the 1961 College Hill report: it saved and rebuilt a truly unique inner-city neighborhood and, in so doing, provided people with an opportunity to live in an extraordinary environment that is markedly different from what is typically experienced in suburban communities. Because of the success of the College Hill planning effort, over 11,000 people are able to live in a neighborhood with a distinctly urban character and with a wide array of housing accommodations, literally only "a stone's throw" away from the heart of the city. Few American cities as large as Providence have such a large, stable and attractive residential neighborhood so close to the downtown core.[8]

College Hill is not for everyone. Because the streets that crisscross College Hill were laid out before the automobile age, they are narrow and parking spaces are hard to find. People who have grown accustomed to having private driveways, and two- and three-car garages, would probably not want to live there. Also, lots are small and buildings are close together; people who need or want large private yards, and don't want to have anything to do with their neighbors, would not want to live in College Hill either. College Hill is a densely developed, congested place. On the other hand, for people who like cities, value history and architecture, like to walk and don't mind the prospect of bumping into and talking to people, there could hardly be a better place.

Some people may be inclined to criticize and dismiss what was achieved at College Hill by observing that the renewal and restoration of the neighborhood displaced low-income people who had come to occupy the badly run-down but cheap tenement apartments of College Hill. However, even more widespread displacement would have occurred had the preservation plan not been prepared and adopted. As this account makes clear, the alternative to preserving and renovating the existing structures was clearance. Indeed, had the city simply adopted a policy of "benign neglect," the prolonged period of disinvestment that would have followed would most certainly have resulted in a widespread loss of structures due to deterioration, abandonment and fire.

The preservation of existing structures in the College Hill area actually had the long-term benefit of preserving and maintaining a wide array of housing types to meet a variety of housing needs. Preservation did not simply produce elegant homes for wealthy people. Many long-time and well-to-do families live on College Hill, but the population of College Hill is remarkably varied in terms of age, income and household characteristics. Over one-quarter of the people who live in the College Hill neighborhood are students.

RECREATING THE CITY'S CENTER
AND MAKING THE CITY WHOLE

Two years after the 1959 College Hill plan was prepared, at a time when conditions in downtown Providence were becoming increasingly bleak, the PRA prepared a plan called *Downtown Providence 1970—A Master Plan for Downtown Providence* ("the 1961 Downtown plan").[9] Two-thirds of the $165,000 cost of preparing the plan was funded by the Federal Urban Renewal Administration. The plan was fairly typical of the kind of urban renewal planning many cities were doing at the time in that it called for massive clearance within the downtown area and for the construction of major new highways into and through the city. Maps and "bird's-eye" view illustrations in the document showed vast areas of surface parking, new parking garages and modern, high-rise office buildings. Most of the major physical changes proposed in the plan (with the exception of the idea of creating a pedestrian precinct along Westminster and

4-9   Row of restored homes on Benefit Street in the College Hill neighborhood.

Source: Gene Bunnell

Mathewson Streets) were designed to make it easier for people to drive cars into the city, to park and then drive out again.

Very little of what was called for in that plan actually came to pass. However, there was *one* major planning idea in the 1961 Downtown plan that did exert a powerful influence in reshaping the city in the future: the idea of relocating the mainline railroad tracks and moving them closer to the State House.

Thirteen years after the 1961 Downtown plan was prepared (in 1974), a second downtown plan was independently prepared by faculty members of RISD. The plan, which was called *Interface Providence* ("the 1974 Interface Providence plan"), was prepared at a time when the U.S. was coping with the "energy crisis" and the shock of sharply rising oil and gasoline prices brought on by the OPEC-led oil embargo. The primary purpose of the 1974 Interface Providence plan was to drastically reduce automobile use in Providence. (In fact, the plan called for excluding automobiles entirely from the core of the downtown.) To promote increased use of public transportation, the plan called for an intermodal bus/rail transportation facility to be built next to the Union Railroad

4-10   Prospect Terrace on College Hill, overlooking downtown Providence.

Source: Gene Bunnell

Station. Interestingly enough, the 1974 Interface Providence plan did not pick up on the idea of relocating the railroad tracks.

As was the case with the 1961 Downtown plan, very little of what was called for in the 1974 Interface Providence plan was implemented. Nevertheless, the 1974 Interface Providence plan did contain a seminal planning idea that, like the idea of relocating the railroad tracks, would resurface later and have a profound influence on the replanning and redevelopment of the downtown. That planning idea was that it was important to recapture the city's waterfront, and to reconnect the city to the rivers that flowed through the downtown.

In 1978, the federal government announced its intention to undertake a major, long-term investment to significantly upgrade and improve the northeast railroad corridor to pave the way for high-speed rail passenger service between New York City and Boston.[10] As part of that commitment, federal funding was earmarked to upgrade the rail corridor through Providence. At the time this commitment was made, it was assumed that the railroad tracks and rail station would remain where they were. However, fairly early on in the process, the idea of relocating the railroad tracks (first broached in the 1961 Downtown plan) surfaced once again.

According to Sam Shamoon, the track relocation idea was recalled and discussed in a meeting that involved the city's chief of planning at the time (Martha Bailey), the chief of the planning division of the Rhode Island Department of Transportation (RIDOT) (Joseph Arruda) and the executive director of the Providence Foundation (Ron Marsella). In the course of that meeting, someone pulled out the 1961 Downtown plan and said, "Why don't we think about relocating the tracks? Maybe now is the time to do it."

Soon after that meeting, the Providence Foundation hired the firm of C. E. Maguire to evaluate the feasibility of relocating the tracks. The Maguire study concluded that the cost of relocating the railroad tracks was not much greater than the cost of completely reconstructing the existing track bed. Equally (if not more) important, it found that relocating the tracks would free up roughly 65 acres of land, which could then be redeveloped in a way that was economically beneficial to Amtrak, the State of Rhode Island, the P & W Railroad and the City of Providence, all of which owned land in the area. Of those four parties, the City of Providence owned the least amount of land. However, the city stood to derive considerable economic benefit from the development of the 65 acres by virtue of the property taxes it stood to collect.

As a result of the findings of the Maguire study, Mayor Vincent "Buddy" Cianci, Jr. became a strong supporter of the plan. State funding was obtained to hire the firm of Skidmore, Owings & Merrill LLP (SOM) to prepare a concept plan that would outline, in broad-brush terms, how the area might be reorganized and redeveloped once the tracks were relocated. SOM's Marilyn Taylor was in charge of this planning effort, which came to be called the "Capital Center project."

The concept plan Taylor produced in 1979, called the *Capital Center Plan* ("the 1979 Capital Center plan"), called for relocating the railroad tracks 600-850 feet to the north, and for burying and covering over the tracks to create an expansive green, open space rising gradually up to the State Capital Building. The plan was decidedly classical in nature in that it established a strong radial axis leading from the State Capital Building toward the downtown. At the downtown end of the axis, the plan established a terminal focal point that was loosely referred to as a "water feature." Initial sketches suggested that the "water feature" might take the form of some kind of monumental fountain in the center of a circular reflecting pool of water.

Over the course of the next two or three years, the major planning proposals and ideas contained in SOM's 1979 Capital Center plan were reviewed, and steps were taken to pave the way for implementing the plan. The Federal Railroad Administration (FRA) approved the plan to move the railroad tracks and construct a new train station at Gaspee Street. The Federal Highway Administration (FHWA), the State of Rhode Island and the City of Providence agreed to cooperate in constructing a new civic center interchange with I-95, as well as connecting roads leading into the city. State legislation was passed establishing the Capital Center Special Development District, encompassing a land area of over 65 acres that would become developable once the railroad tracks and freight yards were removed. State legislation was also passed establishing the Capital Center Commission (jointly appointed by the governor, the mayor and the Providence Foundation) to oversee the development process, and to carry out a mandatory design review process related to all public and private development projects undertaken in the district. Detailed "Design and Development Guidelines" were subsequently drafted and formally adopted by the commission, specifying what could and could not be done on each parcel of land in the district. These Design and Development Guidelines were superimposed as an overlay zoning district, in addition to the requirements imposed by the preexisting zoning.

The method that was used to finance and carry out this large-scale development project has been rarely used in the U.S., although it has been used fairly frequently in other countries such as Japan and Korea. In planning parlance, the Capital Center project was financed and carried out through the method of "Land Readjustment." The four parties with land in the district (Amtrak, the State of Rhode Island, the P & W Railroad and the City of Providence) agreed to pool their land, thereby erasing previously drawn property boundaries, and to designate an entity (the Capital Center Commission) to act on their behalf in carrying out the project according to the adopted Design and Development Guidelines. The parties also agreed that future profits resulting from the development of the land would be apportioned among the four landowners in proportion to the share of the total land area they previously owned and contributed to the project.

The plan that was developed for the Capital Center project created 11 development parcels. Four additional parcels were added later, bringing the total number of parcels to 15. Amtrak developed Parcel 7 for the new railroad station.

Had the Capital Center project been carried out as originally envisioned and authorized, it would probably have fallen well short of what was eventually achieved, because the original SOM plan did not call for uncovering the rivers that flowed through the downtown or for creating parks and walkways along the banks of the rivers. In addition, the original SOM plan did nothing to alleviate traffic problems at Memorial Square, to which, as noted earlier, people in Providence already referred as "Suicide Circle." Indeed, if the 1979 Capital Center plan had been carried out without anything additional being done, it would have made traffic problems in and around Memorial Square even worse.

Planner Sam Shamoon could foresee that the development, which was going to take place in the Capital Center District, and the highways and interchanges that were being built as part of the project, were going to funnel still more traffic into the downtown area at Memorial Square, and was convinced that something needed to be done to alleviate the problem. He approached state highway officials and asked, "You're bringing in a huge volume of traffic here. Where is it going to go?" The response he got, according to Shamoon, was essentially, "That's your job. You people at the city figure it out."

Shamoon, along with two members of his staff, began to sketch out various ways that traffic coming into the Memorial Square area could be handled. The Memorial Square Committee was formed—which included the city traffic engineer and Ken Ornstein (the executive director of the Providence Foundation)—and the firm of Wilbur Smith Associates was hired to carry out a detailed analysis. The analysis showed that the biggest factor contributing to congestion at Memorial Square was traffic funneling through the square to and from the east, through the College Hill area along Angell and Waterman Streets. By February 1983, Wilbur Smith Associates had come up with seven different traffic circulation alternatives for dealing with the problem, most of them calling for extending Memorial Boulevard to the south. One of the alternatives (Alternative #6) called for extending Memorial Boulevard along the west side of the river, utilizing existing decking over the river in some places and constructing additional decking over the river where necessary.[11]

Around the same time, a new player appeared on the scene to contribute yet another key planning concept. Architect/planner William D. Warner was no stranger to Providence, having previously worked for the Providence City Plan Commission as project director for the 1959 College Hill plan. In 1960, he opened a private architectural and planning firm in Providence, which later relocated to nearby Exeter. Warner nevertheless kept track of what was happening in Providence, and kept a particularly close eye on what was being called for in the 1979 Capital Center plan.

Warner was convinced that the city had made a serious mistake years ago when it had allowed the rivers that ran through the city to be almost completely covered over with decking for traffic circulation and parking. He also recognized that the city was about to undertake a major downtown project that was going to help perpetuate the situation. Some people called it "the world's widest bridge." It was really nine separate bridges, all interconnected. The tenth and final insult occurred in 1940 when the city's central post office was constructed over the entire width of the Providence River, just 40 feet south of its confluence.

As noted earlier, the 1979 Capital Center plan that was prepared by SOM did not address the issue of the rivers and kept them as they were—largely covered and out of sight. It also did not attempt to alleviate traffic problems that were going to arise at Memorial Square as a result of the project.

With these issues in mind, Bill Warner went to see Bob Bendick, director of the Rhode Island Department of Environmental Management (RIDEM), to talk about the possibility of taking a look at the larger picture of how highways were cutting the city off from its waterfront. The problem, after all, wasn't limited to the area near Memorial Square and the Capital Center District. I-95 cut the east side of the city off from the Narragansett Bay to the south; continuing west, I-95 crossed the Providence River at Old Harbor, leaving interchange ramps on both shores, from which service roads extended north to downtown.

Bendick agreed with Warner that a comprehensive planning study was needed to produce solutions that would restore the city's connection to its waterfront and minimize the negative impacts of highway traffic on the downtown. The timing seemed right for such a waterfront study. James Rouse, the highly respected developer of Fanieul Hall Marketplace in Boston and Harborplace in Baltimore, had come to Providence in 1982 and delivered a speech that generated a great deal of publicity. Rouse essentially said, "Look at what we're doing in Boston, and look at what we're doing in Baltimore. Everyone wants to be near the water. Go to the water!"

Bendick suggested that a possible source of funding for a waterfront urban design study was the National Endowment for the Arts (NEA). Before going to work on preparing a funding application to NEA, Warner and Bendick went to discuss their ideas with Ed Wood, the director of the RIDOT, who was generally supportive of their proposed approach. Warner and Bendick also went to see Sam Shamoon, the associate director for planning. Shamoon had heard about Warner from his work on College Hill but had not met him before. Shamoon recalls that Warner pulled out some old photographs of the city (including a picture of the Old Cove that used to be in the center of the downtown in front of the State Capital Building) and said, "We have to do something about the river—it's been buried too long."

The Providence Foundation agreed to sponsor the NEA grant application, and to host the meetings that would be part of the planning process and keep minutes. The funding application was completed and submitted to the NEA in the fall of 1982. The proposed study was divided into three areas: the Providence River; Fox and India Point (the southern shoreline of the east side); and the Seekonk River (the eastern shoreline). Somewhat later, the Providence River was further subdivided into Old Harbor (the area south of the Crawford Street Bridge) and the segment north of the Crawford Street Bridge.

On May 18, 1983, the NEA announced a grant award which, when added to the city, state and institutional money that had already been pledged, provided a total of $125,000 for the Providence Waterfront Study, and Warner was engaged as director and designer of the study. In June, a 20-member Waterfront Study Coordinating Committee was established, composed of people from all of the city, state and federal agencies that needed to be involved and had an interest in the project (environment, transportation, historic preservation, city planning and state planning) as well as key private sector and nonprofit organizations (such as the Providence Foundation and the Providence Preservation Society). Ken Ornstein, the executive director of the Providence Foundation, chaired the committee.

Because construction was about to begin on the Capital Center project, and there was some urgency in developing planning recommendations that could be integrated with improvements planned for the Capital Center area, the Providence Waterfront Study initially focused on the portion of the Providence River closest to the Capital Center project—the segment north of the Crawford Street Bridge. In planning for this area, Warner and the Waterfront Study Coordinating Committee confronted the same traffic issues Shamoon and Wilbur Smith Associates had been grappling with and, like Shamoon and Wilbur Smith Associates, developed a number of alternative plans that called for extending Memorial Boulevard south toward the waterfront. Sam Shamoon (associate director for planning and a member of the Waterfront Study Coordinating Committee) strongly urged that the Memorial Boulevard Extension be confined to the west side of the river.

The members of the Waterfront Study Coordinating Committee met twice monthly between June and October 1983. At one of those meetings (July 1983), Warner unveiled a seemingly radical scheme that introduced an altogether new variable: *relocating* the rivers. At first, the idea of moving the rivers seemed crazy and impractical; however, the more people thought about it, the more the idea seemed worth considering. The "River Relocation" scheme Warner developed called for moving the river out from under the post office and relocating the confluence of the rivers nearly 100 yards to the east. It would then be possible to construct an extension of Memorial Boulevard on solid ground between the post office and the rivers' new confluence and, most importantly, *to uncover the rivers.*

Between July and October 1983, the members of the Waterfront Study Coordinating Committee worked collaboratively to overcome potential obstacles and refine the plan. In August 1983, after a lengthy discussion, the members of the committee agreed that the city should amend Wilbur Smith's Memorial Square-Crawford Street design contract to have them look at the traffic implications of the Providence Waterfront Study. They also discussed the importance of trying to keep the Capital Center project "on track . . . without closing the door to the ideas being developed by the Providence Waterfront Study." According to the minutes of that August meeting, Joseph Arruda, who headed the planning division of RIDOT, commented that if the Memorial Boulevard Extension could be classified as an "urban connector" highway, it would be eligible for 85% federal funding. "That was the real breakthrough in thinking about how we could implement and pay for this more ambitious downtown plan," said Shamoon.

By October, the final version of the Memorial Boulevard Extension/River Relocation plan had taken shape and been endorsed by the committee. A little later in the fall of 1983, as construction work on the Capital Center project was about to begin, RIDOT agreed to "pull" the Memorial Boulevard Extension/River Relocation part of the Providence Waterfront Study for the purpose of conducting an Environmental Impact Statement (EIS) on the project—an action that was intended to advance the project closer to the implementation stage so that it could hopefully be coordinated with the Capital Center project.

An influential local businessman and developer, upon learning about the recommendations contained in the Providence Waterfront Study, and the possibility that the rivers through downtown might be relocated, started making telephone calls. Ron Marsella had previously served as executive director of the Providence Foundation but, by the 1980s, had left that position to become a private developer. Marsella was about to develop a major downtown office building right where Warner's plan called for relocating the river and was extremely upset by the prospect that his development project would have to be delayed. Sam Shamoon recalls Marsella angrily saying, "This river relocation is going to stop me in my tracks and I don't want that to happen. And I bet any amount of money this project will never happen!"

For a while, the politics surrounding the project became pretty sticky. Marsella was well known in the Providence business community and knew many people in important positions. Moreover, the city did not want to lose the substantial investment that Marsella was promising to make in the downtown. Marsella did have a point: moving rivers is not a simple matter and raises seri-

STATE HOUSE PARK

RAILROAD RELOCATION
PROJECT
(CAPITAL CENTER PROJECT)

*STATUS OF PARCELS
JANUARY 2001*

1-12	**Development Parcels**
1	Old Railroad Station: *renovated and occupied*
2	Hotel and Condominiums: *on hold*
3	New Bank Headquarters: *occupied*
3 E&W	Office Building: *on hold*
3 E&W	Office Building: *on hold*
5	Apartments: *occupied*
7	Relocated Railroad Station
8	New American Express Headquarters
10	Providence Place Mall: *completed Fall 1999*
11	Convention Center and Hotel: *completed Fall 1994*

RIVER RELOCATION PROJECT

A   Relocated Woonasquatucket River with riverwalks and new bridges
B   Relocated Moshassuck River with riverwalks
C   Relocated confluence
D   Exposed river walls with uncovered river and new bridges
E   Auto-free riverwalk
F   Waterplace
G   New Parcel
H   Memorial Boulevard Extension
J   Pedestrian Concourse
K   Boat Landings
L   Relocated World War I Monument

■   RIVERS AS RELOCATED

▪ ▪ ▪   ORIGINAL RIVER LOCATION

RIVER RELOCATION PLAN

0 20 50 100   200   300

N

4-11   1984 River Relocation plan, prepared by William D. Warner, Architects and Planners, showing the original river location (dotted lines) and the new river location. Also shown are the development parcels created by the 1979 Capital Center plan. Parcel 3 is the Citizens Bank Building that was eventually developed by Ron Marsella.

Source: Courtesy of William D. Warner, Architects and Planners

ous environmental issues. A detailed EIS would have to be prepared and permits from environmental agencies would need to be obtained.

Around this time, Pete Pointner, who had conducted the EIS on the Capital Center project, received a call from an unnamed developer in Providence. Pointner had previously worked for the firm of Delew Cather, but had more recently formed his own planning consulting firm called Planning Resources, Inc. in Wheaton, Illinois. According to Pointner, the telephone conversation

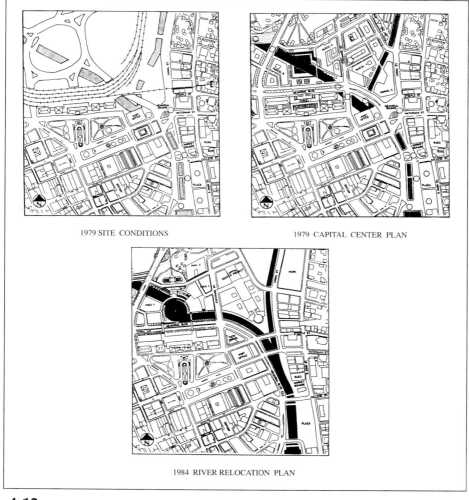

1979 SITE CONDITIONS

1979 CAPITAL CENTER PLAN

1984 RIVER RELOCATION PLAN

4-12   Composite showing evolution of downtown Providence from site conditions that existed in the 1970s, to the reconfigured development pattern called for in the 1979 Capital Center plan, to the 1984 Memorial Boulevard Extension/River Relocation plan, which was implemented.

Source: Courtesy of William D. Warner, Architects and Planners

went like this: "The developer began by asking me, 'What do you think of a project involving moving rivers in a downtown?' I said, 'Well, on the surface, it sounds like it would be impossible to obtain the permits.' It sounded to me at the time like some crazy scheme cooked up by a developer who was intent on screwing the environment to get more building space." The last thing the developer said to Pointner as their telephone conversation ended was, "If you don't bring us together and help us resolve this conflict, we're in trouble."

Pete Pointner was hired and brought back to Providence to assess the environmental issues raised by the proposed river relocation, and to work with Warner and Wilbur Smith Associates on the preparation of a detailed EIS. The EIS evaluated and compared four different traffic alternatives that had been identified by Wilbur Smith Associates—including the one proposed in 1983 by Sam Shamoon (which did *not* relocate the rivers nor remove the decking) and the River Relocation project proposed by the Providence Waterfront Study. Both of these alternatives placed the Memorial Boulevard Extension to the west side of the river.

The EIS was completed in six months and selected the River Relocation plan as the preferred alternative. In August 1984, an official public hearing was held to receive public comments, at which almost all the comments were favorable. In November of that year, the city, state and the FHWA committed to the project's funding. Because of the collaborative planning effort, and the favorable response the plan received at the public hearing, only minor amendments were required and all necessary environmental clearances were obtained not long thereafter. In February 1985, Warner and C. E. Maguire (engineers for the Capital Center project) began preparing detailed design and engineering plans for the Memorial Boulevard Extension/River Relocation project.

The final Memorial Boulevard Extension/River Relocation plan included the following principle features:

- *Providence River Park:* A Y-shaped, landscaped river corridor was created at the center of the city to connect existing parks, and establish an independent walkway system from Capital Center and the State House to Kennedy Plaza and Crawford Street.

- *Circulation:* Boat traffic was accommodated by dredging the rivers and establishing a uniform clearance under the bridges. Three docking places were provided for boats to discharge and take on passengers. Continuous accessibility for visiting boats was provided along the riverwalks between these boat landings by conveniently spaced line cleats.

- *Waterplace Park:* A 4-acre park punctuated the western terminus of the walkway system and included a 30-foot-high fountain, an amphitheater, several smaller plazas with seating, two pedestrian bridges, and a pavilion building to accommodate a restaurant and visitor's center.

- *Memorial Park:* The 2-acre park—framed by the historic brick Market House, courthouse and buildings of RISD—anchored the southern portion of the project. The park provided an ideal setting for the relocated World War I monument, which had to be moved from its long-standing position in the center of Memorial Square (alias "Suicide Circle").[12]

In the fall of 1987, four years after construction began on the Capital Center project, construction work began on the complicated task of uncovering the city's riverfront—an undertaking that would take nine years to complete. The total public cost of the Capital Center and River Relocation projects, including the Memorial Boulevard Extension and all connecting highways (as well as all of the bridges, pedestrian walkways, parks and plazas) was $169 million. Of that total amount, the City of Providence had to pay only $6 million. The FRA paid the $33 million cost of relocating the railroad tracks and constructing the new train station. Relocating the rivers, constructing the highways and highway interchanges, and constructing Waterplace Park and the riverwalk cost $136 million, most of which was paid for by the FHWA.[13]

As a result of the Memorial Boulevard Extension/River Relocation plan being grafted onto the 1979 Capital Center plan, over 11 acres of urban riverfront parks were created for people's enjoyment, along with nearly 1.5 miles of riverwalks. Boats can navigate to and from Waterplace Park, utilizing nearly a mile of downtown river channels, and an amphitheater and smaller plazas provide places for music, theater and other forms of entertainment.

Between 1983 and the spring of 2000, a total of $605 million was privately invested in developing the 65 acres of land within the Capital Center District.[14] Privately financed developments completed within the district included the renovation and adaptive reuse of the old Union Railroad Station Building into offices and restaurants, as well as the construction of a number of major new buildings—the first new buildings built in downtown Providence in many years. Among the new buildings that had been constructed within the Capital Center District by 2001 were: an $18 million office building originally built for American Express, currently occupied by Boston Financial; an 8-story, 225-unit residential apartment building (Center Place); the 13-story, 234,000-square-foot Citizens Plaza Office Building developed by Ron Marsella at the relocated confluence of the two rivers; the $460 million Providence Place Mall; and a 215-room Marriott Courtyard Hotel.

Between 1983 and 2000, every major new structure built in downtown Providence has been built within, or immediately adjacent to, the Capital Center District. The fact that no demolition of buildings has been needed to accommodate all this new construction makes what was accomplished through the Capital Center project all the more remarkable.

DOWNTOWN PROVIDENCE TODAY

People who know first-hand what the city was like 20 or 30 years ago will be especially impressed by the changes that have occurred in Providence. If you stood in front of the Rhode Island State Capital Building in the 1960s and looked out toward the downtown, you mostly saw the busy northeast rail corridor, acres of railroad freight yards and vast areas of surface parking. Because of the railroad tracks, "Suicide Circle" and decking over the river that was used for parking, it was a physically divided and fragmented city—making it difficult and uninviting to walk from one part of the downtown to another, and from downtown to College Hill. Today, the railroad tracks are nowhere to be seen. "Suicide Circle" is gone; instead, one sees rivers and bodies of water lined with parks and pedestrian walkways.

4-13   1994 view of Waterplace Cove Basin from Francis Street stairway.

Source: Courtesy of William D. Warner, Architects and Planners

4-14   Decking being removed from Providence River, 1994. View looking south toward Old Harbor.

Source: Courtesy of William D. Warner, Architects and Planners

4-15 Memorial Boulevard Extension/River Relocation project completed. A wide, landscaped pedestrian walkway now leads past buildings of the Rhode Island School of Design (on left of photo) toward Gardner Jackson Park and the relocated World War II memorial.

Source: Courtesy of William D. Warner, Architects and Planners

4-16   Center Place residential apartment building overlooking the riverwalk along the Woonasquatucket River—one of a number of significant downtown developments completed as a result of the Capital Center and River Relocation plans.

Source: Gene Bunnell

In April 1998, after attending the APA National Conference in Boston, I took some extra time to make the short trip down to Providence. I hadn't been back to Providence in many years and was eager to see how it had changed from the way I had known it. Sam Shamoon offered to meet and walk with me around the downtown, and provided me with a running commentary as we went along. We walked from the planning department offices on Westminster Street, past Providence City Hall overlooking Kennedy Plaza (an imposing Second Empire-style building built in 1878) and through a wide pedestrian underpass under Memorial Boulevard. As we came through the opening of the under-pass, we were immediately facing Waterplace Park which, as Shamoon pointed out, recreates and makes reference to the Old Cove that used to exist in that location in the 19th century, before the marshes and lowlands were filled in with the soil removed from Weybosset Hill.

As we circled around the perimeter of Waterplace Park toward the state cap-ital, Sam described what Marilyn Taylor had in mind when she sketched out her initial concept plan. "Before the Capital Center project, the State House stood on top of a steep hill, looking out over freight yards that covered the flat

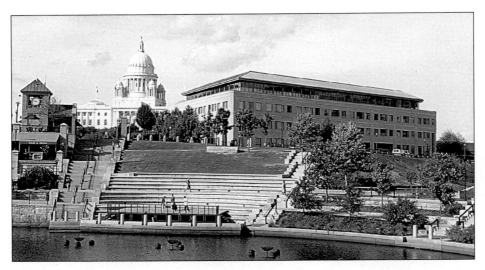

4-17   Looking across Waterplace Park toward the formal staircase and
amphitheater leading up to the Rhode Island State House—a design feature
called for in the 1979 Capital Center plan.

Source: Gene Bunnell

4-18   Looking east down Woonasquatucket River from Waterplace Park on a chilly
April day, 1998. The arched opening on the right is the pedestrian walkway that leads
from the former Union Railroad Station and Kennedy Plaza underneath Memorial
Boulevard to Waterplace Park.

Source: Gene Bunnell

and low land at the base. What Marilyn Taylor's plan did was to anchor the low-lying area with Waterplace Park, and then to create a series of steps leading gradually up to reveal the state capital. It is a dramatic way to approach the state capital because, as you walk up the steps, the State Capital Building is gradually revealed. When you get to the top of the steps, you expect to see the tracks, but you don't because the railroad tracks are buried."

We climbed the grand staircase leading from Waterplace Park and at the top looked out across the large, grassy lawn that now spreads out from the state capital. To the right was the new railroad station building—a modern building with decidedly classical features, which was also designed by Marilyn Taylor and SOM. As we walked along, Sam pointed out the air vents that could be seen protruding above the surface of the lawn, which were installed to vent fumes out of the railroad tunnel. "You can't plant or build anything very deep here. It looks like an ordinary lawn, but the soil here is not very deep, because we're actually standing on a deck that spans over the railroad tunnel below."

After walking through the attractive interior of the new rail passenger terminal, we walked east to the Roger Williams Spring National Park, which provides a welcome buffer between the state capital area and the densely developed College Hill neighborhood.

After walking through the lush green environment of the park, we continued south along the east side of the Moshassuck River to a point where we were looking across the river at the 13-story Citizens Plaza Office Building. The developer of the building, it will be recalled, was extremely unhappy when construction of the building was delayed by William Warner's river relocation plan. However, with the benefit of hindsight, he was probably fortunate that he was unable to build his building when and where he wanted. Had the developer not been delayed, his building would have come on the market around the time of the 1987-88 real estate market collapse, when there was a glut of vacant new office buildings throughout New England. Moreover, the new site on which he was eventually able to build—the point of land formed by the convergence of the relocated Moshassuck and Woonasquatucket Rivers—is arguably the most prestigious private development site in the reconfigured downtown. As a result of the river relocation, the three-sided building that was developed (designed by the firm of Jung-Brannen of Boston) has become downtown Providence's signature building.

From there, Sam and I walked south along the nicely landscaped, brick-paved walkway that runs along the eastern edge of the Providence River, and that leads to a particularly attractive, wide riverwalk segment fronting on buildings of RISD.

Although we were in the heart of the city, the area was remarkably peaceful and free of traffic noise—just as Sam Shamoon hoped it would be when he first proposed that traffic be diverted to the west side of the Providence River,

4-19   Roger Williams Spring National Park.

Source: Gene Bunnell

4-20   Citizens Plaza Office Building.

Source: Gene Bunnell

4-21   View looking south down the Providence River. Picture taken from Citizens Plaza Office Building.

Source: Department of Planning and Development, City of Providence

thereby reserving the east side of the river bordering College Hill for pedestrian walkways, parks, plazas and sitting areas. "I just felt the area was too beautiful to have traffic on both sides of the river," said Shamoon. We ended our walk at Gardner Jackson Park, where the World War I memorial (relocated from the middle of "Suicide Circle") and the statue honoring Verrazano now peacefully coexist.

In place of "the world's widest bridge," a series of attractively designed bridges now span the river at convenient intervals. The large number of bridges has prompted some people to compare Providence to Venice; the fact that each of the bridges is distinctive also encourages the comparison. In Venice, each and every bridge has its own distinctive design and form, so that if you know Venice well, all you need to do is to see a particular bridge to tell where you are in the city. One other striking thing about the bridges bears mentioning: a number of the bridges are exclusively for pedestrians and those that aren't have extra-wide sidewalks. In downtown Providence today, people who are on foot are every bit as important and deserving of consideration as people in automobiles.

4-22   Riverwalk along east side of Providence River leading toward Gardner Jackson Park. Buildings of Rhode Island School of Design on left.

Source: Gene Bunnell

4-23   Quiet surroundings of Gardner Jackson Park. Relocated World War I memorial in background.

Source: Gene Bunnell

THE PROVIDENCE WATERFRONT STUDY:
LOOSENING THE GRIP OF HIGHWAYS IN PROVIDENCE

Although the completion of the Memorial Boulevard Extension/River Relocation plan and the Capital Center softened the impact of highways on the city's
downtown core, Interstate 195 (which ran along the southern edge of the
downtown) continued to exert a decidedly negative impact on the city. Highway engineers who originally chose the alignment for I-195 could not have
done a better job in dividing major parts of the downtown area. As built in
1956, I-195 formed a physical and visual barrier between two historic neighbor-

4-24   Pedestrian bridge over Providence River, connecting College Hill
neighborhood to the commercial core of downtown Providence.

Source: Gene Bunnell

hoods, separating the Fox Point neighborhood from its waterfront, and cutting off the city's jewelry district in the southern third of the downtown from the center city.

When Warner's Providence Waterfront Study was undertaken, highway engineers at RIDOT had intended to completely rebuild I-195 (including a new bridge across the Providence River) because I-195 had reached the end of its useful life. The plan was for the alignment of I-195 to remain the same, and for the new bridge at Old Harbor to be built either slightly north or south of the old bridge. However, Warner's Providence Waterfront Study suggested the possibility that the access ramps leading to and from I-195 at Old Harbor could be relocated, thereby freeing up approximately 44 acres of land along both sides of the Providence River for water-related uses. The engineering and design contract for rebuilding I-195 had already been entered into with the firm of C. E. Maguire. Nevertheless, Joseph Arruda (the head of RIDOT's planning division, who was on the Coordinating Committee that was overseeing the Providence Waterfront Study) recommended that RIDOT hold off putting the I-195 project out to bid while further planning studies were conducted.

In 1991, Bill Warner and Robert E. Freeman, who by then had succeeded Ken Ornstein as the executive director of the Providence Foundation, went through very much the same process that Warner and Ornstein had gone through years earlier to launch the Providence Waterfront Study.[15] This time, the aim was to prepare a comprehensive land use plan for the entire Old Harbor area which addressed the possibility of relocating I-195 to an entirely new alignment (not just relocating the access ramps at Old Harbor), and which specified the land use policies that should be applied to land freed up by the relocation. Working through the Providence Foundation, they prepared another grant application to the NEA, which once again was successful.

The *Old Harbor Plan* ("the 1992 Old Harbor plan") was completed in 1992. As a result of this planning effort, two alternatives emerged for rebuilding I-195: (1) rebuild I-195 essentially along its original alignment; and (2) shift I-195 to the south, to a location just south of the Hurricane Barrier.[16] Once again, Pete Pointner was brought in to assist the Maguire group and Warner in preparing the EIS that evaluated the two highway alternatives. In 1996, the final EIS was completed and concluded that the Hurricane Barrier alignment was the best solution. Relocating I-195 south of the Hurricane Barrier would not only improve traffic flow and safety, but would also repair the damage done to the urban fabric of inner-city neighborhoods by the original alignment. Selecting a new highway alignment also meant that construction of the new highway could proceed while the existing highway remained in use, thereby reducing traffic disruptions.

4-25   1970s aerial photo of I-195. Downtown Providence on upper left of photo. Old Harbor area of Providence is on the west (left) side of the Providence River, where a long exit ramp winds north toward the downtown just after I-195 crosses the river.

Source: William D. Warner, Architects and Planners

The land use recommendations contained in the 1992 Old Harbor plan, and land use policies governing the 44 acres of land freed up by eliminating the Old Harbor/I-195 interchange, were incorporated and adopted as part of *Providence 2000—The Comprehensive Plan of the City of Providence* ("the Providence 2000 plan").[17] The officially adopted plan encourages water-related uses that enhance access to the waterfront and that complement the three surrounding historic neighborhoods of Fox Point, College Hill and the jewelry district, all of which are listed on the National Register of Historic Places. Facilities and improvements constructed along the east bank of the Providence River in Phase One of the I-195 relocation project will extend the pedestrian-oriented amenities and improvements that were part of the Memorial Boulevard Extension/River Relocation project. Improvements called for in the plan include extended riverwalks, a bike path, public greenspace, a boat ramp and several docks.[18]

Many of you who read this will some day find yourself driving into or through Providence on the new I-195. When you do, perhaps you will

LEGEND
DEVELOPMENT PARCELS
RIVERWALKS & PATHWAYS
TREES & STREETSCAPE IMPROVEMENTS
PARKS & R.O.W.
WATER
DREDGED AREA
BOAT & WATER TAXI LANDINGS
DOCKS & BOARDWALKS
RELOCATED MONUMENTS

EXISTING AND PROPOSED
URBAN DESIGN ELEMENTS
HURRICANE
BARRIER
ALIGNMENT
IMPROVEMENTS TO I-195 E.I.S.

CURRENT RHODE ISLAND DEPARTMENT OF TRANSPORTATION I-195 PLAN
FOR THE RELOCATION OF THE INTERSTATE
SHOWING INCORPORATION OF OLD HARBOR PLAN

4-26 Approved plan for the relocation of I-195, incorporating land use recommendations suggested in the 1992 Old Harbor plan.

Source: William D. Warner, Architects and Planners

remember this story of deliberate community change, and take some pleasure in knowing that the alignment of the road on which you are driving is much better for the city and its residents than what was there before.

NOT PERFECT, BUT CERTAINLY BETTER

In 1976, a plan was prepared by the firm of Anderson Notter of Boston calling for renovation and reuse of the old Union Railroad Station for continued use by Amtrak as a railroad station. Unfortunately, that didn't happen because the railroad tracks were relocated and also because a fire in 1987 inflicted major damage to the structure. The old Union Railroad Station Building was instead sold to a private developer who thoroughly rebuilt and renovated the structure for occupancy by a private financial services company.

The RISD faculty members who produced the 1974 Interface Providence plan probably also feel that what was done in Providence fell short of what ideally would have been achieved. The 1974 Interface Providence plan's recommendation that an intermodal transportation center (an integrated facility linking rail and bus service) be developed not only had merit, but was highly attainable at the time, given the fact that the city's main bus station was then located not far from the old railroad station at the other end of Kennedy Plaza. Unfortunately, when the decision was made to develop the Convention Center, the Bonanza (Bus Co.) bus station was displaced from its site in the city's center. As a result, the Bonanza bus station is now inconveniently located off an exit of I-95 (Exit 25), roughly 4 miles from the city's downtown rail station.[19]

Despite these shortcomings, the changes and improvements that have come about in downtown Providence as a result of the Capital Center and College Hill plans are still pretty remarkable and impressive.

OBSERVATIONS AND COMMENTS

Thoughts on Urban Renewal, Highway Building and Planning

Many cities have never recovered from being torn apart by ill-conceived, downtown "urban renewal" clearance projects and interstate highways. If one were to ask who is to blame for the damage inflicted on downtowns and inner-city neighborhoods, many people would probably say "the planners." However, what happened in Providence presents a different picture of what planners have stood for and worked to achieve. Planners like Samuel J. Shamoon and William D. Warner recognized the destructive effects that interstate highways had had on downtown Providence and on in-town neighborhoods, and spent years developing plans to undo their damaging effects. When a preservation-oriented plan was developed for the College Hill neighborhood as an alternative to demolition and clearance, and when the Capital Center and Memorial Boulevard Extension/River Relocation plans were prepared to revitalize downtown Providence without demolishing any existing buildings, professional planners were in the forefront.

People who blame "planners" for the destructive effects of urban renewal and interstate highways in Providence need to be reminded of what Antoinette F. Downing said in 1979 when she was interviewed for a feature article in *The Providence Journal*. She said that the way most project plans for federally funded interstate highways and urban renewal had been developed was "antithetical" to planning. "Both federal programs tried to accomplish their objectives in the shortest amount of time, and displayed little interest in thorough planning or citizens' advice," said Downing. (Wyss, November 4, 1979, 26)

Sound, responsible planning that can stand the test of time *takes time* because it requires recognizing and taking account of competing needs and interests. It also requires being open to alternatives. A major reason why many urban renewal plans went wrong, and why interstate highways often had devastatingly negative effects on cities, is that the people who were in charge of devising and implementing those major undertakings, from the very beginning, committed themselves to a particular approach and did not take into account competing goals and interests. As a result, they failed to develop and evaluate alternatives that could have produced much better outcomes.

Redevelopment agency officials who received federal urban renewal money in the 1950s and 1960s simply assumed that the best way to redevelop old cities was to clear everything away and start over with a clean slate. Likewise, highway engineers assumed that the best highway was the one that moved the most cars as quickly and as safely as possible (and that the secondary impacts of highways on adjacent communities were unimportant). They also assumed that increasing traffic demands had to be met with more highways and increased traffic capacity (*i.e.,* that the "no-build" alternative was not an option). Given these assumptions, it was fairly easy for highway engineers to agree on the "best" highway plan. Uniform highway standards dictated by federal and state highway agencies made it even easier—insulating highway engineers from the need to consider alternatives because it was believed that highway standards could not be compromised without compromising safety. Carl Feiss may have overstated it when he wrote, "Nothing outside of Russia . . . is more dictatorial than the state highway official." (Feiss 1968, 229) However, there was also an element of truth in what he said, particularly back in 1968 when his words were published.

Happily, all that is beginning to change, largely due to the passage of the 1991 federal Intermodal Surface Transportation Efficiency Act (ISTEA), and its successor Transportation Efficiency Act for the 21st century (TEA-21), which mandates that highway and transportation plans take account of land use considerations and impacts. An important message of this case study is that transportation and land use planning considerations *can* be addressed simultaneously, and that planners, if given the opportunity, can work *with* highway engineers to produce plans that have a much more positive impact on the quality of life in cities.

A WILLINGNESS TO ACCEPT RISK

Looking back at the positive changes that have been brought about in downtown Providence, it is easy to forget the uncertainty and sense of risk that citizens and professional planners must have felt when they first began to plan. We look at College Hill and the Capital Center areas today and see glittering success stories—places that are truly special and unique; however, the outcome was far from certain when planning first began.

When the 1959 College Hill plan was prepared, there were few people who thought it made economic sense to invest in College Hill, and few (if any) banks were willing to write mortgages and make major home improvement loans to those who did. Similarly, when Bill Warner unveiled his plans for uncovering and moving rivers in downtown Providence, few people believed that it would ever happen. Even Antoinette F. Downing who, in planning for College Hill, was such a visionary and bold leader, questioned whether the Capital Center project was a good idea. Like many other preservationists, Ms. Downing feared that new commercial buildings developed on the 65 acres of land freed up by relocating the railroad tracks would drain commercial activity and investments away from historic buildings in the city's traditional commercial core (along Westminster Street).

These fears were quieted to some extent by the EIS conducted by Pete Pointner—which calculated the rate at which new commercial space would be built, come on the market and be occupied—and concluded that the Capital Center project would not kill off the adaptive reuse of historic buildings in downtown Providence. Quite to the contrary, Pointner's planning study concluded that the Capital Center project would actually serve as a "relief valve" that *reduced* the pressure and need to tear down historic buildings in the center of the city.[20]

PEOPLE DIDN'T "VOTE WITH THEIR FEET"— THEY STAYED AND MADE THINGS BETTER

When older cities have declined and older neighborhoods in the U.S. have deteriorated, it has almost always been because large numbers of people have "voted with their feet" and moved to places (often in the suburbs) that provided the facilities, services and environmental qualities they wanted. Downtown Providence is the way it is today because there were many people who did *not* "vote with their feet," but stayed and worked together to make their city a better place. People in the business community joined together to form the Providence Foundation, raised money to save landmark institutions such as the Loew's State Theater and the Biltmore Hotel, and supported the lengthy planning and design process that ultimately produced the visionary plan for downtown Providence.

In the College Hill area, people like Beatrice "Happy" Chace, Betty Allen, Tina Regan and many others stayed, organized the Providence Preservation Society and, over the course of many years, worked, fought and lobbied to make College Hill a better place. Committing time and energy to preparing a plan was critically important—a way of effectively and meaningfully expressing their commitment to and love of their community. Once the plan was prepared and officially accepted, these people continued to stay involved and worked energetically to see to it that the aims of the plan were achieved. Ms. Chace did considerably more than that by buying up and renovating 15 properties in the College Hill area when no one else was willing to take on such a risk.

Another factor, which clearly contributed to the successful outcome in Providence, is that talented and dedicated professionals were drawn into the process. People to whom I spoke were unanimous in praising the genius and creativity of William D. Warner. In the words of Sam Shamoon, "Warner was a

4-27   Looking west from the College Hill neighborhood toward the Rhode Island State House in spring 1998. The Providence Mall is under construction (girders on horizon at extreme left of photo).

Source: Gene Bunnell

true visionary." Other skilled and dedicated professionals also played important roles—people like Antoinette F. Downing, Lachlan F. Blair, Stewart Stein, Marilyn Taylor and Pete Pointner.

STILL A ROLE FOR VISIONARY PLANNING

At the beginning of the 20th century, Daniel Burnham urged his countrymen to "make no little plans . . . they have no magic to stir men's blood . . ." Burnham clearly recognized that plans could inspire people to act to make places better. Oddly enough, our sense of what is possible is much more limited today. In cities across the country, there is remarkably little bold thinking and very little of what could be seriously called "visionary planning."

The story of the Capital Center project in Providence reminds us of the power of "big ideas," and the fact that there is still a time and a place for bold and visionary plans like the one that William D. Warner produced for downtown Providence. When Warner first put forward his grand plan, few people felt that it could ever be accomplished and many dismissed it altogether. Today, everyone remotely associated with the Capital Center project is eager to take credit for what was accomplished. Visionary planning—and big and bold ideas—were just what Providence needed at that critical stage in its history.

A SERIES OF PLANS THAT BUILT ON ONE ANOTHER

In certain circles, there is a tendency to characterize planning as inherently undemocratic, bordering on socialism if not outright communism. Consistent with that characterization, people often think of planners as powerful and arrogant bureaucrats who impose plans and regulations on communities by fiat. If that were the case in America, there would be good reason for people to think that planning—and developing a plan—is basically "un-American."

To an outside observer, the unity and coherence of what occurred in Providence might suggest that a single plan was centrally prepared and imposed. In fact, what happened was that a number of plans was prepared at different times by different people, organizations and agencies, each of which contributed new ideas and elements and which, over time, were integrated to produce an overall vision for the downtown. The following is a succinct listing of the sequence of plans and planning:

- the 1959 College Hill plan, which called for the preservation of the College Hill neighborhood and for the creation of Roger Williams Spring National Park along the eastern edge of the Moshassuck River—the first piece of what was to become a network of public open space along the edges of the city's rivers
- the 1961 Downtown plan, which first put forward the idea that the railroad tracks through the downtown should be relocated
- the 1974 Interface Providence plan, prepared by the faculty of RISD, which called for recapturing the city's waterfront
- the planning that was done by C. E. Maguire related to the Northeast Rail Corridor Improvement project, which established the feasibility of relocating the railroad tracks (first proposed in the 1961 Downtown plan), and reported that relocating the tracks would free up 65 acres of underutilized downtown land for redevelopment
- the 1979 Capital Center plan, prepared by SOM
- the seven alternative traffic circulation plans, developed in 1983 by Sam Shamoon and Wilbur Smith Associates, for resolving traffic problems in the Memorial Square area
- the Providence Waterfront Study, by William D. Warner, which led to the development and refinement of the Memorial Boulevard Extension/River Relocation plan, which was ultimately grafted onto the 1979 Capital Center plan and implemented

As the above summary of the sequence of planning in Providence suggests, plans are not rigid and immutable documents. They provide a way of communicating ideas that can evolve and change over time, as new ideas are added to the mix. As the Providence experience suggests, key ideas communicated in plans can also take hold and remain alive in the public consciousness for years, and be resurrected and applied years later when the time is right. The power of a plan ultimately lies in the power of its ideas.

In August 1999, I returned once again to Providence, this time with my wife, to see an unusual outdoor event called "Waterfire" that was being "staged" in Providence. This creation of Barnaby Evans (a local artist) was attracting extraordinarily large numbers of people to downtown Providence and we decided we just had to see it in person.

We drove up to Providence from our home in southern Westchester County on a clear and warm summer Saturday in August. We arrived in Providence around 5 PM and found a precious parking space in the College Hill neighborhood behind a museum. We strolled along the streets of College Hill for a while, admiring the architectural details of the beautifully restored homes nestled close to the street, and soaking up the atmosphere and charm of the area. From College Hill, it was only a short walk down College Street to the Providence River. Families with children and people of all ages were leisurely strolling along the riverwalk. Many others had already staked out places to sit with good views of the water. By 8 PM, there were thousands of people in downtown Providence, and people were standing three and four deep along the full length of both sides of the riverwalks.

When I managed to get close to the edge of the river, I could see that a long line of steel braziers holding stacks of firewood had been placed down the centerline of the river. Within the circular lagoon of Waterplace Park, the wood-filled braziers formed a circle around the perimeter of the lagoon. As darkness descended on the city, black boats with people dressed in black began to come slowly and quietly up the canal, lighting the stacks of wood. Eventually all the braziers were alight. At the same time, I was aware of mysterious and eerie musical sounds. We could not see where the speakers were; it was almost as if the sounds were coming from within the fires themselves. Throughout the evening, black barges stacked with firewood made their way back and forth, refilling the braziers to keep the fires burning at the same high intensity.

The air was filled with the sweet smell of burning wood. (A brochure I picked up states that the wood burned at "Waterfire" is a specially selected mixture of firewood and, from the rich smell that night, I can believe it.) From time to time, sparks exploded in the air from the piles of burning wood, like sparklers set off at the Fourth of July, and were extinguished as they fell into the water.

4-28   1992 aerial view of downtown Providence. The railroad tracks have been relocated, and the Moshassuck and Woonasquatucket Rivers have also been relocated. A new railroad station and four major buildings have been constructed on development parcels created by the 1979 Capital Center plan. The site on which the Providence Mall was later built is the surface parking lot, visible in the top center of this photo.

Source: William D. Warner, Architects and Planners

4-29   "Waterfire" display on a summer night in Providence, as viewed looking across the lagoon of Waterplace Park toward buildings in the Downcity area.

Source: Michael Melford, courtesy of the Providence Tourism Council

The combination of sensations—the bright light and intense heat generated by the fires, the crackling sounds of the burning wood, the reflections of the fires dancing on the water, the pungent smell of wood smoke, and the mysterious and moody sounds coming from various directions—seemed to have a spell-binding effect on the people who were there.

As I think back to what we saw and experienced that night in downtown Providence, I am struck by the extraordinariness of what we observed. Thousands of people had come to sit quietly and watch wood burn in the middle of a river—not the kind of thing one would normally expect would draw a huge crowd in America today. What made the burning piles of wood special, of course, and worth coming to see, was the *place* where the display occurred.

Providence is a very different city than it was in the 1970s and even the mid-1980s. People now care about and are proud of Providence in a way that was not the case years ago. How many people know *how* these changes came about? How many understand the role planning played in making Providence a better place? That is why this story is important.

INTERVIEWEES

Martin Adler, AICP

Lachlan F. Blair, FAICP, consulting planner, Urbana, Illinois

William G. Brody, attorney at law

Thomas E. Deller, AICP, deputy director of planning and development, City of Providence

Debra Melino-Wender, executive director, Capital Center Commission

Pete Pointner, executive officer, Planning Resources, Inc., Wheaton, Illinois

Tina Regan, Providence Preservation Society; chairperson of College Hill Historic District Commission; member, Downcity Design Review Committee

Samuel J. Shamoon, AICP, associate director for planning, City of Providence

William D. Warner, William D. Warner, Architects and Planners, Exeter, Rhode Island

PLANNING STORY CHRONOLOGY

1959	*College Hill: A Demonstration Study and Plan for Historic Area Renewal* ("the 1959 College Hill plan") is completed.
1960	The Providence City Council approves an ordinance creating the College Hill Historic District Commission.
1961	*College Hill 1961—progress after planning* ("the 1961 College Hill report") is completed, documenting the progress that had been made in implementing recommendations contained in the 1959 College Hill plan.

Downtown Providence 1970—A Master Plan for Downtown Providence ("the 1961 Downtown plan") is completed.

1974   *Interface Providence* ("the 1974 Interface Providence plan") is prepared by faculty members at the Rhode Island School of Design.

1978   The federal government announces its intention to undertake a major, long-term infrastructure investment program to upgrade the Northeast Rail Corridor, including station and track improvements serving Providence. The firm of C. E. Maguire is hired by the Providence Foundation to study and evaluate the pros and cons of relocating the tracks through Providence and building a new train station.

1979   *Capital Center Plan* ("the 1979 Capital Center plan") is completed by Skidmore, Owings & Merrill LLP, and calls for the relocation of the railroad tracks 600-850 feet to the north and the construction of a new train station.

1980   Sam Shamoon is hired as associate director for planning.

1982   James Rouse comes to Providence and tells assembled business leaders and citizens that the future of the city can be assured by going "to the water."

1983   Construction of the Capital Center project begins.

1983-86 William D. Warner promotes the idea of uncovering the rivers that flow through the downtown. Warner's ideas gain acceptance. Warner refines his plan and, in the process of integrating it with the previously prepared 1979 Capital Center plan, comes up with the bold idea of *relocating* the rivers.

1989   Design and Development Regulations officially adopted by the Capital Center Commission governing development projects with the Capital Center Project Area.

1992   *Old Harbor Plan* ("the 1992 Old Harbor plan") for Interstate 195 is completed.

1994   The 1992 Old Harbor plan is officially made part of *Providence 2000—The Comprehensive Plan of the City of Providence* ("the Providence 2000 plan").

NOTES

1. The bulky Walter Wilson Laboratory is a good example of the kind of out-of-scale building Brown University seemed to be intent on erecting, and intensified the impression that the university felt no need to build buildings that "fit in" or respected the character and texture of the College Hill area.

2. The citizen-initiated planning effort to save and renew College Hill would not have succeeded but for the fact that *many* individuals (the individuals already named as well as many others) joined and worked together toward a common cause. It must also be said, however, that the leadership provided by John Nicholas Brown over a 23-year period was absolutely critical. In addition to being an original founder of the Providence Preservation Society, John Nicholas Brown was the society's chairman from 1956 to 1979. Brown's roots in the College Hill neighborhood went deep. He was a member of the family after which Brown University was named, and could trace his ancestry back to a follower of Roger Williams who was with Williams in 1636 when Providence was first settled.

3. In 1978, the American Society of Planning Officials and the American Institute of Planners merged to create the American Planning Association.

4. Among the cities studied and, in some cases, visited first-hand, were: Annapolis, Maryland; Boston, Massachusetts; Charleston, South Carolina; Nantucket, Massachusetts; New Castle, Delaware; New Orleans, Louisiana; Newport, Rhode Island; Philadelphia, Pennsylvania; Salem, Massachusetts; San Antonio, Texas; Santa Fe, New Mexico; Savannah, Georgia; Washington, DC; Williamsburg, Virginia; and Winston-Salem, North Carolina. Learning about the way a comprehensive survey of almost 1,200 historic properties was carried out in Charleston, South Carolina in 1941 was particularly helpful, and had a considerable influence on how the survey of historic properties was carried out at College Hill. In the Charleston survey, structures were classified into four historical periods and into five groups according to importance.

5. Antoinette F. Downing moved to Providence from New Mexico in 1936. Perhaps because she was an "outsider" and looked at the city with fresh eyes, she recognized more quickly than many long-time residents the preciousness of the city and the area's historic and architectural resources. Her reputation as an expert in historic preservation was first established when she wrote *Early Homes of Rhode Island* (1937). Her stature in the field of historic preservation was further strengthened by the publication of *The Architectural Heritage of Newport, Rhode Island: 1640-1915* (1952, first edition), which she co-authored with Vincent J. Scully, Jr. A founder of the Providence Preservation Society in 1956, Ms. Downing was also the founder of Stop Wasting Abandoned Properties (SWAP), and was the first chairman of the Rhode Island Historical Preservation Commission when it was established in 1967.

6. The boundaries of the College Hill Historic District were extended in 1977 and again in 1990.

7. Final site work related to the development of Roger Williams Spring National Park was finally completed in 1981. At 4.5 acres, it is the smallest national park in the country, but in an urban neighborhood that has few parks and little greenspace, it has had a hugely positive impact. The park defines the western edge of College Hill, and buffers the neighborhood from the bustle of activity in the City Center and Capital Center District.

8. One of the best places in which to appreciate how close the College Hill neighborhood is to downtown Providence is Prospect Terrace, a lovely little park on College Hill. To get to Prospect Terrace, walk east up College Hill to Angell Street, which runs along the northern edge of the campus of RISD. Turn left (north) up Congdon Street and go two blocks. Prospect Terrace will be on your left.

9. The title of the plan, *Downtown Providence 1970—A Master Plan for Downtown Providence*, may be a source of some confusion. The plan itself was prepared in 1961, but was prepared to show what Providence could be like in 1970.

10. Twenty-three years after the Northeast Corridor Rail Improvement project was announced, high-speed Amtrak Acela trains began operating in 2001 between New York City and Boston, cutting the travel time between the two cities from six hours to approximately four hours.

11. This alternative, which Wilbur Smith Associates called Alternative #6, was included for evaluation as Alternative C in the Memorial Boulevard EIS.

12. According to Bill Warner, Ted Sanderson (the director of the Rhode Island Historic Preservation Commission and a member of the Providence Waterfront Study Design Review Committee) was the person who came up with the idea of relocating the World War I memorial from Memorial Square to the park in front of the courthouse. However, the idea of relocating the World War I memorial to the 2-acre park near the courthouse, which already had a statue honoring the Italian explorer Verrazano, initially aroused considerable opposition from two major segments of the city's population. Italian Americans didn't want to share the site with the veterans' monument; veterans organizations, in turn, didn't like the idea of a monument honoring fallen American soldiers sharing the same square with another memorial, let alone one honoring a person representing a country that had fought against American soldiers in World War II. Luckily, Mayor Cianci, being of Italian descent, was able to convince the Italian American community that it was fine if the World War I monument were moved next to the Verazzano statue. He

was also able to convince veterans groups that the World War I memorial would not be diminished by sharing the space with a memorial honoring the courageous Italian explorer. Everyone could coexist.

13. A new federal program established in 1984 provided 100% funding for independent walkway systems. The balance of the cost of constructing Waterplace Park was funded by the RIDEM.

14. Expenditures associated with constructing the Convention Center and Westin Hotel are not included in this total for three reasons: (1) both the hotel and the Convention Center were financed and paid for entirely by the State of Rhode Island Convention Authority, and the Westin Hotel chain manages the hotel under a contract with the State Convention Authority; (2) the Convention Center Building is *outside* of the Capital Center District planning area, and did not come about as a result of the deliberate planning process that focused on the Capital Center project; and (3) the hotel was built when the State Convention Authority realized that a hotel was needed to support the Convention Center.

15. According to Bill Warner, Freeman had a solid background in planning and architecture and was a brilliant individual.

16. The Hurricane Barrier was built across the mouth of the Providence River to afford a degree of protection to the city from hurricane-driven storm surges—like the ones that inundated and heavily damaged downtown Providence in 1938 and 1954. Construction of the Hurricane Barrier began in 1961 and was completed in 1966.

17. Since 1991, all municipalities in Rhode Island have been *required* by state law to prepare a 10-year comprehensive plan addressing land use, economic development, transportation/circulation/parking, historic and cultural resources, natural resources, community services and facilities, and housing and parks/recreation/open space.

18. Completely realigning I-195 will cost roughly $300 million and take five to seven years to complete.

19. Bonanza operates a shuttle bus service between Kennedy Plaza and its bus station outside of the downtown. Buses operated by the Rhode Island Transit Authority, which provides public transportation in and around Providence, still converge on and operate out of Kennedy Plaza.

20. In a step aimed at reducing the extent to which commercial development in the Capital Center project competed with the downtown commercial core, the Design and Development Guidelines approved for the Capital Center project specifically excluded retail development. However, when developers came forward seeking to build a major downtown shopping mall on the largest remaining undeveloped parcel of land in the Capital Center District, the Design and Development Guidelines were revised to allow retail stores on that portion of the project. This action resurrected concerns on the part of many downtown business and property owners, as well as on the part of planners in the city's planning department, that retail stores in the new mall would drain retail business away from businesses in the downtown core along Westminster Street. Unfortunately, even before the mall opened, retail business along Westminster Street was in decline and the new mall may accelerate that decline in retail activity. On the other hand, there is also a chance that the influx of large numbers of shoppers drawn into downtown Providence by the new mall could have a positive spin-off effect on the older commercial core of the city. What *is* clear is that the Providence Mall would never have been built in downtown Providence had it not been for the Capital Center project.

CHAPTER

5

Charleston, South Carolina

Making a Very Special Place

5-1   South Carolina Society Hall (1803-04) on Meeting Street, just south of Broad Street.

Source: Gene Bunnell

Charles Kuralt had a knack for finding special places and interesting people when he traveled across the country producing profiles for the *On the Road* television series. He consciously avoided reporting about bad news or terrible events; instead, he set out to discover and write about the positive qualities of the different places and people he encountered along the way.

When Kuralt retired from television after a long career, he decided to reward himself with what he called "the perfect year." He would spend an entire year in the places he loved the most, and spend a full month in each one of his 12 most favorite places—enough time to savor the distinct qualities and attributes of each place. To make the year even more perfect, he would plan his year so that he would experience each place at the perfect time of year when its distinctive qualities were best appreciated. Kuralt made sure that he spent the month of March in Charleston, South Carolina.

Kuralt's account of his month-long stay in Charleston is included in *Charles Kuralt's America*, published two years before his death. In it, he conveys a sense of how pleasurable it is to walk throughout Charleston's historic and well-tended neighborhoods. "The pleasure of the city," he notes, "is in the details . . ." (Kuralt 1995, 67)

Wherever he walked, he never seemed to be out of sight of a church steeple. Like many visitors, Kuralt was particularly impressed by the unique housing type invented in Charleston (the "single house") that predominates the historic neighborhoods of the city to this day. The house is narrow (only one room wide) but deep; it is two or three stories high and set on a half-story base, which gives the house an imposing appearance from the street, despite its narrow width. Along the full length of the side of the house (the side toward the shade), there are tiers of galleries or porches supported by slender classical columns. The front façade of the Charleston single house typically extends the full width of the structure to provide a level of privacy for people sitting on the side porches.

Rather than enter the house directly from a central doorway, entrance to the Charleston house is achieved by first passing through a carved, false entryway that leads onto the porch, from which one can then enter the house. This layout of a Charleston single house is ideally suited to South Carolina's warm climate, since it affords maximum cross-ventilation as well as ample, shaded, private outdoor sitting areas that frequently look out over lavishly planted private gardens.

The way in which Charleston single houses are placed on their lots also creates an intimate, pedestrian-oriented streetscape. In his chapter on Charleston, Kuralt quotes David Kludt: "The city appears dense from the street because its houses come up to the sidewalk. What that means is that space, air, sunlight, landscaping, fountains, trees and grass are behind the house or next to the

5-2   Unitarian Church and graveyard.

Source: Gene Bunnell

5-3   An example of a classic Charleston "single house."

Source: Gene Bunnell

5-4 The front façade of a Charleston "single house," which typically extends the full width of the structure, provides privacy for people sitting on the side porch.

Source: Gene Bunnell

house where they ought to be for privacy . . . on the south or west side of the house [shaded] from the sun." (*ibid.*, 54)

Charles Kuralt is certainly not the only person who has come to cherish Charleston's special qualities. In his *A Guide to Great American Public Places*, Gianni Longo calls Charleston "possibly, the most beautiful small city in the country." (Longo 1996, 48)

When I surveyed planners who had been members of the APA for 10 years or more, many of them specifically cited Charleston as one of the "best cities in the U.S. in terms of exemplifying the qualities and outcomes that planning seeks to achieve."[1] Indeed, as the following account will illustrate, planning has played an extremely important role in making Charleston the city it is today.

AN HISTORIC AND PLANNED CITY

Charleston was founded in 1672 and, interestingly enough, the site for the city was chosen by committee. As Jonathan H. Poston reports in his history of *The Buildings of Charleston: A Guide to the City's Architecture*, a committee of the Grand Council of the Carolina colony surveyed the Cooper River area to identify a place that was best suited to the establishment of a town "in a Square" of 12,000 acres fronting as much as possible on navigable rivers. (Poston 1997, 48) Today, it is commonplace to make jokes concerning the poor decisions that are often made by committees, but this committee did its job well in locating the new community on a peninsula formed by the convergence of the Cooper and Ashley Rivers.

When Charleston was established, it was the southernmost English city on the American continent, and was vulnerable to threats of attack from Spanish Florida and from the French. Fortified walls were therefore constructed around the city to protect it, and "by 1704 plans were made for the construction of gates and a drawbridge at Broad Street and a seawall along the Cooper River waterfront." (*ibid.*, 49)

Within the walls of the city, a conscious decision was made to depart from the irregular street pattern that typified English cities at the time; instead, an orderly grid of north-south and east-west streets was laid out. As the position of the city became more secure, and as the city prospered and more development occurred outside the original walled city, the walls were taken down. Removal of the western wall began in the 1720s and the process was completed by 1740.

Once the walls that encircled the original city were removed, a more formal and orderly development pattern was established. Meeting Street (where the city's first Meeting House was built), which ran down the central spine of the peninsula, became the main north-south street. Broad Street, which bisected the peninsula in an east-west direction, became the main east-west street. The intersection of Broad and Meeting Streets thus came to define the center point of the city, and many of the city's most important institutions of public and community life either already stood or were built at this key intersection.

The city hall (a structure originally built as a bank) was on the northeast corner; the county courthouse was on the northwest corner; and St. Michael's Church occupied the southeast corner. Late in the 19th century, the federal courthouse and central post office were built on the southwest corner of the intersection, on the site where the city's first guardhouse had stood. This unique and orderly grouping of civic and religious institutions remains mostly intact to this day. Nearly all of the historic buildings continue to serve the original purposes; modern and tastefully designed additions have been added onto some of the buildings but have not detracted from the historic character or con-

5-5 View looking south down Meeting Street toward Charleston City Hall (left, foreground) and St. Michael's Church (1852-61), which occupy the northeast and southeast corners of the "Four Corners of Law." The other two corners are occupied by the federal and the county courthouses.

Source: Gene Bunnell

tinuity of the area. Indeed, the importance of this central place in the city is reflected by its special name: the "Four Corners of Law."

A HIGHLY REGULATED ENVIRONMENT

In many American cities, the notion has taken hold that public regulation of private land and building use is unnecessary and undesirable, and that local needs and desires are best fulfilled by allowing market forces to play themselves out freely. That is clearly not what people in Charleston have believed.

Charleston's historic neighborhoods have survived—and continue to be places where city residents can live close to where they work and shop—because people in Charleston have recognized that land use and development decisions should not simply be dictated by market forces. Plans and policies limiting the nature and scale of development, and directing development into areas initially shunned by developers, were not imposed on an unwilling populace. Rather, citizens have demanded and supported such policies.

The first step toward regulating land use and development in the city was taken in 1920, when a number of prominent Charleston citizens heard that the historic Joseph Manigault House was about to be demolished to make way for a gas station. The citizens organized in opposition and the net result of this initial skirmish was the formation of the Charleston Preservation Society. The Manigault House was saved and is now a museum; nearly 80 years later, the Charleston Preservation Society remains a powerful force in the community.

Despite the early success of saving the Manigault House, threats to other historic properties continued to arise as automobile use dramatically increased. By 1931, citizen support for regulations to protect the city's built environment became great enough that the City of Charleston adopted its first zoning ordinance, which delineated the boundaries of the "Old and Historic District." Moreover, to assure that the purposes of the ordinance were fulfilled, the city established the Board of Architectural Review (BAR). Initially, the BAR had relatively few powers. Over the years, however, the BAR's powers have steadily increased, and today it is called upon to review and approve all proposed alterations of historic properties and new development proposals within the historic district.

In the late 1930s, funds were obtained by the Carolina Art Association to conduct a city-wide survey of historic properties—the first such comprehensive survey ever conducted in the U.S. The completion of this city-wide survey was extremely important to future planning and regulation of development because it provided preservationists and members of the city's BAR with a crucial baseline record of historically and architecturally significant properties.

Throughout the 1930s and 1940s, the Charleston Preservation Society remained an active and powerful force in advocating historic preservation. In 1947, a second preservation organization was formed in Charleston (the Historic Charleston Foundation) for the purpose of becoming more directly involved in renovating and restoring historic properties. The foundation acquired its first property by way of a donation in 1958: a three-story brick house at 329 East Bay Street.

A key element of the foundation's strategy was the establishment of an Historic Preservation Revolving Fund, which enabled the foundation to utilize revenue derived from the renovation and sale of historic properties to acquire and renovate additional properties. This in turn enabled the foundation to expand its aims from saving individual properties to stabilizing and renovating whole neighborhoods. For example, between 1958 and 1976, the foundation bought, rehabilitated and sold almost 60 historic properties in the run-down and deteriorated Ansonborough neighborhood. Properties acquired, renovated and offered for sale by the foundation have typically been made subject to deed restrictions that, in effect, grant the foundation a conservation easement on the property, and thereby assure that any future renovations undertaken in the

5-6   Cobblestone street, off East Bay Street.

Source: Gene Bunnell

future are compatible with their historic character. As of 1998, the foundation had easements on roughly 200 Charleston properties.

The lengths to which Charleston has gone to preserve the quirky features of its historic urban fabric are almost mind-boggling when compared to most American cities. Charles Kuralt wrote with amazement (and admiration) that Charlestonians cherished their cobblestone lanes so much that "when the power company had to dig one up, the city required that each cobblestone be numbered for replacement just where it had been . . ." (Kuralt 1995, 67)

Indeed, city residents have found that preserving cobblestoned streets serves a practical purpose. While other newer cities have had to invent and design special "traffic-calming" measures to protect downtown neighborhoods from unwelcome through traffic, Charleston's residents and planners have found that the ruggedly uneven surfaces of cobblestoned lanes have the same results. Anyone who drives a car down one of those cobblestoned lanes at a speed of more than 5 miles per hour runs a very real risk of either damaging their vehicle or breaking a tooth!

Other signs of Charleston's extraordinary commitment to preservation are evident throughout the city. In an industrial area currently owned and operated by the South Carolina Port Authority, I saw a jagged section of brick wall, roughly 6-8 feet thick, supported on both sides by steel girders to make sure it didn't fall down, standing in the middle of a vast paved area where a number of trucks were parked. This lone segment of brick wall was all that remained of a colonial-era rice mill which, in the early years of the South Carolina colony, processed rice before it was loaded onto ships for export throughout the world.

Some years ago, a fire ravaged the mill and this section of the building's front façade was all that survived. According to *The Post and Courier* columnist Robert Behre, there was no assurance that the wall would ever be reused. Nevertheless, the possibility that this historic wall fragment *might* be used in some way seemed to provide sufficient reason for going to the considerable effort and expense of stabilizing and protecting the wall. If you visit Charleston in the future, you may find that the wall is still standing there, or you might discover that it has been incorporated into some new development scheme as a reminder of the city's historic past.

In old residential neighborhoods, such as those north of Calhoun Street, I saw the burned-out shells of a number of old homes and commercial buildings. In some cases, a few broken sections of outer walls were all that was left standing. In Charleston, permission to demolish the fragmentary remains of old buildings is not easily obtained; the city goes to extraordinary lengths to encourage (and even require) that historic properties damaged by fire or hurricanes are rebuilt. In a case where the property is a total loss and new construction is required, the city usually insists that the footprint and "envelop" of the original building are replicated.

5-7   A preserved segment of a colonial-era rice mill wall.

Source: Gene Bunnell

5-8   The old County Courthouse Building, which occupies the northwest corner of the "Four Corners of Law," was badly damaged during Hurricane Hugo. Extraordinary steps were taken to stabilize and preserve the exterior walls of the historic structure, and to incorporate them into a new and expanded courthouse.

Source: Gene Bunnell

5-9   The shell of a home badly damaged by fire—still standing, awaiting renovation, not demolition.

Source: Gene Bunnell

5-10   Market Hall (1840) at Market and Meeting Streets—the western end of a long line of market sheds that extends from Meeting Street to East Bay Street.

Source: Gene Bunnell

Maintaining Charleston's historic fabric and character has been far from easy, especially given the number of occasions in the city's history when whole areas have been heavily damaged. Indeed, given the number of catastrophes that have befallen Charleston over the years, the fact that so much of the original historic fabric of the city survives is nothing short of a miracle. A brief overview of some of the major calamities that have struck the city is sufficient to make the point.

For one and one-half years during the Civil War, Charleston was subjected to heavy federal bombardment that wrecked large parts of the city. Fifteen years later (in 1886), the city was devastated by a major earthquake that inflicted massive damage. Six years later (in 1892), not long after the damage of the 1886 earthquake had been repaired, the city was again damaged by a powerful hurricane; another hurricane struck the city in 1911. In 1938, two tornadoes struck the city within 15 minutes—the second tornado devastating the City Market. In 1940, the city was heavily damaged by another hurricane.

For a period of approximately 50 years, Charleston was relatively immune from weather-related damage. In 1989, however, the city experienced its most devastating weather-related event in its history when it was hit with the full force of Hurricane Hugo. The damage the city sustained from Hugo was so great, in fact, that two major local insurance companies (Charleston Insurance and Hibernian Mutual Insurance) went bankrupt as a result. Once again, the people of the city rebuilt their homes, workplaces and public buildings.

PLANNING AS WELL AS PRESERVATION

The historic preservation movement has clearly played an important role in making Charleston the place it is today. It is understandable, therefore, that outside observers frequently assume that the success Charleston has achieved over the years has been due to its single-minded dedication to historic preservation. However, the full story behind Charleston's accomplishments is far richer and more complicated. When one looks carefully, one realizes that the true strength of the city is more than the preservation of the past; rather, it is a story about how, *through careful and continuous planning*, it has been possible to create a city both old and new.

Planning has enabled Charleston to achieve and reconcile a number of different objectives. As the city has created a strong and robust local economy by becoming an increasingly popular tourist destination, it has essentially rebuilt its central core area while at the same time preserving much of its historical and architectural fabric and character. As increasing numbers of tourists have flocked to the city, it has managed to maintain and strengthen in-town neighborhoods, and to maintain and add to its central city population. (Many older neighborhoods that previously had been considered marginal are now viewed as desirable places to live.) These kinds of potentially conflicting objectives have not been achieved and balanced simply by chance.

Experiencing today's Charleston, it may be difficult to fully appreciate how bleak the city's future looked in the early 1970s before Joseph P. Riley became mayor.[2] Over a 20-year period (between the 1950s and 1970s), seven major hotels in the city closed. By 1975, the city's unemployment rate was at about 15%, 27% of the city's roughly 70,000 citizens lived in poverty and gross revenues in the commercial district had fallen 12% in the preceding five years.

Despite these deteriorating conditions, no formal planning was being done in Charleston; there was not even a planning department within city government. The city did have a strong historic preservation ordinance, and its BAR had to review and approve any building alterations and new buildings in the historic district. However, the city had no strategy or plan for improving conditions, apart from the Historic Charleston Foundation's efforts in preserving and restoring historic properties.

In 1975, things began to change. Charleston was designated an "Entitlement Community" by HUD, which meant that the city began to receive an annual appropriation of CDBG funds that it could use for planning and implementing various housing and community development programs and projects. Prompted by this infusion of CDBG funding, the city established the Department of Planning and Urban Development (DPUD) and hired its first full-time professional planners. At the request of the city, the chamber of commerce also committed $10,000 of its own money to hire a private consulting firm (Barton-Aschman Associates of Washington, DC) to conduct an initial study of downtown redevelopment possibilities, and to prepare a report recommending how the city should proceed in attempting to reverse the decline of the downtown area. One of the key people active in the chamber of commerce at the time was Joseph P. Riley, who was running for mayor. Later that year (in November), he was elected.

THE DOWNTOWN PLAN: THE KING STREET DISTRICT AND CHARLESTON PLACE

Soon after he took office in January 1976, Riley announced the creation of the Charleston Commercial Revitalization Program, and appointed a commission of area businessmen to examine ways to bring business back to the central business district (CBD). The commission concluded that a detailed downtown revitalization plan was needed and $100,000 was appropriated by the city for that purpose. The geographic area targeted by the plan was the commercial corridor of King Street, north of Broad Street—the central spine of the peninsula where major department stores and retail activity had traditionally been concentrated.

For purposes of planning and analysis, King Street was broken into five sections (Market Street, Lower King Street, Middle King Street, Upper King Street and North King Street), and a separate plan analyzing current conditions and offering recommendations was prepared for each segment. Of these five segments, Lower King Street appeared to be the best place to begin for a number of reasons. Several buildings and properties in the area of Lower King Street were vacant (including the property formerly occupied by the Belk department store), which made the area seem opportune for redevelopment. Also, the area of Lower King Street was adjacent to the old City Market (a popular shopping destination for tourists). Ideally, a complementary relationship could be developed between the City Market and the proposed redevelopment area that would extend the positive economic impact of tourism to bolster retail activity in the city's traditional retail area. Once Lower King Street was redeveloped, the city could proceed to implement the recommendations for other areas of King Street, moving in a logical progression from south to north.

The Lower King Street District plan that was completed and delivered in March 1977 was a formidable document: when all five sections of the plan were stacked on top of one another, they stood almost 6 inches thick. The plan outlined the elements of an ambitious municipal undertaking. The initial redevelopment project recommended in the plan called for the city to assemble all of the property within the large downtown block north of Market Street between King and Meeting Streets, clear the land of most of the existing structures, and redevelop the area to accommodate a luxury hotel and associated structured parking.

Although the redevelopment plan at this point was preliminary and conceptual in nature, it *was* very specific in describing the kind of outcomes and spin-off benefits it hoped the project would produce. Throughout the report, the consultants noted the lack of "pedestrian-generators," and the lack of features and amenities to encourage people to walk on King Street. The planners hoped to introduce a type of development that fit in with the pedestrian-oriented fabric of the city and stimulate pedestrian activity.

Six months after the Barton-Aschman report was delivered (in October 1977), a plan was publicly unveiled for what was called "the Charleston Place project," which was twice the size (in terms of both land and floor area) than what Barton-Aschman had initially envisioned. The plan also included a number of additional elements: in addition to a luxury hotel with 450 rooms, the plan also included a conference center, retail stores, a department store and structured parking.

Anyone who was a "preservationist" was bound to object to the project. The project called for demolishing some 30 structures, including 17 rated as historically significant in the city's 1972-73 survey of historic properties. Preservationists were also stunned by the height and scale of the proposed new buildings. The plan of Charleston Place called for building a massive complex that in most areas was eight stories high, but the hotel (a major portion of the complex) was to be 11-1/2 stories high.

One of the qualities that unquestionably makes Charleston so special and unique among American cities is its low-scaled environment. Because the tallest structures in the city continue to be church steeples rather than office buildings or hotels, the city's skyline looks more like the 19th century than the 21st century. Because of the strict building height limitations incorporated into the city's zoning ordinances, there are remarkably few buildings more than eight stories tall.[3]

Preservationists were not the only ones with reservations about the proposed project. To many long-time Charlestonians, such a large-scale project was incompatible with Charleston's low-scaled environment. Many other residents expressed fears that building such a large project in the center of the city would make traffic congestion and parking in the downtown unbearable. In fact, because the goal of the project was to stimulate pedestrian activity in the downtown area, planners of the project had made a conscious decision *not* to provide a great deal of parking. The 500 parking spaces called for in the plan were far fewer than the city's zoning ordinance required for a project of that size.

In December 1977, the city's Board of Adjustment granted a zoning variance to the project, permitting the project to be built with fewer than the normally required number of parking spaces. In January 1978, the Charleston City Council gave its support to the issuance of bonds for the project. In April 1978, Charleston was awarded a $4.15 million UDAG to finance land acquisition and demolition activities in the area. In October 1978, the city obtained more federal funding when it was awarded an additional $3 million by the Economic Development Administration (EDA) for the parking garage. Despite concerns raised by opponents of the project, the BAR granted its approval "in concept" for the project.

However, opponents of the project did not give up and filed a series of legal challenges that dragged on for nearly four years, during which time the controversy attracted considerable national media attention. First, an appeal was filed by the Charleston Preservation Society with the president's Advisory Council on Historic Preservation challenging the appropriateness of using federal funds for a project that was contrary to the purposes for which the historic district was established. When that did not derail the project, two additional lawsuits were filed challenging the constitutionality of the project and seeking to bar the use of federal funds. In December 1980, the Fourth U.S. Circuit Court of Appeals in Richmond, Virginia upheld a lower court ruling dismissing the Charleston Preservation Society's legal challenge and, in January 1981, the Charleston Preservation Society voted to drop its suit.

One more hurdle stood in the way: during the years that the project was delayed by lawsuits, the developer who was initially selected for the project encountered financial and legal problems with a project in another city and had to withdraw from the Charleston Place project. This meant that a new developer had to be selected, and a new development agreement had to be negotiated between the city and that developer.

The selection of a new developer (and, in turn, the hiring of a new architect) provided an opportunity to reassess various aspects of the project. Architect John Carl Warnecke (who designed the grave of President John Kennedy and Lafayette Square across from the White House) was hired to review and revise the plans. An agreement in principle was reached to reduce the height of the hotel from 11-1/2 to eight stories, as well as the height of perimeter buildings abutting the street—proposed changes that were welcomed by people who had been opponents of the project. However, this reduction in the project's scale required a substantial reworking of the financing and increased the need for public subsidies to offset the loss in project revenue due to the reduced size of the project. This final obstacle was overcome when Mayor Riley persuaded HUD to make available an additional $10 million in UDAG funding, on top of the $4.15 million in UDAG funding initially granted to the project.

In 1986, Charleston Place finally opened. The completed project comprised a hotel with 450 rooms, a ballroom/conference facility capable of accommodating up to 1,500 people, and retail stores that enveloped the hotel on all four sides that were reachable from street level as well as through an internal arcade leading seamlessly to the hotel lobby. The parking structure for 500 cars that was built as part of the project is largely hidden from view within the complex.

Despite the scale of the project, and the fact that the footprint of the project covers a huge area, Charleston Place fits in well with its surroundings. One particularly marvelous thing about the way the project was designed is that the front portions of historic buildings facing onto Meeting Street, which are actually part of the Charleston Place development, were preserved. In fact, the original buildings themselves—including the façades—were preserved to a depth of 40 feet. As a result of this careful merging of old and new, most people who walk down Meeting Street are unaware that the historic storefronts are really part of the new Charleston Place development. Moreover, because the highest portion of the development is recessed within the interior of the block, most people walking in and around the vicinity of Charleston Place are unaware of the scale of the project.[4]

The success of Charleston Place, and its popularity as a destination and meeting place, has led to the restoration and reuse of other valued downtown landmarks and institutions. The Riviera Theater on the corner of King and Market Streets, which might easily have slipped into oblivion like so many other old downtown movie theaters, was acquired and rehabilitated by

5-11 Charleston Place, overlooking the intersection of Market and King Streets.

Source: Gene Bunnell

5-12 Charleston Place, as viewed looking south down King Street.

Source: Gene Bunnell

5-13   The true scale of Charleston Place is revealed in this photograph, taken from the top of a multistory parking structure south of Charleston Place.

Source: Gene Bunnell

5-14   Despite its size, and the fact that the buildings of Charleston Place are significantly taller than surrounding buildings, the scale of the development is not apparent at street level. Shown here are the preserved historic buildings along Meeting Street that form the eastern side of the development. The tallest portion of Charleston Place is partly visible above the cornices of the historic buildings, in the top center of the photo.

Source: Gene Bunnell

5-15 Saks Fifth Avenue department store, diagonally across from Charleston Place.

Source: Gene Bunnell

Charleston Place and Orient Express Hotels, Inc. This acquisition and renovation of the theater expands the meeting space available at Charleston Place, while at the same time providing 8,000 square feet of renovated gallery retail space.

Another positive spin-off benefit of the Charleston Place project is that Charleston also ended up getting a department store.[5] A handsome new building containing a Saks Fifth Avenue department store now stands on the block diagonally across from Charleston Place.

The Charleston Place project achieved exactly what Mayor Riley and the city's planners and planning consultants had hoped. It has greatly increased pedestrian activity by drawing tourists and visitors from the City Market area onto Meeting and King Streets. In turn, there has been a remarkable resurgence of retail activity up and down King Street. (Across the street from Charleston Place on King Street, for example, I found a Foot Locker store that was doing a

5-16   King Street, south of Charleston Place.

Source: Gene Bunnell

5-17   Activity at the City Market, across the street from Charleston Place to the east.

Source: Gene Bunnell

healthy business selling athletic shoes in what used to be Woolworth's.) In effect, the city's bold plans for developing a major commercial complex in the center of the Charleston peninsula has given Charlestonians back their downtown shopping district—something they very nearly lost. Despite all the controversy the project caused when it was being planned, it is hard to find anyone in Charleston today who does not regard Charleston Place as a wonderful addition to the city, and who does not believe that the city is a better place because of it.

1978 TOURISM IMPACT AND MANAGEMENT STUDY

By the mid-1970s, city and county officials were becoming increasingly aware of the need to do some serious planning related to tourism. Approximately 2.2 million people were visiting the Charleston area each year, and a large majority of those visitors spent a considerable amount of time on the Charleston peninsula. Nevertheless, downtown Charleston was dying. The growing influx of tourists into the city was not having the kind of positive effect on the city's economy city leaders and residents had hoped for. To make matters worse, the large influx of tourists was having an increasingly negative impact on the livability of the city's older historic neighborhoods.

The planning consulting firm of Barton-Aschman Associates was rehired—this time to conduct a *Tourism Impact and Management Study* ("the Tourism study"). This study, which was completed in February 1978, represented the first serious attempt to identify potentially negative impacts that unmanaged and ever-expanding tourism could have on the city, and to devise strategies to minimize those negative impacts.

The Fort Sumter Tour Boat Facility

One of the extremely important and consequential things that resulted from the Tourism study was an understanding of the criteria the city should consider when deciding where to locate major "activity generators." In that regard, the Tourism study had a major impact on land use and development policy even before it was completed.

Planners at Barton-Aschman were in the midst of their study, and the final report was not even in draft form, when it came to the attention of Mayor Riley that the National Parks Service was contemplating constructing a new, expanded and permanent dock facility from which tour boats would take tourists to and from Fort Sumter out in Charleston Harbor. The place where the National Parks Service wanted to build this dock facility was at the southern end of the peninsula, not far from White Point Gardens (where the tour boats had been operating for years). Had the city not been in the midst of preparing its Tourism study, and thinking carefully about where such major "activity generators" should be located, the National Parks Service's plan would undoubtedly have gone ahead. However, because the city was in the midst of developing a plan to manage the impacts of tourism, that is not what happened.

Mayor Riley asked the planning consultants who were preparing the study to analyze the appropriateness of the site that was being proposed for the Fort Sumter tour boats. The consultants' response was that the site the National Parks Service had chosen was definitely in "the wrong part of town" for that kind of tourist facility. The consultants told Riley, "It's not going to do any good for the city because the site [proposed by the National Parks Service] is surrounded by residential land uses, and there's nothing else of a commercial nature around there. Not only is it not going to give you any benefit, but it will have a detrimental impact on the surrounding residential area."

What the consultants said made sense and ultimately had a profound impact on how Riley and the city would approach facility-siting decisions in the future. Unfortunately, the National Parks Service plan had reached a fairly advanced stage. A scale model of the plan encased in glass had already been prepared and had been put on display; everyone seemed to assume that the city would approve the National Parks Service's chosen site. However, Riley had become convinced that it was necessary to stop the project and he did.

Thinking back to how the planning consultant's report changed his thinking and the direction of city development policy, Riley says that he learned an important lesson: "The most important and vastly underappreciated element necessary for successful redevelopment in a city is having a *strategy* and thinking *strategically*. Whoever is in charge—whether it's the mayor, the planning office or the redevelopment agency—has got to ask, 'How is this going to help us achieve our goals?'"

Although the city's rejection of the proposed docking facility was initially viewed by the National Parks Service as a setback, the city and the National Parks Service arrived at a plan which virtually everyone agrees identified a much better location for the Fort Sumter dock facility.

1982 VISITOR ACCOMMODATIONS STUDY

As the legal suits which dogged and delayed the Charleston Place project were finally winding to a close, but well before construction of Charleston Place began, the city undertook a major planning study of visitor accommodations. The *Visitor Accommodations Study* ("the Visitor Accommodations study"), prepared by the city's DPUD, was officially adopted by the city council in January 1982.

The philosophy which guided the planning staff was that new hotels should be allowed in areas where they would have the effect of revitalizing the central commercial core of the city, and should not be allowed in or adjacent to residential areas or in other locations where they would detract from the qualities that made the city a desirable place in which to live. One of the important environmental qualities that made the city a desirable place in which to live, planners reasoned, was that the city was built on a peninsula surrounded by water. It therefore stood to reason that hotels should not be allowed to line the city's waterfront where they would block public access to the water and views of the harbor.

Planners also reasoned that hotels should not be overly concentrated in any one location. This meant that the area within which hotels were allowed had to be fairly large. In this regard, the planning framework that emerged from the Visitor Accommodations study was consistent with the philosophy of the Tourism study—namely, that major activity generators should not be overly concentrated in any one area, but should rather be introduced into underdeveloped and underutilized areas to strengthen and improve those areas.

The planning policy recommended by the Visitor Accommodations study was that an Accommodations Zoning Overlay District should be established designating areas where new hotels might be appropriately located. Areas covered by the new Accommodations Zoning Overlay District basically included a large portion of the center of the Charleston peninsula, extending from the northerly "neck" of the peninsula (where State Highway 17 crosses from west to east) down to Broad Street. In effect, the city decided as a matter of policy that new hotels would generally be allowed within core commercial areas of the city, but would not be approved along the city's waterfront, in residential areas within the Old and Historic District or in residential areas west of King Street.

Once again, the city sought to strike a balance between meeting the needs of visitors and serving the needs and interests of city residents. In the words of the 1982 Visitor Accommodations study, "The livability of Charleston is a concept that is difficult to define or measure but it is responsible for making the city attractive to residents and visitors. The future of the City of Charleston rests on balancing the interests of developers, tourists and residents."

It is important to note that the recommendations of the Visitor Accommodations study built on and reinforced the aims of the *Lower King Street District: District Plan and Program* ("the Lower King Street District plan") as well as those of the Tourism study. The Accommodations Zoning Overlay District adopted by the city encouraged hotels to be built in areas that the city targeted for commercial revitalization in order to help support the revitalization of the city's CBD. New hotels were specifically encouraged in the center of the peninsula in the area where Charleston Place was expected to be built. However, hotels were not going to be approved (and would, in fact, be strongly opposed) in areas where the Tourism study hoped to minimize the impacts of tourism.

By placing the Accommodations Zoning Overlay District down the central spine of the peninsula (in commercial areas), city planners were consciously forcing new hotels to be built in areas that were already densely developed, where little (if any) land was available for surface parking and where the city did not want a great deal of parking provided. Instead, the idea was to encourage hotels to be developed in areas where they would inevitably stimulate pedestrian activity. The whole idea was to have people check into a downtown hotel, forget about their cars and walk from there throughout the city, or travel by public transit.

It is also important to note that the areas designated by the city for hotel development were *not* the areas where developers wanted to develop hotels. In fact, the Accommodations Zoning Overlay District represented nothing less than a bold attempt on the part of the city to oppose and counteract what market forces and developers were pushing for at the time. Not surprisingly, the city's commitment to its plan was severely tested. On a number of occasions, the city was presented with proposals calling for the development of new hotels along the waterfront and, each time, the city turned them down. In one instance, a developer proposed to build a large hotel on a waterfront site at the eastern end of Vendue Range. It was a grand scheme comprised of a number of tall buildings and a marina. The developer said that it would transform Charleston into the "Venice of the South." The development proposal was a difficult one to turn down because of its quality and because of the taxes it would have paid to the city.

Planning director Yvonne Fortenberry recalled that the depressed condition of adjacent areas of the city made it especially tempting to cave in and approve the development. "At the time, that part of the waterfront was pretty crummy and underutilized. There were lots of vacant lots, empty buildings, boarded-up warehouses and parking lots. That section of East Bay Street—where all the nice restaurants are now—was almost entirely empty and devoid of activity."

Nevertheless, the city held firm to its vision of where it wanted hotels to be. "It wasn't the kind of use that we felt was in the best long-term interests of the city, so we turned it down and publicly acquired the property," said Riley. "That decision [to turn down the project] was very controversial at the time, but in retrospect it may very well be the most important decision we've ever made." As a result, an important segment of the city's waterfront was kept open and made available for public enjoyment.

The city used most of the property proposed for the hotel for Waterfront Park—a public park that has become one of the most treasured places in Charleston. The rest of the site between the park and East Bay Street has been committed for the development of modestly scaled, high-quality housing. Because the city owns the land, it is able to assure that whatever housing is built will be of moderate density and height, and be consistent with the objective of maintaining strong residential neighborhoods in the heart of the city.

5-18   Looking east down Vendue Range toward the Cooper River waterfront. Had development of a proposed waterfront hotel been allowed, this view of the water would have been blocked.

Source: Gene Bunnell

The "Venice of the South" proposal was not the only waterfront hotel development scheme that the city turned down. Another waterfront parcel of land (not far from where the South Carolina Aquarium was built) was also proposed for a hotel. "We stopped that one, too," recalled Mayor Riley. "The guy sued us. We would have won the lawsuit, but I figured any time the city could own its waterfront and assure public access, we'd be better off. So we bought the land."

The city subsequently built a recreational pier and the two-story Maritime Center on this property, both of which opened in spring 1998. The pier provides docking facilities for shrimping and fishing boats, as well as other kinds of vessels and sailing ships. The Maritime Center is rented out for meetings, gatherings and various public events, and includes a wide second-floor balcony with an excellent view of the harbor.

1989 CALHOUN STREET CORRIDOR STUDY

In 1989, the *Calhoun Street Corridor Study* ("the Calhoun Street study") was completed. There were a number of reasons why the city decided that it was important to study and develop a plan for Calhoun Street. This street was an important east-west artery through the city and was attracting increased traffic because of the construction of the new James Island Bridge.[6] Calhoun Street was also an important entryway into the city. For many people entering the city, their first impression of Charleston was formed by what they saw along Calhoun Street.

Some of the city's most important institutions and employment centers, such as the Charleston Medical Complex and College of Charleston, were also located along Calhoun Street. Because these institutions backed onto residential neighborhoods to the north and south of Calhoun Street, actions taken by these institutions to increase parking or acquire land for expansion and/or new facilities could threaten the stability and quality of these residential areas. Thus, an additional reason for studying and planning for the Calhoun Street Corridor was to try to minimize future institutional-residential land use conflicts—to anticipate and try to meet institutional needs and, at the same time, insulate adjoining neighborhoods from negative institutional impacts.

The need for studying the corridor and developing a plan was further heightened by the fact that a number of key properties along the street were at risk. The Francis Marion Hotel at the corner of Calhoun and King Streets, formerly the city's largest and most prestigious first-class hotel, was in a spiral of decline and was about to close. Directly across from the Francis Marion Hotel, Marion Square—a potentially grand public space that took up an entire city block—was showing the signs of long-term neglect. Along the north side of Marion Square, the former Citadel Building was being used on an interim basis for county offices. (For a number of years, the Citadel Building housed various school district and local government offices, but eventually the county decided to sell it off.)

By the 1970s and 1980s, Calhoun Street had come to represent a major racial and socioeconomic dividing line within Charleston.[7] Residential areas north of Calhoun Street were poorer than those south of Calhoun Street; likewise, commercial establishments north of Calhoun Street catered to a largely poorer clientele and struggled economically, whereas those south of Calhoun Street catered to a wealthier clientele and were more successful. Developing a plan for Calhoun Street was therefore a way of attempting to bridge a social and psychological divide within the city. It also represented a commitment by the city to invest in facilities and aesthetic improvements in an area that, until then, had not received much positive attention, public investment or benefited much from the city's revitalization.

The Calhoun Street study analyzed the visual, aesthetic and environmental qualities of various parts of the corridor, and compared them to the qualities present in other historic and valued areas of the city. It concluded that, although a small portion of Calhoun Street had the intimate, pedestrian-scale qualities that characterized other historic areas of the city, those qualities were largely absent along most of the Calhoun Street Corridor. Rather, the character and "feel" of Calhoun Street was more like that of an "urban boulevard," with fairly massive buildings lining and framing the corridor. The plan therefore focused on recommending ways to strengthen the boulevard qualities of Calhoun Street, while at the same time making it more pedestrian-friendly.[8]

A number of projects and public investments were recommended by the plan, including measures to improve pedestrian safety at heavily trafficked intersections, the removal of above-grade utility wires and their placement underground, the construction of major drainage improvements, the construction of major public facilities to strengthen and frame Calhoun Street as a major urban boulevard, and the redesign and reconstruction of Marion Square.

Three important public projects undertaken along the eastern third of Calhoun Street—two major public buildings and an infill residential development project—helped achieve the aims of the Calhoun Street study. Indeed, their completion is a clear indication that Calhoun Street is no longer seen as a boundary, but rather as an increasingly important and desirable area in the city.

For many years, the offices of the Charleston County School District (which operates schools for city as well as county schoolchildren) were located in an old school building south of Broad Street. The school district was unhappy with these facilities and was considering moving out of the downtown. Hoping to keep the school district offices in Charleston, the city also saw an opportunity to help achieve the aims articulated in the Calhoun Street study.

The city owned a large tract of land along the south side of Calhoun Street adjacent to the city auditorium, which at the time was used as a surface parking lot. The city approached the Charleston County School District with an offer it could not refuse: the city offered to give the land it owned along Calhoun Street to the county at no cost if the school department would agree to construct a new school district building on the land. To sweeten the offer, the city also agreed to build a parking garage behind the building to provide parking for people employed in the building during the day (as well as for people attending evening events in the auditorium). As a result, the county constructed a large and very attractive office building on the site. The top floor of the office building is leased by the city for the offices of the Departments of Planning and Urban Development, Housing and Community Development, Economic Development, Public Services and Business Licenses.

5-19   New School District Office Building on Calhoun Street.

Source: Gene Bunnell

5-20   New County Library Building on Calhoun Street, across the street from the new School District Office Building.

Source: Gene Bunnell

Directly across from the new School District Office Building, an equally large and imposing new County Library has been built, which has further reinforced the prominence of Calhoun Street in the life of the city. Placing these two massive and important public buildings opposite one another has created a major center of public activity—and also reinforced the boulevard quality of the corridor by framing it in a strong and aesthetically pleasing way. As was the case with the School District Office Building, the new library was built on Calhoun Street because the city offered to give the land to the county for free. (The story of how the city came to acquire the land on which the County Library was built is described later in this chapter.)

The city also strengthened and reinforced the residential character of the neighborhood adjacent to the new School District Office Building by making a third parcel of publicly owned land available for infill residential development. This third parcel of land had previously belonged to the municipal water utility and, for many years, was occupied by a concrete basin used to store water. For a while, the basin was used as a public swimming pool but later fell into disuse. More recently, it had become a popular place for skateboarding.

There are relatively few open, undeveloped sites suitable for the development of new housing on the Charleston peninsula, and the city recognized an

5-21   New homes developed on city-owned land between Calhoun and George Streets, just west of the new School District Office Building.

Source: Gene Bunnell

opportunity to increase the supply of owner-occupied housing in the center of the city and, at the same time, stabilize and improve the Calhoun Street Corridor. The city therefore issued an RFP inviting developers to submit housing development proposals for the site.

According to Robert Behre, the city decided "not to sell the property for the 'highest and best use' or for the most money." Rather, the city sought to encourage the development of high-quality, single-family housing in the city and, to achieve that objective, the city agreed to sell the land to a developer at less than market cost. The city also agreed to take a second mortgage on properties in the development to further write down the cost.

The result is a charming urban neighborhood of modest-sized homes that intimately relate to one another and to the street. Houses are placed closely together on lots that are only about 31 feet wide and comparatively little space is given over to accommodate automobiles. The architecture of the homes resembles the traditional Charleston single house—long and narrow, with porches along the side. Indeed, it is a neighborhood that has many of the qualities and attributes advocated in recent years by New Urbanist planners and designers.

The roadway into the L-shaped neighborhood is narrow and most of the houses have shared driveways. Rather than building a cul-de-sac with a wide turnaround, a one-way road through the neighborhood was built, and a cobblestone alley alongside the old Water Works Building allows cars to exit onto George Street. (When I first saw the development, it looked as if the alley had been there for a hundred years. In fact, the alley was newly built as part of the development and was done in such a high-quality way that it *looked* old.) The development also brought life to the old Water Works Building, which now houses the offices of the Spoleto Festival.

Although the project turned out well in the end, achieving this outcome was not easy. The original developer the city selected for the project went bankrupt and the city ended up being paid even less for the property than it had expected. "The second developer who came in did a nice job of finishing up the development," said Behre, but by that time the cost of the project had risen so much that the homes sold for $200,000 or more. Still, by 1999, all of the homes in the development had been sold.

The Calhoun Street study was completed in 1989; within 10 years, most of the improvements recommended in the plan had been completed or were well on the way to being implemented. As a result, some highly significant, privately financed development projects have come about along the corridor. After being vacant for approximately seven years, the Francis Marion Hotel was thoroughly renovated and reopened for business in 1998. In support of this major hotel renovation project, the city constructed a 400-space parking garage immediately adjacent to the hotel with 9,000 square feet of retail space

5-22 One of the homes in the infill housing development shown in Figure 5-21—a New Urbanist interpretation of the Charleston "single house."

Source: Gene Bunnell

5-23 The Francis Marion Hotel.

Source: Gene Bunnell

fronting on King Street. Moreover, a master plan was prepared to redesign and replant Marion Square, across the street from the Francis Marion Hotel. In the words of Mayor Joseph Riley, the reconstruction of Marion Square, now underway, "will transform the square into Charleston's 'central park.'"

HOW PLANNING MADE A DIFFERENCE

Planning has had a profound effect on land use and development in Charleston. Two factors greatly increased the impact and effectiveness of planning: (1) the various plans that the city prepared were consistent with one another, so that each succeeding plan built on and reinforced the aims of the preceding plan; and (2) the city strategically undertook and invested in projects that accomplished multiple purposes.

The Consistency of Plans

As noted previously, the 1982 Visitor Accommodations study recommended that new hotel development be directed into the center of the peninsula, and not be allowed in residential areas south of Broad Street or west of King Street. The Accommodations Zoning Overlay District adopted as a result of that study also had the effect of encouraging commercial revitalization and retail activity along King and Meeting Streets (north of Broad), which was the goal of the 1978 Lower King Street District plan and of the Charleston Place project.

The goals and recommendations contained in the Tourism study, the Visitor Accommodations study and the Lower King Street District plan were also consistent and supportive of one another. For example, a major aim of the Tourism study was to protect the city's historic residential neighborhoods. Some of the ways that the plan sought to do this have already been mentioned (*i.e.*, by limiting vehicular and tour bus access and parking, and by making sure that major generators of tourism activity were not located in or near those neighborhoods).

Another way that the city minimized the impact of tourism on residential neighborhoods was by limiting the operation of "bed and breakfasts." Soon after the Tourism study was completed, the city began to look at its regulations pertaining to the operation of "bed and breakfast" guest houses in residential neighborhoods, because planners realized that conversions of residential properties to "bed and breakfasts" could eventually undermine the residential character and stability of the city's historic neighborhoods. Regulations were therefore adopted that required *every* "bed and breakfast" to apply for approval to operate (including those already in operation). No "bed and breakfasts" were grandfathered or exempted from having to apply.

Strict limitations were also imposed on the number of guest rooms that could be rented out for transient occupancy, as well as on the proportion of a residential structure that could be devoted to such a use (the intent of these restrictions being to assure that "bed and breakfasts," where allowed, remained an accessory use to the structures' principal use as a private residence). Only homes built prior to 1860 could be used as "bed and breakfasts," and the operator of the "bed and breakfast" has to own and live on the property.

The effect of these new regulations, according to the city's zoning administrator, Lee Batchelder, was to make it impossible to operate a "bed and breakfast" within a majority of residential properties in the city. This, in turn, reinforced the aim of the 1982 Visitor Accommodations study, which was to encourage developers to invest in building hotels in the center of the peninsula. Had the city not been so aggressive in limiting "bed and breakfasts," more residential properties in the city would undoubtedly have been converted and there would have been less market demand for the development of new hotels. In other words, the actions set in motion by the Tourism study and the Visitor Accommodations study were mutually reinforcing.

Similarly, had the Visitor Accommodations study and the Accommodations Zoning Overlay District not limited the ability of developers to build new waterfront hotels, the ability of the city to fulfill the objectives of the Lower King Street District plan would have been seriously undermined. In the words of Mayor Riley, had developers succeeded in building big hotels on waterfront sites, "Our ability to do Charleston Place would have been lost."

Plans and Policies Served Multiple Purposes

When I interviewed Yvonne Fortenberry, Charleston's planning director, she provided an important insight that explains why planning has made such a positive difference in Charleston. "In the planning initiatives and projects we've undertaken, we've consciously tried to address several things at once. That's an important key: not just focusing on a single objective, but thinking about the whole picture and multiple objectives." Fortenberry's observation can be illustrated in a number of ways.

Soon after the Tourism study was completed in 1978, Charleston enacted a strict height limitation ordinance. Height limits vary in different parts of the city. In most areas in the lower peninsula, the maximum building height is 50-55 feet; along the spine of the CBD, a somewhat greater height is allowed. Not only have the city's height limits produced new development that is appropriately scaled and pedestrian-oriented, but they have also helped to preserve one of the city's most treasured historic and aesthetic qualities: its skyline dominated by church steeples. The steeple of St. Matthew's Lutheran Church, overlooking Marion Square, remains the tallest structure in Charleston.

Adoption of the height limitation ordinance also furthered the objectives of the Visitor Accommodations study, which was completed somewhat later. Precluding the possibility of constructing tall, high-density buildings in the down-

5-24   View looking north on Church Street toward St. Philip's Church.

Source: Gene Bunnell

5-25   Former Citadel Building, renovated into a 150-room Embassy Suites Hotel.

Source: Gene Bunnell

town effectively forced those hotel developers who wanted to open new hotels to renovate existing structures instead, such as the previously abandoned Francis Marion Hotel and the old Citadel Building (also overlooking Marion Square), which was converted into an Embassy Suites Hotel.

A Case in Point: The Waterfront Park

The city's decision to develop the new Waterfront Park along the Cooper River, rather than allowing a developer to build a hotel and marina on the site, perfectly illustrates how the city strategically undertook projects that served multiple purposes. First, it was consistent with the principle articulated in the Tourism study (namely, that the impacts of tourism needed to be managed and not undermine the environmental qualities that made the city a desirable and beautiful place in which to live).

Prior to Waterfront Park, people seeking views of the water and peaceful enjoyment of open space inevitably gravitated to the Battery and to White Point Gardens. There was no other public park in or near the downtown and no other place where people could enjoy waterfront views. As a result, the Battery and White Point Gardens were becoming overcrowded and overused which, in turn, was having a negative impact on adjoining residential areas. Building Waterfront Park close to the downtown commercial district and City Market thus took the pressure off White Point Gardens and the Battery by pro-

5-26 Waterfront Park, overlooking the Cooper River.

Source: Gene Bunnell

viding tourists and visitors with a wonderful and inviting place to enjoy views of the water. In this way, the development of Waterfront Park was consistent with a major aim of the Tourism study, which was to insulate residential areas from the impacts of tourism.

The development of Waterfront Park was also consistent with aims of the Visitor Accommodations study and the Lower King Street District plan, in that it prevented development of a major waterfront hotel that would have competed with Charleston Place, and strengthened the market for the development of additional hotels along King and Meeting Streets—thereby reinforcing the aim of the Lower King Street District plan.

Another Case in Point: The Visitors Center

The approach the city took in siting the new Visitors Reception and Transportation Center ("Visitors Center") provides yet another illustration of the city's skill in devising and executing projects that achieved multiple planning objectives. The need for a new Visitors Center in Charleston was first identified by Barton-Aschman in the Tourism study. The study pointed out that the Visitors Center at that time, which was located at the east end of Calhoun Street, was adjacent to an older residential neighborhood, and that any attempt to expand the facility would have adverse impacts on the neighborhood.

The study concluded that the development of a new Visitors Center, in a new location, was extremely important to the management of tourism in Charleston. A new and expanded Visitors Center, it said, would serve a variety of purposes:

- First-time visitors could be oriented and educated regarding the history and qualities of the city through exhibits and films.
- Visitors could learn about and purchase tickets for various city tours.
- It could serve as the departure point and terminus for tour buses, as well as public transit vehicles operated by the city.
- People could find out about places to stay and book accommodations.

The new Visitors Center had to be located in a place that could intercept as many visitors and tourists as possible as soon as they entered the city. Also, because the city hoped to minimize the impact of automobiles on historic and residential areas of the city, the site for the Visitors Center needed to be large enough to accommodate large numbers of cars in structured parking, thereby encouraging people to park their cars and experience the city via a guided tour, by public transportation or on foot.

The Barton-Aschman study identified, evaluated and ranked a number of potential sites for the Visitors Center. The site that was eventually selected was an abandoned railroad property, north of Calhoun Street between Meeting and King Streets. Locating the center in this deteriorated and largely abandoned industrial area achieved multiple planning objectives, including many which

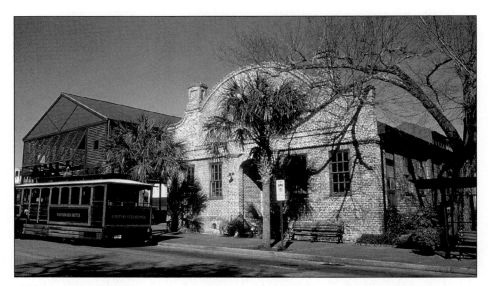

5-27   New Charleston Visitors Center on John Street. The Visitors Center fits perfectly in a former railroad freight warehouse. The structure on the left provides shelter (from rain and sun) for tour buses picking up and dropping off passengers at the Visitors Center.

Source: Gene Bunnell

5-28   The Charleston Museum, across the street from the Visitors Center.

Source: Gene Bunnell

5-29 View looking north toward the Visitors Center bus shed. The building in the foreground (on the right) is a former burlap bag factory, which was renovated into a Hampton Inn Hotel.

Source: Gene Bunnell

were articulated in the Tourism study, in the 1978 Lower King Street District plan and the 1982 Visitor Accommodations study.

Choosing this site minimized the impact of automobiles on residential neighborhoods (an objective of the Tourism study) and made it possible to build a large complex of facilities without displacing or having a negative impact on existing residents and businesses. Second, it enabled the city to intercept visitors before they had ventured too far onto the peninsula. The site was also across the street from the Charleston Museum (which opened in 1979) and was in close proximity to two of the most historically significant and highly revered city properties: the Joseph Manigault House and the Aiken-Rhett House. As a result, visitors arriving at the Visitors Center have some important tourist destinations available to them within a short walking distance.

Locating the center between Meeting and North King Streets also helped to revitalize the North King Street commercial area. For years, the North King Street commercial district had experienced significant disinvestment and had many abandoned buildings and storefronts. Not long after the Visitors Center opened (around 1991), however, commercial buildings along North King Street began to be rehabilitated and occupied by new businesses. One of the first businesses to open on North King Street, a short distance away from the Visitors Center, was the Bookstore Cafe (where Mayor Riley and I ate lunch the day we spent touring the city). Nearby, the American Theater, which had been closed and vacant for decades, was renovated into a 150-seat cinema and a 200-seat restaurant. Indeed, the activity generated by the Visitors Center has clearly had a positive effect on commercial properties along North King Street.

Lastly, locating the Visitors Center north of Calhoun Street advanced the objectives of the Visitor Accommodations study by encouraging the development of hotels in a previously ignored and underappreciated commercial part of the city. As soon as the Visitors Center opened, hotel developers started looking at the area north of King Street in a new and much more positive way. Certainly, it increased the feasibility of renovating and reopening the Francis Marion Hotel at King and Calhoun Streets. It also sparked the renovation of a former burlap bag factory building (located across the street from the new Visitors Center) into a 171-room Hampton Inn. In short, the strategic decision to locate the Visitors Center in a previously underused and underappreciated area of the city—rather than in a part of the city that was already thriving—achieved exactly what the city hoped it would.

THE QUIETNESS OF THE CITY

Charleston is an ideal walking city, and its visual and aesthetic qualities are best experienced and appreciated on foot. While walking through Charleston's historic neighborhoods and commercial areas, it is easy to savor the qualities that so delighted Charles Kuralt, and that have similarly delighted and entranced architectural historians and visitors over the years. It is not just the architectural details and embellishments that make Charleston so inviting; it is the coherence and "intactness" of the environment, the absence of gaps or breaks in the fabric of the city (such as vacant lots and parking lots) and the equally striking absence of automobile-oriented uses such as gas stations, drive-in banks and drive-in restaurants.

Another unique sensation one experiences while walking through the city—something of which many visitors may not be consciously aware—is the stillness and quietness of the historic, almost entirely residential areas of the city south of Broad Street. As I walked down tightly developed residential streets, with buildings that came right up to the sidewalk, I was aware of the sound of my footsteps (and the footsteps of other pedestrians). I heard church bells chiming somewhere in the distance, and the clip-clop of horse-drawn carriages carrying small groups of tourists on slow-paced guided tours of the old city.

I did *not* hear the sound of automobile traffic, so prevalent in most American cities. The only other densely developed urban environment where I recall experiencing a comparable sensation of silence was Venice, Italy—a city where automobiles are entirely absent. Admittedly, there are some American cities and downtowns that are heavy with silence because they have so little remaining commercial activity, with so few people still living in or near the downtown. However, I know of no other thriving American city so densely occupied by residents and tourists that has managed to remain so comfortably quiet and peacefully inviting.

In other historic cities overrun with tourists (such as Savannah, Georgia or Bath, England), one of the most annoying things that residents must endure is the constant noise pollution of tour buses rumbling through, with the voice of a tour guide booming through the public address system on the bus. In Charleston, the operation of tour buses south of Broad Street is strictly limited: only small tour buses are allowed to operate there and only on certain routes, and the number of tour buses is strictly limited. The parking of tour buses along the East Battery and in and around the popular White Point Gardens at the southern end of the peninsula is also prohibited.

Because of these limitations, many people choose to tour historic residential areas of the city in small groups, either on foot or riding in horse-drawn carriages. Outdoor use of sound-amplifying systems by tour guides is also strictly

5-30   A quiet, residential, pedestrian-oriented street, south of Broad Street.

Source: Gene Bunnell

prohibited. If you want to hear what the tour guide is saying, you just have to stand close, lean forward, stop talking and listen closely.

In a further attempt to maintain and protect the residential character of historic neighborhoods, zoning regulations have been adopted to prevent commercial buildings and uses from being introduced into areas south of Broad Street, and requests to convert historic buildings to commercial uses have been consistently denied. When the Fort Sumter tour boats used to operate out of the southern tip of the peninsula, there was actually a considerable amount of commercial activity south of Broad Street. "Twenty to 30 years ago, there were T-shirt and snow-cone vendors operating in White Point Gardens," noted Robert Behre. Moreover, the city's first major hotel, the Fort Sumter House (which was built before the Francis Marion Hotel), was at the western end of the park, overlooking the water and White Point Gardens.

Today, the T-shirt and snow-cone vendors are gone and White Point Gardens is a peaceful oasis. The tranquility of the area is preserved by regulations that prohibit vendors from operating in and around those areas. The Fort Sumter House is no longer a hotel; it has been converted into condominiums.

As recommended in the Barton-Aschman report, the city took a number of actions that were aimed at discouraging tourists from attempting to drive and park cars in historic areas of the city. For example, the city severely restricted on-street parking south of Broad Street and reserved most on-street parking

5-31   Walking along the Battery, overlooking the water.

Source: Gene Bunnell

5-32   East Bay Street—an area that has retained its residential character despite considerable market pressures favoring commercial development.

Source: Gene Bunnell

5-33   A peaceful afternoon in White Point Gardens.

Source: Gene Bunnell

spaces for residents with parking permits.[9] Furthermore, no attempt has been made to increase the number of parking spaces south of Broad Street and the development of structured parking has been confined to areas north of Broad Street.

At the same time, the city has made it as convenient and enticing as possible to travel throughout the city by public transit. As of 1998, the Downtown Area Shuttle (DASH) system had four principal routes providing public transit access to most major destinations and employment centers in the city:

1. The King and Meeting Streets route provides access to the city's main retail shopping district (King Street), the City Market area, city hall, the district court and federal courthouse, and numerous historic downtown churches and institutions.
2. The Medical/Marina Shuttle serves the city's main hospitals and medical facilities, the City Marina and Coast Guard Station, as well as the College of Charleston and the Citadel.
3. The Gateway Loop provides access to Trident Technical College, the headquarters of the Charleston Police Department and the new Joseph P. Riley, Jr. Ballpark.
4. The Market/Waterfront route provides access to the City Market and Waterfront Park area and the eastern end of Calhoun Street.

A fifth DASH route to and from the Battery was added in November 1999. All DASH trolley routes depart from and converge on the Visitors Center at John and Meeting Streets.[10] Trips on most DASH routes are scheduled at 30-minute intervals; service on the King-Meeting route operates every 20 minutes. Moreover, service on two of the DASH routes operates throughout the evening hours until 11 PM.

One other planning policy that has helped create and maintain a quiet, pedestrian-friendly urban environment has been the policy of keeping parking scarce and of discouraging surface parking lots. For example, rather than requiring hotels (which generate a strong demand for parking) to provide large numbers of parking spaces as a condition for obtaining development approval, the city has strictly limited the number of parking spaces that new hotels can provide and control for their exclusive use. Instead, the city encourages hotel guests and patrons to park their cars in multilevel municipal parking garages built by the city, which are adjacent to major business locations and tourist destinations.[11]

At the same time, care has been taken to make sure that commercial uses that do require large amounts of surface parking are placed in locations where they will not do significant harm to the fabric and pedestrian scale of the city. For example, the Harris Teeter supermarket (the largest supermarket in the Charleston peninsula), is located on the eastern edge of the city (along East Bay Street) adjacent to an area of freight transfer yards and dock facilities.

5-34   One of the DASH vehicles operating on King Street.

Source: Gene Bunnell

Further minimizing the intrusiveness of this use, much of the supermarket was accommodated by adaptively reusing and renovating an old freight warehouse.

The beneficial net result of Charleston's integrated land use, parking and transportation policies is readily apparent in the visual appearance and "feel" of the city. More so than practically any other American city of its size, Charleston possesses an intact urban environment that is incredibly hospitable and inviting to pedestrians.

PLANNING FOR AFFORDABLE HOUSING AND AVOIDING DISPLACEMENT

In communities that become especially good places to live and visit (like Charleston), property values and housing prices tend to increase. Planners and locally elected officials working to enhance the livability of communities and neighborhoods therefore often confront two unsettling possibilities: their efforts to improve conditions may fail; or they may succeed, in which case property values and housing costs may increase so much that existing low- and moderate-income residents are displaced.

When the Historic Charleston Foundation first established its Revolving Fund, and began to acquire and restore historic properties and neighborhoods, few people could have foreseen the success of its efforts. Indeed, the biggest fear was that large areas of the downtown would be abandoned by residents of average and above-average incomes as a result of the widespread deterioration of residential properties in older neighborhoods.

To almost everyone's surprise, preservation efforts in Charleston proved so successful that many of the low- and moderate-income people who used to live in historic neighborhoods (such as the Ansonborough neighborhood) could no longer afford to live there and ended up being displaced. Historic preservationists and the Historic Charleston Foundation were blamed by many for the "gentrification" that occurred. As a result of that experience, major changes were eventually made in the way the foundation bought, fixed up and resold homes using its Revolving Fund. In its more recent efforts in Elliottborough, the foundation has made a conscious effort to resell the houses to residents already in the neighborhood or living nearby.

The displacement and gentrification that occurred in many neighborhoods as a result of the success of privately sponsored and publicly encouraged historic preservation efforts taught people in Charleston an important lesson. Ever since, a major planning goal of the city has been to provide and maintain an adequate supply of affordable housing and the widest range of housing types possible. A related planning goal has been to create and maintain a city in which people can both live and work—and to assure that residential neighborhoods close to the downtown meet the needs of the city's socially and economically diverse population.

Planners in Charleston have been well aware that the city's successes in improving its downtown area, and in luring increasing numbers of tourists to the city, could cause economic hardship for low- and moderate-income residents, forcing their displacement. In fact, housing costs in Charleston have significantly increased in recent years. According to a national survey, the median home price in Charleston increased 16.7% between 1996 and 1997 (Grant and Choquette, April 7, 1998, 1A), making Charleston the "hottest" housing market in the country as of the fourth quarter of 1997.

Many popular tourist destinations elsewhere in the country have seemed to accept displacement and gentrification as inevitably associated with having a successful tourism-based economy. Thus, most service workers employed in restaurants, hotels, motels and other tourist-oriented businesses in other popular South Carolina tourist destinations like Myrtle Beach and Hilton Head have to either drive long distances from surrounding communities, or employers have to pay to provide other means of transportation (such as shuttle buses).

Likewise, large numbers of those who work in ski resorts in places like Vail, Colorado must live far outside of Vail and commute long distances to their jobs.

Mayor Riley and city planners had a different vision for Charleston. The planning philosophy they articulated was that improvements in the city should benefit all the residents of the city at all income levels. They recognized that maintaining and increasing the supply of low- and moderate-income housing in the city was very much in the city's economic interest. In the words of the city's historic preservation officer, Charles Chase, "Long-term residents, many of whom are not economically well off, play a vital role in the city's service economy. They are the heart and soul of this city. It does the city no good at all if they are forced out of the city as a result of having their housing units eaten up and gentrified."

Nevertheless, providing an adequate supply of quality housing that low- and moderate-income residents can afford is particularly difficult in Charleston, where nearly one-third of the city's 89,000 residents have incomes below the national poverty line. A number of factors unique to Charleston add to the difficulty. The city's coastal location, which puts it in the path of frequent hurricanes, poses a constant threat to the city's stock of older housing. Indeed, hundreds of old homes inhabited by low- and moderate-income households were badly damaged, and dozens were irreparably destroyed, by Hurricane Hugo in 1989. New building code requirements adopted in the wake of Hurricane Hugo (requiring that new homes be built on elevated foundations, which raise the level of the first floors of habitable space above the anticipated flood level brought about by hurricane- induced storm surges) have significantly added to the cost of building new structures.

Historic preservation restrictions, and the city's insistence that significant structures within the historic district be restored in an historically accurate way and with the proper materials, have increased construction and rehabilitation costs. The cost of maintaining homes has also been raised by regulations preventing property owners from putting vinyl siding on homes—an action which homeowners might favor as a way of avoiding the cost of repainting their homes every few years. (In fact, the need to repaint homes is a frequently recurring expense in Charleston, where the salt sea air has such a corrosive effect on the painted exteriors of buildings that building owners need to paint their structures every three to five years.)

Given the extent to which historic preservation requirements can increase housing costs, Charleston has had to continually try to strike a balance between its commitment to historic preservation and its commitment to maintaining affordable housing. For that very reason, Mayor Riley recommended *against* the expansion of the National Register Historic District. "The local perception at the time was that, by expanding the district, the city was going to provide

Federal Historic Preservation Tax Credits and other financial incentives that would bring about too rapid a pace of gentrification," said Charles Chase.

Few other cities have confronted as squarely or as effectively as Charleston has the need to maintain and increase the supply of affordable housing. In carrying out its affordable housing initiatives, Charleston has followed two tracks: it has sought to maintain and develop new, affordable rental housing units, and has simultaneously tried to expand opportunities for homeownership to moderate-income households who would otherwise not be able to afford to buy their own homes.

In 1996, the city reported that it had exceeded its own goal of creating 1,800 new or rehabilitated affordable housing units by completing an additional 305 units in that year. (City of Charleston 1996) As soon as that goal had been reached, Mayor Riley moved the goal posts back further with a new goal: 2,000 affordable housing units by the year 2000.

Over and above the sheer number of units produced, the affordable housing units that Charleston has built have been of remarkable quality and character. In the 1950s and 1960s, as in other cities, Charleston built some fairly typical, nondescript public housing projects. The standard, bleak brick construction of those projects (typical of federally funded public housing projects of that era) was unmistakable and something that the project's residents could not escape. Ever since then, Charleston has focused on producing affordable housing units in small-scale developments on scattered sites.

One reason why Charleston has been so successful in developing affordable housing is that the city, under Joseph Riley, has been aggressive in taking advantage of available federal and state housing programs, and in layering that funding with local government and other funding. Nevertheless, as federal funding for affordable housing has fallen nationally over the years, such funding has become harder and harder for Charleston to obtain. Federal funding to the City of Charleston Housing Authority declined 65% between 1984 and 1991.

According to Patricia W. Crawford, director of Charleston's Housing and Community Development Department, the city has endeavored to increase the supply of affordable rental housing, and to maintain and expand opportunities for affordable home ownership in a variety of ways. One of the first steps the city took was to establish a program using CDBG funds that made rehabilitation grants available to low-income residents who owned their own homes and who needed to make repairs to their properties, but couldn't qualify for a conventional bank loan. This program enabled low-income residents to keep their homes in decent condition and continue to live in their neighborhoods. From that, the city progressed to taking a more direct and active role by acquiring, stabilizing and rehabilitating abandoned structures.

"In some cases," said Crawford, "we would do urban homesteading, and sell the property for $1 or $5 to those whose incomes did not exceed a certain level," allowing people to secure ownership by living in a structure for a specified number of years and by making improvements to the property. The city also established a revolving property acquisition fund called the Charleston Housing Trust Program, with an initial infusion of $1 million from the city, which was used to acquire, stabilize and redevelop abandoned houses on the Charleston peninsula, and then offer them for sale under a competitive bid process to those who agreed to rehabilitate the houses for occupancy by low- to moderate-income persons. As of December 31, 1996, the Charleston Housing Trust had purchased 88 housing units and had rehabilitated 47 units; in addition, six units were under construction, six units were under contract for sale or rehabilitation and eight units were available for purchase.

The city's housing development initiatives have frequently been used to reinforce and advance various area and neighborhood planning objectives. For example, during the late 1970s and early 1980s, the city used HUD 312 loan funds to renovate a large number of rental housing units on the upper floors above retail stores on King Street. In addition to providing needed affordable housing units, putting housing units into the upper floors of vacant King Street buildings created added activity that encouraged the development of new businesses.

In recent years, the city has been aggressive in acquiring vacant parcels of land and in arranging for the construction of new houses through private contractors. "We try to bring the houses in at an affordable price," said Crawford, "and write down the cost of the land to zero if necessary to accomplish that." The city has also succeeded in getting 10 banks doing business in Charleston to form the Charleston Bank Consortium, and to commit a total of $7.5 million in first mortgage financing to assist low- to moderate-income families in becoming first-time homebuyers. The city extracted this commitment of bank financing by agreeing to provide a second mortgage to back up the first mortgage. "In some cases, we may even have a third mortgage on the property," added Crawford. "In that way, we have been able to make almost a hundred people homeowners who wouldn't otherwise have had the opportunity."

The city has been fortunate in being able to advance its affordable housing goals by working with and through Charleston Affordable Housing, Inc. (CAH), a locally based private, nonprofit housing development organization. As a designated Community Housing Development Organization in Charleston, CAH has received a percentage of the federal and state housing and community development funding that the city has received each year, as well as additional allocations of federal CDBG funding from time to time. An important legally required feature of CAH is that its board must include a number of members who have low and moderate incomes themselves, and/or reside in low- and moderate-income neighborhoods where CAH is undertaking housing developments.

The executive director of CAH is Cathy Kleiman, who grew up in Charleston, studied architecture at the University of North Carolina, went on to work at HUD under Donna Shalala, was hired by the Koch administration to run New York City's low-income housing program for seven years, ran a for-profit housing development corporation and then "came home" to Charleston in 1991 and established CAH.

Developing high-quality, affordable housing units requires considerable creativity, because to make the units affordable to low- and moderate-income persons, the cost must be subsidized and "written down" to a considerable extent. To do that, it is often necessary to combine and "layer" funding from a variety of funding sources. According to Kleiman, some of the developments that CAH has completed took funding from 11 different funding sources. "We make use of every possible funding source," said Kleiman, "including federal CDBG funds, HOME [Home Investment Partnerships program (a program of HUD's Office of Community Planning and Development)] funding obtained from the state and the city, low-income housing tax credits, financing from churches, sweat equity and so on. Another important source of funding is the Federal Home Loan Bank. Each of the Federal Home Loan Bank Districts (there are 12 in the country) put a percentage of their profits into the Affordable Housing Program, and member banks can apply to their districts for housing money. That's been a tremendous source for us."

The quality and character of the affordable housing produced by CAH, and Kleiman's skill and energy in taking advantage of all available funding sources, are well illustrated by some recently completed housing developments. On the city's historic east side, CAH completed a scattered-site project which included four buildings (32 Mary Street, 18 Amherst Street, 72 Nassau Street and 93 Columbus Street), each containing one to four rental units. The total cost of the project was $2.1 million ($210,000 per house and almost $100,000 per rental unit). Approximately $1.2 million of the project's cost was financed through low-income tax credits purchased by NationsBank. The city contributed about $500,000 in federal CDBG funding. Home Depot, South-Trust Bank, the Community Foundation and other private entities also contributed.

Another housing development, which involved infill new construction, was completed by CAH on the city's west side (on the corner of Race and Carondolet Streets, between the two north-south streets of Rutledge and Coming). In this infill project, 10 duplex units were constructed on scattered sites to meet the needs of single-parent households. Among the features incorporated in each unit were a place for kids to study, and storage bins for toys and bicycles.

5-35   Abandoned home at 24 Amherst Street, before renovation, as it appeared in September 1996.

Source: Courtesy of Charleston Affordable Housing, Inc.

Robert Behre showed me other small-scale housing developments completed by CAH in different parts of the city. One of them was a pretty three-story residential structure on Cannon Street. It was painted pink and had porches running along the side of the building off of the second and third floors. It certainly did not resemble what one would expect of "public housing"; it was a house in which people could be proud to live.

A number of the CAH-sponsored affordable housing developments Behre showed me were built in some fairly troubled neighborhoods that suffered from absentee ownership, neglect and fairly high rates of crime. The scattered-site housing developments in these areas, like those in more stable neighborhoods, were very attractive. "The goal is not just to provide safe, attractive and affordable housing units, but also to try to help stabilize these neighborhoods and give them a boost," commented Robert Behre.

Another CAH-initiated project worth mentioning has come to be known as the "South Carolina Model." This project involved scattered-site new construction in the historic district. It was called the "South Carolina Model" because the intent was to design a new residential building that could be built on vacant lots in the city's historic neighborhoods and look like it belonged. The model building plan that was developed reflected the typical layout of the historic Charleston single house—a linear floor plan arrangement from front to

5-36   24 Amherst Street, after renovation.

Source: Courtesy of Charleston Affordable Housing, Inc.

back, with a porch running along the side. Different floor plans were developed to fit on different sized lots—including the small "postage-stamp" size lots that are common in some of Charleston's oldest neighborhoods.

When I toured Charleston with Robert Behre, I saw some additional scattered-site housing developments completed by CAH, such as a remarkable project at 183 Smith Street on Charleston's northwest side. At one point, when CAH acquired the property, all that was left of the building was one wall—the front façade—and the brick foundation. Everything else that one sees today is new construction, matched to the style of what was once there. "Here you have a kind of preservation triumph, because a crumbly old house has been brought back much to the way it was," commented Behre. "However, it's so expensive to do."

Indeed, Cathy Kleiman and CAH have not had an easy time trying to produce attractive, scattered-site affordable housing in Charleston's historically regulated neighborhoods. One building that CAH had initially intended to ren-

5-37   The "South Carolina Model" of scattered site housing—incorporating many of the design features of a traditional Charleston "single house." Note that these structures are built on elevated foundations to meet new building code flood-protection requirements.

Source: Dixson Dunlap, courtesy of Charleston Affordable Housing, Inc.

ovate was an old corner store at Nassau and Columbus Streets. CAH had acquired the building from the Historic Charleston Foundation, which retained a preservation deed restriction on the exterior of the building. The building was going to be extremely difficult to convert to housing because "it needed to be three stories, but the building was a couple of feet short for three stories," said Kleiman. In Charleston, maintaining and replicating the proportions of existing buildings is regarded as extremely important, and therefore the Historic Charleston Foundation was not likely to allow the existing proportions of the building to be changed.

Then, in March 1996, something seemingly disastrous happened. A bad storm hit Charleston and Kleiman got a call that night saying "Cathy, your building at Nassau and Columbus has blown down." Said Kleiman, "That's the best bad news I ever got!" Because the building was made unsalvageable by the storm, CAH was able to build a new, affordable residential structure much less expensively on the site.

COMMUNITY APPEARANCE AND DESIGN

Viewing Charleston today, most outsiders tend to focus on the extent to which the city and its citizenry have preserved the city's historic buildings and historic urban fabric, and to overlook the extent to which the city has regulated other aspects of land use and development. In fact, Charleston's landscape is one of the most highly and carefully regulated environments in the country.

The reason that Charleston established its BAR in 1931, as stated in the City of Charleston zoning ordinance, was to assure "the preservation and protection of the old historic or architecturally worthy structures and quaint neighborhoods which . . . serve as visible reminders of the historical and cultural heritage of the City of Charleston, the state, and the nation." The way the city chose to fulfill that purpose was by establishing the Old and Historic District, and by requiring that all proposed building alterations and other developments in the district be reviewed and approved by the BAR.

Although the central concern that initially led to the establishment of the BAR and the Old and Historic District was historic preservation, the review powers given to the BAR were not limited simply to proposed changes and/or alterations to historic buildings. Rather, the review powers of the BAR were extended to *all* proposed developments and physical changes within the district—including new construction. Indeed, the policy for almost 70 years, according to Charles Chase, has been that any exterior alteration that is visible from any public right of way must be reviewed and approved by the BAR.

Over the years, not only have the boundaries of the Old and Historic District been expanded, but the powers of the BAR have also been successively expanded. Within the Old and Historic District, the BAR must review and approve the demolition or relocation of *any* building, regardless of its age or condition. Furthermore, the review powers of the BAR have been extended to areas beyond the Old and Historic District. North of the Old and Historic District and south of Line Street (within the area called the Old City District), the BAR must review and approve the construction of all new structures or additions to existing structures that are visible from the public right of way. The approval of the BAR must also be obtained to demolish or relocate any structure 75 years or older, or rated 1, 2 or 3 on the Historic Architecture Inventory; or to make any repairs or alterations to structures 100 years or older, or rated 1, 2 or 3 on the Historic Architecture Inventory.

Another design review district has been established, north of Line Street and south of Mount Pleasant Street, wherein approval must be sought from the

WORK REQUIRING APPROVAL BY THE BAR

North of Line St. and South of Mt. Pleasant St.
Demolitions/ Relocations: Structures 75 years of age or older; or rated 1, 2, or 3 on City Architectural Inventory.

Old City District*
Demolitions/ Relocations: Structures 75 years of age or older; or rated 1, 2, or 3 on City Architectural Inventory.

Repairs & Alterations: Structures 100 years of age or older; or rated 1, 2 or 3 on City Architectural Inventory.

New Construction: All proposed structures or additions to existing structures visible from the public right of way.

Old & Historic District
Demolitions/ Relocations: All buildings regardless of age or condition.

Repairs & Alterations: All repairs and alterations visible from the public right of way.

New Construction: All proposed structures or additions to existing structures visible from the public right of way.

The City of Charleston

*Please refer to zoning maps for Old City District west of the Ashley River

5-38   Map of the Charleston peninsula, showing areas where the BAR exercises varying degrees of control over proposed demolitions/relocations, new construction and building repairs and alterations. The shaded area at the southern end of the peninsula is the area of the Old and Historic District, where the powers of the BAR are the greatest.

Source: Courtesy of City of Charleston, Department of Planning and Urban Development

BAR to demolish or relocate any structure 75 years or older, or rated 1, 2 or 3 on the Historic Architecture Inventory. Thus, the BAR now exercises varying degrees of control over design and development throughout virtually the entire Charleston peninsula.

Review and Regulation of the Design of New Buildings

In cities with historic districts and historic resources in need of protection, there is often a tendency to develop and impose very specific design guidelines and regulations—and, in effect, *prescribe* what buildings in the historic district should look like. Indeed, design handbooks have often been developed containing illustrations showing contrasting examples of "good" and "bad" development (*i.e.,* what would be approved versus what would *not* be approved).

The remarkable thing about Charleston's approach to regulating design and development, Robert Behre noted, is that "the marching orders given to the BAR by the ordinance are intentionally vague." All the ordinance establishing the Old and Historic District and Old City District Regulations says is that the purpose of creating districts is "to achieve . . . the continued existence and preservation of historic areas and buildings [and the] continued construction of buildings in the historic styles and a general harmony as to style, form, color, proportion, texture and material between buildings of historic design and those of more modern design." In other words, there are no specific design guidelines per se to indicate how traditional or modern a given building should be. Rather, it is left to the BAR to judge, on a case-by-case basis, whether a given proposed development is sufficiently harmonious and compatible with its surroundings to be approved.

Although the BAR was initially established primarily to protect the city's historic resources and character, the BAR's influence has probably most powerfully been felt in the way it has regulated the siting, scale and appearance of new buildings. Moreover, because the BAR has not been constrained by rigid and prescriptive design guidelines, it has not found it necessary to stifle design creativity by requiring that new buildings replicate the styles and materials of older buildings. "Charleston is not like Santa Fe, New Mexico. Modern buildings are accepted here," observed Behre.

Throughout the city, including areas encompassed by the Old and Historic District, there are buildings representative of a wide range of architectural styles that have been approved by the BAR—including very contemporary and modern building designs. Across from Charleston Place (facing the restored cast-iron building façades fronting on Meeting Street, which hide the parking structure for Charleston Place) is an imposing, post-modern new building that houses the offices of NationsBank. At the eastern end of Calhoun Street is the Charleston Gateway Center—a large commercial building of modern design that sailed through the BAR because of its judged design excellence but which, when built, proved to be somewhat controversial.

In the western segment of Calhoun Street are two additional modern buildings approved by the BAR that have elicited more than a little public comment since their construction. One of the buildings (a three-story brick office building across from what used to be St. Francis Hospital) had just opened when I toured the city with Robert Behre. "It was approved by the BAR because they don't want to stifle design creativity in the city, but is not well loved," said Behre. Another building of modern design I saw was a steel and concrete bank building in the shape of a "T" at 281 Calhoun Street, which was designed by Jeffrey Rosenblum (a local architect who later became the chairman of the BAR).

When he stepped down from the BAR in 1998, after serving on the board since 1989, Rosenblum was interviewed by Robert Behre for his newspaper column on architecture and preservation. Rosenblum was asked for his opinion on the need to allow modern and diverse downtown architecture. His answer, which Behre quoted in his column, was, "If you don't let change and diversity happen, everything becomes so stagnant . . . and the city becomes boring." (Behre, March 16, 1998, 1-B) Rosenblum went on to note that the Riviera Theater and the Bank of Charleston Building at 276 East Bay Street "were modern for their time, but have already become familiar, beloved parts of the cityscape." (*ibid.*)

Building styles in Charleston are far from homogeneous. There are Victorian buildings, Georgian buildings, and buildings representing practically every major period and architectural style. Moreover, buildings in Charleston (particularly in residential neighborhoods) are in widely differing colors. "Paint colors are not prescribed," said Charles Chase. "If people want to put up a very different color, we ask them to put up the paint color on part of the structure as a sample, leave it up for a week or so and ask people to comment."

What makes the environment seem so unified and compatible is the fact that buildings in Charleston respect their surroundings and take their cues from the buildings and environment around them. Although buildings may differ in terms of their architectural styles, materials and colors, they nevertheless relate carefully to one another in terms of their scale and height, and in the way they align with one another and relate to the street.

The Design and Construction of Public Buildings and Facilities

All too often in communities where citizens expect private developers and property owners to meet high standards of design and construction, public buildings are built which fall far short of those standards. In Northampton, Massachusetts (where I once served as planning director), one of the ugliest buildings in the city's Downtown Historic District was the Central Police Station. It was almost grotesque in its plainness—a one-story building in the midst of an area of architectural elegance.

Part of the reason that public buildings are frequently so aesthetically awful, I suspect, is that local officials are sometimes afraid that if the buildings they build look good, taxpayers will get the impression that too much was spent on them. Part of the reason may also be carelessness and a lack of community pride.

In Charleston, a different attitude has prevailed. In the words of Charles Chase, Charleston has had a mayor who "has taken very seriously the notion that the city needs to set a standard, and that the standard of excellence needs to be demonstrated by what the city does with its own buildings and public improvements. The mayor clearly has in mind, 'How can I ask someone to do something that I am not willing to do myself?'"

The city's commitment to design excellence is particularly obvious when one looks at the parking garages it has built in recent years. Parking garages are utilitarian structures that are rarely beautiful and are often so unsightly that they exert a negative impact on their surroundings. However, parking structures in Charleston actually complement and enhance the appearance of their surrounding areas.

The parking structure built on East Bay Street, designed by Sasaki Associates, is an excellent example. According to Robert Behre, "The architects' initial design was 'form follows function'—the building *looked* like a parking garage. When the mayor saw the proposed design, he said, 'That won't cut it here.'" The structure was completely redesigned to look more like an historic warehouse. Openings in the structure above the first floor were screened with wooden louvers, thereby hiding the cars. Ground-floor retail and office space maintains a pedestrian-scaled environment at street level. As a result, walking along East Bay Street, one is completely unaware that the building is a parking structure.

The multilevel parking structure built adjacent to the Visitors Center (also designed by Sasaki Associates) is larger and even more impressive. The exterior of the garage was designed to reflect the architectural features of the railroad warehouse across the street, which was restored and adaptively reused to serve as the city's new Tourism Information and Reception Center. It also has an interior atrium, and was planned and designed to be capable of accommodating first-floor commercial businesses to help to further enliven the area north of the center. "People call it the Garage Majal," commented Robert Behre. A parking structure of more modern design (by Cooper-Cary of Atlanta) was constructed by the city immediately north of the Francis Marion Hotel, which also includes first-floor commercial space. Yet another impressively designed parking structure was built by the city behind the new School District Office Building.

5-39   The East Bay Street parking garage.

Source: Gene Bunnell

5-40   Street-level view of East Bay Street parking garage with ground-level office and retail space.

Source: Gene Bunnell

5-41 The "Garage Majal"—the parking structure built across the street from the new Visitors Center.

Source: Gene Bunnell

5-42 Parking structure, with ground-level retail, built by the city adjacent to the Francis Marion Hotel.

Source: Gene Bunnell

5-43   Parking structure built behind the new School District Office Building on Calhoun Street.

Source: Gene Bunnell

5-44   The federal courthouse at Meeting and Broad Streets. The new addition (on the left) complements and enhances the character of the much older portion of the courthouse.

Source: Gene Bunnell

5-45   The Commissioners of Public Works Building on St. Philip Street.

Source: Gene Bunnell

Building high-quality parking garages that enhance rather than detract from the value of surrounding properties has not been cheap. The cost of two of the most recently constructed parking structures—the Visitors Center Garage in 1995 and the Francis Marion Garage in 1996—averaged over $16,000 per parking space. On the other hand, the revenues generated from parking fees (and leases of commercial space) have been more than sufficient to cover their costs.

Other public buildings in the city also show that great attention has been paid to design. The new addition to the federal courthouse (visible from Meeting Street just south of Broad Street) includes both classical and modern design elements and is perfectly integrated with the historic building to which it was attached.

On the other hand, the city's new Commissioners of Public Works Building at 103 St. Philip Street (at Vanderhorst) is extremely modern and innovative in its design. The exterior of the building, which was designed by LS3P Architects (the largest architectural firm in Charleston), is mostly covered with white concrete; however, along St. Philip Street, the exterior of the building is indented at regular intervals.

According to Robert Behre, the glass indentations along St. Philip Street make the building special and create the same rhythm as a row of Charleston single houses. "The glass indented portions create the sense of the existence of a number of separate buildings, with the reflective glass suggesting the openings between single houses where side porches would be placed." Another daring feature of the building is that the southeast corner of the building (at St. Philip and Vanderhorst) points sharply out at a 45-degree angle.

As radical as the design of the new Commissioners of Public Works Building is, it *does* respect its surroundings. The building may be quite large, taking up most of a city block, but the height of the structure is generally similar to buildings across the street, and articulation and indentations along the street create the impression that there are a number of individual buildings, rather than just one.

The quality of public buildings in Charleston has not come about just because of Mayor Riley's commitment to design excellence and to setting the standard for private sector developers. It has also come about because the city adopted a formal policy requiring that all new public buildings go through a formal process of design review similar to that required of private buildings. Thus, in city districts where the BAR has design review powers, all public buildings must be reviewed and approved by the seven-member BAR, similar to the procedures for private buildings and alterations.

Little Things That Make a Big Difference

As Charles Kuralt wrote about Charleston, "The pleasure of the city is in the details." (Kuralt 1995, 67) Many of these details are largely serendipitous, having come about through the individual decisions and actions of countless numbers of people who have lived in the city over the course of its long history. On the other hand, many of the other little things that make the city so pleasurable have happened more recently as a result of careful planning and deliberate policies.

One of the little things that makes the downtown so attractive and pleasant for pedestrians is the fact that so many trees have been planted along downtown streets and sidewalks. Rows of live oak trees have been planted up and down East Bay Street, and palmetto trees have been planted along Meeting, Market and Broad Streets. Moreover, existing trees are protected by a comprehensive tree protection and landscaping ordinance adopted in 1988. Under the ordinance, permission is needed from the city to remove any tree that is 2 feet or more in diameter.

Another "little thing" that easily goes unnoticed, and which contributes to the simple elegance of Charleston's urban fabric, is that utility poles and overhead utility lines are completely absent in large areas of the city. Throughout

5-46   View looking east on Broad Street toward St. Michael's Church. Palmetto trees line the street.

Source: Gene Bunnell

the Old and Historic District, and most of the central core of the city, utilities (such as electrical, telephone and cable lines) have been placed underground.

Similar attention to detail has been paid to the design of individual buildings and the way buildings relate to one another. Indeed, it is the harmonious blending of small features and details that is responsible for much of Charleston's charm. Robert Behre told me that he has often been struck by the extent to which the BAR is caught up in reviewing small details. Major controversies may occasionally erupt over big issues, such as over the scale of Charleston Place or the height and mass of the new Judicial Center. "However," said Behre, "for the most part, the design matters dealt with by the BAR are over aesthetic fine points, like the pitch of a roof or the kind of windows to be used."

Small features incorporated into the design of Waterfront Park provide another expression of the city's attention to detail. For example, the park includes an informative series of maps of the Charleston peninsula, cast in bronze and set on large granite blocks, which depict the extent of the city's development at various points in its history. Also included along the westerly edge of the park are a number of separate sitting areas surrounded by hedges, each with a different arrangement of chairs and benches (appropriate for different groups and different types of conversation).

When he took me around the city, Mayor Riley made a point of walking me through Waterfront Park, of which he is justly proud. We sat down on a bench that allowed us to look out over a large, raised lawn toward the harbor. While the mayor was telling me about various details in the park's design, I raised my legs and rested my feet on a low granite wall just in front of the bench. Riley stopped talking and exclaimed, "Ah, that's exactly what we hoped you'd do! Isn't that comfortable? That's why we put it there."

A large, formal fountain in the center of the park—sculpted into the form of a golden pineapple and meant to symbolize the city's southern hospitality— serves as the park's centerpiece. Another less formal fountain is provided at the northerly end of the park, which invites children to frolic in the jets of water. The long, wooden pier extending out into the harbor includes a sheltered area with a number of sets of swinging chairs, ideally sized for couples to quietly swing together.

Signs in commercial areas of Charleston are strictly controlled and limited in size, which has also helped to maintain the city's visual and aesthetic quality. Many kinds of signs are prohibited outright, such as free-standing pole signs, signs mounted on pedestals, roof-mounted signs, off-premise signs, portable signs and interior-illuminated signs. Only signs with exterior lighting or back lighting are allowed.

Commercial establishments are thus left with a fairly limited range of choices in terms of signage. Signs that are placed flush to the front façade of a building are allowable, provided that they do not cover more than 15% of the total façade area (although the BAR may restrict the size of a sign to less than the allowed area if it feels that the architectural design, location and physical features of the building façade so requires). Awning and window signs of limited size are also allowed. Custom-designed signs of limited size, hung at a right angle to the building façade, are allowed in certain commercial areas in the Old and Historic City, provided that they do not extend lower than 9 feet above the ground or extend above the sill of second-story windows. However, hanging signs that protrude out from buildings are discouraged by the BAR along King Street.

Neon signs are generally discouraged (but not completely prohibited) within the Old and Historic City District; some historic neon signs have in fact been permitted by the BAR. Perhaps the most well-known and treasured sign in the city is the right-angle neon sign at the Tellis Pharmacy—the oldest neon sign in the city, which has been designated an historic landmark.

One last, small difference that planning regulation has made in Charleston is worth mentioning. If and when you ever fly into Charleston, and drive into the city on I-26 from the airport, you will see dozens of huge advertising billboards. Most of the billboards, and all of the newest ones, are in North Charles-

5-47   Bronze castings of historic maps of the city mounted at Waterfront Park show various stages of Charleston's development.

Source: Gene Bunnell

5-48   Golden pineapple fountain in the center of Waterfront Park.

Source: Gene Bunnell

5-49   The placement of this bench overlooking the lawn of Waterfront Park *invites* people who sit there to put their feet up and relax.

Source: Gene Bunnell

5-50   Fountain at northern end of Waterfront Park.

Source: Gene Bunnell

ton (a separate municipality). Only a very small number of billboards line I-26 once you enter Charleston itself.

Again, this small difference (which easily goes unnoticed because it is marked by the *absence* of something rather than by the presence of something visible) did not come about by accident. Charleston adopted its first comprehensive sign regulations in 1985 that included strict limitations on the placement of billboards. The ordinance also included an amortization schedule for removing existing nonconforming billboards, which was revised and strengthened in 1987. As it turned out, the work of the billboard ordinance was sped up by Hurricane Hugo in 1989, which destroyed a large number of the nonconforming billboards that the ordinance had stated could not be rebuilt.

Officials of the City of Charleston, such as Lee Batchelder (zoning administrator), saw an opportunity in the wake of Hurricane Hugo to achieve the permanent removal of a large number of billboards, particularly those located in visually sensitive locations. They therefore approached representatives of three outdoor advertising companies and began negotiations on an agreement calling for the "voluntary" removal of a specified number of signs in specified locations. The primary aim of the city in this endeavor was to achieve the removal of all billboards from the city's Old and Historic District and all residential neighborhoods, as well as from locations that interfered with views of

5-51   A couple swinging on one of the swinging chairs on the Waterfront Park pier.

Source: Gene Bunnell

5-52 Signs of lawyers' offices along Broad Street.

Source: Gene Bunnell

5-53   Hanging signs of commercial establishments on East Bay Street.

Source: Gene Bunnell

the city, rivers and marshes. In return, the city was willing to grant its assurance that certain other signs could remain permanently in place *and be replaced in case they were ever damaged or destroyed by future hurricanes or other natural disasters.*

After much negotiation, the companies eventually agreed to remove all 45 billboards from downtown Charleston neighborhoods, another 52 billboards that intruded on views of marshes and rivers, and those along federal primary highways leading into the city (such as I-26 and the Mark Clark Expressway). Under the final signed agreement, only 39 of the 136 billboards originally in place within the city limits were allowed to remain.

BEING WILLING TO SAY "NO"

Planning has enabled Charleston to remake and transform itself into a place that is valued and appreciated by residents and visitors alike. However, as Charleston's experience has shown, merely preparing a plan was not enough, in and of itself, to make the difference. Plans made the difference because they were used as guides to decision-making.

Decision-making related to land use and development has two important facets. First, local and community officials must set priorities and decide what needs to be done—where and how to spend limited public resources, and what kinds of development proposals should be encouraged and approved. Second, locally elected officials and members of local planning commissions must be prepared to make hard decisions regarding what should *not* be done and what developments should *not* be approved, which is equally (if not more) important.

In many American communities—particularly those that have no sense of place, and where residents and local leaders have no clear vision of what they want their community to be like in the future—it is extremely rare to say "no" to any development that is proposed. Indeed, it often seems that some communities have never seen a development they didn't like. However, an undiscriminating approach to land use and development is not the way to create communities people value and want to live in. Making good places requires that communities know when to say "no" to development that is at odds with the qualities people value in their community.

One thing clearly stands out about Charleston's planning story: the number of times that local officials and community leaders said "no" to development proposals that conflicted with local plans and desired patterns of land use and development.

What made Charleston's Waterfront Park possible was the city's refusal to permit a major hotel to be built there. Likewise, the city's preparation of a Tourism study led the mayor to oppose the National Parks Service's proposal to build a major embarkation facility for Fort Sumter tour boats at the southerly end of the Charleston peninsula, across from White Point Gardens. An even more impressive instance of the city's willingness to say "no" occurred when the city was presented with a development proposal to reuse the Francis Marion Hotel, which had stood vacant for a number of years, for student housing.

The Visitor Accommodations study (1982) and the Accommodations Zoning Overlay District (adopted by the city in 1987) provided a clear policy framework related to the location of new hotels. As previously noted, the aim of that plan was to encourage hotels in the center of the peninsula to reinforce and strengthen commercial activity along King Street. *Implicit* in that policy was the hope that this policy would eventually bring about the renovation and reopening of the 12-story, 226-room Francis Marion Hotel at the corner of King and Calhoun Streets.

The Francis Marion Hotel was built in the 1920s and for years was the city's crown-jewel hotel. However, during the 1960s and 1970s, the hotel changed owners and operators a number of times, and each time the hotel seemed to decline in quality; in the later 1980s, the hotel finally closed. In the aftermath of Hurricane Hugo, it was used to house roofers who came to Charleston to put people's roofs back on. After that, it was again abandoned and remained vacant between the latter part of 1989 to about 1995-96.

Robert Behre picked up the story from there: "Throughout the early 1990s, there was a debate going on about the College of Charleston's growing impact on city neighborhoods. The college was growing to a population of several thousand students, but was only housing roughly 20-25% of them on campus. The rest of the students lived off campus in surrounding neighborhoods, where they played their stereos loud at night and kept the residents awake. There was a lot of talk that the Francis Marion was right there, only a block away from the college and was vacant. Wouldn't that make an excellent dormitory in which to house college students?"

In many respects, it was a tempting proposal. The building was deteriorating and the longer it stood vacant and unused, the greater the risk that it might not survive. Purchase and renovation of the hotel building by the college would stabilize and protect the building, and would enable the city to avoid the downside risk of losing the building altogether. However, Mayor Riley remembered that the downtown revitalization plan of the late 1970s said that it was important that the Francis Marion continue to be a hotel and therefore said "no" to the dormitory idea.

It is important to realize how courageous the mayor's decision was, given the prevailing conditions at the time. "This was during a major drought in hotel financing. Nobody was financing new hotels in the early 1990s. So the prospects at the time for bringing back the Francis Marion as a hotel seemed bleak. It was just standing there empty—just a shell," said Behre.

In the years that followed, Riley did not simply sit back, waiting and hoping a hotel developer would appear and ask for the city's approval to renovate and reopen the Francis Marion. According to Behre, "The mayor was the catalyst behind the formation of a coalition of banks that agreed to finance the project. At the same time, he succeeded in getting a $4.25 million federal UDAG for the $12 million project, and promised that the city would build a $4 million parking garage adjacent to the hotel if and when it was renovated. The Francis Marion project was not as controversial as Charleston Place but, from a persistence standpoint, the fight to bring back the Francis Marion was almost as difficult and took almost as long."

The thoroughly renovated Francis Marion Hotel today is once again one of the premier hotels in Charleston, joining the Charleston Place Hotel as among the finest places to stay. Robert Behre attended the press conference that was held when the hotel reopened, and vividly recalls hearing the mayor talk passionately about how important it was at times for the city to aim high, to "hold the line" and not compromise. Riley's exact words, as Behre reported them, were: "What we did here was refuse to compromise, and what we've been doing in our city is refusing to compromise. Compromise is too prevalent in our society." It occurred to Behre that it was not the kind statement that one usually heard from a politician.

As it turned out, a much better site was found to accommodate the need for student housing. Not long after the Francis Marion Hotel reopened, the vacant upper floors of two large commercial buildings (formerly occupied by Condon's department store) were renovated into 84 apartments. Seven thousand square feet on the ground floor fronting on North King Street was retained for retail space.

In yet another situation, the city said "no" to a proposed hotel development that conflicted with the goals of the 1989 Calhoun Street study. Mayor Riley told me what happened: "A couple of local developers came in with a plan to put a cheap McSleep Inn on the north side of Calhoun Street, on the site where the new County Library has since been built. They had a lot of political muscle. Because the project conflicted with the plan that we had prepared for Calhoun Street, as well as with the Visitor Accommodations study, we were able to stop it. They needed a zoning change for a motel, and the city council rejected the zoning change by one vote. Not long after that proposed use of the site was defeated, the city bought the land and gave it to the county in return for its commitment to build a new library on the property."

In Mayor Riley's opinion, the city's experience with the McSleep Inn proposal clearly demonstrates the practical importance of having prepared a formal plan. "If we hadn't had a plan, and had simply said, 'We don't think that building an automobile-oriented motel is a good idea,' the developer could have easily steamrolled over us and gotten the project approved. They had a

5-54   The renovated former Condon's department store building on North King Street. In addition to ground-level retail, the building contains 84 apartments.

Source: Gene Bunnell

lot of political clout. However, we were able to say, 'The community has done a study of Calhoun Street, and has prepared a plan with the benefit of a lot of community input. The plan says this is what we need here, and this is what we don't need.' Having a plan at least gave us a fighting chance."

REVISITING AND REVISING PREVIOUSLY PREPARED PLANS

Communities often make the mistake of thinking that once a plan has been prepared, the problem or issue that prompted preparation of the plan has been solved. However, plans can never be perfect in all respects and, with the passage of time, citizens and local officials often recognize the need to make modifications and refinements. Also, as conditions change, the plan itself may need to be changed. In other words, *for planning to be truly effective, it cannot simply be a one-time exercise.* To be relevant and effectual, plans need to be kept up to date. Indeed, an important factor that has contributed to the effectiveness and relevance of planning in Charleston is that plans and regulations have been routinely reviewed and updated as necessary. As a result, they have remained current and have continued to earn public support so that they can be enforced.

For example, the Accommodations Zoning Overlay District was not simply adopted in 1987 and set in stone. The boundaries and certain provisions of the Accommodations Zoning Overlay District were revised as experience in implementing the provisions brought to light new issues and as conditions changed.

The reason why planners revisited and revised the Accommodations Zoning Overlay District was that, in the years following the adoption of the Overlay District, there had been a spate of new hotel construction in Charleston—because Charleston had become such a desirable tourist destination and because the hotel financing had been available. As a result, the concern arose that the city was possibly allowing itself to be overrun by tourists and hotels. Also, some citizens reacted negatively to proposed developments that were allowed under the ordinance. Charles Chase recounted how a developer (and his architect) came before the BAR asking the board to review the proposed design for a new hotel.

"It was one of the best designed projects that I've seen presented to us in the 11 years I've been here, but the hotel use of the site became an issue because of the number of rooms and the proposed height of the building, which the neighborhood association objected to—even though it was allowed by the ordinance."

The philosophy that Charleston planners have adhered to throughout the Riley administration is that planning regulations should provide a clear indication to property owners and developers of the city's desires and the kind of development they will approve. Said Chase, "We don't want a project that meets our adopted zoning and design criteria not to be approved just because it gets pushed aside by special interests. On the other hand, we don't want neighborhoods negatively impacted. What we need to do is continually balance the two." Thus, the decision was made to revisit and openly discuss and revise the provisions of the ordinance.

"There was a good deal of give and take [between these citizens and the mayor] when the city undertook a recent study and reassessment of hotel development," reported Robert Behre. "The residents wrested some concessions from the city—like insisting on a maximum of 50 rooms in new hotels south of Calhoun Street, with one or two exceptions." At the same time, however, certain areas were added to the Accommodations Zoning Overlay District to encourage new hotel development of those sites.

Interestingly enough, one of the sites added to the Accommodations Zoning Overlay District is occupied by the Mendell Rivers Federal Building—the highly unpopular, seven-story, white granite building of modern design built in the 1960s that seems uncomfortably out of place as it looks out over Marion Square and clashes with neighboring historic buildings.

The city, with the support of historic preservationists and citizens, has been trying for years to get the federal offices moved so that the Mendell Rivers Fed-

5-55   The Mendell Rivers Federal Building, overlooking Marion Square—one of the least loved buildings in the city. Plans are underway to have the building demolished.

Source: Gene Bunnell

eral Building can be torn down. The discovery of widespread asbestos throughout this building has given new strength to these efforts. Thus, in the course of revising the Accommodations Zoning Overlay District, the possibility of including the Mendell Rivers Federal Building site in the district was raised—and the neighborhood accepted the idea. As a result, that parcel is now included in and covered by the Accommodations Zoning Overlay District.

USING PLANNING TO BENEFIT DISADVANTAGED AREAS

In developing and implementing plans for community and economic development, planners in Charleston were continually aware that the plans they were developing and the projects they were planning were not merely ends in themselves, but would and should produce positive spin-off effects. As a result, a conscious attempt was made to spread facilities and improvements throughout the city, so that their beneficial effects were shared with residents and property owners in different parts of the city. In particular, the city consciously located community facilities, made improvements and invested in parts of the city that, in a purely market-driven economy, would very likely have been overlooked. The decisions the city made to locate the new City/County Library and new School District Office Building on Calhoun Street and to locate the Visitors Center on John Street (well north of Calhoun Street) are prime examples.

Because Charleston's special qualities are so widely recognized today, there may be a tendency to downplay what Charleston has accomplished, as if all that has happened were somehow preordained and inevitable. Admittedly, Charleston's location along the coast, its beautiful harbor and its impressive supply of historic buildings (almost unparalleled in this country) gave it certain advantages. However, nothing has come easily in Charleston. The city's vulnerability to hurricanes, tornadoes and earthquakes—which, over the years, have inflicted immense damage and pain on the city—forced city residents to rebuild their city again and again. Moreover, as the preceding account makes clear, none of the truly dramatic and positive changes that occurred in Charleston in recent decades came about by chance. Charleston is the way it is today largely as a result of *careful and deliberate planning*.

It might even be argued that Charleston was actually at somewhat of a disadvantage when it first began planning with the aim of revitalizing its downtown core since, unlike Chattanooga and Wichita, it did not have any big local corporations or foundations to financially support its planning and redevelopment efforts. In Wichita, for example, the downtown planning and revitalization program was spearheaded and supported by wealthy business leaders and the heads of major national corporations based in Wichita. Chattanooga's planning and revitalization effort was supported to a remarkable degree by the Lyndhurst Foundation, which was established and funded by Coca-Cola.

Charleston was not in a position to benefit from such private sector leadership because no major corporations or industries are located in Charleston. The largest employer in the area was the Charleston Naval and Air Base. Tourism accounts for most of the local employment in the trade and service sectors, and most of the businesses in these sectors employ relatively few people. Indeed, in the beginning at least, the city as a public entity was very much on its own.

THE FUTURE OF PLANNING IN CHARLESTON

As I talked to people about the difference planning had made in Charleston, I frequently asked whether the dramatic changes and improvements of the last 25 years had taught citizens something about the value of planning and the importance of continuing to plan; would planning continue to be practiced and relied upon under future mayors when Joseph P. Riley eventually leaves office? Riley, after all, has been a strong proponent and supporter of planning throughout his terms in office, and has elevated planning to a level of importance that has been matched in few American cities. Riley's personal involvement in shaping the planning agenda has been so direct and personal that, in many people's minds, Riley has been the city's master planner.

The extent to which Joseph Riley's vision has shaped Charleston is well illustrated by the role he played in planning and siting the South Carolina Aquarium. "It really came out of the mayor's vision of what makes a city great," observed Robert Behre. Riley had seen what the aquarium in Baltimore had done for that city, and felt that building a major aquarium that reinforced the city's connection to the sea would be especially good for Charleston. Not everyone in the city agreed with the mayor that there was a need to build yet another tourist attraction, but that didn't discourage Riley from pushing the aquarium idea.

The site that Riley had in mind for the aquarium was a contaminated, 4-acre industrial site at the eastern end of Calhoun Street. The key element in the mayor's planning strategy was getting the National Parks Service to agree to build its new Fort Sumter tour boat facility, next to the aquarium. Once the National Parks Service agreed, a strong case could be made that the federal government should pay to acquire the site.

The strategy worked. The National Parks Service agreed to build its new Fort Sumter tour boat facility at the eastern end of Calhoun Street, next to the proposed aquarium, and Riley succeeded in persuading Congress to buy the site. "In that one bold stroke, the aquarium was sited well away from historic neighborhoods and in such a way as to help revitalize a section of the city's waterfront so polluted that no mortal would venture into that water," said Behre.

Building the aquarium on a contaminated Superfund site greatly increased the cost and complexity of the project. As of 1998, the expected total project cost had risen to approximately $62 million. The upside was that locating the aquarium project on a brownfield site provided the impetus for cleaning up a site that the city had been wanting to clean up for a long time. The net public cost to the city was significantly reduced when the city negotiated a settlement with South Carolina Electric and Gas in which the utility agreed to pay $26 million to the city over four years to settle pollution-related problems in and around the site. The city has also undertaken legal negotiations with the U.S. Navy regarding its possible liability for the site's pollution.

A national competition was held to select a firm to design the aquarium. As Riley took me to survey the site where construction of the aquarium was underway in 1998, it was clear that he had taken an active interest in the project's planning and the details of its design. Standing on the derelict site, Riley pointed out toward the water and described what the facility was going to be like. "The aquarium will be built out into the harbor. To enter it, you will walk along the side of the building on a covered ramp 335 feet long, which will lead up to a raised deck overlooking the harbor. The view of the harbor from there will be breathtaking."

The South Carolina Aquarium opened in 2000. Construction of the National Parks Service's new Fort Sumter tour boat facility was completed in the summer of 2001. An 1,100-space, multilevel parking facility at the end of Calhoun Street handles the parking demands generated by the facilities and development in the area. Between the parking structure and the aquarium/tour boat facility is a broad expanse of lawn, trees and landscaping, providing an attractive and serene setting for the two facilities. Along the northern edge of the site, between the parking garage and the aquarium, and overlooking the landscaped square, the abandoned power plant that formerly stood on the site has been renovated to accommodate an IMAX-3D Theater and "food court"; a new office building ("Fountain Walk") has also been constructed, which is connected to the renovated power plant. The administrative offices of the aquarium are located in that new office building.

One of the wonderful indirect benefits of siting the South Carolina Aquarium and Fort Sumter tour boat facilities together along the eastern shore of the peninsula, well north of Waterfront Park, has been that it has helped move the city much closer to fulfilling its goal of creating a continuous waterfront promenade north from Waterfront Park.

Yvonne Fortenberry recounted how the pieces have gradually fallen into place. "The aquarium has a waterfront promenade as part of it. South of that is the Maritime Center, built and owned by the city, which has a waterfront promenade. Between the aquarium and the Maritime Center are the Dockside condominiums, which are privately owned. I never thought it would happen (although I hoped that it would), but the Dockside Condominium Association has agreed to let the city build a waterfront access connection in front of their condominiums, linking the aquarium and the Maritime Center."

With that piece of waterfront access in place, the only missing link was the Union Pier property—a large container ship cargo facility operated by the South Carolina Port Authority. As it happens, the South Carolina Port Authority is planning to relocate these cargo ship facilities and operations to Daniel Island across the Cooper River, which will open up the Union Pier site for redevelopment. A master plan (prepared for the Union Pier property in 1996 by Ehrenkrantz and Eckstut) calls for the site to be developed largely for housing, as well as for some associated mixed-use development. An important element of the plan, which has the support of the city and the South Carolina Port Authority, is for continuing the waterfront promenade through the entire Union Pier property. The plan also calls for a large park to be provided in the center of the development.

Thus, by fully embracing the goal of increasing public access to the water, and by pressing to achieve this goal on specific sites as the opportunity has

5-56   The new South Carolina Aquarium.

Source: Robert Behre

5-57   View of the formerly abandoned power plant (left), which was renovated to accommodate an IMAX-3D Theater, food court and offices. The front of the South Carolina Aquarium is visible at the extreme right of the photo.

Source: Robert Behre

arisen, Charleston is on the brink of achieving something truly wonderful: a mile-long promenade that people will be making use of and enjoying for years to come.

THE LEGACY OF A MAYOR
WHO THINKS AND ACTS LIKE A PLANNER

In the spring of 1999 when I was last in Charleston, Joseph P. Riley had been mayor of Charleston for 24 years. In November 1999, he was re-elected to a seventh four-year term. As city council member Yvonne Evans observed, "There is a whole generation living in this city that does not know a time when Riley was not mayor. They take a lot for granted."

One of Riley's major skills has been his ability to communicate a sense of the value and importance of the public realm, and to persuade people of the strategic importance of planning in achieving and maintaining the qualities people value in Charleston. Succeeding mayors may not be equally supportive of planning, or possibly may not be as persuasive or as capable of putting together the coalitions needed to develop and implement effective plans.

When I asked Charles Chase whether he thought planning would endure after Joseph Riley left office, he said he thought it would. "You have to remember," Chase pointed out, "this city has had restrictive regulations in place through the BAR since 1931. Architectural controls [and public control of what development is allowed] have been around for a long, long time." On the other hand, he shared Yvonne Evans' fear that more recent arrivals to Charleston tend to take things for granted, and do not recognize or appreciate the fact that the qualities that attracted them to Charleston did not come about or survive by chance.

"Newcomers do not realize how much effort went into making the city's streets and neighborhoods good places," Chase continued. "They have not experienced what this place was like 20 years ago. As a result, they do not recognize the energy that it took to accomplish what we accomplished."

Robert Behre offered the following assessment: "History, I think, will show that Mayor Riley needed to act decisively. The downtown was dying. There was a crisis, and he responded with a series of bold and somewhat controversial moves, starting with the Lower King Street District plan, fighting for Charleston Place, and fighting the other battles that followed, taking the plan up the street."

Charleston has changed significantly over the last 25 years. The city has grown much bigger in population and in terms of its geographic size as a result of a number of annexations. Although the number of people living on the Charleston peninsula has grown in recent years, many more residents of Charleston now live in peripheral areas that until recently were not part of the city. Charleston today is a more metropolitan city and, as a result, the planning and land issues with which the city must deal in the future have in some ways become even more complex and challenging.

One of the areas annexed by Charleston in recent years was Daniel Island— an island about the size of the Charleston peninsula that has only recently been connected to the mainland by a bridge. It is also where the South Carolina Port Authority is relocating and expanding its port and cargo-handling facilities. Once completed, the new port facilities on Daniel Island will make Charleston the biggest and most active container port in the south, second only to New York on the east coast.

The new bridge and expanded port facilities are major stimuli for new growth and development on the island. They also present the city with a unique planning opportunity to guide and shape development in an area which, until now, has been largely undeveloped. The city has welcomed this opportunity by joining with the island's owners in hiring a team of outside planning consultants, which has prepared a comprehensive master plan for what may eventually turn out to be a new planned community on the island.

Even without additional major planning initiatives being undertaken, the planning that has already been done will continue to leave a lasting legacy. As Robert Behre observed, "A lot of what the mayor has brought about won't even be felt until after he's left office—like the whole makeover of the eastern waterfront, including the redevelopment of the Union Pier property. Another major project is the construction of a County Judicial Center at Meeting and Broad Streets, tucked in behind the old historic courthouse, which will contain 160,000 square feet of space and bring a lot more people downtown. Then there is the federal courthouse expansion going on across the street."

In light of all that has been accomplished during such a relatively short period of time, and the major planning initiatives and projects still in the pipeline, it is understandable that the pace of planned change in Charleston might eventually slow down. "Perhaps we just need a little time to catch our breath," observed Robert Behre.

INTERVIEWEES

Lee Batchelder, AICP, zoning administrator, City of Charleston
Robert Behre, newspaper reporter and columnist, *The Post and Courier*
Charles Chase, architect, preservation officer and staff person to the Board of
    Architectural Review
Patricia W. Crawford, director of Housing and Community Development
Yvonne Evans, city council member, Chair of Planning and Zoning
    Commission
Yvonne Fortenberry, AICP, director of planning, City of Charleston
Cathy Kleiman, executive director, Charleston Affordable Housing, Inc.
Joseph P. Riley, mayor of Charleston (1976–present)

PLANNING STORY CHRONOLOGY

1920   A number of prominent Charleston citizens are outraged to learn that the Joseph Manigault House is about to be demolished to make way for a gas station. The Society for the Preservation of Old Dwellings is formed.

1924   The Francis Marion Hotel opens at Calhoun and King Streets, overlooking Marion Square.

1931   The first formal planning study of the city is completed. The city's first zoning ordinance is adopted, establishing the "Old and Historic District." The Board of Architectural Review (BAR), the first municipally appointed architectural/design review body in America, is established.

1947   The Historic Charleston Foundation is established.

1959   The 1931 zoning ordinance is amended, giving the BAR the power to delay demolitions of pre-1860 buildings and to review exterior alterations.

1962   The Charleston Hotel on Meeting Street, once one of the city's grandest structures, is razed.

1966   The city's first general development plan is prepared and adopted. The city council expands the Old and Historic District to include the Ansonborough neighborhood, and expands the BAR's membership and powers.

1971   Historic Architecture Inventory completed.

1972   Sears Roebuck closes its main downtown retail store on King Street, which opened in 1929.

1974   An *Historic Preservation Plan* is prepared and adopted.

1975   Joseph P. Riley is elected Mayor of Charleston. Charleston is designated a Community Development Block Grant Entitlement Community by the U.S. Department of Housing and Urban Development. The Old and Historic District is expanded yet again, extending it north to Calhoun Street to include the Radcliffeborough and Mazyck-Wraggsborough neighborhoods.

1976   Joseph P. Riley takes office. The Department of Planning and Urban Development is established. At the request of the City, the Chamber of Commerce commits $10,000 of its own money to hire a private consulting firm to study downtown redevelopment possibilities and to prepare a report recommending how the city should proceed in attempting to reverse the decline of the downtown area.

1977   The *Lower King Street District: District Plan and Program* ("the Lower King Street District plan") is completed.

1978   The *Tourism Impact and Management Study* ("the Tourism study") is completed and adopted. The city council adopts an ordinance limiting the height of new buildings. The adopted height limits are largely consistent with the height limits recommended in the 1974 *Historic Preservation Plan*. A Land Use and Housing plan is completed. Twelve neighborhood plans are also completed.

1982   The *Visitor Accommodations Study* ("the Visitor Accommodations study") is completed.

1983   First scattered site public housing is built.

1984   Condon's department store on North King Street closes.

1985   Comprehensive signage amendment to zoning ordinance is adopted.

1986   Charleston Place opens. A national design competition is held to select the designer of the South Carolina Aquarium.

1987   The Accommodations Zoning Overlay District Ordinance is adopted.

1988   The Charleston Housing Trust is formed. Homesteading Program is initiated.
Tree Preservation and Landscape Ordinance is adopted.

1989   The *Calhoun Street Corridor Study* ("the Calhoun Street study") is completed.
Hurricane Hugo inflicts massive damage on Charleston. Property losses are so great that Charleston Insurance and Hibernian Mutual Insurance go out of business. Charleston 2000 Steering Committee is organized.

1990   Waterfront Park is completed. The Old and Historic District, and the Old City Height District, are extended across the Ashley River to include the Albemarle Road area.

1991   The new Visitors Reception and Transportation Center opens on a site north of Calhoun Street. *Charleston 2000—A Plan to Preserve and Enhance the Quality of LIfe of the Citizens of Charleston* is completed and adopted.

1996   Saks Fifth Avenue opens a new department store at King and Market Streets, diagonally across from Charleston Place. In addition to the 30,000 square feet of retail space in Saks, the project includes 40,000 square feet of Class A office space, 5,000 square feet of other retail space and a 450-space parking garage. The Old Citadel Building at Marion Square is renovated into a 150-room Embassy Suites Hotel. The city council passes an ordinance calling for the imposition of a 2% accommodation tax on gross proceeds derived from the rental of transient accommodations within the city—half of the proceeds to be applied to property tax relief and half to finance visitor-related capital projects. The South Carolina Port Authority, working in cooperation with the city, prepares a plan for the reuse and redevelopment of 60 acres of Port Authority-owned land on the Cooper River waterfront.

1997   Two buildings on North King Street (formerly occupied by Condon's department store) that stood vacant for 12 years are renovated to accommodate 84 apartment units on the upper floors, and 7,000 square feet of retail space on the ground floor. The Francis Marion Hotel (vacant for over seven years) is renovated at a cost of $12 million and reopens. The Charleston Maritime Center is completed overlooking the Cooper River, just south of the site of the planned new South Carolina Aquarium. The $13.4 million project completes a key section of the planned HarborWalk.

1998   The new main County Library opens on Calhoun Street. A revised *Visitor Accommodations Study* is completed.

1999   Joseph P. Riley, having already served as the city's mayor for 24 years, is re-elected to a seventh four-year term.

2000   The South Carolina Aquarium opens.

2001   The National Park Service's new Fort Sumter tour boat facility is completed, on a site adjacent to the South Carolina Aquarium.

NOTES

1. Charleston came in sixth as the city most often mentioned, and the only city among the 10 most frequently mentioned with a population of less than 100,000. The only cities more frequently mentioned by planners as good places were: Portland, Oregon; San Francisco, California; Seattle, Washington; Boston, Massachusetts; and Minneapolis/St. Paul, Minnesota.

2. Joseph P. Riley first took office as mayor of Charleston in 1976.

3. You can count the number of buildings of 10 or more stories on the fingers of one hand. One of those tall buildings is the beloved Francis Marion Hotel. Another tall building on the peninsula, much less loved, is the Mendell Rivers Federal Building.

4. The scale of Charleston Place is deceiving when viewed at street level. In order to get a clear view of Charleston Place and fully grasp its scale, I had to go to the top of a six-level parking structure south of Charleston Place.

5. A department store was initially included in the original plan for Charleston Place but had to be omitted when the project was scaled down.

6. Originally, state highway engineers wanted to bring the bridge into Charleston at the western end of Broad Street, but this proposed alignment was strenuously opposed by the city and Charleston residents because of the large numbers of cars it would have brought into the lower half of the peninsula. After many years of debate and study, the route was changed and the new bridge was constructed further north to connect with Calhoun Street.

7. In the 19th and first half of the 20th century, the social dividing line in Charleston had been Broad Street (those with higher incomes lived south of Broad). An excellent restaurant in Charleston has taken a name that playfully refers to this previously important social and physical dividing line: the name of the restaurant, Slightly North of Broad (SNOB, for short), is also its location.

8. The plan was prepared by Buckhurst Fish Hutton Katz, Inc. and Thomas & Means Associates.

9. For on-street spaces not reserved for neighborhood residents with permits, parking is limited to one or two hours.

10. To encourage people to use the DASH system, fares have intentionally been kept low. In 1999, the cost of a ticket for all-day, unlimited use of DASH vehicles was only $2; the cost of a single ride was $.75.

11. The city's policy of prohibiting and limiting the development of on-street parking has actually been implemented in a way that has been supportive of new hotel development. For example, to assist the development of two new hotels close to the Visitors Center, the city built a multilevel parking facility that serves both the new Hampton Inn (developed within the shell of an old Burlap Bag Factory) and the new Embassy Suites Hotel (developed in the Citadel Building, formerly occupied and used by the Citadel Military School to house and parade its cadets). Similarly, to encourage the restoration and reopening of the Francis Marion Hotel (for decades, the city's premier hotel, which closed in 1990 and stood vacant and deteriorating for roughly eight years), the city built a municipal parking garage adjacent to the Francis Marion Hotel for use by hotel guests. These newly constructed parking facilities were in addition to the huge multilevel parking facility that the city built immediately north of the Visitors Center.

6

Duluth, Minnesota

Making a Special Place in the Face of Decline

PREFACE

Most Americans seem to agree that growth is good. Accordingly, we often assume that cities which are growing the fastest must be the *best* places to live (why else would so many people be moving there?) and that cities that have lost population must not be good places to live. The following story makes it clear that we need to stop stereotyping communities in that way. Cities that have not grown—and even those that have lost population—can be great places, and planning can play an important role in bringing about positive changes in such communities.

CONTEXT AND HISTORY

Duluth's story is potentially instructive to many other American cities that, like Duluth, experienced tremendous growth and prosperity long ago, but are now having to adjust to a very different kind of reality.

As the 19th century came to a close and the 20th century began, many of the fastest growing—and the most prosperous and admired—cities in the country were on the Great Lakes: Buffalo, New York; Cleveland, Ohio; Detroit, Michigan; Chicago, Illinois; and Milwaukee, Wisconsin. Little wonder that the 1893 Colombian Exposition—showcasing American technology and industry as well as skill in architecture and design—was held in Chicago, and that the Pan American Exposition at the beginning of the 20th century was in Buffalo.

The first major event that spurred the growth of Great Lakes cities was the opening of the Erie Canal in 1825. Virtually overnight, Buffalo became the principal gateway for transporting people and goods back and forth between eastern states (via New York City) and the vast, largely undeveloped midsection of the continental U.S. Once the canal was completed, goods could be transported by boat and barge to Buffalo, where they were transferred to ships, which took them even further west to port cities along the shores of Lake Erie, Lake Huron and Lake Michigan. Railroads eventually replaced the Erie Canal as the principal means of carrying goods east and west, but did not replace Buffalo's importance as a transfer point. Indeed, Buffalo went on to become the #2 rail center in the country—second only to Chicago.[1]

Today, we largely take for granted the fact that ships can travel from Lake Ontario (at the eastern end of the Great Lakes) to Lake Superior (the westernmost of the Great Lakes). Nevertheless, significant physical and geographic barriers needed to be overcome to fully make use of the Great Lakes as a way of transporting goods and material between the midwest and the east. One of those significant barriers was the fact that Lake Superior—by far the largest and deepest of the Great Lakes—was cut off from the lower lakes (Lake Michigan and Lake Huron) by 1.25 miles of rapids at Sault Ste. Marie. Goods and passengers transported between the two lakes had to be "unloaded and hauled across on a tramway to be reloaded on the opposite side . . . at enormous labor and expense." (Wolff, Jr. 1976, 144) In addition, there was no way for ships to travel from Lake Erie to Lake Ontario because the Niagara River and Niagara Falls made the water connection between the two lakes unnavigable.

In 1855, the forerunner of the present-day Soo Canal at Sault St. Marie was completed which, for the first time, allowed ships to move between Lake Superior and the other Great Lakes, greatly expanding opportunities for settlement and trade. Up until that time, only a handful of people lived in the area now known as Duluth.

In 1869, the Lake Superior and Mississippi Railroad built a rail line to Duluth, and other railroads soon followed. As these rail lines were being built, work was feverishly undertaken to develop port facilities capable of handling Great Lakes ships. Not long thereafter, Duluth became a major transshipment point for shipping goods from the midsection of the country to cities in the east. By the end of 1870, there were 3,500 people living in Duluth; by the middle of 1873, the city's population had grown to nearly 6,000.

The settlement of the Great Plains, and the transformation of the vast prairies to the west and south into farms producing huge amounts of grain, propelled further growth of the port and the City of Duluth. As the shipment of grain through Duluth increased, a number of huge grain elevators were built in the city, and Duluth became a major gateway for shipping agricultural products from the heartland to the east. Around the same time, vast U.S. timber reserves in Minnesota and Wisconsin were opened for logging, and sawmills in Duluth began to do a booming business. Once again, Duluth experienced a period of explosive growth. The population of the city (which had been 13,000 in 1883) rose to 30,000 by 1887, making it by far the largest and most important city in the entire Lake Superior watershed.

The optimism about Duluth's future, which pervaded the city in the 1880s, can be clearly discerned by looking at the grand Central High School that the city built and opened in 1892. To meet the educational needs of the growing number of school-age children (during the five-year period of 1886 and 1991, Duluth's student body increased from 1,600 to more than 5,000), the city built a truly impressive structure: a four-story, red stone building that was the "talk of the Midwest" (Hertzel 1993, 86), a building with a 230-foot-high clock tower that was visible for miles, as well as chandeliers, oak woodwork, and carved stone gargoyles and cherubs. Newspapers at the time praised it as "the most complete high school in America." (*ibid.*) The building, which now houses school district administrative offices, remains a major landmark in the city (110 years after its construction) and the clock tower of Central High School is still one of the most visible and recognizable features of the city's skyline.

In Duluth's early years, ships that came in and out of the Port of Duluth carried primarily grains (wheat, corn and rye), furs, timber and coal. However, in the late 1880s and 1890s, new forces came on the scene to propel another development surge: the discovery of iron ore in the Mesabi Iron Range (60 miles north of Duluth), the rise of the American steel industry and the growing demand for iron ore in steel-making industrial cities further to the east. The Duluth, Mesabi and Iron Range Company built a railroad from the Iron Range to Duluth, the U.S. Army Corps of Engineers dredged and enlarged the Duluth-Superior Harbor, and major docking facilities were built in Duluth (as well as in nearby Superior) to handle the transfer of iron ore to Great Lakes ships.[2]

By the turn of the century, Duluth had a population of almost 53,000 and was one of the nation's 50 largest cities. During World War I, Duluth's harbor was loading more cargo than any other harbor in the world. In 1913 alone, nearly 12,000 ships entered the Duluth-Superior Harbor, where the principal goods being shipped through Duluth were wheat and Iron Range ore. In 1915, the U.S. Steel Corporation opened a factory in what is now known as the Gary-New Duluth neighborhood, manufacturing tin plate, sheet metal, wire and nails.[3]

In 1917, the Duluth, Mesabi and Iron Range Company built a massive ore dock extending nearly one-half mile into St. Louis Bay, so that taconite (the name applied to the low-grade iron ore deposits that come out of the Lake Superior region) could be transferred from railroad freight cars directly into the holds of Great Lakes freighters. In that same year, the population of Duluth reached 90,000.

Duluth's growth during the early part of the 20th century was so explosive that many thought Duluth would eventually become one of the nation's great cities and rival, if not eclipse, Pittsburgh, Cleveland and Chicago. The scale and grandeur of many of the public and private buildings built during the early 20th century seemed to confidently express that expectation. Around the same time that he was completing work on his famous plan for Chicago, Daniel Burnham was commissioned by Marshall Alworth (a wealthy businessman who had made his fortune in real estate and iron ore) to design a "skyscraper" office building for the city's Board of Trade. When the 16-story Alworth Building was completed in 1910, it was the tallest building in the entire State of Minnesota; it is still the tallest building in Duluth.

Burnham was also hired to design Duluth's new county courthouse. Being a planner as well as an architect, Burnham gave careful consideration to the courthouse's location, and chose a site at 1st Street and 5th Avenue, just up the hill from the city's bustling train depot. Burnham did more than simply design a single public building. As a proponent of the "City Beautiful" movement,

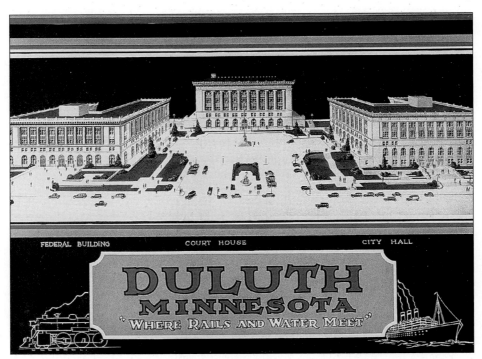

6-1   Illustration on the cover of a 1930s City of Duluth publication showing the Civic Center group of public buildings planned by Daniel Burnham. The St. Louis County courthouse is the center building. Duluth City Hall is the building on the right. The Federal Building is on the left.

Source: Courtesy of Thomas D. Cotruvo, City of Duluth Office of Business Development

Burnham believed that great cities should have monumental and classically designed public buildings, and that such buildings should be grouped around monumental public spaces to create a more orderly and uplifting urban environment. Toward that end, Burnham developed a plan that made the courthouse the centerpiece of the Civic Center complex (composed of three major public buildings grouped around a landscaped square) and called for a broad, landscaped parkway boulevard to lead down the hill from the Civic Center toward the bay.

Although it took many years, Burnham's vision was largely realized. The impressive and ornately designed new St. Louis County courthouse was completed in 1911 at a cost of $1 million—an astoundingly large sum at the time. Duluth City Hall, the easternmost building, was completed in 1928; the Federal Building, framing the west side of the square, was completed in 1930. The broad, landscaped boulevard designed by Burnham (now referred to as the 5th Avenue Mall) was constructed as part of a federally funded urban renewal project in the 1950s.

6-2   St. Louis County courthouse, overlooking landscaped greenspace framed by three major public buildings (1998).

Source: Gene Bunnell

All three public buildings that make up the Civic Center are still used for their originally intended purposes. The carefully tended and landscaped square framed by the three buildings (planted with flower beds, gardens and apple trees, which flower in spring) remains one of the most pleasant spaces in the downtown.

CREATING A DULUTH LANDMARK: THE DULUTH AERIAL LIFT BRIDGE

In their haste to capture the burgeoning amount of ship traffic on the Great Lakes, and make Duluth a major Great Lakes port, a canal was dug in 1870 through Minnesota Point (a 9-mile-long peninsula that extends out from Duluth into Lake Superior). The canal allowed ships to sail directly into Duluth's sheltered harbor (St. Louis Bay) instead of sailing all the way around the peninsula (and possibly diverting to port facilities in Superior, Wisconsin). As port traffic increased and the City of Duluth grew, however, the fact that Minnesota Point had been severed from the rest of the city became more and more of a problem. During the summer, ferries operated on a frequent basis, carrying passengers back and forth between the mainland and Minnesota Point; however, during the winter, when the lake and canal were frozen, people had to try to make their way on their own as best as they could over uneven, slippery and treacherous ice formations.

City engineers set about to try to devise a solution that would allow people to be transported between the city and Minnesota Point year-round, without interfering with or restricting the ability of ships to move through the ship canal. Their solution was a "Rube Goldberg" kind of structure. Two vertical steel towers were built on the opposite sides of the canal, and a long steel span was anchored to the tops of the two towers to span the canal. Embedded within this interconnecting span was a grooved track. A gondola was suspended by means of cables from the track, which could then move back and forth between the two sides of the canal. "Cars and pedestrians boarded at one side and the trolley [or gondola] slowly traveled across the channel to the other side. . . . During its first year, the bridge reportedly transported 33,000 people to and from Park Point on one summer day." (*ibid.*, 95)

As Duluth grew, and as automobile ownership and use increased, the ingenious gondola became increasingly inadequate. Because the capacity of the gondola was limited (a maximum of six cars at one time), and because increasing numbers of people in cars wanted to travel to and from Minnesota Point, the gondola system was unable to keep up with the demand and there were often long waiting lines and delays. Some kind of innovative lift bridge design was needed—one that would essentially reconnect Minnesota Point to the mainland (allowing cars and people to cross), and that could also be raised out of the way to allow ships to pass in and out of the harbor.

6-3   Ocean-going "salties" and Great Lakes freighters anchored outside the canal leading to St. Louis Bay, framed by the Duluth Aerial Lift Bridge.

Source: Jerry Bielicki

As it turned out, the perfect model that Duluth's bridge engineers found was in Rouen, France. In fact, the contraption that had been built in Duluth in 1905 already looked somewhat like the lift bridge in Rouen. After the side towers were raised and reinforced, and the suspended gondola that formerly ran from one end to the other was removed, a suspended roadway was constructed that could be raised (in a horizontal position) to allow ships to pass through the canal, and then be lowered back into place to allow cars and pedestrians to pass back and forth at ground level. That same remodeled Aerial Lift Bridge is still in operation today and, over the years, has become Duluth's best-known landmark, marking the gateway to the city's inner harbor like a giant erector set.

Although Duluth was shaped by many of the same forces that shaped the growth of other Great Lakes industrial cities, in at least one respect Duluth was (and is) very different from the other Great Lakes cities mentioned above. Duluth is a remarkably isolated city. Located at the extreme western end of the Great Lakes, Duluth is halfway between the east and west coasts and is the farthest inland seaport in the world (2,342 miles from the Atlantic Ocean).

To this day, very little urban development has occurred within the Lake Superior basin; vast areas of the upper peninsula of Michigan, northeastern Minnesota and southwest Ontario surrounding Duluth are either wilderness or very sparsely populated. Superior, Wisconsin (population 27,000) is just across the St. Louis River from Duluth. Otherwise, one has to travel a long way to reach another significant concentration of population and urban development. Minnesota's largest metropolitan area (Minneapolis-St. Paul) is 151 miles away, and St. Cloud (population 48,812) is 135 miles away. Thunder Bay, Ontario (population 113,700) is 122 miles to the east. The closest city of any appreciable size in Wisconsin is Eau Claire (1990 population 56,856), 157 miles to the south.

THE CITY'S DECLINE

After World War I and during the 1920s, the vulnerability of the city's economy began to be exposed. Duluth was highly dependent on a small number of commodities and industries (lumber, agricultural products and steel), which were highly cyclical and which were entering a prolonged period of decline.

"Located on the fringes of the American economy, Duluth . . . depended on the most unstable elements to provide it with an economic base: lumbering, mining, and the transshipment of agricultural commodities. The juxtaposition of these three unstable elements . . . contributed to the creation of a perpetually fluctuating local economy with a propensity to long-range decline." (Elazar 1965, 50)

The lumber industry had pretty well exhausted the lumber supply of the North Woods (as it had previously done in lower Michigan and New England), leading to a sharp decline in the volume of timber processed in Duluth sawmills and shipped through its port. There was the long, postwar agricultural depression, which began in the 1920s and intensified in the 1930s. "Settlers who had homesteaded millions of acres of marginal lands in Duluth's hinterland in the previous two decades were forced to abandon those lands as the bottom fell out of the wheat market." (*ibid.*, 53) As a result, less and less grain was being shipped out of Duluth. Iron ore operations on the Mesabi Range also leveled off during the 1920s and the railroads, which had conferred such importance on Duluth, began to move their operations to Minneapolis and St. Paul, making the Twin Cities the region's primary rail center.

Another underlying condition made Duluth's economic situation even more precarious. When businesses are headquartered in a city, they typically invest in, and have some commitment to, that city. However, from the beginning, Duluth's economy was dependent on and ruled by industries and companies that were headquartered in eastern industrial cities, notably Cleveland and Pittsburgh (even the three banks in the city at the turn of the century were absentee-owned). As a result, during its years of greatest prosperity, more money undoubtedly flowed out of Duluth to eastern cities than was retained and invested in Duluth. Likewise, many of the people in the private sector who could have exerted leadership were remarkably complacent as the city's economic situation worsened.

People did not realize it at the time, but the opening of the Panama Canal in 1914 probably sealed Duluth's fate and hastened its decline. Before the Panama Canal, the Port of Duluth was the preferred gateway to the western U.S. and ports in the Orient. The Northern Pacific Railroad built a railroad line directly from Duluth to the Pacific coast to capture that lucrative transportation market. However, once the Panama Canal was opened, transporting goods by rail to Buffalo, then on ships to Duluth, and then by rail to the west coast was no longer as attractive as simply having ships sail from east to west coast ports through the Panama Canal, without the time and expense of splitting transportation modes.

Even the completion of the Welland Canal in 1932 (allowing large ships to pass between Lake Erie and Lake Ontario), and the St. Lawrence Seaway in 1959 (which made it possible for ocean-going ships to reach Lake Ontario and sail halfway across the U.S. to Duluth) did not result in the increase of shipping activity that was anticipated and expected.[4] Goods shipped through Duluth on ocean-going "salties" bound for foreign ports account for only 15-20% of the total cargo handled by the port. As the amount of tonnage handled by major U.S. ports on the east and west coasts has grown, Duluth's ranking relative to other American ports has fallen.[5] Nevertheless, the fact remains that Duluth continues to handle more total tonnage of cargo, more iron ore and more grain than any other Great Lakes port.

6-4   Halfway between the east and west coasts, and 2,342 miles from the Atlantic Ocean, a Great Lakes freighter starts its long journey out of Duluth.

Source: Gene Bunnell

6-5   Downtown Duluth, nestled in along the shore of Lake Superior at the base of a steep escarpment. Much of the land within the city's municipal boundaries is urban wilderness.

Source: Gene Bunnell

Returning World War II veterans and the postwar building boom caused Duluth's population to increase to 104,500 and to reach an all-time high of 106,800 in 1960. However, production and employment at U.S. Steel Corporation's Morgan Park plant began to decline in the 1950s and, by the 1960s, a number of major industrial employers (Interlake Steel, Universal Atlas Cement and the Coolerator plant) closed down their Duluth operations. Between 1960 and 1970, the city's population fell 6% to 100,500. In 1971, U.S. Steel laid off 1,300 employees; not long thereafter, the entire plant was shut down. Between 1970 and 1980, Duluth's population fell another 8% to 92,800.

As domestic steel production fell, taconite plants on the Iron Range reduced production. In 1979, 14,400 people were employed at the eight taconite-producing facilities in the Iron Range. Just five years later (in 1984), employment in the Iron Range had fallen to around 7,300. (Olsen and Witzig 1984, 4) To make matters worse, grain shipments through the Port of Duluth likewise declined as farmers, faced with rising production costs and decreased prices for their goods, cut back on production and went bankrupt in growing numbers. By 1983, the unemployment rate in Duluth was over 16%, at a time when the unemployment rate in the state was 7.5%. In 1987, it was estimated that Duluth's population had fallen to 82,000—a drop of over 10% from 1980.

Many American central cities in the 1970s and 1980s were losing population but, in most cases, it was lost to the suburbs. Other "rust-belt" cities on the Great Lakes like Detroit, Cleveland and Buffalo lost population, but the populations of their respective metropolitan areas remained fairly steady. In Duluth, however, the population of the metropolitan area as a whole was in decline. "People were leaving the area entirely. We truly had a mass out-migration," said Darrell Lewis (manager of the City of Duluth Physical Planning Division).

A UNIQUE PLACE

Between 14,000 and 20,000 years ago, a huge, thick glacier extended down from Lake Superior that covered the upper two-thirds of what we now know as Wisconsin. When the glacier finally melted and receded (about 12,000-14,000 years ago), the vast quantities of water released by the glacier collected and formed the Great Lakes. Roughly 10,000 years ago, the biggest of these Great Lakes—Lake Superior—was 600 feet deeper than it is today. The water level of Lake Superior gradually dropped and left behind a rocky, 600- to 800-foot-high escarpment steeply sloping down to the lake's present level. The first settlers who arrived in Duluth built homes, sawmills, piers and commercial buildings at the base of this steep escarpment. Although the municipal boundaries of Duluth encompass a nearly 68-square-mile area, most of the heavily developed and settled area of the city today occupies a fairly narrow linear strip of land at the base of the escarpment, along the north shore of Lake Superior and the St. Louis Bay.

Over the course of a century's development, a series of separate communities evolved (Fond du Lac, New Duluth, Gary, Morgan Park, Smithville, Riverside, West Duluth, West End, Central Hillside, East Hillside, Endion, Congdon Park, Lakeside and Lester Park) like a string of pearls strung together along the shore of the lake.[6] In the 1960s, a second major strand of development began spreading out to the northwest along the Miller Hill Corridor (Route 53/194) in the direction of the airport. As a result of this second strand of development, the urban form of the city has come to resemble an upside-down "T," with the stem of the "T" tilted at approximately 45 degrees, running straight up and down the escarpment that overlooks and circumscribes the city's downtown and oldest neighborhoods.

As you drive into Duluth from the airport, you quickly appreciate the city's unique geography. Suddenly, you find yourself passing over the crest of the escarpment. Stretching out before you, far below, you see the harbor, grain elevators, iron ore loading piers, the downtown core area of Duluth, the Aerial Lift Bridge and Minnesota Point (the 9-mile-long peninsula extending out into the lake that is connected to the city's downtown by the Aerial Lift Bridge). You will also be able to see the City of Superior and the Wisconsin shoreline.

Approaching Duluth from the south, the view is very different but no less stunning. I will never forget my first glimpse of Duluth as I approached from the south at the end of a long drive from Madison, Wisconsin. The sun had set and there was a pinkish hue in the sky. A few miles south of Superior, I drove over the crest of a hill and saw a band of lights twinkling on the horizon. The texture of lights against a dark background was not unlike what one might see looking down from an airplane at night while flying over an urban area. However, in this case, the twinkling lights were not below me but directly in front, on a 600- to 800-foot-high escarpment that rose steeply and dramatically up from the shores of Lake Superior.

Words are not adequate to describe the qualities that make the geographic setting of Duluth so alluring and spellbinding. One of the most overused words in the English language is "beautiful"—a word we commonly use to describe the landscapes of places that visually appeal to us. It might therefore be said that Duluth, too, is beautiful, but the characteristics that make Duluth so striking are not the soft, sugar-coated qualities we normally associate with beautiful places. What makes Duluth so unique and entrancing is the ruggedness of the topography and surrounding environment, which contrasts so dramatically against the city's urban fabric.

Few cities have had to contend with the kind of impenetrable subsurface conditions and steep slopes that exist in Duluth. In many places, the linear pattern of urban development along the shoreline is interrupted by streams that flow down the escarpment to Lake Superior, through deep canyons and ravines that over thousands of years have been carved into the landscape. (This explains why Duluth began as a collection of discrete urban settlements, and why the various neighborhoods that make up the city—such as Morgan Park, West Duluth, West End, Central Hillside and East End—have retained their distinct identities.)

From the time Duluth was first settled, the most formidable physical (and psychological) barrier of all was the "Point of Rocks"—a rugged, rocky formation that extended from the escarpment in a southeasterly direction to almost the edge of the bay, thereby separating the West End and West Duluth from the city's downtown and neighborhoods to the east.

Even in areas of Duluth with the least geologic and topographic obstacles to development, building structures and laying infrastructure is typically difficult. Most water and sewer lines that have been laid in the city (and most structures with basements) have required rock blasting. There is also the complication of steep slopes. Avenues in Duluth run from the lake up the escarpment and most are built on very steep grades. 5th Avenue West, directly above the Duluth Civic Center, is the steepest street in the city (a 26% slope), but there are many other streets that are almost as steep.

The fact that avenues tend to intersect with the shoreline at a roughly 90-degree angle increases one's appreciation of the sloping terrain by continually drawing attention to the lake. Indeed, the layout of city streets seems intended to maximize the number of vantage points for looking out at the lake. Standing at the top of one of the many steep streets looking out toward Lake Superior, the visual effect is not unlike what one experiences in San Francisco looking down one of that city's steep streets toward San Francisco Bay. The climates of the two cities are very different, but the visual drama is very much the same!

THE PLANNING OF THE DULUTH
PARKWAY SYSTEM AND SKYLINE DRIVE

Sometimes when I become discouraged, I say to myself, "I should have gone to another city to seek my fortune." But when I look over these hills and see the great natural beauties of our community, I console myself and wonder, "Where in all this wide world could I find such a view as this?"

—SAMUEL F. SNIVELY (AS QUOTED FROM DULUTH
HERITAGE PRESERVATION COMMISSION, 1997, 1)

Everyone who lives in Duluth, and anyone who visits for any length of time, cannot help but recognize two outstanding features of the city: (1) the Skyline Parkway (a winding, 23-mile-long scenic road that runs through a continuous band of parkland at the top of the escarpment, high above the city and Lake Superior); and (2) the remarkably extensive Duluth parkway system.[7]

According to an unpublished history written in the mid-1970s by Charles Aguar, the person who first proposed the idea of creating a Skyline Parkway (or "Terrace Drive," as it was first called) was William K. Rogers, the president of the city's Public Works Commission. Rogers came up with the idea around 1887, when the City of Duluth was first organized as a city. Aguar wrote that the parkway Rogers envisioned "was not an isolated project, but part of a brilliant plan for the city's open space system." (City of Duluth Department of Research and Planning 1977, unpublished)

Indeed, the hilltop parkway provided the backbone for the Duluth parkway system. There were four parts to Rogers' plan: (1) a hilltop parkway widening into occasional parks; (2) lakefront and bayfront parks joined by parkways; (3) park strips connecting the hillside and waterfront systems; and (4) supplementary playgrounds and community parks.

"Rogers emphasized an urban park system that established linkage between open spaces. It was a flexible plan that did not require extensive expenditures and allowed for dynamic growth that could respond to changing urban patterns without changing the basic concept." (*ibid.*) Rogers personally supervised the construction of a key section of the Terrace Parkway between Lincoln and Chester Parks and, according to Aguar, deserves to be remembered as the "father" of the Duluth parkway system. (*ibid.*)

Two former mayors of the city were also closely associated with the development of the Duluth parkway system and deserve considerable credit as well. Clarence R. Magney was Duluth's mayor from 1917 through 1920 and, during that short time, managed to add 1,433 acres to the city's park system. Samuel F. Snively followed Magney as mayor and, over the course of the 16 consecutive years he held that office (from 1921 until 1937), he made expansion of the city's park system and completion of Skyline Parkway the centerpiece of his administration. Snively was a genius at raising private funds for the acquisition of parklands and the right of way for Skyline Parkway. During his term, both ends of the present Skyline Parkway—as well as the Mission Creek extension begun by Magney and the Snively Boulevard portion of the parkway in the east—were completed. (*ibid.*)

Mayor Snively took an active role in acquiring land, and in planning and designing the parkway system. According to Aguar, Snively personally supervised construction of 20 miles of the scenic parkway "at times walking ahead of the horseteams while establishing grades for new alignments." (*ibid.*) Snively made sure that lookouts and observation points were strategically placed to provide attractive views of the lake, forests and the city below. He also had a hand in designing the bridges that were needed to span the creeks and ravines along the course of the parkway, and specified that they be built of stone (because stone was indigenous to the region and would survive long into the future). The stone bridges of the Duluth Parkway were originally built in the

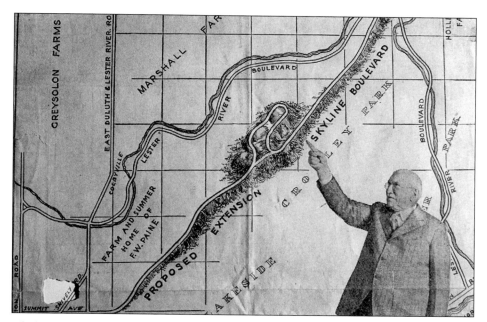

6-6   Illustration depicting Mayor Samuel F. Snively pointing to a map showing the proposed extension of Skyline Boulevard.

Source: Reprinted with permission from the *Duluth News-Tribune*

6-7   One of the stone bridges along Skyline Parkway, in 1998.

Source: Gene Bunnell

1930s under the Works Progress Administration (WPA) and are now listed on the National Register of Historic Places.

Snively's vision of a network of parks and forests surrounding the city encouraged a number of large gifts of land to the city from wealthy landowners. The Hartley Field property (donated to the city by the Hartley family in the 1930s) provides a large, open space resource area with nature and hiking trails (cross-country ski trails in winter) and an informal nature center.

Another major private gift of protected land in the 1930s, which significantly enlarged the city's parkway system, was made by Bert Enger, a Norwegian immigrant who made his fortune in the furniture business. Enger donated two-thirds of his hilltop estate to the City of Duluth as a park, and embellished the gift by constructing Enger Tower—an octagonal stone tower with an internal winding staircase leading to an observation level, which affords a panoramic view of Duluth and the harbor. Enger Park, restored and improved in the 1980s, is one of the most beautiful parks in the city today. "The many flower beds, brilliant with color in the summer, along with the frilly wooden gazebo, give the park a civilized air. People get married here, or come here for family reunions, or just sit and daydream in quiet reflection." (Hertzel 1993, 8-9) Down the road from Enger Park is Enger Park Golf Course—a 27-hole, hilltop golf course carved out of the woods, which offers many captivating views of the harbor.

Another noteworthy and extraordinary private gift of land to the city for open space preservation was made by Chester Congdon, an attorney who made his wealth working for the mining companies that operated in the region. As a result of Congdon's gift of land, the city owns miles of shoreline property between Congdon Parkway and Lake Superior.

MAKING PLANNING AN ESSENTIAL FUNCTION OF LOCAL GOVERNMENT

During Snively's tenure as mayor, city planning came to be recognized as an important function of city government. In 1926, the city hired its first city planner, A. B. Horowitz, who oversaw the completion of the city's first comprehensive plan in 1928 and a major updating of the city's zoning ordinance.[8]

John Hunner became Duluth's second planning director in 1944, and served in the position for 23 years (until 1967). Under Hunner's direction, the city prepared and completed a second comprehensive plan in 1958, which called for confining future development largely to previously developed areas and for preserving large areas of open space beyond. Pursuant to the recommendations of the 1958 comprehensive plan, a major rezoning of the city was accomplished, which included the adoption of an altogether new zoning category: "S-Suburban." (The importance of S-Suburban zoning in preserving open space in Duluth is discussed further later in this chapter.)

Another very important event occurred in 1958: the passage of a new city charter establishing a strong mayor form of government. Prior to this charter revision, Duluth had a commission form of government and had been governed by a board of commissioners.

MAJOR PROJECTS AIMED AT
REVERSING THE CITY'S DECLINE

During the 1950s and 1960s, Duluth suffered so many closures in the manufacturing wholesale and retail sectors that it almost became a backwater. People here and elsewhere saw it as a city in decline!

—Frederick T. Witzig

Urban Renewal

As in other cities, large-scale, federally funded highway and urban renewal clearance projects were undertaken in Duluth in the 1960s in an attempt to reverse the city's decline. A major interstate highway extension of I-35 into Duluth was planned, engineered and built by the Minnesota Department of Transportation (MNDOT) and was largely funded with federal highway money. (The impacts of the I-35 extension on West Duluth are discussed later in this chapter.)

Urban renewal clearance projects were also carried out by the city's federally funded Housing and Redevelopment Agency (HRA). Indeed, the HRA was the highest funded agency in the city—the one city agency that had sufficient money at its disposal to do essentially whatever it wanted. The staff of the HRA included Bob Reichardt, who had previously worked for Harland Bartholomew's planning consulting firm on the preparation of the city's 1958 comprehensive plan. The problem was that the HRA was entirely independent from the city's professional planning staff in city hall and from the Duluth Planning Commission.

Two major urban renewal clearance projects were carried out under the direction of the HRA. The first involved the clearance of the St. Croix District—an area of warehouses, docks, scrap yards and miscellaneous structures along the city's waterfront. William Majewski, who has worked as a planner for the City of Duluth for over 30 years, recalled that, when he first moved to Duluth in 1965, the Arena Auditorium had just been built on land that had been cleared in the St. Croix District. (The construction of the Arena Auditorium, which was funded largely by an EDA grant, was at the time one of the most expensive publicly funded projects ever undertaken in Duluth.) However, most of the remaining cleared land was left vacant for many years.

A second urban renewal clearance project (the Gateway) was undertaken in the mid-1960s in the area between the bay and the Burnham-designed Civic

Center. In the 1970s, another large city block was demolished to build an enclosed downtown shopping mall, structured parking and a hotel (currently a Holiday Inn).[9] One building that fortunately wasn't cleared away was the old Duluth Union Depot (circa 1892), a French chateau-style structure designed by the Boston architectural firm of Peabody and Stearns.

The Interstate 35 Extension

Throughout Duluth's history, the massive rock outcropping that extended from the escarpment to the lake—known as the "Point of Rocks"—had marked a major dividing line in Duluth, separating the western half of the city (largely blue-collar and industrial neighborhoods) from the eastern half (the downtown core and the largely white-collar, middle- and upper-class neighborhoods). However, in the 1950s, state highway engineers developed a plan that called for extending Interstate 35 into Duluth by blasting through and obliterating the Point of Rocks.

Extending and constructing I-35 into the city had a devastating effect on abutting neighborhoods. "The Oneota neighborhood of West Duluth was literally ripped apart by the freeway," said planner James E. Mohn. In the 1960s and 1970s, residential structures and neighborhood businesses were demolished, and at least 114 household residents were forced to move. Excess property acquired in the process of clearing the path for the freeway was transferred to the city and is now the Oneota Industrial Park. "West Duluth has yet to fully recover from the impact of the highway construction," said Mohn. "The scars are still there."

At the time I-35 was extended into the city through West Duluth, highway engineers had intended that the highway would be extended completely through the city, although the exact route the highway would take had not yet been decided.[10] A glimpse of the path that the I-35 extension might have taken through the city was provided in a 1967 document with the innocuous title of "Shore Protection Study."

Had the MNDOT succeeded in building the freeway the way they wanted, I-35 would have usurped every bit of the city's waterfront and permanently separated the city from the lake. Public access to the lake would have been completely cut off. The impact the proposed freeway would have had on the downtown and on East Side neighborhoods would have been equally dire.

MNDOT's proposed plan for the I-35 extension was finally completed and ready for construction in the early 1970s. With millions of dollars of federally and state-funded construction jobs at stake, there was considerable pressure on the city to accept the plan. Consequently, the mayor and a majority of city council members acquiesced and voiced little or no opposition. However, residents of city neighborhoods did speak out and filed suit against the federal government and MNDOT. Federal money for building the highway had already been reserved, but nothing got built because the project was hung up in court for years.

Establishing the University of Minnesota at Duluth

There was, however, one major development project undertaken in the 1950s and 1960s that unquestionably had a positive impact on Duluth: the establishment and building of the University of Minnesota at Duluth (UMD). There is an interesting planning story behind the development of the UMD campus.

Before the UMD campus existed, there was a State Teachers College in Duluth. The first building of the Duluth Normal School, as it was called, was built in 1898 on a site at 6th Street and 22nd Avenue East. Around 1946-47, a movement was initiated by local business leaders seeking the establishment of a full-fledged university in Duluth. University proponents drafted legislation (and got it passed by the state legislature) that authorized the establishment of a branch campus of the state university in Duluth.

Interestingly enough, Duluth's first city planner, A. B. Horowitz, had already recognized the desirability of having a university in Duluth and many years

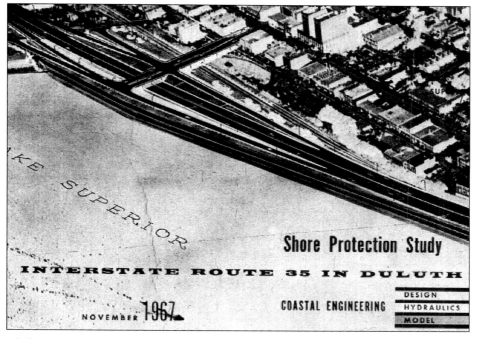

6-8 Illustration showing what highway engineers originally intended the extension of Interstate 35 through downtown Duluth to look like. The illustration was contained in a 1967 document innocuously dubbed the "Shore Protection Study."

Source: Thomas D. Cotruvo, City of Duluth Office of Business Development

earlier had assembled land for a university campus. According to Daniel J. Elazar, "The city planner was a man of vision who foresaw the needs of the civil community and not only drew up plans for their implementation but put the city government in a position to implement those plans." (Elazar 1965, 60) Accordingly, he "acquired and set aside land for the new campus of the University of Minnesota . . . in the 1930s, holding [it] in readiness against the time that [it] would be needed for just [that] purpose." (*ibid.*) (Horowitz also reserved and set aside land for public projects such as schools, parks, playgrounds and fire stations, as well as for the development and expansion of the city's port facilities.)

The actions Horowitz took greatly facilitated and sped up the development of the UMD campus in the heart of the city. Had land not been reserved ahead of time for the university campus, the development of the university would undoubtedly have been delayed, and there is a good chance that the university would have been much less well located. The site Horowitz reserved for the new university campus was only three-quarters of a mile from the old Duluth Normal School. Construction of the first university buildings began around 1947 and the first faculty began arriving in 1948.[11]

Among the many new faculty people who came in the early 1950s to teach at UMD (and who stayed) were Frederick T. Witzig (a geographer) and Dale Olsen (a political scientist). Witzig and Olsen went on to set up an interdisciplinary urban and regional studies degree program at UMD and, over the years, it was common for students enrolled in that program to work as interns on various specific planning projects and processes. (Student involvement in connection with the preparation of plans for the Duluth waterfront and West Duluth is noted in later portions of this chapter.)

A Major Political Commitment to Strengthening Local Planning Capacity

Between the end of the 1960s and the end of the 1990s, Duluth had four mayors: Ben Boo was elected mayor in 1967 and served in the office until 1974; Robert Beaudin was Duluth's mayor from 1974 through 1979; Beaudin was followed by John Fedo, who was Duluth's mayor between 1980 and 1992; Gary L. Doty was elected mayor in 1992 and still held office in 2000. There were important planning accomplishments during the terms of all four mayors. With the benefit of hindsight, however, it is clear that the actions Ben Boo took—in terms of increasing the city's commitment to planning, and in recruiting a handful of skilled and dedicated professional planners—laid the foundation for the significant municipal accomplishments that were achieved during the terms of the three mayors who held office after him.

"When I became mayor, there was no planning department," remembered Ben Boo. "There was just one gentleman—a very competent architect—who held the position of city planner, and that was it. It seemed to me that if we were going to get anything going and achieve positive changes in the city, it had to be by doing more planning." Selling planning to the council, however, was nearly impossible. "They wouldn't accept anything unless it involved bricks and mortar," continued Boo. Consequently, Boo attempted to conceal what he was doing by creating a departmental structure—and four new staff positions—that was only indirectly and secondarily associated with planning.

Boo's new department was called the Department of Research and Planning, and he named Donn Wiski as the director. Within the new department, there were three divisions—one of which was the Division of Current Planning (later renamed the Physical Planning Division). Under Wiski's direction, a search was undertaken to fill the physical planning position that was vacated when John Hunner retired. Jerry Kimball, an architecture and planning graduate who was working in St. Paul at the time, was hired. Kimball was attracted to living in a city close to the Boundary Waters canoeing area of northern Minnesota, and ended up working as Duluth's chief physical planner for 26 years (from 1968 until 1995).

"I threw a lot of planning stuff into the budget as 'projects' and 'programs,'" recalled Boo. "It sounds like subterfuge, but it was necessary. It was important that the members of the city council not pick up the city budget and see the names of these people listed under the heading of 'Planning,' but that's what they were doing."

When Jerry Kimball first started working in Duluth in 1968, the most hotly debated land use issue was billboards. "The League of Women Voters was pushing the idea that there were too many billboards and that a billboard ordinance was needed," Kimball told me. "I identified a number of important scenic views and viewsheds that needed protection, and drafted an ordinance prohibiting billboards in those districts. When the ordinance went before the city council for a vote, it lost 2 to 1, but we didn't give up. Every five or six years, we would get everyone organized and submit it again. We finally got a fairly tough ordinance onto the books. Many billboards were removed through attrition and by special purchases by the city over the years. As a result, instead of seeing one billboard after another, you can enjoy clear, unobstructed views of the lake. I feel very proud of that accomplishment."

In 1969, UMD faculty member Fred Witzig was appointed by Ben Boo to the Duluth Planning Commission and served as a member of the commission until 1983. Fred Witzig recollected how contentious things were back then, and how difficult it was to get members of the city council to recognize the importance of planning. "I'll never forget my first meeting as a member of the Duluth Planning Commission in 1969. After a public hearing, the first thing on the agenda was a proposed resolution, which the commission went on to approve, which declared that the members of the commission were going to resign *en masse*

6-9   People looking out from atop the escarpment at ships waiting to make their way through the Ship Canal, and under the Aerial Lift Bridge, into the sheltered docking facilities along St. Louis Bay.

Source: Sam Alvar, Seaquest Photo

unless the city council began to take the commission's recommendations more seriously."

Relations with the council flared again in the 1970s and the commission passed another resolution. "The Duluth Planning Commission resolved that if the city council was going to overrule us on zoning and land use policy matters that, out of common courtesy, we wanted to know *why,*" Witzig recalled. "The resolution wasn't altogether successful. The city council often avoided explaining their actions because, in their minds, the issues being considered were *political* in nature. However, passing the resolution did help somewhat stem the flow of reversals and improve our relationship with the council. Most members of the commission firmly believed we were adhering to fundamental principles of good planning, and saw the resolution as a way of registering our hope that the council would pay greater attention to those same principles."

Up to that point, "People were building houses on 'paper streets' (not shown on any official city maps) that no one knew existed, and often put more than one house on a lot," said Witzig. If they applied for permission from the Duluth Planning Commission, it was often as an afterthought.

"I can recall coming to a Duluth Planning Commission meeting during my first years as a member and looking out toward the harbor from a window in the hearing room of city hall," Witzig remembered. "I noticed that a rectangular portion of the bay had been separated off with rock material to create a small boat basin. I looked again at the meeting agenda and packet of explanatory material describing petitions and requests, and sure enough, there it was: a request for a permit to do the very thing that I saw out in the lake. We were being asked to approve something that was already constructed!"

Gradually things began to change. As the professionalism of the city's new planning staff began to rub off on the new members of the Duluth Planning Commission, the planning commissioners began to expect and insist that property owners and developers abide by the city's land use and zoning regulations. According to Witzig, "The new members of the commission read all the staff reports and asked a lot of questions. When we went on a site visit, they'd ask Jerry Kimball and/or Tom Cotruvo a lot of questions, and then the next day at the public hearing, they'd ask the questions again. It was an exciting time. There was a sense that things were changing. We had leadership at the staff level, and planning commissioners were developing a better understanding and appreciation of sound land use and zoning principles."

When Ben Boo took office, much of the western side of the downtown that had been cleared away by the HRA was still vacant and undeveloped. In a move designed to energize the redevelopment of the downtown, and diminish the independence of the HRA, Boo and his staff established a downtown planning function within city hall and good things began to happen. Among the physical developments completed during Boo's term were the construction of the new Duluth Public Library (a modern structure with an elongated form that resembles a Great Lakes freighter), the development of a new downtown (Radisson) hotel, and the restoration of the old Duluth Union Depot and its conversion into a museum of local history.

Another important downtown planning initiative undertaken during Boo's term in office was the Central Hillside Model City program, which was developed and carried out under the direction of planner Mark Flaherty, a former assistant to John Hunner. Duluth, in fact, was one of the first two cities in the country to apply for Model Cities designation, placing it very much on the cutting edge.

As Kimball pointed out, "The Central Hillside Model City program was designed to provide coordinated decision-making for an array of programs in a depressed neighborhood, ranging from day care and 'Meals on Wheels,' to residential rehabilitation and street reconstruction, and much more. Seventy-five projects were initiated under the Model City program, all but one of which continue today."

6-10   The Duluth Public Library.

Source: Gene Bunnell

6-11   The old Duluth Union Depot, preserved and reused to house the St. Louis County Heritage and Arts Center.

Source: Gene Bunnell

The city also started planning and building enclosed skywalks connecting commercial buildings and activity centers in the downtown. Not all planners think building skywalks is a good idea, since they can produce a downtown that is less lively at street level. However, if skywalks make sense anywhere, they certainly do in a northern city like Duluth, where it can be bitterly cold for prolonged periods of time during the winter. "We started building the skywalks during my administration, and every mayor since then has carried it on," said Ben Boo.

In 1972, Boo hired Dick Loraas to succeed Donn Wiski as the city's director of the Department of Research and Planning. Like Wiski before him, Loraas had a strong background in planning. He allowed Jerry Kimball to operate the Physical Planning Division largely as he saw fit, with close coordination but a minimum of direct day-to-day supervision.[12]

Loraas headed the Department of Research and Planning until 1980 and, throughout the years that Robert Beaudin was Duluth's mayor (1974-1979), a close working relationship developed between Loraas and Beaudin. Under Beaudin and Loraas' leadership, a workable compromise was achieved regarding the alignment and design of the bitterly opposed and long-delayed downtown freeway. Loraas facilitated a citizens committee, consisting of people active in fighting both for and against the project. The creative design solutions

6-12   Downtown skywalks that span Superior Street, part of a downtown circulation system that began to be planned and built in the late 1960s and 1970s.

Source: Gene Bunnell

that were worked out through this process made the freeway a connector (rather than a barrier) to the lake. (For a further description of the final compromise plan, see the section titled "The Downtown Waterfront Plan and Strategy.") Beaudin and Loraas also positioned the city to be able to use the money freed up by de-designating the interstate freeway stretch east of 26th Avenue East for downtown skywalks, parks and pathways.

Another outcome achieved by Beaudin and Loraas was the expansion of the downtown skywalk system, including a 1,600-foot extension (called the Northwest Passage) linking downtown hotels and commercial buildings to the Duluth Entertainment and Convention Center (DECC) (formerly called the Arena Auditorium). The Northwest Passage, which was completed in 1976, was initially conceived for the convenience of out-of-town people attending conventions, meetings and trade shows at the DECC who were staying in downtown hotels. However, the Northwest Passage has also proven to be a major amenity for local residents. "You should see it in the wintertime in the morning, and between 11 AM and 2 PM other times during the year. It's full of people walking for exercise," said Jerry Kimball.

Other cities (like Minneapolis, Minnesota) have skywalks linking buildings, so the fact that Duluth has skywalks does not make the city unique. What *is* noteworthy about Duluth's skywalks is that they were planned to operate as a *system* of downtown pedestrian circulation, and to interconnect most major buildings and activity centers in the downtown area.

Building Upon Rogers' Parkway Plan

The real and lasting power of a plan lies in the power of its ideas. There is no other explanation why William K. Rogers' four-part plan, calling for the establishment and preservation of an extensive network of parks, exerted such a powerful force in shaping land use plans and policies in Duluth over more than seven decades to the present day.

As noted earlier, major additions to the city's park system, and Skyline Parkway, were accomplished between 1917 and 1937 by augmenting public land purchases and actively soliciting gifts of land from wealthy landowners and business leaders. However, in the 1930s and 1940s, two new tools for protecting land for conservation emerged. In 1933, a Minnesota state law was passed that authorized the zoning of land for "Municipal Forests." In the 1940s, Clarence Magney (the former Duluth mayor who, by then, had become a district judge) drafted a law that gave cities like Duluth the authority to withhold certain tax-forfeited lands for conservation purposes.[13] That law, applied in combination with the zoning of land for municipal forests, provided planners and planning commission members in Duluth with an effective way of enlarging the city's open space system and conservation land holdings.

Under Minnesota law, if a property owner is delinquent in paying property taxes for a period of three or more years, ownership of that property reverts to the state. After a reasonable period of time, the state can then proceed to sell the property at auction and keep the proceeds from the sale. During the interim period, before tax-forfeited properties are put out to auction, they are managed by the counties in which they are located. The law, drafted by Judge Magney and enacted in 1944, gave cities like Duluth the authority to intervene in the process to prevent the auctioning of tax-forfeited properties deemed to have conservation value.

Taking full advantage of the provisions of the 1944 law, for over 55 years the Duluth Planning Commission has reviewed lists of tax-forfeited properties on a regular basis, and has recommended that certain of those properties on the list (particularly those in areas zoned "Municipal Forest") be "withheld from sale" and dedicated for conservation. In practice, the law has allowed the city to "hold" and set aside any land that the Duluth Planning Commission decides might be needed in the future for some public purpose.[14]

In his unpublished manuscript, Charles Aguar writes, "Using the tax-forfeited land law, Duluth has assembled more than 9000 acres of land that is too steep, of excessive rock content, beyond utility limits or otherwise unsuitable for urban development. The total acreage in permanent open space now amounts to almost a quarter of the incorporated area. Of the forest parks, about a third of the land is owned by the City in fee title, having been conveyed by the state, while the remaining are tax-forfeited conservation lands. Recommendations for conservation lands were originally made by the City Planning Commission in 1943 with advice from the Citizen Planning Association, 150 citizens representing about 70 local organizations. In addition to the forest parks, lands were withheld for other public purposes, including flood protection, watershed management, expansion of the UMD campus, reservations for future schools, beach access, and for the consolidation of communications towers in the Central Hillside area." (City of Duluth Department of Research and Planning 1977, unpublished)

The last use of tax-forfeited conservation land listed above (the consolidation of communications towers) I believe requires some explanation. In the 1940s, the Federal Aviation Agency came up with the idea of encouraging cities to cluster radio and television broadcast towers in one area, as opposed to allowing them to be placed in scattered locations that would increase the hazard to airplanes. Because of Duluth's success in acquiring tax-forfeited land for conservation, it was one of the few cities in the country that succeeded in implementing the scheme. During the day, the clustered antennas are hardly noticeable, but if you look up behind the Burnham-designed Civic Center at night, the blinking red lights of the clustered antennas will be very visible along the ridge of the escarpment.[15]

Another conservation goal that the city achieved by withholding state tax-forfeited land from sale has been the protection and maintenance of views of the city and the lake from Skyline Parkway. "Whenever any land became tax-forfeited along the lower side of Skyline Parkway, the Duluth Planning Commission recommended that the land be withheld from sale and reserved for conservation," said Kimball.

The city-wide 1958 comprehensive plan prepared under the supervision of John Hunner (the planning director at that time) went even further in seeking to expand conservation land holdings. Large areas of the city recommended for conservation—existing publicly owned and tax-forfeited property held in conservation, and large areas of adjoining privately owned land—were shown on maps in the plan as "Municipal Forest." The plan also called for the creation of a new zoning district, called "S-Suburban," and for placing all land designated as "Municipal Forest," and private lands outside the existing network of sewer and water infrastructure, in the S-Suburban zone. Within this S-Suburban zone, only single-family detached homes were allowed, and the minimum lot size was set at 5 acres—a density 30 times lower than what was allowed in other standard residential zones. Although 5-acre minimum lot zoning has been adopted in rural communities and prosperous suburban communities, it is virtually unheard of in cities with declining populations of Duluth's size, age and character.

In suburban communities and rural areas which *have* adopted 5-acre minimum zoning in an apparent attempt to preserve open space, the measure has almost always backfired and accelerated sprawl. However, in Duluth, it *did* preserve open space because of Duluth's depressed economy, weak housing market and rocky substrata. If developers had been able to build at higher densities, they might have been able to justify the expense of blasting through rock to extend water and sewer lines to new development; however, they couldn't justify that expense when they could only build one home per 5 acres.

When Jerry Kimball came to Duluth in 1968 to direct the city's Physical Planning Division, it did not take him long to realize that this gritty, struggling city had something special that hardly any other American city had: a greenbelt of pristine forests and conservation lands that completely enveloped the city. The term "greenbelt" never appeared in any official city plan, but it was very much on Kimball's mind as he worked with the Duluth Planning Commission to identify tax-forfeited property that should be held in conservation.

The Duluth Planning Commission established a permanent "standing committee" whose sole responsibility was to review lists of tax-forfeited property on a quarterly basis, and identify parcels of environmental and scenic importance and/or that could serve a long-term public purpose if set aside for conservation. That subcommittee's recommendations were then brought to the full Duluth Planning Commission which, in most cases, affirmed its recommendations. The Duluth Planning Commission's recommendations were then forwarded to the city council, and then on to the Board of County Commissioners, which is required to honor the city's action. After these steps have been taken, the list of protected tax-title properties goes back to the County Land Office, which manages the land for the state.

From time to time, petitions were submitted requesting that the Duluth Planning Commission allow certain tax-forfeited lands previously "withheld from sale" and set aside for conservation, to be released for sale and development. According to Fred Witzig, "petitioners came before the commission and often made extremely passionate appeals. Sometimes, the commission did agree to release lands from conservation, but there had to be a good reason for doing so—greater than to simply serve the financial interests of a private individual. Jerry took this responsibility very seriously, and would continually remind us to think carefully before agreeing to release tax-forfeited land from conservation. He would say, 'You may think there is no need to keep this land in conservation now, but you don't really know for sure because you don't know what the future holds. Don't give it up if you think there may be a public use down the line. Think carefully, because once it is released, [the city] won't ever be able to buy it back.'"

At these hearings, Jerry Kimball was often the only person who was there to speak *against* releasing land from conservation. "Who else was going to look out and speak up for the public interest—and the interest of the public that will come on the scene long after we're gone?" Witzig noted.

Being an advocate for the interests of future generations (as opposed to taking positions that benefited people who had an immediate financial interest in acquiring and developing tax-forfeited property) did not increase Kimball's popularity with Duluth's real estate, development and business communities. Builders, realtors and local business people often said that Kimball and the city's planning department were *against* development, and that keeping so much land out of development was making it difficult to develop housing in the city.

In May 1976, an article appeared in the *Duluth Budgeteer* that detailed the concerns of a group called the "Duluth Let Us Grow Committee" related to the lack of growth and development in the city. According to the group, the main reason for the city's slow growth was the application of "unreasonable planning and zoning standards" by the city's Physical Planning Division. (*Duluth Budgeteer,* May 5, 1976) The criticism was deemed serious enough at the time that, on May 11, 1976, the Duluth Planning Commission passed a resolution expressing its "confidence in the Planning staff by commending them for their excellent record of impartial interpretation and administration of city ordinances relating to matters of planning and zoning." The Duluth Planning Commission's resolution did not put the matter to rest.

"Another time, there was a big flap in the newspapers to the effect that the Physical Planning Division was restricting development. The newspaper was particularly critical of Jerry," said Witzig. "He had a set of principles he adhered to and defended, and often took quite a lot of heat for his positions. I used to say to him, 'Jerry, how in the world do you take it?'"

The charge that the policies of the Physical Planning Division and Duluth Planning Commission were the reason why so little development was occurring in Duluth was a bit of an exaggeration. As planner Bill Majewski put it, "There wasn't a whole lot being built in Duluth because we weren't growing. If we built 30 or 40 houses in the city, that was a boom for us. There were years when we only built half a dozen new homes. That was all. There weren't a lot of things changing."

To counter the charge that zoning policies were overly restrictive, the Physical Planning Division carried out a study that identified all the vacant developable parcels of land outside of the S-Suburban zone where new housing could be built. The study found that there was enough open land outside the S-Suburban zone to accommodate 7,000 housing units. At the rate at which new housing was being built in Duluth, that represented at least a 50-year supply of developable land.

Over a 70-year period, more than 20,000 acres of wilderness, forests and conservation land have been preserved *within the city limits* of Duluth; 35% of the land is undeveloped and 50% of all the land in the S-Suburban zone (which encompasses the area designated in the 1958 comprehensive plan as "Municipal Forest") is publicly owned. The scale of the conservation land holdings in relation to the city's population is truly impressive. As senior planner, Jill Fisher, rightly pointed out, "Duluth's parkway system—which stretches 30 miles—is on a par with Chicago's lakefront park system, but Duluth is only a fraction of the size of Chicago."

Some who read this chapter might be inclined to minimize the significance of the open space network that has been created and preserved in Duluth, and assume that it was relatively easy to increase the city's conservation land holdings because the city's population decreased. I would argue that Duluth's success in preserving forests and wilderness areas is all the more remarkable given the fact that the city has not grown.

An examination of American history teaches us that environmental and natural resources have typically been most at risk—and wasted—in places and during times when such resources are regarded as plentiful. As William H. Whyte observed in *The Last Landscape*, "The less of our landscape there is to save, the better our chances of saving it. It is a shame to have to lose so much land to learn the lesson, but desecration does seem to be a prerequisite for action." (Whyte 1968, 2) When you consider the truth of what Whyte was saying, Duluth's success in preserving forests, wilderness areas and parks within the city's borders is even more exemplary. Duluth's conservation land holdings did not increase simply because the city did not grow. Farsighted plans were developed and actions were taken to protect large tracts of land in conservation at a time when people could well have argued that there was no need to do so.

Midway through my time in Duluth, Jerry Kimball took me on a drive around the perimeter of the city. We drove east out London Road (Route 61) and, at Lester Park, headed north on Seven Bridges Road (named for the seven stone bridges built by the WPA) as we made our way up the escarpment.[16] After about 2 miles of climbing and negotiating one sharp curve after another along Seven Bridges Road, we reached the top of the escarpment and turned left (west) onto Skyline Parkway. After driving along a stretch of gravel road that hugged the cliff, we reached an area known as Hawk Ridge, where Jerry pulled over and parked the car so we could get out and take in the view. "In the fall, the hawk migrations here are unbelievable," Kimball declared. "According to bird watchers, this is the second best place in the country for watching hawks—the first being a ridge in Pennsylvania."

The place where we were standing was roughly 700 feet above the level of Lake Superior, which was about a mile away. "I've been here 30 years and I'm still amazed by the constantly changing patterns and colors on the lake," said

6-13   Former Duluth planner Jerry Kimball at Hawk Ridge, looking out over the wilderness land in the Duluth greenbelt toward Lake Superior.

Source: Gene Bunnell

Kimball. The view of the lake was truly breathtaking. It was made even more beautiful by the lush green landscape that spread out in all directions below us.

"Isn't it amazing?" Kimball asked. "Here we are, in the middle of the city, and we're standing in the midst of forest and wilderness. I'm convinced that the acquisition and protection of land for conservation and parks have done as much as anything to define the city and make it a special place."

THE BIG STORM AND THE MILLER HILL CORRIDOR PLAN

During the 1950s and 1960s, a considerable amount of highway-oriented development began to occur on top of the escarpment along the Miller Trunk Highway and Central Entrance Highway (the state highway that leads northwest out from the center of the city to the airport and the Iron Range) in the area known as "Duluth Heights." The largest single development that occurred along the corridor was the Miller Hill Mall (an enclosed shopping mall on a 40-acre site surrounded by paved parking). "They blasted away part of a hillside to fit the mall in there," said planner Jim Mohn. The first Target store in Minnesota was built along the Miller Hill Corridor in the middle or late 1960s—a huge, "big-box" retail store that was also surrounded by acres of paved parking. "They filled in a large area of wetlands to build the parking lot for that store and re-routed Miller Creek. Miller Creek went from being a blue-ribbon trout stream to a muddy, narrow drainage ditch," recalled Mohn.

As the name Duluth Heights suggests, the area where all this highway-oriented commercial development took place was at a much higher elevation than the rest of the city and, as every plumber and homeowner knows, water runs downhill. On August 20, 1972, a major storm took place in Duluth that is supposed to occur only once in a hundred years. Water, which in the past would have been absorbed by wetlands, began sheeting off the rocky subsurface and the hundreds of acres of paved surfaces.

Creeks, streams and drainage ditches leading from the Miller Hill Corridor quickly filled with water and began cascading downhill. Unfortunately, a number of individual property owners had decided over the years to cover over the streams with various types of planking and build over them. When the huge rainstorm hit in 1972, and massive amounts of water started surging down the streambeds, a disaster was in the making. "Everything that was built over the streams just blew off. It all erupted," Ben Boo remembered.

A powerful surge of stormwater runoff carrying tons of silt and debris flowed down the escarpment, burying the business district of West Duluth under 2 feet of mud and muck; another major surge of stormwater, silt and debris was carried down Brewery Creek. The powerful surge of stormwater also caused a devastating amount of erosion along the way. (Along 6th Avenue East, the surging stormwater runoff left behind a 14-foot-deep hole and all of the material gouged out along the way wound up at the bottom of the hill.)

6-14 Target store parking lot in Miller Hill area during August 20, 1972 flood.

Source: Jerry Kimball

6-15 Erosion damage sustained along 1st Avenue West, looking up the hill from 4th Street after the August 20, 1972 flood.

Source: Jerry Kimball

When the flood occurred, Ben Boo was Duluth's mayor, Wendell Anderson was Minnesota's governor and Walter "Fritz" Mondale was a state senator. A news photo taken in the aftermath of the flood, published in the *Duluth Herald* on August 22, 1972, showed Mayor Boo, Governor Anderson, Walter Mondale and federal disaster relief officials standing on the edge of a deep crevice in the Central Hillside neighborhood, where 1st Avenue West used to be before it was sheared and eroded away. One month later (on September 20, 1972), another "100-year" rainfall occurred, inflicting even more damage.

These two major flood events in 1972 were a badly needed wake-up call telling Duluth citizens that new land use policies were needed to curb development along the Miller Hill Corridor and in Duluth Heights; unfortunately, people in Duluth were not ready to listen. Between 1972 and 1979, a substantial amount of additional development took place in the Duluth Heights area, including 16 drive-in restaurants and other drive-in businesses, five office buildings, four auto dealers, a large discount department store, the Village Mall, a motel, four branch banks and a variety of other commercial establishments. In the process, additional wetlands were filled in, creating a substantial expansion of paved surfaces and further increasing flood risks to low-lying areas.

On June 22, 1978, the Duluth Planning Commission recommended to the city council that intensive planning for the area of Duluth Heights begin immediately and that a moratorium on development along the Miller Hill Corridor be imposed until a plan for the area was completed. The city council finally agreed and a moratorium on development in the Duluth Heights area was imposed until December 31, 1979.

The Miller Hill Corridor Plan Committee was created, consisting of seven members of the Duluth Planning Commission and Thomas D. Cotruvo (the project manager), who was acting under the direction of Jerry Kimball. The process of preparing the *Miller Hill Corridor Plan* ("the Miller Hill Corridor plan") took a little over a year and, while it was being prepared, another "100-year" storm (the third such event in seven years) occurred on May 10, 1979, causing major flooding and property damage once again.

City planners produced six alternative scenarios depicting what the future could be like in 1995:

1. No Change (existing conditions with minor changes)
2. Current Rate of Development Extended
3. Development Boom
4. Energy Crisis
5. Environmental Concern
6. Planned/Controlled Development

Concise, two-paragraph descriptions of each of the six scenarios were included in the Miller Hill Corridor plan, enabling citizens and local officials to clearly understand the qualities associated with each scenario and the actions that would be required to achieve them. After the six scenarios were evaluated and compared, a preferred outcome was chosen that represented somewhat of a compromise. Rather than selecting a pure form of one of the six scenarios, planners recommended an approach which combined elements of three of the scenarios: the "Planned/Controlled Development" scenario combined with elements from the "Energy Crisis" and "Environmental Concern" scenarios.

Public hearings on the proposed Miller Hill Corridor plan were held in the fall of 1979 and the plan was adopted by the Duluth City Council on December 10, 1979. Rezonings recommended in the plan were approved by the city council in January 1980.

A number of concrete outcomes came about as a result of the Miller Hill Corridor plan. Commercial zoning along the Miller Trunk Highway was substantially reduced, particularly along the north side of the highway. One hundred and sixty acres of land, which previously could have been intensively developed for highway commercial development, were downzoned. In addition, a new and highly restrictive zoning classification was developed (C-5/Planned Commercial District) and imposed on areas that remained commercially zoned. Within the C-5/Planned Commercial District, no development could occur without first applying to the Duluth Planning Commission for detailed site plan approval (related to overall site design, landscaping, drainage, building elevations, parking lot design and signage). A water resource management ordinance was also adopted as an overlay zone, which prevented property owners and developers from undertaking any development that increased stormwater runoff and flood risks or adversely affected streams and wetlands.

"All of these protections were tied into the C-5 zone and C-5 plan review," Jim Mohn explained. "So we have stormwater detention requirements, severe restrictions on altering or filling wetlands, erosion and sedimentation control requirements, open space requirements and landscaping requirements."

When the Miller Hill Corridor plan was prepared, there was no Minnesota state statute that protected wetlands. In fact, a state wetlands protection statute was not adopted in Minnesota until 1992—12 years after Duluth adopted its own local regulations protecting wetlands. Planners in Duluth were therefore very much in the forefront in terms of developing and implementing wetland protection measures—the need for which is much more widely appreciated today.

The Miller Hill Corridor plan did not succeed in turning back the clock. The design quality of physical development along the corridor today is far from perfect and is largely characterized by mediocre, automobile-oriented strip development. Nevertheless, the importance of the plan and what it has achieved should not be underestimated. "It's probably been the most adhered to plan I have ever worked with in my 25 years here. It's been chewed on, chewed up and shot at, but it's still in place and still working. My copy of the plan is badly worn because I've referred to it so much," said Jim Mohn.

Before the Miller Hill Corridor plan was adopted, 70 acres of wetlands were lost along the highway corridor, significantly increasing the flood risk to low-lying areas of the city. In the 20-year period following the adoption of the Miller Hill Corridor plan, only 2 acres of the roughly 400 acres of wetlands that remained were filled in, and specific mitigation measures were required to off-set the impacts of those minor losses. Indeed, the package of zoning provisions, site plan review requirements and stormwater management regulations in the C-5 zone along the Miller Hill Corridor have gone a long way toward protect-ing and restoring the Miller Hill Corridor environment, and toward reducing the risk of flooding to lower lying areas.

"Every time we have a major rainfall," observed Jim Mohn, "we hold our breath and hope that we've done enough along the Miller Hill Corridor to pre-vent a recurrence of the severe flooding that occurred in the 1970s. So far it has."

When I drove along the Miller Hill Corridor with Jerry Kimball in 1998, he pointed out a number of large, undeveloped parcels of land along the north side of the highway that were taken out of commercial zoning as a result of the plan—parcels that surely would have been developed by now had the zoning not been changed. "We had a definite policy in mind in the plan to create some breaks in development—to stop commercial development from continuously extending to the mall and from spreading further into Duluth Heights," said Kimball.

The cutbacks in commercial zoning and tighter regulations pertaining to new development have had the additional benefit of encouraging private investment in improving and upgrading previously vacant and/or marginal commercial properties along the strip. "We're beginning to see vacant commer-cial properties in the older part of the corridor being redeveloped," said Jim Mohn. "There are still about a dozen eyesores along the corridor, but fewer than before. So the plan has had the effect of focusing development and invest-ment on existing properties, rather than expanding out and building new."

A NEW MAYOR SKEPTICAL OF PLANNING

In November 1979, Duluthians elected John Fedo as the city's new mayor and, in January 1980 (the same month the Miller Hill Corridor plan was adopted), he took office. The election of John Fedo did not initially seem to bode well for planning in Duluth. During his campaign, Fedo said that his #1 goal as mayor would be to stimulate development. He also charged that plans and regula-tions developed by the city's Physical Planning Division were a major cause of the city's economic malaise and that the Department of Planning and Develop-ment (DPD) was "bloated."

Once in office, Fedo seemed intent on weakening the Physical Planning Division's influence on city land use policy. Members of the Duluth Planning Commission learned that the mayor was about to move the city's planners into the Public Works Department. "We went in to have a long talk with the mayor and told him it was a bad idea," said Witzig. "We told him, 'It's too transparent. Anyway, planning can be good politics.'"

In 1983, a new departmental structure was created in city hall that brought planning and development-related programs more closely under the control of the mayor. A new DPD was created with four divisions: (1) Development; (2) Housing; (3) Job Training; and (4) Physical Planning. At the same time, two key staff members were removed from the Physical Planning Division.[17]

One of the planners removed from the Physical Planning Division was David Sebok, who had been hired by and worked for Kimball.[18] Fedo appointed Sebok as the director of the newly formed department. The other planner transferred out of the Physical Planning Division was Tom Cotruvo, who had provided staff support to the Duluth Planning Commission. According to Fred Witzig, "Tom staffed the Duluth Planning Commission for five or six years. He'd prepare the staff reports and take us on field trips. He's very talented and we were fortunate to have him." Cotruvo was transferred from the Physical Planning Division to the mayor's Office of Business Development.

The loss of these two planners could have been a serious blow to the Physical Planning Division's influence on city policy. Nevertheless, Sebok, Fedo and Kimball worked closely together in the coming years to achieve a number of important projects that changed the face and image of the city. "Fedo was a hands-on leader, and took a personal interest in planning and design issues," Jerry Kimball told me. "He even helped choose the plants in the Rose Garden and light fixtures downtown. The guy actually had a pretty good sense of design. What really matters is that he was truly interested and was good at getting funding resources, as was Dave Sebok. Of the four Duluth mayors for whom I worked, Fedo was the best at getting things done."

FUTURE CITY, DULUTH TOMORROW VISIONING PROGRAM

The early 1980s were not good years in Duluth. The city's population was still dropping, economic conditions were worsening and there was no sign whatsoever that things were ever going to get any better. On the other hand, the city had been in decline for so long, and people in Duluth were so used to it, that no one panicked. As Bill Majewski perceptively observed, "There wasn't a sense of crisis; it was more like a chronic illness."

With little new development occurring in the city, the Physical Planning Division's staff turned their attention to encouraging housing rehabilitation and historic preservation. A demonstration project was carried out in the Portland Square area of the East Hillside neighborhood, which resulted in the rehabilitation of a number of structures, and the positive visible changes that occurred in the neighborhood encouraged historically appropriate restorations outside the demonstration area. Kimball and the staff of the depleted Physical Planning Division also worked with the members of the Duluth Planning Commission to plan and carry out a six-month "visioning" process called *Future City, Duluth Tomorrow.*

Six public forums were held over a six-month period (between March and August 1983). At the first session, Jerry Kimball and Duluth Planning Commission members Dale Olsen and Fred Witzig made presentations which described the city's changing population, demographic characteristics and changing economic conditions.[19] To stimulate discussion, and generate new ideas and perspectives, a number of nationally recognized experts (the author William H. Whyte, urban law expert Robert Freilich, journalist Neal R. Peirce, futurist Luther P. Gerlach and geographer John Borchert) were brought to Duluth to speak at later sessions.

The initial thought in bringing these outside experts to Duluth was to generate new ideas and raise people's horizons regarding future possibilities. Even more important, however, was the fact that all of the outside "experts" who came to Duluth (most of them for the first time) were truly impressed by the inherent qualities of the city. Thus, in the course of delivering their remarks, they all delivered a message with a common theme: "Look at what you have. Look at your assets. Build on your unique qualities. Build on your strengths. Build on what is Duluth."

After each of the presentations, round-table discussions were held that invited people to react to the ideas presented by the speakers and offer ideas of their own. Out of this process, a broad-based consensus emerged that it was important to concentrate municipal planning efforts on the city's largely neglected downtown waterfront.

The six-month *Future City, Duluth Tomorrow* visioning exercise not only succeeded in building public understanding and agreement on key areas of land use and development policy, but also seemed to have an effect on the way Mayor Fedo thought about planning. "When John Fedo was first elected mayor, he was young and energetic and wanted to get things done quickly," said Jill Fisher. "He slowly came to realize that planning can be an asset, and that when you want to accomplish something important, it's a good idea to have a plan."

THE DOWNTOWN WATERFRONT PLAN AND STRATEGY

In the fall of 1983, Mayor Fedo called a press conference to announce that he was calling upon the Duluth Planning Commission to prepare a plan for the downtown waterfront, called the *Downtown Waterfront Plan and Strategy* ("the

Downtown Waterfront plan"). "He finally realized that planning was good politics," said Witzig.

Because Jerry Kimball staffed the Duluth Planning Commission, responsibility for leading the waterfront planning effort largely fell on his shoulders. However, in this case, because of the high priority the mayor placed on the preparation of a waterfront plan, Kimball and the Duluth Planning Commission were provided with a generous amount of funding to accomplish the task.

$110,000 was committed to the overall planning effort, including money to hire specialized outside consultants to assist in the preparation of the plan. City funding was also provided to enable Kimball to travel to a number of cities in the U.S. and Canada, which had redeveloped their waterfronts, to study what they had done and to try to learn from their successes and mistakes. Over the course of six weeks, Kimball traveled to New Bedford, Massachusetts; Baltimore, Maryland; Charleston, South Carolina; New York, New York; Boston, Massachusetts; Seattle, Washington; Vancouver, British Columbia; San Francisco, California; Toronto, Ontario; and other Great Lakes cities closer in size to Duluth. Along the way, he took hundreds of photographs and showed them to people in Duluth so they could see what other cities had done to take advantage of their waterfronts. These pictures helped spur peoples' imaginations and stimulate public interest in developing the Downtown Waterfront plan.

A detailed RFP was prepared and nationally advertised, outlining the aims of the planning effort, the tasks the city expected consultants to perform and the specific products consultants were expected to deliver. Six firms submitted formal proposals in response to the RFP, and Buckhurst Fish Hutton Katz (New York City) and Pei Property Development Corporation (headed by the son of architect I. M. Pei) were eventually awarded the contract.

An intense, 18-month planning effort ensued. A "Contact Group" of 28 people was formed (composed of representatives of organizations and groups having an interest in the waterfront) to review the work of the consultants, and offer advice and input. A series of four major planning "events" (open to the public) were also held (round-table discussions and brainstorming sessions). Most of these open planning events were attended by between 100 and 125 people, although one particular planning event held at the Convention Center attracted 200 people.

To keep citizens who were not participating directly in the planning process informed about its progress, and about specific issues that were being addressed, a series of reports was prepared and distributed on issues such as economics and urban design. Planning ideas and proposals under consideration were also described and disseminated in the form of fold-out inserts in the *Duluth News-Tribune* daily newspaper. Focus groups were used to identify key themes that the plan should seek to reinforce, and students from the UMD

Urban and Regional Studies Program worked as interns, researching the history of the waterfront and performing related background research.

In his travels to various coastal cities, Jerry Kimball saw a number of waterfront areas that had been redeveloped into settings for largely commercial purposes ("Festival Marketplaces" like Baltimore's Harborplace, Boston's Fanieul Hall Marketplace and San Diego's Seaport Village). However, it seemed to Kimball that to try to imitate the festival marketplace approach in Duluth would be a mistake. Duluth's waterfront was still a very active, working waterfront.

Although the Port of Duluth has declined in importance relative to other U.S. ports, it still handles more large freighters and more total volume of cargo than any other Great Lakes port. No other Great Lakes port ships more iron ore or more grain on an annual basis.[20] In a typical year, roughly 1,300 vessels pass through Duluth. There is no better place in the midwest (or anywhere else in the U.S., for that matter) to watch huge ships that are coming from (or going to) distant ports. When you stand along the side of the Duluth Ship Canal, the ships are so close that it seems like you could reach out and touch them; you can certainly smell their smoke, feel the vibrations of the engines and the lake water pulsing from the propellers, and yell greetings to the sailors standing at the railings of the passing ships.

"Our thinking was that people would not be coming to Duluth's waterfront to shop, but rather because it was an authentic, working waterfront—a real place," said Kimball. As a result, the Downtown Waterfront plan minimized the importance of retail activity along the waterfront. Instead of encouraging the construction of new commercial structures, it was expected and hoped that new retail and commercial uses introduced into the district would be accommodated primarily by renovating and reusing the existing commercial and industrial buildings. The plan also placed emphasis on encouraging pedestrian activity and pedestrian-oriented businesses. Fast-food restaurants with drive-in windows were specifically disallowed and a number of commercial uses that could have proven privately profitable were also discouraged.

Another reason for not placing more emphasis on expanding retail activity along the waterfront was that planners were mindful of the limited retail market potential in Duluth (a four-page section of the Downtown Waterfront plan focused on "The Need for Realism") and didn't want to do anything on the waterfront that would undermine the viability of the city's traditional CBD. Indeed, the city's traditional CBD along Superior Street has capitalized on the growing popularity of the waterfront and Canal Park by marketing itself as the "Downtown Waterfront" area.

The Downtown Waterfront plan recognized that different segments of the waterfront had different characteristics, and broke down the waterfront area into subareas (the Bayfront area; the Hotel, Convention Center and Arena

Complex; the Minnesota Slip area; the Canal Park area; and the Lake Place area) in order to address the problems and opportunities specific to each. Key recommendations in the plan were to:

- retain and preserve major buildings along the waterfront and Canal Park area, particularly buildings of historic and architectural significance
- provide a continuous public promenade along the harbor and lakefront extending from Bayfront to Leif Erikson Park
- encourage specialty retail uses in the Canal Park area
- develop a boat basin and marina near the Bayfront area
- develop a spacious Festival Grounds area (overlooking the harbor) to accommodate leisure activities and major public events like the Fourth of July and Bayfront Friday music events
- encourage the development of a limited number of new, low-rise, two-story, attached housing units in the Bayfront area
- expand parking facilities at important tourist destinations
- provide pedestrian linkages between the downtown and the waterfront
- develop a landscaped park (Corner-of-Lake Park) and relocate an old suburban railroad depot (the Endion Railroad Station, built in 1899 by the Duluth and Iron Range Railroad) to the park
- establish design guidelines for small- and large-scale developments that occur in the waterfront planning area

THE DOWNTOWN LAKEWALK

You can now get on the Downtown Lakewalk at 27th Avenue East and walk 27 blocks, and then walk along the area that was filled in [with boulders blasted out in the course of depressing I-35], along the east side of Canal Park to the Marine Museum, and then under the Aerial Lift Bridge, and all along the west side of the canal facing the Minnesota Slip, then cross the little blue lift bridge and walk to 10th Avenue West. That's a walk of about 3.5 miles. We accomplished that in seven years which, when you think about it, is not all that long.

—WILLIAM MAJEWSKI

Fred Witzig remembers the day Mayor Fedo publicly announced that planning for the waterfront was going to begin, because he attended the press conference and because it was held on the very same day that he retired from the Duluth Planning Commission and attended his last commission meeting. The setting for the mayor's press conference was the old Fitgers Brewery, which had been renovated and converted into a complex of stores, restaurants, drinking establishments and a hotel. Witzig distinctly remembers that, while the mayor was speaking, construction was underway on the I-35 freeway extension behind Fitgers. What was being built was very different from what the MNDOT had initially wanted to build.

As noted earlier, neighborhood groups filed suit against MNDOT's original highway plan. While the highway project was held up in court, the city's director of planning and development, Dick Loraas, formed a citizens committee consisting of people active in fighting both for and against the project. He then proceeded to facilitate a negotiation process, involving representatives of MNDOT, to see if MNDOT's plan could be modified in a way that satisfied the opposing sides.

One of the first concessions MNDOT made was to agree to terminate the freeway at 26th Avenue East, and to allow the city to use money that would have been spent on making the freeway longer ("Interstate Substitution Money") for other transportation-related improvements. Some of this money was used to pay for extending the downtown skywalk system; other portions of the money were used to pay for downtown street, sidewalk and streetscape improvements.

6-16   Aerial view looking west toward St. Louis Bay in the early 1980s, with Minnesota Point and the Aerial Lift Bridge in the foreground. The shoreline at the base of Minnesota Point (to the right of the Aerial Lift Bridge) is full of low-grade industrial uses with no public access to the water. Construction of the I-35 freeway extension through Duluth has begun (right side of photo).

Source: Jerry Kimball

In their negotiations with MNDOT, Duluth's planners insisted that the highway be depressed to make it possible to create physical connections between the city and the lake by decking over the highway. To bolster the argument, planners pointed out that decking over the highway would protect the surface of the highway from freezing lake spray during winter storms.

Divided highways and freeways have often been depressed in an attempt to minimize impacts on surrounding communities and the results have not always been positive. Not uncommonly, a depressed highway produces a wide, unsightly trench dividing areas on opposite sides; however, in Duluth, depressing the highway was extraordinarily beneficial because the topography of the city slopes down to the lake. "The topography of the city was working in our favor," observed Bill Majewski.

The most troubling problem facing the city planners was the fact that Leif Erikson Park and its treasured Rose Garden lay in the path of the least intrusive highway alignment. "Leif Erikson Park was created by the WPA during the 1930s, and losing the Rose Garden was unthinkable," said Jerry Kimball.

6-17 Streetscape improvements made to the 5th Avenue Mall that leads up from Superior Street to the Civic Center Group planned by Daniel Burnham. The improvements were funded by "Interstate Substitution Money," which was freed up when MNDOT agreed to terminate the freeway through Duluth at 26th Avenue East.

Source: Gene Bunnell

6-18   The redesigned, depressed freeway ultimately constructed through downtown Duluth, as photographed in 1992. The decked area over the freeway in the foreground, linking the downtown to the waterfront, is Lake Place Park.

Source: Jeff Frey Photos

Duluth's planners got MNDOT to agree to relocate the rose bushes and create a new Rose Garden in a park above the new highway. The rose bushes were dug up, saved and tended in the interim, and were eventually replanted in a recreated Rose Garden twice the size of the original one. When I was in Duluth in 1998, I saw people carefully tending the rose bushes, giving reason to hope that the Rose Garden will, in time, approach its former beauty.

The revised plan that was finally negotiated with MNDOT bore little resemblance to the initial proposal. It required bringing the freeway into the city below grade and constructing decking over the highway at a number of points. As built, the freeway runs under Superior Street, opens into a trench, goes back under Superior Street, opens up into a trench, goes into a tunnel underneath Leif Erikson Park and then opens again.

MAKING THE DOWNTOWN LAKEWALK POSSIBLE

In planning cities, as in life, one thing often leads to another. In this case, the city planners' insistence that I-35 be depressed meant that contractors building the highway had to blast away thousands of tons of rock.

The highway engineers and builders needed to find somewhere to put all the rock. According to Jerry Kimball, a local landscape architect named Kent Worley, who contributed some wonderful ideas and designs for the waterfront, suggested, "Why not use the rock removed from the highway trench to fill in the shoreline and extend it into the lake to create a walkway and parkland along the lake?"

The idea of developing parkland along the shore of Lake Superior had actually been around for quite some time. According to Jill Fisher, the idea of developing a park along the lake was put forward in the city's first comprehensive plan, prepared in 1927 by Harland Bartholomew, and had been discussed as early as 1910. "People in Duluth at the turn of the century were very much taken with the idea of developing a lakefront park. Park planning was in the ascendance in big cities like Chicago and Boston, and the thought here was, 'If we're going to be a great city, like those other cities, we should have that, too,'" said Fisher.

The possibility of reshaping the waterfront to provide a strip of continuous public open space along the lake had also been something that Jerry Kimball considered long before work began on preparing the Downtown Waterfront plan. In the 1970s, Kimball tried to interest the Junior Chamber of Commerce in taking on the project of creating a .4-mile-long park between the Ship Canal and the end of the lake; however, nothing came of it. The idea resurfaced during plan review and design review sessions with MNDOT related to the modified I-35 freeway.

The concept of using the rock that was blasted away to fill in and extend the shoreline presented two principal benefits: (1) it was a way to increase the amount of public open space along the shoreline and create a park-like setting for a walkway along the lake; and (2) it helped provide an increased measure of protection for adjacent properties from surging lake waters during storms. "When the St. Croix urban renewal project was carried out in the 1950s," remembered Jerry Kimball, "a new hotel was allowed to be built too close to the water. It was so close that, every five to six years, they'd lose two or three rooms because of the waves bashing in."

Placing rock and stone boulders along the shoreline solved a third problem by providing the impetus for removing a substantial amount of unauthorized filling that had taken place over the years. "One or two businesses located along the lakefront had dumped car bodies and other junk into the lake to try to protect their properties against erosion," said Kimball. Reconstituting and rebuilding the shoreline provided an occasion for disposing of this environmentally damaging and unsightly situation.

Lastly, allowing rock blasted from the highway to be placed along the city's shoreline saved MNDOT a great deal of money. Had highway contractors not been able to dispose of the rock along the city's shoreline, highway contractors would have had to transport the rock a much greater distance, adding at least $3 million to the highway cost. By coming up with a plan that saved MNDOT this amount, Duluth's planners were able to secure the money they needed to plan, design and construct the Downtown Lakewalk.

6-19 Car bodies dumped along the Duluth waterfront in the 1960s.

Source: Charles Aguar

Donated easements were obtained from owners of property along the lake allowing MNDOT to place the rock along the shore, and the shoreline was extended into the lake (60-80 feet in most places, and 100 feet or more in other places). Rocks removed by blasting were cleaned (dirt and miscellaneous debris were removed) and then placed along the shoreline in a carefully pre-scribed way, providing level surfaces so that people could use the boulders as stepping stones down to the lake.

THE TRANSFORMATION OF THE DULUTH WATERFRONT

The 48-page Downtown Waterfront plan, which contained colored land use maps, illustrations and photographs, was completed in December 1985 and copies were widely distributed. It was not long before positive things started to happen.

In 1986:

- The Minnesota Slip bulkhead is repaired at a cost of $400,000.
- The William A. Irvin, a 600-foot-long iron ore carrier, which had been in storage upriver and which was about to be dismantled for scrap, is purchased for $140,000, restored at a cost of $250,000, brought to the Minnesota Slip alongside Canal Park and opened as a floating maritime museum. The Irvin soon becomes a major attraction.[21]
- The 1899 Endion Railroad Station (weighing 400 tons) is moved 1 mile to the Corner-of-Lake Park, and renovated to accommodate the offices of the city's Visitors and Convention Bureau.
- A 230-car parking area is constructed by acquiring and clearing away an old scrap yard.

In 1987:

- Bayfront Festival Park (an 11-acre park for public events with a tensile structure stage and stage canopy) is completed at a cost of $700,000 (the cost was shared by the city and the private Bayfront Park Development Association). Major events are held at Bayfront Festival Park (16 in the first year; 60 by the third year).
- The historic Aerial Lift Bridge is illuminated to showcase it at night, with a $30,000 grant from the Rotary Club.
- A Saturday Farmer's Market is established at Canal Park (operating between July and October).
- A public charter fishing dock is established at the Minnesota Slip. (There were four boats in the Duluth Charter fishing fleet in 1986; by 1990, there were 48.)

6-20   The Duluth waterfront as it existed in 1986.

Source: Jerry Kimball

6-21   Rear view of the William A. Irvin, tied up at the Minnesota Slip, restored and opened as a floating maritime museum.

Source: Jerry Kimball

6-22 Bayfront Festival Park.

Source: Jerry Kimball

6-23 A tour boat passing through the Ship Canal and under the Aerial Lift Bridge from St. Louis Bay out into Lake Superior.

Source: Gene Bunnell

6-24   Downtown Lakewalk, 1990.

Source: Jerry Kimball

- The U.S. Army Corps of Engineers completes a $12 million reconstruction of shipping canal piers. As part of the project, public walkways along the Ship Canal are significantly widened.

- State legislation is passed approving special Duluth legislation for the Downtown Waterfront Mixed-Use Design Review District.

In 1988:

- The first section of the Downtown Lakewalk is completed (a .5-mile-long stretch between the Ship Canal and Corner-of-Lake Park) consisting of a boardwalk, a separate bike/skating path and a third path for horse carriages.

- The Vista Star, a dinner cruiser, is added to the excursion fleet based in Duluth.

- A 1,000-foot-long, offshore, underwater, lake trout habitat reef is created utilizing more freeway tunnel rock.

- The "pilot house" from a former Great Lakes freighter is donated to the city and installed along the Downtown Lakewalk as a storm-watch pavilion.

6-25   Entrance to the Downtown Lakewalk at Corner-of-Lake Park. The 1899 former Endion Railroad Station (on right of photo) was moved one mile to the Corner-of-Lake Park and was renovated to accommodate the offices of the Visitors and Convention Bureau.

Source: Gene Bunnell

6-26   The "pilot house" from a former Great Lakes freighter was installed along the Downtown Lakewalk as a storm-watch pavilion—the perfect place in which to take refuge and watch the waves crashing ashore during a furious Lake Superior storm.

Source: Gene Bunnell

6-27   55-foot entry tower at the entrance to Canal Park.

Source: Gene Bunnell

In 1989:

- The city establishes a program of design assistance and reconstruction subsidies to encourage the renovation of historic building façades in the Canal Park area.
- A large parking area is constructed alongside Bayfront Park.
- The Waterfront Plaza Marina opens for charter fishing boats at Minnesota Slip.

In 1990:

- The waterfront design review zoning ordinance is officially adopted by the city, and the Waterfront Design Review Board is established.
- Playfront Park (a 10,000-square-foot playground) is constructed over a four-day period by 2,000 volunteers.
- The "Lake Place Image Wall" is completed (a 580- by 12-foot mosaic wall utilizing computer interpretations of photos of historic local shipping scenes).[22]
- A new $18 million State Convention Center is opened, further expanding the DECC/Arena Auditorium complex.

- A 55-foot-high entry tower is constructed at the entrance to Canal Park, at the intersection of Lake Avenue and Commerce Street. The lantern at the top of the tower makes reference to the light at the end of the pier, which guides ships into the Duluth Ship Canal.[23]

In 1991:

- Lake Avenue (the main highway leading from downtown Duluth into the Canal Park waterfront area) is reconstructed.
- Major utility reconstruction in the Canal Park area is completed (new stormwater sewers and new water/gas lines; overhead power lines placed underground).
- Sidewalks throughout the Canal Park area are reconstructed and widened. Canal Park Streetscape project is 95% complete.
- The Buchanon Street boardwalk is constructed connecting the DECC, Arena Auditorium and Convention Center to the Downtown Lakewalk.
- The Minnesota Slip Pedestrian Drawbridge is constructed, connecting Canal Park with the Bayfront Area.
- The construction of Lake Place (a 2.5-acre, $10 million park) is completed over I-35, providing an attractive physical connection between downtown and the waterfront.
- The air-driven "diaphone" foghorn, which had operated for decades at the entrance to Duluth's harbor but was replaced in the 1970s by a more modern (and shrill-sounding) "peanut whistle," is restored by a citizens group, and the city agrees to assume responsibility for operating and maintaining it. The old foghorn is reinstalled as the main fog warning device in Duluth's harbor. (An air-driven "diaphone" foghorn gives off a deep, throaty baritone sound that is the perfect accompaniment to dark, fog-shrouded nights on the Great Lakes.)

In 1992:

- 11 major public art pieces, including a number of bronze sculptures, are installed in Canal Park.[24]
- 78 major events are held at Bayfront Festival Park, including the Bayfront Blues Festival—one of the premier blues music events in the country.

In 1993:

- Two additional major sculpture pieces are added to Lake Place's International Sculpture Garden.
- The City of Duluth is awarded the national Waterfront Center's top honor award for "Excellence in Waterfront Development."

6-28   The Minnesota Slip Pedestrian Drawbridge connecting Canal Park with the Bayfront Area.

Source: Jerry Kimball

6-29   View of Lake Superior from landscaped park space atop the decking over the depressed freeway.

Source: Gene Bunnell

6-30   A totem pole-like sculpture at the entrance to the Downtown Lakewalk near the entry tower. "We placed that particular piece there because we wanted people to enter Canal Park with a smile on their faces," said Jerry Kimball.

Source: Gene Bunnell

6-31   Sculpture of the "Determined Mariner" at one of the entrances to the Downtown Lakewalk.

Source: Jerry Kimball

6-32   The Great Lakes Aquarium, viewed across the snow.

Source: Jerry Kimball

In 1994:

- The Rose Garden, which had to be relocated because of the construction of the I-35 freeway, is reopened.

In 1996:

- A new IMAX-3D Theater opens adjacent to the DECC.
- The Downtown Lakewalk is extended another 1,000 feet to the east.

In August 2000, another important benchmark was reached: the opening of the $32 million Great Lakes Aquarium on a prominent waterfront site—a short walking distance from Canal Park. The aquarium, although not called for specifically in the Downtown Waterfront plan, was very much inspired by the plan, the aim of which was to cement the connection between Duluth and Lake Superior. Indeed, the first steps aimed at developing an aquarium were taken around the time work began on the Downtown Waterfront plan.[25] The land for the aquarium was acquired and donated by the Marshall sisters—descendants of a long-time Duluth family that became wealthy operating the Marshall-Wells Hardware Company.

According to Tom Cotruvo, "One of the sisters had studied art in Paris and knew how wonderful a waterfront could be. When some vacant property along the Duluth waterfront became available (a junkyard, actually), she and her sister bought it—not to make money from it but to see that it was used for a good public purpose. They formed a nonprofit organization to take custody of the site, established a board of directors and hired consultants to develop alternative plans."

Roughly half of the money needed for the project ($16 million) was provided by the State of Minnesota; approximately $11 million was committed by the city by issuing bonds through its Economic Development Authority and through tax increment financing (TIF). The balance of the funding (approximately $5 million) was raised privately.

By all accounts, the money that the city has spent on planning for and developing the Duluth waterfront, and on infrastructure improvements and amenities in the Canal Park area, has been a very good investment. Property values throughout the Canal Park area have increased appreciably as old industrial buildings have been renovated and occupied by shops, restaurants and a variety of other commercial businesses (such as the former mattress factory that has become the DeWitt-Seitz Marketplace). Moreover, in the three-year period after the Canal Park and waterfront improvements were completed, the amount of sales tax revenue collected by the city increased 90%. In 1999, the city collected $1,861,000 from its 1.5% food and beverage tax (compared to $1,082,696 in 1996), and most of that tax revenue increase was generated by businesses in and near Canal Park.

Most of the city's downtown hotels have changed their names to incorporate references to the lake—a good indication of how the changes that have occurred along Duluth's waterfront have changed people's perception of Duluth. The hotel in the renovated Fitgers Brewery is now called "Fitgers Head of the Lake," while other recently adopted hotel names include "Lakewalk Holiday Inn," "Downtown Waterfront Hotel," "Hotel Duluth Harborview" and "Lakewalk Inn."

While the changes that have occurred along the Duluth waterfront have made it an increasingly popular place to visit, they have also made Duluth a much more pleasant and enjoyable place in which to live. The construction of the Downtown Lakewalk, in particular, has benefited the residents of city neighborhoods. Every time I walked along the Downtown Lakewalk (and I did so at least once a day), I encountered dozens of local people (young and old, mothers with children, young couples, the elderly, joggers, bicyclists, and people sitting in quiet contemplation of the beauty and constantly changing appearance of the lake).

CLEAR DESIGN GUIDELINES

An important reason why the Canal Park waterfront area turned out as well as it did is because the Downtown Waterfront plan called for the adoption of a Downtown Waterfront Mixed-Use Design Review District overlapping the Design Review District (created pursuant to Chapter 84 of the Laws of Minnesota, 1987). The purpose of the Downtown Waterfront Mixed-Use Design Review District was to "preserve and enhance the unique visual character and environmental quality of the area" by allowing and encouraging "flexible and creative approaches to development with mixed land uses that would not be permitted within standard zoning districts." The formal design review process and design guidelines adopted applied to all new construction and exterior building alterations, signs and landscaping.

A gas station and convenience store that occupies the visible corner parcel at the entrance to Canal Park is a good example of how the appearance of the most ordinary kind of commercial development has been improved by going through design review. The design of the gas station, which was carefully scrutinized during a formal design review process, is attractive and unobtrusive. The pay counter and convenience store of the gas station are housed in a renovated building. Brick columns that support the canopy over the gas pumps match the brick of the structure.

As Canal Park has become increasingly successful, and as developers have conjured up novel ways of trying to capitalize on the success of the area, design

6-33   The design and appearance of this gas station/convenience store in Canal Park was improved by going through a mandatory design review process.

Source: Gene Bunnell

review has become even more important. "Had we not done the architectural and historic studies, and written the ordinance to specify exactly the character of development we wanted," commented Jill Fisher, "something very different would have happened. We could have lost our old buildings. We would have ended up with a row of fast-food, national franchise restaurants with drive-in windows. Within a short time, all the good we did by investing $10 million in the area would have been undone by a few people putting up their blimps, flashing signs and drive-in windows."

Fisher offered the following case in point to illustrate the kind of unsightly and inappropriate development that *might have* occurred in the Canal Park area had mixed-use zoning and design review not been adopted: "Someone came in wanting to put in a mini-golf course along the Downtown Lakewalk. He wanted to bring in fill and make a little mountain for mini-golf. The Design Review Committee and staff looked at the proposal and concluded it wasn't consistent with the plan. 'That doesn't fit on the Duluth waterfront. That's Anywhere U.S.A. You can do it up on the Miller Hill Corridor, but you're not going to do it on our scarce, beautiful waterfront.'"

6-34   A manhole cover in Canal Park, which incorporates the logo that was developed during the Duluth waterfront planning process to apply to a whole range of improvements associated with the Downtown Waterfront plan. The logo was used on directional signs, information kiosks, street furniture and advertising displays, as well as in publications, press releases and brochures focusing on the waterfront. The Downtown Waterfront plan had such a profound impact on the city that the logo has subsequently come to symbolize the city as a whole, and is now widely used by the city government, private groups and organizations in their various promotional efforts related to the city.

Source: Gene Bunnell

In a 1997 presentation, Jerry Kimball summarized the critical elements that contributed to the success of Duluth's waterfront planning effort: "We took it one step at a time. Before doing anything, we undertook a thorough planning process which included real and meaningful citizen involvement. There was no 'quick fix'—just eight years of concentrated effort and commitment to the strategy. We tried to be true to our strengths and produce an authentic interpretation of what constitutes our uniqueness. We studied waterfronts throughout this country and Canada, but concentrated on what would work in Duluth, Minnesota. We wanted change, but only if it nurtured our uniqueness. We wanted quality, which we addressed through attention to detail and concentration on our historic industrial and nautical image. Although expansion of tourism was a major goal, a more important one [was] giving Duluthians more reasons to be proud of living in the city. We tried to remember that the star of the show was and is the lake. Access to the lake and historic and working vessels were and are of prime importance."

LOCAL ECONOMIC DEVELOPMENT

The Lake Superior Paper Plant

In 1986, it was announced that a huge, $425 million paper-making plant was going to be built on the site of a former salvage yard and factory in West Duluth. The announcement didn't come about simply because a paper company happened to decide to build a plant in Duluth; rather, the announcement was the culmination of an industrial recruitment effort that began in the mid-1970s—and of nearly 10 years of attempting to entice such a major facility to be built in Duluth.

"No one was asking to build a paper mill here," recalled Tom Cotruvo, "but this office (the Business Development Division) thought that a paper mill on the site might work and went out looking for one. There was an old power plant near the site that could be used to produce steam for paper. So we put together a brochure and went around to paper companies. We found one business that was going to do it, but it fell through when they were taken over. Eventually Minnesota Power (the local power company) agreed to be a partner in the project and helped to interest Pentair, a Minneapolis-based paper company."

To secure the paper-making plant, the city offered a package of incentives totaling roughly $64 million. City contributions toward the project consisted of TIF-backed revenue bonds, sewer revenue bonds, steam revenue bonds, federal funds (CDBG funds for two years totalling $3.1 million and a federal EDA grant of $1.2 million) and forgiveness of city sales tax revenue. Despite the apparent size of the public subsidy, the real cost to the city and its exposure to risk were relatively minor. According to Pagano and Bowman, "Only the city's forgiven sales tax revenues (which were approximately $1.5 million) and fore-gone property tax revenues from the cleared site in the TIF district can be con-sidered true city costs or concessions. And neither of those city investments put Duluth's General Fund (or taxpayer) at risk . . . The remaining subsidies took the form of revenues foregone by the State of Minnesota: enterprise zone tax credits (nearly $5.5 million in state sales tax forgiveness); $1.5 million for employee training; and $0.3 million for site clean-up." (Pagano and Bowman 1989, 12-13)

Construction of the Lake Superior Paper Industries (LSPI) plant was com-pleted in 1987 and, when hiring began, there were 24,000 applicants for the 325 high-paying jobs at the plant. The one major disadvantage associated with building the state-of-the-art paper factory project was that, once again, West Duluth bore its negative impacts. In order for the plant to be built, the city had to publicly acquire and clear an area of 50-60 acres, and take a large number of homes by eminent domain. At least 114 West Duluth household residents were forced out.

A Downtown Casino

In 1988, a gambling casino opened in downtown Duluth. According to Pagano and Bowman, the Fond-du-Luth Casino was the brainchild of the mayor [John Fedo was mayor at that time] who thought it would "attract tourists and give life to the east end of the CBD." (Pagano and Bowman 1995, 118)

The site chosen for the Fond-du-Luth Casino was an old Sears Roebuck department store, which occupied a whole city block on Superior Street. Ini-tially, the city had tried to attract another retail outlet as a replacement but, when these efforts failed, the idea of a downtown casino surfaced as a fallback option.

Somehow Mayor Fedo, with the help of David Sebok (the planning and development director), managed to convince the federal government to allow most of the former Sears property to be deeded to the Fond du Lac Band of the Chippewa Indian tribe. The fact that the city managed to gain federal and state approval for a downtown casino is really quite extraordinary, given the fact that the property, in effect, was attached to a reservation roughly 20 miles away.

"[T]he Band bought the building and renovated the first floor as a gambling casino. The Band agreed to create a joint City-Band gaming commission to act as the governing board for the casino with four Band members and three city appointed members. The agreement also called for the city to raze some adja-cent buildings, which housed primarily adult entertainment stores, and build a parking garage to be financed by city issuance of an IRB [Industrial Revenue Bond] to serve the casino. The casino agreed to repay the debt which the city incurred for construction of the garage." (*ibid.*)

Because of the tribe's sovereign status, the city was unable to collect property taxes from properties owned by the Fond du Lac Band. However, the formal legal agreement, which created the Fond-du-Luth Gaming Commission, called for an "in lieu of" payment to the city based on a percentage of the earnings from the casino. Under the original terms of the agreement, the City of Duluth received 24.5% of the net proceeds (profits) and the Band received 25.5%. "The remaining 50 percent [was] retained by the commission for other 'economic development' projects. The city's share [was] earmarked for its economic development fund and insulated from the city's general fund revenues." (*ibid.*, 25)

"In 1994, the terms of the agreement were modified," Kimball told me. "Under the modified agreement, the city receives a 'rent payment' that is equal to 19% of all the casino slot machine revenue, after payouts."

Each year, the amount of money collected by the city from the casino has grown. In 1999, the City of Duluth received $4.8 million from the operating profits of the casino. Although profiting directly from the operation of a gambling casino may strike some readers as unseemly, the city has taken steps to assure that the money received from the casino has not been simply frittered away. To the contrary, the city's approach to handling the revenue received from the casino has reflected the kind of concern for the long-term future of the city that is commonly associated with planning. Each year since the casino opened, money received by the city from the casino has been deposited into a dedicated fund called the "Community Investment Trust Fund."

As of August 2000, over $25 million had accumulated in the Community Investment Trust Fund. Instead of depleting the principal of the fund, the city has committed itself to spending only the *interest* earned annually from the fund, and has used this money to fund an ongoing street improvement program. In 1999, $1.2 million in interest was earned by the Community Investment Trust Fund and spent on street improvements.

Although the Fond-du-Luth Casino has succeeded in generating a considerable amount of revenue for Duluth's city government (money which the city seems to have handled and invested wisely), my sense is that the casino has had a relatively minor impact on the city as a whole and produced relatively few spin-off benefits in terms of local economic development. The casino has kept a major block of downtown buildings occupied, and generated a certain amount of street and pedestrian activity. However, it is certainly not the main reason for the increased pride that Duluthians now seem to feel about their city and their increased optimism about the future. In all of my interviews with people and planners in Duluth, hardly anyone mentioned the casino and no one seemed to place much importance on the casino as a contributing factor to the city's renaissance.

The building of the LSPI plant and the Fond-du-Luth Casino in downtown Duluth are clear indications of the importance that Duluth's city government has placed on economic development, on attracting investment and in creating jobs. However, Jerry Kimball reminded people that, in order to strengthen and diversify the city's economy, it was necessary to do more than recruit a paper plant and build a casino. It was necessary to make the city a better place to live by preserving and drawing attention to its unique qualities and sense of place.

A PLAN FOR WEST DULUTH

If there were one part of Duluth that deserved and needed something good to happen, it was West Duluth—a traditionally working-class area where nearly two-thirds of the developed land was in industrial use. Over a 25- to 30-year period, one bad thing after another occurred in West Duluth: (1) the I-35 freeway was driven through the Oneota neighborhood; (2) as travel patterns shifted and a major, new retail shopping area developed along the Miller Hill Corridor in the 1970s, commercial and retail establishments up and down West Grand Avenue in West Duluth began to go out of business; and (3) the decision was made to site the LSPI plant in West Duluth, which forced over a hundred additional West Duluth household residents out of their homes.

For many of the people who called West Duluth home, the LSPI plant was the last straw. Not long after the LSPI plant was built, citizens in West Duluth formed the Spirit Valley Neighborhood Development Association (SVNDA).[26] Jeanne Koneczny is a long-time resident of West Duluth and played a key role in creating SVNDA. When I spoke with her in August 2000, she was working as the housing coordinator of SVNDA, which has become the lead agency responsible for planning, initiating and overseeing housing development and rehabilitation projects throughout West Duluth.

"We realized that nothing positive was ever going happen in West Duluth unless and until we had a plan," said Koneczny. "People in West Duluth were constantly living in fear of the next industrial expansion or project that would displace more people from their homes. The zoning in West Duluth was also atrocious—a hodgepodge that afforded no protection whatsoever to residential areas. People were never going to buy homes, get mortgages or be able to borrow money to fix up homes in West Duluth until we had a plan. Without a plan, their investments in their homes were just going to go down the drain."

From a city-wide perspective, the need for planning to improve the livability of West Duluth neighborhoods was undeniable. The fact that West Duluth was losing population was not necessarily surprising, since the population of the city as a whole was declining. However, between 1960 and 1980, the population of West Duluth fell 50% (from 5,257 to 2,667)—a rate of population decline three times greater than the rate of decline in the city as a whole. Still, the people who remained continued to have a strong attachment to West Duluth. When 114 household residents were forced out of their homes by the building of the LSPI plant, three-quarters of those households chose to relocate and remain in West Duluth rather than move to another part of the city.

In 1985, the city's Office of Planning and Development placed a high priority on working with West Duluth residents and SVNDA to prepare a plan. Four staff planners (two from the Physical Planning Division and two from the Community Development and Housing Division) were assigned to the West Duluth planning process, and these staff members were supplemented by student interns from the UMD Urban and Regional Studies Program. A 19-member Plan Steering Committee was formed, which was composed of West Duluth residents and two city councilors.

Planners first had to gain the trust of local residents. Many residents blamed them for the dislocations caused by the building of I-35 through West Duluth (even though they were not responsible for the route the freeway took). They were also bitter about the siting of the LSPI plant in West Duluth, which Jerry Kimball admits he *did* have something to do with. "I supported the LSPI project because it was badly needed, and got into hot water with people in West Duluth because of it. I remember that one time I brought a group of city council members and Duluth Planning Commission members out to view the site of the Oneota Industrial Park. There was a group of protesters waiting with signs that said 'Kimball Realty Company—Land Cheap.'"

Over the course of a year and one-half (between 1986 and 1987), a series of neighborhood meetings and open-ended, round-table discussions were held. Residents picked various topics and sat around tables talking about them, while people wrote down the key points. Planners played a supporting and facilitating role in the process. "We wrote down people's comments, took them back to the office to digest and synthesize them, and developed them into ideas for physical improvements and land use changes which we then brought back to the group for further discussion," said Jim Mohn.

Over the course of these meetings and discussions, a consensus emerged on two main points: (1) people accepted that industry was an important part of the heritage and character of West Duluth; and (2) additional industrial development was appropriate and desirable in certain areas. However, they also felt strongly that West Duluth should be a place where people could live in decent residential neighborhoods, and that the residential qualities and amenities of West Duluth neighborhoods needed to be respected and strengthened.

Out of these discussions, a consensus emerged on a set of priority issues, which led to the formulation of six goals:

1. Enhance the economic base of the neighborhood through the creation of new businesses and jobs.
2. Expand the number and type of housing units and provide housing incentives for all age groups.

3. Upgrade the neighborhood by improving streets, adding sidewalks and storm sewers, as well as solving traffic safety-related problems.

4. Improve the quality of life in the neighborhood through the removal of dilapidated buildings; the rehabilitation of deteriorated housing units; the creation of wage-producing jobs; access to the waterfront; reduction of air, noise and water pollution; development of appropriate private recreational facilities; and recognition of the value of existing natural resources.

5. Provide a greater sense of stability to the neighborhood through the plan process, rezoning, and other efforts to stabilize existing land uses and separate conflicting land uses.

6. Offer opportunities for increased citizen participation in the decision-making process on issues which directly affect the residents.

West Duluth—Opportunities for Change ("the West Duluth plan") was completed in 1987. "When the plan was done, they took it as *their* plan," said Bill Majewski, who was the project manager. "We have used the plan as a guide to action," added Jeanne Koneczny. "Before we do anything, we look at the plan. People here carry copies of the plan with them to all our meetings, and our copies are getting pretty worn out. I tell people that if they see a copy of the plan at a yard sale or flea market to be sure and buy it. We could use some more copies of the plan that are in decent condition."

One reason why so many of the recommendations contained in the West Duluth plan have been implemented is because the core group of people who participated in the planning process are still involved. "Over 15 years later, they meet just about every Monday at noon at one of the local restaurants. Most of their meetings now deal with the implementation of the plan," said Majewski. Although it has certainly not happened overnight, a number of positive changes and developments have been brought about to fulfill the key aims of the West Duluth plan.

Economic Development

- The plan authorized the expansion of the Oneota Industrial Park to provide increased sites for business and industry. By the middle of 2000, all of the new industrial sites created by the expansion of the park had been developed and occupied.

- A derelict area of old boat slips, previously owned by the Hallett Dock Company, was subdivided and redeveloped, creating six new sites for business and industry. A truck route was extended to the area using state aid money, but was routed around—rather than through—the adjoining neighborhood.

Significant Rezonings of Commercial to Residential

- Commercial strip zoning was eliminated along Grand Avenue from the Ore Docks at 35th Avenue West to 75th Avenue West, and the corridor was rezoned "residential." Before I-35 was constructed through the Point of Rocks, Grand Avenue was the principal highway corridor leading into the city from the west. Because it carried a great deal of traffic, commercial uses developed along much of its length. However, when I-35 was constructed, traffic along Grand Avenue decreased dramatically, and the only traffic along the corridor was local traffic destined for points in West Duluth or neighborhoods immediately to the south and west.

- To accommodate needed commercial uses in West Duluth, commercial zoning was compressed into a 10- to 12-block area in the center of Spirit Valley, and commercial development within this area has since intensified. Existing commercial uses along portions of Grand Avenue were grandfathered and allowed to continue to operate. However, expansions of commercial use, and changes to other commercial uses along Grand Avenue, are discouraged. The hope is that nonconforming commercial areas will gradually transition to less intensive uses more residential in character. There are indications that this is beginning to happen: on Grand Avenue near 67th Avenue West, a structure that formerly housed a small neighborhood grocery store has been rebuilt and converted into a house.

Housing and Neighborhoods

- A program of matching grants (up to $4,000) was established and administered by SVNDA to encourage the rehabilitation of existing homes in West Duluth.

- SVNDA obtained two state grants (totaling $510,000) to finance the voluntary acquisition of derelict residential properties so badly deteriorated that renovation was not feasible. Many of the lots acquired under this voluntary acquisition program were only 25 feet wide; in some cases, the cleared land from these lots was combined with adjacent lots or tax-forfeited property to create larger and more appealing lots.

- New housing has been built in West Duluth for the first time in years. A number of scattered, tax-forfeited properties in the Fremont neighborhood that had been held in conservation were released by the city to SVNDA, which in turn made the lots available for the development of new housing under what it called its "Home Start" program. According to Jeanne Koneczny, "We got four banks to each agree to grant eight mortgages of up to a maximum of $55,000. Lots were sold for a dollar to income-qualified households, who could use the land as their equity for securing financing. Following this initial housing venture in the Fremont neighborhood, the city released a large triangular tract of conservation land just south of where the first phase of housing had been developed. The city then developed a subdivision plan, constructed roads, utilities and other site improvements, and made the lots available for purchase for roughly $15,000. A TIF district was established as a way of financing the project. In the Ramsey neighborhood, a 44-unit townhome development (composed of two- and three-bedroom rental units for low- and moderate-income households) was built with financing from the Duluth Economic Development Authority. A handful of infill single-family homes have also been built on scattered sites in the Irving neighborhood. A former elementary school in the Irving neighborhood was renovated into 43 rental units.

- An "Urban Village" housing scheme is about to be undertaken in the Ramsey neighborhood, and financing from the Minnesota Housing Agency has been obtained for new housing in the Irving neighborhood.

- Prior to the West Duluth plan, there were only three streets in the Irving neighborhood that weren't oil and dirt roads. Now, all the streets in the Irving neighborhood are paved, curbed and lined with trees.

Parks and Open Space

- "You see a lot more green in West Duluth these days," observed Jim Mohn. A park and recreation area was developed where Grand, Central, Cody and Ramsey Avenues come together. A mile-long extension of the Western Waterfront Trail was constructed along the St. Louis River from 75th Avenue West to 63rd Avenue West. Grassy Point (a promontory of land extending into St. Louis Bay) was cleaned up and restored to make it more of an amenity for passive recreation. The property, which was acquired by the Department of National Resources (DNR) and designated a state wildlife refuge, had previously been occupied by loading docks for loading lumber onto ships. "Vast numbers of logs had just been dumped there over the years and had sunk into the ground. They rotted and smelled pretty bad. A few years ago, the DNR started digging the logs out and restoring the area," said Jeanne Koneczny. A trail has since been constructed along Keene Creek connecting the Irving neighborhood playground to the restored Grassy Point Wildlife Refuge.

Many of the changes described above took years to accomplish. As Jim Mohn observed, "One of the things I've learned about being a planner is that it takes a lot of patience. The Keene Creek trail was envisioned in the 1985 West Duluth plan, and 14 years later, it got built." The process of replatting land and getting new homes built on former city-owned land in the Fremont neighborhood took nearly a decade. Nevertheless, 10 years later, all of the lots created had been sold and built upon, producing 31 new, single-family homes in West Duluth.

What *Did Not* Happen

The outcomes listed above are one way of measuring the positive impact of the West Duluth plan. However, the positive difference the plan has made for West Duluth can also be measured in terms of the things that *did not* happen. One of the main reasons why a plan was needed in West Duluth was to confront the issue of possible future industrial expansion in West Duluth and determine where such expansion should—and should *not*—occur. Only in that way could residential areas in West Duluth achieve the kind of stability needed to retain and attract new residents, potential homebuyers and new residential investment.

The West Duluth plan has, in fact, afforded older residential areas a degree of certainty and protection from unplanned and unwanted industrial expansion that they never had before. The protection afforded to West Duluth by the plan is perfectly illustrated by the LSPI plant, which was built on a 92-acre site created by displacing 114 West Duluth households.

According to Jeanne Koneczny, "After the [LSPI] plant was in operation for a while, it turned out that they wanted *more* land. Luckily, we had the plan, and the plan said they could not expand west of Central Avenue. Had we not had the plan, neighboring residents would have continually been threatened with displacement."

THE *2001 AND BEYOND* VISIONING PROCESS

In 1992, a new mayor took office. Throughout his campaign for office, Gary L. Doty made clear (as his predecessor had done) that his first and foremost goal was to promote business and economic development. Not long after Doty took office, Jerry Kimball and Karl Nollenberger (the city's administrative assistant) went to see the new mayor to discuss the concept of "community visioning" and to propose that a visioning process be carried out in Duluth.

Mayor Doty tended to view plans and regulations as obstacles to growth and development, but nevertheless found the idea of engaging members of the community in a visioning process appealing. In March 1993, Doty called together a group of corporate representatives and business leaders to seek their support for a fairly elaborate visioning process. In July 1993, a 25-member steering committee was formed, composed of the "movers and shakers" in town, to recommend how the visioning process should unfold and to raise money to cover expenses related to the process.

Roughly a year later (in September 1994), the "kick-off session" for what was to turn out to be a lengthy visioning process was held at the DECC. Later that fall, a series of 14 "cracker-barrel chats" was held, at which participants were divided into groups and asked to identify Duluth's positive attributes as well as problems and issues they felt needed to be addressed. To supplement the input obtained from these chats, the *Duluth News-Tribune* and *Duluth Budgeteer* published and distributed a community survey as an insert to their newspapers.

Analysis of the content of the cracker-barrel chats and community surveys produced three alternative visions or scenarios for Duluth:

1. Duluth as an Urban Wilderness
2. Duluth as a Neighborly Place
3. A Duluth that Embraces Innovation

In January 1995, a city-wide "Town Meeting" was held at the DECC where the findings of the two-year-long process and three future scenarios were presented. As a follow-up to this event, an "Electronic Town Meeting" was held that enabled people to respond to and ask questions about the three scenarios.

At the end of the lengthy *2001 and Beyond* process, a vision statement was produced that focused public attention on three "guiding principles" that embraced and expressed the key features of all three scenarios:

1. Investing in People, Neighborhoods and Communities
2. Building a Strong Economic Base
3. Preserving and Enhancing the Environment

A number of specific actions and investments were also identified and proposed that, if implemented, would help advance the three principles. The vision statement, guiding principles and recommendations were printed on a glossy 2- by 3-foot poster that was published and widely distributed throughout the city. Like the vision statement developed in Chattanooga, the three principles incorporated in the Duluth vision statement articulated the core principles underlying sustainable development.

While this city-wide visioning process was going on, planners in the Physical Planning Division were also working to prepare the *Old Downtown Strategic Plan* ("the Old Downtown plan") for the "Old Downtown" area (a 4.5-block-long stretch of the city's CBD, centered on Superior Street) that backs onto Lake Place (the pedestrian plaza, park and sculpture garden that was developed above the I-35 freeway).[27] There were several reasons for focusing planning attention on the Old Downtown area:

1. A number of buildings of architectural and historic significance were concentrated in the area.
2. The area included the old Nor-Shore and Strand Theaters, and the Fond-du-Luth Casino.
3. The Old Downtown area was the part of the downtown closest to Canal Park and the Downtown Lakewalk. (Unless one is arriving by boat, it is necessary to pass through the Old Downtown area to get to Canal Park.)

It was therefore a logical area in which to try to capitalize on the spin-off benefits of previous waterfront and Canal Park improvements. The Old Downtown plan was completed in February 1995 and had the following goals:

- Strengthen the identity of the Old Downtown area and preserve its historic character.
- Preserve and enhance arts and entertainment.
- Preserve and revitalize important buildings.
- Develop housing on vacant upper floors of existing buildings and encourage the development of new housing.
- Support a diverse mix of development.

Plans which seek to bring about significant changes can take years—sometime decades—to fully implement and realize. It is therefore not necessarily surprising that, roughly six years after the Old Downtown plan was completed, success in achieving the goals of the plan has been spotty and uneven. As of 2001, no new housing had been developed in the Old Downtown area, although the city was trying to achieve that goal by offering grants and low-interest loans to building owners to defray the cost of renovating upper floors and meeting building code requirements. The old Strand Theater, which the plan had hoped would be preserved, reached the point of such serious deterioration that it had to be taken down. The "Central Plaza" that was envisioned (a wide, midblock opening that was recommended to connect Superior Street to Lake Place) had also not happened.[28]

However, other actions consistent with the goals and recommendations of the plan had been taken. The city established three low-interest loan programs to encourage building owners to restore and renovate existing buildings in the Old Downtown area (loans for bringing buildings into code compliance, for interior improvements and for the restoration of historic façades). Each of these three types of loans can be for a maximum of $50,000. The maximum total loan for any building qualifying for all three loan programs is $150,000. According to planner John Judd, as of the end of July 2000, the façades of eight buildings within the project area had been restored under the storefront loan program.

An even more dramatic and visible outcome, consistent with the Old Downtown plan, was the city's decision to site and construct a 200,000-square-foot "Technology Village" (described more fully later in the chapter) on the corner of Lake Avenue and Superior Street, right where the plan called for the development of a new building. Lake Avenue is the principal gateway to the Canal Park area, and the Old Downtown plan recognized that the northeast corner of Lake Avenue and Superior Street was a highly visible and prestigious location that needed to be reinforced through more intense development. The main difference between what the plan called for—and what happened—is that the Technology Village/Soft Center structure is much larger than what was envisioned, taking up practically the entire city block between Lake Avenue and 1st

6-35   The 200,000-square-foot "Technology Village" on the corner of Lake Avenue and Superior Street, under construction.

Source: Courtesy of LHB Engineers & Architects, by Jeff Frey & Associates Photography

Avenue East. As a result, building the structure necessitated the demolition of some buildings that the Old Downtown plan had recommended for preservation. An attempt was made to soften these architectural losses by incorporating portions of the front façades of some of the demolished old buildings into the exterior of the new building.

PLANNING AND THE BUSINESS COMMUNITY

For over 30 years, from the time that Jerry Kimball arrived in Duluth, there has been a lively public debate about how to achieve a healthy community and a strong local economy. Many leaders of the city's business community have argued that the best way to bring about economic development is to minimize regulatory restraints and make development as easy as possible. Planners, on the other hand, have argued that the best way to achieve an economically successful city in the long run is to protect the city's environmental and historic resources, reinforce Duluth's unique identity and sense of place, and introduce positive qualities and features that make people want to live in Duluth—and make businesses want to locate in, stay in and invest in Duluth.

Critics charged that Jerry Kimball didn't care about economic development, but that wasn't true. He just felt that there was a better way to go about it. He recognized that meaningful, sustainable economic development required more than simply adopting a pro-business, "anything-goes" attitude. When people told him that all the city needed to do to create more jobs was to loosen the city's development regulations, he would answer, "There's more to economic development than that!" As Jill Fisher put it, "The economic development folks just don't seem to understand, or don't want to understand, that preserving a city's historic and environmental resources is, in itself, an effective, proven strategy for economic revitalization."

Building a sound and enduring local economy can and must be an important consideration in planning a city, but that does not mean that planning for "business and economic development" is the same as planning a city. Planning for business development is only *part* of what it takes to create a successful community—a fact that was explicitly recognized during the *2001 and Beyond* visioning process in Duluth, which identified three essential principles for a successful future: (1) Investing in People, Neighborhoods and Communities; (2) Building a Strong Economic Base; and (3) Preserving and Enhancing the Environment.

There are other important differences between planning a city and encouraging business development. The aims of business development tend to be mostly focused on achieving fairly immediate, near-term results (such as increasing jobs or investment), whereas planning tends to be characterized by longer term thinking. The phrase "business development" also tends to suggest that all businesses, and all forms and types of development, are equally desirable (*i.e.*, a job is a job). Planners, on the other hand, typically adopt a more discriminating point of view by asking, "What kind of place do we want our community to be in the future, and how can we make it a better place to live?" Lastly, framing the municipal agenda as "business development" rather than "city planning" suggests that the most important constituency in the community—the one to which we need to listen the most—is the business community rather than *all* the people of the city.

AN EDUCATED AND AROUSED CITIZENRY

Early in 1995, around the same time as the Old Downtown plan and the *2001 and Beyond* visioning process were being completed, Jerry Kimball took advantage of the opportunity to retire early. Over the course of a 30-year planning career, Kimball worked under six different mayors—most of whom came to recognize and warm to the benefits of planning during their years in office, even if they had been skeptical of the value of planning when they first took office. "The only mayor for whom I worked who didn't warm to the benefits of planning was Mayor Doty," said Kimball.

In a newspaper article that appeared soon after Jerry Kimball's retirement was announced, Kimball was quoted as saying, "My basic interest as a planner is to get people to think further ahead. There are very few constituencies for that type of thinking. I wish more Duluthians would be amateur planners and think about long-range issues." (Lincoln, February 19, 1995, 2B)

Under state and local law, if at least 4% of registered voters in the City of Duluth sign a petition challenging an ordinance or official vote of the city council, a referendum is held which, if approved, can overturn that city council action. In the years following Jerry Kimball's retirement, citizens in Duluth exercised this right of petition with increasing frequency; the number of land use-related lawsuits filed against the city also increased.[29]

A Proposed Waterfront Outlet Mall

In 1994, the first citizen-initiated petition was filed seeking to overturn the city council's approval of a large outlet mall along the Duluth waterfront—a major development and land use change that was most definitely *not* recommended in the Downtown Waterfront plan. The Downtown Council and the Greater Duluth Chamber of Commerce both strongly supported the Outlet Mall project, saying it would bring people to downtown Duluth and create economic development. However, other people in the community soon began to question whether devoting precious waterfront property to an automobile-oriented outlet mall made sense. They noted that most outlet malls were developed on large, expansive tracts of flat land near major interchanges of interstate and state highways, and that an outlet mall did not require a prime waterfront location.

Critics also questioned the idea that an outlet mall would produce economic benefits for the city. Since they tend to be large, self-contained, automobile-oriented developments requiring huge surface parking lots, such developments attract people in cars from long distances away but tend to generate little positive spin-off business for adjacent areas (except perhaps for gas stations and drive-in convenience stores). Also, despite their huge size, outlet malls tend to produce relatively few jobs (retail outlets economize by minimizing sales staff) and the jobs they create are relatively low paying. In addition, citizens argued that an outlet mall was out of character with the historic qualities of the city's Old Downtown and Canal Park areas—the very opposite of the type of development that the Downtown Waterfront plan was seeking to achieve.

According to Fred Witzig, "It would have been an atrocious use of waterfront property. People in the city who had seen the Duluth waterfront become a special place really got up in arms. It became an extremely unpopular proposal and, when it became unpopular, the developer couldn't get the money he needed because the people who were going to fund it got nervous. So it's not going to happen."

Proposed Expansion of Miller Hill Corridor Commercial Zoning

Two more citizen-initiative petitions were filed in 1995 appealing zoning changes granted by the city council for two major commercial developments along the Miller Hill Corridor. Both developments needed to be zoned C-5 to proceed. One of the zoning changes was requested to pave the way for a "big-box" retail mall (the Opus Mall) on a large, undeveloped property along the north side of Miller Trunk Highway. The other zoning change was requested by the operators of the Miller Hill Mall to allow the mall to increase from 40 to 70 acres.[30] The city council, which has the final authority over zoning changes, approved both zoning changes.

Petitions containing the signatures of over 4% of the registered voters in the city were filed, seeking to overturn both rezonings, and referenda were held on both matters in April 1996. The local newspaper ran a series of articles on the proposed developments and referenda questions. Indeed, the newspaper's balanced coverage, which included lengthy published interviews with Jerry Kimball (who opposed both rezonings) and a representative of the chamber of commerce (which supported them), helped voters understand the issues that were at stake. The results of the referenda produced a split decision and a partial victory for the city's planners and Duluth Planning Commission. The zoning change approved for the new Opus Mall was defeated by a wide margin—an important and encouraging vindication of the Miller Hill Corridor plan. The zoning change needed for the expansion of the Miller Hill Mall was narrowly approved by a 51 to 49% margin.

Fortunately, the C-5 zoning regulations adopted as a result of the Miller Hill Corridor plan gave the Duluth Planning Commission strong control over *how* the mall expansion was designed and carried out. "We required the Miller Hill Mall to retrofit the storm drainage system serving their site and the surrounding area," said Jim Mohn. "We got them to totally redo their circulation system and parking lot, and got a ring road developed around the mall. We got landscaping and landscaped islands incorporated for traffic control as well as for aesthetics and better drainage, and we got 40% of the site dedicated for stormwater management and detention."

As a further condition of approval, the city required the developers of the mall to set aside $20,000 into a fund to be administered by the city with the consent of the Pollution Control Agency and the Minnesota DNR for the restoration and improvement of Miller Creek. A Miller Creek Task Force, chaired by David Zentner (a local environmentalist) was formed to advise on how the money should be spent. People on the task force included mayors from affected adjoining communities, a Hermantown High School teacher, a Hermantown Elementary School teacher, and representatives from Trout Unlimited, DNR Fisheries, DNR Wildlife and DNR Water Resources. The task force decided to use most of the $20,000 exaction to undertake a concentrated tree-planting program along the banks of Miller Creek, and install traps in storm drains feeding into the creek to reduce sedimentation and erosion.

"During the last two or three years," said Jim Mohn, "we've planted 2,000 trees along the Miller Creek stream to get back some shade cover and to lower its temperature in the summer. We are also working with consultants to design sediment traps for storm drain systems in the area."

THE IMPACT OF A PLANNER ON A COMMUNITY

Fred Witzig is convinced that the planning principles for which Jerry Kimball stood and fought have served the City of Duluth well. At a gathering honoring Kimball when he retired, Witzig gave a speech in which he listed a number of the positive things planning had achieved in Duluth. He summed up by saying, "Good planning protects the amenities of a city, and this city is blessed with amenities in spades. We should never forget that. Jerry really introduced that important principle. Every plan and every proposal he developed was devoted to that idea."

The planning principles and ideals Kimball put forward and defended did not simply go quietly into the night. People listened to what he said and, in the process, Kimball became a lightning rod for the public debate of important land use and development issues. In turn, people who opposed Kimball's planning goals and programs, rather than debating the issues themselves, frequently tried to make Kimball the issue. "Jerry had some pretty strong convictions and the stands he took often became election issues," recalled Jim Mohn. "People just lined up, either for or against Jerry Kimball," said Jim Halquist, the owner of the Ellery House Bed and Breakfast where I stayed when I was in Duluth.

While highlighting his many planning accomplishments, a feature article on Jerry Kimball in the *Duluth News-Tribune* at the time of Kimball's announced retirement also drew attention to the fact that Kimball's planning efforts and positions often aroused harsh criticism from the business community. According to the article, "To business people, his beautiful streets, public artwork and historic preservation regulations stifle the essential foundation of the city's commerce." (Lincoln, February 19, 1995, 1B) The fact that some people in the city's business community criticized him did not cause Kimball to question the soundness of his ideas and principles. As Kimball told me, "Someone in my position is inevitably going to be somewhat controversial. It's the '90% is not enough' rule. A planner can satisfy developers or the business community 90% of the time, but it's the other 10% they remember."

In 1999, roughly three years after Jerry Kimball retired, the Physical Planning Division was effectively shut down when the position of physical planning division manager was eliminated, and the planners who formerly staffed the division (such as Bill Majewski, Jim Mohn and Jill Fisher) were shifted to the

Office of Business Development. When I interviewed Darrell Lewis (the person who was hired to replace Kimball), it was made very clear to me that a major shift in purpose and style of practice had taken place. Early on in the interview, Lewis went out of his way to distance himself from previous planning efforts. "My aims are different from my predecessors. My aim is to get Duluth back to a stable economic footing. A lot of what was done in the past in the name of planning stood in the way of that."

Lewis' pro-business, pro-development stance earned him considerable praise from Duluth's business community. An article that appeared in the June 1995 issue of *Business North* (a local business magazine) gleefully proclaimed "New Duluth Planner Talks Like a Developer."

The fact that the person who occupied the city's most senior planning position in Duluth in 1998 was so openly critical of past planning efforts was not what I had expected to discover when I traveled to Duluth. Nevertheless, it is something that I must report, since it is highly relevant to the point of this book: planning *does* and *can* make a difference in communities, and the *way* it is conducted *does matter*.

Lewis' conscious effort to be seen as pro-development could not have been more different from the message Jerry Kimball sought to convey. To Kimball, it was important to be able to discriminate between "good" and "bad" development. He prided himself on trying to achieve a balanced approach to land use and development. In an article in the *Duluth News-Tribune*, Kimball is quoted as saying, "My planning division took controversial stands for job-producing projects. It was important to support projects like the Oneota and Airport industrial parks, the paper mill and Minneapolis Electric foundry. But it was also important for us to help initiate improvements that lift the human spirit. Projects like the Downtown Lakewalk, Bayfront Park, the William A. Irvin, Public Arts Commission, Heritage Preservation Commission and the downtown renaissance make Duluth more inviting to investors and rekindle civic pride." (Kimball, January 31, 1998)

To me, one of the most important obligations of being a professional planner is to try to strike a balance between the need for development (and for building and maintaining a healthy economy) and the need for environmental conservation and historic preservation. Darrell Lewis' approach for land use and development issues, in my opinion, fell short of that standard. However, I don't think for a moment that Darrell Lewis was solely responsible for the shift in planning policy that occurred following Jerry Kimball's departure. It was simply another manifestation of the long-standing battle between planning and economic development that has been playing itself out in Duluth for almost half a century. The positions that Lewis took on land use and development issues were ones the city's mayor hoped and expected him to take—and Mayor Doty must have believed that such pro-economic development policies would play well with the electorate. However, the mayor may have misread public opinion.[31]

THE USS DES MOINES IN DULUTH?

The dust had only just settled from the results of the two 1996 referenda (discussed earlier) when another development idea came out of left field that had no basis in any plan. A group of Duluthians convinced the governor of Minnesota, Arne Carlson, that it would be a great idea to bring the USS Des Moines (a heavy cruiser that was in mothballs in Philadelphia) to Duluth and put it on display. The governor, like any good politician anxious to do something for his constituents, ran with the idea. Not only was the USS Des Moines going to become a permanent fixture on Duluth's waterfront, but the immediate area surrounding the USS Des Moines was going be a veterans' memorial, which the governor said could then be made into a state park.

Making the USS Des Moines the centerpiece of a "veterans memorial" seemed to assure that the project would sail through the local approval process. The fact that the governor was prepared to commit $10 million in state money to the project was also a powerful inducement. However, once again, many residents in Duluth—educated and sensitized by planners regarding the importance of preserving the city's unique sense of place and identity, and who were reinforced in thinking that way by the success of the Downtown Waterfront plan—were not impressed. The proposal just didn't ring true to the city's identity as a Great Lakes port.

"This is a fresh water port," claimed Fred Witzig, "and we're developing a theme here. The USS Des Moines just doesn't fit that theme. The Irvin fits down there, and we can find other ships that will fit the history of the city. What does the Des Moines have to do with Duluth?"

The city's mayor and city council lined up behind the governor's proposal in favor of bringing the Des Moines to Duluth. However, the project generated so much controversy that, while it was working its way through the state legislature, the city council decided to put it to a city-wide advisory referendum. The referendum on the USS Des Moines and Veterans Park project was held in March 1998. Most people in the city's business community, and most owners of businesses and restaurants downtown and in Canal Park, were in favor of the project. According to the *Duluth News-Tribune*, the local and state interest groups that backed the ship/veterans memorial project outspent the opponents 11 to 1. (*Duluth News-Tribune*, March 28, 1998) Nevertheless, by a 2 to 1 margin, voters said "no" to bringing the USS Des Moines to Duluth.

According to Fred Witzig, "The newspaper, to its credit, did a lot of research on this issue and ran articles about other navy ships in other cities. They told how costly they were to maintain, how they rusted and how most of them received some subsidy from the federal government."

It is a very encouraging sign, I think, that citizens in Duluth are now willing to vote to overturn major developments and projects which conflict with adopted plans and policies. It suggests that planners like Jerry Kimball have done more than simply develop plans and policies that have been good for the city's physical environment. They have also been community educators, and have taught people in Duluth to appreciate and celebrate what is special about their city. In so doing, they have helped raise the collective self-esteem of the community. People in Duluth now have enough confidence in their community's future that they know the city can and must be selective in what it approves. No longer are Duluthians so desperate for development that they feel compelled to accept any and every proposal that comes along. They even feel confident enough to say "No, thank you!" to Governor Carlson's offer of a heavy cruiser and $10 million.

THE ECONOMIC BENEFITS OF A
BALANCED APPROACH TO PLANNING

Today's businesses are much more foot-loose than they ever were in the past. They can find offices in almost any location, which also means that the environmental and aesthetic qualities of places often loom large in corporate siting decisions.

Not long ago, Cirrus Aircraft (a fledgling company that had been based in southern Wisconsin) decided it would relocate its operations to Duluth. "The principal owner of the company just happened to drive through Duluth on his way somewhere else and liked what he saw. He decided then and there that he would move the company to Duluth," said Bill Majewski.

Fingerhut and United Healthcare have also opened offices in Duluth in recent years. "Both companies are headquartered in the Twin Cities and had never dreamed of having operations in Duluth," explained Tom Cotruvo, "but we finally got their attention. When we got them to take a look, they saw that our downtown was cleaned up. When they found out that there were a lot of people who wanted to live here, they both decided to establish offices. Between them, they now probably employ around 1,000 people."

In an article he wrote for the *Duluth News-Tribune*, Jerry Kimball summarized Duluth's locational advantage in this way: "Duluth's economic advantage is so close we often overlook it, so simple we often view it as simplistic . . . Duluth's economic grail is our civic spirit, our individuality, and our unique identity . . . Our local identity is indeed unique. It is what so many American cities would love to have and what more and more astute investors and developers are looking for: a city that looks good and has a good feel; one that has good schools and relatively low crime; one that has memorable natural features of hills, water, rock, wetlands, parks and a greenbelt better than the famous British ones; a city having the will to dare to preserve those natural features as well as its solid downtown, proud waterfront and clearly defined neighborhoods." (Kimball, September 23, 1995)

The qualities to which Kimball drew attention in his article are particularly valued by educated, skilled professionals who place a high value on quality of life and who want to live in places that have qualities and amenities that make them special. That should help improve the chances of success of the $32 million Technology Village which opened in the heart of downtown Duluth in the summer of 2000.[32] Dubbed by many as the "Soft Center Duluth," the project's aim is to broaden Duluth's economic base by making it "a major port city for information technology as it has long been for timber, grain and iron ore." (Honan, July 8, 2000, C4)

The inspiration for Duluth's Technology Village came from a sister-city exchange trip that Mayor Doty took to Växjö, Sweden in 1995. On his way to Växjö, Doty passed through the City of Ronneby where he stumbled upon "a technology campus that brought together under one roof about 100 high-technology businesses, branches of academic institutions, professors working as research and development consultants, and students taking classes and serving internships." (*ibid.*) To Doty, it was a "school-to-work" model that seemed potentially applicable to Duluth in that it afforded a way to capitalize on the talents of UMD faculty, and provide training and work opportunities in Duluth for bright and talented university students in growing fields of information technology (and not lose them to other cities after graduation).

It is impossible to tell at this point whether the center will succeed in achieving its grandiose aim of strengthening Duluth's position as a center for emerging technology-based businesses. (As of July 2000, the Technology Village was roughly 30% occupied.) However, the chances that the center will attract and retain talented people with skills in information technology *have been greatly increased* by the positive changes brought about in Duluth in the 1970s, 1980s and 1990s.

The transformation and revitalization of the city's waterfront has most certainly increased the drawing power of Duluth as a tourist destination, and made it an increasingly popular location for major conferences, professional meetings, trade shows and entertainment events. In 1987, roughly 12 statewide conventions were held in Duluth; in 1998, approximately 45 major conventions and conferences were held.

"Some of the growth in the convention business is obviously due to the improvement and expansion of the convention facilities themselves," commented Jerry Kimball. (In the early 1990s, the DECC was dramatically expanded by constructing a convention center adjacent to the original arena/auditorium.) "However," Kimball continued, "a lot of it has to do with the city's improved image and the improvements that have been made along the waterfront."

6-36 View from the top of the staircase and platform leading down to the Downtown Lakewalk.

Source: Gene Bunnell

AN INCREASINGLY APPEALING PLACE TO LIVE

The transformation of Duluth has not gone unnoticed nationally. *Money Magazine's* 1990 "Best Places to Live" survey (taken one year after the first section of the Downtown Lakewalk was completed) ranked Duluth #51 out of 300 cities nationwide; one year later (in 1991), Duluth was ranked #21; in its 1992 "Best Places" survey, Duluth was ranked #14.

Feature articles describing Duluth's positive qualities have also appeared in national newspapers and publications such as *The New York Times* and *The Chicago Tribune*. An article that appeared in a magazine published by the Farmers Insurance Company typified the positive tone of most of these articles. The article spotlighted three "Favorite Destinations": Carmel and San Francisco, California; and Duluth, Minnesota. Not bad company!

One evening at sunset, toward the end of my stay in Duluth, I bought an ice cream cone at a stand in a renovated, vintage gas station on Superior Street and walked a short distance to a platform and staircase that led down to the Downtown Lakewalk. The staircase had a broad platform that provided an excellent spot for viewing the lake and Downtown Lakewalk below.

As I stood gazing out at the lake, I noticed a couple in their late 50s or early 60s standing nearby who were also enjoying the sunset. As we ate our ice cream cones, we began talking. When I told them I had driven up from Madi-

6-37   Walking along the Downtown Lakewalk, with Aerial Lift Bridge far in the distance.

Source: Gene Bunnell

son, I learned that they were also from Madison. They had lived in Madison for most of their working lives but, when they recently retired, they decided to move to Duluth. They said they loved being in Duluth, looking out at the lake and walking on the Downtown Lakewalk.

Few people have probably ever thought of Duluth as a retirement place, but they might be on to something. Why retire to Florida or Arizona just because it's warm there? Why not retire to some place special—like Duluth!

INTERVIEWEES

Ben Boo, long-time resident and mayor of Duluth (1967-1974)

Thomas D. Cotruvo, manager, City of Duluth Office of Business Development

Jill Fisher, senior planner (and interim manager of physical planning), City of Duluth Physical Planning Division

Jim Halquist, city resident, owner of the Ellery House Bed and Breakfast

John Judd, City of Duluth Community Development Division, Office of Planning and Development

Gerald M. (Jerry) Kimball, City of Duluth, manager of City of Duluth Physical Planning Division (1968-1995)

Jeanne Koneczny, West Duluth resident and Spirit Valley Neighborhood Development Association Housing Coordinator

Patrick Labadie, U.S. Army Corps of Engineers, head, Duluth Marine Museum

Darrell Lewis, manager of City of Duluth Physical Planning Division (1995-98)
William Majewski, senior planner, City of Duluth Physical Planning Division
James E. Mohn, senior planner, City of Duluth Physical Planning Division
Kathy Severson, City of Duluth, Community Development and Housing
    Division
Frederick T. Witzig, professor of geography and urban and regional studies
    program, University of Minnesota at Duluth (retired), and member of the
    Duluth Planning Commission (1969-83)

PLANNING STORY CHRONOLOGY

1887   William K. Rogers envisions the creation of a hilltop parkway
        running through a greenbelt of parks along the top of the steep
        escarpment overlooking the city and Lake Superior, as well as
        bayfront and lakefront parks along the length of the city's
        shoreline. Rogers' vision proves so compelling that it is eventually
        fulfilled through the development of the Duluth parkway system
        and Skyline Drive.

1907   Daniel Burnham prepares the plan for the Duluth Civic Center—
        three classically designed government buildings grouped around a
        landscaped park. He also designs the first building—the St. Louis
        County courthouse. Burnham proposes that the Civic Center be
        built on an elevated site on 5th Avenue, a short distance from the
        city's main railroad depot.

1909   The 16-story Alworth Building, designed by Daniel Burnham, is
        completed in the same year as Burnham completes his famous
        1909 Chicago plan. At the time, the Alworth Building was the
        tallest building in Minnesota.

1911   Construction of the St. Louis County courthouse is completed at a
        cost of $1 million.

1912   Duluth adopts a commission form of government.

1917-20 Inspired by William K. Rogers' vision of a hilltop parkway and
        park system, 1,433 acres of land is added to the park system.

1921   Samuel F. Snively is elected mayor of Duluth, serves as mayor for
        four terms until 1937 and makes expansion of the city's park
        system and completion of Skyline Drive the centerpiece of his
        administration. Snively plays a key role in raising private funds for
        the acquisition of parklands and the right of way for Skyline Drive,
        and personally supervises the construction of 20 miles of the scenic
        parkway.

1922   The city's planning department is created by ordinance, and a 13-
        member City Planning Commission is appointed.

1926   A. B. Horowitz is hired as the city's first city planner.

1928	Duluth City Hall is completed, the second of three buildings at the Civic Center. The city's first comprehensive plan is completed by planning consultant Harland Bartholomew.
1930	The third of three proposed buildings at the Civic Center, the Federal Building, is completed.
1930s	City planner Horowitz reserves land for a future campus of the University of Minnesota at Duluth (UMD).
1937	An updated zoning ordinance, developed with the assistance of planning and zoning consultant Edward Bassett, is adopted.
1944	John Hunner becomes Duluth's second city planner.
1947	Construction work begins on the first university buildings on the new campus of UMD.
1956	Duluth changes its structure of government from a commission form to a strong mayor/council form. Subsequent reorganizations during the next two decades place the planning director much closer to the mayor.
1958	A second comprehensive plan is prepared, calling for future development to be confined largely to previously developed areas and for preserving large areas of open space. The city's zoning ordinance is thoroughly revised.
1967	Ben Boo is elected mayor, and creates the Department of Research and Planning. Donn Wiski is appointed as the department's director.
1968	Jerry Kimball is hired to direct physical planning in the city, filling the position vacated by John Hunner.
1972	Immense quantities of stormwater runoff cascade down into the city, causing enormous damage ("The Big Storm").
1979	The *Miller Hill Corridor Plan* ("the Miller Hill Corridor plan") is completed and adopted by the city council. John Fedo is elected mayor. During his mayoral campaign, Fedo criticizes the city's Planning and Development Department and says it is "bloated."
1980	Mayor Fedo splits the Department of Planning and Development into a Business Development Office (reporting directly to him), and a truncated Planning Office headed by a manager who reports to the mayor's administrative assistant. Staff transfers out of the Planning Office leave it with a staff of only two full-time professionals, two clerical positions and a handful of student interns.
1983	The Duluth Planning Office and Duluth Planning Commission organize a series of vision forums called *Future City, Duluth Tomorrow*. Six vision forums are held over a six-month period. Nationally recognized outside experts (such as William H. Whyte,

Robert Freilich, Neal Peirce, Luther P. Gerlach and John Borchert) are brought to Duluth to make presentations. A major outcome of the visioning process is that a consensus develops that the city's waterfront is the top planning and development priority. Mayor Fedo calls a press conference to announce that he is calling upon the Duluth Planning Commission to prepare a plan for the downtown waterfront.

1986   *Downtown Waterfront Plan and Strategy* ("the Downtown Waterfront plan") is completed and published. The William A. Irvin, a 600-foot-long iron ore carrier, which was about to be dismantled for scrap, is purchased for $140,000, restored at a cost of $250,000, brought to the Minnesota Slip alongside Canal Park and opened as a floating maritime museum.

1987   *West Duluth—Opportunities for Change* ("the West Duluth plan"), a plan for West Duluth, is completed. State legislation is passed approving special Duluth legislation calling for the establishment of the Downtown Waterfront Mixed-Use Design Review District. Bayfront Festival Park, an 11-acre park for public events, is completed.

1989   The first section of the Downtown Lakewalk is completed—a one-half mile stretch between the Ship Canal and "Corner-of-Lake" Park.

1990   The waterfront design review zoning ordinance is officially adopted, and the Waterfront Design Review Board is established.

1991   Lake Place, a 2.5-acre park constructed on top of Interstate 35 at a cost of $10 million, is completed.

1994   Kick-off session of *2001 and Beyond* visioning process.

1995   *Old Downtown Strategic Plan* ("the Old Downtown plan") is completed. Jerry Kimball retires after directing physical planning in the city for 26 years.

1998   Voters vote down a proposal to move the USS Des Moines to Duluth.

2000 $32 million Great Lakes Aquarium opens.

NOTES

1. The completion of the St. Lawrence Seaway effectively brought an end to Buffalo's role as an important Great Lakes port. Business leaders in Buffalo hailed the completion of the seaway, saying that it would make Buffalo a world port. It actually did the opposite, because it eliminated Buffalo's role as a "break-in-bulk" point where goods were transferred between rail and ships. Once the seaway was completed, there was no need whatsoever for ships to stop in the Port of Buffalo; they simply sailed past Buffalo toward Great Lakes ports further inland.

2. The port facilities at Duluth, Minnesota and Superior, Wisconsin effectively function as a single port, the operations of which are overseen by a single port authority—the Twin Ports Authority. However, despite the functional integration of the port and the close proximity of Duluth and Superior, the two city governments have historically operated independently of each other and, as far as I can tell, there has been no attempt whatsoever to coordinate municipal planning efforts. One factor that has undoubtedly increased the gulf between the two cities is that they are in different states, with different tax structures and systems of state and local finance that are essentially in competition with each another for economic development. For these and other reasons, perhaps, Duluth and Superior have essentially come to see themselves as rivals rather than partners and have largely gone their separate ways.

3. U.S. Steel Corporation's production facilities were built as part of a model planned community named Morgan Park (after J. P. Morgan). In addition to the steel plant and associated industrial facilities, Morgan Park included attractively laid out residential neighborhoods (composed of single-family detached dwellings, two-family and attached dwellings and boarding house units) as well as a general store, a cafe, a school, a children's playground, churches (Catholic and Protestant), a hospital, company offices and workshops.

4. The St. Lawrence and Great Lakes Waterway is the longest inland navigation system on the North American continent.

5. In 1961, the Duluth-Superior Harbor shipped 31,376,472 tons of cargo, making it the ninth busiest port in the nation. In 1991, the amount of cargo transported through the port had risen to 40,802,451 tons, but that total ranked Duluth-Superior #14, relative to other ports in the U.S. In 1997, Duluth-Superior ranked #18 nationally in terms of total cargo volume handled, even though it once again handled more than 40 million metric tons of cargo.

6. Many of the neighborhoods that now comprise Duluth were at one time separate municipalities. Six previously separate municipalities were annexed to create what we now know as the City of Duluth. The last annexation occurred in 1912.

7. An Historic Landscape Evaluation Study of the Duluth parkway system was completed in 1997 by the Duluth Preservation Commission, with funds provided by the National Parks Service through the Minnesota Historical Society.

8. In the process of preparing the city's first comprehensive plan and city-wide zoning ordinance, A. B. Horowitz brought two of the most highly respected planning and zoning consultants of the time to Duluth. The 1928 comprehensive plan was prepared by Harland Bartholomew. The updated zoning ordinance adopted in 1937 was developed with the assistance of Edward Bassett. Horowitz served as Duluth's planning director from 1926 until 1944. After Duluth, Horowitz went on to work as a planner in Cleveland and, after World War II, in Israel.

9. The complex, which was constructed on the land that was cleared, has enjoyed only mixed results. The hotel has done well, but the retail portion of the development has not been successful and retail stores in the mall have struggled.

10. A late 1960s plan that called for bringing the freeway up and over the city, miles away from the lake, was aborted after 10 planning commissioners took a much-publicized, 15-mile snowmobile ride over the proposed route to see for themselves the devastating impact the route would have on the city's valleys and greenbelt.

11. Total student enrollment at UMD now stands at roughly 5,000.

12. Loraas held a master's degree in urban planning from the University of Illinois. Wiski's graduate and undergraduate degrees were in public administration and geography.

13. After serving as mayor of Duluth from 1917-1920, Magney served for 23

years as a district judge and later became an associate justice of the Minnesota Supreme Court.

14. The fact that economic conditions were so bad in Duluth for so long made the tax-forfeited land provision an even more important tool for conserving land than it would have been in a city with a healthy and growing economy. As the city's population declined and the local economy weakened, many property owners (believing that there was little or no prospect of ever profitably developing the land they owned—especially land on which it was difficult to build) simply decided not to pay the property taxes that were owed and walked away, thereby adding to the list of tax-forfeited property.

15. A local law, passed in the mid-1980s, outlawed the placement of strobe lights—so irritatingly pervasive in other cities—on broadcasting antenna and other communications towers, and instead required that the lights be a flashing red (much easier on the eye).

16. The seven stone bridges, which are listed on the National Register of Historic Places, were restored and rebuilt in 1997 and 1998, largely due to the efforts of planners in the city's Physical Planning Division. According to Jerry Kimball, "We [in the Physical Planning Division] had a hard time convincing the city engineer and highway engineers at the MNDOT that the bridges should be restored rather than replaced with new bridges. The highway engineers wanted to tear down the old bridges to straighten and widen the road, and increase its design speed." Fortunately, in this case, scenic and historic preservation considerations raised by planners won out.

17. With the loss of these two planners, the Physical Planning Division was left with a staff that consisted of three, full-time professional planners and two clerical positions.

18. Sebok had professional training in both urban planning and landscape architecture.

19. The findings and observations Olsen and Witzig presented to citizens at the 1983 *Future City, Duluth Tomorrow* visioning program were summarized in a paper they presented at the 1984 Annual Meeting of the Urban Affairs Association in Portland, Oregon. The title of the paper was "Coming to Grips with a City in Decline: The Role of the City Planning Commission." Video copies of the *Future City* sessions are on file for viewing at Duluth City Hall.

20. In 1998, shipments of iron ore and taconite accounted for 32% of the nation's total tonnage; over 25% of the cargo handled through the Port of Duluth-Superior in 1998 was involved in international trade—nearly half of which was accounted for by bulk grain shipments. In addition to wheat, corn and rye, the agricultural goods shipped out of Duluth include soybeans, sunflower seeds, flax, sugar beet pellets, onions and potatoes. Although iron ore and taconite continue to account for the largest amount of tonnage, other commodities are also shipped through the port in significant quantities, such as low sulfur coal from Montana and limestone.

21. The cost of acquiring and restoring the Irvin was paid for by the DECC, but these costs have been easily defrayed by income generated from admission fees paid by visitors to the ship. The Irvin has generated an annual operating profit for the DECC of no less than $70,000 since it first opened.

22. The "Lake Place Image Wall" was constructed to mitigate the sound and visual impacts of the I-35 freeway, and was funded with highway funds.

23. The color, pattern and texture of the exterior surface of the lantern tower match that of the clock tower of the old Central High School—another indication of the considerable attention to detail given in the execution of the Downtown Waterfront plan.

24. "We defined the locations where pieces of art or sculpture would be placed, and specified what we wanted works of art in specific locations to achieve," said Jerry Kimball. An RFP was then issued and sent to artists across the country, inviting them to submit their proposed works. The RFP elicited over 600 different proposals, and a committee was established to review them and choose specific works for specific sites. Roughly 5% of the $10 million spent on streetscape improvements in the Canal Park area between 1990 and 1992 was for sculpture and art.

25. During the first eight years of the planning effort on the aquarium, Robert Bruce (a senior planner in the city's Physical Planning Division) was the project manager.

26. There are seven neighborhoods in West Duluth: Spirit Valley (located in the geographic center of West Duluth), Fremont, Fairmont, Irving, Cody, Denfield and Oneota. However, it is important to make clear that SVNDA does not only represent the interests of the Spirit Valley neighborhood; rather, it was formed to represent the interests of *all* West Duluth neighborhoods.

27. The preparation of the *Old Downtown Strategic Plan* was completed by planners of the city's Physical Planning Division, working with an eight-member Plan Steering Committee and approximately 40 other people on six different task forces.

28. The "Central Plaza" would not have required any demolition of any significant downtown structures. Rather, it was planned to utilize the property of a one-story muffler repair shop and parking area (that replaced the former Sears muffler repair shop). However, the city has been unable, as of this date, to reach an agreement with the property owner on an acceptable purchase price, so prospects for the plaza are currently on the "back burner."

29. According to Jerry Kimball, more land use lawsuits were filed against the city in the five years after he retired than during his entire 26-year tenure as the head of the city's Physical Planning Division.

30. Citizen members of the Duluth Planning Commission were bitterly divided when the two proposed zoning changes were brought before them for a recommendation. One planning commissioner said that what the developers were attempting to do was like "trying to stuff 15 pounds into a 5-pound bag." Nevertheless, upon Darrell Lewis' recommendation, the commission narrowly approved the rezoning for the Opus Mall; the commission's vote on the rezoning for the expansion of the existing Miller Hill Mall was a tie, which was officially recorded as "no action."

31. In June 1998, after a little more than three years working as Duluth's director of planning and development, Darrell Lewis resigned to take a new position in Pasadena, California.

32. The Technology Village/Soft Center was privately developed by A & L Development. Approximately two-thirds of the cost of the project was privately financed with public funding contributing the balance. The city's contribution to the project was principally toward the cost of land acquisition and clearance, and toward the cost of constructing an adjacent 600-car parking structure.

7

San Diego, California

A Hundred-Year Planning Legacy
(Periodically Interrupted)

Author's Note: In writing about San Diego's early history, I have relied heavily on *San Diego: Perfecting Paradise* (1999) by Roger M. Showley—a wonderful and beautifully illustrated book that devotes considerable attention to San Diego's long and distinguished planning legacy.

I am equally indebted to Michael Stepner for his valuable assistance and insights. Before becoming the dean of the NewSchool of Architecture and Design, Stepner worked for 26 years for the City of San Diego (1971-97), first as an urban designer/planner, then as assistant planning director, acting planning director, city architect, assistant to the city manager/special projects coordinator, and finally as city urban design coordinator. Michael Stepner spent almost an entire day taking me to far-flung places, projects, neighborhoods and landscapes that provided visible proof of the positive difference planning has made in San Diego. I had the tape recorder running throughout the day, and many of the comments Stepner made are quoted in the chapter that follows. Michael Stepner has also written a number of articles on the subject of planning in San Diego, some of which are also quoted in this chapter. Quotes from those articles and papers are accompanied by the date of publication. Statements made by Stepner during our 1998 tour are *not* accompanied by a date.

INTRODUCTION

San Diego's emergence as a major American city is a remarkably recent phenomenon. Prior to 1940, San Diego was a fairly minor port and industrial city

7-1   Downtown San Diego as viewed from across San Diego Bay.

Source: Port of San Diego/Dale Frost

7-2   Mission Beach, one of the many long stretches of sandy beaches in San Diego, which encloses Mission Bay to the right. Photographed shortly after taking off from Lindbergh Field in downtown San Diego.

Source: Gene Bunnell

with a population of approximately 200,000—its growth apparently hampered by its location at the southernmost point of the American Pacific Coast, and the perception that it was remote and out of the way. Even San Diegans seemed to embrace the notion that their city was "on the edge"—as if North America somehow dropped off at the Mexican border.

However, with the outbreak of World War II, San Diego was quickly brought into the center of activity as a result of a dramatic upsurge in war-related employment and a consequent dramatic inflow of population. In 1950, after World War II ended, San Diego's population stood at 557,000—over two and one-half times what it was only 10 years before. Between 1950 and 1970, the city continued to grow, but at a more moderate rate. In the 1970s, a new upsurge in population growth and development activity occurred and San Diego's population increased from 697,640 in 1970 to 1,110,549 in 1990—an almost 60% increase in 20 years. By 2000, the population of the City of San Diego was 1,223,400, making it the seventh largest city in terms of population in the U.S.

San Diego encompasses an area of over 320 square miles and is the 11th largest municipality in the U.S. in terms of land area. San Diego County (which includes the City of San Diego and 17 other municipalities) is super-sized as well, encompassing a 4,200-square-mile area (slightly less than the size of the State of Connecticut). Approximately half of the roughly 2.5 million people living in San Diego County live in the City of San Diego.

Viewed purely in terms of its natural and environmental qualities, it is easy to understand why people have been drawn to San Diego. Seventy miles of sandy beaches extend north from San Diego Bay to Oceanside and south toward Tijuana, Mexico, luring swimmers, surfers and sun-bathers. San Diego has a sunny, dry, mild Mediterranean climate. Along the coast, where most of San Diego's population is concentrated, it hardly ever rains (the annual rainfall is usually less than 10 inches) and temperatures are remarkably stable (the annual average high temperature throughout the year is 70 degrees F, and the annual average low is 55 degrees F). As John Gunther cleverly put it, San Diego has "the shortest thermometer in the United States." (Gunther 1947, 55)

In the center of this natural paradise (and in the heart of the City of San Diego) lies Balboa Park, which is 1,400 acres—50% larger than New York City's Central Park. The following description, written over a quarter century ago, provides a sense of what Balboa Park has meant to San Diego.

"On the mesa and canyons just above downtown, happy crowds wander through this masterfully planned pleasure ground. Next door to the zoo, carefully maintained remains of two world's fairs form another unmatched outdoor setting for public life. Among the youth, inner-city folk, Chicanos, and out-of-town visitors mingling in this urbane place, a well-turned-out Tijuana family reacted, 'Balboa Park is the most beautiful park in the world.'" (Montgomery, August 21, 1976, 26)

THE UNIQUE GEOGRAPHY OF THE REGION

Two features of San Diego's geography immediately distinguish it from other cities and regions in the country. The first is the tremendous diversity of landscapes and microclimates. As Thomas T. Story (a planner with the City of San Diego) explained, there are more microclimates in San Diego than any other place in the country. The juxtaposition of different types of landscapes within a relatively compressed geographic area—mountains, mesas, valleys and canyons, coastal bluffs and sandy beaches along the sea—makes the San Diego region unique.

Kevin Lynch and Donald Appleyard provided the following description the area's unusually diverse landscape: "Upland from the shore, above the first bluffs, the flat mesas rise gradually to the mountains. The ground is dry, and the soil, for the most part, thin and poor, covered with a tough, dull brush. What water there is is in the valleys . . . The streams are quite small, but on occasion they will fill their valley with a wild torrent. The mesa tops are intersected almost everywhere by a branching network of deep, dry, V-shaped canyons, leading down to the flat-bottomed valleys, and so breaking up what otherwise might be a rather monotonous terrain. Behind all this lie the mountains, with their picturesque ridges and green valleys. Behind them is the desert."

Other major cities in the U.S. (such as Portland, Oregon and Los Angeles, California) have developed within a valley. However, as William Anderson (a long-time member of the San Diego Planning Commission) reminded me, San Diego is the only major city in the U.S. that has superimposed itself upon and grown within a *system* of canyons and valleys. "Having this intricate system of canyons and valleys does quite a few things," Anderson said. "First, it helps define communities and neighborhoods. Second, it provides natural systems that are very close to, and integrated with, the urban system, bringing people into much closer contact with the natural environment."

Mission Valley (roughly 3 miles north of downtown San Diego) is the largest of the valleys in San Diego and extends roughly 11 miles in an east-west direction. A number of other valleys and canyons, not as large as Mission Valley, also run east-west and drain into the Pacific Ocean; others run north-south and directions in between.

Moving inland, the mesas gradually rise in elevation, to foothills and eventually to 6,000-foot mountains. In the eastern third of San Diego County, the mountains drop off abruptly into the Anza-Borrego Desert. These dramatic changes in the physical landscape are accompanied by equally striking changes in climatic conditions and vegetation. Leaving the mesas along the coast and moving east into the foothills and toward the mountains, the climate becomes progressively more extreme—hotter in the summer and colder in the winter. Likewise, chaparral and coastal sage scrub along the mesas and within the valleys and canyons give way to oaks in the foothills and coniferous forest in the mountains. The variety and diversity of landscapes and climates, all within relatively close proximity, is astounding. As John Gunther observed, "You can pick oranges in the morning, ski at noon, and swim at dusk." (Gunther 1947, 55)

Another important aspect of San Diego's geography, which has clearly shaped the city's character and identity, is its location—125 miles south of Los Angeles and only 18 miles from downtown San Diego to the Mexican border. To appreciate the importance of San Diego's position vis-à-vis Mexico, all one has to do is to spend time watching the steady flow of traffic (cars, trucks and pedestrians) at the border crossing at San Ysidro—the busiest border crossing in the world. To appreciate the extent to which San Diego is tied to Los Angeles, all one has to do is to drive on the Los Angeles-San Diego (I-5) freeway, which carries tens of thousands of cars and trucks roaring back and forth between the two cities around the clock every day.

Based on trade, market and employment statistics, a strong case could be made that San Diego and Los Angeles already constitute a single regional city—just as the French geographer Jean Gottmann contended in the 1950s that the nearly continuous urban corridor stretching between Boston and Washington was "Megalopolis." Most San Diegans, however, find the idea of San Diego being part of Los Angeles to be deeply disturbing.[1]

People in San Diego may not always have agreed on what they want their city to be in the future, but they have had much more success agreeing on what they *don't* want San Diego to become. Ask San Diegans what they would like their city to be in the future and, more times than not, you will get the following answer: *"Not* like Los Angeles."[2]

Fortunately, for those who are comforted by the sense of San Diego's separateness from the looming metropolis to the north, there is the huge Camp Pendleton Marine Corps base in northern San Diego County. Stepner and Fiske describe Camp Pendleton as an "armed border" and a "line of defense against the encroachment of Orange County and Los Angeles." (Stepner and Fiske 2000, 80)

In addition to the natural geographic features and characteristics that San Diego has inherited, there is a man-made feature of the city's geography that is also important to note: Lindbergh Field (San Diego's centrally located airport). With winds typically blowing inland from the ocean, planes coming in to land at Lindbergh Field fly in low over neighborhoods built on hillsides to the east of the end of the airport runway, providing a thrilling approach for airline passengers. One national travel guide to San Diego describes the landing approach to Lindbergh Field as "right over the central business district, creating the familiar sight of planes threading through high-rise buildings on their way to the airport." (Yates 2001, 52)[3]

Lindbergh Field's in-town location makes it ideal if your destination or point of origin is downtown San Diego. The problem is that, at 464 acres, it is the smallest airport serving a major American city, and its 9,400-foot-long runway is not long enough to handle fully loaded 747s and other wide-body jet planes. As a result, airlines flying long-distance, intercontinental routes across the Pacific have concentrated their operations at Los Angeles International airport (LAX), and people in San Diego flying to Pacific Rim destinations must travel to Los Angeles to begin their journeys. Likewise, goods manufactured by San Diego area firms intended for Pacific Rim markets cannot be shipped directly out of San Diego, but must first be shipped by truck to Los Angeles and then shipped out of LAX. In addition, an 11:30 pm to 6:30 am curfew has been adopted, preventing planes from taking off from Lindbergh Field during that seven-hour period, in an effort to reduce noise impacts on nearby neighborhoods.[4]

Because the airport is surrounded by water or urban development on all sides, expanding Lindbergh Field's size and capacity to any significant extent (lengthening the one main runway and/or adding new runways) is highly problematic. A number of studies have been conducted over the years that have identified and evaluated alternative locations where a new and larger airport could be developed.[5] However, as the 20th century came to a close, little progress had been made toward embracing a workable alternative to Lindbergh Field. In the meantime, the San Diego Unified Port Authority, which owns and operates the airport, has looked for ways to marginally expand the airport so that it can continue to serve as the city's main airport until 2020. Land acquired from the adjacent Naval Training Center (now closed) has made it possible to add 18 gates to the airport terminal building.

One other nongeographic factor deserves mention because it has had a major bearing on the ability of the city to implement plans requiring a significant level of public investment. The passage of Proposition 13 by California voters in 1978 rolled back property assessments to their 1975 market value and limited property taxes to 1% of property value. As a result, when Proposition 13 took effect in 1979, the amount of revenue collected from property taxes by local governments in California was cut in half.

As this is written, Proposition 13 has been in effect for over 20 years. As a result, the property taxes levied and collected by local government units in California (like the City of San Diego) have fallen further and further behind what cities elsewhere in the country are able to collect. Taxes collected by the City of San Diego during the 1990s amounted to only $335 per city resident—placing San Diego 60th out of 77 major cities in the U.S. in terms of tax collections. (Stepner and Fiske 2000, 84)[6]

"Taxes are low and services aren't there as a result. Our public libraries and schools are falling apart. There is a real fiscal squeeze. In the entire city budget a few years back, only $200,000 was budgeted for maintenance—which is nothing. No wonder public buildings are in such poor condition," said Michael Stepner.

The City of San Diego's long-standing inability to come up with the resources to build a new main city library provides a case in point. "When the current city library building was built in the 1950s," Stepner remembered, "it was planned and designed to occupy an entire block in downtown San Diego. However, when the project was put out to bid, the decision was made to build only half of it, and to come back later and do the rest. Later hasn't arrived yet."

In the 1980s, it looked like the city was finally going to replace its inadequate main library. A 12-acre property in the Hillcrest area was acquired by the city and plans were developed for building a new main library on the site. However, when the projected cost of the project was deemed too high, plans for building the library on the site were dropped. No further progress was made toward building a new main library for a number of years. Finally, in 1997, the city's mayor, Susan Golding, declared that, after years of delay, the city was going to get planning a new main library back on track.

"The city acquired a site next to the Santa Fe Depot," recounted Stepner. "A carefully thought-out planning and design process was undertaken that generated a number of different plans and design schemes, proposed by different architects and design firms. A panel of design experts and city officials reviewed all the proposals and narrowed the number of schemes down to four or five. An all-day program, open to the public, was then held at the Lyceum Theater in Horton Plaza. Each proposer had an hour to make their presentation to a full house of 600 people, who wrote questions on pieces of paper and handed them to the moderator. People in the audience were asked for straw votes on the various schemes. It was a wonderful process."

Unfortunately, elected city officials were still not sufficiently committed to funding the construction of the new library to ensure that the chosen and endorsed plan got built. "We had set an in-house budget of around $110 million for the project," Stepner continued. "Then somebody came along who said we could do it for $65 million, and the mayor appeared to buy into that lower figure. Actually, in fairness to the mayor, the mayor said $65 million was a 'starting point,' but most people interpreted that to mean that it was the amount we had to work with. So we started the planning and design process with an internal budget of $110 million but a political budget of $65 million. Then, of course, the project came in 'over budget' and was pushed aside."

Planning for a new library was back to square one.

WHY THE SAN DIEGO STORY IS IMPORTANT

For a number of reasons, it is fitting that the story of San Diego serves as the capstone for the case studies presented in this book. First, even though San Diego is a relatively young city, it has a long and distinguished planning legacy and has benefited from some brilliant and far-sighted planning. Moreover, as the following chapter will demonstrate, plans and planners have exerted a strong influence on how San Diego has developed and changed.

Second, planners in San Diego have had to confront extremely complex and vexing land use and development issues, due in large part to the region's extraordinarily rapid rate of growth. Indeed, planners in San Diego have confronted a wide range of problems and challenges (growth management, environmental conservation and habitat protection, the coordination of development and transportation, and the preservation and development of affordable housing, to name a few) and devised some remarkably imaginative approaches and solutions that can serve as models for fast-growing communities across the country.

Third, this San Diego case study substantiates a number of key points made in a previous chapter, namely that:

- Planning can and frequently does produce positive outcomes.
- The likelihood of successful planning is greatly increased when people *want* it to succeed and when planners have the support of elected officials and the private sector.
- The benefits that can be achieved by investing in and supporting planning institutions and processes are frequently and easily overlooked.

During particular periods in San Diego's history (most notably during the first and last quarters of the 20th century), there was extraordinarily strong public and private support for planning. Even during those periods, however, there were powerful and influential voices in the San Diego community that remained fundamentally and vigorously opposed to planning. Indeed, the picture that emerges from an examination of San Diego's 20th century history is that of a city that has undergone a series of alternating mood swings—at one time supportive of planning, then rejecting planning, then embracing planning again during a time of crisis and then turning its back on planning once again when the crisis seemed to have passed.

During the 1970s and most of the 1980s, there were few U.S. cities where the city's mayor was more supportive of planning than San Diego. Nevertheless, by 1991, the pendulum had swung the other way and political and public support for planning was at a low ebb. Writing in 1991, Herbert H. Smith reported that, "Planners in San Diego . . . are not highly regarded as influential professionals by the officials and the general public." (Smith 1991, 218)

Indeed, when I made my field research visit to San Diego in 1998, the City of San Diego had been governing itself, and trying to cope with the enormous growth pressures it was facing, without the benefit of a planning department for seven years. By the new millennium, however, the city had a professionally staffed planning department and planning director once again, and a mayor strongly committed to planning. If nothing else, the ebb and flow of public and political support for planning in San Diego provides an important reminder of the tenuous position that planning occupies in many American cities.

EARLY HISTORY

Although San Diego is one of the oldest settlements in California (Spanish exploration along the coast of San Diego dates back to the 16th century), the city we know today did not really begin to be established until the 1860s—well after other cities described in this book had come into existence and achieved a level of maturity. As in the case of Madison, Wisconsin, the planning and development of San Diego was carried out by a single individual—a land speculator by the name of Alonzo Horton.

Alonzo Horton was born in Connecticut in 1813, raised in New York State and eventually moved to Wisconsin, where he traded in land and cattle and founded the town of Hortonville (20 miles from Oshkosh).

In 1851, lured by news of the California gold rush, Horton journeyed from Wisconsin to California. Instead of making a fortune mining for gold, he established and operated a furniture and household goods shop in San Francisco. In 1867, while still in San Francisco, he attended a lecture which "changed his life and that of his adopted city." (Showley 1999, 57) The subject of the talk was the question of which ports along the Pacific coast would make great cities. After going systematically down the Pacific coast (beginning with Seattle and then San Francisco and evaluating the potential of each port city), the speaker finally got to San Diego, which Horton heard him say was "one of the healthiest places in the world, and . . . had one of the best harbors in the world . . ." (*ibid.*)

In a letter, Horton described the impact that the presentation had on him: "I could not sleep that night for thinking about San Diego, and at two o'clock in the morning I got up and looked on the map to see where San Diego was, and then went back to bed satisfied. In the morning I said to my wife, 'I am going to sell my goods and go to San Diego and build a city.'" (as quoted by Showley 1999, 57)

Horton arrived in San Diego in April 1867 aboard a Pacific mail steamer. Within a month, he had bought 800 acres of land adjoining San Diego Bay for $265. Horton then took a steamer back to San Francisco, where he began selling lots in what he called "Horton's Addition." The pattern of development Horton chose for his new community was simple and straightforward.

He divided the land into blocks of 200 by 300 feet containing twelve 50- by 100-foot lots and no alleys, ensuring a plentiful supply of desirable corner lots. He numbered the streets starting at the boundary of his holdings; thus, 1st Avenue is not at the water's edge but inland nine city blocks. Alphabetic streets started at the edge of what was soon to be reserved as City (later Balboa) Park and proceeded south; to the north, streets were named for trees and flowers in alphabetical order from Ash to Upas. (*ibid.*, 59)[7]

Like James Doty in Madison, Horton was an astute developer. In 1868, he built a wharf at the foot of 5th Avenue at a cost of $45,000; in January 1870, he began building the 100-room Horton House Hotel at 4th and D Streets (later renamed Broadway).[8] The first clerk of the Horton House Hotel (who, like Horton, came to San Diego from Wisconsin) was a 20-year-old man named George W. Marston, "who would succeed Horton as San Diego's No. 1 citizen 30 years later." (*ibid.*)

Horton took other carefully calculated actions to advance the development of the city. "Horton traded lots for services, donated land to churches and paid to whitewash the south and west facing sides of buildings to improve the city's appearance for visitors arriving by sea. He supported the *San Diego Weekly Bulletin* until *The San Diego Union* [was] founded . . . [I]n 1870 . . . Horton joined others in founding the San Diego Chamber of Commerce, the Bank of San Diego and the Horton Library Association." (*ibid.*)

Horton had the foresight to reserve 1,400 acres of city-owned land, immediately north of the land he was developing, for what is now known as Balboa Park. Back in 1868, few people other than Horton probably thought that setting aside such a large amount of open space was necessary. "San Diego (population less than 2,000) was only the second American municipality to lay out such a large piece of centrally located land as permanent open space parkland; the first was New York (population 700,000 in 1850) which had established Central Park just 10 years earlier. It is all the more remarkable that San Diego protected the park for more than 40 years before major improvements were ready to commence." (*ibid.*, 61)

Because of its extraordinary size, Balboa Park is able to accommodate a wide range of recreational facilities (such as baseball, tennis, soccer and swimming) as well as the world-famous San Diego Zoo and numerous museums, theaters and cultural venues (such as the Old Globe Theatre and the Spreckels Organ Pavilion), and still leave hundreds of acres of landscaped grounds for passive recreation and quiet enjoyment. Balboa Park is so important to San Diego that it is almost impossible to imagine San Diego *without* it—like trying to imagine Manhattan without Central Park.

A CITY WITH A HEAD START IN PLANNING

Knowing what planners, city officials and civic leaders hoped would happen makes it easier to measure their goals against present realities and to measure which ideas materialized and which did not, which are still relevant and which are not.

—LYNNE CARRIER (*IMAGINE A GREAT CITY—
DRAFTING A 'WORKING VISION' FOR SAN DIEGO*, 1998, 2)

At the beginning of the 20th century, San Diego's population stood at only 17,700 (55 of whom were real estate agents). Within the San Diego business community, there was fortunately, however, a forceful advocate for planning: George W. Marston, the young man Alonzo Horton hired to be the first clerk of his Horton House Hotel, who went on to found and head the Marston department store (now part of the Macy's chain). In 1903, at the urging of George Marston, the Civic Improvement Committee of the chamber of commerce hired John Nolen to prepare a plan for the city. Nolen, whose practice was based in Cambridge, Massachusetts, had never experienced a place like San Diego and was entranced by its qualities.

In the plan delivered to the city in 1908, Nolen observed that, "The climate defies description. Dry, fresh, equable, wholly without extremes of heat or cold . . . A disinterested visitor has remarked that 'If nervous prostration is wanted, it must be brought here, and it cannot be relied on to continue long . . .' The scenery is varied and exquisitely beautiful . . . The great, broad, quiet mesas, the picturesque canyons, the bold line of distant mountains, the wide hard ocean beaches, the great Bay, its beauty crowned by the islands of Coronado, the caves and coves of La Jolla, the unique Torrey Pines, the lovely Mission Valley—these are but some of the features of the landscape that should be looked upon as precious assets to be preserved and enhanced."

Nolen was *not* at all impressed, however, by San Diego's built environment, or by its plans and policies related to land use and development. In the 109-page plan, Nolen observed that "Notwithstanding its [natural] advantages . . . San Diego is, today, neither interesting nor beautiful. Its city plan is not thoughtful but, on the contrary, ignorant and wasteful."

Nolen's 1908 plan sought to remedy the city's immediate shortcomings but, even more importantly, to put forward a compelling vision of the wonderful city it could become in the future. In Nolen's words, "It is not the intention of this report to rehearse nor dwell upon the mistakes of the past . . . Each generation has spent too much time in lamenting the errors of the past, and has given too little attention to the opportunities of the present."

Nolen said there were four general principles of landscape design that should guide the replanning of San Diego:

1. to conform, so far as possible, to the topography
2. to use places for what they are naturally most fit
3. to conserve, develop and utilize all natural resources, aesthetic as well as commercial
4. to aim to secure beauty by organic arrangement rather than by mere embellishment

Among the specific recommendations Nolen made in his 1908 report were that industrial uses be limited to the southern end of the city's waterfront, and that the balance of the city's waterfront be kept open and developed as a recreational resource and public amenity for the people of the city. Broad boulevards and avenues, he said, should also be developed leading to and along the waterfront, and public buildings should be grouped around a square at Front Street and Broadway to form a public plaza and civic center (in line with "City Beautiful" planning principles).[9]

Nolen also urged that the city develop a multitiered park system (composed of large regional parks, smaller parks scattered throughout the city, and small open spaces and playgrounds associated with neighborhood schools). Nolen's recommendations regarding specific areas that needed to be permanently protected and kept as open space were particularly prescient. For example, Nolen recognized that Torrey Pines was a unique resource area that the city could not afford to omit from the regional park system. Presidio Hill in Old Town, he said, should also be developed by making use of city-owned property "to form another center in this wonderful park system."

Nolen acknowledged at the end of his report that, "These recommendations may appear to present a heavy task for a city the size of San Diego." Nevertheless, he argued, "When they are looked at from the point of view of 25 years hence, so far as that can be brought before the imagination, they will in many respects be considered inadequate. No city regrets its acquisition of parks, but many cities regret their failure to act in time."

Roger Showley put it well when he wrote that Nolen's 1908 plan "bears re-reading by elected officials, city planners and interested citizens." (Showley 1999, 81) In Showley's opinion, "No statement of San Diego's potential has ever been so inspiring as Nolen's. Twenty-first century San Diego would do well to read Nolen and to improve and enlarge on his challenge, still relevant after 90 years." (*ibid.*)

The 1908 Nolen plan was never officially adopted by the city and it initially looked like that plan's recommendations would largely be ignored. Instead of reserving the Bayfront north of E Street for open space and recreation (linked to Balboa Park by a 12-block landscaped promenade, as Nolen recommended), the city council in 1911 approved filling in the bay west of Pacific Highway and the construction of waterfront piers for shipping and commerce at Broadway and B Streets. Instead of taking action on many of Nolen's recommendations, the chamber of commerce proposed something else entirely: that San Diego host an exposition to coincide with and celebrate the opening of the Panama Canal in 1915.

George Marston ran unsuccessfully for mayor in 1913 and 1917, espousing Nolen's planning vision for San Diego, losing badly to banker/developer Louis J. Wilde in his second attempt. Throughout the campaign, Wilde referred derisively to Marston as "Geranium George," because he favored civic beauty rather than smokestacks, jobs and economic growth. Ever since, the phrase "smokestacks vs. geraniums" has symbolized the struggle that has been waged in San Diego between competing visions of the city's future. With Wilde occupying the mayor's office, all thoughts of planning were swept aside.

The 1915-16 Panama-California Exposition, which took place in City Park (renamed Balboa Park in 1910), turned out to be a major success. During its two-year run, the Panama-California Exposition attracted more than 3.7 million people. In addition to being a commercial success in its own right, the exposition helped spur the development of the U. S. Grant Hotel (which opened in 1910), the development of the Spreckels Theater in 1912 and the Mission Revival-styled Santa Fe Depot (which opened in 1915), just in time to receive the many visitors attracted to San Diego by the exposition.

All the structures built for the exposition were of Spanish-Colonial/Moorish design—an architectural style that was dictated by a city ordinance, which required Spanish Revival-style architecture for all exposition buildings and for public and private developments throughout the city.[10] The way exposition buildings were sited and grouped together along the main avenue (called the Prado) further contributed to the creation of a sense of place.[11]

Most world's fairs leave few physical remnants behind, and architect Bertram Goodhue strongly recommended that all the temporary buildings be razed and replaced by gardens as originally intended. However, San Diegans had fallen in love with their dream city and objected to plans to demolish most of the buildings. New uses were found for them and, out of those makeshift institutions, many of San Diego's key cultural institutions grew, including the Museum of Man, the San Diego Museum of Art and the San Diego Zoo. (*ibid.*, 97)

By 1921, San Diego had a new mayor, John Bacon (publisher of the old *San Diego Independent* newspaper) who, like Marston, was a strong supporter of planning. In 1923, a planning department was established. Kenneth Gardner (who had worked for Nolen on the 1908 plan) was hired as the department's first planning director and Glenn Rick was hired as assistant city planning engineer.

John Nolen was brought back to San Diego to prepare a City, Harbor and Parks plan. This second plan afforded Nolen an opportunity to reiterate and expand upon a number of his earlier recommendations, modify others and put forward a few new ones. Nolen reiterated his recommendation that a civic center be developed on the waterfront, and elaborated on his earlier neighborhood planning recommendation that playgrounds, libraries and schools be grouped together to create neighborhood centers.

He recommended that an integrated parkway system be developed extending across Mission Valley, along Mission Bay, up the coast and through several canyons and river valleys. In the plan, Nolen also called for parks and recreational centers to be established at Mission Bay, La Jolla Shores, Pacific Beach, Ocean Beach and Silver Strand, Torrey Pines Mesa and around various reservoirs and dams. He urged that an historic preservation effort be undertaken in Old Town and Presidio Park, that comprehensive zoning and subdivision regulations be formulated and adopted, and that the city undertake capital improvement budgeting. Lastly, Nolen recommended that an airport be developed adjoining San Diego Bay.[12]

At least 1,000 citizens attended a public presentation unveiling Nolen's plan in February 1926. Speaking to the crowd, Will Rogers commented, "Now you have a real plan prepared by Nolen. Don't let any prominent citizen get up and talk you out of it." (Showley 1989, 6)

The plan was officially adopted in 1926. In 1927, San Diego's city council passed a comprehensive zoning ordinance, initiated neighborhood planning studies and appropriated $15,000 for traffic maps. In 1929, Glenn Rick replaced Gardner as the city's planning director. (Rick went on to serve as San Diego's planning director for 26 years, until 1955.) In 1931, a new city charter was ratified which established a council/manager form of government and empowered the city's planning commission to review public as well as private projects.[13]

In 1935-36, the California-Pacific International Exposition was held in Balboa Park. According to Showley, this second exposition was "the brainchild" of Frank Drugan, a former field representative of the *Scripps-Howard* newspaper chain, who had seen Chicago's Century of Progress Exposition in 1933-34 and got the idea of moving the exhibits to San Diego. (Showley 1999, 109) The plan for the 1935-36 exposition, developed by architect Richard Requa, added a number of new buildings that complemented the Spanish-Colonial style buildings left over from the 1915-16 exposition. Again, most of the new buildings erected for the exposition were retained and used to accommodate museums and cultural facilities.

Not long after the Japanese bombing of Pearl Harbor, Balboa Park was turned over to the U.S. Navy and named Camp Kidd. In 1942, the U.S. Marine Corps seized the 121,400-acre Santa Margarita y Flores Rancho north of Oceanside and named it Camp Pendleton. (*ibid.*, 114, 115) Within a fairly short period of time, the various aircraft manufacturing companies based in San Diego started turning out large numbers of airplanes for the military. The Convair

Corporation manufactured over 33,000 aircraft during the war years, such as B-24 Liberator bombers and PBY flying boats.

"In July 1941, *The Saturday Evening Post* termed the rapid growth [in San Diego] a 'boom blitz.' Author Frank J. Taylor followed Mayor Percy Benbough around town, describing the nightmare that accompanied the war buildup. 'Today, San Diego is a rip snorting Little Detroit,' Taylor wrote, 'booming with defense industry.' Benbough drove Taylor past the naval Training Center in Point Loma, where houses were painted alternately green, pink and buff to help enlistees distinguish one from another. In Mission Valley were auto trailers connected to temporary gas meters . . ." (*ibid.*, 110)

POST-WORLD WAR II SAN DIEGO

With the end of World War II, America's citizen soldiers and sailors returned home, got married and started families. Those new families started buying homes and automobiles, sparking a surge of suburban development. Initially, development took place on the fringes of previously developed areas. Before long, however, development was expanding outward into more remote, previously untouched areas, such as Mission Valley—a lush, agricultural valley roughly 3 miles north of downtown San Diego that until then had been ". . . the site of truck farms and dairies that served the City and was unofficially viewed as an open space preserve." (Stepner 1997a, 35)

If you didn't observe its transformation (desecration) first-hand, the best way to grasp what happened to Mission Valley in a 20-year period is to pick up a copy of Kevin Lynch's book, *Managing the Sense of a Region* (1980). The first page contains two photographs, taken from essentially the same elevated location and the same angle. The first photograph was taken toward the end of the 1950s; the second photograph was taken at the end of the 1970s. The two photographs are accompanied by the following narrative:

"Twenty years ago [in the 1950s] Mission Valley was open countryside, passing through the city of San Diego like a broad green river in that arid urban landscape. Houses looked over the high bluffs on either side. On the valley floor there were dairy farms, strung along the line of trees that marked the little stream. Now the valley is a breathtaking giant shopping strip, with its freeway, parking lots, offices, stadium, two major shopping centers, and a yard for old car bodies. The stream itself is no longer visible (but given a flood, it may show to better advantage). The bluffs are scraped bare. There is a new smell to the air. The sounds have changed, and the asphalt surfaces reflect the heat . . . The story of this change is not unusual for any North American city. It is a tale of locating a new freeway, of a shift in the central business district to meet parking demands and urban growth, of large land profits, tax windfalls, a zoning battle, and a brief, belated, isolated, 'unreasonable' resistance." (Lynch 1980, 1-3)

Had it been up to planner Harry Haelsig (who replaced Glenn Rick as San Diego's planning director in 1955), Mission Valley would have been kept as an open space preserve and "developed . . . as a recreational greenbelt leading to Mission Bay." (Showley 1999, 126) However, the people whose opinions apparently mattered the most to members of San Diego's city council (real estate developers and pro-development business interests) had an altogether different vision for Mission Valley.

In 1958, the city council, under intense pressure from the May department stores (and over the objections of the city's planning director) unanimously approved the rezoning of a large tract of land in the heart of Mission Valley for the development of a major shopping center. Arthur Jessop, a downtown merchant, is reported to have said at the time, "We might as well tattoo on the Council wall, 'Here died planning in San Diego.'" (Stepner 1997a, 35) The construction of the I-8 freeway through Mission Valley further sealed the valley's fate.

When it opened in 1961, the Mission Valley shopping center attracted further waves of commercial and residential development to the valley, and hastened the decline of downtown San Diego, which was further amplified when San Diego's economy slid into recession in the early 1960s. One of the biggest blows came as a result of the failure of San Diego-based General Dynamics to gain customers for its Convair 880 (a four-engine jet aircraft that was in direct competition with Boeing's 707). Between August 1959 and June 1960, General Dynamics cut its workforce from 56,400 to 47,600. Within a short period, new housing starts in San Diego fell dramatically. *Time* magazine, in its August 17, 1962 issue, quoted a parking lot operator in downtown San Diego, who regularly netted $800 a month: "Hell, business is so dead I won't take home more than $130 this month." (as reported and quoted by Showley 1999, 128)

When economic conditions worsen, it usually follows that people begin calling for *less* planning and land use regulation, not more. That was certainly the case in Duluth, Minnesota as well as in San Diego when that city experienced hard times. Thankfully, efforts aimed at undermining planning in San Diego were blunted by the formation of a nonprofit, grass-roots planning advocacy organization called Citizens Coordinate for Century Three (C3) in 1961.

The 1926 Nolen plan was still the official plan of San Diego and C3 urged that the city prepare a new plan.[14] A new general plan was prepared that called for stronger land use regulations to control fringe development, and for the use of federal urban renewal funds to redevelop and revitalize downtown San Diego; however, that plan went nowhere. Opponents, spearheaded by a group called the "Jobs and Growth Association" (led by Martin J. Montroy and backed by Mission Valley land interests) argued that planning was "a step toward creeping socialism" (as reported by Showley 1999, 134) and succeeded in derailing the plan.

Another city plan was subsequently prepared titled the *Progress Guide and General Plan* ("the 1967 general plan"), this time with greater citizen participation and the active involvement of many community-based organizations. This plan modified a number of the recommendations contained in the earlier plan and rejected the idea of undertaking federally funded urban renewal in downtown San Diego. (Stepner 1997a, 35)

The same interest groups that opposed the earlier plan rallied in opposition to the new plan and filed petitions requiring that referenda be held on two separate ballot measures—the first on the proposed plan itself and the second on whether there should be an independent planning department. The two referenda questions were voted on in 1967. To the surprise of many, a majority of voters cast votes in support of the 1967 general plan, and in support of the principle that the city's planning department should be largely independent and insulated from direct political pressure from the city council, the mayor and the city manager.

A BURST OF PLANNING ACTIVITY IN THE 1970S

In 1971, San Diego elected Pete Wilson as the city's new mayor. The election of Pete Wilson proved to be pivotal in terms of re-establishing the importance of planning in San Diego. Throughout his campaign, Wilson had focused attention on two key planning-related issues: the need to manage and control growth in peripheral areas and the need to revitalize downtown San Diego.

During his campaign, Wilson repeated, "We don't want to be another sprawled-out Los Angeles Monster." (as quoted by Montgomery, August 21, 1976, 26) In his inaugural address (December 1971), the new mayor called San Diego a dynamic and changing city—a "City in Motion." However, he reminded citizens that, "We must see to it that the 'City in Motion' gives *direction* [italics added] to its motion. We must plan now for tomorrow ... [and that planning] must integrate social, economic and political—as well as physical factors ..." (as quoted by Showley 1999, 138) In explaining the policies he intended to pursue, Wilson observed, "The critical point ... is that though growth may be inevitable, the way in which growth occurs is by no means inevitable ..." (as quoted by Montgomery, August 21, 1976, 26)

Planning received a further boost in 1973 when the grandson and daughter of George W. Marston committed $10,000 for a planning study to assess the state of the region, and make recommendations on what should be done to manage growth and protect the region's special environmental qualities and resources. Kevin Lynch (Massachusetts Institute of Technology) and Donald Appleyard (University of California at Berkeley) were chosen to prepare the study.

Roughly three decades later, San Diego is a much bigger city than it was in 1971, both in terms of its total population and in developed land area. As cities get bigger, problems often multiply and intensify—and San Diego is no exception. Nevertheless, many positive developments and changes have occurred since 1971. Even though it has become a bigger city, San Diego has become a *better* city in a number of ways. The story of how planning contributed to making San Diego a better place is told in the pages that follow.

Temporary Paradise?

Kevin Lynch and Donald Appleyard spent a year and one-half conducting a thorough reconnaissance of the San Diego region, meeting with and polling citizens and working with a 15-member resource panel. Staff members from the city's planning department were in particularly close contact with Lynch and Appleyard throughout the period.

The planning report Lynch and Appleyard prepared for San Diego was titled *Temporary Paradise?—A Look at the Special Landscape of the San Diego Region* ("*Temporary Paradise?*") and was delivered in 1974. *Temporary Paradise?* was not a "plan" in the formal sense; rather, it was a "sketchbook" of observations and ideas written for a general readership. Limited to 50 pages, it was laid out in the format of a tabloid, with approximately 130 illustrations and photographs; 25,000 copies of the report were published and distributed.

Temporary Paradise? reiterated many of the themes put forward in the much earlier Nolen plans. It urged the removal of all uses "which are not water-related" from shoreline areas, and that priority be given to reserving coastal areas for public recreational use and enjoyment. Housing was also a use that Lynch and Appleyard felt was "water-related" and therefore suitable as a land use along the coast, as long as it was kept well back from the water's edge, as long as beaches and coastal areas were accessible to the public on foot as well as by public transit and as long as it was low rise rather than high rise.[15]

Lynch and Appleyard were extremely critical of the uncontrolled, sprawling suburban development that had been allowed to take place in San Diego in the 1950s and 1960s. "Present suburban growth [tends to be] too rapid, too poorly coordinated with public services, too extensive and homogeneous, too destructive of the land, inappropriate in form, and in the wrong place," they said.

They were even more pointedly critical that San Diegans had allowed the beautiful and bountiful farmland in the Mission Valley to be converted into "a chaos of highways, parking lots, and scattered commercial buildings," and called on the city to take strong measures to preserve remaining undeveloped areas of open space in all of the region's canyons and valleys. "Keep the valleys and canyons, and their rims, out of development, using public purchase, and floodplain and hillside zoning with real teeth in them," they said. Instead, development should be concentrated on the elevated, flat mesas overlooking the bay and canyons. Remaining undeveloped valley areas, they said, should become ecological preserves, which could be linked together to create green fingers of open space capable of accommodating trails for walking, cycling and horseback riding.

In addition to urging the city to do everything possible to discourage development in environmentally sensitive areas, Lynch and Appleyard said that it was important to *encourage and support development* in areas where development was suitable. Transportation infrastructure improvements were a particularly powerful tool for encouraging more compact development. Toward that end, Lynch and Appleyard strongly recommended that a fixed rail transit system be developed, and urged that no further freeways be constructed until the rail rapid transit system was in place.

The location of [transit] routes and stations, they argued, should be planned to "affect the form of regional growth," and a broad array of community planning and environmental considerations needed to be taken into account when determining the locations of transit routes and stations. "The location and form of transit lines and stations should respect the local fabric and environment. Routing decisions cannot be based solely on engineering criteria. Environmental surveys of the corridors, locating sensitive areas, areas of change, neighborhood and community territories, valued places, and good crossing points must also be factored in."

Taking many of these factors into account, and their judgment that the mesas overlooking the coast were especially well suited to accommodate additional development, Lynch and Appleyard stated that "the highest priority rail transit line, from our viewpoint, is that which will run from Mission Bay to Tijuana . . ."

Indeed, *Temporary Paradise?* includes a number of striking and bold recommendations suggesting ways to strengthen what Lynch and Appleyard called "The Mexican Connection," including the recommendation that a new international airport be developed adjoining the Mexican border to serve the needs of both San Diego and Tijuana, Mexico. "A border airport will be no more than 30 minutes from downtown San Diego, and could have a transit connection. It would encourage the industrial development needed to employ residents of Tijuana and of the South Bay Communities."

Once this new regional and international airport was in place, Lynch and Appleyard pointed out, the land occupied by Lindbergh Field, as well as the adjacent U.S. Marine Corps Recruit Depot and Naval Training Center and the U.S. Naval Air Station at the northern end of North Island (across the bay from Lindbergh Field) could be freed up and redeveloped into a new Bayfront community.

"Vast areas of land by the Bay could thus be opened up for residence and recreation—some 2500 acres and six miles of beach in North Island alone (which is sufficient for a population of 100,000 to 150,000 people, at moderate densities).

Lindbergh Field and the Marine Corps Depot . . . would furnish another 2000 acres in a strategic location . . ."

It was, Lynch and Appleyard said, "a magnificent opportunity for revitalizing the great Bay of San Diego—the kind of transformation that is only very rarely afforded to a major city." Planning commission member William Anderson thinks what Lynch and Appleyard said decades ago still holds true. "The area where the airport is now would be a wonderful location for an in-town community—akin to the Back Bay area in Boston," said Anderson.

Temporary Paradise? was never officially adopted by the city, and Donald Appleyard died in 1982; Kevin Lynch died in 1984. Nevertheless, *Temporary Paradise?* had a profound effect on the growth management plans, policies and ordinances that were developed and implemented beginning in the late 1970s.

While Lynch and Appleyard were completing their report, planners in San Diego's planning department were also in the process of preparing *Progress Guide and General Plan* ("the 1979 general plan"). This new general plan would directly address the two land use planning and development issues Pete Wilson focused on during his campaign for mayor: the management and control of growth on the periphery and the revitalization of downtown San Diego. Although the issuance of *Temporary Paradise?* preceded the completion and adoption of a new general plan by five years, to a large extent they were parallel planning efforts. Indeed, the planning concepts and principles contained in *Temporary Paradise?* provided the justification and planning rationale for many of the key land use policies that were incorporated in the 1979 general plan.

Without minimizing the importance of Lynch and Appleyard's planning contribution, it should not be assumed that all of the ideas and recommendations in *Temporary Paradise?* originated with Lynch and Appleyard. "They were very patient and attentive, and listened to the proposed growth management strategies we had developed up to that point," urban planner/designer Max Schmidt told me. Reading between the lines, it is probably fair to say that many of the ideas that found their way into *Temporary Paradise?* were actually contributed by members of the city's planning staff.

After *Temporary Paradise?* was issued, planners working for the city turned their attention toward developing a strategy to encourage development in areas where infrastructure and facilities were already in place, and/or where it was relatively cost-effective to provide or improve such facilities, and to discourage development in peripheral areas where it was outstripping the capacity of local infrastructure and public facilities. In focusing on the adequacy of infrastructure and facilities, planners were in fact picking up on one of the major issues that Pete Wilson had repeatedly spoken about when he was campaigning for mayor.

"One of Wilson's favorite targets during his 1971 campaign was Mira Mesa, a distant suburb in the early stages of development. Hundreds of residents were moving into the 10,700-acre community north of the Miramar Naval Air Station. But public services were nowhere in sight . . . Schools were in trailers and unoccupied homes. Dirt lots doubled as playgrounds." (Showley 1999, 138)

Land use lawyer and planning consultant Robert Freilich was brought to San Diego to work with the planning department on the growth management strategy. By the time Freilich arrived on the scene, the basic form the growth management strategy would take had pretty much been decided. Freilich's involvement, however, was crucial in fine-tuning the strategy and in establishing its legal basis.[16]

The city was divided into a series of tiers and different policies were devised for the different tiers. The first tier (called the "urbanized area") encompassed developed areas where infrastructure and public facilities were already in place. To encourage infill development within this tier, the city proposed to pay all development-related infrastructure costs within the area and no development impact fees were to be imposed.

The second tier (called the "planned urbanizing area") was where all peripheral development over the next 20 years was to be accommodated. In this tier, developers were required to pay impact fees to cover the cost of roads, parks, branch libraries, schools and other public facilities and services *in advance,* as a precondition for receiving project approval. Mayor Pete Wilson called it "pay-as-you-grow."

The third tier (called the "future urbanizing area") was off limits for development for at least 20 years, and was not to be released for development until all or most of the "planned urbanizing area" had been developed.

Although it did not become part of the officially adopted growth management strategy, serious consideration was also given to establishing a fourth tier. As Max Schmidt explained, "The growth management strategy we originally developed with Robert Freilich called for establishing an additional tier beyond the 'future urbanizing area'—a *permanently* preserved area." However, when the plan was submitted for formal adoption, the fourth tier was eliminated from the plan.

According to Douglas Porter, the main reason why the fourth tier was dropped was because policymakers and elected officials concluded that designating privately owned land for permanent preservation was "legally insupportable." (Porter 1996, 83) Thus, when the general plan was officially adopted, all land not included in the "planned urbanizing area" or "urbanized area" was lumped into the "future urbanizing area."

AN UPSURGE IN INFILL DEVELOPMENT

The 1979 general plan imposed fairly high development impact fees on developments in the "planned urbanizing area." In the "urbanized area," however, no development impact fees were imposed in order to encourage development in already developed, closer-in areas.

The plan worked as intended, producing an upsurge in infill development in older neighborhoods of San Diego in the 1980s. One infill development—particularly worthy of mention because it came about as a direct result of a planning process carried out by San Diego's planning department—is the Uptown District development in the Hillcrest area. The site where this infill development took place had previously been occupied by a large Sears store, which had closed. The boarded-up Sears store was surrounded by a vast paved surface parking lot, and the area surrounding the Sears property had been in decline for so long that a master plan had been prepared, which slated the site for redevelopment. Eventually, an opportunity to redevelop the site presented itself when the 12-acre property was acquired by the city as the site for the proposed new main library.

When the city decided *not* to go ahead with the library project because it was going to be too expensive, the task of deciding what to do with the former Sears property fell to the city's planning department. "We worked with the community and determined that a mixed-use project was most appropriate and desirable on the site," Michael Stepner remembered. "People in the neighborhood wanted housing, if it was done right, and also some commercial, but not too much. They definitely didn't want strip commercial. They wanted to rebuild a neighborhood by creating a pedestrian-oriented streetscape and by bringing the street system back into the site. They also wanted a supermarket."

What the community and planning department agreed should ideally happen on the site was spelled out in an RFP. Three developers submitted development proposals for the site in response to the RFP, one of which was chosen. The compact, mixed-use development that has resulted ("the Uptown District") is both urban in character and pedestrian oriented, with attractively landscaped and shaded walkways that encourage casual strolling. Indeed, the Uptown District is an excellent example of the kind of classic "pedestrian pocket" that architect/designer Peter Calthorpe and other New Urbanists have been saying we should be building more of. Townhouses ring the outer edges of the Uptown District, while higher density housing and commercial establishments—a Ralph's supermarket, Trader Joe's, and other smaller stores and offices—are located in the center. Also located in the center of the Uptown District is a community center and a small park. Bus service is conveniently located on adjacent streets, a short walk away.

One of the key specifications contained in the RFP was that the development should contain a supermarket. Not only did planners succeed in getting a supermarket to be included in the Uptown District, but they got it built in the *center* of the district rather than on a heavily traveled street on the edge of the development.

7-3   The pedestrian-oriented plan of the Uptown District encourages walking.

Source: Gene Bunnell

7-4   Ralph's Supermarket (in the background) is in the very center of the Uptown District, hidden from view from major traffic arteries bounding the neighborhood.

Source: Gene Bunnell

7-5 Multistory structures in the center of the Uptown District, containing a mixture of retail and office space and housing.

Source: Gene Bunnell

7-6 The Uptown Community Center in the heart of the Uptown District.

Source: Gene Bunnell

As I walked through the Uptown District with Michael Stepner, I confided to him, "I'm not sure I would ever have found this interior commercial area had you not brought me here." The supermarket was generally hidden and out of view, and there was only one very small sign for Ralph's out on the main street to let people know there was a supermarket somewhere in the center of the development. "Ralph's supermarket was very concerned about moving in here," said Stepner, "but the deal the supermarket entered into with the developer protected them from any losses they might incur, so they had nothing to lose. As it turned out, the supermarket broke all sales records in the first month they were open and has continued to generate an extremely high rate of sales per square foot ever since."

Had the city sought to maximize its economic return by awarding the property to the developer who offered to pay the most money for the property, the Uptown District would probably not have turned out as well and not included as many pedestrian amenities and attractive design features, but it didn't. "As long as the developer promised to do what we wanted on the site, and made us whole by paying what the city paid for the property plus our planning costs, that was all we really cared about," said Stepner.

The Untoward Effects of Proposition 13

What planners and policymakers in San Diego did not foresee (and were powerless to do anything about, even if they had) was the extent to which the benefits of encouraging infill development in existing neighborhoods would be undermined by Proposition 13. When Proposition 13 took effect in 1979 (the same year as the second general plan was adopted), the amount of property tax revenue that the City of San Diego collected was effectively cut in half, thereby denying the city the revenues it needed to make infrastructure and facility improvements in existing neighborhoods that were experiencing accelerated development activity. As a result, as more and more infill development took place in existing neighborhoods, schools and public facilities in those areas became increasingly inadequate.

Ironically, in the planned urbanizing area where developers paid hefty impact fees that enabled the city to pay for needed public infrastructure and facilities, the adverse effects of the fiscal squeeze caused by Proposition 13 were not nearly as apparent. "The facilities were much better in outlying areas," reported Michael Stepner. Moreover, with each passing year, the infrastructure and facility disparities between older inner-city neighborhoods and newly developed areas on the outskirts widened. Ultimately, city officials concluded that to address the problem, and keep facility and service disparities from widening still further, impact fees needed to be extended to urbanized areas as well—which the city did in 1987.

THE REVITALIZATION OF DOWNTOWN SAN DIEGO

"By the 1970s, we didn't have any downtown retail activity to speak of. It had all gone to Mission Valley and the suburbs," Donna L. Alm explained. "Nor did we have any downtown housing to speak of, except perhaps a thousand scattered units of mostly low-income housing. People didn't live downtown and didn't come downtown if they could help it. They came downtown to work and then went home."

Almost all of the land along the bay in the center of the city was given over to naval and military-related port facilities, military air bases, the city airport (Lindbergh Field) and scattered private industrial uses. Downtown San Diego largely reflected the gritty character of the city's waterfront.[17] Buildings south of Broadway (especially those located between 4th and 6th Streets) were largely occupied by bars, adult book stores, massage parlors, tattoo shops and Navy "locker clubs." "Sailors couldn't bring civilian clothes on board ship in those days, so they would get these lockers to keep their civilian clothes. If they got back from leave on shore after 11 PM after the gates had closed, they would sleep there," said Michael Stepner.

The downtown revitalization strategy Pete Wilson envisioned when he became mayor of San Diego had five components:
1. Bring retail activity back downtown.
2. Bring more businesses downtown by constructing downtown office buildings.
3. Expand the employment base downtown by building a downtown convention center.
4. Build downtown housing.
5. Build a transit system connecting downtown to outlying areas.

Donna Alm worked on Mayor Wilson's staff during his first term of office, and therefore had first-hand knowledge of what was discussed and the steps that were taken in the early years of Wilson's administration. When I interviewed her in 1998, Alm reflected on the importance that was placed on planning during those years. "A great deal of time and effort was put into planning before we ever started any development," Alm remembered. "I think that was the key to our success. When you look at each redevelopment project that has been completed, you'll also be able to find a redevelopment plan that carefully analyzed the area and talked about the kind of development that was going to be put where. There was a very careful inventory of existing conditions, and a very clear idea of the kind of development that was being aimed for."

Another thing, in Alm's opinion, that distinguished the way San Diego went about trying to revitalize its downtown was the multifaceted and comprehensive nature of San Diego's downtown revitalization strategy. "If you look at other cities, nobody else took on the kind of master planning approach we took on in the 1970s. When other cities talked about downtown redevelopment, they were talking about doing single projects composed of a single use—such as either retail or office development," said Alm. San Diego, on the other hand, was talking about bringing together a number of different uses, all within a relatively small geographic area.

The third key to the success of San Diego's downtown revitalization strategy was the creation of a new institutional entity that was responsible for developing plans and was also in a position to implement them. The entity that was officially created in 1975 was called Centre City Development Corporation (CCDC).

"People call CCDC a 'quasi-public' agency, but we are a 'public agency' under California law," explained Donna Alm. "We are a public, nonprofit corporation formed to guide the development of downtown. We have a seven-member board of directors that is appointed by the mayor and city council, who serve without remuneration—business people from throughout San Diego. The board of directors hires the president of the corporation."

When CCDC was created, it became the official planning agency for downtown San Diego—taking over that responsibility from the city's planning department. It also became responsible for development review and permitting, design review, infrastructure planning and construction, code enforcement and various other functions.

To enable it to carry out its broad responsibilities, CCDC was provided with funding to hire professional staff.[18] It was also given the legal and financial tools it needed to carry out its redevelopment activities. Among the most important financial tools conferred on CCDC was the ability to finance projects and improvements by means of TIF (*i.e.,* to borrow money in anticipation of the increased tax revenues that would be collected due to increasing property and land values produced by public investments and redevelopment activities in the district).

When CCDC was formed, Donna Alm moved from the mayor's staff to join the staff of CCDC.[19] Planner Max Schmidt also joined the staff of CCDC early on; prior to transferring to CCDC, he had been on the staff of the San Diego Planning Department from 1956 to 1977.[20]

I asked Schmidt why he decided to transfer from the city's planning department to CCDC. Basically, he replied, it was because many of the plans he had worked on while in the planning department had been ignored or only half-heartedly or partially implemented by the city. "I had become disenchanted with the lack of implementation," he replied. CCDC, on the other hand, was a planning agency that was also capable of *implementing* its plans. "So I decided I would travel with the plan and go to CCDC."

Those who were involved in establishing CCDC had hoped to make the agency responsible for planning and development throughout the entire downtown area. However, there was considerable political pressure on the city council to limit CCDC's jurisdiction to a relatively small portion of the downtown. "We had several very conservative people on the city council who could not go along with that idea," said Schmidt. "The most they would do was to support a portion of the area." As a result, CCDC started out with a project area of 325 acres—only about one-quarter of the Centre City area.

Within that initial area, three separate redevelopment project areas were established: the Marina, Columbia and Horton Plaza redevelopment areas. A fourth project area was subsequently created, which became known as the Gaslamp Quarter. "It wasn't until much later [1992], after they conceded that we were successful in redeveloping downtown, that they [the city council] considered expanding CCDC's jurisdiction and designating the entire Centre City area as a redevelopment area," said Schmidt.

Today, the geographic area for which CCDC is responsible encompasses 1,500 acres and is referred to as the "Centre City." "When you look at a map, it is easy to identify the Centre City because Interstate 5 creates a lazy 'S' to form the northern and eastern boundary, and the waterfront bounds the other part of it," said Alm.

Horton Plaza

Almost everyone to whom I spoke agreed that the planning and development of Horton Plaza was pivotal to turning around downtown San Diego. As Max Schmidt put it, Horton Plaza was "the catalyst" for the revitalization of downtown San Diego.

Viewed from outside, Horton Plaza does not look all that exceptional. However, once you enter from one of the principal entryways, the development lures you further and further into a succession of surprising and delightful vistas. Although Horton Plaza is an immense project (the footprint of the development covers six and one-half city blocks), the environment created for pedestrians as they circulate through Horton Plaza's interior is fine grained and surprisingly intimate, with irregularly shaped openings and plazas, unfolding vistas and overlooks, and playful architectural embellishments and colors that continually delight and amuse.

From the time it opened in 1985, Horton Plaza drew huge crowds, attracting suburbanites and visitors to downtown San Diego as never before. One popular travel guide to San Diego described Horton Plaza this way: ". . . Horton Plaza is far from what one would imagine a shopping center—or city center to be. A collage of pastels with elaborate, colorful tile work on benches and stairways, cloth banners swaying in the air, and modern sculptures marking the entrances, Horton Plaza rises in uneven, staggered levels to six floors; great views of downtown from the harbor to Balboa Park and beyond can be had here." (Mangin 1996, 29) Another travel guide put it this way: "[Y]ou could skip the stores altogether and ... while away the better part of a day just finding your way around. At each corner is yet another spectacle." (Wurman 1996, 47)

"The process of planning and negotiation that led to the development of Horton Plaza was tortuous, and took 13 years. With Pete Wilson's election as mayor, planning for downtown San Diego got a political boost, and in 1972, with Wilson's support, the city council approved a redevelopment plan for a fifteen block area around Horton Plaza park." (Frieden and Segalyn 1990, 124)

One of the most difficult hurdles in developing a plan for Horton Plaza was deciding what mixture of uses should be included. Mayor Pete Wilson thought that re-establishing retail activity was essential to revitalizing downtown San Diego and many planners shared that hope. However, as Frieden and Segalyn point out, "San Diego was a discouraging place for a downtown mall. In comparison with Boston, Seattle, and St. Paul, the city hardly had a recognizable center." (*ibid.*, 125)

7-7 This photograph, looking south down 4th Street toward San Diego Bay, shows the area where Horton Plaza was built as it looked in the late 1970s. Horton Park is in the foreground. All of the buildings to the right of 4th Street were demolished—with the exception of the old Balboa Theater (the building with the elevated turret and dome in the left center of the photo), which was preserved by wrapping Horton Plaza around it. For years, the mummified Balboa Theater (a former vaudeville theater built in 1923) stood empty and unused, anchoring a corner of Horton Plaza. By 2001, plans were underway to renovate the theater at a cost of $15 million so that it can reopen as a performing arts center.

Source: Courtesy of Centre City Development Corporation

Indeed, there were many people in the real estate and development communities who questioned whether it was feasible to re-establish retail activity in the downtown area. Their skepticism seemed to be born out by market studies, which indicated that office space was the most marketable use for land in the project area and that hotels were the second.

Max Schmidt remained unconvinced that the market for downtown office space was strong enough to support major office developments. In an attempt to resolve the question of what uses should be included in the project, the city invited developers to submit development proposals for the property. The city gave developers wide latitude to propose what *they* considered to be the best way of developing the property. Three developers submitted proposals (James Rouse, Ernest Hahn and Lyman Jee) and all three proposed to develop a significant amount of retail space. Rouse eventually removed his firm from consideration, leaving the choice between Hahn and Jee. Hahn proposed to build between 500,000 and 750,000 square feet of retail space; Jee proposed to develop 1 million square feet in a mixed office and retail center, plus low- and moderate-income housing.

In the contest between Jee and Hahn, Hahn had the edge on two counts. First, he was proposing to bring more retail space into downtown San Diego (*i.e.,* the use that Mayor Wilson was convinced was most essential to revitalize downtown). Hahn also had the edge based on his previous experience and the number of development projects he had already completed.[21] Indeed, Hahn's reputation and prior track record made people believe that if anyone could develop a successful shopping center in downtown San Diego, it was Hahn.

However, Hahn's development proposal came with a set of preconditions. Before he was going to fully commit to developing a downtown shopping center, he wanted the city to commit to building several thousand downtown housing units as well as a convention center and hotels. As Mike Madigan (who, when I interviewed him in 1998, was senior vice president and development coordinator of Pardee Construction) explained to me, Hahn felt that the city was "significantly underestimating" what needed to happen in downtown San Diego to make it a vital city center.

According to Max Schmidt, Hahn told the city, "I will commit to Horton Plaza *if* you build a convention center, *if* you clean up the general environment in the surrounding area [by which he was specifically referring to the rundown and seedy Gaslamp District], *if* you build housing downtown and *if* you build a transit system."

The actions to which Hahn wanted the city to commit were things that were already on the city's planning agenda; however, the commitments Hahn extracted probably led the city to undertake and complete those actions sooner and in a more orchestrated fashion than otherwise might have been the case.

In May 1974, Hahn was officially designated as the developer of Horton Plaza. "The city started negotiating with Ernie Hahn before we [CCDC] were in place, and before a detailed plan for the project had been developed and approved," reported Donna Alm, "but we [CCDC] closed the deal." Still, all that the parties had done was to reach an agreement in principle that a shopping center of a certain threshold size would be built overlooking Horton Plaza. There was no clear idea of exactly what the shopping center was going to contain or look like."

The point person who negotiated with Hahn on behalf of the city was Gerald Trimble, the executive director of CCDC. Trimble was a forceful negotiator, and had the strong backing of both Dean Dunphy (the chairman of the board of CCDC and a key advocate of the Horton Plaza project) and of Mayor Wilson. Another key person at CCDC, who was less publicly visible but nevertheless exerted considerable influence on the negotiations, was urban planner/designer Max Schmidt.

"As originally presented to us," said Schmidt, "the proposed project was a typical, self-contained retail mall dropped into downtown San Diego—completely enclosed, no outlets, no pedestrian access from the perimeter, and no design details or attention to the appearance of the structure's various façades. It was like a fortified city. Our concept for Horton Plaza was that it should be—in addition to a retail center—a place for recreation with a community orientation. It should be a special place."

Schmidt worked long and hard to try to keep Horton Plaza from making the same mistake made by other downtown shopping centers of solely looking inward and turning away from the surrounding area. "It was a tremendous struggle," said Schmidt. "It often seemed to Trimble that I was being hopelessly impractical. He used to say to me, 'Think like a developer!' We were constantly arguing. To his credit, he put up with me and eventually we made a good team. It took a lot of back-and-forth negotiations, and something like 15 or 16 iterations of both the plan and the financing." Indeed, there were undoubtedly times during the negotiations when the principal actors must have wondered whether the project would ever get built and, if it did, whether it would turn out to have been worth all the effort. The pressure on Trimble and the CCDC board to pull back from insisting on major concessions and changes in the project was increased by the fact that city council support for the project was shaky.

"The city council at the time was not a happy partner and was very reluctant," said Schmidt. As Frieden and Segalyn report, "Some city council members voted consistently against the project because they were flatly opposed to spending public money for redevelopment no matter what the economic justifications might be. With two members unshakable in their disapproval, the

7-8   A fancifully designed obelisk at one of the entrances to Horton Plaza.

Source: Gene Bunnell

7-9   Walkways at various levels provide multiple vantage points for viewing and partaking of the hustle and bustle in the center of Horton Plaza.

Source: Gene Bunnell

7-10   The central space of Horton Plaza functions very much like a public square.

Source: Gene Bunnell

7-11   Carefully articulated openings in walls surrounding the central space of Horton Plaza create delightful patterns of light and shadow.

Source: Gene Bunnell

7-12   The atmosphere within Horton Plaza is more like a festive, open-air market than a shopping center. The sense of enclosure, and continually unfolding views created by oddly angled walls and narrowings and openings, makes it feel like walking through an Italian hilltown run amok with Post-Modernist Architecture.

Source: Gene Bunnell

project came within a hair of losing the two-thirds vote it needed for a renegotiated agreement in 1979." (*ibid.*, 130)

Fortunately, Trimble did press for major design changes in the project, and Hahn was open-minded enough to listen and consider the city's requests. As Michael Stepner put it, Hahn showed himself to be "a real statesman."

Jon Jerde (Hahn's architect) was also instrumental in making Horton Plaza into a special place. "It was Jerde who convinced Hahn that he needed to do something that left his mark on San Diego," observed Schmidt. When Jerde was hired by Hahn to design Horton Plaza, he was the most famous shopping-center architect in America, but still had not produced anything very distinguished. The following revealing account is provided by author Jerry Adler:

"Jerde had an astonishing tale of woe to account for his winding up as the most famous shopping-center architect in America. After graduating from U.S.C. in 1964, he was tempted by a Los Angeles firm with that dream of every young architect in those days, a five-figure salary. He planned on spending a year there and then living off what he had saved, but his wife had other plans and at the end of the year handed him divorce papers. The settlement essentially trapped him in his high-paying job indefinitely. Over the next decade

Jerde directly or indirectly was responsible for millions of square feet of shopping centers, all of them deplorable. 'Hissing, grim tubes,' he called them, down which shoppers were made to trudge until, with nothing left to spend, they were spit out into the parking lot.

"Yet gradually an idea was taking shape within him for a different kind of shopping center. It would be a celebration of civic life instead of a cynical machine for evacuating wallets. It would be open to the community instead of isolated in its asphalt meadow . . .

"Jerde quit his job and opened his own practice, with Hahn as his first and for a time only client. Horton Plaza . . . became Jerde's revenge on the shopping center. He set about conscientiously breaking every rule the Hahn Company had. It was axiomatic in shopping-center design that you created an environment with as few references as possible to the world outside, where there were things to do besides shop and eat. Exits were as obscure as the fire code allowed, it being assumed that shoppers were too stupid to leave unless they smacked their noses on a door. Jerde did the unthinkable and opened the mall to the city around it; he flayed off the roof and took its venerable H-plan and twisted its spine like a sadistic child. He slathered the walls with phony Tuscan mosaics and absurdly rusticated stucco in pale blue-greens and desert pinks and ochers." (Adler 1993, 156)

Downtown Housing

Unlike in Charleston, South Carolina and Providence, Rhode Island, there was no established tradition in San Diego of people living in or near downtown. San Diego's attempts at developing housing and encouraging people to live downtown therefore faced greater obstacles than many other cities have faced. Nevertheless, the development of housing from the beginning was a key element in the city's downtown revitalization strategy. Developing downtown housing was also one of the things that the city agreed to do to get Ernie Hahn to commit to developing Horton Plaza. The idea was that the development of Horton Plaza and the development of downtown housing would occur at the same time. As things turned out, the housing came first and Horton Plaza followed.

The first two downtown housing developments to be built (Park Row and Marina Park) were completed and first occupied in 1983. Both were subsidized to a significant extent by CCDC because, without the subsidies, they would not have been built. "No one knew whether or not they could be successfully marketed, and whether buyers and renters would materialize to occupy the units," said Michael Stepner. In fact, it took five years for the first two projects to be fully occupied. However, by the time later downtown developments came on line, the idea of living downtown appealed to so many people that "they didn't

7-13   New housing in downtown San Diego. The tower of the San Diego Hyatt Hotel is in the background.

Source: Gene Bunnell

even build models," said Stepner. "The units at Columbia Place [a later development] were fully sold before the sticks were up."

In the first decade of downtown housing development, most of the new housing was built on cleared land west and south of Horton Plaza. The housing developments built ranged from attached single-family dwellings (rowhouses); to garden-style apartment buildings; to higher density, high-rise apartment and condominium structures. Despite the variety of development styles, however, there was a remarkable unity and cohesiveness to the area. One thing that contributed greatly to the unified "feel" of the downtown residential precinct was that planners made a conscious effort to interconnect different developments by means of a network of greenspaces with footpaths and walkways.

Had city planners not done that, developers would no doubt have built a series of separate, unconnected developments arranged around dead-end cul-de-sacs. Indeed, in our tour of the downtown housing precinct, Michael Stepner showed me a more recent residential development where city planners had called for a connecting walkway through the development, "but where the city had allowed the building owners to gate it off for parking on an interim basis.

7-14   A lush greenspace surrounded by housing in the heart of downtown San Diego. A planned network of greenspaces and walkways provides convenient pedestrian connections between adjoining residential developments.

Source: Gene Bunnell

Once it was done, the walkway through was gone," said Stepner, "and once it's gone, it's gone. We'll never get it back."

By 1998, there were over 20,000 people living in over 5,000 new housing units in downtown San Diego that had been built over a 15-year period. Over time, the supply of housing units produced in downtown San Diego has in fact become increasingly diverse. For example, loft-style housing has begun to appear on the market as developers have renovated and converted the vacant upper floors of old downtown buildings, such as along C Street and 4th and 5th Streets. Distinctively designed loft-style units have also been produced by means of new construction.

Little Italy (north and west of the city's CBD) is one area that, for probably 50 years, had not seen any significant amount of housing construction, but which was beginning to see some new housing development activity by 1998. In my tour of the city, Michael Stepner took me to see the recently completed first phase of what was called the Little Italy Neighborhood Project.

Having prepared a plan for the Little Italy Redevelopment District, CCDC acquired and assembled properties in the area in anticipation of soliciting development proposals from private developers that were consistent with the plan. Had CCDC not played this role, it is highly unlikely that a single private developer could have succeeded in acquiring all the properties within a given

7-15   Areas of downtown residential development with interconnecting greenspaces—as photographed from the top floor of the Hyatt Hotel. The tracks of the San Diego Trolley run diagonally through the area.

Source: Gene Bunnell

7-16   The upper floors of this downtown building have been renovated into loft-style housing.

Source: Gene Bunnell

block and, if a private developer *had* managed to gain control of the entire area, the housing development would probably not have fit in with the scale of a neighborhood. Had a developer gained control of only part of a block, it was questionable whether such a small-scale housing development, in the midst of an unimproved block, would be feasible and marketable. There needed to be a critical mass of housing to make it work.

Because of these varied considerations, CCDC approached the development of this first phase of Little Italy in an unusual way. Instead of putting the entire block out to bid to a single developer (the way that public agencies typically approach redevelopment), CCDC developed an urban-scale housing plan that divided the block into a number of different parcels and then parceled them out to different developers. The result is a row of abutting developments that forms a continuous frontage facing the street and presents the appearance of a unified housing development. However, due to the fact that different components were built by different developers, there is a variety of building styles that gives the development a more complex character than would have been the case had it been carried out by a single developer. The market-rate units produced in the first phase of development are modern-looking, townhouse-style units, with a garage on the ground floor and two three-story residential units on top. Construction of housing on a second block in Little Italy was just beginning when I was in San Diego in 1998 and has since been completed.

Most of the new housing units in downtown San Diego have been created through new construction. However, a significant number of units have been produced by renovating and reusing existing buildings, such as the former 1920s-style El Cortez Hotel at 7th and Ash, which was renovated and converted to accommodate 85 apartments. The ground-floor level of the former hotel contains space that is leased out for private functions and events as well as for neighborhood-serving retail space.

As the number of downtown housing units has increased, so too has the diversity of housing types and styles. A review of residential projects completed or under construction between 1998 and 2000 reveals that a growing number of loft-style, live-work units have been produced by new construction as well as a growing number of senior citizen and assisted-living housing units. High-rise condominium and apartment developments, as well as high-rise developments including both residential and nonresidential uses, have also begun to punctuate the city's downtown skyline.

When planning for the encouragement of downtown housing began, planners at CCDC hoped that up to 50,000 people would ultimately live downtown. As the pace of downtown housing development has accelerated, that goal seems more and more within reach.

7-17   New housing in Little Italy, just north of the central business district.

Source: Gene Bunnell

7-18   Sign on a construction site, announcing the construction of housing on a second block in Little Italy.

Source: Gene Bunnell

The Gaslamp Quarter

Another element in the revitalization strategy for downtown San Diego was aimed at the transformation of the city's Gaslamp Quarter—the area between 4th and 6th Streets, which contained the largest concentration of turn-of-the-century commercial buildings in the city. By the 1970s, the future of the Gaslamp Quarter seemed dim. In 1976, Roger Montgomery wrote, "Whether they [the turn-of-the-century commercial buildings] will last much longer seems problematical. The area, locally called the Gaslamp Quarter, looks to many in the city like a prime target for urban renewal. Too bad." (Montgomery, August 21, 1976, 26)

Montgomery's pessimistic outlook turns out to have been unfounded. Today, the old buildings throughout the Gaslamp Quarter have been renovated, new buildings have been added, and the area contains a lively mixture of shops, restaurants, bars, night clubs and theaters. There are probably even one or two tattoo parlors and risqué activities to make sailors still feel at home.

In the 1970s, historic preservation was beginning to receive attention in American cities. Historic areas (such as the Pioneer Square area in Seattle and the Fanieul Hall Market area in Boston) were becoming focal points for downtown revitalization. Historic preservation efforts in San Diego lagged somewhat behind what was happening in other cities, in part because San Diego was a relatively young city and citizens in San Diego were less vocal in pressing for historic preservation.

Around 1975, the city's planning department turned its attention to planning for the area just east of where Horton Plaza was to be built—an area of historic significance which was to become known as the Gaslamp Quarter. One reason for focusing attention on this area, of course, was the fact that the city had promised Ernie Hahn that it would address the deteriorated conditions that existed in the area and try to spruce it up. However, not much progress was being made in moving the Horton Plaza project forward. As Michael Stepner sees it, Hahn was telling the city that he wanted the area cleaned up before he would go forward with Horton Plaza, but what Hahn was really doing was "buying time."

In 1976 (the year of the nation's bicentennial), a plan for the Gaslamp Quarter was completed and adopted by the city council. A major component of the plan was the *Planned District Ordinance and Urban Design and Development Manual*. The Gaslamp Quarter plan, ordinance and manual considerably tightened development and design regulations in the district, requiring that before "any work" commenced (related to erecting any new building or structure, moving a structure, remodeling, altering, adding to or demolishing any existing building, or changing the use of a structure in the district), it was first necessary to apply for and obtain a special permit from the city. It also set out design and development guidelines to which applicants had to conform to obtain a special

7-19 The Gaslamp Quarter.

Source: Gene Bunnell

7-20 This renovated historic building in the Gaslamp Quarter was once San Diego's city hall.

Source: Gene Bunnell

7-21   One of many distinguished Victorian-era commercial structures in the Gaslamp Quarter.

Source: Gene Bunnell

7-22   The upper portion of this commercial building in the Gaslamp Quarter has been embellished by a mural.

Source: Gene Bunnell

7-23   The Horton Grand Hotel in the Gaslamp Quarter.

Source: Gene Bunnell

permit. CCDC and the city's planning department also inventoried and documented the historic significance of all buildings in the district.

Michael Stepner looks upon the efforts that were undertaken in an attempt to revitalize the Gaslamp Quarter as a learning process. "We experimented with all sorts of tools, and learned a lot about the community and economic development process," said Stepner. "We started out with zoning and sign control, but discovered that it was going to take a lot more than that."

In addition to tightening development regulations, the city offered low-interest loans to building owners for façade improvements and to small businesses in the district. The Gaslamp Quarter was also where San Diego's first Business Improvement District was established, which became a model for what has now become a large number of little Business Improvement Districts throughout the city. Moreover, on the national level, "What was done in the Gaslamp Quarter became a model for the National Trust's Main Street Program," said Stepner. In 1980, the 16-block Gaslamp Quarter area was officially designated as a National Historic District on the National Register of Historic Places.

Today, the Gaslamp Quarter is one of the liveliest places in San Diego—an area that most tourists, visitors and conventioneers make a point of visiting at some point in their stay. It is also extremely popular with and much frequented by young San Diegans. However, as Mike Madigan pointed out, the Gaslamp Quarter would not be what it is today had the other land use and development changes in downtown not come about. "There are dependent variables and there are independent variables," explained Madigan. "The Gaslamp District was a dependent variable in that it was going to succeed when the rest of downtown came along—not before. People had to see downtown as a safe and comfortable place first. Now the Gaslamp District is a big hit, but it was utterly dependent on other things happening, like Horton Plaza."

It is interesting to note that one of the most well-known Victorian-era structures in the Gaslamp Quarter—the Horton Grand Hotel—wasn't actually in the Gaslamp Quarter when the area was threatened by urban renewal. Moreover, only part of the structure can accurately be described as being the Horton Grand Hotel (circa 1888), which was slated for demolition because it stood in the footprint of what today is Horton Plaza. The rest of the Horton Grand Hotel is composed of another historic hotel—the former Brooklyn Hotel (also known as the Kahle Saddlery Hotel)—which was taken down when the Salvation Army expanded onto *its* site. The two structures survived and stand today because architect Wayne Donaldson dismantled them, brick by brick, and eventually relocated and rebuilt them in the heart of the Gaslamp Quarter, joining them together to create a 108-room hotel that, by all accounts, has been a smashing success.

The San Diego Convention Center

The other key component of the downtown strategy was the development of a downtown convention center. When CCDC first began planning for a downtown convention center, the idea was that it would be located near the Santa Fe Depot, and fairly detailed plans and cost estimates were developed based on that expectation. However, because that convention plan required a significant commitment of city funding, it had to be approved by the voters in a referendum. When the referendum was held, it was voted down.

After an extensive study of alternative sites and possible funding mechanisms, a solution to the impasse materialized when the San Diego Unified Port Authority—a public agency that, unlike the city, had the financial resources and wherewithal to develop the convention center without relying on city funds and without obtaining the specific approval of the voters—agreed to pay for and develop the convention center on land that it owned and controlled along San Diego Bay.

The property that was chosen for the convention center was directly south of Horton Plaza. The 760,000-square-foot San Diego Convention Center opened and hosted its first events in 1990. The design of the building by architect Arthur Erickson won considerable praise and has made it an important city landmark, particularly as viewed from the harbor. Despite the building's huge size and length, the mock sails incorporated along the length of the top of the structure give its roof line a delicacy and distinctiveness not normally found in such structures. From an economic standpoint, and in terms of attracting visitors to downtown San Diego, the convention center has clearly been a success. It has proven so successful that a $216 million expansion was approved, doubling its total size and length.

In the opinion of Donna Alm, the site where the convention center was built is far better than the one CCDC originally identified next to the Santa Fe Depot. The direct alignment of the convention center to Horton Plaza (along 1st, 2nd, 3rd and 4th Avenues) has encouraged convention attendees to walk a short way to the north, thereby achieving a positive synergistic effect between the convention center and Horton Plaza. The site of the convention center also fronts on a line of the San Diego Trolley, making it conveniently accessible by means of public transit from other parts of the city.

The thousands of out-of-town visitors coming downtown to attend conferences and conventions spurred a veritable explosion of hotel development in downtown San Diego. Two of the largest and most visually dramatic new hotels (the Hyatt Regency and the San Diego Marriott) were developed adjacent to the convention center, on land also under the ownership and control of the San Diego Unified Port District.[22] Toward the end of the 1990s, new hotels began to be built in other parts of the downtown area, including areas of the downtown core that had seen little or no previous hotel development. By 1998,

7-24   The original portion of the San Diego Convention Center, designed by Arthur Erickson.

Source: Port of San Diego/Dale Frost

more than 3,700 new hotel rooms had been built in downtown San Diego and many more were in the process of being built.

From a planning perspective, however, the convention center does have one serious failure. It physically walls off a major portion of the downtown from the waterfront, obstructing views of the water and restricting the points at which people can gain access to the waterfront. Many people to whom I talked said they felt that the city had been diminished by allowing the downtown to be cut off from the water.

As *The San Diego Union-Tribune*'s architectural critic Ann Jarmusch commented, "There's been a lot of criticism, and I count myself among the critics, of how the waterfront has been treated. The hotels, combined with the convention center and Seaport Village, wall the city off from the bay. If you're a conventioneer, it's great; if you're a citizen, it's not. There are two lovely parks behind [on the bay side of] the convention center that extend out into the water, but most people who live and work in the city don't know they're there. They're inaccessible and invisible, because there are no view corridors through to the bay. I didn't know they were there when I moved here. Somebody had to

7-25   Construction of the San Diego Convention Center sparked the development of high-rise hotels on adjacent waterfront property also owned by the Unified Port District. The tallest structure (on the left) is the Hyatt Hotel. A second 22-story tower of the Hyatt Hotel, containing another 750 rooms, has been constructed since this photo was taken. The Marriott Hotel is on the right. The twin towers in the center are condominiums.

Source: Port of San Diego/Dale Frost

7-26   New addition to the San Diego Convention Center, completed in 2001.

Source: Port of San Diego/Dale Frost

7-27   A continuous waterfront promenade extends from Seaport Village, alongside the Marriott Hotel, and all along the full length of the expanded San Diego Convention Center—but is invisible to most people and hard to reach.

Source: Gene Bunnell

7-28   View looking south from the top of the Hyatt Hotel. Waterfront Park, which is part of the Embarcadero Marina Park and is mentioned by *The San Diego Union-Tribune* architecture critic Ann Jarmusch, is visible in the upper right.

Source: Gene Bunnell

7-29 San Diego has changed but it is still a Navy town. In this photo, an aircraft carrier—part of a fleet of naval ships—returns to port after a six-month tour of duty. Sailors in white dress uniform line the length of the flight deck. Seaport Village, a tourist-oriented commercial development on Unified Port District land, is visible in the extreme right of the photo.

Source: Gene Bunnell

tell me."[23] The expansion of the convention center, completed in the fall of 2001, has made the obstruction even worse.

As Ann Jarmusch noted above, there is a continuous promenade and band of public space that run along the full length of the convention center overlooking San Diego Bay. Unfortunately, it is very difficult to reach unless you have a boat. The only way you can get to the promenade is by circling around the southerly end of the convention center or by circling around to the north and entering near Seaport Village and/or the Marriott Hotel. Either way, it can require going a mile or more out of one's way.

The only other way of getting to the waterfront promenade from downtown is to climb up and down a steep staircase that leads up and over the convention center. When the plans for the convention center expansion were approved, city planners asked that the staircase leading up and over the convention center be doubled in width, and that platforms be constructed at various levels to provide places where people could stop and rest. This was done.

One factor that probably goes a long way toward explaining why development has been so intense along San Diego's waterfront is that the city's professional planners and planning commission have virtually no authority or control whatsoever over shoreline development. When I told William Anderson about the planning that was done in Charleston (limiting the density of development along its waterfront so as to maintain views and increase public access to the water), this is what he said: "If the waterfront of San Diego were within the city's jurisdiction, it certainly would have been in the city's interest to have followed Charleston's example. Unfortunately, the tidelands and shoreline property in San Diego are all under the control of the Unified Port District, and the incentive for the Unified Port District has been to put up high-density, lucrative development on their land—despite what the city's planning objective is. City-wide, the incentive would be for us to do what Charleston did. If you stepped building heights up as you moved inland [instead of putting the tallest buildings closest to the water], you'd have more rooms and total floor area with views of the water, and greater total land and property values."

Attracting a Major Downtown Supermarket

In 1997, a large supermarket opened in downtown San Diego, on a site bordering the southern edge of Horton Plaza. From one perspective, the opening of the downtown supermarket (operated by the Ralph's supermarket chain—the same chain that operates the supermarket in the Uptown District development, previously described) is proof of the tremendous progress the city has made in making downtown San Diego an appealing place for people to live, and in creating a fairly large downtown residential population.

However, the development of a Ralph's supermarket in downtown San Diego didn't just happen on its own. It came about because the city worked long and hard to get a major supermarket built downtown as part of its overall strategy of making downtown an appealing and convenient place to live. "Getting a downtown supermarket was one of the hardest things we [CCDC] did," recalled Donna Alm. "It took 15 years to get Ralph's. It was very difficult because supermarkets have this incredible market testing process they go through and we just didn't meet their criteria. We didn't have the size of residential base they require, at least at this point in time. We pointed out that 75,000 people work downtown on a daily basis, in addition to the 20,000 that now live downtown, in addition to all of the people staying in hotels and attending conventions. What we offered wasn't their conventional shopping base. It was a hard sell."

In the end, the secret to getting a downtown supermarket was that the staff at CCDC just kept working on it. After many years, they got Ralph's and two other supermarket chains to consider the possibility of operating a downtown supermarket. "We just kept talking to them," said Alm, "and finally, when the right developer came along to work with Ralph's, we were able to put the project together." CCDC acquired and assembled the property needed for the supermarket, mostly through friendly purchases, and sold the land to Ralph's at the agreed-upon price.

On the inside, Ralph's supermarket in downtown San Diego looks and feels like its suburban counterparts. However, unlike supermarkets in suburban areas, Ralph's downtown San Diego supermarket does not look out onto acres of paved surface parking. Instead, the building is built fairly close to G Street and fronts onto a wide sidewalk. Because it is close to Horton Plaza (right across the street) and to thousands of downtown housing units, the supermarket gets a lot of foot traffic. On the other hand, people *can* drive to Ralph's. The only difference is that the parking is below grade, underneath the supermarket building. An angled moving sidewalk carries people from the below-grade parking area up to the supermarket at grade level, making it easy for shoppers to roll their shopping carts full of goods down to their parked cars when they are done shopping.

The urban-oriented site planning approach of placing parking *underneath* a supermarket was not something Ralph's would have done on its own had it not been urged to do so by CCDC's planners. Ralph's was used to building suburban-style supermarkets fronting on lots of surface parking; placing parking underneath a supermarket therefore seemed highly unconventional. In acceding to CCDC's plan, the executives at Ralph's learned something important and useful. According to Michael Stepner, "They've found that it is cheaper to buy a smaller site and build underground parking than to buy extra land to put in surface parking."

Downtown Amenities and Design Treatments

Across the street from the San Diego Convention Center and the San Diego Marriott Hotel, and a short walk from Horton Plaza, is a remarkable linear park called the Martin Luther King, Jr. Promenade, which runs parallel to the tracks of the San Diego Trolley and Harbor Drive. The rows of palm trees planted along both sides of Harbor Drive, and down Harbor Drive's center median, make the promenade feel even more spacious.

Walking across Harbor Drive from the convention center and hotel, I found myself in a remarkably beautiful urban park called Children's Park, the centerpiece of which was a large circular body of water, bisected by the tracks of the San Diego Trolley as well as by a pedestrian path and bikeway, which seem to float on the water. Despite all the trolleys, bicyclists and surrounding activity, I can't think of another space in the center of a city more tranquil and enjoyable in which to sit.

When I told Michael Stepner how impressed I was by Children's Park, and the pedestrian path and bikeway paralleling the trolley tracks that were part of the Martin Luther King, Jr. Promenade, he indicated that the person who really deserved the credit was Max Schmidt. "Max just pushed and pushed for the

7-30   The Martin Luther King, Jr. Promenade.

Source: Courtesy of Centre City Development Corporation/Skip Jurus

7-31   The pedestrian path and bikeway through Children's Park.

Source: Gene Bunnell

bikeway and the park and the landscaping of the Martin Luther King, Jr. Promenade," Stepner explained. "He put forward the ideas, got people to buy into them and got them included in the downtown plan. Each time a project came forward, he would push to make sure improvements called for in the plan got included and implemented."

That segment of Harbor Drive could easily have turned into one of the ugliest and most desolate traffic arteries in the city. As Max Schmidt put it, "There were too many barriers between the city and the waterfront. Large-scale developments [like the convention center and the Marriott Hotel] had created a wall. Harbor Drive and the railroad right of way also formed a wall."

As he thought about what could be done, Schmidt realized that there was a good deal of excess railroad property there, which presented an opportunity to do something that would really transform the area. The hard part was getting the different property owners—the Unified Port District, the Santa Fe Railroad, California Department of Transportation (Caltrans), Metropolitan Transit Development Board (MTDB), CCDC, the city and a number of private property owners—all of whom had different interests to work cooperatively toward the development of an agreed-upon plan. "We all got together under the auspices of CCDC and developed a plan that mitigated the barrier of the railroad and Harbor Drive, and created an attractive setting for residential development in the area, which has subsequently occurred," said Schmidt.

Schmidt brought in Peter Walker (a landscape architect from San Francisco) to help develop the plan. "I encouraged him to be creative. I didn't realize how creative he would be," said Schmidt. The design plan he came up with showed a large circular pond of water, 207 feet across, which the trolley and the bikepath would pass over. "The plan was so wonderful," said Schmidt, "that everyone bought into it." Schmidt continued: "We had to negotiate with the Santa Fe Railroad to get them to allow the bikepath on their right of way. We call it a bikeway. They call it a paved pathway, which is open to the public but which the railroad's service vehicles can also use if need be to service their rails."

The circular pond of water is only part of what makes Children's Park special. Behind the pond, there is a sculpted mound with plantings and palm trees—a tranquil area in which to sit, read or just look at the water.

Schmidt admitted to me that "Children's Park" is a bit of a misnomer. "It wasn't designed just for children, but CCDC board members suggested to the mayor and the business community that it be named 'Children's Park.' Actually, the 'p.r.' the opening of the park generated was fantastic. It opened on a very hot July day and we had thousands of people there. Hundreds of kids were in the water, jumping between the stones and having a great time."

Piecing together the funding for the construction of the Martin Luther King, Jr. Promenade and Children's Park required almost as much creativity and persistence as the act of preparing a plan to which all the parties involved could agree. The cost of constructing the park and promenade ran about $25 million. Part of the cost was funded by TIF (with increased tax revenues generated by increased property values in the district pledged toward project costs); other portions of project costs were paid for by adjoining private developments.

"You can't tell at Harbor Club or at Cityfront Terrace [major developments adjoining the park] where the public park ends and private property begins," commented Schmidt. "That's the way we designed it. In some cases, we got outright contributions for park improvements from developers. In all cases, where private developments adjoin the park, we have a 30-year agreement that the owners of the adjoining property will maintain the park according to very specific design criteria and maintenance standards. It's been a cooperative venture all the way."

PLANNING AND DEVELOPING A RAIL TRANSIT SYSTEM

One of the most significant accomplishments in San Diego in the last quarter of the 20th century, made possible by planning, was the development of an extensive rail transit system—much like the kind of rail transit system that Lynch and Appleyard recommended in *Temporary Paradise?*

The first part of the San Diego Trolley system (later known as the Blue Line), which became operational in the summer of 1981, was the 15.9-mile-long segment from downtown San Diego south to San Ysidro at the U.S./Mexican bor-

7-32 Children's Park, as viewed from many stories above—an oasis in the center of the city.

Source: Gene Bunnell

7-33 Low-rise housing in downtown San Diego, not far from Children's Park. The brightly painted exteriors of these structures (with large blocks of orange, purple and red) express a brash southern California style and a new sense of confidence in the future of downtown San Diego.

Source: Gene Bunnell

der. Before long, service began on the second line (the East Line from downtown to El Cajon). In 1995, service on the East Line (renamed the Orange Line) was extended another 3.6 miles from El Cajon to Santee; a year later, service on the Blue Line was extended 3.2 miles from the Santa Fe Depot to Old Town. By 1997, when the 6.1-mile Mission Valley segment opened, the trolley route system had grown to 47.8 miles and 48 stations, ridership on the trolley system had grown to an average of 50,100 on weekdays, and total annual ridership had reached 18.3 million.

By 2001, average weekday trolley ridership had risen to 83,000. A 5.9-mile easterly extension of the Mission Valley line (from Mission Valley Centre to La Mesa, to be completed in 2004) will add an additional four stations (including a stop serving the campus of San Diego State University) and will connect the Mission Valley Line to the El Cajon and Santee Orange Lines, thereby completing a large circular rail loop encompassing the city's northern tier. A further extension north from the Old Town Transit Center will add another nine stations, including stations serving La Jolla Village Square, the campus of the University of California at San Diego and the "Golden Triangle"/University Towne Centre area.

The region's evolving rail transit network has been further augmented by commuter passenger rail service, which began operating in 1995 between downtown San Diego and Oceanside (41 miles to the north). The San Diego-Oceanside commuter rail service (called the Coaster), which stops at six newly developed stations between San Diego's Santa Fe Depot and Oceanside, consists of double-decker passenger cars with bicycle accommodations on every train.

A further 23.7-mile extension of commuter rail line service from Oceanside to Escondido (providing service to an additional 14 stations) is expected to be completed in 2005. The same 1987 Transportation Sales Tax Initiative (Trans-Net), which helped finance extensions of the San Diego Trolley system undertaken since 1987, helped pay for the development of these new commuter rail lines.

To learn how San Diego's ambitious and evolving rail transit network came about, and how the San Diego Trolley in particular—which started it all—got planned and built, I went to see William Lieberman, director of planning and operations for the MTDB of San Diego at that time (the public agency that planned, built and operates the San Diego Trolley system). Mike Madigan (a close aide to Mayor Peter Wilson when many crucial transit planning and finance decisions were made) and Kenneth E. Sulzer (executive director of the San Diego Association of Governments (SANDAG)) also provided helpful insights and background information.

The first important step toward planning a transit system in San Diego, according to Ken Sulzer, was taken in 1975, when the San Diego Comprehen-

7-34 People boarding the Coaster at the Santa Fe Depot, at the beginning of its 41-mile run from San Diego north to Oceanside. The San Diego Trolley stops at a parallel platform.

Source: Gene Bunnell

sive Planning Organization (CPO)—the predecessor to the present-day SAN-DAG—completed a *Comprehensive Regional Transportation Plan* that represented a radical departure from the almost exclusive focus that had been placed on promoting highways and automobile transportation prior to that time.

As it happened, the plan was completed the same year Lynch and Appleyard's *Temporary Paradise?* was released. It was, said Sulzer, "the first *balanced* transportation plan ever prepared in the San Diego area," and called for one-third of all transportation spending to be directed toward rail transit improvements, with the other two-thirds split between state highways and local road improvements. The plan also identified and evaluated various potential transit corridors. "It took 25 years," said Sulzer, "but the plan did get implemented." According to Sulzer, the transit corridors identified in the plan were generally adhered to when it came time to actually build the city's transit system.

When I interviewed him in 1998, William Lieberman had been involved in transit planning in San Diego for 14 years. He came to San Diego in 1984—three years after the first line of the San Diego Trolley to San Ysidro/Tijuana opened—and was therefore not involved in the earliest stages of transit planning. Nevertheless, he was extremely knowledgeable about the events that shaped transit planning in San Diego, including those that preceded his arrival.

Two bills passed by the California legislature made planning and development of a transit system in San Diego possible. Both of them passed largely due to the efforts and leadership of Jim Mills. "Jim Mills had been a history teacher before running for state senator," said Lieberman, "and was a very cultured and articulate person." Mills was elected to the California Senate and then went on to become the president pro tem of the Senate.

According to Lieberman, "A lot of what happened here is really explained by the Great Man Theory of History, because Jim Mills really was the spark that pushed the whole thing along. I'm not sure how much progress we would have made if he hadn't been so interested [in improving transit] and hadn't been in the powerful position he was."

The first bill, passed by the California legislature in 1971, was the Transportation Development Act (TDA). Under the TDA, a quarter cent of the state sales tax was earmarked and distributed to local units of government, exclusively for the purpose of improving public transportation. (An increase in the state sales tax on gasoline was also approved, so the state didn't lose revenue in the process.) The second bill authorized the formation of the MTDB.

The importance of the two above-mentioned bills is best appreciated by considering the state of public transit in San Diego during the 1960s, when the only public transit available was an increasingly unsatisfactory bus service operated by San Diego Transit (a private company). As more people moved to the suburbs and bought cars, and as bus ridership plummeted, San Diego Transit was on the verge of bankruptcy. To avoid the loss of all remaining bus service, the City of San Diego took over San Diego Transit in 1967 and assumed responsibility for its operations.

Under city ownership, San Diego Transit also contracted to provide bus service to and within other surrounding communities. However, San Diego Transit continued to lose money and ridership, and the federal transit subsidies that the city received did little to keep bus service from continuing to deteriorate. A good deal of the federal money went to salary increases for bus drivers rather than into service increases. "Bus drivers in San Diego were reportedly the highest paid bus drivers in the country, but the bus service was still deteriorating," said Lieberman.

Meanwhile, nearby cities such as Chula Vista and National City and some other communities in the county, reluctant to see their TDA money siphoned off by San Diego Transit, formed their own bus companies, which they felt could operate in a more cost-effective manner than San Diego Transit. In each case, the municipalities bought a fleet of buses and contracted with private companies through a bidding process to operate the buses independent of San Diego Transit. "We had four or five transit systems in the region with minimal coordination between them," said Lieberman.

One of the most pressing reasons behind passing the legislation establishing the MTDB was to try to coordinate the different transit operations that had evolved in the region (*i.e.,* to try to create some order out of the chaos). "By the late 1970s, we had accomplished getting contracts in order with all the different bus companies so that the separate entities essentially functioned as a single system," said Lieberman. "There was one set of fares, one route map and a central telephone information system."[24]

The other reason for establishing the MTDB was to study and evaluate alternative transit technologies and systems, and determine what type of system would best meet San Diego's long-range transportation needs. "Mills was convinced that we were never going to get out of the box with just a bus system, and that somebody—some agency—needed to look at alternatives other than buses," said Lieberman.

During the 1960s and 1970s, cities across the country were considering developing new transit systems. Other cities were talking about significantly upgrading and expanding their existing transit systems. Indeed, transit planning activity was increasing due to the availability of federal Urban Mass Transit Administration funding which could potentially cover a substantial portion of the costs of developing new systems. Technologically advanced transportation systems, like the one that was being planned in the San Francisco Bay Area (called BART), were also becoming extremely popular.

Many of the new transportation technologies and systems being discussed nationally at the time were also being talked about in San Diego, such as monorails and so-called "people movers" (unmanned vehicles that looked like trains but had rubber wheels and operated on an elevated guideway). "Mayor Wilson was actually very keen on the 'people mover' scheme for downtown at one time. Consultants were also coming to town encouraging the city to develop a grandiose, expensive heavy rail metro-style system," said Lieberman, and encouraging San Diego to apply for federal funding to pay for it.

In fact, during the mid-1970s, the CPO (the regional planning organization that preceded SANDAG) conducted a study of fixed guideway transit systems and actually recommended that a system modeled on BART should be built in San Diego.[25] Meanwhile, San Diego Transit came up with a proposal for operating articulated express buses on reserved bus lanes.

"A lot of alternatives were considered," remembered William Lieberman, "and it was very contentious planning. Planning has to be passionate if it's going to mean something—and it certainly was quite passionate here. I gather that the MTDB had some big fights with SANDAG's predecessor, the CPO. It's hard for me to believe, given the good relationship we have now. Nevertheless, by the time I arrived here [in 1984], the dust had somewhat settled and the warring factions had pretty much come to terms."

Eventually, the decision was made to develop a light rail trolley system, rather than a much more expensive heavy rail system that probably would have had the capacity to carry much heavier volumes of ridership than San Diego would be likely to generate. Again, Jim Mills seems to have played a role in that decision.

Lieberman recalled, "I remember Jim telling me that he had been kind of amused in the early 1970s when somebody approached him with the idea that some day you might want to ride a streetcar in San Diego, but when he studied the light rail systems that other cities were developing, he was impressed by what he saw."

By 1977, Mayor Wilson (like Mills) had become convinced that light rail was the way to go, and directed the city's planning department to lay out trolley routes and include them in the general plan that was adopted in 1979. "Wilson became a staunch supporter of light rail," said Bill Lieberman.

Two other strategic decisions were made that were critically important to the success of San Diego's transit planning and development effort. The first was the decision *not* to use technologically advanced light rail transit vehicles, but instead to use transit vehicles that had been proven reliable in other cities. Around the time that San Diego was deciding what kind of light rail vehicle to use, for example, the Boeing Corporation was marketing a highly technologically advanced light rail transit vehicle to transit systems around the country, and sold large numbers of vehicles to the Massachusetts Bay Transportation Authority (MBTA) in Boston. However, when these sleek, space-age vehicles were put into service to replace the MBTA's aging fleet of trolley cars, numerous operational problems were encountered. San Diego avoided those problems by going the low-tech route and by ordering "off-the-shelf" transit vehicles.

The other strategically important planning decision was *not* to seek federal funding to establish the transit system. As subsequent events proved, it was a brilliant decision that, in the long run, saved a great deal of time and money. As Mike Madigan explained, "Initially, we did what everybody else did. We organized an effort to try to qualify for federal funding."

A man by the name of General Lipscomb, who had been involved in constructing the Lindenwold rail line in New Jersey, was hired to help in that regard. Nevertheless, the city's application to qualify for federal funding to establish a transit system was not approved and prospects for obtaining a commitment of federal funding in the future remained uncertain. Instead of putting everything on hold until federal funding approval was finally obtained, the decision was made to proceed *without* federal approval.

"Eventually, a group of people and I got together and decided to try a different approach," explained Mike Madigan. "We decided to build the first section on our own, and then go back to get federal funding to *expand* the system once it was in place and running. Jim Mills had come up with sufficient funding from the state to build the first line."

"We decided to build a transit system as cheaply as we could, *and on time*, to defy the notion that a big public works project always has to be over budget and late," said Lieberman. To keep costs down and avoid delays, the first line of the transit system was run along an existing right of way and built entirely at grade, thereby avoiding costly tunneling and the need to construct expensive underground stations. The cost of acquiring the existing railroad right of way (formerly owned by the Southern Pacific Railroad) was further reduced when a hurricane hit the southern California coast, heavily damaging and undermining the tracks. "We were able to buy 90% of the right of way that we needed for the first line to the south, as well as 90% of the right of way that we were going to need for the second line to the east, very inexpensively," explained Madigan.

The emphasis placed on getting the trolley line up and running, on time and on budget, meant that San Diego's trolley system had few frills. "It was a basic system, with no fancy bells and whistles. However, it was clean and reliable— the kind of system people feel comfortable using," said Mike Madigan. Dubbed the "Tijuana Trolley," San Diego's new trolley system immediately attracted national attention and rave reviews. "Once we got the line built, the feds came to town and gave it the award as the best new transit system in the country—which was only possible because they weren't involved in funding it," said Madigan. Moreover, once the system was up and running, it *did* qualify for federal funding because it was an *existing* system and not an entirely *new* system.

One way to appreciate the tradeoffs that were made in San Diego is to compare San Diego's trolley system to the light rail system that was planned and built in the Portland, Oregon metropolitan area. Comparing the two systems is especially appropriate, given the fact that the legislation establishing the MTDB (the agency that planned and built San Diego's trolley system) was passed around the same time that the Oregon state legislature passed legislation establishing Tri-Met (the regional agency that planned and built Portland's light rail system). Actually, the two cities started planning their transit systems at roughly the same time.

After attending the national APA conference in Seattle in 1998, I took a short side trip down to Portland to see the changes that had occurred since I was last there (nearly 20 years earlier). While in Portland, I rode the new Westside MAX light rail line, which had recently opened. At each of the 20 stations along the line, there were unique art treatments and installations. A brochure titled "Art on Westside MAX," prepared by Tri-Met, explained that eight design team artists and 15 project artists had collaborated with a team of architects and engineers to create over 100 permanent art elements in order to "bring individual identity to each of the 20 stations and honor the history, culture and landscape along the line." (Portland Metro/Tri-Met, 1998)

No such elaborate design effort went into making individual stations unique in San Diego, and San Diego has nothing to compare to the attractive, carefully planned and designed Transit Mall in Portland. As William Lieberman readily admitted, "Our stations are very simple—sometimes too simple. We should probably have made them look better because, as a component of total project cost, the additional cost would have been relatively small."

The system that was planned and built in San Diego is far from the optimal system that might have been produced, had saving money and building a system on time and on budget not been such overriding considerations. Indeed, Bill Lieberman admitted that he often reflects back on what might have been done to produce a better transit system. "It could possibly have turned out better if we had been able to push the trolley line under Broadway in a subway, or had we been able to take two lanes of traffic off of Broadway instead of putting the transit line one block north on C Street, which is what we did," said Lieberman. "However, the politics of the day ruled against seriously considering those options, so we did the best we could."

Having been closely involved in the planning of both Portland and San Diego's transit systems, William Lieberman is in a good position to compare the pros and cons of both. In his opinion, Portland succeeded more than San Diego because they integrated the planning of transit and development. "They worked much more carefully and did a much better job than we did in the beginning in getting land uses properly planned around the rail system, so the two were working in concert. Our focus as an agency when we started, on the other hand, was simply to build a light rail system as cheaply as we could and on time." In this regard, there was definitely a downside to the decision to route the trolley along an existing freight rail line, because it meant that the first line of the San Diego Trolley went through industrial areas. As a result, station stops along that first line tended to be on the edges rather than in the centers of populated areas.

On the other hand, there were also disadvantages to the approach that Portland took in planning its transit system. Unlike San Diego, Portland went through the process of getting federal approval and funding before ever starting to build its system. "They also combined transit planning with highway planning, and had a much more extensive planning and public involvement process," said Lieberman. Because of these differences, Portland's light rail system took a great deal longer to build and get operational than did San Diego's—a difference which Lieberman can clearly document in terms of his own work history.

William Lieberman came to San Diego to work for the MTDB in 1984, having previously worked for nine years at Tri-Met in Portland planning that city's light rail system. When Lieberman arrived in San Diego, the trolley line from downtown to San Ysidro/Tijuana had been operating for three years, but Portland's first transit line was still not operating. It wasn't until 1986 (two years after Lieberman starting working in San Diego) that the first segment of Portland's transit system opened.

In 1998, Portland's second transit line (the Westside line to Hillsboro) opened. "I started work on planning that second line in 1978," said Lieberman. "It took 20 years from the time I started planning that line to the time it got built." Twenty years of planning and careful attention to detail in Portland has produced a transit system that is widely admired and envied. However, if San Diego had taken 20 years to open its first transit line, the system would never have gotten built.

Although the economical way that San Diego went about planning its transit system had disadvantages, it also appears to have been absolutely the right strategy for San Diego to have pursued. "It helped us gain credibility, which allowed us to expand the system," said Lieberman. "Had we not built and operated the system in such a cost-effective manner, we would never have had a local mandate to expand the system, nor would the federal government have been so interested in helping fund the expansion of the system."

As I talked with William Lieberman, it was clear that he had done a good deal of thinking and soul searching in comparing the planning approaches taken in Portland and San Diego and the respective outcomes they produced in the two cities. "I've learned a lot about looking backwards. You can do a lot of retrospective thinking about, 'Wouldn't it have been nice if we had done this, that or the other?' However, you may never have gotten to where you are today had you done those things," said Lieberman.

Portland planned a lot longer and more thoroughly than San Diego did on its first transit line and it shows. On the other hand, as Bill Lieberman observed, "When you look at what we got *for what we paid*, it wasn't too bad a deal—sort of like a *Consumer Reports* article that concludes that the best performer isn't necessarily the 'best buy,' given the difference in price. What we lost out from not being in a more optimal location and having fancier stations, I think we gained in other ways. You can either front load a project [like Portland did], or you can do what we did less than perfectly, and then go back afterwards and make it better. There are pros and cons to both approaches."

STRENGTHENING THE TRANSIT/LAND USE CONNECTION

When transit planning began in San Diego in 1970s, it was hoped that the development of a transit system would exert a major influence on patterns of land use and development. As noted earlier, the development of a rail transit system was a key element in the regional growth management strategy recommended by Lynch and Appleyard in their 1974 *Temporary Paradise?* report. The development of a rail transit system was also one of the five key elements in the strategy to revitalize and redevelop downtown San Diego. Indeed, in few cities has the goal of connecting transportation improvements and desired land use outcomes been as clearly articulated. However, getting development to concentrate and cluster around transit stations proved harder to achieve than had been expected.

As Bill Lieberman explained, "There was this notion that it would become obvious to everyone that concentrating development around transit stations was a good deal—not just for transit riders, but also for developers and people looking for homes and places to live. However, it just didn't happen. 'Carrots and sticks' were needed. We found that we needed to advertise to promote station sites as desirable places for joint development. There needed to be land use regulations that, if they didn't mandate relatively dense development around transit stations, at least made it more advantageous to the developer. Unfortunately, those things weren't in place when we started out."

Nevertheless, remarkable progress *has* been made in recent years in coordinating development with transit stations. In 1998, I saw a number of impressive examples—one of them being the 10-story building at 1255 Imperial Avenue, where the MTDB's offices are located and where I interviewed William Lieberman. The building, which straddles a busy transfer station of the San Diego Trolley, was planned and developed by the MTDB.

"We owned the property and were going to put up a little office building here because we were renting office space downtown," said Lieberman. "However, the office building got bigger as other agencies said they were looking for space. Originally, the building was going to be alongside the tracks, but I had seen a photo of a development in Germany where a trolley line was brought into a department store, and it seemed to me we needed to do something like that to show the community what the possibilities were [for joint development]. It was our project, so we could do it."

The 10-story, 180,000-square-foot building, built above the tracks of two transit lines that join at the Imperial Avenue transfer station, was named after James R. Mills and called the Mills/MTS [Metropolitan Transit System] Building.

"A lot of people have gotten ideas from it," said Lieberman. Among them is the developer of One America Plaza—the first major, privately initiated joint development project in downtown San Diego. At One America Plaza, an important downtown transit station across the street from the Santa Fe Depot was incorporated into the base of a 34-story, 555,630-square-foot office tower. There, passengers wait for trains under a crescent-shaped glass and steel canopy that Bernick and Cervero have described as having been "designed with an eye to the grand train stations of Europe" (Bernick and Cervero 1997, 258) on a station platform lined on both sides by stores—a convenience store, a

7-35   This photograph was taken looking directly down from the offices of the MTDB. It shows trolleys on three different tracks converging on the 12th and Imperial transfer station at the base of the Mills/MTS Building.

Source: Gene Bunnell

sandwich/lunch shop and a small restaurant—as well as a branch of the San Diego Museum of Contemporary Art and the museum's gift shop. Nearly four-fifths of the $5.2 million capital cost for the station was funded by One America Plaza's developer. (*ibid.*)

Unfortunately, municipalities outside of San Diego served by the San Diego Trolley have often been reluctant to reserve land around transit stations for high-density, transit-oriented, mixed-use development. "Many of them favor the idea, in principle," said Lieberman, "but if a developer comes along who puts money on the table and wants to put up a 'big-box' retail development, where people will buy things in huge quantities and therefore not be likely to want to take transit, then they willingly go along."

Proposition 13 has made it even more difficult for transit and land use planners to get communities along the transit corridor to commit to encouraging mixed-use developments around stations that include a substantial amount of housing. "When Proposition 13 was passed in 1978," recalled William Lieber-

7-36   The tracks of the San Diego Trolley pass through the middle of the Mills/ MTS Building. The 12th and Imperial transfer station occupies a major portion of the lower level of the structure.

Source: W. Lieberman/San Diego Metropolitan Transportation Development Board

7-37   The San Diego Trolley station at the base of One America Plaza.

Source: Gene Bunnell

man, "it put a cap on what a municipality could collect in property taxes. The only other real revenue source is the sales tax. So when 'big-box' retailers come to town, most municipalities are not very likely to put them off in order to possibly achieve a more transit-oriented land use later on. That's what happened in Chula Vista around the Palomar station. After the transit line was built, a 'big-box' retail development was proposed for the land around the station. We went to the planning commission and city council to argue that it wasn't the best use of land near the transit station. We urged that they encourage fairly high-density residential development, combined with some transit-serving retail space and offices. They weren't interested because they needed the sales tax income."

As traffic congestion on San Diego highways has gotten progressively worse—it increased 54% in San Diego between 1982 and 1991, over twice the rate of increase experienced in Portland, Oregon during the same period (Dunphy, July 1995, 32)—the need to locate new housing and employment centers in close proximity to transit stations has become increasingly obvious. SANDAG's projection (that, if land continues to be developed at the same rate as in the 1990s, the region could run out of land suitable for residential development as early as 2008) has added a note of urgency. "We just can't continue to go on developing quarter-acre lots. There *has* to be intensification of development around transit stations," said Lieberman. "Each station is a precious resource. When you lose one to a less-than-optimal use, it's like losing another bead in the necklace."[26]

Despite a number of lost opportunities, there have been some successes in co-locating significant developments with transit stations. In *Transit Villages in the 21st Century* (1997, 254) Bernick and Cervero report the following completed transit-oriented developments (TODs):

- Villages of La Mesa (a 384-unit apartment development completed in 1989) adjacent to the Amaya Street trolley station
- La Mesa Village Plaza (99 condominium units and retail space, completed in 1991) adjacent to the La Mesa Boulevard trolley station
- Creekside Villas (144 apartment units, completed in 1989) adjacent to the 47th Street trolley station
- The Mercado (144 apartment units, completed in 1992) adjacent to the Barrio Logan trolley station. (The Mercado housing development, planned by the San Diego Housing Commission (SDHC), is discussed again in the following section titled "Planning for Affordable Housing.")

In 1992-93, San Diego became one of the first cities in the country to draft and adopt a formal set of transit-oriented development and design guidelines.[27] The planning process that led to the adoption of those guidelines and policies (supervised by Michael Stepner) had actually begun a couple of years before, encouraged by passage of a 1990 California law requiring municipalities to develop plans to reduce congestion. "We had all these policies developed and ready to go," Michael Stepner told me, "but couldn't get them officially adopted." It occurred to Stepner that a major reason why it was proving so difficult to muster the political support needed for passage could be the fact that the policies and guidelines had been developed locally and not by some well-known outside "expert." "So we brought in Peter Calthorpe—Peter and I go way back—and carried out this tremendous public process," Stepner explained.

A Land Guidance Subcommittee was formed, composed of transportation planners, air quality specialists, architects, developers, urban planners, community activists, community group leaders and environmentalists, whose responsibility it was to work with city staff and the consultant to recommend land development policies, programs and regulations to reduce demands on the transportation system.

A case study (prepared as part of a Surface Transportation Policy Project Resource Guide) described the process Stepner and the subcommittee followed as follows: "With the Land Guidance Subcommittee members participating in the selection process, the City hired architect Peter Calthorpe to prepare specific design guidelines so that developers and builders would know exactly what the city was looking for . . . The City staff made presentations about the TOD guidelines to over 45 community groups in order to gain their input and held a two-day workshop for all citizens to answer questions and gather ideas. The resolutions that came out of these efforts reconfirmed the direction of the Land Guidance Subcommittee and were important in building the community consensus for the eventual adoption of the guidelines by the City Council." (Corbett 1993, 2) "After that, the ideas we had developed became acceptable," said Stepner, and they were officially adopted.[28]

The first TOD to fall under the guidelines was Rio Vista West, a mixed-use development proposed for a 90-acre site adjacent to a station on the Mission Valley trolley line. The plan submitted to and approved by the city and the MTDB called for building up to 1,000 units of moderate-density housing, 165,000 square feet of office space and 325,000 square feet of retail space.

Unfortunately, the development I saw at Rio Vista West in 1998 appeared to be falling well short of the walkable, transit-oriented community that planners had hoped would be created. In fact, the first thing built was a suburban-style, "big-box" shopping center (including a K-Mart and Office Depot) fronting onto a 1,000-car surface parking lot. The Spanish-style grouping of pedestrian-oriented small shops surrounding an open-air plaza overlooking the trolley station that had been called for in the plan had not yet been built. "There was supposed to be a town square over here, with the trolley station opening up on the town square," Stepner observed, but it hadn't yet materialized. The most encouraging sign of progress toward creating a transit-oriented community at Rio Vista was that the first phase of housing construction (240 units of apartments, 600-700 feet from the trolley station) was nearing completion.

Three years later, the long-awaited development adjacent to the station was finally taking shape and the pedestrian plaza/town square was also under construction. "The plaza extends north from the trolley station to the shopping center, flanked by high-density housing. It's been a long time coming, but it should turn out to be one of our best examples of TOD," said Bill Lieberman.

Another site of a proposed TOD project I saw with Michael Stepner in 1998 was one that had been approved for a site next to the Morena Linda Vista station on the Mission Valley line—a mixed-use housing/commercial development on a roughly 8-acre site. According to Stepner, the planning that produced the project was jointly carried out by the city's planning department, the housing commission and the MTDB. "We held a national competition to pick a design concept for the area, invited development proposals and selected a developer," Stepner explained as we looked over the site. However, three years later, the project that the developer proposed to build was stalled and nothing had been built.[29]

While the Rio Vista West development had fallen somewhat short of what planners at the city and the MTDB had hoped for, and while the TOD at Morena Linda Vista was still just a plan on the drawing board, the next place Michael Stepner took me to was a good example of what planners had been striving to achieve: a mixed-use development centered around the Hazard Center station, also along the Mission Valley trolley line. The land for the trolley right of way, which runs through the development, was donated by the developer, who also contributed to the cost of building the trolley station. In return, the development was granted a density bonus that allowed more housing units to be built than would otherwise have been allowed. The number of parking spaces that the developer had to provide was also reduced because of the availability of trolley service.[30]

The new housing at Hazard Center is dense and compact, but there is also a spacious and open quality to the site due to an attractively designed and landscaped pedestrian walkway that leads into the development and then along the San Diego River, onto which the housing backs up. The walkway along the banks of the river is remarkably quiet and secluded.

Across the street is a neighborhood shopping center with a grocery store, a movie theater, various other shops and a Barnes and Noble bookstore. "It provides a bit of an urban experience," said Stepner, "not quite there, but getting there." Like the residential development across the street, the shopping center was developed because the trolley station was planned to be built there. "We have development agreements with the developers of both projects, and contributions toward the cost of the trolley were obtained from both as a condition for approving the projects," Stepner explained.[31]

Hazard Center is an indication that the TOD policies and guidelines adopted by the city and the MTDB are beginning to work, and that developers are recognizing that coordinating their developments with trolley lines and stations is very much in their interest. I saw further evidence to that effect when Michael Stepner took me to the Fashion Valley shopping center.

When it opened in 1969, Fashion Valley was accessible only by automobile and was surrounded by acres of paved parking. Today, paved parking areas have been replaced by structured parking, and the shopping center is physically connected to a major station along the Mission Valley trolley line, which is also a bus transfer hub where a number of feeder bus lines converge.

Until recently, the conventional wisdom among most shopping center developers and managers (including those in San Diego) was that making it easy for people to reach their premises by means of public transportation simply brought so-called "undesirable" categories of people who did little shopping and just milled around, creating a nuisance. According to William Lieberman, "getting the transit/transfer station at Fashion Valley was a real battle. Initially, they didn't want it [the transit station] anywhere near them. In fact, the reason

7-38 Transit-oriented residential development centered around the Hazard Center East trolley station in Mission Valley.

Source: W. Lieberman/San Diego Metropolitan Transportation Development Board

7-39 Transit-oriented commercial development directly opposite the Hazard Center East trolley station.

Source: W. Lieberman/San Diego Metropolitan Transportation Development Board

why the transit station is at the corner, and not in the center of the development, is because, to quote someone who worked for the company managing the center, 'You might as well go down to the end where Woolworth's and J. C. Penney are, because that's probably the only kind of clientele that will come here by public transit.'"

Nevertheless, planners at the MTDB and in the city's planning department kept pushing for a major transit hub to be developed at Fashion Valley and eventually succeeded. They even got the company that owned and managed the shopping center to donate land for the trolley line and transit hub, in exchange for being able to expand the shopping center. Feeder buses arriving at and departing from the transit hub at Fashion Valley pick up and discharge their passengers at ground level, below the elevated trolley station. People arriving at Fashion Valley by trolley, on the other hand, can walk directly from the elevated trolley station platform to the mall, without having to make their way down to ground level. Michael Stepner admitted that the Fashion Valley transit station that ended up being built reminds him a little of the "El" in Chicago. "I grew up in Chicago, as did Tom Larwin [the general manager of the MTDB]. So I guess we tried to make it look as much like the 'El' as possible."

The people who worked for the company that managed the shopping mall greatly underestimated the number of people who would come to Fashion Valley on the trolley and the substantial amount of shopping they would do at the mall. A survey of trolley riders at the Fashion Valley and Mission Valley trolley stations conducted by SANDAG in December 1997 produced the following findings:

- Nearly 80% shopped, banked, dined or went to a movie at the mall, and almost all of them made a purchase at the mall.
- Trolley riders who made purchases at the mall spent an average of $75.57 and 17% spent more than $200.
- When asked whether they would have shopped at the mall had trolley service not been available, 57% said "no."

When I rode the trolley on the Mission Valley line, I noticed a fairly large number of people getting on with many shopping bags that were obviously full of purchases they had made at the mall. Recalling the comment of the person at the shopping mall management company (reported above) who stereotyped the people expected to come to the mall by trolley, I was interested to notice that a number of the shopping bags people were carrying were from high-end retailers like Neiman Marcus and Nordstrom.

PLANNING FOR AFFORDABLE HOUSING

When areas improve and become more desirable places in which to live and work, property values inevitably increase and living expenses rise. As a result, plans and public policies that have succeeded in reviving downtowns and inner-city neighborhoods have frequently been criticized for contributing to the displacement of low- and moderate-income persons.

This criticism is both troubling and perplexing. If developing plans and policies to reverse spiraling decay, disinvestment and abandonment is wrong, then the only alternative is a policy of "benign neglect" that consciously allows areas to deteriorate to the point that they become so bad that the only people who inhabit them are those who have no other choice and can't leave. Following that path seems to me to border on irresponsibility.

Throughout much of the 20th century, the federal government played a major role in helping to fund the provision of housing needed by people with low and moderate incomes. This federal funding role was reasonable and equitable from a number of standpoints. First, the federal government has broader sources of revenue available to it than do local governments. Moreover, the revenue sources at its disposal are less regressive and less burdensome on persons with low and moderate incomes than the principal revenue sources relied on by local governments (property and sales taxes). Having the federal government fund affordable housing is also reasonable because federal policies (fiscal, tax, budgetary, monetary, trade and immigration) have a much greater bearing on the number and percentage of low-income persons living in American communities than do local policies.

Local government policies themselves are rarely the cause of widespread unemployment and poverty. Localities are just the places where disadvantaged people find themselves at a given point in time. The fact that low-income populations are more concentrated in some municipalities than others doesn't mean that the places with the highest concentrations of low-income persons should bear a disproportionate share of the cost of meeting the nationwide need for decent, safe and sanitary housing.

However, the fact remains that, during the 1980s and 1990s, the federal government, to a remarkable extent, withdrew itself from its long-standing practice of providing funding for the provision of low- and moderate-income housing at the state and local levels. Calavita and Grimes have described the dramatic shift in federal housing policy that occurred during the 1980s in the following stark terms: "... [F]ederal government expenditure for assisted housing, the major source of revenue for affordable housing since the 1940's, was reduced by more than 75% ..., the federally funded public housing program was brought to a near standstill, and federal subsidies to private developers building affordable housing were virtually eliminated." (Calavita and Grimes 1992, 173)

The conditions that argue for some form of public intervention to address the shortage of affordable housing are, in fact, a good deal more pressing in San Diego than in many other cities. When housing costs are compared to incomes, San Diego has one of the least affordable housing markets in the country. According to recent statistics, over 51% of all housing units in San Diego are occupied by renters, and more than 50% of San Diego renters pay over 30% of their income on rent. (25% of San Diego renters pay over 40% of their income on rent.) Only one-fifth of San Diego households can afford a median-priced new home; only one-third of households can afford a median-priced resale home. As Elizabeth Morris (executive director of the SDHC) explained, "Our wages are depressed while our housing prices are toward the higher end."

The housing affordability problem is further exacerbated by people moving into San Diego from other parts of the U.S. "People who come here from the outside have money and bid up housing prices," commented William Anderson. "However, those costs can't be sustained by the incomes of local people, because a big part of our economy is tourism, which doesn't pay a lot."

Tourism, in fact, is the third most important sector in San Diego's economy, and planning efforts undertaken in downtown San Diego between the 1970s and 1990s have strengthened that segment of the city's economy, further compounding the problem. One in three jobs in San Diego are presently in the service sector. "If the region's job base continues to change in this direction, per capita income will drop 20% below the state and national average between 2000 and 2020." (Stepner and Fiske 2000, 83) If that happens, the housing affordability gap will probably become even wider in the future. "When we talk about growing certain industries and attracting jobs, it is often forgotten that the people who come for those jobs need to live somewhere," said Elizabeth Morris.

It might be argued that the practice of imposing development impact fees on new residential developments—first in the "planned urbanizing area" and now in "urbanized areas"—has also increased the cost of housing, and that one way to make housing more affordable would be to reduce or eliminate the fees imposed on developers. As Elizabeth Morris pointed out, that seems unlikely to happen. "The real reason we impose those high developer fees is because we have an aversion to taxing ourselves to pay for things. We can't reduce the developer fees because no one else is going to pay for the needed facilities and infrastructure."

To learn about what had been done in San Diego to help meet the need for affordable housing for low- and moderate-income persons, I interviewed Elizabeth Morris in 1998. She started working at the SDHC in 1979—the same year that the commission was established—and became its executive director in 1994.

When I asked Morris what planning initiatives related to housing had made a positive difference in San Diego, she identified and described three particular initiatives: the Balanced Communities Policy, the Housing Trust Fund (HTF)

7-40 Vista Verde Apartments—an infill housing development for low-income families, built in an older neighborhood by a private developer with funding provided by the San Diego Housing Commission.

Source: San Diego Housing Commission

and the SDHC's encouragement and support of nonprofit housing development corporations.

The Balanced Communities Policy

In 1972, the San Diego City Council adopted what was called the Balanced Communities Policy which, according to Morris, said that every community should incorporate housing for all economic groups. "One of the things we have tried to do, as difficult as it might be, has been to try to implement the intent of that policy," said Morris. As a result, the commission has made a conscious effort not to concentrate public housing in particular neighborhoods, to develop small-scale public housing developments intermingled

7-41 The 2.36-acre site of this San Diego Housing Commission public housing development is in a middle-class suburban neighborhood in the community of Linda Vista, not far from shopping and schools. The site's location at the end of a cul-de-sac, in close proximity to a freeway (Highway 163), required the construction of a wall to reduce noise levels.

Source: San Diego Housing Commission

7-42 This San Diego Housing Commission's housing development (on Saranac Street) in the College Area of San Diego is in a middle-class neighborhood consisting of a mixture of apartments, duplexes and single-family residences.

Source: San Diego Housing Commission

7-43 This housing development (on Golfcrest Drive in the community of San Carlos) was developed on the site of an abandoned, boarded-up convenience store. The site is flanked by a suburban single-family neighborhood on one side and a large regional park (Mission Trails Park) on two other sides. The Golfcrest Drive site is in close proximity to schools and shopping and is served by public transportation.

Source: San Diego Housing Commission

with other types of housing, and to do everything possible to disprove the notion that public housing needs to be ugly and stigmatizing. "You will find conventional public housing developments in garden apartment or town-house configurations in many different neighborhoods, such as the Mission Terrace development that won a number of design awards, and others in the College Area [near the campus of San Diego State University] and Pacific Beach area," said Morris.

Another way the commission achieved the aims of the Balanced Communities Policy was by devising and administering a municipal bond financing program that encouraged developers to include affordable housing units in privately developed new housing developments. "In the early 1980s, before the tax laws changed, we geared up a municipal bond financing program that helped finance literally thousands of housing units," said Morris. To illustrate the impact that the program had, Morris noted that 20% of the housing units constructed by private developers in the University City and Golden Triangle areas during that period were set aside for low- and moderate-income persons.

The SDHC's Fulton, Golfcrest and Saranac public housing developments are outcomes of the agency's Balanced Communities Policy. Instead of building a single, large public housing development, the commission identified three separate sites in relatively affluent areas of the city north of Interstate 8, where smaller scale, subsidized housing developments could fit into the fabrics of existing neighborhoods.

Despite these notable successes, promoting and implementing the Balanced Communities Policy has not been easy. "It's been a hard sell, because you have to battle a lot of powerful constituencies, like developers and people in upscale communities, to make it happen," observed Morris.

The Housing Trust Fund

"Many people probably wouldn't think of the HTF as having been produced by planning, because no planning document was produced," said Elizabeth Morris. "However, what got the HTF established was a planning process," she added.

When I called Nico Calavita (a professor in the Graduate City Planning Program in the School of Public Administration and Urban Studies at San Diego State University) and asked him to identify an area where planning had made a positive difference in San Diego, the HTF was the first thing he mentioned. Not long after we talked, I received a copy of a 1992 article that Calavita co-authored with Kenneth Grimes, which carefully reconstructed and documented the planning process that produced the HTF.

According to Calavita and Grimes, planners at the SDHC were the central figures in orchestrating the planning process that led to the creation of the HTF. Planners at the commission recognized that the shortage of affordable housing was so severe and pervasive that individual housing projects undertaken here and there were inadequate to address the problem. A more comprehensive and systematic solution was needed.

The comprehensive solution they envisioned was the establishment of a well-funded HTF. SDHC planners also recognized, however, that the commission, acting alone, had little hope of acquiring the resources needed to implement a comprehensive solution. A broader base of support, and a broader coalition of interest groups and organizations, were required.

By virtue of their sheer numbers, low-income persons (who stood to be the primary beneficiaries of an HTF) should have been an important constituency; however, acting alone, they lacked the political power to influence the positions taken by elected officials on housing policy. Moreover, "community-based groups and non-profit organizations representing the interests of lower-income [people] . . . were atomized, only dimly aware of each other's existence, and politically unorganized." (Calavita and Grimes 1992, 176)

The first thing that housing planners did, therefore, was to identify all the various community-based groups and nonprofit organizations in San Diego that claimed to represent the interests of low-income persons, and sought out and met individually with representatives of those organizations. At these one-on-one meetings, they described what an HTF was and how it could operate in San Diego. ". . . Commission planners stressed that if the HTF was administered by a board of trustees, it could be created as a fund over which non-profit organizations might have a measure of control. Financially strapped non-profits thus came to see the HTF as a mechanism that not only could provide low-income housing, but could also help stabilize their organizations, increase their influence, and fund their activities." (*ibid.*)

After an extended period of behind-the-scenes networking and community outreach, a meeting was held at the SDHC offices that was attended by representatives of more than 30 community groups. At this large group meeting, the commission staff made its pitch describing, as they had in the individual meetings, how an HTF could help systematically address San Diego's persistent and widespread affordable housing shortage. Mary Brooks (from the Housing Trust Fund Project/Center for Community Change) was also invited to attend as an independent expert, and she elaborated on and corroborated the advantages of establishing an HTF. The groups that attended the meeting subsequently formed what was called the San Diego Housing Trust Fund Coalition, which ". . . eventually became a broad alliance of more than 50 community groups, religious organizations, service providers and labor unions." (*ibid.*, 177)

Calavita and Grimes note that, "The San Diego planners took some risk in acting as catalysts in bringing together potential support groups . . ." and had to try to avoid ". . . the appearance of engaging in outright political organizing." (*ibid.*, 173) They note that the SDHC also took a risk in empowering other housing groups and organizations, and in providing the information and assistance that allowed the Coalition to function independently of the commission. Taking these risks paid off, however. "The Coalition became an essential force in the process that led to the establishment of the HTF in San Diego; it is doubtful that the HTF would exist in San Diego today without the initial meeting organized by the San Diego planners that brought the community organizations together." (*ibid.*)

With this broad coalition in place, the SDHC established a 17-member Housing Trust Fund Task Force. Five members of the Coalition were appointed to the task force. The chairman of the task force, Pat Kruer, was the head of a local development company. It was at this point that a more formal and structured planning process unfolded.

The commission staff started the planning process by conducting a comprehensive assessment of housing needs in San Diego. According to Elizabeth Morris, "The findings of the needs assessment were a real eye-opener for a lot of members on the task force," and served as a reminder of the huge amount of money that would need to be raised to seriously address the affordable housing shortage. Based on the findings of the needs assessment, the task force concluded that $54 million would be needed to meet one-third of the need by the year 2000. (*ibid., 179-180*)

The task force then identified and evaluated various revenue sources that could possibly be tapped to help fund the HTF. It also worked to develop policy guidelines (specifying, for example, the kinds of housing that the HTF should support and who might qualify for such housing) and developed an administrative plan.[32] Two key principles on which the task force members agreed were that the primary beneficiaries of the HTF should be persons with low incomes, and that the funding of the HTF should be as broad-based as possible so that homeowners, corporations, businesses and developers—as well as visitors to the city—all contributed. "The rationale was that this is everybody's problem, and so everyone should pay something," said Elizabeth Morris.

Roughly two dozen different potential funding sources for the HTF were identified and evaluated. The task force ultimately recommended that the HTF be funded by the following five revenue sources:

1. a linkage fee imposed on a per-square-foot basis on new commercial and industrial developments—with a different fee imposed on different types of commercial/industrial uses
2. two-thirds of the annual increase in transient occupancy tax (TOT) collections—a tax paid by people staying in hotels and motels
3. a tax on gross business receipts
4. a landscape, lighting and park maintenance fee paid by owners of residential properties, which would free up money from the general fund that could be pledged to the HTF

5. a 2% utility users' fee, with lower income households exempted

One revenue source that the task force would have liked to recommend to help fund the HTF (but didn't) was a tax on the sale and transfer of real estate. "If a real estate transfer tax had been proposed, the realtors would have gone ballistic," observed Morris. "The realtors and real estate lobby in southern California is one of the strongest lobbies in the nation," she added. As Ken Sulzer put it, speaking in another context, "If you have the real estate sector behind you, you've got one out of two people behind you."

The Housing Trust Fund Task Force completed its work in 1989 and submitted its report to the city council. After wrestling with it for a while, the city council eventually agreed to have the SDHC draft a formal ordinance establishing the HTF and designating revenue sources. However, when the ordinance was brought back to the council, it approved only two of the five recommended revenue sources (the TOT and the developer linkage fee).

"During the first year that the fund was in place, the annual revenue stream just from developers was between $7 and $8 million," said Morris. "The incremental growth in the TOT pledged to the HTF added another $2 million, and would have continued to grow because the amount of revenue the city collects from the TOT has increased steadily and significantly year after year." However, a year after the HTF started operating, the city council abruptly voted to eliminate the TOT as a source of revenue for the HTF. "So we ended up with an HTF that was funded only by developers of commercial and industrial floorspace."[33]

The fact that the HTF was only funded by linkage fees levied on new commercial and industrial developments also meant that the amount of money going into the HTF varied from year to year. For example, when development activity slumped during the late 1980s and early 1990s, the amount of revenue that went into the HTF fell significantly. In 1998, when I interviewed Morris, she reported that development activity had begun to pick up and the revenue stream going into the HTF was back up to around $3 million a year.

Elizabeth Morris expressed her frustration and disappointment that the HTF had fallen so far short of the comprehensive solution that the task force had recommended be implemented. Nevertheless, the fact remains that the San Diego HTF is one of the largest of its kind in the country. Moreover, as Calavita and Grimes state, ". . . the success of the San Diego Housing Commission planners in establishing such a redistributive housing program is especially remarkable considering that . . . approval was given at a time when the city was facing a budget shortfall of $60 million." (*ibid.*, 170)

Planning for Single-Room Occupancy Housing

One type of affordable housing that is badly needed in cities like San Diego—where a high proportion of jobs are in the service, retail and hospitality sectors—is single-room-occupancy (SRO) housing. Prior to going to San Diego, I had been made aware of San Diego's efforts related to preserving and developing new SRO housing by a 1993 article by Mary Lou Gallagher in *Planning* magazine. I was reminded of it when Michael Stepner pointed out an old-fashioned, working-persons hotel located at 4th and G Streets in the Gaslamp Quarter that had been renovated with funding provided by the SDHC. I later learned from Elizabeth Morris that the building (called the Golden West Hotel) had been designed by a son of Frank Lloyd Wright. "If you look up around the top of the building, you will see reliefs of different kinds of workmen," said Morris.

San Diego's city council first started paying attention to the need for SRO housing units around the time that a nine-block area of downtown San Diego, which contained numerous SRO units, was being bulldozed to make way for Horton Plaza. The city council addressed the issue by imposing a moratorium on any further SRO demolition and conversion, and asked the city's planning department to develop a longer term strategy that would preserve SROs without dampening downtown development.

Gallagher's article quotes Judith Lenthall, a former senior planner in the planning department, as saying "They wanted a miracle." (Gallagher, June 1993, 21) To some extent, that is what they got. By 1993, San Diego was seeing more new SRO housing units being created than any other city in the country. As of 1993, 2,262 new SROs had been developed in San Diego in 18 different properties; another 388 units in nine existing buildings had been substantially renovated.

Lenthall put together a task force that included housing advocates, developers and representatives of city departments and commissions like the city's fire and police departments and the SDHC. Meanwhile, as the task force was beginning its work, the commission was conducting a study which found that 1,247 units in 30 SRO hotels had been lost by 1985 due to demolition or conversion, and that rents for the remaining SROs had increased by 80% between 1980 and 1985.

The first aspect of the SRO problem addressed by the task force was how best to preserve the existing supply of SRO housing once the moratorium expired. According to Elizabeth Morris, "San Francisco had a very tough ordinance that said existing SROs could not be eliminated under any circumstances, but objections were raised that the ordinance constituted a 'taking' and it was taken to court. So we didn't go quite that far. Instead, we established a threshold level, which said that if an existing, low-cost SRO was eliminated through demolition or conversion, it had to be replaced with [the developer also paying] relocation costs."

The SRO Housing Preservation Ordinance, drafted by the task force, was adopted by the city council in 1987. The ordinance specified that the supply of

SRO housing should not be allowed to fall below a certain threshold amount. "It was sort of like having to maintain a certain amount of money in a bank account. If new SROs were developed, we could credit the bank account; when units were lost due to demolition or conversion, we would debit the account," said Morris.

Six months into the process, the task force started to redefine the problem. "We realized that the issue was not just preservation . . . The real issue was the *lack of supply* and *the failure to produce new units*," said Morris. Around that time, Bud Fischer (a local developer who, up to that point, had specialized in renovating historic buildings) came to one of the task force meetings. Fischer, whom Morris said was a "very sharp developer," had come to believe that "it might actually be economically feasible to develop certain kinds of SRO housing and make a profit."

Fischer eventually hired architect Rob Wellington Quigley to "design a low-cost building that would offer amenities not available in old transient hotels." (*ibid.*) The task force had hoped that Fischer and Quigley would produce a prototype that could serve as a model for other SRO developments in San Diego. However, before the design process could progress too far, the developer and his architect realized that various zoning and building code regulations that applied to SRO housing made building a new SRO virtually impossible.

Prompted by this finding, the task force undertook an intensive study of the zoning and building code regulations that applied to SRO housing in the hope that ways could be found to revise those regulations to remove unnecessary barriers. Eventually, the task force came up with a novel solution. It proposed to reclassify SROs in the city's *zoning code* from a multifamily residential use to a commercial use (commercial hotel), but to continue to classify SROs as a multifamily residential use in its *building code*. Considering an SRO building to be a *residential use* for building code purposes made it easier to meet access requirements for the disabled and allowed sprinkler systems to be introduced to reduce the number of required fire exits. Considering an SRO building to be a *commercial use* for purposes of zoning made it much easier to meet the required rear- and side-yard setbacks and parking requirements.

Other recommendations made by the task force were also implemented. Statewide legislation was passed changing the Uniform Building Code to permit a "living unit" of 150 to 400 square feet for two people. The city's water department reduced water and sewer connection fees and usage rates to reflect the low-use levels of SRO units. Zoning provisions were modified to allow developers of SROs to apply for a waiver or reduction of the amount of required parking—the rationale being that automobile ownership by occupants of SRO housing, typically located in areas served by public transit, is very low.

7-44   Peachtree Inn—a single-room occupancy development financed in part by the San Diego Housing Commission.

Source: San Diego Housing Commission

There are actually three different types of SROs in San Diego. The first type, Elizabeth Morris explained, are "real working-persons hotels—the old model, like a lodging house—that serve the needs of people working in minimum-wage jobs." Two examples of this type of SRO housing are the working-persons hotel I saw in the Gaslamp District and the 24-room Island Hotel at 5th and Island. "People working 40 hours a week in minimum-wage jobs in downtown establishments can only afford to pay about $200 per month," explained Morris, "so we've tried to set up and maintain structures that meet that need. The financing of such hotels has to be structured in a certain way, because operating costs are so high. Just about all the money collected in rents is paid out toward operating costs." To get new SRO housing developments of this type to be built, very deep subsidies from the SDHC and HTF have been necessary.

The second type of SRO, said Morris, is at the other end of the scale—"a pretty nice, small room in the Centre City area of San Diego, within walking distance of downtown hotels, restaurants and the convention center, for around $500 a month." Back in 1993, senior planner Lenthall reported that such an SRO unit could be constructed for about $20,000—much less than the cost of standard types of housing accommodations but, on a per-square-foot basis, still not inexpensive. Indeed, once the building and zoning code regulations that applied to SRO housing were revised, as per the task force's recommendations, it was usually economically feasible for private developers to build and market this kind of SRO housing without a public subsidy.

The third type of SRO, Morris explained, is a mixed-income SRO. "This kind of SRO receives some subsidy from the SDHC in exchange for renting out a certain percentage of units at a reduced rate." Three notable examples of this mixed-income type of newly constructed SRO housing in downtown San Diego are the Baltic Inn at 521 6th Avenue (completed in 1987), 202 Island Inn and the Peachtree Inn at 915 F Street.

- The Baltic Inn contains 207 units, 41 of which are restricted to very low-income tenants. The total development cost of the project was $3.6 million, with the SDHC loaning the developer $500,000 at 3%, which is payable annually. Repayment of the principal was deferred for 10 years, with options to renew for successive five-year periods, up to 30 years.

- 202 Island Inn (also in downtown San Diego) contains 199 rooms, 40 of which are restricted to very low-income tenants. The total cost of 202 Island Inn was $8.6 million, which was offset by a $2.4 million HUD grant and a $582,000 loan from CCDC. The 202 Island Inn development won a national AIA honor award and a design award from *Time* magazine.

- The 300-room Peachtree Inn, completed in 1990, is the largest new residential hotel yet developed in San Diego—a four-story building that contains 300 rooms and 4,200 square feet of retail and office space on the first floor. Sixty of the 300 residential units are leased to very low-income per-

7-45 A family sits on the front steps of their unit at the Mercado Apartments.

Source: San Diego Housing Commission

sons at $258 a month; 240 units are leased to low-income persons with slightly higher incomes at $330 per month. The total development cost of the Peachtree Inn, including land acquisition, was $7.1 million. Secondary financing of $750,000 was provided by the SDHC under favorable terms.

Unfortunately, the remarkable success that the SDHC had in developing new SRO housing was abruptly brought to a halt. "We aren't building SROs anymore," Morris told me, "because the city council changed the SRO Housing Preservation Ordinance to require one parking space for every unit. With a one-to-one parking requirement, you just can't do them."

I asked Morris if the council's vote to increase the SRO parking requirement came as a result of some new study. "No, it just came on the recommendation of the council member from the Hillcrest area. Michael Stepner and I both happen to live in the Hillcrest area. It's a nice, old neighborhood with lots of

7-46 The Mercado Apartments—a 140-unit housing development produced by a nonprofit housing development corporation. Financing for the project was obtained from a variety of sources, including the Housing Trust Fund. The development was built in the shadow of the San Diego-Coronado Bay Bridge.

Source: San Diego Housing Commission

'granny flats' that were built in the years following World War II. The minute that certain people in the neighborhood raised concerns about parking, the council member's knee-jerk reaction was to recommend that the parking requirement be increased and the council agreed. There haven't been any SROs built since."

Support of Nonprofit Housing Development Corporations

"As recently as 1990, San Diego had only a couple of nonprofits that pretty much limited their activities to developing a senior [citizen] housing project here and there, and that was about it," said Elizabeth Morris. Meanwhile, in San Francisco, there were scores of nonprofits actively involved in developing affordable housing.

"We went to talk to various folks in San Francisco to try to figure out why they had so many nonprofit housing developers and we didn't," Morris continued. "What we found was that the city government in San Francisco had subsidized the formation of these groups. So we decided to do that, too. We developed a program to fund nonprofits to hire staff and tailored some programs specifically to the needs of nonprofits. If you look around the city now, you will find that we have lots of nonprofit housing development corporations."

The commission's efforts aimed at aiding the formation of nonprofits has helped produce a number of nonprofit-sponsored housing developments (like the Mercado Apartments—a 140-unit housing development next to the San Diego-Coronado Bay Bridge that was funded from a variety of sources, including funds from the HTF). "It was built in an area of the city that hadn't seen any new housing developed in 70 years, and it's really nice," said Morris. It was also built very close to a station stop of the San Diego Trolley, which makes the site even more advantageous as a place to live.

Inclusionary Zoning and Density Bonuses

Like many other cities, San Diego has also developed and passed land use regulations aimed at encouraging the development of affordable housing. "We worked with the California Coastal Commission, which has adopted an inclusionary zoning ordinance that requires the inclusion of low- and moderate-income housing units in new residential developments in the coastal zone," said Morris. An inclusionary zoning provision also applies throughout the Centre City redevelopment area overseen by CCDC, and within the roughly 10 other redevelopment areas outside the downtown area. Also, under San Diego law, 20% of all public spending funded by means of TIF must be devoted to affordable housing.

"We also wrote the policies and zoning provisions that grant developers a density bonus in exchange for making a certain percentage of units affordable to low- and moderate-income persons," Morris explained. "If a developer agrees to make 20% of the housing units affordable, the development can qualify for a density bonus of up to 25% on that site." Moreover, San Diego's zoning provisions afford developers considerable flexibility in terms of how much of that density bonus they take advantage of. "If all the bonus units can't fit on a site because of limitations in space and parking, the developer can opt for a partial density bonus. As of 1998, about 500 density bonus units had been built around the city as a result of that ordinance—all of them rent- and price-restricted to assure they were affordable to low- and moderate-income persons," Morris added.

Unfortunately, the above-described density bonus provisions have not been utilized by developers in outlying areas, where low-density, suburban-style housing has been able to command a market premium. As William Anderson told me, "The density bonus only works if there is an economic incentive to build at an increased density. Many developers have said they would rather pay a fee-in-lieu to the San Diego Housing Commission for *them* [the SDHC] to build affordable housing *elsewhere*, than to receive a density bonus and include affordable housing units in their developments. We [the planning commission] have actually received *down*-zoning requests from a number of large developers. If developers are willing to *pay more* to build *fewer* units, offering a density bonus won't work."

PLANNING IN THE 1990s

The Demise of the City's Planning Department

Despite the many positive outcomes that planning helped to achieve during the 20th century, by the 1990s the value of planning was once again being publicly questioned. In 1991, the status of planning in San Diego seemed to reach a low ebb, when half of the staff members in the city's planning department were transferred to other city departments to work on nonplanning issues. Remaining staff members were put under the direct supervision of Jack McGrory, the city manager. Planning no longer had the status of a city department and was no longer to be found in the city's organizational chart displaying the essential functions of local government.

The action the city manager and city council took in 1991 to disband the city's planning department was presumably precipitated by the revelation that the city's planning director had been having an affair with one of his employees. When news of the affair became public knowledge, the planning director was forced to resign. However, the city manager and council apparently felt the need to take even sterner action to punish the planning department as a whole for the indiscretion.

Interviews I have conducted, and articles written by Roger Showley, suggest that McGrory and certain members of the city council had actually been wanting to limit the independence and visibility of the city's planning staff for some time. According to Showley, McGrory and some members on the city council had long felt that having an independent planning director and staff ran counter to the purpose of a city manager-run form of government. Dismantling the planning department was also "a way to demonstrate the city's 'business-friendly' attitude." (Showley, August 26, 2001, I4)

The scandal involving the city's planning director and employee appears therefore to have simply provided a convenient excuse for exacting retribution; subsequent events seem consistent with that interpretation. To quote again from one of Showley's columns in *The San Diego Union-Tribune*, once the planning staff was put under McGrory's direction, he "gutted the staff, moved key people elsewhere and hired Ernie Freeman from Baltimore, who proved to be a nearly invisible, silent and ineffective director." (*ibid.*, February 13, 1997, B3)

In 1995, the city manager went a step further and dismissed the city's remaining planning staff (50 members). The city's director of planning, having no one left to supervise, subsequently resigned, and the planning director position was left vacant. In 1996, City Manager Jack McGrory declared that, "Planning has gone the way of the horse and buggy." (*ibid.*, October 6, 1996, H1)

The fact that the City of San Diego operated for most of the 1990s without the benefit of a professionally staffed planning department does not mean there was *no* planning being done in San Diego:

- The MTDB was still planning transit extensions and working to coordinate station stops with surrounding land use.
- The SDHC was still planning for affordable housing.
- SANDAG was as active as ever in developing regional plans.
- An innovative plan for environmental conservation and habitat protection plan—the *Multiple Species Conservation Program* ("the MSCP")—was developed. (The MSCP is discussed at length at the end of the chapter.)

At the neighborhood and district levels, a good deal of planning was also occurring. The following section describes a planning process that was undertaken in the City Heights neighborhood of San Diego, instigated by an unusual set of actors, that produced a number of positive results and dramatically changed that community's outlook for the future. Meanwhile, throughout San Diego as a whole, there were 44 officially recognized neighborhood planning groups (composed of people elected from within those neighborhoods), with which city agencies and the planning commission consulted when development and land use issues arose affecting their respective neighborhoods. In addition, CCDC was still planning redevelopment projects and land use changes in the 1,500-acre Centre City area of San Diego.

As Roger Showley observed in 1997, ". . . [W]e have plenty of planning going on. The problem is it is proceeding issue by issue, project by project, and no one seems to be making sure everything ties together." (*ibid.*, July 13, 1997, H7)

City Heights Urban Village Planning Initiative

City Heights (in the Mid-City area of San Diego, roughly 6 miles northeast of downtown) was the last place to which Michael Stepner took me during our day-long tour of San Diego in 1998. When City Heights was first developed and settled, it was primarily a single-family neighborhood. A trolley operated along University Avenue (the main east-west avenue) providing residents easy access to core areas of the city.

During the 1940s, the character of the neighborhood changed dramatically as homes were subdivided to provide housing for military personnel and workers who flocked to San Diego to work in war-related industries; the area never regained its equilibrium after that. When growth began surging into Mission Valley in the 1960s with the completion of Interstate 8, businesses and house-holds started leaving City Heights in droves—an evacuation that was further encouraged when Caltrans announced plans to build a freeway (I-15) through the area, and started acquiring and clearing away land.[34]

By the 1990s, City Heights had essentially become San Diego's "port of entry" and its population was the most diverse of any neighborhood in the city—including people of Hispanic, Vietnamese, Laotian, Korean and North African (Ethiopian, Eritrean and Somali) heritage. "Over 30 different languages are spoken in City Heights," Stepner told me.[35]

As City Heights was becoming increasingly diverse, its population was also becoming increasingly transient and low income. By the 1990s, City Heights had become one of the most economically and socially distressed areas in the city, and residents had to cope with rising crime and violence. Many people regarded it as one of the most dangerous neighborhoods in San Diego. To make matters worse, the closest police substation was far away in Kearny Mesa, so that there was little police presence and response times were slow. City officials were aware of the need for a police substation to serve the area, but no progress had been made toward addressing that need because of a lack of public funds.

The growing frustration and desperation that local residents and business people felt over the failure of the city to provide the area with greater police protection came to a head in June 1993, when the University Avenue Business Improvement Association decided to put up as many as 10 billboards along University Avenue with the message, "Welcome to City Heights, Crime Capital of San Diego. Won't Anybody Help Us?" The association's decision to mount the billboard campaign provoked a storm of criticism, particularly from people outside of City Heights, and the association eventually dropped the idea. However, because of the public attention and controversy generated by the proposed billboard campaign, the association's message and cry for help was effectively delivered anyway.

One person who got the message was City Manager Jack McGrory, who responded by forming the City Heights Partnership—a citizens group composed of community residents, business leaders and city government representatives. "I was assigned to the partnership as a representative of the city," said Michael Stepner. (By this time, the planning department no longer existed, and Stepner's position was that of assistant to the city manager and special projects coordinator/urban policy advisor.)

Residents in the partnership suggested holding a "Crime Summit" in City Heights. The police who, according to Stepner, "were acting as the lead city agency at that point, argued that if a summit meeting were held, it needed to focus on more than just crime. It also had to focus on job development and fixing up the area. Eventually, the community agreed that it should be called the 'Crime and Economic Summit.'"

As the City Heights Partnership was meeting and planning the Crime and Economic Summit, two private entrepreneurs were in the process of teaming up to play a prominent role in the planning and redevelopment process that was about to unfold. The first of those entrepreneurs was Sol Price, who grew up in the Mid-City area of San Diego and went on to found the Price Club (a highly successful chain of discount warehouse superstores), which was eventually sold to and merged with the Costco chain. Price's tremendous business success, interestingly enough, made him even more driven to use his entrepreneurial abilities—as well as much of the wealth he had acquired—to help regenerate down-trodden, inner-city neighborhoods like City Heights. Toward the end, he established a charitable foundation called Price Entities (often referred to as Price Charities) to administer the Weingart-Price Fund (an advised fund of the San Diego Foundation).

The second entrepreneur who teamed up with Sol Price was William Jones. At one time, Jones had represented a portion of the City Heights area as its city councilor and had subsequently earned a scholarship to study at the Kennedy School of Government at Harvard University. During the early 1990s, while working for Prudential Insurance, Jones and Price came in contact with one another and had conversations during which Price described his idea of establishing a socially responsible corporation that would invest in inner-city neighborhoods. Jones was so taken with Price's ideas that he moved back to San Diego and joined forces with Price.

Jones and Price began by conducting a series of neighborhood meetings with residents of neighborhoods in the Mid-City area to identify the kinds of investments people in those communities felt were needed. These neighborhood meetings revealed that one of the most difficult aspects of living in inner-city neighborhoods was the lack of affordable and accessible shopping and consumer services. With no major chain stores in the area, people had to travel long distances to other parts of the city to purchase groceries and other necessities, or had to shop at small "mom-and-pop" stores, where prices were high and the quality and selection of goods were poor.

To make matters worse, around the time that these neighborhood meetings were being held, it was reported in *The San Diego Union-Tribune* that the Von's supermarket in City Heights was about to be closed. The closure of Von's was a devastating blow. The one positive result was that it helped to focus Price and Jones' attention on investing in the City Heights neighborhood. When Jones and Price learned that the Von's supermarket was going to close, their first thought was that the Von's property was perfect for the kind of community-oriented commercial development they wanted to undertake and that people had told them was needed in the Mid-City area. They therefore began making inquiries about the possibility of acquiring the Von's property. They also created a formal development entity that could take on such a project, which they called the CityLink Investment Corporation.

Around the same time, Jack McGrory received a call from a City Heights resident and member of the City Heights Partnership, suggesting that the Von's store could possibly be converted into a police substation. Before long, McGrory had contacted the corporate people at Von's and negotiated a price at which the city could acquire the property. The only problem was that McGrory didn't know where the money would come from to build the police substation.

When Jones and Price learned that the city had already expressed interest in the property, they quickly concluded that nothing would be gained by appearing to compete with the city's plans to build a police substation, which the community obviously needed and wanted. It was at this point that Price and Jones came up with the idea of studying the area surrounding the Von's site in a comprehensive manner and of developing a long-range plan for the entire neighborhood.

In April 1994, representatives of CityLink Investment Corporation held a series of brainstorming sessions and focus group discussions with City Heights residents. Two outside parties were brought in to participate in these meetings (architect Anthony Cutri of Martinez + Cutri; and Jerry Trimble, the former CEO of CCDC who, by then, was working as a real estate and redevelopment consultant). At these sessions, Cutri provided an overview of existing physical, infrastructure, economic and housing conditions in the area; Jones described CityLink's general ideas about inner-city investment and neighborhood participation; and community members were invited to express their ideas and concerns.

Two weeks after the first focus group discussion was held by CityLink, the Crime and Economic Summit was held. Instead of being a one-day event, the summit was planned and organized as a charette that extended over a three-day period. According to Michael Stepner, "We held the charette at one of the local junior high schools and planned it so everyone would stay overnight in the community. We spent two nights and two and one-half days there. The charette was scheduled to coincide with 'Earthquake Preparedness Week,' which is an annual event in California. During Earthquake Preparedness Week, all public agencies run drills, and the schools are set up as emergency shelters with cots and soup kitchens. Separate male and female dormitories were set up in the school and shower rooms that hadn't worked in 20 years were fixed."

Up until the time of the charette, most people in City Heights were still focused almost exclusively on the crime issue and on getting a police substation built in the neighborhood. However, the charette got people talking about other needs as well, such as the need for a skills training center in the area.

William Jones played a critical role at the charette by encouraging people to consider a wider range of needs and to develop a broader vision of what was possible. According to Stepner, "William Jones spoke up and said, 'Maybe there's a better way of doing this thing. More is needed here than just one building. Lots of things are needed and the community should get involved. What is needed is a master plan for an urban village.' The call for planning came from the *private sector*. Those of us representing the city were just brought along. We did our part, at first reluctantly, and then as one of the players on the team."

On June 23, CityLink met with Mayor Susan Golding to brief her on its activities in the City Heights area, to receive her feedback and encourage the city's participation in the planning process. Five days later, CityLink made a presentation to the city council and submitted a draft Memorandum of Understanding (which the city council approved) authorizing CityLink to hire a team of architects and planners to prepare a master plan ("the City Heights master plan") for a nine-block area, and to plan and design a police substation. The San Diego firm of Martinez + Cutri was hired, and a planning and design team headed by Anthony Cutri began work. The master planning effort was subsequently expanded to encompass a 20-block area bounded by 43rd Street on the west, University Avenue on the north, Shamoune Avenue on the east and Landis Street on the south.

Early on in the process, Cutri recognized that the former Von's building contained more space than the police substation was going to need, and that some other use or uses could be incorporated. One unusual possibility, suggested by William Jones, was to combine the police substation with a community gymnasium for local youth. Jones came up with the idea while walking through the City Heights neighborhood one day, when he heard some young boys complaining that the older and bigger kids monopolized the basketball court and never gave them a chance to play. Jones asked the kids a theoretical question: "If a gymnasium were built next to the police substation, would you go there to play?" The kids answered, "Yes, definitely." Jones went back to his office and tried to figure out what the requirements were for a gymnasium. He then passed the idea on to Cutri.

Other public and community facilities identified as needed and desirable by the master plan were a new neighborhood elementary school; a park with recreational fields for softball and soccer adjacent to the elementary school; a neighborhood library; a community center; a swimming pool; soccer fields; basketball and tennis courts; and a theater that could be used for live performances as well as for the showing of films, lectures and presentations.

In addition to showing how and where these public and community facilities should be provided, the City Heights master plan also identified areas where neighborhood-serving retail and commercial business should be developed, and where new housing and mixed-use development could be undertaken. It recommended, however, that the plan be implemented in phases. The building of public and community facilities, especially the police substation, needed to happen first. After the public and community facilities were in place, the focus could turn to neighborhood commercial development and the development of new housing.

Because the city did not have the upfront funding it needed to acquire and remodel the Von's building into a police substation, Sol Price's Price Entities agreed to loan CityLink $3.3 million so that the corporation could acquire and renovate the structure into a police substation on the city's behalf—with the understanding that once the construction was completed, the city would take over ownership of the building and reimburse CityLink for the cost. In this way, the police substation would be able to be in place at least two or three years faster than if the city had to finance the project. The new police substation and Mid-City gymnasium connected to the police substation were completed and opened in 1996.

The money that Price Charities loaned the city for the police substation and attached gymnasium was not the only major investment it made in City Heights. Price Charities also provided a $5.25 million grant that paid for the construction of the Weingart Library, which opened its doors to the City Heights community in November 1998. The 15,000-square-foot facility (designed by Martinez + Cutri) has shelf capacity for 60,000 books. It contains reading rooms, public meeting rooms and an Internet technology room, and is one of the most heavily utilized branch libraries in San Diego.

When Price Charities and CityLink began investing in City Heights, the hope was that the city and public agencies like the Unified School District and the community college system would follow suit by also making major facility investments in the area. The strategy worked, and a number of new public facilities were in place when I visited City Heights with Michael Stepner in 1998. Among the prominent new public buildings I saw was the new Rosa Parks Elementary School, constructed by the San Diego Unified School District, next to a large park and recreation area.

A short distance away was the Mid-City Community Service and Recreation Center—a 8,800-square-foot, single-story facility which opened in 1998 and contains a child-care center operated by Head Start, a teen center, meeting rooms and the offices of the City Heights Town Council.[36]

Adjacent to the community center site were two outdoor swimming pools (an adult pool and a children's pool) and water slide, a tennis center, and an open-air amphitheater around an elevated stage. The city's park and recreation department, which has an office in the Mid-City Community Service and Recreation Center, maintains the tennis courts and swimming pools as well as the nearby park and recreation area. A joint-use agreement was developed between the school district and the city that allows the area to be used as a school yard during school hours and as a public recreation area during non-school hours.

Meanwhile, construction had begun on the Mid-City Continuing Education Center (a branch of the community college system) in City Heights. The 58,400-square-foot facility, containing 34 classrooms (including computer and language labs), opened its doors in November 2000. A significant proportion of the many courses and skills taught at the center are specifically tailored to the needs of City Heights and Mid-City residents, who speak different languages and for whom English is a second language.

In many ways, the role that Price Charities played in City Heights is reminiscent of the role that the Lyndhurst Foundation played in Chattanooga. Both charitable foundations invested millions of dollars in their respective communities. Both also funded the hiring of planning consultants and the preparation of plans, and then provided funding to enable recommended actions and initiatives in those plans to be carried out. In some ways, Sol Price and Price Charities went even further. As Elizabeth Morris explained, "Price didn't just pay to build the library. He also funded the town council and the staff for the town council, so there is a place for the community to come together. He was so committed to the school making a difference in the community that he paid the salary of the school principal for an entire year before the school opened, so she could work with parents in the community and organize programs."

As a new phase of development activity (focusing on neighborhood commercial development and housing) was about to begin, Sol Price decided that it was time to separate his nonprofit community development activities from the profit-oriented development activities of CityLink. He therefore sold his interests in CityLink to William Jones. In 2000, CityLink (under Jones' direction) began construction of a shopping center two blocks north of the new Weingart Library, aided by a $16.4 million San Diego Redevelopment Agency bond issue that paid for land acquisition, relocation assistance to displaced residents and businesses, and for removing lead and asbestos from the site. The shopping center—containing an Albertson's grocery store, a drug store, a McDonald's restaurant, a bank, an auto parts store and a Starbucks—opened in the summer of 2001.

Meanwhile, Sol Price formed a new nonprofit entity called City Heights Revitalization Limited Partnership for the purpose of developing a large-scale, mixed-use project on University Avenue (at Fairmount Avenue) composed of 116 two-, three- and four-bedroom townhome housing units, 34 of which will be affordable to low- and moderate-income households; a six-story commercial building with retail space and a child-care center at ground level, and five floors of office space for occupancy by nonprofit and government agencies; and a 371-car parking structure.[37] Construction of the project, estimated to cost $43 million, began in the summer of 2001 and should be completed in 2002.

Lastly, efforts have begun to upgrade and stabilize City Heights' existing housing stock. The SDHC has provided funding to a nonprofit Community Development Corporation to buy bank-owned (foreclosed) properties and boarded-up buildings, and to do some major rehabilitation of those properties. The first existing home in City Heights was rehabilitated in May 2001. The rehabilitation work was funded with a $25,000 subsidy from the SDHC, and a $25,000 grant from Price Charities in the form of a second mortgage administered by Neighborhood Housing Services—one of two nonprofits that are active in City Heights. Under the provisions set by Price Charities, the owner of the rehabilitated home can reduce the amount of the second mortgage by doing community service work, which is counted at $12 per hour.

A Bold Environmental Planning Initiative:
The Multiple Species Conservation Program

Undoubtedly the most daunting planning issue facing San Diego has been (and will continue to be) how to accommodate a steadily increasing population without totally destroying the region's unique environmental qualities. Forecasts indicate that an additional 1 to 1.2 million people will be living in San Diego County in 2020 than lived there in 2000—an annual population increase during that period of 50,000-60,000. Roughly half of those new residents are expected to settle within the City of San Diego.

Meanwhile, the amount of vacant undeveloped land is shrinking. As of 2000, only 5.6% of the city's total land area was still vacant and available for residential development. If vacant land continues to be developed at the same rate as it was in the 1990s, all of the land set aside by the 1979 general plan in the "planned urbanizing area" will probably have been developed by 2008.[38] The stark reality has begun to sink in that, in the not too distant future, all of the remaining undeveloped land in the region, including all of the land that was set aside in the "future urbanizing area," could be developed.

The environmental tragedy that is certain to occur if all of the remaining vacant land in the city and county is allowed to be developed is impossible to overstate. Because of the region's remarkably varied topography, climatic conditions, soils and vegetation, San Diego is one of the most biologically diverse environments in the country. It is also inhabited by an unusually large number of endangered species.

As Tom Story explained, "San Diego County has more endangered species than any county in the contiguous 48 states. There are over 200 plant and animal species currently listed as endangered in San Diego County, or seriously threatened and rare, and close to being placed on the list. The City of San Diego itself has 20 species on the endangered species list, which I believe is the highest number of listed species of any city in the continental U.S."

Not surprisingly, as development has pushed further out into peripheral areas, and as remaining parcels of undeveloped land in between have also been developed, proposed developments have increasingly impinged on the habitats of endangered species, and run afoul of the federal Endangered Species Act, which "prohibits a private party from killing (actually called a 'taking' under federal law) a federally listed endangered species without first obtaining a permit from the U.S. Fish & Wildlife Service." (Fulton 1991, 184)

California also has an endangered species law. "The state law parallels the federal act, and appears to serve two purposes. First, it permits the state to take action on species that are threatened statewide, but not nationally. And second, it permits the California Department of Fish & Game to work in conjunction with the federal Fish & Wildlife Service in protecting federally endangered species." (*ibid.*, 185)

The federal Endangered Species Act (along with the companion state act) has been the last line of defense in attempting to prevent the extinction of individual species. When citizens hoping to prevent certain parcels of land from being developed find that the property they hope to preserve is inhabited by an endangered species, the act's provisions can seem like a godsend. Across the State of California, in fact, there are bits and pieces of property where development has been stopped in its tracks. Unfortunately, these forceful, last-minute interventions seem to have produced little net environmental benefit. Each year, areas of rare forms of vegetation providing habitat for endangered species have become smaller and more fragmented, and the list of endangered species has become longer.

One factor that has clearly limited the effectiveness of efforts aimed at preserving endangered species is that the provisions of the act can only be invoked when a species—already officially designated as endangered—is threatened. "Once a species is placed on the endangered list, the agency [the U.S. Fish & Wildlife Service] has the power to halt all development that might place that species' future existence in jeopardy." (*ibid.*) Unfortunately, that power cannot be exercised *until* the species is put on the list *and* is threatened by a particular action. "Biologists usually have a good idea of which species are likely to be placed on the U.S. Fish & Wildlife Service's endangered list in the near future. But until that listing actually takes place, Fish & Wildlife cannot take action, nor can it make any guarantees that current preservation efforts will be sufficient in the future." (*ibid.*)

The unpredictable and ad-hoc way in which the provisions of the Endangered Species Act have been applied has been particularly frustrating to developers and land owners. As Tom Story explained, "When property owners and developers discovered some particular species or habitat on their property, which was on the endangered species list, they didn't know what they had on their hands; they didn't know what they could or couldn't do with the property until they prepared and submitted a development plan for the property. Essentially, what the government was telling developers and landowners was, 'You tell us first what you want to do, and then we'll tell you what you've got on your property and what you've got to do.' The issue was dealt with on a case-by-case basis. It was a pretty impossible situation to be in."

The situation facing developers was made even more unpredictable due to the fact that the provisions of the Endangered Species Act could be invoked well after a development plan had been officially approved and after construction was well underway. As William Fulton explains, ". . . projects can be stopped in mid-stream if a [new] species in the area is suddenly placed on the list." (*ibid.*, 173)

Developers were often not the only ones placed at risk by the Endangered Species Act. For example, ". . . when Fish & Wildlife concluded that rapid home construction in western Riverside County [California] would place the Stephen's kangaroo rat in jeopardy, the agency was able to threaten local officials with criminal prosecution if they permitted those developments to proceed." (*ibid.*, 185)

By the end of the 1980s, planners in San Diego had come to the conclusion that a new way of approaching the problem of protecting endangered species was necessary. "We needed to get ahead of the curve," said Story. "Planning, up until then, had focused on protecting a single species or habitat type at a time, related to a particular property." The important conceptual breakthrough was in beginning to think more comprehensively at a much larger scale about the preservation of *multiple* species—rather than simply reacting when a proposed development threatened a particular species on a particular property. As Ken Sulzer put it, "When you step back and look at the big picture, the only way you're going to protect endangered species is to protect their *habitats*. If you protect different types of habitats, and if those habitats are interconnected and not just in fragmented bits and pieces, you preserve many endangered species, not just one."

Political support for undertaking a comprehensive planned approach to the preservation of endangered species might not have coalesced had it not been for an unexpected turn of events. Toward the end of the 1980s, the City of San Diego signed a settlement agreement with the U.S. EPA in which the city agreed to construct a new multibillion dollar sewage treatment system to bring the quality of treated effluent being pumped into the ocean into compliance with the Clean Water Act. The city also agreed to build outfalls a couple of miles out into the ocean, and to construct reclamation plants and install new sewer pipes throughout the 900-square-mile sewer service district. "It was the largest and most expensive public improvement project in the city's history, if not in the state," said Tom Story.

What the city did not foresee was that, by agreeing to undertake a major capital spending plan to upgrade its sewage treatment system to improve water quality, it was also making itself subject to additional federal environmental requirements. When the EIS was prepared (evaluating the environmental impacts of the proposed sewage system project), it attributed a substantial "growth-inducing impact" to the project. According to reasoning set out in the EIS, the construction of an improved sewer system meant that the sewer district had a greater capacity to accommodate growth. The impacts of that additional growth therefore had to be mitigated.

"It was a real double whammy and totally unexpected," said Tom Story. The way Story and other San Diego planners viewed it, the construction of the new sewage treatment plant wasn't going to *cause* additional growth. Rather, the new treatment facilities were going to lessen the potentially adverse environmental impacts of growth. "We weren't revising our general plan or increasing allowed densities. We were simply being mandated by federal law to bring our system up to meet the standards of the Clean Water Act," Story added.

Nevertheless, the EPA's stipulation that the city and region needed to come up with a plan to mitigate the environmental impacts to future growth did produce a beneficial result: it essentially forced the city to undertake a comprehensive environmental planning process and to produce a bold and innovative plan for environmental conservation—the *Multiple Species Conservation Program* (MSCP).

The planning process that produced the MSCP was spearheaded and orchestrated by two key staff persons working in the office of Mayor Susan Golding (Tom Story, a landscape architect by training, whose position was deputy director of the MSCP; and Karen Scarborough, the mayor's senior policy advisor). The study area chosen for planning purposes was the 900-square-mile San Diego sewer district—an area that included the City of San Diego, several small cities (such as Chula Vista, Coronado, Del Mar, El Cajon, La Mesa, Lemon Grove, Imperial Beach, National City, Poway and Santee) as well as unincorporated areas of San Diego County. A private engineering firm was hired (Ogden Environmental Consulting) and, using geographic information system (GIS) computer mapping technology, all types of vegetation and wildlife habitats in the region (areas of coastal sage scrub, desert scrub, chaparral, grasslands, marshes, etc.) were mapped.[39]

According to Tom Story, "From the detailed biological resource information that was compiled and mapped at a regional scale, we were able to identify areas we *absolutely* needed to preserve: areas that contained rare species, areas with the greatest diversity of species, and biological corridors and linkages that could potentially connect relatively isolated resource areas to areas that were large enough to maintain adequate gene-pool diversity."

Using this graphically displayed and very detailed environmental information as the basis, a number of different regional plans were developed based on different sets of assumptions. One of the first plans that was prepared focused on preserving the habitat of the coastal California gnatcatcher, which was listed as threatened in 1993. "The coastal California gnatcatcher," Janet Fairbanks (senior planner at SANDAG) explained, "is our poster child of endangered species. Its primary habitat is in the few concentrations of coastal sage scrub that remain in the San Diego region, which also happens to be prime real estate."

Developing a habitat conservation plan that preserved the California gnatcatcher seemed a good way to start the planning process. "We knew a good deal about the habitat requirements of the California gnatcatcher—a good deal more than we did about many other species," said Tom Story. "If we were going to assure the perpetuation of that species, then we had to preserve a majority of that vegetation type, and provide connectivity between remaining areas. If we developed a plan that assured the perpetuation of the California gnatcatcher, there was a good chance we would also help protect other species as well."

Additional plan iterations were subsequently prepared, using somewhat the same conceptual approach but focusing on additional species and habitats. As Tom Story explained, "At the time, we had a list of 93 endangered species. The problem was that we had more knowledge about the habitat needs of some species than about others, and knew much more about what we could do to preserve certain species than others. The species we knew the most about we called 'target species.' So we developed another plan that did the best we could to preserve the target species—based on the assumption that habitats supportive of target species were probably also of some value to other species we knew less about."

Throughout the process of developing alternative plans, planners had the benefit of input from both a scientific review panel and a larger group, called the MSCP Working Group. "The MSCP Working Group included a whole range of stakeholders—including homebuilders and developers, representatives of various environmental organizations such as San Diego Gas and Electric—as well as representatives of municipalities and public agencies," Story continued. It took roughly six years, meeting on an average of once a month, before a draft of the final plan was developed and accepted. Public review and comment on that draft resulted in further modifications being made to the plan. "The responses and comments we received were so extensive that we actually went back and produced a new plan and recirculated that plan for public review," said Story.

A careful and time-consuming process was followed to make sure that property owners of affected properties were notified about public hearings that were held regarding the proposed plan, so that they had an opportunity to comment and express their opinions. "We sent out individual notices four times to every property owner to make sure that, at the final hearing, no one could come in and say they were not notified and did not have adequate opportunity to comment or object," said Tom Story. "More than 30,000 notices went out at four different times."

When the plan came up for official approval and adoption, elected officials were fully informed regarding the implications of the plan and the actions that were required to carry it out. As Tom Story explained, "The council did not want to adopt the plan in concept without knowing its full ramifications. What we brought to the council [for its approval] was not only the plan, but also the General Plan Amendments, Community Plan Amendments, and the Implementing Regulations and Guidelines for the California Environmental Quality Act and the Environmental Review Process. Everything was laid out for them," said Story.

The City of San Diego's MSCP plan was unanimously approved and adopted by the San Diego City Council in the spring of 1997. San Diego County approved and adopted the MSCP plan for the unincorporated areas of the county covered by the plan shortly thereafter. Adoption of the plan commits the city, several small cities and the county to work together to create a 172,000-acre contiguous and interconnected habitat preserve. *The New York Times* has called San Diego's MSCP, "The nation's most ambitious attempt to reconcile the preservation of nature with urban development," and a potential "model for [the] nation." (Stevens, February 16, 1997, 12)

The key to getting the MSCP approved was producing a plan that could gain the support of environmentalists as well as people in the real estate and development communities. People on opposite sides of the issue had to find something of value in the plan. "What landowners and developers wanted and needed most was certainty. What we tried to do was put together a plan that preserved enough habitat to protect endangered species and our important natural resource areas, yet allowed development to occur outside those areas," said Ken Sulzer. "What the environmental community wanted was assurance that the resource areas being set aside would be protected and preserved in perpetuity—not just protected for five, 10 or 20 years and then it's gone" [a reference to the previously established "future urbanizing" tier].

The MSCP plan did not give either developers *or* environmentalists everything they wanted. Many environmentalists feel that the MSCP enables too much of the region's remaining vacant land to be developed. Meanwhile, there are developers who feel that the MSCP has gone too far in restricting opportunities to develop land. Story admitted to me that there are even some planners who feel that the MSCP has placed greater importance on maintaining biological diversity than on developing and planning communities that are good for *people*. "What I would say in response," said Story, "is that this is probably the first time we've put biological conservation and open space planning on an *equal* footing with the concerns of people. Up to now, we've always dealt with conservation and open space preservation as if it were of secondary importance."

One key element of the plan that some environmentalists have criticized is the provision that absolves landowners of further responsibility for protecting endangered species after the habitat preserve is established. Another key element of the MSCP, also criticized by ardent environmentalists, is that the state and federal governments have delegated to local governments that have adopted the MSCP the authority to meet the goals of the MSCP and to, in certain cases, permit a developer to disturb an endangered species habitat (*i.e.*, an area where the Endangered Species Act would otherwise not have allowed development to occur) in exchange for substantial dedications of land for permanent habitat conservation and other mitigation measures that more than offset the development's adverse impacts.

"For example, a developer might be permitted to develop a relatively small area occupied by an endangered species in return for setting aside the remaining land for habitat conservation," said Janet Fairbanks. Agreeing to these provisions was the quid pro quo necessary to get property owners to agree to commit thousands of acres of privately owned land to be included in the permanent habitat preserve. It is estimated that 63,000 acres of the permanent habitat preserve will be acquired by imposing open space requirements and mitigation measures on private landowners and developers.

A number of factors and considerations make it likely that the MSCP that San Diego and neighboring local governments adopted will be implemented. "We [the local governments in the region that have approved the plan] are obligated to preserve 90% of the remaining habitats throughout this wide area. It is what *needs* to be done in order for development to be able to occur on adjoining lands," said Story.

Janet Fairbanks further explained: "The local governments [covered by the MSCP] have signed an implementation agreement with the state and federal governments. It is a *contract*. Also, progress in implementing the plan is monitored on a yearly basis. Every year, the local governments must report on what they have implemented. The federal and state governments haven't gone away and can step in if the local governments falter. If San Diego and the other local governments don't do what they say they're committed to doing, the permit-granting authority [over lands covered by the Endangered Species Act] would go back to the federal government. There are a lot of checks and balances."

In addition, the state and federal governments have pledged to pay for half of the land acquisition cost, which is expected to run somewhere between $263 million and $360 million, with local governments being responsible for the other cost.

The MSCP is a boldly conceived plan that provides a responsible way of managing growth and development in San Diego in the future. However, it also represents a compromise. As Janet Fairbanks observed, "There are a lot of people who just can't seem to accept the notion of compromise. The fact is that a compromise [like the one struck in the MSCP] is the only responsible course of action. We are living in an area where people want to live and where more people will be living in the future, because we have a young population with lots of young families. We're going to see a significant natural increase in popu-lation—a baby boom—even without the factor of in-migration. We have a pre-cariously fragile environment and have to be good stewards of the habitats and species that are left. Both needs are undeniably important."

Although creating a 172,000-acre, metropolitan-wide, integrated conserva-tion preserve is an enormous undertaking, San Diego is not starting from scratch. Considerable progress has been made over the years in terms of pre-serving networks of open space within canyons and valleys throughout the city—in line with the recommendations that Lynch and Appleyard made in *Temporary Paradise?* Eighty-one thousand acres of land were already in public ownership when the MSCP plan was approved—in areas such as the Marian Bear Natural Park that runs through San Clemente Canyon, and the huge Los Peñasquitos Canyon Preserve north of the Miramar Naval Air Station. This existing open space network provides the foundation for the more extensive conservation preserve that is being created. Thousands of other acres of land have been preserved by land use regulations preventing development along steep slopes and canyon walls.

During our day-long tour of San Diego, one of the places to which Michael Stepner took me was Tecolote Canyon (a north-south canyon that roughly par-allels Mission Bay). Much of the land running through Tecolote Canyon is now part of Tecolote Canyon Natural Park. "This major canyon was once threatened by development and could have been completely filled in with development, but that didn't happen," explained Michael Stepner. "Over there is a bluff with no development on it and, at the base of the bluff, there is a park. This canyon extends about 6 or 7 miles and includes miles of hiking trails. The trails weave along the edges of large and small neighborhoods. Sometimes, the development is at eye level; at other points, you are so low in the canyon that you wouldn't know there is any development at all. It has been a struggle, but the net result is a network of protected open space that includes nature preserves as well as open space for passive and active recreation. There are systems and networks of open space like this throughout the city."

PLANNING RETURNS FROM THE WOODSHED TO PLAY AN IMPORTANT ROLE IN CITY GOVERNMENT

At the time that I conducted my field research and face-to-face interviews in San Diego in 1998, the city had been without a professionally staffed planning department for nearly seven years; however, the important role that planning had once played in the city was not completely forgotten. In columns that appeared in *The San Diego Union-Tribune,* Roger Showley repeatedly drew attention to the void in city government left by the demise of the city's planning department. He also reminded readers that one of the important things a professional planner can and should do is to provide independent advice and speak publicly on important planning-related issues—and to be in a position to suggest policies and courses of action that might not otherwise be considered.

"It would be nice, for once, if somebody at City Hall had the official task of reminding successive mayors and councils that there is a right way and a wrong way of planning a city. And it would be even nicer if the person who tells the truth does not get fired or demoted for speaking his or her mind, in public as well as in private." (Showley, July 13, 1997, H7)

Given that the future of planning seemed so much up in the air when I carried out my field research, I made a point of keeping track of what was happening in San Diego during the years that followed, while I was completing work on this book. I conducted a number of telephone interviews between 1999 and 2001 with people I did not have the opportunity to interview in person in 1998, as well as follow-up interviews with people with whom I had previously spoken. I also continued to monitor the Web sites of the City of San Diego (http://www.ci.san-diego.ca.us), the Centre City Development Corporation (http://www.ccdc.org) and the Mid-City planning initiative in City Heights (http://www.midtowncenter.org).

The first indication that planning might once again be viewed as necessary and valuable came in the early summer of 1997, when the San Diego City Council appropriated $129,000 in the budget for the 1998 fiscal year to enable the city to begin rewriting their 18-year-old *Progress Guide and General Plan.* Not long thereafter, a new city manager, Mike Uberuaga, was named to replace Jack McGrory. In a column that appeared in *The San Diego Union-Tribune* in July 1997, Roger Showley observed that, "Planning has returned from the woodshed at City Hall after five years of being out of favor." (*ibid.,* July 13, 1997, H1)

Nevertheless, the extent of the commitment being made to planning was still tepid at best. In a column written in the form of an open letter to the new city manager, Roger Showley noted that the amount of money the city had set aside ($129,000) for updating the general plan amounted to only 10.9 cents per city resident. "By contrast, the county Board of Supervisors is prepared to spend $3.1 million to rewrite its equally outdated general plan for the unincorporated area. Cost per resident affected by the plan: $7.23." (*ibid.*, October 26, 1997, H1)

To further drive the point home, Showley pointed out that, in Huntington Beach, California (a community one-sixth the size of San Diego) *where Uberuaga had been city manager prior to coming to San Diego*, Uberuaga had approved nearly $800,000 to rewrite that city's plan and conduct an extensive outreach program to engage citizens in the process. (*ibid.*)

Some time after Uberuaga became San Diego's city manager, Gail Goldberg was hired to work on updating the city's 1979 general plan.[40] The key to updating the general plan, Goldberg determined, was to develop and add a new element: the Strategic Framework Element. In the fall of 1999, a 40-person Strategic Framework Citizen Committee was assembled, composed of planning commission members and people from throughout the community. The committee was divided into four subcommittees: Economic Prosperity, Urban Form and the Environment, Neighborhood Quality, and Public Facilities and Infrastructure. It should be noted that when this work began on updating the city's general plan, there was still no planning department.[41] For a year or two, Goldberg's work remained fairly low profile.

The election of Dick Murphy (a former judge) as San Diego's new mayor at the end of 2000 proved to be pivotal in bringing about a renewed commitment to planning. One of the clearest indications of the importance Murphy placed on planning was that, prior to being elected and while campaigning for the office of mayor, Murphy attended a number of the community outreach meetings that Goldberg was holding in various parts of the city related to updating the city's general plan. After he was elected mayor, Murphy continued to attend the community planning outreach meetings. "The mayor is out there, going to every meeting and standing there next to community planners as they interact with citizens," said Goldberg.

One of the first things Murphy did during his first months in office was to re-establish the city's planning department and make Goldberg its director. The "State of the City Address" that Mayor Murphy delivered in January 2001, titled "A Vision for San Diego in the Year 2020: A City Worthy of Our Affection," provided a good indication of the importance that the new mayor placed on planning. The new mayor laid out 10 goals, which he proposed be accomplished by 2005—eight of which were planning- and land use-related:

1. Create Neighborhoods We Can Be Proud Of
2. Reduce Traffic Congestion

3. Pursue Energy Independence
4. Clean Up Our Beaches and Bays
5. Construct a New Regional Airport
6. Build a Library System and a New Main Library
7. Complete the Downtown Ballpark
8. Complete MSCP Open Space Acquisitions

In elaborating on these various planning-related goals, the new mayor repeatedly emphasized that it was essential to think about the city's long-term future, and to plan and act in ways that serve the interests of *future* inhabitants of San Diego, as well as those presently living in the city.

On the subject of reducing traffic congestion, the mayor acknowledged that additional freeway construction was necessary. However, he also noted that it was important to reduce traffic congestion by developing "a land use strategy that discourages urban sprawl and reduces commute distances." Murphy underscored the importance of increasing the percentage of commuters using mass transit. Toward that end he endorsed MTDB's recently adopted *Transit First Plan* (aimed at making San Diego's transit system the transportation mode of choice, rather than just an option), and called for the extension of the San Diego Mission Valley East Line to San Diego State University and East County to be completed by the year 2004.

Regarding the goal of building a library system, the mayor observed, "To have a city worthy of our affection in the year 2020, we need a library system that will serve the needs of all San Diegans. That means a new main library and a great branch system . . . First, we need to build a new main library. Virtually from the moment it was finished in the 1950s, the main library at 8th and E downtown has been inadequate to meet San Diego's needs. Proposals and locations to build a new main library have bounced around town like a ping pong ball for years. The time has come to stop procrastinating and move forward this year."[42]

Regarding the goal of completing the MSCP open space acquisitions, the mayor said, "To have a city worthy of our affection in the year 2020, we need to have preserved our canyons, hillsides and wildlife habitat for future generations. The city's MSCP plan provides us this opportunity. At more than 50,000 acres [the area to be preserved within the City of San Diego], it is the largest urban open space system ever devised. It will provide permanent protection for some of our most precious hillsides, canyons and wildlife habitat . . . During the early 1980s, I chaired the Mission Trails Regional Park Task Force and the San Diego City Council Public Facilities and Recreation Committee, when much of the land was purchased to create the Mission Trails Regional Park and Los Peñasquitos Canyon Preserve. Today, San Diego is applauded for the visionary decision to make those investments 20 years ago. We have the same

496 Making Places Special

opportunity today with the MSCP open space acquisitions to leave a legacy that will be applauded in the year 2020 and by all future generations."[43]

On the matter of building a new airport, the mayor said, "To have a city worthy of our affection in the year 2020, San Diego needs a 21st century airport. All studies demonstrate that Lindbergh Field will reach capacity before the year 2020. The result will be inconvenience to local travelers, limitations on our economy and diminished air safety."

Unfortunately, he said, current units of local government (the City and County of San Diego) and current governmental agencies with responsibilities related to transportation and transportation planning (such as SANDAG, the MTDB and the San Diego Unified Port District which operates Lindbergh Field) were incapable of resolving the airport dilemma. He therefore urged that a regional airport authority be created that could focus exclusively on the airport problem, and that had the power to select an airport site, secure the site, and build and operate the airport.

When I interviewed Donna Alm in her office in 1998, CCDC was actively involved in developing a plan for a new baseball stadium, which was to be built in downtown San Diego at the foot of 12th Avenue. Alm was in the thick of that planning process and, while speaking with me, had to duck out of the office from time to time to field calls from reporters pressing her for details on the proposed project.

Construction work on the ballpark eventually began, but was suspended because of lawsuits challenging the amount of city funds going into the project. In his "State of the City Address," Mayor Murphy urged that construction of the downtown ballpark resume, and drew an analogy to Horton Plaza which, in its time, was also extremely controversial. "I was on the San Diego City Council when Horton Plaza was approved and built almost two decades ago. It too faced many obstacles. Today, it is the pride of downtown. Twenty years from now, in the year 2020, San Diegans will point to the ballpark with similar pride."[44]

When I spoke with Gail Goldberg by phone in June 2001, she reported that the city's planning department had just been approved for a significant increase in staffing and funding for the next fiscal year. "We just went through a budgetary process that was fairly brutal on many other city departments," said Goldberg. Most city departments saw their budgets kept level, or cut back or held to a modest increase. The planning department, however, had its overall budget increased from $8.9 million to $10.6 million, and received approval to add 16 new staff positions to its existing 96-person staff (nine new planner positions and seven support staff positions). "I was able to make the case for increasing the planning department's budget by pointing out that, throughout the 1990s, while the city had been growing and while the budgets of other city departments had been growing as well, the city's planning department had lost 50 positions—30 professionals and 20 support staff," said Goldberg.

What accounts for this renewed political and financial commitment to planning? Goldberg offered a simple explanation: "Planning and land use-related issues simply became too serious to ignore," she said.

The new Strategic Framework Element is not viewed as a repudiation of past plans; rather, it is seen as a way of building on them. Indeed, many of the planning principles and policies emphasized in previous plans are likely to be reiterated in the new Strategic Framework Element. Goldberg expects, for example, that the new plan will call for the development of "a city of villages," and for promoting fairly intense mixed-use development clustered around and/or with easy access to transit. "Our goal is to plan and develop communities, not just to develop plans," she said. "The Strategic Framework Element will describe a process for selecting village projects, and set out a five-year action plan for implementing the first phase of new village development."

A great deal of the time that planners have spent working on the new Strategic Framework Element has been devoted to engaging citizens and neighborhood planning groups in the process. As mentioned earlier, the City of San Diego has 44 designated community planning areas—each served by a community planning group, which is officially recognized by the city, composed of citizens representing the area, who are elected. "The purpose of these community planning groups," Goldberg explained, "is to advise the city, the city council, the planning department and the planning commission on land use and development issues and policies that pertain to those neighborhoods."

Goldberg knew that it was extremely important to consult with each of the neighborhood planning groups related to the preparation of the Strategic Framework Element. However, she also recognized that meeting separately with each neighborhood planning group could produce fragmented and competing visions of the future. "The problem has been that the neighborhood planning groups in the past have not been very generous with one another, and have tended to fight with one another for resources and favorable treatment," said Goldberg. "We wanted instead to try to get people to think about the city as a whole, and to begin talking about developing a strategy for the entire city."

Instead of meeting separately with individual neighborhood planning groups, the planning department adopted the practice of bringing several (usually four or five) neighborhood planning groups together at one time. "Meeting with four or five groups at one time has been a way of getting people to think about more than just what is happening in *their* neighborhood—to think about the city as a whole and realize that, in terms of trying to shape the future, we are all tied together," said Goldberg. Getting different neighborhood groups to meet with one another helped make people aware of land use problems and issues in neighborhoods other than their own, and was a way to get people thinking and talking about more than one issue. "If we hadn't done that," said Goldberg, "entire meetings could have been devoted to a single issue, like traffic congestion, to the exclusion of every other planning issue."

Planners also conducted a series of Town Hall meetings designed to get people thinking and talking about the future. One way planners got people to participate and share their thoughts and feelings was to ask questions like, "What really frightens you about San Diego's future?" and "What exciting things do you think might happen?"

Planners also used the Town Hall meetings to make citizens aware of equity considerations that they might not otherwise have thought much about. For example, at a number of the meetings, Goldberg presented a short slide presentation showing public facilities in different parts of the city (such as in older, in-town neighborhoods and in more recently developed areas on the periphery). "Without providing much commentary and by simply looking at the pictures, people could see that there were wide disparities in the quality of public facilities and schools, and that the quality of facilities was generally much better in peripheral areas than in older, in-town neighborhoods," said Goldberg. "All of a sudden, people woke up to the need to address these facility disparities," she said.

When planners described some the major population and demographic trends that were unfolding, and the likelihood that an additional 1 to 1.2 million people would be living in San Diego County by 2020, the response people gave was almost invariably that, "We don't want one million more people living in San Diego." When people said that, the planners at the meeting did not disagree or argue with them. Instead, they responded by asking follow-up questions that produced discussions which helped raise citizens' awareness of the complexity of the issues facing the region and of the need for planning.

"One of the important things we learned through this process," said Goldberg, "was that most people believed that future population growth of the city could be stopped." The reason people believed that it was possible to stop future population growth was that they did not understand the sources of the city's projected future population growth. "People did not understand that 60% of the city's projected future population growth will be coming from the natural population increase of existing residents," Goldberg explained, "and 40% of the city's future growth will be coming from in-migration. Half of the in-migration will be domestic in-migrants—people moving to San Diego from other parts of the U.S. The other half of the in-migration (accounting for only 20% of the population increase) will be due to foreign in-migration, most notably from Asia, Mexico and South America."

When people said they didn't want one million more people living in San Diego, planners responded by trotting out statistics on the sources of the city's future population growth, and by saying, "OK, then tell us how to stop it!"

"People came up with all kinds of proposals for stopping growth. However, when they thought about and discussed them, they realized that either they wouldn't work or that the measures they proposed would be impossible to implement. In the end, people came around to the conclusion that, in fact, future population growth could not be stopped and, if that were the case, it was better to plan for it than to have it happen and not plan for it."

There is no guarantee that the planning effort described above will succeed. There is also no guarantee that San Diego voters will continue to back elected officials and leaders who have the courage to put themselves on the line by supporting and participating in such a planning process. Planning is never easy, and in a city as populous and as fast-growing as San Diego, it is even more difficult. As the city reaches the outer limits of growth, and as voters face fiscal realities and the costs of upgrading public infrastructure and facilities in already developed areas, some difficult and potentially unpleasant choices are going to have to be made.

Planning is unlikely to reclaim San Diego as "paradise." Perfection is impossible in such a heavily urbanized and rapidly urbanizing region. However, if past is prologue, San Diego in 2020 and beyond will be a *better* place if the city's commitment to planning is sustained. Bold and visionary planning produced a number of positive changes in San Diego in the preceding century. It can do so again in the 21st century—*if* people want it and enable it.

INTERVIEWEES

Donna L. Alm, deputy director, Centre City Development Corporation

William Anderson, AICP, member, San Diego Planning Commission and past president of Citizens Coordinate for Century Three

William J. Briggs, planner, San Diego Unified Port District

Nico Calavita, professor, School of Public Administration and Urban Studies, San Diego State University

William B. Chopyk, AICP, manager, Planning Services, Port of San Diego

Anthony Cutri, Martinez + Cutri, Architects

Janet Fairbanks, AICP, senior planner, San Diego Association of Governments

Gail Goldberg, AICP, director of planning, City of San Diego

Ann Jarmusch, architecture critic, *The San Diego Union-Tribune*

William Lieberman, AICP, director of planning and operations, Metropolitan Transit Development Board (1984-2001)

James LoBue, redevelopment, City of San Diego Redevelopment Division, project manager / City Heights Urban Village

Mike Madigan, senior vice president and development coordinator, Pardee Construction; staff assistant to former San Diego Mayor Pete Wilson in the 1970s; special assistant to Mayor Dick Murphy related to the development of a downtown ballpark

Elizabeth Morris, executive director, San Diego Housing Commission

Ella Isabel Paris, senior planner, City of San Diego Planning Department

Max Schmidt, urban planner/designer, City of San Diego Planning Department (1956-1977); supervising planner, Centre City Development Corporation (1977-97)

Roger M. Showley, writer, *The San Diego Union-Tribune,* and author of various books on San Diego

Michael Stepner, FAIA, FAICP, dean, NewSchool of Architecture and Design, San Diego (1997-2001); urban designer/planner, assistant planning director, acting planning director, city architect, and special assistant to the city manager for special projects (1971-1997), City of San Diego[45]

Thomas T. Story, ASLA, deputy director, Strategic Planning Division, City of San Diego

Kenneth E. Sulzer, FAICP, executive director, San Diego Association of Governments; past president of Citizens Coordinate for Century Three

PLANNING STORY CHRONOLOGY

1903   Civic Improvement Committee of the chamber of commerce hires John Nolen to prepare a plan for the city at the urging of George W. Marston.

1908   Plan of San Diego, prepared by John Nolen, is delivered to the city, but not officially adopted.

1915   The Panama-California Exposition is held in Balboa Park.

1923   The San Diego Planning Department is established. Kenneth Gardner is hired from Nolen's office to become the city's first planning director. Glenn Rick is hired as assistant city planning engineer.

1926   John Nolen completes a second plan for San Diego ("the City, Harbor and Parks plan"). This plan is officially adopted and becomes the cornerstone of all master planning of the city for the next 42 years.

1929   Glenn Rick assumes the position of planning director—a position he will hold for 26 years (until 1955).

1931   A new city charter is approved by voters, establishing a council/manager form of government. A planning commission is also established independent from the city manager. The city's first zoning ordinance is adopted.

1958   Under intense pressure from the May department stores, the city council approves the rezoning of a large tract of land in Mission Valley area to allow construction of the Mission Valley shopping center.

1961   The Mission Valley shopping center opens. Citizens Coordinate for Century Three (C3), a grass-roots planning advocacy organization, is formed.

1967   *Progress Guide and General Plan* ("the 1967 general plan") is approved by the voters in a city-wide referendum. Voters also approve maintaining an independent planning department and reject a proposal to place the planning function under the city manager.

1971   Pete Wilson campaigns for mayor on a platform that calls for managing growth and revitalizing downtown San Diego, and is elected. Transportation Development Act passed, earmarking a quarter-cent state sales tax, solely for the purpose of improving public transportation. A bill is also passed establishing the Metropolitan Transportation Development Board.

1972   The Balanced Communities Policy is adopted by the San Diego City Council. A redevelopment plan for a 15-block area around Horton Plaza is approved by the city council, but goes nowhere.

1973   Kevin Lynch and Donald Appleyard are hired to conduct a reconnaissance of the San Diego region and offer recommendations related to growth management.

1974   Lynch and Appleyard deliver *Temporary Paradise?—A Look at the Special Landscape of the San Diego Region*.

1975   The San Diego City Council adopts policies related to the phasing and timing of new development, and requires that new development pay its own way. Centre City Development Corporation is created to oversee planning and development of downtown. The *Comprehensive Regional Transportation Plan* is prepared—"the first balanced transportation plan ever prepared in the San Diego area."

1976   *Planned District Ordinance and Urban Design and Development Manual* for the Gaslamp Quarter is completed.

1978   Proposition 13 is approved in a statewide referendum.

1979   *Progress Guide and General Plan* ("the 1979 general plan") is completed and adopted— incorporating many of the growth management policies and principles called for in *Temporary Paradise?* The plan includes lines on a map showing proposed rail transit routes. Ernie Hahn is officially designated the developer of Horton Plaza. The provisions of Proposition 13 take effect.

1980   The 16-block Gaslamp Quarter area is officially designated as a National Historic District on the National Register of Historic Places.

1981   First 15.9-mile-long segment of the San Diego Trolley begins operating between downtown San Diego and San Ysidro at the U.S./Mexico border.

1983   The first new housing developments in downtown San Diego (Park Row and Marina Park) are completed and occupied.

1985   Horton Plaza opens.

1987   Single-Room Occupancy Housing Preservation Ordinance is adopted by San Diego City Council. Transportation Sales Tax Initiative (TransNet) is passed to finance extensions of the San Diego Trolley system and the establishment of commuter rail service.

1989   Housing Trust Fund Task Force delivers its report to the city council, which passes an ordinance establishing a Housing Trust Fund to finance the development of affordable housing.

1991   The city's planning department, in existence for 52 years, is disbanded.

1992   Transit-Oriented Development and Design Guidelines are officially adopted.

1994   Crime and Economic Summit held in City Heights. Martinez + Cutri (Anthony Cutri, principal-in-charge) is hired to prepare a master plan (*City Heights Master Plan*) for a nine-block area of City Heights and design a police substation.

1995   San Diego Trolley Orange Line extended 3.6 miles from El Cajon to Santee. San Diego-Oceanside commuter rail service (the Coaster) begins operating.

1996   San Diego Trolley Blue Line extended 3.2 miles from Santa Fe Depot (downtown) to Old Town.

1997   A new city manager, Michael Uberuaga, is appointed. Planning returns from the woodshed. Work begins on updating the 1979 *Progress Guide and General Plan*. Mission Valley Trolley Line of the San Diego Trolley is completed and begins operating. Comprehensive *Multiple Species Habitat Conservation Program* (MSCP) is unanimously approved by San Diego City Council. *The New York Times* terms San Diego's MSCP "the nation's most ambitious attempt to reconcile the preservation of nature with urban development" and "a model for [the] nation."

2000   Dick Murphy is elected mayor.

2001   Mayor Murphy re-establishes the city's planning department.

NOTES

1. Given its size, one might have thought that San Diego would have become an important headquarters city for major corporations based in southern California. However, as a general rule, when large corporations have decided to locate or build a headquarters or regional office in southern California, they have almost always decided to locate in Los Angeles rather than in San Diego, which is perceived as being more remote.

2. The name of the San Diego citizens organization that was formed in the 1970s to fight suburban sprawl was Prevent Los Angelization Now (PLAN). In the 1970s, when the U.S. Army Corps of Engineers proposed to put San Diego's rivers and streams into V-shaped concrete channels, public opposition to the "L.A.-style" river channelization scheme was so intense that the project was dropped.

3. The airplane that Charles Lindbergh flew on his solo flight across the Atlantic

Ocean in 1927, the "Spirit of St. Louis," was manufactured by the Ryan Aeronautical Company of San Diego. Lindbergh conducted extensive test flights of the "Spirit of St. Louis" in San Diego, prior to flying across the U.S. to Roosevelt Field on Long Island, New York, where he began his history-making trans-Atlantic flight.

4. During the hours of the curfew, planes are allowed to land but are not allowed to take off.

5. One solution, which has been proposed and studied, is to build a joint international airport facility with Tijuana at the U.S.-Mexico border, linking Tijuana's Rodriguez International airport and Brown Field. Another proposed solution is to develop a new airport on the huge tract of land occupied by the Miramar Naval Air Station (now a Marine Corps Air Station).

6. Among the 77 American cities surveyed, Washington, DC ranked first in property taxes: $3,978 per resident. (Stepner and Fiske 2000, 84)

7. The short blocks that characterize downtown San Diego as a result of Horton's plan are not unlike the 200- by 200-foot blocks that characterize downtown Portland, Oregon, which are widely believed to have been inspired by the short blocks in older east coast and New England cities. Many of the people who initially settled in and developed Portland came from New England, and Alonzo Horton's decision to lay out San Diego with short blocks may also have reflected his east coast origins.

Laying out a city with short blocks (as was done in imposing "The World's Greatest Grid" from one end of Manhattan island to the other) has traditionally been seen by land speculators as a way to maximize land values by maximizing visibility and frontage. However, urban planners and researchers have also noted that short blocks can be a key ingredient in creating and maintaining healthy and vital urban places. (See, for example, Jane Jacobs' chapters in *The Death and Life of Great American Cities* (1961) on "The uses of sidewalks: contact" and "The need for small blocks.")

Indeed, a number of urban planners who have studied the changes that have occurred in downtown Portland believe that the city's decision to maintain its original street layout (and not to consolidate short blocks into larger blocks or "superblocks") played an important role in creating and maintaining a vital downtown.

8. In 1905, the 1870 Horton House Hotel was razed to make way for the $1 million U.S. Grant Hotel, a venerable downtown San Diego landmark, which still operates as a hotel.

9. Nolen envisioned that Bayfront Boulevard (now Harbor Drive) would have such extensive planting and landscaping that it would "virtually become a park." Nolen also called for a wide, east-west mall of greenspace to be developed along Cedar Street (somewhat like the mall in Washington, DC) linking Balboa Park to the waterfront.

10. The idea that Spanish-style architecture was appropriate and desirable in San Diego was so widely accepted that this architectural design requirement, enforced by a design review process, remained in force for over 40 years. (Stepner 1997a, 34)

11. In this respect, the Panama-California Exposition seems to have had somewhat the same intoxicating effect on visitors as the extraordinarily popular "White City" of the 1893 Chicago Exposition, planned by a team of architects and planners headed by Daniel Burnham.

12. Given the primitive state of aviation at the time, Nolen's recommendation that an airport be developed where Lindbergh Field is today was really quite farsighted. Unfortunately, Nolen did not foresee the tremendous advances in aviation that would be made later in the 20th century, and greatly underestimated the airport size and runway length required to meet the operational demands of modern jet aircraft.

13. Michael Stepner points out that the new city charter also made the planning department "independent of the City Manager to allow it to focus on the long-term without being constrained by the day-to-day decisions of the manager." (Stepner 1997a, 34)

14. C3 also worked to oppose and overturn the proposed widening of Highway 395 (now 163) through Balboa Park. Largely as a result of C3's efforts, Highway 163 was kept as a parkway rather than a freeway. "Keeping Highway 163 as a parkway was an important and wonderful outcome," Ann Jarmusch (architecture critic for *The San Diego Union-Tribune*) told me. Michael Stepner agrees, having called the stretch of Highway 163 through Balboa Park "the region's most scenic stretch of highway." (Stepner 1997a, 35)

15. Except for the tall hotels that have been built along the San Diego waterfront on land owned by the Unified Port District, there is remarkably little high-rise residential development along San Diego's coast. This is because the height of residential structures immediately overlooking the coast is limited to 30 feet. According to William Anderson (a member of the San Diego Planning Commission and past president of C3), a large-scale condominium development built on Coronado Island in the early 1970s (the first development of that scale built on the California coast) made people realize that, if building heights were not limited, San Diego could end up looking like Miami Beach.

16. Freilich had gained national attention by devising the phased growth strategy that was initiated by Ramapo, New York in 1969, and successfully defending it in court.

17. In the aftermath of World War II, in a move designed to facilitate the development of the city's port facilities as well as serve the needs of the U.S. Navy, the cities of San Diego, Coronado, National City, Chula Vista and Imperial Beach gave up their authority and control over their waterfronts to the San Diego Unified Port

District (an independent agency formed by the state legislature to manage bayfront and tidelands development). Once the transfer of authority was completed, the city's planning department lost its ability to plan for and regulate the development of the city's waterfront—the area which, in many ways, was the city's most precious asset and which the 1908 Nolen plan urged be protected and enhanced for recreation and public access.

18. In 1998, CCDC's budget provided funding for 34 full-time staff.

19. When I interviewed her in 1998, Donna Alm had worked at CCDC for 23 years and was deputy director of the agency.

20. The name and reputation of planner John Nolen is more widely known, but among those who know San Diego well—and particularly among planners in San Diego—the name and reputation of Max Schmidt looms almost as large. According to *The San Diego Union-Tribune* architecture critic Ann Jarmusch, Schmidt is regarded so highly that planners in San Diego call him "the father of planning in San Diego" and send him a card each Father's Day to remind him of his honorary title. Schmidt retired from CCDC in 1997.

21. "By 1975, Hahn's firm owned eleven regional shopping malls, and had thirty more under way." (Frieden and Segalyn 1990, 126) One shopping center Hahn developed that proved to be particularly successful was the University Town Centre, near the University of California San Diego campus. When Hahn's initial plan for building a shopping center in the university area met with opposition, he produced a revised plan, which was approved, that called for the development of both a retail center and 300 adjacent housing units, connected to the center by means of pedestrian and bicycle paths. The University Town Centre in San Diego is a perfect, real-world demonstration of the feasibility and desirability of bringing nonresidential and residential uses into closer proximity. As Michael Stepner pointed out, "You can walk right from your home to the shopping center. It's a very desirable area in which to live and proves that mixed-use development can work."

22. The San Diego Unified Port District was created by state legislation passed in 1962 that authorized the cities of San Diego, National City, Chula Vista, Imperial Beach and Coronado to form a special district for the purpose of developing the tidelands and industrial areas along the shorelines of the five municipalities on San Diego Bay. A seven-member board was created. Each of the four bay communities has one representative on the board; San Diego, which accounts for more than 80% of the population of the San Diego Unified Port District, has three commissioners on the board.

23. As this is written, a plan has been developed calling for streetscape improvements along 12th Street (pedestrian amenities such as widened sidewalks, tree planting, landscaping and street furniture) and for a new diagonal landscaped "Park Boulevard" to be constructed leading from lower 12th Street to the bay. Completion of these pedestrian-oriented streetscape projects will create a continuously landscaped corridor from Balboa Park to the bay which, in turn, will connect with the promenades along the waterfront and Martin Luther King, Jr. Boulevard—going a long way toward helping to reconnect the city to its waterfront and San Diego Bay.

24. Transit operations in San Diego continued to be operated in this improvised manner for a number of years. In 1985, the umbrella organization which, as a practical matter, had existed for about six years, was finally given an official name—the Metropolitan Transit System (MTS)—and the San Diego City Council asked MTDB to take over San Diego Transit's operations. Soon thereafter, the MTS logo started appearing on buses in the region.

25. SANDAG was formally established in 1972. It is organized as a "Joint Powers Authority" under California state law, which means that it is a voluntary association of local governments. In addition to being the center and clearinghouse for regional data and information, SANDAG also has important responsibilities for transportation and environmental planning. It is designated by the federal government as the Metropolitan Planning Organization for transportation planning and as the Regional Transportation Planning Agency by the state.

26. At a ribbon-cutting ceremony for a new stretch of freeway near Los Angeles, Governor Gray Davis' announcement in August 2001 that this would be the *last* new major freeway built in California further underscores the importance of the planning that is being done to expand public transit in San Diego and cluster, and concentrate future development around transit stations. The State of California once built new freeways with abandon, but building new freeways is no longer a plausible option. "There are no new California freeways in the planning . . ." (Editorial, *The New York Times*, August 22, 2001, A18)

27. Under the guidelines that were adopted, a TOD is defined as a mixed-use community within an average 2,000 feet walking distance of a transit stop and core commercial area, in which the design, configuration and mix of uses emphasize a pedestrian-oriented environment and reinforce the use of public transportation.

28. In an effort to market and promote the concept of TODs to citizens and developers, William Lieberman and the MTDB produced a 24-minute video in 1993 called *Cities in the Balance: Creating the Transit-Friendly Environment* (a joint venture with the U.S. Department of Transportation). They also prepared and distributed *Designing For Transit—A Manual for Integrating Public Transportation and Land Development in the San Diego Metropolitan Area* (July 1993)—a highly readable and informative manual containing photographs and illustrations, which shows ways that communities can be made more transit-oriented.

29. Bill Lieberman provided the following sad update on the proposed Morena Linda Vista joint development project at the end of August 2001: "First, there was intense neighborhood opposition about the amount of housing proposed. Residents of surrounding areas were concerned about the traffic that it would generate and wanted retail/commercial instead. Our studies showed that the latter would actually generate more traffic than residential, but the developer modified the project anyway with fewer housing units and more retail. That seemed to solve that problem, but then the city came up with the idea of constructing a roundabout at one corner of the site. This not only took up some of the developable land, but also put the proposed anchor retail tenant out of the line of sight [of the trolley stop], so the tenant pulled out. The developer is still trying to regroup."

30. Prior to the Mission Valley line, almost all portions of the San Diego Trolley had been built on existing railroad rights of way acquired from the Southern Pacific Railroad. However, there was no such existing railroad right of way running through Mission Valley, so the land for the right of way had to be acquired and pieced together. On the one hand, having to create a right of way made planning and building the Mission Valley line a considerable challenge. On the other hand, it meant that planners had much greater flexibility in deciding where the railroad right of way should go—and, more particularly, the ability to base those routing decisions at least in part on the outcomes of negotiations with property owners and developers interested in having a station stop located on their property. In many ways, it gave planners greater leverage with developers to achieve the goal of achieving TOD.

31. In working to achieve the goal of TOD, there has actually been a remarkable degree of interagency cooperation and coordination, with planners in the city's planning department working closely with transit planners at the MTDB. "We had a very close working relationship between and among all the public agencies that were involved in planning. The MTDB would rent planners from the city," said Stepner, "and we also worked closely with the SDHC on a number of their projects." Not every cooperative planning effort produced a happy ending, however. In the early 1990s, planners at the commission, the MTDB and in the city's planning department worked together to try to locate a proposed housing development at the Marina Boulevard trolley stop. "Unfortunately, it just fell apart because we had a city manager at the time who didn't believe in planning, and a city council that wasn't very interested in planning either," said Stepner.

32. David Paul Rosen & Associates was brought in to advise the task force regarding these matters.

33. It should also be noted that the developer linkage fee is not imposed in the downtown redevelopment area overseen by CCDC, or in any of the other approximately 10 officially established redevelopment areas outside of downtown. In addition, the linkage fee does not apply to nonprofit developers.

34. Mission Valley seems worlds away from City Heights. Nevertheless, Mission Valley is actually less than 2 miles north of City Heights "as the crow flies."

35. Between 1990 and 1995, San Diego's Hispanic and Asian population increased roughly 20%, while the region's black population increased by 9%. By 2000, 25% of the people living in San Diego County were of Hispanic origin, 11% were of Asian descent and 6% were black.

36. The City Heights Town Council is the neighborhood governing body of City Heights, and provides a public forum for discussing and addressing a wide range of neighborhood issues. It also organizes and oversees various neighborhood activities such as neighborhood crime watch, community cleanups and voluntary code enforcement.

37. Each of the townhomes are two-story units. However, in this project, one row of townhome units has been placed on top of another row, thereby creating what is effectively a four-story residential structure. Below the four-story residential structure is a level of below-grade parking.

38. According to statistics compiled by SANDAG, while the average density of development throughout San Diego is five units per acre, new developments built and proposed in the "planned urbanizing area" in the 1990s averaged only about two units per acre.

39. Funding for the region-wide biological inventory and mapping of environmental resources was obtained from a variety of sources—the City of San Diego Water Department, San Diego County and SANDAG, and the U.S. Department of the Interior.

40. Gail Goldberg holds a degree in urban studies and planning from the University of California at San Diego. She began working for the City of San Diego in 1989, in the planning department, as a community planner to the Otay Mesa Community Planning Area. She later served as the planning department's project manager for the Bi-National Airport Planning Project; after that study was completed, she served as the city's airport planning project manager. For four years, she served as director for the Naval Training Center Reuse Planning Project.

41. Goldberg's position at the time was listed as being part of the Department of Development Services—a large, roughly 500-person multifaceted department, which was headed by a nonplanner.

42. As of August 2001, a site for the proposed new main library had been selected by the city, near the proposed new downtown ballpark in the East Village section of downtown; however, funding had not yet been secured.

43. As of 2001, Tom Story was senior policy advisor to Mayor Dick Murphy (the same position Karen Scarborough held previously during Mayor Susan Golding's administration, when planning began on the MSCP). In that new position, Story will likely continue to be involved in advising on and overseeing the implementation of the MSCP.

44. In 2001, Mike Madigan became special assistant to Mayor Dick Murphy related to the development of the ballpark.

45. In August 2001, Michael Stepner stepped down as dean of the NewSchool of Architecture to become director of land use and housing for the San Diego Regional Economic Development Corporation, a corporation funded by the cities in San Diego County, the County of San Diego, the Port of San Diego and private sector businesses.

8

Lessons Learned

Critics have commonly portrayed planners as faceless, uncaring bureaucrats with a penchant for imposing rigid and obscure rules and regulations for no apparent good reason and to no particular advantage. The stories presented in this book paint a very different picture and put a human face on planning that is much easier with which to identify. The planners whose efforts are described in the case studies cared deeply about the communities in which they lived and for which they worked.

They didn't come into situations armed with ready-made solutions. They knew that planning is a journey of learning and discovery. They were open and receptive to new ideas and approaches and were eager to share them with people in their communities. In short, they know that, in planning, what is most important is not to be the originator of an idea, but to know how to integrate and synthesize many ideas.

Before work began on developing a plan for the Duluth waterfront, the head of the city's Physical Planning Division traveled to port cities throughout North America to study and learn from them. During his travels to cities in other parts of the country, Westminster's community development director took pictures of projects and developments that illustrated lessons related to both good and bad development. Before transit planners at Madison Metro set about replanning and restructuring their city-wide bus route system, they studied what other cities of comparable size had done and tried to learn from their mistakes.

Planners in many of the case-study communities brought in outside experts as speakers, organized visioning sessions and forums that expanded people's horizons and a sense of what was possible, and devised planning processes that encouraged a free and open exchange of ideas. They also developed plans that challenged people in their communities to strive for outcomes that must have seemed wildly ambitious and unattainable at the time. As Wichita archi-tect/planner Bill Livingston put it, "There is more to planning than being prac-tical. You also have to be inspirational."

Planning critics have frequently contended that planning is a waste of time and money, and rarely, if ever, achieves positive results. The fact that my research uncovered evidence that planning had produced a number of positive outcomes in all of the cities I studied should help put that argument to rest.

Considerable emphasis in the case studies has admittedly been placed on documenting land use changes and development outcomes brought about by planning that are physically observable (an emphasis that is no doubt under-scored by the large number of photographs included in each case study). How-ever, physically observable outcomes are certainly not the whole story of what planning produced in these communities.

In many ways, the most positive and significant outcomes brought about by planning were the changes inside people—in the way people feel about their communities, themselves and their fellow citizens. Reflecting back on the changes brought about in Chattanooga, Dave Crockett (city council member and director of the Chattanooga Institute) told me, "We've recaptured a sense of civic pride, a belief in the community and respect for each other." Michael Stepner (who, when I interviewed him, was dean of the NewSchool of Archi-tecture and Design in San Diego) said essentially the same thing when he offered the simple observation that "Planning brings people together."

There is, therefore, a great deal of "good news" in these case studies. How-ever, the bad news is that planning is extremely hard work and involves a con-siderable amount of risk-taking. When people engage in planning, they are attempting to shape the future in some desired way, but there can never be any assurance that planning will achieve what people hope it will achieve. People who engage in planning are continually aware of the possibility of failure—that, at any time throughout a process of planning, some unforeseen turn of events can put the whole effort at risk. The risks elected officials take when they closely identify themselves with specific planning initiatives are particu-larly obvious and should not be underestimated.

Having said this, these case studies suggest that the risk is worth taking. After you read these stories, I urge you to analyze the odds of whether plan-ning can help your community achieve a better future against the likelihood that your community will become better by simply leaving matters to chance. Think about the kind of place you want your community to be in the future and the kind of surroundings you want for your children and grandchildren. Think about the outcomes and results that the communities featured in this book produced by planning, and consider what could be achieved in your community through enlightened, skillful and courageous planning.

INGREDIENTS FOR SUCCESSFUL PLANNING

The stories and accounts of planning processes and outcomes in these 10 case-study communities are remarkably varied. In each of the communities, different planning issues and problems were identified and addressed, different sets of actors stepped forward and the process of planning unfolded in a different way. Professional planners who worked on staff and as consultants also used different skills and played different roles. In each case, planning was approached in a way that was specifically tailored to the needs, constraints and opportunities of a particular place at a particular point in time. Indeed, one of the most important lessons that these case studies should therefore teach us is that there is no single approach or technique of planning that is ideal or workable in all situations.

Planning is the creative process—more of an art than a science—of devising novel solutions to unique problems in unique contexts. When people engage in planning, they are attempting to confront issues and problems that have never presented themselves in exactly the same way in the same context before. The whole purpose of planning is to devise processes, plans and strategies that take account of the unique needs, constraints and opportunities of particular places. (If a planning consultant comes to your community hyping a particular planning approach or technique that he or she says has worked well in any number of places, and proposes to apply the same approach to your community, think twice about hiring that consultant. Look instead for a consultant with varied experiences, and with a demonstrated ability to devise plans and strategies tailored to the specific needs and special qualities of different places.)

While there is no simple formula to successful planning, there do appear to be a number of common threads running through the case studies, which suggest that the likelihood of success in planning is greatly increased when certain ingredients are present. The more of these ingredients that are present, the more likely that planning will be able to achieve positive results. Just consider the following ingredients that were present in the case-study communities:

Invested in Planning

In 1992, while still living in Northampton, Massachusetts, I came across a headline in the local *Daily Hampshire Gazette* that provided another reminder of the precariousness of planning in American communities. The headline read, "The planner's job should go, panel says." (Yurko, April 6, 1992) The main body of the article quoted the chairman of the Town of Easthampton's finance committee as saying that the recommendation to eliminate the planner position, which had been held since 1989 by Stuart Beckley, was "no reflection on Beckley's performance in the post." (*ibid.*) Rather, she said, it was simply that, "We can't afford to fund the planning position . . . It's just a matter of priorities." (*ibid.*) The article went on to explain that the town's proposed budget for the following year was $17.3 million, and that eliminating the town's planning department would "save the town $39,000, including the planner's expense account." (*ibid.*)

Given the reluctance of many communities to spend anything at all on planning, the fact that the communities written about in this book spent an average of $9.04 per capita annually on planning is certainly worth noting. The number of professionals employed on local planning staffs, and the amounts spent on planning in a recent budget year (the total amount as well as the amount per capita) are shown on the community profiles that can be found in the Appendix.

Each of the 10 case-study communities—with the exception of Block Island, Rhode Island (winter population approximately 1,000)—employed professionally trained, full-time planners on staff. In a number of cities, the professional capacities of local planning staff were augmented by also employing urban designers, architects and landscape architects. Indeed, a careful reading of these stories suggests that employing capable, professionally trained planners on staff is almost without exception a prerequisite for successful planning.

A Sustained Planning Effort—Not Just One Plan

The positive outcomes achieved by these case-study communities were not simply the result of a single project or policy; rather, they undertook a series of planning initiatives that were intentionally complementary and mutually reinforcing.

These communities did not simply develop one plan and then slavishly adhere to and implement that plan. Instead, they engaged in a series of planning processes and developed a number of plans over an extended period of time, each of which built on and reinforced the aims of previous planning efforts. The succession of planning studies and plans produced in Charleston and Chattanooga illustrate this point.

In Charleston:

* The *Tourism Impact and Management Study* (completed in 1978) reinforced the aims of the Lower King Street District plan (completed a year earlier) that led to the development of Charleston Place.
* The Accommodations Zoning Overlay District ordinance finalized in 1987 (based on the recommendations of the Visitor Accommodations study of 1982), and the actions recommended in the 1989 Calhoun Street study, were consistent with one another, and further complemented and reinforced the aims of the *Tourism Impact and Management Study* and the Lower King Street District plan.

In Chattanooga, five different plans prepared over a 15-year period were mutually complementary and reinforcing:

* the 1982 Structure plan developed by the Urban Design Studio

- the 1985 Riverpark master plan developed by Carr, Lynch Associates, Inc., under the guidance of the Moccasin Bend Task Force
- the 1985 Miller Park District plan
- the 1992 plan for the Tennessee State Aquarium and Ross's Landing Park and Public Plaza
- the 1997 Southside plan

Planning for the revitalization of downtown San Diego was successful because Mayor Pete Wilson and his staff realized that no one project—no matter how well planned and designed—would be capable of turning the downtown around. What was needed instead was to develop, integrate and implement at least seven different but highly complementary and mutually reinforcing plan elements:

- the development of a rail transit system (the San Diego Trolley)
- the development of a major center of retail activity (Horton Plaza)
- the development of a significant amount of downtown housing
- the development of a large downtown supermarket to add to the convenience of living and working downtown
- the restoration and redevelopment of the Gaslamp Quarter next to Horton Plaza
- the development of a downtown convention center which would produce spin-off demand for downtown hotels and restaurants
- the planning and design of downtown amenities like Children's Park and the Martin Luther King, Jr. Promenade

In committing itself to achieve all of these distinct plan elements, the city was in effect committing itself to a long-term vision that would take 15-20 years to fully realize and that, in many ways, is still unfolding.

Gianni Longo was essentially saying the same thing when he wrote that "Charleston's achievement is due not to any single major project but to many small ones: a height-restriction ordinance, which has preserved the striking skyline of church spires and trees; an ordinance limiting hotel construction, even in commercially zoned areas; an ordinance drastically limiting tour-bus routes, which keeps the streets of the historic areas serene; and aggressive programs to increase home ownership in the historic district, which have enabled longtime low- and middle-income residents to buy and restore deteriorating houses, in turn adding to the area's racial and economic diversity. The list goes on . . ." (Longo 1996, 48-49)

Many different elements go into creating places that have the qualities people value. The importance of planning is that it can enable communities to balance competing interests and achieve multiple objectives. It can also enable communities to gradually put a number of different pieces together (like a jigsaw puzzle), so that when all the pieces are in place, there is a discernible pattern and a sense of wholeness. The planning and design projects described in the various case studies were not isolated undertakings, unconnected to planning initiatives being carried out in adjoining areas. Rather, the overall planning strategy in the case-study communities was to weave together initiatives and projects developed for different geographic areas.

- The Capital Center and Memorial Boulevard Extension/River Relocation projects in Providence interconnected previously disparate parts of the city's downtown and also integrated the College Hill neighborhood more compatibly into the fabric of downtown.
- Much of the success of the Charleston Place project in Charleston was due to the fact that it achieved multiple objectives: it went a long way toward revitalizing the Lower King Street retail area, revitalized the City Market area and provided a badly needed physical connection between the two.

Continuity of Planning Effort

While reviewing the planning chronologies compiled for these stories, the remarkable continuity and stability of the planning staffs in most of the cities I had studied made a strong impression. The length of service of planning directors was particularly striking:

- Over the course of 75 years (from the 1920s when Duluth's planning department was established until 1995 when Jerry Kimball retired), Duluth had had only three planning directors. Kimball himself directed physical planning in Duluth for 26 years.
- Over a period of more than 32 years (from 1969 through 2001), the Wichita-Sedgwick County MAPD had only two planning directors. Robert Lakin was the Wichita-Sedgwick County MAPD director for 17 years (from 1969 until 1986); Marvin Krout became MAPD's planning director in 1986 and, as of 2001, was still in that position.
- Max Schmidt worked as a planner and urban designer for San Diego in the city's planning department and then in the Centre City Development Corporation for a total of 41 years.
- Michael Stepner worked for San Diego in various planning-related positions for 26 years.
- George Austin was the director of planning and development for the City of Madison for 16 years.
- T. D. Harden directed the Chattanooga-Hamilton County RPA for 30 years.
- As of 2001, John Carpenter had been director of Westminster's Department of Community Development for 11 years.

The fact that continuity and stability in the staffing of planning agencies were associated with planning success should not be that surprising. It can take years—sometimes decades—for visionary plans to be implemented. Frequent staff turnovers and changes at the helm of a city's planning agency certainly are not helpful in carrying out a consistent and sustained planning effort.

Another way continuity was maintained was by not allowing the pace of planning to be dictated or altered by the ups and downs of real estate markets. In all too many communities, planning activity only increases when there is a sharp upturn in development activity, and then decreases when development activity falls. In other words, in these communities, planning is simply undertaken *in reaction* to what is already happening, and is not *anticipatory.*

The only way planning can get ahead of the curve is if it is sustained even when there is a marked downturn in development activity. Lulls in development activity, in fact, present marvelous opportunities for getting ahead of the curve:

- The planning efforts that produced the Legacy Ridge Golf Course and Promenade projects in Westminster were actually begun during a pronounced slowdown in development activity. Indeed, during much of the time the city was engaged in planning these projects, the real estate market was so weak that it would have been impossible to attract the private capital necessary to build them. However, because planning was sustained throughout this down period, when market conditions finally did improve, the planning had been completed and the plans were ready. Had planners in Westminster waited for market conditions to improve before they did the planning, they would have fallen behind the curve, and the projects would have taken much longer to realize and very possibly might not have come to fruition at all.

Projects Not Ends in Themselves

Communities are rarely, if ever, transformed by a single project or action. To be transformed, and create an identity and sense of place all their own, cities need to be able to develop more sophisticated plans and strategies, calling for actions and initiatives on a number of different fronts, and in different geographic areas, which complement and reinforce one another.

The $45 million Tennessee State Aquarium is the most visible manifestation of the revival of downtown Chattanooga and has become one of the most frequently visited sites in the city. However, it was not simply the building's design or the quality of its exhibits that made the activity generated by the aquarium so beneficial to Chattanooga. Rather, it was because the aquarium was part of, and was inspired by, a much larger, more encompassing plan or vision of the city. It was not a stand-alone project—an end unto itself. Its strategic value and significance is that it created a focal point destination at Ross's Landing (a goal of the city's Structure plan that was completed by the Urban Design Studio in 1982), and reconnected the city to the Tennessee River (a goal strongly endorsed by the 1984 *Vision 2000* process and the 1985 Riverpark master plan).

- The 1989 RTKL plan for downtown Wichita identified distinct downtown districts and recommended different types of projects and initiatives for each of these districts—the ultimate aim being to accentuate the unique characteristics and qualities of each district, and thereby create a core area that was more than the sum of its parts.

- The complementary projects and mutually reinforcing initiatives undertaken in Westminster provide another good example. When City Park was planned and developed in Westminster, it was intended to be that city's central park, but it was not a stand-alone project. Later planning initiatives made it the focal point of an integrated network of open space and trails running diagonally through the city. The planning and development of the city's new Recreation Center overlooking City Park on one side, and the development of the Promenade (a retail, office, conference and entertainment center) overlooking City Park on the opposite side, further reinforced the importance of City Park as defining the center of the city. In other words, each individual project and initiative complemented that which had been done before, and represented yet another step toward creating an economically, socially and environmentally successful and balanced community.

Another valuable lesson that can be learned from the case-study communities is that planning is necessary to achieve connectivity and make sure that development is not allowed to occur in a way that separates and divides communities, and imposes needless barriers.

- Planners in Westminster made sure that walkways and greenbelts in private residential developments were interconnected with the city's public trail and open space network. They also insisted that alterations be made in the planning and design of major shopping center developments that backed up onto adjoining residential areas to make the rears of those developments less hostile and more attractive, and to create midpoint openings so that residents living in those residential areas had easier access to the shopping centers.

- The attractive pedestrian bridge that was planned and built in connection with the Uptown District infill project in San Diego, that made stores in the Uptown District accessible to residents living in a neighborhood on the other side of a busy freeway, is another indication of the way that planning can help to build connectivity and avoid isolation.

Made Good Use of Consultants

Another common thread running through the planning stories was that all of the case-study communities made excellent use of outside planning and design consultants.

- On a number of occasions, city government officials in Westminster approved appropriations of public funds to obtain specialized planning and design consultant services related to special projects like the City Center Marketplace, Legacy Ridge Golf Course and the Promenade.

In fact, the case-study communities typically went to great lengths to hire extremely qualified and talented outside consultants by issuing nationally advertised RFPs and Request for Qualifications (RFQs), and by interviewing a number of finalists before making a choice.

- The wide-ranging national search conducted in Wichita before selecting Moishe Safdie to design Exploration Place is indicative of the painstaking and involved consultant selection processes that were frequently undertaken.

The list of planning consultants and firms hired by the case-study communities includes some of the most highly respected and well-known planning and design consultants and design firms in the country:

- Harland Bartholomew, Daniel Burnham and Buckhurst Fish Hutton Katz, Inc. (Duluth)
- John Nolen, Frank Lloyd Wright, Taliesin Architects (Wright's successor firm in Spring Green, Wisconsin) and Cesar Pelli (Madison)
- John Nolen, Kevin Lynch and Donald Appleyard (San Diego)
- Gianni Longo/ACP; Cambridge Seven Architects; Carr, Lynch Associates, Inc.; Peter Calthorpe; and Anton Nelessen Associates, Inc. (Chattanooga)
- Barton-Aschman Associates, Sasaki Associates, and Ehrenkrantz and Eckstut (Charleston)
- Skidmore, Owings & Merrill LLP (Providence)
- RTKL Associates, Inc. and Moishe Safdie (Wichita)

Hiring outside experts for advice on how to address particular problems or issues can be extremely valuable and constructive for a number of reasons:

- Because of their range of experience and knowledge of solutions and approaches devised in other places, they can expand people's horizons and open their eyes to new possibilities.
- Outside consultants and experts tend to be perceived in a more neutral light than staff planners (whose positions on issues may be well known), which allows them to say things that staff planners could not and to challenge prevailing assumptions and beliefs.

Having noted the importance of the work performed in the case-study communities by outside consultants, it is also important to note that it is difficult (if not impossible) for planning consultants—no matter how skillful they are—to produce plans and reports that are implemented and have a positive impact without capable and knowledgeable staff planners working in a supporting role behind the scenes.

When I teach courses to students training to become planners, I have always felt it important to describe and distinguish the respective roles played by staff planners (who work for a unit of government in a planning department or agency) and those who work as private planning consultants. When I do, students invariably find the role played by the planning consultant to be the more glamorous and appealing of the two. To them, as well as to many other observers, private consultants appear to play the role of the "good guy in the white hat" who rides into town on a white horse, lays out some brilliant ideas and strategies no one there had thought of before, and then rides off into the sunset as the problem is finally solved—while the local staff planners sit by as passive observers. However, such a portrayal ignores interdependency of the roles of staff planners and planning consultants.

One reason why the consultant role appears so much more appealing is that planners employed on the staffs of public agencies typically receive very little recognition for their work, whereas outside planning consultants frequently appear to play very prominent roles, at least for a relatively short period of time. Indeed, in the absence of documented stories like those in this book, it is easy to overlook the importance of the work that planners employed at the local level perform on a day-to-day basis, largely out of public view.

In the first place, planners working on staff at the local level typically play an important role in identifying the local problems and framing the issues that eventually become the subject of consultant studies, and drafting the RFPs or RFQs that are issued to solicit consultant submissions and proposals. Local staff planners are often heavily involved in the consultant selection process. Once the consultant is selected, staff planners are the ones who draft the scope of consultant services that serves as the basis of the consultant contract, and subsequently direct and review the consultants' work throughout the duration of the contract.

Indeed, smart planning consultants know that local planners are an important source of information, and are typically eager to turn to local planners to help orient and advise them.

- As the San Diego case study suggests, the source of many of the key planning concepts and ideas in consultant plans (such as in Lynch and Appleyard's *Temporary Paradise?* and in the tiered approach to growth management recommended by consultant Robert Freilich) came from the city's own planning staff. Had planning consultants been hired by communities to perform similar planning tasks without the benefit of having highly knowledgeable and capable planners working full time on staff to anchor and validate their work, the plans and reports they prepared would undoubtedly have been nowhere near as excellent or effective.

Given the well-trained and experienced professional planners working on staff in the case-study communities, some might be surprised that these communities made such frequent use of outside consultants. Indeed, it is probably fair to say that local planners who worked on staff were often capable of doing the work that outside consultants were hired to do.

- In the San Diego example, we learn that the staff of the city's planning department had been working for a number of years on developing transit-oriented development guidelines, but had been unable to get them approved by the city council. To break the log jam, it was decided to bring in consultant Peter Calthorpe to put the finishing touches on those guidelines. Hiring Calthorpe was a strategic move on the part of the city's planning department and proved crucial to getting the city council to approve them, because Calthorpe's reputation and stature carried greater weight with the council than that of the city's own planning staff.

The Bible says, "A prophet is not without honour, save in his own country." (Matthew XIII, 57) Or, as T. D. Harden observed, acknowledging the limited visibility of the role that staff planners play, "Always the bridesmaid, never the bride."

Executive Leadership and Political Support for Planning

Strong and courageous executive leadership and support for planning is clearly an important ingredient of successful planning.

- A key turning point in the story of Chattanooga's planning can be traced back to the election of Ralph Kelly as mayor of Chattanooga in 1963. Kelly then hired T. D. Harden to be Chattanooga's first professionally trained planner, and gained voter approval for a ballot measure that increased the city and county sales tax and earmarked the revenue to fund a joint city/county planning agency as well as other joint city/county agencies.

- The ability of planning to have a major impact in terms of shaping the urban landscape of San Diego was greatly increased when Pete Wilson was elected mayor in 1971 and threw the full weight of his office behind the development of plans and policies to manage peripheral growth and revitalize downtown San Diego. Conversely, the demise of planning in San Diego in the 1990s occurred at a time of greatly diminished executive support for planning.

- Few mayors in this country have been more visible and steadfast in their support of planning than Charleston's Joseph P. Riley, and more willing to take on opposing interests in defense of recommended planning regulations and strategies. His strong and unwavering support of planning is undoubtedly a major reason why planning has been able to produce such impressive results in that city. Indeed, Riley has identified and involved himself with the planning of his city so much that, when he spoke to the

South Carolina APA Chapter in July 1994, he began his speech by saying, "I feel that I am one of you." (Knack, September 1994, 21)

- Between 1983 and 1997, the 14-year period during which many of the planning efforts which transformed Chattanooga were undertaken, Gene Roberts was mayor of Chattanooga.[1] The message here is not necessarily that re-electing incumbent mayors, and keeping the same individual as mayor for a long time, is always beneficial to a city. It is simply to say that if we want planning to succeed, and want people who run for elected office to speak out in support of planning, mayors who have supported planning must be able to gain re-election and not be voted out of office. It can take years for planning to produce readily discernible positive results. The chances that planning can produce positive results are therefore greatly increased when mayors who have encouraged and supported planning (as Gene Roberts did) have their positions validated and reinforced by the electorate. In Robert's case, he was re-elected enough times that he remained in office long enough to see many of the planning efforts that were launched during his first years as mayor bear fruit.

- In the two case-study communities with a city manager form of government, city managers Chris Cherches (Wichita) and Bill Christopher (Westminster) were extremely supportive of planning, and helped deflect a good deal of the political pressure that otherwise could have impaired the work of planning staff members who worked under them. The fact that Cherches and Christopher were so supportive of planning and held their positions for a fairly long period of time was clearly a positive factor. When I traveled to Westminster and Wichita in 1998, Bill Christopher had been Westminster's city manager for 20 years and Chris Cherches had been Wichita's city manager for 12 years. The extent to which Bill Christopher deflected criticism away from the city's planning staff, and kept people focused on issues, is particularly noteworthy. When people associated with the development industry would complain about various planning requirements and development standards, Christopher did not allow the city's planning staff to take the brunt of the criticisms. Instead, he would bring developers, realtors, builders and members of the city council into his office and ask them simple questions like, "Do you really want to go back to the way things were?" After these kinds of sessions, people usually came away agreeing that development was being managed better than in the past and they didn't want to turn back the clock.

A Culture of Planning

As of 2001, roughly one-fifth of all states in the U.S. have adopted legislation either encouraging or requiring local governments to prepare comprehensive plans; in some of those states, the legislation also includes a requirement that local plans be reviewed at a higher level to assure their consistency with other local plans and with county, regional and statewide planning goals. Nevertheless, in the vast majority of states, the question of whether or not there is any planning is left entirely up to local governments. There is no requirement that plans be prepared (and no incentive for engaging in planning), and no requirement that local governments make an honest attempt to implement and adhere to their plans. The fact that most local governments are quite small in land area and have very small populations, with relatively small budgets, have also been factors which have discouraged local governments from investing in planning.

For all these reasons, a large proportion of local governments have never employed a full-time professional planner or planning consultant. Moreover, in a large proportion of towns and villages (and even small cities) that have established full-time planning offices, the local planning office is a one-person operation. Having personally known many planners who have worked in such one-person planning offices, and having worked in a very small planning office myself, I know how lonely it can feel. Trying to plan in such situations, without the support and encouragement of other professional colleagues, and in the absence of much overt citizen support, requires a great deal of inner strength and courage. A lone planner speaking out about the importance of long-term thinking, when everyone else is talking and worrying about things that are happening right now, can feel very much like the proverbial "voice in the wilderness."

One of the important lessons to be learned from the planning stories in this book is that, when planning succeeds in American communities, it is rarely because of the efforts of just one person, or even a handful of people, and is rarely confined to just the staff of the city's planning department.

- In the story of Providence, a remarkable cast of characters played leading roles in planning for the College Hill neighborhood and the city's adjoining downtown area: Lachlan F. Blair, Antoinette F. Downing, William D. Warner, Marilyn Taylor, Pete Pointner, Samuel J. Shamoon and various members of the faculty of the RISD. Equally important roles in the planning of Providence were played by Ken Ornstein and Robert E. Freeman when they directed the Providence Foundation; by the College Hill residents who came together to form the Providence Preservation Society; citizens like Tina Regan who became active in the work of the society and served on the Downcity Design Review Committee; and many, many others.

- In Madison, planning for bicycle and pedestrian transportation and safety was carried out in the city's transportation department, while parks and open space planning was carried out in the Parks Division of the Department of Public Works.

- In Wichita, responsibility for coordinating projects related to the implementation of the $100 million Core Area Initiative, and for reviewing and approving the design of all publicly funded projects, was delegated to the downtown development coordinator in the city engineer's office.
- In San Diego, the MTDB and the San Diego Housing Commission (two agencies not normally thought of as planning agencies) did a great deal of planning, and worked closely with the staff of the city's planning department to coordinate plans for specific housing developments and transit stations with the city's land use plans and policies.
- William D. Warner's plan for minimizing the negative impacts of highway traffic on downtown Providence and for restoring the city's connection to its waterfront might not have become a reality had not Bob Bendick (director of the RIDEM) supported the idea of a comprehensive planning study and worked with Warner on a grant application to the NEA to fund the study. Joseph Arruda (head of the planning division of the RIDOT) also played a key role in enabling the Memorial Boulevard Extension/River Relocation plan to become a reality by authorizing a separate EIS to be conducted on the project—a move that enabled the project to obtain fast-track approval and to be coordinated with the Capital Center project, which was already under construction.

In practically every one of the case-study communities, a culture of planning developed that, in fact, encouraged large numbers of people who never thought of themselves as "planners" (such as citizens and neighborhood residents, business leaders, property owners, preservationists, environmentalists and college teachers) to participate in planning processes and to feel that they had an important stake in seeing positive, concrete outcomes come about as a result.

- In Chattanooga, more than 2,000 citizens came together in the *Vision 2000* planning process, which produced a Portfolio of Commitments to provide the framework for an action agenda that guided that city over a period of years.
- In the case study of Block Island (Rhode Island) by Philip B. Herr & Associates, the real planners were the citizens of that island who came together to develop plans and strategies for managing the pressures of growth and change.

Private Sector Support for Planning

Having support for planning from the private sector was also a crucial ingredient to the success of planning.

- The initial impetus for cleaning up Chattanooga's foul air and environmental problems came from the private business community. The preparation of the 1967 Better Environment plan for Chattanooga and

Hamilton County was overseen by the chairperson of the Beautification Committee of the chamber of commerce. Key funding for planning, and for the implementation of key planning initiatives and projects related to the revitalization of downtown Chattanooga, came from the private Lyndhurst Foundation.

- In Wichita, the impetus for developing a plan for downtown Wichita came from the WI/SE Partnership for Growth, composed primarily of the heads and representatives of local businesses, banks and other private-sector interests as well as local government representatives. Further evidence of the degree of private-sector support for the development of a plan came when Wichita entrepreneur Jack DeBoer stepped forward and paid for the preparation of an alternative plan that was even more ambitious and costly than the first plan, which had the effect of encouraging the city and county to commit an even larger amount of public funding to plan implementation than they might otherwise have been willing to approve.

- Much of the impetus for preparing a master plan for the City Heights neighborhood in San Diego came from a private, nonprofit development corporation.

An Asset-Based Approach to Planning

Rather than focusing on problems, the eight cities I studied chose to take an *asset-based* approach to planning. In the course of thinking about what they wanted their communities to be like in the future, they thought long and hard about the qualities and assets that made their cities special and that contributed to a unique sense of place and identity. They translated their analyses into plans and policies aimed at protecting and enhancing those distinctive qualities and assets.

The preservation and protection of historic and architectural resources was a central aim of planning in Charleston, but I found equally important examples of an asset-based approach to planning in the other communities:

- In Chattanooga, the resource planning focused on protecting and enhancing was the Tennessee River.

- In Duluth, the asset that planning sought to preserve and enhance was the city's waterfront.

- An asset-based approach to planning was also clearly evident in San Diego, where plans were developed calling for preserving networks of open space within the many canyons and valleys crisscrossing the city, and for preserving coastal areas primarily for recreation and public enjoyment.

Willingness to Say "No" to Proposed Developments

Planning is about making choices regarding where development should and should not occur. To have the process of making such choices mean anything, communities must be willing to say "no" to proposed developments that are contrary to publicly stated planning objectives and the goals and objectives articulated in approved plans.

In practically every one of these case studies, there were key instances when communities had the courage and confidence to say "no" to developments that might have been acceptable and even desirable in certain locations, but which conflicted with plans and planning objectives for specific areas.

- As Duluth's real estate market contracted and the city's population declined, builders and real estate interests continued to want to build new houses in rugged, semi-wilderness areas unconnected to existing neighborhoods. To discourage and counter that trend, land use regulations were developed and adopted, and procedures were put into place, that enabled the city's planning commission to secure tax-title property for conservation. In the Duluth parkway system, these actions, over time, added to, expanded and helped secure the extraordinary greenbelt and park system that provides the backdrop and setting for Duluth's many distinct neighborhoods and downtown area.

- The most obvious place that developers thought of building hotels in Charleston was along the city's waterfront. However, planning studies concluded that it would be an undesirable outcome for two reasons: (1) such high-rise hotels would obstruct public access and views of the water; and (2) locating hotels along the waterfront would undermine the commercial core of the city along King Street. Acting on the recommendations of these planning studies, areas closest to the water were zoned for low-density development. When developers proposed to develop large-scale hotels along the waterfront, the city refused to approve them, and closed the door to future proposals by publicly acquiring key parcels on and close to the water for parks and walkways.

- City officials in Charleston said "no" to the idea of converting the Francis Marion Hotel into student housing for the College of Charleston, even though the hotel had stood vacant for a number of years, because it was felt that a much better outcome would be for the hotel to be renovated and reopened as a hotel—an outcome that was eventually realized.

- The first (and in many ways, the most) important step toward realizing Westminster's City Center Marketplace project was taken when planners in the city's DCD, with the backing of the city manager and city council, said "no" to an ugly but potentially lucrative proposed highway-oriented, "big-box" development. The planning process that produced the Westminster Promenade, which defines the city's new city center, also

came about because city planners said "no" to a proposed suburban-style, multiscreen theater complex.
- The Town of Burlington (Massachusetts) turned down a proposal to develop a huge "big-box" store on a vacant industrial site.
- In perhaps the most remarkable turn of events of all, a majority of voters in Duluth (a city that had been losing population and jobs for years, where voters could possibly be forgiven for feeling the need to say "yes" to anything that came their way) voted "no" to the idea of bringing the battleship USS Des Moines to the Duluth waterfront.

Committed to Implementation

The planners whom I got to know in my research were not simply dreamers. They were pragmatic in their approach to planning, and worked diligently and creatively to find ways to translate plans into reality.

The communities whose stories I've told didn't prepare plans because they thought it would just be nice to have them. They prepared plans because they intended to use them as the basis for making choices about where development should and should not occur, and about the types and densities of development that were appropriate in different areas.

Once the plans were prepared, they developed and adopted land use regulations and policies consistent with the public purposes stated in those plans. They were also extremely creative and enterprising in identifying sources of public and private funding to implement plans, and in coming up with innovative ways of paying for proposed projects and improvements. In both Providence and Duluth, planners came up with creative ways of using federal and state highway funding programs to fund pedestrian-oriented improvements and amenities.

A number of the case-study communities established new public/private institutional entities capable of implementing key plan elements and provided substantial amounts of funding to those entities.
- In Chattanooga, the city created the RiverCity Company—a quasi-public, nonprofit corporation for the purpose of implementing land use and development recommendations contained in the 1985 Riverpark master plan, and provided a good deal of the funding that the company needed to fulfill its charge.
- The planning commitments endorsed during Chattanooga's *Vision 2000* process, related to the development of affordable housing and the revitalization of city neighborhoods, led to the creation of another nonprofit corporation (CNE), which received public funds from the city as well as from other sources.
- San Diego created CCDC to plan and coordinate the implementation of a multifaceted plan for the revitalization of downtown San Diego.

- The planning objectives set out in Westminster's comprehensive park, open space and recreation plan were achieved because voters in Westminster approved a sales tax increase to establish a dedicated fund for open space acquisition. Westminster's City Center Marketplace project was realized because the city did more than just reject a bad plan for the site. It hired outside planners and designers at public expense to help the developer come up with an approvable project site plan and project design. When the cost estimates of the project increased as the site plan and project design became more elaborate and unique, the city agreed to rebate sales tax revenue generated by the project up to an agreed-upon amount to help offset the additional costs associated with the redesigned project.

- The City of Wichita went to even more extraordinary lengths to get a downtown hotel built next to its expanded convention center. The city itself actually financed the construction of the hotel and then contracted with the Hyatt Hotel chain to operate the hotel. The city also provided city-owned land for the development of Exploration Place and assumed the cost of relocating a major highway to improve the site.

- When extensive subsurface soil contamination was discovered in downtown Wichita (threatening to derail implementation of the city's downtown revitalization plan), local government officials and planners came up with the novel idea of locally financing much of the cost of the environmental cleanup by means of TIF—a solution that avoided the cumbersome and time-consuming process of having the downtown area declared a federal Superfund site.

- When voters in Westminster failed to approve a bond issue to build a planned new city library, the city's planning staff went back to the drawing board and came up with a new and less costly way of accomplishing the same goal. They devised an innovative plan which called for the city and Front Range Community College to join together in developing a library that could be used both by residents of the city and students of the college.

- An impressive example of the persistence and ingenuity that is often required to be able to translate plans into reality is the incredible 59-year-long planning saga of Monona Terrace in Madison. Three successive plans for Monona Terrace were developed by Frank Lloyd Wright between 1938 and 1959—the last plan being completed one month before Wright died—but each of these plans fell by the wayside. Thirty-one years after Wright's death, another effort was undertaken to resurrect Wright's Monona Terrace plan. In 1997, the doors of Monona Terrace finally opened, the project having been realized through a combination of city, county, state and private funding.

Thinking Big and Paying Attention to Details

While in San Diego researching the difference that planning had made there, I attended a conference on the morning of July 16, 1998 at the Embarcadero Planning Center on the future of San Diego's waterfront. The program featured four guest speakers, including Helene Fried, whose presentation was titled "What makes a place authentic?" Ms. Fried (a planning consultant based in San Francisco and a member of the consultant team that prepared the master plan for Wichita's Water Walk) said that the key to successful planning and to making places authentic lies in being able to come up with a "big idea"—a concept that encapsulates and communicates what is truly special and unique about a particular place. As she was speaking, I was reminded of some of the cities whose stories I was uncovering.

- The "big idea" on which the Duluth waterfront, Canal Park and Downtown Lakewalk plans were based was the idea that what made Duluth special and unique was its "working waterfront."

- In Chattanooga, the "big idea" was the importance of reconnecting the city to the river.

Helene Fried said something else that morning in San Diego that also seems to have been corroborated by these case studies: "What I've learned over the years is that it's the big thing that attracts people initially, but it's the *little* things that create a positive experience and that keep people coming back." Looking back at the case studies, one can find a good deal of evidence that the eight communities I studied paid a good deal of attention to detail. The following come to mind:

- the art and sculpture in the Canal Park area and the design details of the Downtown Lakewalk (Duluth)

- the many design features and amenities that make Waterfront Park such a wonderfully enjoyable place (Charleston)

- the quality of design and construction of utilitarian public structures like parking garages (Charleston)

- the extraordinary design of the serpentine walkway leading down from the Bluff View Art District to the Tennessee Riverwalk (Chattanooga)

- the exquisite design details added to the bridges spanning the Arkansas River (Wichita)

- the elaborate design details incorporated throughout the City Center Marketplace and the Promenade (Westminster)

- the Martin Luther King, Jr. Promenade to Children's Park (San Diego)

- the care that went into designing individual and distinctive bridges along the uncovered and relocated rivers in downtown Providence

The Important Role of the Media

At the beginning of this book, I reflected on how my interest in city planning, and my decision to train and work as an urban planner, were influenced by the books and magazine articles that were published during the years I was in high school and college. Thinking back to how my own attitudes toward planning had been shaped by the media, I was interested to examine the role that the local media in the case-study communities played in informing citizens about ongoing planning processes and in encouraging them to view planning efforts in a positive light.

The way local newspapers and local television stations portrayed local planning efforts, and their detailed and in-depth coverage of local land use and development issues, does appear to have been a key ingredient to successful planning.

- The coverage that *The Chattanooga Times* gave to planning, land use and development issues, and to planning processes such as the *Vision 2000* process and the 1997 Futurescape visual preference survey, was particularly informative and supportive of planning. According to people I interviewed in Chattanooga, the detailed coverage that local television stations provided of the six-month-long *Vision 2000* process was also extremely helpful in encouraging large numbers of Chattanoogans to participate in the process, and in getting many others who did not personally participate to follow its progress and to take its results seriously.

- In San Diego, articles and columns by Roger M. Showley in *The San Diego Union-Tribune* continually reminded San Diego readers of the city's rich planning legacy and of the need for continued planning if the qualities that made San Diego such a paradise were to endure.

- In Charleston, the columns of Robert Behre (a regular feature in *The Post and Courier*) kept readers well informed regarding development issues and projects that were being reviewed by city planners and the city's BAR.

- The extent and quality of the *Duluth News-Tribune*'s coverage of planning and development issues was particularly noteworthy. Among the materials I gathered from Duluth, I have photocopies of a number of lengthy news articles focusing on various planning issues, as well as copies of guest columns by people expressing opposing points of view. The balanced and informative coverage the *Duluth News-Tribune* gave to issues and controversies related to land use planning and development issues went a long way toward creating the kind of informed and engaged citizenry that increased the chances that the principles planners in Duluth were articulating and defending would be heard and eventually win public support.

- Prior to the referendum that was held to decide whether the USS Des Moines should be brought to permanently reside at the Duluth waterfront, the *Duluth News-Tribune* sent a team of reporters to analyze and report on the experiences of other cities where decommissioned navy ships had been put on permanent display. Due in large part to the resulting newspaper articles, a majority of Duluth voters rejected the idea of bringing the Des Moines to Duluth.

Unfortunately, more and more locally owned newspapers have been acquired by national newspaper chains that are much less inclined to invest the amount of time and effort required to provide in-depth, high-quality local news coverage. The rise and growing ubiquitousness of *USA Today* (which distributes the same newspaper everywhere in the U.S.) is a good example of this trend. (In a gesture toward providing news with a local flavor, *USA Today* devotes roughly a half page of each issue to a single news item, usually no more than a paragraph long, from each of the 50 states.)

The number of people who watch locally produced news programs on local television stations is also declining, making it even more difficult for citizens to be well informed about local land use and development issues. Noting these trends, and the importance that local newspaper and television coverage played in enabling Chattanooga's *Vision 2000* to capture public attention, Ron Littlefield honestly wondered whether, if the same *Vision 2000* process were undertaken today, it would be anywhere as successful as the one that was undertaken back in 1984.

The declining presence and importance of local newspapers and television stations is certainly not making the task of keeping local citizens informed and involved in planning any easier. However, even in places with little or no newspaper coverage of local planning issues, there are other outlets available.

- In Westminster (a community that does not have a newspaper of its own), the city has made an effort to keep citizens informed by publishing a bimonthly newspaper called *City Edition*, which is sent to every residence and business in the city—approximately 35,000 in all.[2] In a 1997 issue of *City Edition*, citizens were provided with a summary draft of the proposed comprehensive plan in advance of a public hearing on the plan. *City Edition*'s summer 1998 issue included a lengthy story about the Promenade project then under construction. Other stories in *City Edition* have informed citizens about the planning of Legacy Ridge, Westmoor Business Park and Golf Course, and the Westminster/Front Range Community College Public Library. Westminster also publishes and distributes a biweekly newsletter called *City-Link* to business leaders, city council members, members of city boards and committees, the press and other key opinion leaders.

- City governments, like those in San Diego, Westminster and Providence, and public/private entities like CCDC in San Diego and the RiverCity Company in Chattanooga, have developed informative Web sites that provide an excellent source of up-to-date information on planning activities and initiatives.
- Local cable television station coverage of special planning processes like charettes and visioning sessions, and public meetings at which land use and development issues are discussed, provides an excellent way of keeping people informed and involved.

You've Got to Believe

One of the most important ingredients for successful planning is for people to *believe* that planning matters—that taking the time to try to think through and envision the kind of places we want our communities to be in the future is important, and that time spent developing plans aimed at fulfilling our deepest aspirations is not wasted. If we are skeptical about the likelihood that projects and improvements envisioned in plans will ever be realized, we are much less likely to take planning seriously. When we don't take the plans we prepare seriously, we undermine the ability of planning to bring about positive

Inspirational message incorporated in public art on the pedestrian bridge leading to and from the Uptown District in San Diego.

Source: Gene Bunnell

change. Indeed, an inability to believe in planning, and in the possibilities for translating plans into reality, can itself become a major impediment to successful planning.

- At one point, the plan that had been developed for the proposed Tennessee State Aquarium in Chattanooga (an outgrowth of the plan for the Tennessee Riverwalk) seemed hopelessly stymied. Critics of the project were emboldened by increased doubts as to whether enough money would be able to be raised to finance its $40 million cost. Had those doubts led city and private-sector leaders to retreat in fear, and put the project on hold until all the money was in, the project might have fallen by the wayside. Instead, they launched a well-publicized "ground-breaking" ceremony, after which the public controversy that had surrounded the project dissipated and the money needed for the project magically appeared.

FINAL THOUGHTS

The case studies in this book take the planning stories of 10 communities up to a certain point in time. Events in these communities are obviously continuing to unfold.

Please do not make the mistake of assuming that, as the events chronicled in these chapters recede more and more into the past, these stories somehow become less relevant and instructive. The events and outcomes described in these case studies may have happened in the past, but the people who were major participants in these unfolding planning processes lived and experienced those unfolding events very much *in the present*; the doubts, fears, hopes and uncertainties they felt at the time are very much the same as we would feel today confronting new and as yet unsolved planning problems.

It is tempting to think that today's issues are more complex and difficult than those in the past, but people have always thought that is the case. Each time people engage in planning, there is always a sense that the issues being confronted and addressed are not only different and unique, but more difficult to solve than those any community has ever faced before.

Another mistake would be to believe that the planning outcomes documented in these case studies were somehow inevitable (or, if not inevitable, then not that hard to bring about). These case studies have been written as stories, rather than in the traditional form that case studies usually take, to specifically dispel that notion. The story lines in the case studies continually remind readers of the doubts and uncertainties that surrounded various planning efforts that eventually proved successful.

There is yet one other reason for writing these accounts in the form of stories: to enable readers to sense the satisfaction that people feel when they look back years later and realize that something wonderful has been accomplished by planning . . . something greater than people ever thought possible at the outset. In that aspect, these stories should never lose their ability to communicate valuable lessons about the meaning of planning and its benefits.

NOTES

1. Between 1983 and 1989, Chattanooga still had a commission form of government, and Roberts held his office by virtue of being elected by a majority of the members of the city commission. In 1990 (the year that Chattanooga changed to a mayor-council form of government), Roberts became the city's first popularly elected mayor. He was subsequently re-elected and continued in office until 1997, providing political leadership and support that was extremely helpful to maintaining the momentum of the city's ongoing planning effort.

2. Westminster newspaper readers must depend on Denver newspapers for their news, and those papers rarely cover local public affairs and planning in Westminster.

References

Adler, Jerry. 1993. *High Rise.* New York: HarperCollins.

AIA Cleveland Chapter of the American Institute of Architects. 1997. *Guide to Cleveland Architecture.* Cleveland, OH: Cleveland Chapter of the American Institute of Architects, p. 16.

American Architectural Foundation. 1996. *Back From the Brink: Saving America's Cities by Design.* Washington, DC: American Architectural Foundation. 56-minute VHS videotape describing the experiences of three cities: Chattanooga, Tennessee; Portland, Oregon; and Suisun City, California.

Apple, R. W., Jr. "Pocket-Size Providence, Built of Hope." *The New York Times,* April 24, 1998, pp. B29, B37.

____. "Blessings of a City Beside The Sea." *The New York Times,* September 18, 1998, pp. B29, B38.

____. "A Southern Legacy and a New Spirit." *The New York Times,* November 26, 1999, pp. E37, E45.

Arrandale, Tom. "Wichita, Kansas: The No-Wait Cleanup." *Governing,* October 1992, p. 36.

Austin, George E. and Mark E. Appell. 1995. "Profile in Quality: Frank Lloyd Wright's Monona Terrace." *The Total Quality Review.* November/December 1995, pp. 15-19.

Beatley, Timothy and Kristy Manning. 1997. *The Ecology of Place: Planning for Environment, Economy and Community.* Washington, DC: Island Press.

Behre, Robert. "Despite exit, architect has Charleston on his mind." *The Post and Courier,* March 16, 1998, pp. 1-B, 4-B.

Bernick, Michael and Robert Cervero. 1997. *Transit Villages in the 21st Century.* New York: McGraw-Hill.

Blake, Peter. 1964. *God's Own Junkyard.* New York: Holt, Rinehart and Winston.

Bradley, Jeff. 1997. *Tennessee Handbook.* Chico, CA: Moon Publications, Inc.

Brannon, Anthony. "Architecture: Experts Pick the Buffalo Buildings They Like Least, With Surprising Results and Some Fascinating Reasoning." *Buffalo Evening News* (Gusto Magazine section), March 29, 1985, pp. 3, 14.

Bunnell, Gene. 1977. *Built To Last.* Washington, DC: The Preservation Press, National Trust for Historic Preservation.

Calavita, Nico. "Vale of Tiers." *Planning,* March 1997, pp. 18-21.

Calavita, Nico and Kenneth Grimes. 1992. "The Establishment of the San Diego Housing Trust Fund: Lessons for Theory and Practice," *Journal of Planning Education and Research* 11:170-184.

Cameron, Robert, with text by Neil Morgan. 1991. *Above San Diego.* San Francisco, CA: Cameron and Company.

Campbell, Robert. "Memo to the Mayor on City Hall: Fix it, don't forsake it." *The Boston Globe,* April 10, 1998, pp. A1, B8.

Campbell, Robert and Peter Vanderwarker. *Cityscapes of Boston: An American City Through Time.* Boston, MA: Houghton Mifflin Co.

Carrier, Lynne. "San Diego: Looking to the Future." In *Imagine a Great City— Drafting a 'Working Vision' for San Diego.* A publication prepared for a San Diego Planning Commission Workshop, July 23, 1998.

Citizens Coordinate for Century Three (C3). 1995. *Toward Permanent Paradise.*

Citizens Coordinate for Century Three. *C3 News.* December 1996/January 1997, pp. 1-7.

City of Charleston, South Carolina, Finance Division of the Department of Administrative Services. "Comprehensive Annual Financial Report for the Year Ended December 31, 1996."

City of Duluth, Department of Research and Planning (Gerald M. Kimball, editor). 1974. *Duluth's Legacy—Architecture, Volume 1.* Duluth, MN: City of Duluth.

City of Duluth Department of Research and Planning (Charles Aguar, author and Gerald M. Kimball, editor). 1977. *Duluth's Legacy, Volume 2, Urban Wilderness.* Duluth, MN: City of Duluth (unpublished).

City of Duluth, Physical Planning Division. 1989. *The Historic Zenith Industrial District—The Development of Canal Park.*

City of Madison, Department of Planning and Development and Urban Design Commission. 1985. *Urban Design—Guidelines for Downtown Madison.* Madison, WI: City of Madison, Department of Planning and Development.

Clark, Jayne. "Charleston Shuffle—Y'all come back? This cradle of Southern hospitality is having some second thoughts." *USA Today,* May 14, 1999, pp. 1D-2D.

Clay, Grady. 1973. *Close-Up: How to Read the American City.* Chicago, IL: The University of Chicago Press.

Codrescu, Andrei. 1998. *Hail Babylon—In Search of the American City at the End of the Millennium.* New York: St. Martin's Press.

5

Conley, Patrick T. and Paul Campbell. 1982. *Providence: A Pictorial History.* Norfolk/Virginia Beach, VA: Donning Company.

Corbett, Judith. 1993. "San Diego Gets a Grip on Gridlock—City Ordinance Helps Region Manage Growth." A case study in the Surface Transportation Policy Project Resource Guide. Washington, DC: Surface Transportation Policy Project, pp. 1-6.

Cutri, Anthony G. "The City Heights Urban Village Planning Initiative." Paper presented at the national conference on Livable Cities, Savannah, GA, March 4-8, 2001.

Daniels, Thomas. 1999. *When City and Country Collide.* Washington, DC: Island Press.

Department of Community Affairs, Planning Division, Community Assistance Program, *Town of New Shoreham, Rhode Island: Inventory and Analysis*, 1968, p. 2.

Dillon, David. "Providence Renewed." *American Way,* May 1990, pp. 46-50.

Dorius, Noah. "Land Use Negotiation: Reducing Conflict and Creating Wanted Land Uses," *Journal of the American Planning Association*, Vol. 59, No. 1, Winter 1993.

Downing, Antoinette F. and Vincent J. Scully, Jr. 1952. *The Architectural Heritage of Newport, Rhode Island: 1640-1915.* Cambridge, MA: Harvard University Press.

____. 1967. *The Architectural Heritage of Newport, Rhode Island: 1640-1915* (Second edition, revised and expanded). New York: C. N. Potter.

Downing Antoinette Forrester; drawings by Helen Mason Grose. 1937. *Early Homes of Rhode Island.* Richmond, VA: Garrett and Massie.

Duluth Heritage Preservation Commission. 1997. *Jewel of the North: Duluth's Parkway System, A Historic Landscape Evaluation Study.*

Dunphy, Robert T. "Transportation-Oriented Development: Making a Difference? *Urban Land,* July 1995, pp. 32-48.

Editorial, *The Chattanooga Times.* "Futurescape results describe community's vision for its future." December 26, 1997, p. A10.

Editorial, *The New York Times.* "The Last Freeway." August 22, 2001, p. A18.

Eisen, Marc. "The end of an era—George Austin leaves a rich legacy as the city's top planner." *Madison Isthmus*, September 18, 1998, pp. 5-6.

Elazar, Daniel J. "Constitutional Change in a Long-Depressed Community: A Case Study of Duluth, Minnesota." *Journal of The Minnesota Academy of Science.* Vol. 33:1 (1965), pp. 49-66.

____. 1970. *Cities of the Prairie—The Metropolitan Frontier and American Politics.* New York: Basic Books.

____. 1986. *Cities of the Prairie Revisited—The Closing of the Metropolitan Frontier.* Lincoln, NE: University of Nebraska Press.

Ericson, Jody. "Island of Hope," *Nature Conservancy,* January/February 1992, pp. 14-21.

Feiss, Carl. "Taking Stock: A Resume of Planning Accomplishments in the United States." In *Environment and Change—The Next Fifty Years* (William R. Ewald, Jr., editor). Bloomington, IN: Indiana University Press, 1968, pp. 214-236.

Flint, Anthony. "Menino's goal: Go replace City Hall," *The Boston Globe*, April 9, 1995, pp. A1, A24.

Frederick, Chuck. 1994. *Duluth—The City and The People*. Helena, MT: American & World Geographic Publishing.

Frieden, Bernard J. and Lynne B. Segalyn. 1990. *Downtown, Inc.—How America Rebuilds Cities*. Cambridge, MA: M.I.T. Press.

Fulton, William. 1991. *Guide to California Planning*. Point Arena, CA: Solano Press Books.

Gallagher, Mary Lou. "SRO's in San Diego—A small room at the inn." *Planning,* June 1993, pp. 20-25.

Garreau, Joel. 1991. *Edge City—Life on the New Frontier*. New York: Doubleday.

Garvin, Alexander. 1996. *The American City—What Works, What Doesn't*. New York: McGraw Hill.

Glaser, Mark and Chris Cherches. "A Case for Aggressive Local Government Environmental Policy." *National Civic Review,* Spring 1991, pp. 169-174.

____. "Local Government's Role in Groundwater Cleanup—Preempting Superfund and Protecting the Local Economy." *Public Management*, 74:2, pp. 4-10.

Gottmann, Jean. 1964. *Megalopolis: The Urbanized Northeastern Seaboard of the United States*. Cambridge, MA: M.I.T. Press.

Govan, Gilbert E. and James W. Livingood. 1952. *The Chattanooga Country 1540-1951—From Tomahawks to TVA*. New York: E. P. Dutton and Company, Inc.

Grant, Lorrie and Kara K. Choquette. "Strong economy, low rates fuel coast-to-coast frenzy." *USA Today,* April 7, 1998, p. 1A.

Gratz, Roberta Grandes with Norman Mintz. 1998. *Cities Back From the Edge—new life for downtown*. New York: John Wiley & Sons, Inc.

Grogan, Paul and Tony Proscio. 2000. *Comeback Cities—A Blueprint for Urban Neighborhood Revival*. Boulder, CO: Westview Press.

Guinther, John. 1996. *The Direction of Cities*. New York: Penguin Books.

Gunther, John. 1947. *Inside U.S.A*. New York: Harper and Brothers.

Hall, Peter. 1975. *Urban and Regional Planning*. London: George Allen and Unwin.

____. 1982. *Great Planning Disasters*. Berkeley and Los Angeles, CA: University of California Press.

Hammerschlag, Dieter. 1963. "A Tale of Two Cities: College Hill and Downtown Providence 1970." *AIA Journal*, November 1963, pp. 35-43.

Hancock, John. 1996. "'Smokestacks and Geraniums'—Planning and Politics in San Diego." In *Planning the Twentieth-Century American City* (Mary Corbin

Sies and Christopher Silver, editors). Baltimore, MD: The Johns Hopkins University Press.

Hertzel, Laurie. 1993. *Boomtown Landmarks.* Duluth, MN: Pfeifer-Hamilton.

Historic Preservation Plan, Charleston, South Carolina. City Planning and Architectural Associates, Russell Wright, Carl Feiss and the National Heritage Corporation, June 1974.

Honan, William H. "Duluth Finds a Key To the Global Economy, And Cultural Ties, Too." *The New York Times,* July 8, 2000, pp. C1, C4.

Hund-Milne, Susan, editor. *Spotlight on Wichita '98—Guide and Reference Book to Greater Wichita.* Wichita, KS: Advanced Publishing, L.C.

Huxtable, Ada Louise. 1970. *Will They Ever Finish Bruckner Boulevard?* New York: The MacMillan Company.

Hylton, Thomas. 1995. *Save Our Land, Save Our Towns—A Plan for Pennsylvania.* Harrisburg, PA: Richly Beautiful Books.

Isserman, Andrew M. "Dare to Plan." *Town Planning Review.* 1985. Vol. 56, No. 4, pp. 483-491.

Jacobs, Allan. 1980. *Making City Planning Work.* Chicago, IL: APA Planners Press.

Jacobs, Jane. 1961. *The Death and Life of Great American Cities.* New York: Random House.

Jacobson, Louis. "Tennessee Triumph." *Planning,* May 1997, pp. 20-22.

Jensen, Peter. "San Diego's Vision Quest." *Planning,* March 1997, pp. 5-11.

Kelly, Eric Damian. 1993. *Managing Community Growth—Policies, Techniques and Impacts.* Westport, CT: Praeger Publishers.

Kimball, Gerald M. "Duluth can secure its future by retaining past, character." *Duluth News-Tribune,* September 23, 1995.

____. "Don't tip planning balance toward Develop-Above-All." *Duluth News-Tribune,* January 31, 1998.

Knack, Ruth Eckdish. "Charleston at a Crossroads." *Planning,* September 1994, pp. 21-26.

Kouwenhoven, John A. 1961. *The Beer Can By the Highway—Essays on What's American about America.* Baltimore, MD: The Johns Hopkins University Press.

Kunstler, James Howard. 1993. *Geography of Nowhere.* New York: Simon and Schuster.

____. 1996. *Home From Nowhere.* New York: Simon and Schuster.

Kuralt, Charles. 1995. *Charles Kuralt's America.* New York: G. P. Putnam's Sons.

Larrabee, John. "Providence, R.I., comes back with 'pizazz,'" *USA Today,* December 30, 1998, p. 8A.

Leopold, Aldo. 1949. *a Sand County almanac.* London: Oxford University Press.

Lincoln, Craig. "Powerful, controversial official retires." *Duluth News-Tribune,* February 19, 1995, pp. 1B, 2B.

Lindsey, Greg. "Commentary on Our Relationship with the Earth: Environmental Ethics in Planning Education." *Journal of Planning Education and Research*, Fall 1993, 13:1, pp. 54-56.

Longo, Gianni. 1996. *A Guide to Great American Public Places.* New York: Urban Initiatives.

Lundberg, Kristin. "Mayor Joseph P. Riley, Charleston, South Carolina: The Politics of Preservation." Harvard University, Kennedy School of Government Case Program, Case C16-89-905.0

Lynch, Kevin. 1960. *The Image of the City.* Cambridge, MA: M.I.T. Press.

____. 1972. *What Time Is This Place?* Cambridge, MA: M.I.T. Press.

____. 1980. *Managing the Sense of a Region.* Cambridge, MA: M.I.T. Press.

Madison Metro Planning and Scheduling Unit. 1997. "Madison Metro Transfer Point System—Metro Rethinks, Revises, Restructures, The History 1989-1997."

Madison Newspapers, Incorporated. 1997. (Margo O'Brien Hokanson, editor) *Monona Terrace—Frank Lloyd Wright's Vision on the Lake.* Madison, WI: Madison Newspapers.

Mangin, Daniel, editor. 1996. *Fodors '97 San Diego.* New York: Fodors Travel Publications, Inc.

Master Plan for Arkansas Riverbank Improvements and McLean Boulevard, Wichita Kansas. Prepared by McCluggage VanSickle & Perry; LDR International; Savoy, Ruggles and Bohm; Roy Mann Associates; and Helene Fried Associates (August 1996).

McKenzie, Evan. 1994. *Privatopia—Homeowner Associations and the Rise of Residential Private Government.* New Haven, CT: Yale University Press.

Metropolitan Transit Development Board, San Diego. 1993. *Cities in the Balance: Creating the Transit-Friendly Environment.* Videotape (time 23:45).

____. July 1993. *Designing for Transit—A Manual for Integrating Public Transportation and Land Development in the San Diego Metropolitan Area.*

Miner, Craig. 1988. *Wichita—The Magic City: An Illustrated History.* Wichita, KS: Wichita-Sedgwick County Historical Museum Association.

Mollenhoff, David V. 1982. *Madison: A History of the Formative Years.* Dubuque, IA: Kendall/Hunt Publishing Co.

Mollenhoff, David V. and Mary Jane Hamilton. 1999. *Frank Lloyd Wright's Monona Terrace: The Enduring Power of a Civic Vision.* Madison, WI: The University of Wisconsin Press.

Montgomery, Roger. "San Diego—A Southern California Paradise Not Yet Lost." *The Saturday Review,* August 21, 1976, pp. 23-26.

Morris, Philip. "Building a Good Foundation." *Southern Living, Tennessee Living Section,* February 1996, pp. 3 tl-8 tl.

Murphy Communications. 1997. "Frank Lloyd Wright's Last Dream—The Story of Monona Terrace." 46-minute VHS videotape, shown on Discovery Channel.

Murphy, Dick, "A Vision for San Diego in the Year 2020: A City Worthy of Our Affection." City of San Diego State of the City Address, January 8, 2001. www.ci.san-diego.ca.us/mayor

Olbrich Botanical Gardens (undated brochure). "Olbrich Botanical Gardens—A Brief History, 1916-1991."

Olsen, Dale W. and Fred T. Witzig. 1984. "Coming to Grips with a City in Decline: The Role of the City Planning Commission." A paper presented at the 1984 Annual Meeting of the Urban Affairs Association, Portland, Oregon.

Pagano, Michael A. and Ann O'M. Bowman. 1989. "Financing Duluth's Development Programs: Back to the Future." A case study prepared for the Lincoln Institute of Land Policy (Cambridge, MA).

____. 1995. *Cityscapes and Capital: The Politics of Urban Development.* Baltimore, MD: The Johns Hopkins University Press.

Peirce, Neal R. and Robert Guskind. 1993. *Breakthroughs: Re-Creating the American City.* New Brunswick, NJ: Center for Urban Policy Research, Rutgers University.

Pindell, Terry. 1995. *A Good Place to Live—America's Last Migration.* New York: Owl Books, Henry Holt and Co.

Porter, Douglas R. 1997. *Managing Growth in America's Communities.* Washington, DC: Island Press.

Porter, Douglas R., et al. 1996. "Case Study: San Diego, California." *Profiles in Growth Management: An Assessment of Current Programs and Guidelines for Effective Management.* Washington, DC: Urban Land Institute.

Portland Metro/Tri-Met brochure. 1998. "On track to explore: a great place to live" (a field guide to features along Westside MAX).

Poston, Jonathan H. 1997. *The Buildings of Charleston: A Guide to the City's Architecture.* Columbia, SC: University of South Carolina.

Rawls, Jr., Wendell. "City Seeks Share in Growth of Sun Belt." *The New York Times,* July 27, 1980, p. 20.

Reps, John W. 1965. *The Making of Urban America—A History of City Planning in the United States.* Princeton, NJ: Princeton University Press.

Rhode Island Historical Preservation Commission. "Downtown Providence—Statewide Historical Preservation Report P-P-5." May 1981.

Rusk, David. 1993. *Cities Without Suburbs.* Washington, DC: The Woodrow Wilson Center Press.

____. 1999. *Inside Game, Outside Game—Winning Strategies for Saving Urban America.* Washington, DC: Brookings Institution Press.

Sachse, Nancy D. 1974. *A Thousand Ages.* Madison, WI: The University of Wisconsin Arboretum.

Schon, Donald. 1983. *The Reflective Practitioner—How Professionals Think in Action.* New York: Basic Books, Inc.

Scientific American. 1965. *Cities.* New York: Alfred A. Knopf.

Segoe, Ladislas, editor. 1941. *Local Planning Administration.* Chicago, IL: International City Managers' Association.

Showley, Roger M. 1989. Preface to the updated and reprinted *Progress Guide and General Plan* of 1979, as subsequently amended. San Diego, CA: City of San Diego Planning Department.

____. "At a crossroads, planners grope for San Diego solution." *The San Diego Union-Tribune,* September 15, 1991, p. B1.

____. "Traditional city planning? Not in S.D." *The San Diego Union-Tribune,* October 6, 1996, pp. H1, H4.

____. "City launches major revision of master plan." *The San Diego Union-Tribune,* February 13, 1997, pp. B1, B3.

____. "Planners fault McGrory for lessening role." *The San Diego Union-Tribune,* April 10, 1997, pp. B1, B4.

____. "Put planning squarely in the office of the mayor." *The San Diego Union-Tribune,* July 13, 1997, pp. H1, H7.

____. "City's future worth more than pennies." *The San Diego Union-Tribune,* October 26, 1997, pp. H1, H7.

____. "Is return to 'sleepy navy town' the fate of a myopic San Diego?" *The San Diego Union-Tribune,* December 14, 1997, pp. H1, H7.

____. 1999. *San Diego: Perfecting Paradise.* Carlsbad, CA: Heritage Media.

____. "Smarting over growth: Are we masters of our destiny or destruction?" *The San Diego Union-Tribune,* February 28, 1999, p. H1.

____. "NewSchool dean steps down to guide housing policy for agency." *The San Diego Union-Tribune,* August 26, 2001, p. I4.

Siemon, Charles. 1997. "Successful Growth Management Techniques: Observations From the Monkey Cage." *The Urban Lawyer.* Vol. 29, No. 2, pp. 233-250.

Smith, Herbert H. 1991. *Planning America's Communities—Paradise Found? Paradise Lost?* Chicago, IL: Planners Press, American Planning Association.

Smith, Paul Bryan. "Conserving Charleston's Architectural Heritage." *Town Planning Review,* Vol. 50, No. 4 (October 1979), pp. 459-476.

Southworth, Susan and Michael Southworth. 1992. *AIA Guide to Boston.* Old Saybrook, CT: The Globe Pequot Press.

Stepner, Michael. 1997a. "Looking Back: A Short History of San Diego Planning." In *At This Moment: Planning in the San Diego Region—Where we are and where we aren't.* A collection of articles published by the San Diego Section of the American Planning Association for the APA National Conference, San Diego, CA, April 1997.

_____. 1997b. "The Ten Things San Diego Needs to Consider for the Future." *The Planning Journal,* San Diego Section of the American Planning Association (December 1997).

Stepner, Michael and Paul Fiske. 2000. "San Diego and Tijuana." In *Global City Regions—Their emerging forms* (Roger Simmonds and Gary Hack, editors). London: Spon Press.

Stevens, William K. "Conservation Plan for Southern California Could Be Model for Nation," *The New York Times* (National Edition), February 16, 1997, p. 12.

Stoddard, Brooke. 1991. "Providence Rediscovers Its Rivers—and Itself." *Waterfront World Spotlight,* Vol. 16, No. 4 (Fall 1998), pp. 9-11.

Sutro, Dirk. "Righting Wrongs in San Diego." *Planning,* February 2001, p. 23.

WDSE-TV. 1997. *Working Waterfront: A Harbor Portrait.* 73-minute documentary video of the operations of Duluth-Superior Harbor.

Weber, Bruce. "A Cultural Windfall Sets a City Astir." *The New York Times,* November 24, 1998, pp. El, E8.

Whyte, William H. 1968. *The Last Landscape.* New York: Doubleday Anchor Books.

Wichita-Sedgwick County Metropolitan Area Planning Department. *Planning in Wichita-Sedgwick County* (January 1997).

Wille, Lois. 1972. *Forever Open, Clear and Free: The Struggle for Chicago's Lakefront.* Chicago, IL: University of Chicago Press.

Williams, Charles deV. "Charleston Place cornerstone of downtown growth." *The Post and Courier,* February 28, 1999, Sec. 2, p. 8.

WI/SE Education, Entertainment and Construction Initiative. Prepared by Law/ Kingdon, Inc. (Architects, Engineers, Planners) for the Wichita-Sedgwick County Partnership for Growth, Inc. (May 1990).

Witzig, Frederick T. 1979. "The City Planning Commission: How Relevant for Modern City Planning." A paper presented at the 1979 Annual Meeting of the Council of University Institutes for Urban Affairs, Toronto, Ontario.

_____. 1983. "Duluth—Some Population Trends and Some Suggestions for Revitalizing the Planning Process in the City." Manuscript of presentation to the First Session of the Conference on *Future City—Duluth Tomorrow,* March 16, 1983.

Wolff, Jr., Julius. 1976. "The Ships and Duluth." In *Duluth: sketches of the past—a bicentennial collection.* Lydecker and Sommer (editors). Duluth, MN: American Revolution Bicentennial Commission, pp. 143-163.

Woodworth, Steven E. 1998. *Six Armies in Tennessee—The Chickamauga and Chattanooga Campaigns.* Lincoln, NE: University of Nebraska Press.

Wurman, Richard Saul. 1996. *Access San Diego.* New York: Harper Reference.

Wyss, Bob. "She Fights for Heritage—And Wins." *Sunday Providence Journal Magazine,* November 4, 1979, pp. 22-31.

Yates, Stephanie Avnet. 2001. *Frommers San Diego 2001*. Foster City, CA: IDG Books Worldwide, Inc.

Yurko, Chris. "The planner's job should go, panel says," *Daily Hampshire Gazette*, April 6, 1992.

Appendix

CHATTANOOGA, TENNESSEE PROFILE
(Chapter 3 in book and CD-ROM)

Location

Southeast corner of Tennessee, on the Tennessee River,
   just north of the Tennessee/Georgia border
County: Hamilton County
Land area: 118.4 square miles

Population

	City of Chattanooga		Hamilton County	
	Population	**% Change**	**Population**	**% Change**
1960	130,009		237,905	
1970	118,082	−9.2%	255,077	+7.2%
1980	169,626*	+43.6%*	287,740	+12.8%
1990	152,210	−10.9%	285,536	−.07%
2000	155,554	+2.2%	307,896	+7.8%

* The major increase in city population between 1970 and 1980 was not the result of an increase in the number of people living within the city's original boundaries, but rather was brought about by major land annexations.

1990 city racial composition:
   White: 65%
   Black: 34%
   Other: 1%
Population density: 1,539 persons per square mile

Housing

Total number of housing units (1990): 69,593
   % owner-occupied: 43.4%
   % renter-occupied: 44.7%

Form of Government

Mayor-council form of government
    Mayor elected for 4-year term
    9-member city council; council members elected by district

Who Plans?

- *Regional Planning Agency (RPA) of Chattanooga/Hamilton County*
  Total RPA staff (1998): 30
  Total RPA budget (1998): $1.2 million (funded by the City of Chattanooga and
      Hamilton County through sales tax revenue, and by federal transportation
      planning funds)
  Expenditure per capita on planning: $6.58

- *15-member City Planning Commission:* Members largely appointed by the mayor of the
  City of Chattanooga and the county executive for staggered 3-year terms

PROVIDENCE, RHODE ISLAND PROFILE
(Chapter 4 in book and CD-ROM)

Location

51 miles from Boston, MA; 74 miles from Hartford, CT; 183 miles from New York City
County: Providence County
City land area: 18.5 square miles
County land area: 416 square miles
The entire state of Rhode Island is only 1,055 square miles in area.

Population

	City of Providence		State of Rhode Island	
	Population	**% Change**	**Population**	**% Change**
1960	207,498		859,488	
1970	179,116	−14%	949,723	+10.5%
1980	156,804	−12%	947,154	−0.2%
1990	160,728	+2%	1,003,464	+5.9%
2000	173,618	+8%	1,048,319	+4.5%

Population density:
   8,688 persons per square mile (1990)
   9,384 persons per square mile (2000)

Housing

Total number of housing units (1990): 66,794
      % owner-occupied: 36%
      % renter-occupied: 63%
      % single-family detached units: 22%
      % two-family units: 23%
      % three- and four-family units: 31%
      % multifamily units: 21%

Form and Structure of Local Government

Mayor-council form of government
      16 council members, elected by district

Who Plans?

- *Department of Planning and Development, City of Providence*
  Total full-time staff (1998): 55
     Professional staff: 45
     Administration: 10
  Total budget for planning (1998): $716,745 ($4.34 per capita)

- *7-member City Planning Commission:* 5 members of the City Planning Commission
  appointed by the mayor; mayor and city council president ex-officio members,
  and each appoint a designee to represent them on the commission

CHARLESTON, SOUTH CAROLINA PROFILE
(Chapter 5 in book and CD-ROM)

Location

Southeast coast of South Carolina
114 miles from Columbia (the state capital) and 104 miles from Savannah, GA
County: Charleston County
City land area (1996): 88.8 square miles

From 1848 until 1960, the corporate limits of Charleston remained fixed, and encompassed only 5.71 square miles (the originally settled area of the Charleston peninsula). Between 1960 and 1996, areas totaling approximately 82 square miles were annexed by the city, bringing the city's total land area to almost 89 square miles.

Population

	City of Charleston		Charleston Metropolitan Area (Standard Metropolitan Statistical Area)	
	Population	% Change	Population	% Change
1970	66,945		330,849	
1980	69,859	+4%	430,346	+30%
1990	80,414	+15%	506,877	+18%
2000	96,650	+20%	549,033	+8%

Population density: 1,088 persons per square mile (2000)

Housing

Total housing units (1990): 34,322
 % owner-occupied: 48%
 % single family: 88%
Median value of an existing owner-occupied home: $140,000 (2000)

Form and Structure of Local Government

Mayor-council form of government
City council composed of 12 alderman elected to staggered 4-year terms, plus the mayor

Who Plans?

- *Charleston Department of Planning and Urban Development**
  Number of staff members (2000)
   Professional staff: 21
   Total staff: 25
  Total annual budget (2000): 1,112,850 ($11.51 per capita)

*In 2000, the Department of Planning and Urban Development was reorganized into two separate departments: the Department of Planning and Neighborhoods (headed by Tim Keane) and the Department of Design, Development and Preservation (headed by Yvonne Fortenberry).

- *Charleston Planning Commission:* 9 citizen members, representing different areas of the city, and having different areas of expertise
- *Charleston Board of Architectural Review:* 7 members

DULUTH, MINNESOTA PROFILE
(Chapter 6 in book and CD-ROM)

Location

Northeast corner of Minnesota, at the very western end of Lake Superior
151 miles northeast of Minneapolis/St. Paul
County: St. Louis County
City land area: 67.6 square miles
County land area: 6,125 square miles (one of the largest counties in the country)

Population

	City of Duluth	
	Population	**% Change**
1950	104,511	
1960	106,884	+2.3%
1970	100,578	−5.9%
1980	92,811	−7.7%
1990	85,493	−7.9%
2000	86,918	+1.7%

Population density:
    1,264 persons per square mile (1990)
    1,285 persons per square mile (2000)

Housing

Total number of housing units (1990): 35,934
    % owner-occupied: 64%
    % renter-occupied: 34%
    % single-family detached units: 86%
Change in housing units (1980-1990): −5.4%
Average price of single-family homes (2000): $105,638
Median price of single-family homes (2000): $91,500

Form and Structure of Local Government

Strong mayor form of government
9-member city council
    4 elected at-large; 5 elected by district

Who Plans?

- *13-member City Planning Commission:* all members appointed at large by the mayor and confirmed by the city council

- *Department of Planning and Development (DPD):* including divisions of Physical Planning, Building Inspection, Business Development, Community Development and Housing and Job Training
    Total DPD staff (1998): 35

Total DPD budget (1998): $1,962,900
Physical Planning Division staff (1998): 7
Physical Planning budget (1998): $405,500*
Local government spending per capita on Physical Planning = $4.74 per capita

As of December 1999, the Physical Planning Division was dissolved and the 5 remaining physical planners were folded into a new Division of DPD called "Urban Development."

SAN DIEGO, CALIFORNIA PROFILE
(Chapter 7 in book and CD-ROM)

Location

San Diego County, southern California
125 miles south of Los Angeles; 18 miles north of Tijuana, Mexico
City land area: over 320 square miles

Population

	City of San Diego	
	Population	**% Change**
1950	557,000	
1960	573,224	+2.9%
1970	697,640	+21.7%
1980	875,538	+25.4%
1990	1,110,549	+26.7%
2000	1,223,400	+10.2%

Housing

Total housing units, City of San Diego (1990): 431,722
Total housing units, City of San Diego (1997): 457,231
    % renter-occupied: over 51%
    % single family: 55%
    % multifamily: 43%
    % mobile homes: 1%
% of total housing units that were vacant (1997): 6%
Median value of existing owner-occupied homes (2000): $237,000

Form and Structure of Local Government

City manager with a mayor and city council

Planning Budget

San Diego Planning Department (2001): $8.9 million or $7.22 per person*

* The amount of money budgeted by the City of San Diego for planning reached a high of $11.8 million in 1991 ($10.62 per person), but had fallen to $5.2 million by 1995. In January 1996, the city's planning department was officially abolished. It was re-established by Mayor Dick Murphy in 2001.

Who Plans?

- *City of San Diego Planning Department:* 96-person staff; $8.3 million overall budget as of the first half of 2001

- *San Diego Planning Commission:* 7 members, appointed by the mayor, confirmed by the city council. Members of the commission are appointed for 4 years and can be reappointed to a second 4-year term. According to William Anderson, chairman of the commission as of 2001 and an economic planner, individuals appointed to the commission have had professional experience in planning or other planning-related fields.

- *Centre City Development Corporation (CCDC)*

- *San Diego Housing Commission:* composed of 3 city council members and 4 citizens, 2 of whom represent low-income tenants. Commission members are appointed by the mayor and confirmed by the city council. An annual budget appropriation from the city covers the administrative expenses of the agency and pays for staff who work for the commission.

- *San Diego Association of Governments (SANDAG):* a "joint-powers agency" created under California state law by a formal agreement signed by each of the local government members. It is a regional body governed by a board of directors composed of mayors, council members and a county supervisor from each of the region's 19 local governments. Supplementing these voting members are advisory representatives from the U.S. Department of Defense, Caltrans, the San Diego Unified Port District, the San Diego County Water Authority, and Tijuana/Baja, Mexico/California. The board of directors is assisted by a professional staff of planners, engineers and research specialists. Regional planning issues addressed by SANDAG include growth management, transportation, air quality, open space, environmental management, hazardous waste management and recycling, housing, energy, fiscal management, economic development and criminal justice.

MADISON, WISCONSIN PROFILE
(Chapter 8 in CD-ROM)

Location

South central Wisconsin
Approximately 77 miles west of Milwaukee; 144 miles from Chicago, Illinois
County: Dane County
City land area: Madison is one of David Rusk's "elastic cities"—a city which has been
able to grow outward spatially by annexing peripheral land. In 1970, the city covered
an area of 48.6 square miles; by 1990, it covered an area of 58 square miles; by 2000,
the land area of the city had increased 68.8 square miles.

Population

	City of Madison		Dane County	
	Population	**% Change**	**Population**	**% Change**
1970	171,769		290,272	
1980	170,616	−.06%	323,545	+11.5%
1990	191,262	+12.1%	367,085	+13.5%
2000	206,965	+8.2%	416,088	+13.3%

Population density: 3,008 persons per square mile (2000)

Housing

Total housing units (1990)
    % owner-occupied units: 40.3%
    % renter-occupied units: 51.2%
    % single-family detached homes: 40.6%
Median sales price of a single-family home (2000): $115,000

Form and Structure of Local Government

Mayor-council form of government
    22 elected city alderpersons, elected by district

Who Plans?

- *City of Madison, Office of Planning and Development (OPD):* a 175-person city
  department with wide-ranging planning and planning-related responsibilities.
  Among the many functions performed by the department are: physical planning
  and special projects; comprehensive land use planning; neighborhood planning and
  neighborhood enhancement; community and economic development; transportation
  planning (the agency is the designated Metropolitan Planning Organization—MPO);
  planning and administration of tax increment financing; administration of the
  Capital Revolving Fund; urban design and design review (staff to Urban Design
  Commission); historic preservation (staff to Landmarks Commission); real estate
  and public facilities planning; development review and zoning administration (staff
  to Planning Commission); administration of the federally funded Community
  Development Block Grant (CDBG) program; and building permits and inspections.

Amount spent on planning in 2000: $3,529,528 ($17.05 per resident)*

* The amount shown here only includes money budgeted by the City of Madison for planning-related activities in the city's OPD, parks and open space planning in the city's public works department, and bicycle and pedestrian planning in the city's transportation department. It does not include the value of staff time committed to the planning process of capital budgeting—a process in which all city departments engage, and which is overseen by an appointed capital budgeting review committee. It also does not include $10,311,000 in federal funding received and administered by the city's OPD—$9,800,000 in CDBG funding and a $511,000 grant which OPD received for transportation and land-use planning as the area's officially designated MPO; nor does it include $3,020,000 budgeted by the city for OPD's inspection unit for expenses related to building and sanitation inspections, code enforcement, and zoning administration and enforcement—expenditures which are recouped by fees and charges for services that are paid back into the city's general fund.

- *Madison Planning Commission:* 9 members
  5 citizen members (appointed by mayor)
  3 alderpersons
  mayor or mayor's designee

WICHITA, KANSAS PROFILE
(Chapter 9 in CD-ROM)

Location

South central Kansas, approximately in the center of Sedgwick County
Land area of city: 300 separate annexations of land between 1980 and 1998 expanded
    the land area of Wichita from 105 to 134.8 square miles (an increase of 28%)

Population

	City of Wichita		Sedgwick County	
	Population	**% Change**	**Population**	**% Change**
1960	254,698		325,399	
1970	276,554	+8.6%	350,694	+7.8%
1980	279,835	+1.1%	366,531	+4.5%
1990	304,011	+8.6%	403,662	+10.1%
2000	344,284	+13.2%	452,869	+12.2%

Population density in city (2000): 2,554 persons per square mile

Housing

Total housing units (2000): 152,119
    % owner-occupied: 61.6%
    % renter-occupied: 38.3%
    % vacant: 9.4%
Median value of owner-occupied, single-family homes (April 2000): $77,000

Form and Structure of Local Government

City manager form of government

Who Plans?

- *Wichita-Sedgwick County Metropolitan Area Planning Department (MAPD):* MAPD also
  serves as the designated Metropolitan Transportation Organization for the region.
      18 full-time planning staff (including director)
      11 clerical/technical staff
      29 total staff

- *Wichita-Sedgwick County Metropolitan Area Planning Commission:* 14 members. The
  governing bodies of the City of Wichita and Sedgwick County each appoint 7
  members to the planning commission. The mayor and the six Wichita City Council
  members each appoint representatives to the commission. Each of the 5 members of
  the Sedgwick County Board of Commissioners also appoint representatives to the
  commission. Another 2 members of the commission are appointed by the county
  commission on an "at large" basis, to make a total of 7 county appointees.

MAPD budget total (1998): $1.73 million, including grant funds administered (included approximately $40,000 spent on outside consultant services, and $80,000 spent on project oversight, coordination and administration).

Per capita amount spent on planning: $5.35

WESTMINSTER, COLORADO PROFILE
(Chapter 10 in CD-ROM)

Location

Northwest of the City of Denver
Roughly halfway between Denver and Boulder,
    along the Denver-Boulder Turnpike (US 36)
Land area: 30 square miles (1998)

Population

	City of Westminster	
	Population	% Change
1950	1,686	
1960	13,850	+721%
1970	19,432	+40%
1980	50,211	+158%
1990	74,625	+49%
2000	100,940	+35%

Population density (2000): 3,364 persons per square mile

Housing

Total number of housing units (2000)
    % owner-occupied: 70%
    % renter-occupied: 30%
Mix of housing types (1990)
    Single-family detached: 59%
    Townhomes, condominiums (single-family attached): 8%
    Multifamily apartments: 31%
The average sales list price of all new and existing single-family homes in Westminster
    (including townhomes) in 1995 was $167,000, compared to a metro-wide average
    of $238,000. The average list price of condominiums in Westminster was $88,000,
    compared to the metro-wide average of $143,000.

Form and Structure of Local Government

City manager form of government
City council composed of 6 at-large council members and one elected mayor

Who Plans?

- *Westminster Department of Community Development (DCD)*
    Total number full-time staff (1998): 57
        Professional staff: 53
        Administration: 4
    Total DCD budget (1998): $2,608,368
    DCD budget per capita: $27.40

BURLINGTON, MASSACHUSETTS PROFILE
(Chapter 11 in CD-ROM)

Location

13 miles northwest of Boston; 12 miles south of Lowell
Interstate 95 (State Highway 128) runs east-west through the southern portion of
   the town; Interstate 93 runs north-south through the western portion of the town
City land area: 11.88 square miles

Population

	City of Burlington	
	Population	**% Change**
1960	12,852	
1970	22,150	+72%
1980	23,687	+7%
1990	22,662	−4%
2000 (est.)	22,876	—

Population density: 1,923 persons per square mile (2000)

Housing

Total number of housing units (2000): 8,492
   % single-family detached units: 77%
   % multifamily units: 23%
Average price of existing single-family home (2000): $265,000

Form and Structure of Local Government

Town meeting form of government
A Board of Selectmen composed of 5 members
A town administrator appointed by the Board of Selectmen

Who Plans?

Town of Burlington Planning Board, consisting of 7 elected citizen members
Town of Burlington Planning Department
   Full-time staff: 3
   Part-time staff: 1
Total planning department budget (1998): $143,825
Local government spending on planning = $6.29 per capita

BLOCK ISLAND, RHODE ISLAND PROFILE
(Chapter 11 in CD-ROM)

Location

12 miles south of the mainland Rhode Island coast; 40 miles south of Providence
County: Washington County
Town land area: 9.4 square miles

Population

	1980	1990	2000
Winter	600	800	1,000
Summer overnight	7,800	9,900	11,600
Summer daytrippers	2,000	2,000	2,000

Housing

Tenure (2000 Census)
Winter-occupied: 470
    Owner: 320
    Renter: 150
Winter vacant: 1,130
    Second home: 1,110
    Other: 20
Median value single-family dwelling (1998): $406,000

Economy

	1999	% Change 1989-1999
Private employment		
Agriculture, forestry, fisheries	19	?
Construction	76	+29%
Transport, communications, utilities	46	−22%
Retail trade	314	+39%
Finance, insurance, real estate	31	+138%
Services	207	+2%
Total	**696**	**+ 21%**

Labor Force

	1999	% Change 1989-1999
Total	533	+37%
Employed	484	+34%
Unemployed	49	+37%
Unemployment rate	9.2%	

Government Structure

Manager-town council
  5 councilors: first warden, second warden, plus 3 others

Who Plans?

Planning Board: 5 appointed members
  Staff: land use administrative officer, occasional consultants
Other planning-related town agencies:
  Historic District Commission
  Conservation Commission
  Land Trust
  Zoning Board of Review
  Economic & Industrial Development

Amount Spent on Planning

Annual budget of Planning Board: $20,000
    $20 per year-round resident
    $1.72 per person (summertime population)
Amount budgeted for comprehensive plan update: $15,000
    $15 per year-round resident

Index

Illustrations are indicated by **boldface** page numbers.